D1739432

The Labour Government and the End of Empire

1945–1951

A

The British Documents on
the End of Empire Project
gratefully acknowledges
the generous assistance of
the Leverhulme Trust.

BRITISH DOCUMENTS ON THE END OF EMPIRE
General Editors D J Murray and S R Ashton
Project Chairman D A Low

Series A Volume 2

The Labour Government and the End of Empire 1945–1951

Editor
RONALD HYAM

Part IV
RACE RELATIONS AND THE COMMONWEALTH

Published for the Institute of Commonwealth Studies
in the University of London

LONDON : HMSO

© *Crown copyright 1992*
Applications for reproduction should be made to HMSO
First published 1992

ISBN 0 11 290524 2

British Library Cataloguing in Publication Data

A CIP catalogue record for this book
is available from the British Library

HMSO publications are available from:

HMSO Publications Centre
(Mail and telephone orders only)
PO Box 276, London, SW8 5DT
Telephone orders 071-873 9090
General enquiries 071-873 0011
(queuing system in operation for both numbers)

HMSO Bookshops
49 High Holborn, London, WC1V 6HB 071-873 0011 (counter service only)
258 Broad Street, Birmingham, B1 2HE 021-643 3740
Southey House, 33 Wine Street, Bristol, BS1 2BQ 0272-264306
9–21 Princess Street, Manchester, M60 8AS 061-834 7201
80 Chichester Street, Belfast, BT1 4JY 0232-238451
71 Lothian Road, Edinburgh, EH3 9AZ 031-228 4181

HMSO's Accredited Agents
(see Yellow Pages)

and through good booksellers

Printed in the United Kingdom by HMSO
Dd 2294214 5/92 C7 803128 19585

Contents

The Labour Government and the End of Empire 1945–1951

Schedule of contents: parts I–IV

Abbreviations: part IV

BBC	British Broadcasting Corporation
BDEEP	British Documents on the End of Empire Project
CAS	Colonial Administrative Service
CD(&)W	Colonial Development and Welfare (Act)
C-in-C	commander-in-chief
CM	Cabinet conclusions (minutes), Labour government, 1945–1951
CO	Colonial Office
Col	Colonial
COI	Central Office of Information
Con	Conservative (Party)
Co-op	Co-operative (Party)
COS	Chiefs of Staff
CP	Cabinet memoranda, Labour government, 1945–1951
CRO	Commonwealth Relations Office
Dept	department
DO	Dominions Office
FO	Foreign Office
FRS	Fellow of the Royal Society
GOC-in-C	general officer commanding-in-chief
GNWR	(Patrick) Gordon Walker Papers (diary)
gov	governor
gov-gen	governor-general
govt	government
HCTs	High Commission Territories (Basutoland, Bechuanaland Protectorate and Swaziland)
ICFTU	International Confederation of Free Trade Unions
ILO	International Labour Organisation

IRD	International Relations Department (Colonial Office)
JPS	Joint Planning Staff (COS)
KCB	Knight Commander of the Bath
KCMG	Knight Commander of St Michael and St George
Kt	Knight Bachelor
Lab	Labour (Party)
Lib	Liberal (Party)
LSE	London School of Economics
memo	memorandum
MP	member of parliament
Nat Govt	National Government
Nat Lab	National Labour (Party)
OEEC	Organisation for European Economic Co-operation
PM	prime minister
RNVR	Royal Naval Volunteer Reserve
SA	South Africa
SANF	South African Naval Forces
S of S	secretary of state
SNA	secretary for native affairs
SWA	South-West Africa
tel	telegram
TUC	Trades Union Congress
UN(O)	United Nations (Organisation)
WEA	Workers' Educational Association
WFTU	World Federation of Trade Unions
WT	water transport/warrant travel

Summary of Documents: Part IV

Chapter 7 Social, racial and research policies

(1) Race: general issues

(2) Social Welfare Policy

Chapter 8 The Commonwealth

(1) The Commonwealth relationship: India and Ireland

(2) Smaller colonial territories: future status

(3) Southern African issues: relations with the Union government

CHAPTER 7

Social, Racial and Research Policies

Document numbers 344–379

---

344 CO 537/1523, no 32A [Oct 1945]

'East Africa: control of immigration': CO departmental note

[Although this paper was not drafted by Cohen (the probable author was J S Bennett), he strongly favoured some restriction of immigration into East Africa. He regarded this as necessary if there was not to be sacrifice of the 'interests of a large number of Africans'. The paper was discussed by the secretary of state and Sir P Mitchell on 6 Nov 1945, and general approval given to the CO proposals. Hall made it clear 'that if there is to be a row with India on East Africa immigration policy, he would prefer it to be early rather than late' (CO 537/1523 minutes by Cohen, 30 Oct, and G Creasy, 6 Nov 1945).]

Immigration into the East African Territories is at present restricted by Defence Regulations which were imposed during the war for economic reasons. We are committed publicly to withdrawing these regulations as soon as war-time conditions have disappeared. The Government of India (who are principally affected) have already enquired when the regulations are to be withdrawn. No reply has yet been given pending the current discussions with Sir Philip Mitchell, but the position is that the war conditions which made the restrictions necessary have not been relieved by the end of the war and that, on the contrary, the strain on transport, accommodation and supplies will be increased by demobilisation. The existing restrictions cannot be removed or seriously relaxed until demobilisation has been completed or at any rate much further advanced. In the meantime the regulations will continue to be carefully and sympathetically administered with a view to avoiding hardship and particularly in the case of business and professional men permits will not be withheld in cases of genuine need.

2. The three East African Governments recognise that the war-time regulations must come off within the next year, but they wish to replace them by a permanent system of control. Some restriction is clearly necessary in the interests of the advancement of the African population. The control is intended to be general and non-discriminatory, but the particular problems which make it necessary are the immigration of Indians and to a lesser extent of Southern Europeans. The Africans are advancing in education and technical training and have reached or are reaching a point where if they are to progress they must enter the trades and employments which have hitherto been almost an exclusive preserve of the Indians. Further Indian immigration, backed by the low standards of living which Indians are willing to accept, would progressively impede African progress and sooner or later create serious discontent. Equally, Indian immigration for the purposes of settlement on the land would compete with urgent African needs. (It may be mentioned that there is no such economic conflict at the present stage between the African population and

the small numbers of European immigrants who engage in primary production, industry, and other skilled occupations in which the Africans do not yet compete).

3. Control of immigration has, therefore, become necessary in the paramount interests of the native inhabitants of East Africa. This principle has recently been reinforced in the Colonial and Trusteeship Chapters of the United Nations Charter.

4. There are two main external factors to be considered:—

(a) The attitude of the Government of India, who are anxious to preserve opportunities for the settlement of Indians overseas, particularly in view of the acute over-population problem in India (which, however, is so large that emigration to East Africa would virtually not affect it at all);
(b) The existence in Tanganyika of the Mandate (or Trusteeship Agreement when this replaces the Mandate), which necessitates equal treatment for nationals of all members of the United Nations in respect of rights of entry into the territory.

5. For geographical and administrative reasons, a uniform policy throughout East Africa is necessary. It is not necessary, however, for it to be centrally administered and indeed, in the view of Sir Philip Mitchell and Sir Charles Lockhart,[1] this would be impracticable.

6. For the purpose of the present discussions, Sir Philip Mitchell wishes to obtain from the Secretary of State guidance as to the general principles of a system of control of immigration which would be acceptable to H.M.G. In the light of this, he will discuss with the other Governors on his return and joint detailed proposals will be submitted. These will involve legislation in East Africa. The time-table which it is desired to follow would be publication of the proposed legislation about next March and enactment in June, after which the present war-time regulations would be withdrawn.

7. Preliminary proposals have been received from the three East African Governments and have been discussed on the official level with Sir Philip Mitchell and Sir Charles Lockhart. All the suggestions submitted agree on the first principle that no specific restriction can be aimed at Indians as such. Subject to this, there are broadly speaking two alternative proposals in the field:—

(a) One, proposed by Sir Charles Lockhart and accepted as a basis for discussion by the Kenya and Uganda Governments, involving the enactment of a law restricting immigration to the following categories of people:—

(i) visitors and persons whose maintenance is assured;
(ii) persons entering to engage in some form of large-scale production, i.e. agriculture, mining, business or industry, for each of which a minimum capital qualification would be required to ensure in the first place that it is a type of production which will not interfere with African advancement and in the second place that the person concerned will be able to carry it on effectively and is not likely to become an economic liability;
(iii) persons entering to take up employment, subject to the advice of a Board that opportunities for such employment exist and that there are no adequately qualified residents available in the particular occupation concerned. Details of the proposed qualifications are given in a note by Sir Charles Lockhart, of which

[1] Chief secretary, East African Governors' Conference, 1944–1946.

a copy is attached.[2] The Uganda Government have put forward proposals which are on similar lines, but considerably more restrictive and these will be considered at the same time as Sir Charles Lockhart's proposals.

(b) A proposal by the Tanganyika Government that instead of prescribing the conditions of entry by Ordinance or Regulations, each individual case should be examined by an inter-territorial Board and dealt [with by deciding them administratively on the basis of general directions received from the Governments.][3]

8. These proposals have been discussed at two meetings in the office, the first under Mr. Creasy's[4] chairmanship and the second under Sir George Gater's. While it is for the East African Governments to work out the details of any scheme among themselves, the view of those who have so far considered the matter here is that the Uganda Government, and also the Tanganyika Government, are approaching the problem in too restrictive a way, but that Sir Charles Lockhart's proposals are both workable and defensible, besides being compatible with the provisions of the mandate and trusteeship and justifiable on that basis. The Tanganyika proposal for a board operating under administrative directions does not appear to be defensible and would be likely to lead to endless difficulties and complaints in practice. The administrative instructions under which the board would act, although they would be published, would be subject to change by executive action and the whole procedure would savour far too much of bureaucratic control. The procedure suggested by Sir Charles Lockhart would have the practical advantage that intending immigrants would be able to tell clearly in advance by reference to the law and regulations what the conditions of entry were, while appeals from aggrieved persons could be directed to the courts and not to the executive. Sir Philip Mitchell is particularly anxious to include the safeguard of an appeal to the courts from executive decisions.

9. If the general principles of the above are agreed, it is also necessary to consider what interim reply should be sent to the Government of India. It is proposed to inform them that the war-time regulations will be withdrawn some time in the middle of next year. If nothing further is said, however, the Government of India will interpret this as meaning a return to the status quo and it will be necessary to add that future policy is under consideration by the East African Governments. The Government of India will certainly demand the chance to express their views before new legislation is enacted. The publication of the proposed Bill for discussion in the three East African Legislative Councils would give them an opportunity for this and it is considered that no approach should be made to them in advance of publication regarding the new proposals.

---

[2] Not printed.

[3] Editor's conjectural reconstruction. The original portion is missing as a result of trimming with scissors. The reconstruction has been made by reference to related papers in the file, particularly no 40.

[4] (Sir) Gerald H Creasy, assistant under-secretary of state, 1943–1945; chief secretary to West African Council, 1945–1947; gov, Gold Coast, 1947–1949.

345 CO 83/241/1, no 2 8 Mar 1946

[Fiji]: proposed stricter immigration restriction policy: despatch from Governor Sir A Grantham to S of S. *Minutes* by S Caine, J B Sidebotham, A B Cohen, Sir G Gater and Mr Creech Jones

[In reply to this despatch, the governor's demographic projection was queried, and it was suggested that economically the introduction of *enterprising* immigrants was generally beneficial to colonies (CO 83/241/1, no 5, 31 July 1946). The governor's reply (ibid, no 8, 19 Sept 1946) nevertheless convinced the CO, and a reply was sent (23 Oct 1946) agreeing in principle to enforce stricter control of immigration. However, once Cohen heard of this, a telegram was sent (ibid, no 11, 4 Jan 1947) asking the governor to postpone action. During the course of the discussion Sir C Jeffries asked if there was any general 'philosophy' on this 'rather important matter'. Poynton said there was not, except the old basic trusteeship doctrine of doing what was best for a colony; since this differed for every colony, they should on the whole be left (in accordance with the statement of the 1921 Imperial Conference) to settle their own composition.]

I have the honour to inform you that I have recently had under consideration the need for introducing stricter measures of control of immigration into Fiji. A memorandum summarizing the present policy in respect of the admission of new immigrants is attached.[1]

2. There has been a rapid increase in the population of the Colony in the last 25 years and the increase in the next 25 is likely to be even more marked. From a total of 157,260 at the 1921 census, the population had risen (according to the Registrar-General's estimate) to 246,485 by the end of 1944 and now is almost certainly over 250,000. Assuming that the rate of increase in the past four or five years, during which there has been a considerable decrease in immigration into the Colony, is maintained, it may be expected that the population will, in 25 years' time, have reached the half million mark without any further additions from overseas. The question therefore arises whether or not the Colony will have sufficient resources to provide a livelihood for immigrants as well as for the increased local population. I am sure you will agree that it is imperative that the rate of increase in population should not be allowed to outrun the rate of economic development.

3. The great majority of the population is dependent upon agriculture for a livelihood, but it is now established that the amount of cultivable land available for further development is limited. There is no scope here for the influx of further agriculturists from overseas.

4. Similarly, in industry and the professions it is not likely that there will be any difficulty in providing, from the local population, all the labour and most of the skilled and semi-skilled staff required, except for a few specially trained men. Once abnormal post-war conditions have been removed, there will be no shortage of labour for existing industries and no need to bring in labour for new industries, for which the rising population will itself provide the manpower required. The chief need in the Colony at present is for skilled men but plans are being prepared which, by making training facilities available locally, will eliminate the necessity for overseas recruitment even in this field.

5. It is therefore in the interests of the local population as a whole that the

---

[1] Not printed.

immigration of further competitors in the manpower market should be strictly controlled. The alternative to control would be to allow economic laws to regulate the ebb and flow of immigration, but this would lead only to a lowering of the standard of living and to unemployment, destitution, crime and possibly political disturbance. Control is essential if these consequences are to be avoided.

6. I therefore seek your authority to make it known that in future no new immigrants will be admitted to the Colony unless it can be shown that they will not be entering into competition with local residents in the employment market. It is proposed that this rule should be applied without discrimination against, or in favour of, any particular race, although it is probable that it will be interpreted in some quarters as an effort to check the further immigration of Indians and Chinese and undoubtedly those two races will be most affected by such a policy. The policy I have outlined has been approved unanimously by my Executive Council which, as you are aware, now includes an Indian member. The powers necessary for the enforcement of the policy are already provided in Section 14 of the Immigrants Ordinance, Cap. 57.

Minutes on 345

. . . The issues involved in immigration policy are political or sociological rather than economic in the narrower sense . . . . The alleged economic objections to immigration ought normally to be looked at with considerable suspicion. They are most frequently merely a smoke screen for political or sociological objections which people prefer to keep in the background. From the purely economic point of view the introduction of active, vigorous and enterprising people, such as immigrants most commonly are, is generally beneficial rather than the opposite unless there is clearly over-population in the sense of more people than the land can support. In the particular case of Fiji, it is very doubtful indeed whether economic considerations point against rather than in favour of immigration . . . .

S.C.
4.6.46

. . . the Governor seems to me to make a good case, in reply to our despatch, on political and other grounds for limiting immigration, not only from the point of view of the Fijian . . . but also in the interests of gradually assimilating Indians into the population of Fiji. As the Governor points out, the present immigrants are largely Gujeratis and Punjabis, who never regard themselves as more than temporary citizens, and the Fijian bred Indian and the young Fijian are quite unable to compete with them . . . finding many possible avenues of employment already filled by Asiatics. The Governor also, with I think, justification, refers to various more general pronouncements which have a bearing on immigration . . . . I feel that the Governor has made out his case . . . .

J.B.S.
14.10.46

. . . In my view he has made out his case and his proposal should be approved, although I agree with Sir C. Jeffries some clarification is required in regard to practical administration of the policy.

It must be recognised that, in spite of the fact that the statement will make no discrimination between races, protest from the Government of India is likely as the Indian immigrants will be the chief sufferers.

G.H.G.
17.10.46

We must anticipate criticism from the Govt. of India but I can see no objection to what the Governor proposes provided the regulations are not based on racial grounds but on economic grounds and are necessary for the welfare of the local inhabitants with special regard to the Fijis [sic]. I think we should see the new regulations when they are in draft & I agree with Sir Chas Jeffries' point.

A.C.J.
18.10.46

Mr. Sidebotham

I am most grateful to you for giving me the opportunity of commenting on this. I have not had time to study the bill in detail but have examined its salient features. From the East African point of view I think that it would be very undesirable indeed for the Fiji Bill to be published at the present time. We have recently received a strong protest from the Government of India on the East African bills, both as regards principle and detail, and we are at present engaged in doing what we can to meet this criticism in order to avoid a major row with the Government of India. It was evident from a long conversation which I had yesterday with Mr. Bannerjee and Mr. Jha, representatives of the Government of India, that the subject is taken very seriously indeed in India and we have got to be most careful what we do, especially in the light of the recent Indian South African dispute which was ventilated at UNO and on which the Indians secured a partial victory.

From the point of view of general policy I feel that we should look upon these immigration problems as part of a single picture and from this point of view I imagine that it is important to get the East African issue out of the way before action is taken elsewhere. We hope to get the East African bills into Select Committees within two months, in which case they might be finally passed within 6 months, but not I should think earlier. I do not know whether it would be possible for Fiji to wait as long as that – I may say that we have recently discouraged Northern Rhodesia from going ahead with a new Immigration bill for the same reason. If the Fiji bill were published now, the Government of India would undoubtedly protest and their attitude to the East African bills would almost certainly be hardened.

Another consideration is that as far as I can see the Fiji bill is much stiffer than the East African bills in that in Clause 17 it gives the Principal Immigration Officer power to issue permits or refuse, apparently at his discretion and not in the light of any settled provisions of the law.

I hope that it may be possible to wait until the East African bills are passed before proceeding with legislation elsewhere. I realise that this may not be possible but I suggest at any rate that we should discuss the matter after Christmas among ourselves in view of the extreme importance of the immigration issue in East Africa and the delicate stage which it has now reached.

A.B.C.
24.12.46

346 CO 323/1879/5, no 4 8 Jan 1947

[Racial prejudice]: general policy regarding colour discrimination: circular despatch from Mr Creech Jones to governors

[When in September 1946 Sir G Gater urged that the moment was opportune for making a survey of racial discrimination in the social and economic fields, Creech Jones minuted: 'Yes, such an enquiry is of much importance. The matter has been on my own mind for some time & I am glad this beginning has been suggested. Whatever the difficulties, we must encourage the local government to do this' (16 Sept 1946).]

I have the honour to transmit to you for your consideration the enclosed memorandum,[1] which results from a study of the extent to which legislation in Colonial territories discriminates between different races, more especially between Europeans and non-Europeans.

2. You may be aware that racial discrimination is one of the subjects which has been specifically remitted for examination by the United Nations Organization to the Commission on Human Rights appointed in pursuance of Articles 1(3) and 68 of the Charter. The Commission have not yet begun detailed consideration of this subject. But their Terms of Reference enjoin them to draft an international "Bill of Human Rights", and also to consider "Racial Discrimination", so that it is likely that they will wish to include provisions relating to racial discrimination in this "Bill" or Convention. While it is not possible at this stage to suggest the way in which this matter may be approached by the Commission, it is reasonably safe to assume that the question of removing discriminatory legislation will be one of the subjects for discussion, and that it will be necessary for the United Kingdom representatives on the Commission to be fully seized of the implications of this question in relation to Colonial territories.

3. For this reason, as well as on account of the general political importance of the matter, I feel that it is desirable that Colonial Governments should undertake a factual survey of the present position in regard to discriminatory legislation, and I hope that the enclosed memorandum (which, it is recognised, is not exhaustive or completely up-to-date, nor possibly in all respects accurate) will be useful as a basis for the survey. I am far from suggesting that all discriminatory legislation can be immediately swept away in Colonial territories. Some may be required in the interests of the local or non-European races. Some might be defended as being necessary for the protection of the health and living conditions of sections of the community who have at present widely differing standards in these matters. Some may be incapable on broad political grounds of any immediate change. The purpose of the survey would be to list the provisions of the law which are, or can be regarded as, discriminating between different races, to establish which of these provisions would be susceptible of modification or repeal; and, in cases in which repeal is not considered possible, to state the reasons.

I would suggest that at the same time discrimination in the administrative, social and economic fields should also be examined, even though in some of these fields the scope for effective official action must necessarily be more restricted.

4. I appreciate that a survey of the kind suggested above will in many Colonial

---

[1] Not printed.

Territories entail much research, and will take a considerable time to complete. For the reasons which I have indicated, however, it is likely that enquiries into this subject will in any case be proposed before long, and I feel sure that it will be found to be of advantage to have set them on foot in good time.

347 CO 554/152/1, no 6 14 Mar 1947

[Gold Coast]: Africanisation of the public service and relations with the Africans: circular minute by Governor Sir A Burns to his Colonial Service staff

[Burns was inspired to produce this plain-speaking circular by a directive issued by the Sudan government to its officials (a copy of which was sent him by Sir C Jeffries), and he thought the secretary of state might issue a similar circular: it would have 'more effect than anything a governor could do' (CO 554/152/1, no 1, letter to Sir T Lloyd, 11 Feb 1947). Cohen minuted: 'I like Burns' minute and the procedure and spirit behind it *v. much*' (24 Feb 1947). Lloyd agreed that it was 'an admirable document'; so did Mr Thomas (26 and 27 Feb). Creech Jones minuted: 'I think the draft excellent and forthright. I have a very small point. Some excellent service has been rendered in the territory already (& is being rendered) by a large number of officers & a friendly reference to their devotion would not be out of place in this general exhortation which I thoroughly approve of' [nd]. Lloyd told Burns that the secretary of state in regarding this circular as admirable was 'speaking for everyone here who has seen your draft minute'. Formal approval was given in a letter from Lloyd (1 Mar 1947), Creech Jones's reference to the devotion of service officers being added. A copy was then sent personally to every European officer serving in the Gold Coast. It was, however, decided not to circulate it in other colonies, where circumstances were different; nor to send something similar to commercial firms and banks. Cartland minuted: 'The sort of reactions which it provoked in the Gold Coast included:— (1) A certain amount of resentment among European officers on varying grounds. (2) A feeling among some Africans that it was a score off the Europeans. This feeling was to some extent responsible for the feeling recorded above among European officers. (3) A feeling that this document was an expression of the paternal attitude. . . . I am not pretending that the feelings recorded above were universal, or even very widely felt, but they are indicative of the sort of danger we run when we attempt this sort of thing' (CO 554/161/4, 17 Dec 1948).]

1. On the 17th August, 1942, I addressed a confidential minute to the senior members of the Colonial Service in the Gold Coast, explaining to them some aspects of the policy which I intended to pursue in the government of the Gold Coast. There is nothing in that minute which I wish to retract or modify, but, with the coming of peace and the opening of what I hope will be an era of rapid economic, social and political development, it may be that I can usefully amplify, for the benefit of all European officers in the Service, some of the points I referred to in my earlier minute.

2. The fundamental policy of this Government has been stated on many occasions. It is to educate the people of the Gold Coast, both individually and collectively, so that they may be able to stand on their own feet without support, to manage their own affairs without supervision, and to determine their own future for themselves. They must be trained in all technical and administrative work until they are able to conduct the public service without the assistance of European officers. Self-governing institutions, the Native Authorities and Town Councils, must be fostered and developed, so that through them the African may learn the difficult art of government. The people must be encouraged to take a greater share in the day to

day business of governing the country by the inclusion of an increasing number of African members in Advisory Committees, Commissions of Enquiry, and bodies of this kind. Our policy can achieve lasting results only if we carry the people with us, and give them the opportunity by constant discussion to share in the planning of their own future.

3. All officers are aware that the steady Africanisation of the Public Service is the settled policy of Government, but there are still a few who are not prepared to face this fact and accept its implications. While none of us wishes to see any falling off in the efficiency of any department, or of any branch of the Government, and while it is the duty of all officers to exercise their administrative, professional and technical skill to the best advantage, we must all realise that our principal duty is to use such superior training or qualifications as we may possess to help and educate our African colleagues to take an ever-increasing share of public responsibility. I expect all officers, and especially those in the more responsible posts, to co-operate to the full in promoting this policy, and in impressing its importance on those subordinate to them. Any individual officer who does not take the educational side of his work seriously, and make a constructive effort to assist in the carrying out of Government's policy in this matter, fails in an essential part of his duty. I fully realise that it will be some time before the Gold Coast people will be able efficiently to man all the posts in the Public Service of their Country, but I expect all European officials to work loyally towards this goal.

4. Considerable progress in Africanisation has already been made and there are numbers of scholars now receiving a higher education in the United Kingdom to fit them for senior posts in the Service. For all these men, our present colleagues and those who will join the Service later, I bespeak the sympathy and assistance of all European officers. We shall be failing in our duty if we do not give them all the help that lies in our power. It is easy enough to find faults in Africans, to point out examples of African officials who have failed in character and integrity, and to demonstrate their incapacity for difficult and responsible work—but there have also been European officials who have done no credit to the Service. There are bound to be failures in any Civil Service which sets itself a high standard, whether in Africa or elsewhere; the more generous our attitude and the more sympathetic our understanding of the difficulties of our African colleagues, the fewer will those failures be. I must here particularly emphasise the duty of senior Administrative Officers and Heads of Departments to help along (and not to obstruct) the Government policy of Africanisation of the Service, and to set their subordinates a good example in the treatment of African staff, and particularly in their training.

5. The role of many European officials in the Gold Coast is in fact gradually changing from an executive to an advisory one, and it must be clearly realised that with the acceleration of the process of Africanisation in the Administration and in all Departments, there will soon be little room for officials who do not regard the training of African staff as their primary responsibility.

6. Nor must this training be confined to the Civil Service alone. It is our duty to educate the whole population, and this duty is by no means confined to the members of the Education Department. Education is not given only in schools and colleges. The mass of the people must be taught new and healthier ways of living, improved methods of agriculture and other work, and a greater sense of public responsibility. A fundamental characteristic of British colonial policy is that we do not try to

assimilate the colonial peoples, nor to turn them into imitation Scotsmen or Englishmen, but to help them to develop a higher civilisation of their own, soundly based on their own traditional institutions and culture.

7. Most officers realise that they have an educational mission to carry out, but some are so anxious to promote efficiency at all costs that they tend to become impatient and to do things themselves, instead of showing the African how to do them, and giving him the opportunity to learn by his own mistakes. I realise that in spite of the end of the war staff is still desperately short, and that many officers are still working at great pressure and have little time for teaching their juniors. I know also that it is often quicker to do a piece of work oneself than to show an inexperienced subordinate how to do it, but first things must come first, and the duty of teaching must have first priority.

8. The maintenance and development of sound administration in a colony depends almost entirely on the personal relationship that exists between the European officials (and unofficials) and the people of the country. There is a very good tradition in this respect in the Gold Coast, and we must see to it that it is preserved and developed. If the African believes that the European official seeks honestly to assist and teach him, he will be receptive of ideas and the teaching will endure. The African, like anyone else, is naturally reluctant to admit his shortcomings to unsympathetic persons, but he knows quite well in his own mind that he has much to learn, and he is anxious to learn whatever he can. Like ourselves, while he is willing to be led by a friend, he will not be driven by anybody, and least of all by one whom he does not trust. He is very sensitive and the bad manners, or even the unsympathetic attitude, of one official may be sufficient to undo a great deal of the good work done by a number of others. Every Government officer must bear this constantly in mind.

9. I am aware that there are some "die-hards" who consider that we are moving too fast in giving greater political power to the Colonial peoples and in the Africanisation of the Service. If there are any such "die-hards" in the Public Service of the Gold Coast I suggest to them that they should consider seriously whether they can conscientiously continue to serve a Government with whose policy they are in fundamental disagreement. For this policy is clear and there is no prospect of it being changed except in the direction of still faster progress.

10. Considerable progress has already been made towards the goal of responsible government, and I hope and believe that further progress in inevitable. There is now a Legislative Council with a majority of elected members representing both the Gold Coast Colony and Ashanti; it will not be very long before the Northern Territories also are represented in this Council by elected members. The Governor still retains "reserve powers" which he can use in an emergency to over-ride the wishes of the elected majority, but if, as I think they will, the members of Legislative Council exercise their new responsibilities with discretion it should seldom be necessary for the Governor to use his own powers. On the Executive Council there are three unofficial members. In four municipalities there are Town Councils with elected majorities, and more and more Africans are serving on Advisory Committees where their services are of great value. There is no one who can explain the African point of view so well as the African himself, and no Government can hope to govern well unless it pays careful attention to the wishes of the people it is governing. We must make sure that the African understands our motives, and to do so we must take into

our confidence the leaders of the people, and discuss with them, patiently and with sympathy, all our plans. It is only by the exercise of the greatest patience and tact that we can hope to attain success in our task.

11. Native Authorities (performing many of the functions which in England are the duty of Local Authorities) are making rapid progress, and these, with the municipal Councils, are the best schools for self-government available to the Africans. They must be helped in every way, and officers must bear in mind that it is intended that these forms of local government should, as they become more experienced, bear an increasing share of responsibility for all those services which from their nature can properly be administered locally. Educative and sympathetic assistance should be given to those organs of local government as a prime duty by all officers. I must emphasise that Native Authorities are not independent administrations, but a part of the Government of the Gold Coast, and as such are entitled to the full and sympathetic co-operation of every Civil Servant.

12. In conclusion I wish to record my appreciation of what the Gold Coast Service has already achieved. Recent political advances in the Central and Local Governments and in the Native Administrations have been possible only because of the confidence which exists between the various sections of the community and have in no small measure been due to the fact that many individual members of the Service have displayed those very qualities in their relationship with the Africans which it is the purpose of this minute to emphasise and encourage.

I am, indeed, glad that the writing of this minute gives me an opportunity of paying tribute to the devotion to duty of so many officers of this Government and to recognise the excellent service which they have given, and are still giving, to the people of this country.

13. The Secretary of State for the Colonies has approved the terms of this minute, which should be carefully noted and acted upon by all serving European officers. It will be shown to all overseas candidates for appointment to the Gold Coast Service before they are appointed, since anyone who is not prepared to serve in the spirit of the terms set out in this minute is not the type of official required by this Government.

348 CO 537/1917 22 Mar 1947

[Nigeria]: colour discrimination incident in a Lagos hotel involving I G Cummings (CO): minute by Sir T Lloyd

[J L Keith, director of colonial scholars, and I G Cummings, CO Welfare Department, were booked for five nights into the Bristol Hotel, Lagos. (Cummings was the first coloured man appointed in the Colonial Office; his father was an African doctor who married a Yorkshire woman.) On arrival, the hotel manager queried admitting Cummings because he was 'an African', relenting only to the extent of saying he could stay for one night. Keith protested, and, having seen that the room was only a small double room, he and Cummings decided to go elsewhere. The manager had spoken loudly, with Europeans listening, and the incident resulted in an explosion in the Nigerian press. Keith was inclined to blame government officials in the Nigerian secretariat for not having checked out the hotel. The governor, Sir A Richards, seemed comparatively unmoved, but Sir T Lloyd thought Cummings had been 'very reasonable over this most unhappy business', and suggested that the secretary of state should write to him, which Creech Jones did (8 Apr 1947), sympathising with him in his 'disgraceful treatment' in this 'regrettable affair', but explaining that legal action could not be taken because the

Nigerian government were not paying the expenses; he hoped that good might come out of it, and stop such incidents happening again (CO 537/1917, no 15).]

I had a talk of over an hour with Mr. Cummings yesterday. The first part of this was taken up with a most interesting account of his impressions of all four West African territories, particularly on the point of race relations. In that respect the Gold Coast is, of course, by far the best. Partly because that territory has a much higher proportion of educated Africans, partly because the Administration has shown goodwill by promoting Africans to quite senior appointments, but mainly through the personal influence and efforts of Sir Alan Burns and a few others who think with him, race relations in the Gold Coast are incomparably better than in any other territory Mr. Cummings knows.

In Sierra Leone matters have much improved in this respect since Mr. Cummings was last there in 1945. But present policy over higher education and over the Municipality are still strongly resented by many even of the better disposed Africans. In the Gambia Mr. Cummings thought that race relationships were reasonably good.

Mr. Cummings presents a quite different picture in Nigeria. He agrees that relationships are most embittered in and near Lagos but feels that a similar feeling is gradually pervading the whole country. He agrees that this is in part due to the influence of the Zik press but regards the attitude which a very large number of European officers take up towards Africans as contributing at least as much to present troubles. Several of the examples which he gave of that attitude are touched upon in the attached Reuters report (No. 13) of Sir A. Richards'[1] speech at the opening of the Nigerian Legislature. Sir A. Richards did not, however, mention the European Club at Ikeja[2] which, so Mr. Cummings told me, will not admit Africans of whatever position even as visitors for a single meal. For example, Mr. Macarthy,[3] when visiting Nigeria as a member of the West African Court of Appeal, is accommodated at Ikeja but not admitted to the Club and has to bring his own cook with him. Mr. Cummings mentioned this, together with the past exclusion of all Africans from the European Hospital at Lagos, as making for the embitterment of the more educated coloured people.

We spent the last half hour of our talk in discussing the Bristol Hotel incident. While Mr. Cummings naturally feels strongly over this, I am satisfied from my talk with him that he has no wish to be vindictive and would prefer not to cause embarrassment to the Secretary of State or the Nigerian Government. But he did represent strongly to me his view that the Greek proprietor of the hotel deserved to be expelled from Nigeria and that, if the Nigerian Government really wished to make it plain to the people of the country that they would not tolerate race discrimination, they ought to use powers which (as Mr. Cummings represents) they do possess to deport the proprietor without taking any preliminary legal proceedings against him. I said this would be a strong measure and told Mr. Cummings of the substance of the Governor's view in the telegram at No. 9. I also told him of the advice given to the Governor, and (as I understand it) upheld here, that as Mr. Cummings did not seek a remedy at law while in Nigeria, it would be difficult, in the absence of some

---

[1] Gov of Nigeria, 1943–1947; created Lord Milverton on retirement.

[2] Sir T Lloyd noted in the margin: 'This may be wrongly spelt'. However, there is an Ikeja near Lagos.

[3] (Sir) Leslie Macarthy, puisne judge of the Gold Coast since 1939.

conviction against the proprietor, to take punitive action. Mr. Cummings represents that the Nigerian Government could at least proceed against the proprietor for breach of contract in having at the instance of that Government reserved accommodation for Mr. Keith and Mr. Cummings on which reservation he later went back. This point should now be examined though I doubt whether there can be anything in it.

As the Governor has (see the third page of No. 13) now stated publicly that the future arrangements for the licensing of hotels and bars in Nigeria are to be based on the principle of no discrimination on account of race, I think that this unfortunate incident must be regarded as having served its purpose and that, subject to such further consideration as can be given to it in the light of the point raised in the preceding paragraph, no further action should be required in Nigeria.

One point about which Mr. Cummings naturally feels badly is that not a single word of apology was ever spoken to him by the Governor, the Chief Secretary or the Administrative Secretary, all of whom were closely involved in this unhappy business. This point must be brought out in the reply which eventually goes to Sir A. Richards' letter at No. 12; I should like the Department to consider and to advise whether, as the Nigerian Government failed in what seems to me to be its elementary duty in this matter, Mr. Cummings should not have some letter of regret on this incident from the Secretary of State. I, of course, made my own views plain in the talk yesterday.

349 CO 537/2572, no 1 [July 1947]

'The political significance of African students in Great Britain': memorandum by G B Cartland. *Minute* by H T Bourdillon on Malayan aspects of the problem

One of the most pressing of our colonial political problems is to find a place in the scheme of development for the comparatively small but increasingly important educated classes. In many ways the appearance of this class has upset our calculations and disturbed the even tenour [sic] of political development among the slow moving masses. The new literate classes claim an important part in the affairs of their countries and in shaping their future.

There is a real need for a policy of co-operation with this class. It will become an increasingly important element in the population however small its numbers and the time would seem ripe for a review of policy on two vital matters:

(1) the incorporation of this class in a realistic way in the social, political and economic scheme;
(2) the education of this class for their high calling as leaders and eventually rulers of their people.

The object of this note is not to deal with (1) but with one most important aspect of (2). The literate classes fall into very many groups according to their degree of literacy and their circumstances. For convenience we can divide them into those with higher or university education and those with a lower standard. In East Africa the numbers of the former class are as yet very limited but in West Africa they are much more numerous; but in both East and West Africa they are a growing body. Practically all these men have been to the United Kingdom and educationally and in general breadth of experience have acquired superior advantages which cannot fail to make them generally an outstanding and influential element in the "ruling class" of the future. They will be moreover one of the most important vehicles of culture and thought between the Western world and Africa. What these men and women see and learn in this country is therefore of vital importance to the future of Africa generally and to the future relations between British Colonial Governments in Africa and their peoples. It would scarcely be too much to say that the whole political future of the African colonies is bound up with these few men whether it is as the heirs to government in West Africa or leaders of the principal race in the future partnership governments of East Africa.

The proper political training of this class is, therefore, of the utmost importance. It is not sufficient to teach them civics in their African schools before they come to a British University and to rely on finding a professional niche for them on their return to teach them good citizenship if we let them run intellectually wild during the important formative years at an English University. It is of little value our directing the attention of colonial governments and their officers to the educational and other needs of the literate if we do not at the same time pay attention to the most important element of this class during its vital years in this country.

A great deal has already been done on the Welfare side by the Colonial Office for Africa but the political side of the Office has not yet directed its attention adequately to the political problem which these people represent. There is a good deal of evidence to suggest that they are subject to many undesirable influences and that study of the situation from the broad political view point is required.

The needs of the situation appear to be

(1) a careful survey of the problem,
(2) a definition of needs and objectives based on the survey and
(3) the translation of this policy into terms of practical steps to be taken.

Assuming that the survey confirms the need for an active policy of civic education among African students, I suggest that the following lines of action should be considered.

In general terms our aim should be to ensure that students obtain an appreciation of British culture and a balanced political understanding. This cannot be done purely by teaching, by any prescription of other influences or by any obvious propaganda work which would merely defeat its own ends. The objective presentation of facts is needed rather than any clumsy propaganda.

With this in mind it might be considered inadvisable for the Colonial Office to take any active steps and it may be preferable for non-official bodies to undertake the practical arrangements required. It is probably desirable however that the survey of the situation and any general co-ordination, direction and organisation of steps required should be carried out by the Colonial Office, which should however, make liberal use of other agencies for particular projects.

As regards detailed steps to be taken these might be divided under (a) social (b) educational and (c) political heads. On the social side I consider that the most important need is to increase the contact between the African students and cultured Englishmen and women and to gain access for them to the best type of English homes. Secondly every effort should be made to enlarge the possibilities for social intercourse offered by permanent membership of (as opposed to casual visits to) churches, societies, sports and social clubs. Africans keep far too much to their own society and they should receive every encouragement and help to broaden their field of acquaintances. Thirdly I consider that great establishment of personal contact [sic], and it would be well worth considering whether anything more can be done to assist students by individuals' meeting them either one or two at a time and maintaining a fairly regular contact with them. For this purpose a large roster of volunteers prepared to give some time to fostering these contacts would be required. I am quite certain that a nucleus of this roster could be found among the members of the Colonial Office and particularly among the beachcombers. Such contacts by members of the office would greatly assist in breaking down the suspicion with which the African often views the office. But the main effort could not be made by the members of the Colonial Office and must come from enlisting the support of a large number of outside people all over the country. Although I put this suggestion forward particularly in connection with social activities I think it also has an important political aspect, as personal contact with members of the office will help to impress on the students that the Colonial Office is not merely an inanimate bogey but an institution with a strong human and African sympathies. Colonial Service officers on leave should also be brought in on this side of the work and arrangements made for them to visit and meet students from their own territories. A certain amount of this sort of thing is already done, and a number of officers on leave have gone to some trouble to pay such visits. This however should be put on a properly organised footing and arrangements should be made for regular visits by such men to all centres where colonial students are in residence. In addition to organising this system of visits it would be most helpful if the Colonial Office could produce a comprehensive list or "Who's Who" each year to be brought up to date by monthly or quarterly additions of colonial students in the United Kingdom. Such a list should at least be in the hands of all geographical departments working in much closer contact with the welfare department than has been the case in the past. One of the great difficulties of course is the pressure of work, shortage of staff and the lack of time for such activities by officers engaged on other duties. This difficulty might to some extent be met and useful contacts established if by developing and extending the idea periodic entertainment offered by the Colonial Office to students in this country, possibly on the lines of the monthly Corona Club tea-parties. At these, members of the Colonial Office, Colonial Service officers on leave and other persons interested would have an opportunity of mixing with and meeting African students in this country.

On the educational side it is most important that, in addition to their particular professional studies, students should make the most of their time in this country to see and visit places of interest and to meet and hear experts in various fields of learning. This could be done possibly in some cases directly by arranging visits or tours or specific lectures or series of lectures, or alternatively by informing students of the facilities available in London and in the provinces. Holiday tours could possibly be arranged or advice given on the best means of spending vacations.

The political side of this work is possibly the most difficult and delicate but at the same time the most important. It seems to me that possibly two aims should be kept in view, (1) to present facts objectively, and (2) to counter if possible the extremist political propaganda and atmosphere to which African students are subjected in this country. It may well be that the way to achieve the second aim will be by pursuing the first. It is most important that no semblance of propaganda should appear in this work and any direct activity by the Colonial Office will have to be pursued with great circumspection. I think, however, that there are a number of things which we can do to assist; not the least important would be the activities which I have suggested in the social and educational fields. These should help the students to widen their horizon, give them other outlets for their activities than under-graduate politics and help them to establish contacts with the sort of people who by general conversation and personal contacts may exercise considerable influence on the general attitude of students and help them to a sensible approach to the racial problem and to British colonial policy generally.

I think that a great deal more could be done to provide students with authentic information about Government policy and activities in their own territories and not leave them to gain their impressions and information from their own local press and correspondence. This might be done in a number of ways, possibly by the circulation of a monthly broadsheet of colonial news, possibly by arranging visits to the Universities either by members of the Colonial Office or by Colonial Government officers on leave to explain what is happening in the territories and to inform them about Government policies. When I was in Edinburgh recently lecturing on behalf of the Royal African Society there were in the audience about a dozen African students who cross-questioned me very closely on many aspects of Government policy in West Africa. I spoke to them plainly about some of the extremist views they expressed and I am convinced that they appreciated both authoritative information and straight speaking on some of their views. At least they went so far as to invite me to address a conference they are holding in the new year. I had a long talk with Colonel Beatty the Colonial Office Welfare Officer in Edinburgh and his assistant in charge of the hostel. They were very conscious of the need to put across more authentic information about the colonies and to arrange discussions between the Africans and people sufficiently well-informed to talk to them and counter some of the extremist arguments they put forward. They both urge very strongly that members of the departments concerned with African territories in the Colonial Office should visit Edinburgh and other centres from time to time to have informal talks with the African students in residence both to give them information and to help them to a better understanding of our policy. Both Colonel Beatty and his assistant said they felt unable themselves to do this as they had neither the knowledge nor sufficient up-to-date experience to inspire the attention of the students on these matters. Such visits could be made both by Colonial Office officers and by Colonial officers on leave in conjunction with the social contact visits which I suggested earlier.

Two [sic] other aspects on the political side are the objective provision of information on general political matters. I have in mind possibly lectures on the broad aspects of political philosophy such as the elements of democracy and other forms of Government, studies of the Central Government machine including the work of Parliament and the Civil Service. These students are going back to work a machine which although much simpler is modelled to a large extent upon the organisation and practice of the English constitution and administration and it should be most useful to them to gain some insight into workings of the institutions in this country.

I am not in favour of stressing too strongly the Central Government side in the political education of the African peoples at this particular stage. We should as far as possible divert attention from the light phrases of politics and direct it to the gaining of real political competence and administrative experience. These can be gained best through local government activities. I believe that in the next phase of political development we should aim at training the future political leaders in colonial territories in the practical school of local government. There they can gain experience in handling their own affairs in administration, in responsibility for finance and in grappling with the real problems of government as opposed to the shouting of unsubstantial and dangerous political catchwords in the field of elected politics. In many territories we shall have a short time in which to prepare the people for the next stage of political advance and it is of tremendous importance that we should lay solid foundations of political experience and education. I think therefore that we should make a special effort in this country to show British local government to the African student. This might be done by arranging through outside agencies a series of lectures, by arranging visits to local councils at different levels and by attempting to explain to these people that our system of native administration in Africa is designed on parallel lines with the local district councils and parish councils in this country. Broadly speaking the educated elements are suspicious in many places of our policy of native administration and the emphasis on it as a form of local government needs to be brought home to them.

Although I feel very strongly about the importance of concentrating on the political education of Africans in the immediate future on local Government, I think with these more highly educated elements we must give some attention to the theoretical side of politics and to Central Government politics. They will have to participate in the Central Government of their own territories either now or in the near future and should know something of its background. Moreover the political influences to which they are at present subject are very much concerned with these aspects of politics and some attempt must be made to present more objective and authoritative information and to encourage a balanced point of view.

There are a number of other suggestions which could be made to assist in putting over the policy I have suggested. For instance a hand-book or guide for colonial students coming to this country, would merit attention. This might include advice on general subjects, information about educational possibilities, places to visit, things to do and things to avoid. Something on the lines of the booklets which were issued to American troops and to our own troops in foreign territories which help them to find their bearings and to make their adjustments to a new society more quickly than they otherwise would.

Minute to 349

I am sorry to have delayed this. The subject is of intense interest to my Department (as it must be to most Geographical Departments), and I was anxious to give it proper study.

I have read Mr. Cartland's memorandum with great appreciation. I entirely agree with his principal contention that wise and sympathetic handling of the Colonial student in this country, during the formative years when he is all too susceptible to mischievous propaganda, may be of incalculable importance in the whole future political development of the Colonial Empire. I am certain that this is no less true of Malaya than it is of Africa. We may hope that Malaya, now that constitutional difficulties are virtually settled, will develop quite rapidly towards self-government. It will be for Malaya to decide whether that development is friendly or hostile towards Britain, whether the self-government is inside or outside the Commonwealth; and the decision may depend, as much as on any other single factor, on the treatment which we accord to that limited class who study in this country before going back to qualify for influential positions in their own.

The fundamental problem, then, is the same, but I do not think it works out in quite the same way in the case of Malaya as it does in the case of Africa. I gather from Mr. Dussek[1] (with whom I have discussed the question) that the tendency of Malayan students in this country to go Communist is not very marked—not nearly as marked as one might suppose. Amongst the Chinese, however, (and these form the majority) there is a very real tendency to revolve round the Chinese Embassy and the Chinese colony here, at the expense of the Malayan connection. With the Malays, who are comparatively few in number, there is no such positive danger, but there is always the negative danger of failing to cement friendship with Britain. The opportunity is there, since I understand that the students are ready and willing to draw closer, but it is in danger of being missed. If it is missed, the situation will deteriorate. The reason why it is in danger of being missed is interesting. Asiatic students in this country do not, I understand, mix readily with Africans, and I do not think they can be expected to do so. In any central, undifferentiated scheme for looking after colonial students, whether on the social or political plane, Africans are bound to predominate, and this inevitably gives the Asiatic student, unless he has his own separate facilities, the impression that he is being left out in the cold and that the whole problem is being looked [at] from an exclusively African angle. At present this is happening with a vengeance, because no separate facilities for Asiatic students exist. The students are doing what they can by their own initiative (I am now speaking only of Malaya), and have formed a Malayan Students Union, for which they are raising funds by subscriptions from members. I attended the inaugural dinner a week or two ago. But they are terribly hampered without premises, and the acquisition of suitable premises would of course be far beyond their means. Some months ago we approached the Governor General to find out whether the Governments of the territories within his sphere would be willing to contribute towards the finances of such a project, on a modest scale to start with. We have as yet had no reply. We have already sent one reminder, but I am now arranging to send another.

I heartily welcome the proposal to establish a small ad hoc Committee which would pursue the points raised in Mr. Cartland's memorandum. I am not sure from the previous minutes whether it is now intended that the Secretary should be provided by the Welfare Department or the African Division. If the latter, I would only express the hope (and I am sure there is no need for me to do so) that the problems would not be viewed from too exclusively African an angle, since I fear, for the reasons stated above, that any such tendency, though it would no doubt be very

[1] O T Dussek, Malayan Education Service, CO liaison officer for Malayan and Hong Kong students; formerly principal of the Sultan Idris Training College (at Tanjong Malim) and assistant director of education in charge of Malay schools.

useful for Africa, would be positively harmful for the Far East. I hope also that those of us whose work is connected with the Far East would have the opportunity of giving evidence before the Committee.

As regards the three suggestions in Mr. Cohen's minute of 9/9/47, I am not sure whether it is desired in relation to the first of these (see para. 2 of Sir Thomas Lloyd's minute of 18/9) that members of non-African Departments should join the voluntary panel for meeting *African* students, or merely that they should consider similar arrangements for students from their own territories. If the former, then I should certainly be willing to be called upon from time to time, though I don't know how much use I should be. If the latter, then I definitely agree that contact between members of the Office and Malayan students should be encouraged. By "members of the Office", I mean particularly members of the Political Department concerned, since the Welfare Department already have numerous and valuable contacts. I regard this development as very important, but I think it should begin on completely informal, "unorganised" lines. The moment we are suspected of organising a "drive", or of indulging in propaganda, the whole good effect is lost and we only succeed in engendering suspicion. I am at present engaged in widening my circle of acquaintances amongst the Malayan students in this country, and I understand that other members of Eastern Department A (e.g. Mr. Morris) are doing the same. The process will certainly be continued and encouraged. When and if we get the separate centre for Asiatic students in London, progress will be facilitated, and I think the time will then come to consider whether more organised contact, at the wish of the students themselves, would be desirable.

H.T.B.
17.10.47

350 CO 537/2110, no 42 — 7 Aug 1947

[The Kabaka of Buganda]: colour bar incident in a London hotel restaurant: letter from Mr Creech Jones to Mr Strachey (minister of food)

[The Kabaka of Buganda (HH Edward Frederick Mutesa II) was, at the age of 21, admitted as an undergraduate at Magdalene College, Cambridge. His progress both in term-time and in vacations was carefully monitored by the Colonial Office Welfare Department, who were nurturing him as 'the most important African ruler in East Africa, and indeed one of the more important rulers . . . in the Colonial Empire'. In July 1947 a letter was received in the Office from Oliver Messel (a well-known artist) reporting that he and a friend, who were entertaining Mutesa in London, had been refused entry to a hotel restaurant by the maître d'hotel. Messel explained to him that the Kabaka was an official guest in Britain, and had been received by His Majesty the King; to which the maître (apparently an Italian) had retorted that 'he couldn't care less'—he was 'far from polite regarding the whole question'. Poynton's reaction was: 'This is a disgraceful case'; Cohen's that 'this is really shocking!'. Cohen drafted a protest from the secretary of state to the minister of food. Strachey summoned the directors of the restaurant to explain. They put the blame wholly on the maître d'hotel, and sent a written apology to Mutesa. Mutesa himself never at any time made any comment on or reference to the incident.]

I feel that I must bring to your personal attention a very regrettable incident of colour bar in a restaurant, which has been reported to the Colonial Office.

I think you may know already that we have in this country His Highness The Kabaka of Buganda, Mutesa II, a sovereign ruler of a large territory in Uganda, who is an under-graduate at Magdalen[e] College, Cambridge. The Kabaka was recently the guest of Captain Oliver Messel, the well-known artist who, together with a friend, Mr. Reis-Hansen, was taking the Kabaka out to dinner. They went to the Restaurant Le Cerf, 151, Fulham Road, S.W.5., where the Maitre d'Hotel refused them service on the grounds that they were in the company of a coloured person. I do not think I can do better than enclose a copy of Captain Messel's report[1] on what happened.

I am sure you will appreciate the political implications involved here, and I think I should say that in the Colonial Office everything possible is being done to see that the Kabaka is well treated over here and returns to his own country with a good impression of England and English life. He has in fact done very well at Cambridge and it would be politically disastrous if shocking incidents of this sort were to spoil all our efforts. Naturally I take the strongest exception to this most blatant example of colour prejudice to which he has been subjected. The fact that this incident involved the Kabaka is, of course, the more embarrassing because of his position, but I am sure you will agree that it is the principle of the matter which should be raised, because there are large numbers of coloured Colonial people in this country and this kind of thing might spread, unless it is checked in the early stages.

I do not think that there is any doubt but that the incident as described by Captain Messel is accurate. Do you think there is any action that can be taken against this particular restaurant proprietor?

---

[1] Not printed.

351 CO 537/2573, no 63 — 24 Mar 1948

[Student welfare]: report on the political significance of colonial students in the UK, by the CO informal investigating group (chairman, Sir C Jeffries). *Minute* by A B Cohen (no 85)

[As a result of Cartland's memo (see 349), an *ad hoc* informal Advisory Committee was set up to consider it and to make recommendations, the remit being widened beyond Africa. This Committee was chaired by Sir C Jeffries. It included, from the CO, J L Keith (head of Welfare Dept and director of colonial scholars), A MacKintosh, K E Robinson, G B Cartland and W S Morgan (on secondment from the Malayan Education Service); together with Dr Rita Hinden (secretary, Fabian Colonial Bureau), Miss M Perham, Dr K L Little (lecturer in anthropology at the London School of Economics), R E Wraith (lecturer at the Institute of Local Government Studies, Birmingham University, with a specialist interest in West African administration) and J E Longland (Dorset County education officer). They met first on 13 Jan 1948, rapidly deciding that British colour prejudice was a major issue. Keith did not agree with this conclusion, however, arguing that it was the political situation in Africa which was at the heart of the problem: there was discontent because government there was not democratic and there was widespread disbelief in the policy of Africanisation, especially in East Africa and Nigeria (CO 537/2573, minute, 3 June 1948). Meanwhile Rees-Williams declared himself very worried by the attitude of the African and West Indian students he met. They clearly distrusted British economic policy, thinking 'it is imperialism and intended solely for the benefit of the United Kingdom', and 'much of the good work we are now doing in the Colonies will be upset if these students go back in the frame of mind they are in now'. He noticed that at student gatherings the communists attempted with colonial students to counteract what he had said: 'I hear too that the Communists are working through prostitutes in London and other big cities in order to get their policy across' (CO 537/2574, minutes, 13 and 16, Feb 1948). In the summer of 1951 it was decided to set up a CO Consultative Committee on the welfare of colonial students in the UK; it included MPs and students among its members (CO 537/6702).]

I. Much of the political discontent apparent amongst Colonial students in this country is due to a strong sense of dissatisfaction with the political and social conditions in the Colonies from which they come. In many cases, the students arrive here with ready-made prejudices against European domination in general and against British Colonial administration in particular.

Recommendations

Public relations (i.e. the promotion of mutual confidence between government and people) in the Colonies themselves, are the essential key to the problem. If local public relations are unsatisfactory, any work done with the students in this country must be rendered largely ineffective. Steps should be taken to impress this upon Colonial Governments. (See also VII below).

II. The Colonial student's ready-formed prejudice against British Colonial policy provides excellent material for those who seek to increase his sense of dissatisfaction, not out of consideration for the Colonial peoples but in the desire to hamper and weaken the British Government.

Recommendations

A concentrated effort should be made to correct this prejudice by putting forward to the students the true aims and methods of Colonial policy. Any suggestion of "propaganda" or "direction of consciences" will be strongly resented; therefore, a great deal of the work must be done through the co-operation of organisations other than the Colonial Office.

1. The Colonial Office Information Department, in co-operation with the British Council and the Workers' Educational Association, should prepare a panel of lecturers willing to visit Colonial students' clubs and hostels, W.E.A. and British Council centres, and other places where students congregate. Such a panel should include:–

(a) Responsible visitors from the Colonies;
(b) Colonial Civil Servants on leave;
(c) Members of the Colonial Office staff;
(d) Non-official speakers with or without some experience of Colonial affairs who can give well-informed expositions of British life and thought.

Suitable subjects might include specialist subjects such as Educational Development; general subjects such as British Institutions, the British way of life, British achievements in the fields of government, social services, arts and sciences; and political subjects including the various aspects of British Colonial policy. In this latter connection the presentation of facts is considered to be of primary importance, but discretion has to be exercised in choosing speakers from categories (b) and (c) above, as Government officials cannot take part in political debate with the freedom which may be necessary if effective results are to be obtained.

2. The Colonial Office Information Department should organise regular monthly film shows mainly for the benefit of Colonial students. Many of the British Council films prepared for projecting Britain to foreign countries would be very suitable. The

British Council and the W.E.A. will co-operate with regard to the loan of suitable films and theatres. The Parliamentary Private Secretary has offered to investigate the possibility of using the House of Commons film theatre for this purpose.

3. A Fund should be set up to enable Colonial students to attend Vacation and Week-end courses organised by the British Council and the W.E.A. and to meet any other expenses which might be incurred in connection with paragraph IV Recommendation 3 below.

4. The Colonial Service Journal (which will contain much valuable information about the aims and methods of British Colonial Policy) should be made available to Colonial students in this country and to the "intelligentsia" in the Colonies.

5. Tea parties should be held in the Colonial Office at regular intervals during vacation periods to enable members of the Colonial Office staff, in particular those serving Geographical Departments, to meet Colonial students on an informal basis.

III. The existence of colour prejudice in the United Kingdom greatly increases anti-British feeling amongst Colonial students, and enhances the attraction of Communism as a political creed which repudiates the colour bar.

Recommendations

1. The possibility of dealing with open racial discrimination by legislation, if only as a gesture, should be reconsidered. For instance, those clauses which frequently appear in leases preventing sub-letting to coloured tenants might be made illegal.

2. An effort should be made to improve the standard of education in British schools on Colonial matters, and should include the revision of out-of-date text books.

3. When providing hostel accommodation for Colonial students, greater emphasis should be placed on the value of the inter-racial type of hostel, where coloured and white students of several nationalities can live together.

4. The film industry should be aked to consider the possibility of a judicious censorship of films (especially American films) which show the stereotyped Negro in a derogatory light.

IV. Adherence to the simple and plausible doctrines of Communism is a general symptom of youth, as the apparently positive and dynamic approach appeals to the inexperienced enthusiasm of young people. The special problem of Colonial students is that they are not subject to the same corrective influences of home and social life which help the British student to preserve a more balanced political outlook.

Recomendations

1. An appeal should be made to the British public through the W.E.A. for vacation and week-end hospitality for Colonial students. Existing contacts through the Victoria League, East and West Friendship Council, etc., should be developed.

2. Colonial students should be encouraged to make contacts with British students through the British Council's London and Provincial Centres, if necessary by special invitation. (See also paragraphs III and V).

3. The opportunity should be given for Colonial students to observe the machinery of democratic Government through visits to:–

(a) Local authorities in the United Kingdom;
(b) Parliament;
(c) The Colonial Office;

(d) Trades Union meetings;
(e) Factories.

In connection with (a), an approach should be made to the Association of Local Authorities, and the detailed arrangements made by the British Council in co-operation with the Association. In connection with (d), the W.E.A. should introduce Colonial students to British members of Trade Unions willing to accompany them to branch meetings. In connection with (e), the Industrial Welfare Society should be asked to co-operate with the British Council.

V. Much of the political ferment amongst Colonial students here is due to a growing sense of nationhood. This is the proper result of British Colonial policy, and is to be welcomed as such. The unsatisfactory feature of it is that it tends to find expression in a desire for power or prestige for the individual or his class, and not in a sense of obligation to serve the community.

Recommendations

This national enthusiasm should be encouraged, but at the same time steps should be taken to make both coloured and European students (including Service Probationers) realise their responsibility, in the hope that through a better understanding of the problems and of one another, they may bring the Colonial peoples to full democratic self-government within the British Commonwealth of Nations.

1. Provision of hostels and clubs in which Colonial students will be under healthy influences and responsible guidance, should be given as great a measure of priority as possible. Wherever practicable, racial segregation should be avoided. (See also paragraphs III and IV).

2. At Oxford and Cambridge the Colonial Service Clubs should be expanded to include all types of Colonial students either in Government Service or intending to enter Government Service. At Oxford in particular, where there is no Colonial students' club, new and larger premises should be sought to accommodate a joint Colonial Service and Colonial Students' Club.

3. Colonial Service Summer Vacation Schools should be re-organised if possible, to include Colonial students. (The students' expenses could be met from the Fund mentioned in recommendation 2, paragraph III above).

VI. The attitude of the British public towards the Colonies, as indicated in the Press, contributes very largely to the Colonial student's belief that Britain is concerned only with the welfare and development of the Colonies, insofar as they can be exploited to her own advantage. This belief is often confirmed by Press reports of Ministerial speeches, and by the wrong sort of publicity in the Press.

Recommendations

1. The Secretary of State for the Colonies should invite the Prime Minister to advise Ministers, as opportunity offers, to denounce colour prejudice, and in particular, to stress the concern of His Majesty's Government as a whole for the advancement of the Colonial peoples.

2. The Press should be urged to bear in mind the fact that their journals are read by Colonials and to avoid, if possible, commenting *only* on Colonial events in their relation to the economic situation in Britain, or the more sensational items of Colonial news.

VII. Any good that may be done by the above measures will be nullified if, on the student's return to the Colony he is treated as a "nigger" or inferior, and is not permitted to assume the responsibilities for which his education has fitted him or to enjoy the equality of social status which he has experienced in this country.
Recommendations

1. The attention of Colonial Governments should be drawn to the importance of making very careful arrangements for re-absorbing students into the life of the Colony on their return, and the necessity of giving them the opportunity to make full use of the knowledge gained by higher education in this country.
2. Colonial Governors and senior officers should be urged to make more determined efforts to discourage social manifestations of colour prejudice and to promote a better understanding between the coloured races and Europeans residing in the Colonies.
3. The function of the British Council as an agency for promoting better race relations should be recognised, and more funds provided for this aspect of its work in the Colonies.

VIII. This is a long-term problem and should be continuously watched.
Recommendations
The present informal group should meet again in, say, six months, to review the situation. It may be that the Secretary of State will then think it desirable to set up some standing advisory body.

Minute on 351

I am extremely grateful for the opportunity of commenting on the report of the informal group which has investigated the Political Significance of Colonial Students in the United Kingdom. I was very sorry myself not to have been able to attend the meetings of the group, some of which at any rate unfortunately clashed with other meetings which I had to attend. As you know, I was partly responsible for the suggestion which led to the setting up of the group. I welcome the recommendations in the group's report but do not think that they go far enough or that merely on the basis of the action proposed we shall really succeed in dealing with the problem. I admit immediately that the problem is a particularly difficult one. The Communist Party are in a far stronger position to influence these students than we or anyone we encourage are. As things are at present the students are undoubtedly doing a lot of harm in their own countries (at any rate as far as Africa is concerned). I admit of course that young men and women are bound to be against the Government. But it is the introduction of the racial issue as well and the dead set which the Communists are now making to capture the minds and imaginations of these students which are so dangerous. In London I gather that there are regular weekly seminars by a member of the Communist organisation to indoctrinate a group of students.

I am not sufficiently informed of the position to have any views which carry any weight, but I should like to make the following additional suggestions, all of which are, I think, in the spirit of the report:–

(1) I think that we must have more general and tutorial supervision of these students. I do not think that there are enough liaison officers. The Gold Coast have two, Nigeria one, and Sierra Leone one, and I understand that we are considering

one for East Africa. There are over 200 students from East Africa now in this country and they are probably a good deal greener than the West Africans. There ought in my view to be at least one for every 50 students both for E & W Africa and we ought not to allow the Treasury or anybody else to oppose this. In any case possibly the Governments themselves pay. I think it is a false economy to limit the numbers and that these people by their personal influence can do an immense amount.

(2) We ought to try and get more students into the residential universities, or at any rate the universities away from London. I know how difficult this would be as regards Oxford and Cambridge. Cambridge at any rate are already worried about the relatively high proportion of students from abroad. But on the whole the students do extremely well at Cambridge at any rate and the influences are far more healthy. Also they have made far more real contacts with other students.

(3) We ought to have a more definite policy about students' clubs on a completely inter-racial basis as the report suggests, and I think that we ought to spend more money on these clubs.

(4) We ought to make more determined efforts to get students into British homes.

(5) I think that in addition to the W.E.A. we ought to ask the Labour Party through its local agents to interest themselves in the students. This would be a most healthy corrective to the Communist Party and in spite of possible theoretical political objections I think that we ought to consider this very seriously.

(6) Major Hastings, the Secretary of the Royal African Society, would be prepared to press the Society to do much more for colonial students and in fact to re-orientate its work in this direction. I am strongly in favour of this and one thing which the Society might do is to promote more sports facilities for colonial students. This is Major Hastings' idea. I should like to suggest that you [ie, Sir C Jeffries] and I should have a discussion with Major Hastings fairly soon. I promised him that I would arrange this and am afraid that I have been dilatory.

I hope in any case that there will be an office discussion on this whole subject. I think that unless we can frame a very active policy on it we are going to find ourselves in an even worse position than we are now. In spite of all the quite admirable work being done by the Welfare Department and others the forces against us are very strong and I believe that radical measures are needed.

A.B.C.
21.4.48

352 CAB 129/28, CP(48)154 18 June 1948

'Arrival in the United Kingdom of Jamaican unemployed': Cabinet memorandum by Mr Creech Jones

In view of the interest which is being shown in Parliament and in the press in the matter of the 417 Jamaicans who are due to arrive at Tilbury on 21st June on the *S.S. Empire Windrush*, I think it is desirable that the Cabinet should be aware of the arrangements which the various Departments concerned are making to deal with the situation. I should, however, first like to explain the circumstances in which these men decided to come to Great Britain.

2. *Circumstances of arrival.* It will be appreciated that the men concerned are all

British subjects. The Government of Jamaica has no legal power to prevent their departure from Jamaica and the Government of the United Kingdom has no legal power to prevent their landing. This is a spontaneous movement by Jamaicans who have saved up enough money to pay for their own passages to England, on the chance of finding employment, as they are free to do now that Government allocation of berths has been discontinued. We do not know who were the ringleaders in the enterprise, but I have asked the Governor of Jamaica for a report on this point. It was certainly not organised or encouraged by the Colonial Office or the Jamaica Government. On the contrary, every possible step has been taken by the Colonial Office and by the Jamaica Government to discourage these influxes. Not only has the position about employment and accommodation in the United Kingdom been explained by me to the Governors in correspondence but a senior officer of my Department visited Jamaica and certain of the other West Indian Islands last year and made great efforts to explain the difficulties at this end and to discourage people from coming over to this country on the chance of finding work. There was ample publicity in the Jamaica press of the difficulties which men might meet if they came to England. Before this party of 417 left Jamaica they were warned by the Jamaica Government about the difficulties which would beset them on their arrival in this country, but they decided, as they are free to decide, to take the risk. As I say, the Jamaican Government has no legal power to prevent them leaving the Island, and I doubt the wisdom of authorising a British Colonial Government to take such power in peace-time. In any case, Jamaica has reached such an advanced stage on the road to self-government that it would be impossible to compel them to legislate in this sense by directions from London. I do not think that a similar mass movement will take place again because the transport is unlikely to be available, though we shall be faced with a steady trickle, which, however, can be dealt with without undue difficulty. The immediate point however is that these 417 men are due to arrive on 21st June, and unless there is to be a public scandal and the possibilities of disorder, some arrangements must be made to deal with the situation.

3. *Underlying causes.* Until the economic situation in Jamaica improves there is bound to be a desire among many persons there to seek work elsewhere. The Jamaica Government is doing everything it can to deal with unemployment in a situation of over-population and high birth rate. There are at present some 50,000 unemployed or underemployed in the Island. Some limited relief is given by the recruitment of West Indians for work in the United States of America but most external fields of employment no longer exist. The problem is a long-term one and, for the constitutional reason given above, the internal economy of Jamaica cannot be planned from London. The economic developments now going forward in Jamaica are mainly agricultural and most of the unemployed are men who are unfitted or unwilling to enter agricultural employment. Work of the kind they want might be afforded by extensive industrial development but, even apart from the limitations placed on such development by the extent of the local market, we have hitherto found it impossible to get the machinery, structural steel and other equipment necessary for such development on any large scale. For example, various proposals for cement production have all so far foundered on that difficulty. We have now the Report of the Commission to British Guiana and projects are being examined in the hope that some relief may be given by settlement both in British Guiana and British Honduras.

4. *Size of immediate problem in United Kingdom.* The Colonial Office itself has no executive powers in the United Kingdom and must of course rely on the services of other Departments. The Colonial Office administers a number of hostels, primarily but not exclusively, for colonial students, and can accommodate approximately 70 of these arrivals in their hostel in Wimpole Street for a few days. This hostel is, strictly speaking, for colonial Servicemen only, and if the vacancies are filled up by non-Servicemen there are likely to be protests from Servicemen who will have to use other Service hostels for the time being. But in view of the emergency this risk must be taken. It may allay criticism to some extent if, as I intend, *ex-Servicemen* are selected to go to this hostel. It is probable that about 350 out of the 417 will be without accommodation on arrival, so that some arrangements will have to be made for the balance of about 280, for whom Colonial Office hostel accommodation is not available.

5. *Measures proposed.* The matter has been discussed between the various Departments concerned, and I think it is clear that the problem has got to be tackled, as one outside ordinary provision such as the Poor Law and as a combined operation without too much insistence on normal departmental responsibilities. I need not recount all the possibilities which have been considered and rejected as impracticable on one ground or another. The most helpful solution is that the men should be provided with transport from Tilbury to some central point which can be used as a "clearing house" or "transit camp"; and the War Office have agreed to make available for this purpose the Deep Shelter at South Clapham. The immediate problem of accommodation is therefore met and arrangements to cover transport and food are in hand. This is not ideal, but ordinary surface accommodation for so large a number is apparently unobtainable; and there is considerable convenience in having the men (other than the odd 70 at the Colonial Office hostel) all together.

6. Arrangements are being made for the boat to be met by representatives of the Colonial Office and the Ministry of Labour, and the Ministry of Labour have undertaken to do everything in their power to help the men to find employment in England as quickly as possible. It is understood that some at any rate of the arrivals are anxious to join the Armed Forces. About two-thirds of the total are in fact ex-Servicemen. Many of the men will arrive with only a limited amount of funds, having spent most of their savings on buying their passages to England. It may therefore be necessary to grant them public assistance until they find employment, but there is machinery for dealing with this particular problem through the Assistance Board. They may also need assistance towards railway fares to their ultimate destinations. The whole matter is being vigorously dealt with by the Departments concerned under the chairmanship of the Ministry of Health.

7. *Possibility of employment overeas.* The doors of Cuba and Panama are now closed and employment in the United States of America is very restricted. These men want work in *England*. We shall try to open out possibilities in British Guiana and British Honduras. There have been psychological difficulties about employment in Africa and I am informed that it is doubtful if these men have the skills that are wanted there from time to time. But that problem will be explored further though my present enquiries are not encouraging.

353 CAB 128/17, CM 13(50)7 20 Mar 1950

'Coloured people from British colonial territories': Cabinet conclusions

[On 27 July 1949 the Cabinet discussed the possibility that they might need to reconsider the time-honoured principle that British nationality carried the fundamental right to reside in British territory. The beginnings of West Indian immigration were referred to, but more worrying was the fact the Canadian communist seamen had 'inflicted serious economic damage' in fomenting recent London dock strikes. Perhaps communists would take advantage of the fact that they could not be deported? (CAB 128/16, CM 49 (49) 5). From this point onwards the problem of immigration was regularly before British cabinets. A committee chaired by the home secretary recommended in February 1951 that no legislation should be introduced, partly because the problem was comparatively small scale, and partly because controversial issues were involved (CAB 129/44, CP (51)51, 12 Feb 1951). The Cabinet approved this report, agreeing that legislative control of the immigration of British subjects into the UK would not 'at present be justified' (CAB 128/19, CM 15 (51) 4, 22 Feb 1951).]

In connection with the discussion recorded in the preceding Minute[1] the Cabinet were informed that, at a deputation on behalf of Seretse Khama which Mr. Leary Constantine[2] had recently brought to the Secretaries of State for the Colonies and Commonwealth Relations, instances had been given of racial discrimination against coloured people in the United Kingdom. In the Cabinet's discussion of this question reference was made to the difficulties of finding suitable employment for the coloured people who had come to this country in recent years from the West Indies; and the view was expressed that serious difficulties would arise if this immigration of coloured people from British Colonial possessions were to continue or increase.

The Cabinet:—

Invited the Secretary of State for the Colonies, after consultation with the Home Secretary, the Minister of Labour and the Minister of Health, to submit for their consideration a memorandum on the problems arising from the immigration into this country of coloured people (other than students) from the West Indies and other British Colonial territories.

---

[1] Concerning adverse press comment on the government's handling of the Seretse Khama affair (see notes to 422 and 424).

[2] West Indian cricketer. See 354, para 3(b).

354 CAB 129/40, CP(50)113 18 May 1950

'Coloured people from British colonial territories': Cabinet memorandum by Mr Griffiths

Introduction

(a) At the Cabinet's meeting on 20th March (C.M. (50) 13th Conclusions, Minute 7),[1] I was invited to submit, after consultation with the Home Secretary, the Minister of Labour and the Minister of Health, a memorandum on the problems arising from

---

[1] See 353.

the immigration into this country of coloured people from British Colonial territories.

(b) In this paper the word "colonial" refers collectively to all the Colonies, Protectorates and Trust Territories administered under the Colonial Office.

General background

1. The community of colonial people and their families in this country is estimated to number from 20,000 to 30,000. For the most part these persons live in Liverpool, Cardiff and Manchester, on Tyneside and in the East End of London: there are smaller groups in other centres, notably in Birmingham, Leeds, Hull and Bolton. Although they tend to congregate together and to prefer their own society, the great majority look on themselves as residents of the United Kingdom and have no intention of returning to their Colonies of origin.

Pre-war position

2. Before the 1914–18 war, few coloured people of colonial origin lived here. During that war many colonials served in the Merchant Navy and later settled down in this country. Some were able to remain in sea-going employment, but up to the beginning of the 1939 war, there was a steady fall in the demand for colonial firemen [sic], and the majority had to find employment ashore. This was not easy owing to prevalent unemployment, and there were racial difficulties which led to occasional riots.

Developments during the war

3. On the outbreak of the 1939 war, coloured colonials were recruited in the Colonies and were brought over to this country for war service. Others came over voluntarily. The main developments were—

(a) A group of 1,200 British Honduranians were brought here to fell timber in Scotland. Of these only 700 accepted repatriation. Most of the rest have settled down in Scotland and the North of England.

(b) About 1,000 West Indian technicians and trainees were recruited for service in war factories on Merseyside and in Lancashire. (Mr. L. Constantine was employed by the Ministry of Labour as a Welfare Officer to look after this group of men during their war service.)

(c) 10,000 West Indians were recruited for service in the Royal Air Force to serve in Britain as ground crews. When the war ended, approximately 8,000 of these men were repatriated, and the rest took their discharge here.

(d) Some thousands of men were either recruited or enlisted in the Merchant Navy. Large numbers of them were engaged to fill casual vacancies and not all of them were based on United Kingdom ports. With the return to normal conditions the demand for the services of coloured colonial seamen has been much reduced.

4. All the men recruited under special schemes were eligible for repatriation; but though persistent efforts were made to induce as many of them as possible to return home, a good many preferred to remain in this country. Some of these have not settled down satisfactorily and are unemployed from time to time.

5. Another reinforcement of the colonial population came from stowaways, chiefly from the West Indies and West Africa. Before the war, the number of coloured

stowaways was not large, and most were refused permission to land because they could not satisfy Immigration Officers by producing passports that they were British or British-protected persons. From 1941 onwards, however, the number increased. At about the same time it was being represented to the Government that the treatment of coloured protected persons was out of keeping with the circumstances of the times and the policy of His Majesty's Government as regards colonial peoples, and that it contrasted unfavourably with the fact that these protected persons were treated by British Consulates in foreign territories in the same way as British subjects, and were also subject to the same war-time discipline as United Kingdom seamen. In 1942, therefore, the special restrictions as to registration, &c., of coloured seamen from the Protectorates were abolished and coloured persons coming here as seamen for discharge, as passengers, or as stowaways were not refused admission for lack of documentary evidence as to their national status. They had at that time no difficulty in finding employment here.

Developments since the war

6. Since 1945 there has been a substantial increase in the number of coloured persons arriving in the United Kingdom. They comprise fare-paying passengers and stowaways, mainly from the West Indies and West Africa, and coloured seamen signed on in overseas ports who take their discharge here in the hope of finding regular sea employment. The causes of the influx are complex: in the case of the West Indies it appears to be due to unemployment and under-employment in that area, and the presumption that the labour shortage here was so acute that employment could be easily found: in the case of West Africa, the higher standard of living and social services here appear to be the main attraction.

7. A large number of the immigrant workers who have arrived here since the war comprise West Indians who served in the Royal Air Force during the war and used their gratuities to pay their passages back to the United Kingdom. They are not handicapped by language difficulties and have a much better understanding of British ways of life than the average West African. There are no statistics available but it is understood that approximately 2,000 migrant workers have arrived from the West Indies, chiefly from Jamaica, since 1945, mostly in large parties travelling in troopships at cheap rates. In 1949, the number of such arrivals dropped considerably. This was due partly to shipping difficulties and partly to the fact that fewer men could now afford the cost of passages. Nevertheless until unemployment in Jamaica is reduced there is bound to be a desire among many persons there to seek work overseas.

8. In response to representations from the colonies themselves, my predecessor set up a Departmental Committee in 1948 to advise whether there was any scope in the United Kingdom for the introduction under official auspices of surplus colonial labour. It was not found possible to promote any schemes which would give substantial help to the colonies, but two small groups of people have been recruited from St. Helena and Barbados.

9. Since the war there have been three occasions upon which disturbances between groups of coloured persons and others have called for special police action to restore law and order. These were at Liverpool from 31st July to 2nd August, 1948, at Deptford on 18th July, 1949, and at an industrial hostel near Birmingham from 6th to 8th August, 1949. Isolated disturbances occur from time to time involving

individual coloured men, and the police in the areas with aggregations of coloured persons keep a special watch for any incidents likely to provoke a general disturbance.

The present situation

10. It is among the new voluntary arrivals and persons who came here for war service and did not return that the main problems of housing, employment and relief of distress now arise.

11. In view of the continuing influx, an inter-Departmental meeting was held at the Home Office on 18th February, 1949, to consider what action could be taken by the Government Departments concerned, namely the Colonial Office, the Home Office, the Ministry of Labour, the Ministry of Health, the Ministry of Transport and the National Assistance Board. It was decided to concentrate action under the following heads:—

(a) To press Colonial Governments to reduce the flow at the source by making it known that jobs and accommodation in the United Kingdom are not too easily found, by not issuing passports to persons who cannot pay their passages or are obviously of the type who do not welcome regular employment, and by imposing greater controls at the ports to prevent stowing away.

(b) To stiffen up immigration practice at United Kingdom ports by a return to the pre-1942 practice of requiring all arrivals from any destination to produce satisfactory evidence of British nationality.

(c) To set up a working party of representatives of the Government Departments concerned to tackle the problem of those colonials already here by dispersal, by finding employment and accommodation, and by arranging for voluntary repatriation of the misfits.

Action taken

12. Action so far taken under these heads is briefly as follows:—

(a) (i) In general Colonial Governments have made it their practice to warn potential immigrants of conditions in the United Kingdom and to refuse passports in proper cases. My predecessor sent a despatch to the Governors of the Colonies suggesting ways and means of preventing stowing away in colonial ports. It is too early yet to say how far Colonial Governments will be able to take effective measures.

(ii) Many stowaways from West Africa have produced British Travel Certificates. These documents are issued by the British authorities in West African territories only for travel between those territories, but, as they certify the holder's nationality, Immigration Officers in the United Kingdom have had no option but to accept them. I am seeing whether these Certificates can be changed into documents merely certifying identity and place of residence, without any reference to national status: if this can be done it should reduce substantially the number of stowaways from West Africa who are admitted here.

(b) (i) On 19th September, 1949, the Home Office issued revised instructions to Immigration Officers enabling them to refuse leave to land to persons who cannot provide satisfactory evidence that they are British subjects or British protected persons. This was in effect a return to the pre-1942 practice, and as a result there has been a slight decline in the number of stowaways given leave to land.

(ii) I have sent a despatch to all maritime Colonies recommending the introduction of a standard certificate of nationality and identity for all colonial seamen and the verification of these men's nationality before the document is issued. If this standard document is brought into use it will reduce the possibility of aliens entering the United Kingdom as British subjects with forged or improperly issued certificates.

(c) The inter-Departmental working party began work in May 1949. The questions with which it is mainly concerned are:—

(i) *Accommodation*. The stowaways and migrant workers have settled in the main centres of colonial population and have thus aggravated the poor conditions under which coloured people are living. An added difficulty is that, in places such as Liverpool and Cardiff, there is a general lack of employment. Many of the men are unmarried and are not eligible for housing by local authorities. There is some prejudice on the part of landladies and others against accommodating coloured people.

(ii) *Employment*. This prejudice is exacerbated in areas where there is substantial general unemployment or in establishments where white women are employed.

The principal obstacle, however, is the attitude of some of the coloured colonials themselves and their undisciplined behaviour when they secure employment. This applies to the men who are new to this country and not to the second generation. Nevertheless, the problem of unemployment is comparatively small. A special enquiry undertaken by the Ministry of Labour last July showed that in the main centres there were about 1,200 men out of work. The majority of these were in Liverpool (540), London (East End) (278), Wales (mainly Cardiff) (101) and Manchester (129). Of this total of 1,200 nearly 500 were men who represented themselves as seamen.

There is a constant turnover of men, and except in Liverpool, and to some extent Cardiff, the total of unemployed does not represent a static figure of men who are unable to obtain work. For example, while there were 137 coloured colonial unemployed in Manchester in November, the Ministry of Labour had placed 262 in employment in the previous six months, 82 had obtained seagoing employment and 56 had found work by their own efforts. At Stepney, where there is a relatively large coloured colonial community, 203 men had been found employment in the month ended 6th February this year.

The Ministry of Labour are trying to transfer men in areas such as Liverpool and London to areas in the country where there are acute labour shortages. In spite of accommodation difficulties some success has already been achieved with the help of the National Service Hostels Corporation [sic].

The most difficult problem is that of seamen, genuine or otherwise, who cannot get seagoing employment and who are often neither suitable for, nor willing to take, shore employment away from the ports.

(iii) *Repatriation*. Destitute or incapacitated persons who would otherwise be likely to become a continual charge on public funds can now be repatriated to their colonies at public expense. The cost of repatriation is met by the National Assistance Board if it can be established that the cost cannot be met from any other source. Before men are sent home, enquiries are made in the colonies to see if the next-of-kin can meet the whole or part of the cost.

There are some individuals who are outside the scope of the present repatriation arrangements. Generally these are able-bodied men for whom work can be found by the Ministry of Labour. Men in this category are only offered repatriation when they are likely to become a continual charge on public funds and it is clearly in the public interest that they should be sent home. Some difficulty has been caused by shipowners who engage colonial seamen in foreign or Dominion ports without a repatriation clause in the articles of agreement. In general, it is not possible to exercise control over the recruitment of these men in foreign ships, but a despatch is being sent to Colonial Governments to see if any effective measures can be taken locally to obtain this control. A bigger difficulty arises from the fact that a number of colonial seamen on arrival in the United Kingdom have forfeited or voluntarily waived their repatriation rights. These men are usually paid off here, but, as there is no shortage of labour in the shipping industry, it has not been possible for more than a handful of them to be absorbed in seagoing employment. The Ministry of Transport and the shipping industry have recently reminded overseas representatives and the Masters of ships respectively to see that in all cases where colonial seamen are signed on there should be a repatriation clause in the articles of agreement, so that on arrival in this country the men may be repatriated at the expense of the shipping company concerned. No British coloured person can, however, be compelled to accept repatriation if he does not wish to go, and in many cases men recruited in this way decide to stay and try their luck.

(iv) *Colour discrimination*. As already mentioned, there is a certain amount of prejudice in this country against coloured people; for example, reluctance on the part of landladies to accept them as lodgers, and other manifestations on the part of private employers and workers and in social activities. This prejudice is not, however, capable of being overcome by direct legislative or administrative action. The Information Department of the Colonial Office is carrying out a planned programme of work designed to make the British public better informed about the Colonies and their peoples and to promote mutual understanding. Apart from this, the best service which the Colonial Office and other Departments of Government can render in this field is to grapple with the administrative problems in connection with the immigration, residence and employment of the relatively small group of coloured people who have not yet been absorbed into the normal life and work of the country, to see that they have their fair share of the amenities and opportunities available to the community in general, and to stimulate voluntary interest and service on their behalf.

Future Action

13. My Department has been under some pressure from Parliamentary and public sources to take special action in the way of setting up clubs and providing welfare officers to attend to the special needs of these people. It would, however, be a wrong policy to treat the colonial residents as a class apart from the community in general, though it must be recognised that they do need special guidance. Apart from the settled colonial community only some three or four thousand persons are involved, and by careful and continual attention to their needs I am confident that the problem can be kept within bounds without resort to any drastic measures. There are, however, certain lines of action which my Department can follow to prevent the

problem from growing in size and getting out of hand. These lines are generally as follows:—

(i) Pressure will be maintained on Colonial Governments to take all possible measures to prevent the embarkation of stowaways in Colonial ports. It will not be possible for any action to be taken to control their embarkation in foreign ports, apart from pressure on shipping companies.
(ii) The Colonial Office will, in consultation with Colonial Governments, continue to discourage the migration of unskilled workers from the West Indies, and to reduce the opportunities for aliens to obtain irregular documents which might gain them entry to the United Kingdom. Colonial Governments will be kept fully informed of the difficulties which men may expect to find on arrival in this country and will be asked to make them widely known among the public.
(iii) Efforts will continue to be made in consultation with voluntary organisations and local authorities to deal effectively with the social welfare of new additions to the colonial communities in the United Kingdom, particularly in regard to housing and social amenities. With this object in view, I propose to consult with non-official voluntary organisations such as the British Council of Churches and the National Council of Social Service.
(iv) The Colonial Office will continue to co-operate with the Ministry of Labour in their efforts to reduce by dispersal the number of unemployed colonials living in areas where work is not readily available.

355 CAB 128/17, CM 37(50)2 19 June 1950
'Coloured people from British colonial territories': Cabinet conclusions[1]

The Cabinet had before them a memorandum by the Secretary of State for the Colonies (C.P. (50) 113),[2] submitted in accordance with their request of 20th March, on the problems arising from the immigration into the United Kingdom of coloured people from British Colonial territories.

The Secretary of State for the Colonies said that social problems were more likely to arise if coloured immigrants into this country formed themselves into residential colonies, and his Department therefore sought to disperse these people over as wide an area as possible. In this they had the full support and assistance of the Ministry of Labour. Thus, the current policy was one of dispersal and assimilation; but the policy of assimilation undoubtedly presented great difficulties and, in order to overcome these, a concerted effort was needed on the part of the Government Departments and voluntary organisations concerned. The Secretary of State said that he had taken steps to convene a conference for this purpose on 10th July, which, he hoped, would lead to the establishment of a national advisory committee on which each of the official and unofficial agencies concerned with this problem would be represented.

A number of coloured people continued to find their way into this country from the Colonies as stowaways. Thus, information had just been received that a ship from

---

[1] Previous reference: see 353.

[2] See 354.

the West Indies was due to arrive at Bristol on the following day which had at least fourteen coloured stowaways on board.

The Cabinet's discussion turned mainly on the means of preventing any further increase in the coloured population of this country. Ministers were apprehensive lest the higher standards of social service in this country should attract here an undue proportion of the surplus population of the West Indies and other Colonial territories. They were doubtful whether the existing methods of administration, as described in C.P. (50) 113, were sufficient to keep within reasonable bounds the numbers who contrived to enter this country as stowaways. Was it clear that Colonial Governments and steamship companies were doing everything possible to prevent coloured people from stowing away on vessels bound for this country? If so, should further powers be taken to deal with stowaways? Should there be amending legislation to give the appropriate Minister discretion to require the owners of the vessel in which a stowaway arrived in this country to take him back, whatever his nationality, to the port at which he stowed away? Should not consideration also be given to the wider question whether the time had come to restrict the existing right of any British subject to enter the United Kingdom? In almost all other Commonwealth countries power had been taken to restrict the admission of British subjects from other parts of the Commonwealth. Was it certain that the balance of advantage still lay against taking this course in the United Kingdom itself?

The Cabinet agreed that a further review of these questions should be undertaken and that, at the appropriate stage in that review, the Law Officers should be consulted on the legal and constitutional issues involved.

The Cabinet:—

(1) Took note of C.P. (50) 113.

(2) Invited the Prime Minister to arrange for a review to be made of the further means which might be adopted to check the immigration into this country of coloured people from British Colonial territories, if legislation were passed limiting the right of British subjects, or of any class of British subjects, to enter and reside in the United Kingdom, and of the issues of policy involved in making such a change in the existing law.

356 CAB 129/41, CP(50)171 17 July 1950

'Employment of native-born administrators in the higher grades of colonial civil services': Cabinet memorandum by Mr Griffiths

At the Cabinet's meeting on 11th May (Con. [sic] (50) 30th Conclusions, Minute 6),[1] I was invited to submit a memorandum indicating what steps were being taken to introduce an adequate proportion of native-born administrators into the higher grades of the Colonial Civil Service, particularly in African and other colonies which are progressing towards self-government.

General

It has long been recognised that self-government in the Colonial territories will not

[1] See part 3 of this volume, 222.

be a reality until the administrative and executive machinery of government is operated by the people of the country. Most of the junior ranks of the Colonial civil services are already filled by locally born officers. Progress in increasing local appointments to the higher grades has inevitably varied in different territories. The desirability of such appointments is taken for granted. The limiting factor is the supply of suitably qualified local candidates who can take over the work without undue sacrifice of efficiency. The best way of attacking the problem, therefore, is to increase the sources of supply.

2. During the post-war years, particularly in West Africa, Malaya and the West Indies, there has been great progress in the provision of higher and technical education facilities, and further important developments in those territories are taking place.

3. In all Colonial territories there are scholarship schemes to enable students to train for posts of higher responsibility in Government Service. In addition £1 million has been allocated under the Colonial Development and Welfare Act, 1945 for similar scholarships. For the most part scholarships are tenable in the United Kingdom, but when possible scholars are placed at Universities or other institutions of higher education in the Colonial territories. Scholarships are granted to candidates already in Government service as well as to applicants straight from the schools. In awarding these scholarships care is taken to use them so as to encourage Colonial people to qualify themselves in branches of knowledge which will be of practical value in the economic and cultural progress of their communities. At present there are 1,713 Colonial students at Universities and 2,480 at non-university institutions in the United Kingdom; of these 1,500 are Colonial Government or Colonial Development and Welfare Scholars; the rest are private students, many of whom will take up higher grade Government posts. Details of those students holding Colonial Scholarships are given in Appendix A.[2]

There are also special schemes for Colonial Service training (details are given in Appendix B) some of which are designed to enable members of the public services to qualify for higher appointments. A separate allocation of £1½ million has been made for this purpose under the Colonial Development and Welfare Act.

4. In the following paragraphs details are given of the steps taken to introduce native-born officers into the higher ranks of the Colonial Service in all the African territories and those other Colonial territories which are moving towards self-government. Throughout this memorandum reference to "officers in the higher ranks of the Colonial Service" includes both administrative officers in the strict sense and those holding professional and technical posts, such as accountants and auditors, agricultural and forestry officers, customs officers, education officers, electrical, civil, mechanical, marine and mining engineers, labour officers, legal and judicial officers, surveyors and medical and veterinary officers.

West Africa

5. There has been a rapid increase in the last three years in the number of appointments of Africans to the higher ranks in the West African Colonies, and this rate of increase is being steadily accelerated. In Nigeria there are at present 364 (as against 26 in 1938 and 172 in 1948) Africans in the higher ranks as compared with

[2] Appendixes A and B not printed.

some 1,800 expatriates; in the Gold Coast the corresponding figures are 276 (as against 17 in 1928, 31 in 1938 and 98 in 1948) and 1,100; in Sierra Leone the figures in 1949 were 54 and 417. It will, however, be some time before there are enough qualified Africans to fill a majority of the higher posts in any of the West African Colonies.

6. Since 1948 the reports of local Committees or Commissions on the Africanisation of the higher civil service in Nigeria, the Gold Coast and Sierra Leone have been accepted by the Governments concerned. It is now officially recognised that expatriate candidates should only be recruited for Government posts when no suitable and qualified African is available, and that the policy of Africanisation should be pursued as rapidly as is consistent with the maintenance of present standards of efficiency.

7. In Nigeria, Public Service Boards with a majority of unofficial members were set up in 1949 with the object of selecting candidates for higher civil service posts and for scholarship and training schemes. Departmental selection boards have also been established to recommend junior officers for training and for promotion to the higher ranks. An Assistant Civil Service Commissioner for Nigeria is posted in London; he is specially concerned with the recruitment into the civil service of Nigerians who are undergoing training in the United Kingdom. Up to February, 1950, 243 scholarships or training awards had been made and provision of £250,000 for the three year period 1948–1951 has been made to meet the cost of scholarships and training for higher posts.

8. The progress of Africanisation of the Government Service of the Gold Coast was reviewed in 1949 by a Select Committee with a majority of African members, and recommendations for further Africanisation were made. These recommendations included the appointment of an African Commissioner for Africanisation whose duties would include the co-ordination of recruitment and scholarship policy. The further recommendation for the appointment of a Commission of Enquiry into the organisation of the whole Gold Coast service is now being implemented. In the Gold Coast 626 Government scholarship awards have been made since 1947.

9. In Sierra Leone, the Africanisation Committee recommend, as a short-term policy, the employment of suitable Africans from the junior grades in higher posts. The Committee's main recommendation was however concerned with measures for training suitable candidates by means of scholarship schemes. Ninety Government scholarships for overseas higher education courses have already been granted since 1947.

10. Facilities for higher education at University level have been developed in Nigeria and the Gold Coast since the end of the war and in 1948 a University College was established in each territory. The University College at Ibadan in Nigeria now has Faculties of Arts, Science, Medicine and Veterinary Science, and there are at present 295 students. The University College of the Gold Coast has departments of theology, philosophy, geology and economics and there are over 100 students. It is being developed as rapidly as possible, on the recommendation of the Africanisation Committee, to produce the highest possible number of graduates for the Africanisation programme. Faculties of Agriculture will be opened in both Colleges in October 1950 and in the course of the next few years each of the Colleges will provide facilities for degree course training for about 600 students. The two Colleges expect eventually to accommodate 2,000–3,000 students each.

11. Colleges of Arts, Science and Technology for higher technical education are also to be established shortly in Nigeria and the Gold Coast. They will provide, *inter alia*, courses in engineering, building, and surveying, accountancy, telecommunications, agriculture, forestry, veterinary science and secretarial and commercial practice. Within a few years, there will be about 600 students in the Nigerian College and 300 (eventually there will be 2,000) in the Gold Coast College. The students will come not only from the schools but also from the public services, and the colleges will take over much of the training now carried out by Government Departments. In Sierra Leone, Fourah Bay College is being reconstituted. It will continue to provide certain degree courses and in addition will establish training facilities similar to those proposed for the Nigerian and Gold Coast Colleges. There are at present over 200 students; eventually there will be 1,200.

12. It is the University Colleges and the new Colleges of Arts, Science and Technology which will in the future supply a large proportion of qualified candidates for appointment to the higher ranks in the West African Colonies.

Other African territories

13. With one exception in Tanganyika, there are no African officers holding higher administrative, professional or technical posts in any of the African territories outside West Africa. There are, however, a number of Africans carrying out important executive functions in all the East African territories, though they do not occupy posts which would otherwise be filled by Europeans. In Nyasaland, Northern Rhodesia and Somaliland, the policy of the local governments is first to educate Africans to fill the more responsible clerical posts. In the Somaliland Protectorate a number of Somalis have been appointed to the junior grades and the policy for the immediate future is to provide training to fit them for appointment to the middle grades, e.g., a few Somalis have recently been appointed as Administrative Assistants.

14. These East and Central African territories were in an exceedingly primitive state when they first came under British rule some fifty years ago, and the provision of adequate educational facilities has been and remains an enormous problem. It is, therefore, not surprising that there are no Africans in the higher Governments posts. More primary schools and some secondary and vocational schools are however now being built. At Makerere College, courses of University "intermediate" standard, open to students from all East African territories, are available in Arts, Science, Education, Medicine, Agriculture and Veterinary Science; certain courses for London University degrees are also now available. All the Colonial Governments grant scholarships for higher education to qualified students; these scholarships are for the most part tenable in University institutions in the United Kingdom. Many of the successful students may be expected to qualify for higher posts in Government Service. It will, however, be many years before appreciable numbers of qualified Africans with the necessary standards of integrity and the sense of responsible public service will be ready to hold senior Government appointments.

West Indies

15. About 50 per cent. of the higher posts in the administrative services in the West Indies are held by West Indian-born officers (in Barbados, the percentage is as much as 60). A very large number of medical, legal and technical posts are also held by West Indians. Expatriate officers are only appointed when West Indians of suitable

quality are not available.

16. The policy of appointing West Indian officers in the higher grades is well established and increasing numbers are being appointed.

17. The local governments also grant scholarships to students and serving officers with a view to appointing successful scholars to the higher ranks of the Colonial Service. These scholarships are tenable for the most part in the United Kingdom and Canada, but also, where suitable courses are available, at the University College of the West Indies.

18. Teaching at the University College of the West Indies began in 1948, and there are now Faculties of Medicine and Science, and a Faculty of Arts will be opened in October 1950. There are at present 70 students, but it is hoped that there will be as many as 2,000 when the College has been fully established.

Singapore and Malaya

19. The latest figures available show that, in the highest division in the Federation of Malaya Government Service, there were 181 substantive and acting posts filled by local officers, representing approximately 15 per cent. of the establishment. The corresponding figures in the Singapore Government Service were 102 and 23 per cent. In addition, the Malayan Civil Service, which is confined to high-grade administrative officers occupying the more senior appointments in both territories, had 30 Malays representing approximately 12 per cent. of the total membership.

20. In Singapore a Public Service Commission has now been established to advise on training, recruitment and promotion of local candidates, and it is the declared ultimate aim of Government policy to fill all senior posts by local appointments. In the Federation a Select Committee of Enquiry has been set up to examine the structure of the Public Service. The appointment of Malays is being encouraged by the promotion of suitable officers, by direct recruitment and by scholarship schemes although progress has been delayed in part by the reluctance of the Malay Rulers to consider the admission of non-Malays (e.g., Malayan-born Chinese) to senior posts.

21. In 1949, the University of Malaya was formally constituted. The University has faculties in Arts, Science and Medicine (including Dentistry). There are at present approximately 650 students, and it is hoped that the University will eventually provide higher education for 1,000 students.

22. Facilities for higher technical education in Malaya are provided at the Technical College, Kuala Lumpur. This College provides three-year courses of study in Civil, Mechanical, Electrical and Telecommunications Engineering, and in Surveying. At present there are approximately 200 students attending the College, but when new buildings, now in course of erection, are completed, it is hoped to provide courses for up to 700 students.

Hong Kong

23. In Hong Kong there are 395 higher civil service posts, of which 51 are at present held by local officers, most in the educational, medical, nursing and other professional services. There is one local-born member of the Administrative Service.

24. In correspondence concerning a Bill to authorise the appointment of a Public Services Commission the Governor expressed the opinion that for some years to come the majority of Hong Kong vacancies in the higher posts would have to be filled

from the United Kingdom; he emphasised in particular the difficulty of finding good local material for the Administrative Service and the Police.

25. The University of Hong Kong, which was opened in 1912 and which has faculties of Medicine, Engineering, Arts and Science, had an enrolment of 638 students for the year 1949–50. It is hoped to expand the capacity of the University shortly and also to increase the number of subjects provided for. Courses in building and wireless telegraphy and engineering are provided by the Technical College.

Other territories

26. (a) *Cyprus*. In Cyprus most of the junior posts and a third of the middle grade posts (e.g., District Judge, District Medical Officer, District Commissioner, &c.) are filled by local-born officers. In the higher posts there are six local-born officers (all in legal and judicial posts) and 34 expatriates.

27. There has been little progress towards increasing the number of local-born officers, but the Governor is about to recommend a reduction in the total number of expatriates.

28. In the ten-year priod 1946–1956, 150 scholarships will be granted for candidates who will fill Government posts on the successful completion of their training. All but fourteen of those so far awarded are tenable in the United Kingdom. A number of scholars have already been appointed to posts in the Government service, but the majority will not qualify until later in the period.

29. (b) *Mauritius and Seychelles*. Local officers have already largely replaced expatriates, and now occupy 75 per cent. and 40 per cent. respectively of the senior appointments in these two territories. No further rapid development is to be looked for in this direction, though there will be a gradual increase in these proportions as technically qualified officers gain further administrative experience. Scholarships for higher and technical education overseas are provided from local revenues and from Colonial Development and Welfare funds.

30. (c) *Fiji*. In Fiji there is one native-born head of a government department; there are also two Fijian Administrative Officers and seven other native-born officers who hold higher rank posts.

31. In Fiji and the Western Pacific High Commission territories, approved C.D. and W. schemes providing scholarships for secondary and university education will increase the numbers of locally-born persons who will in future be qualified for higher appointments.

Conclusion

32. From this survey it will be gathered that progress is being made all along the line in encouraging the flow of Colonial people into their own civil services. The key to the problem is education, not merely at the higher level but at all levels. The developments in the Colonial educational services during the last twenty-five years are now beginning to bear fruit, and the supply of suitably qualified Colonials for the higher posts will greatly increase as time goes on. But there is also a continuous increase in the demands of the territories for higher staff as the activities of government broaden out in proportion to the social and political progress of the Colonial communities. In the Colonial field as a whole, therefore, we shall for very many years to come need considerable numbers of qualified men and women from Britain and other parts of the Commonwealth.

357 CAB 128/18, CM 48(50)6 — 20 July 1950

'Native-born administrators in the colonial civil service': Cabinet conclusions

The Cabinet had before them a memorandum by the Secretary of State for the Colonies (C.P. (50) 171)[1] on the steps which were being taken to introduce an adequate proportion of native-born administrators into the higher grades of the Colonial Civil Service, particularly in Colonies which were progressing towards self-government.

The Secretary of State for the Colonies reminded his colleagues that the Cabinet had asked for this information when discussing on 11th May the progress of Nigeria towards self-government.[2] The application of the policy of employing native-born administrators was somewhat uneven, because of differing conditions in different Colonies. It largely depended on the provision of educational facilities for the training of students, either through scholarships tenable in the United Kingdom, or by establishing Universities in the Colonies concerned, which was the preferable course where practicable. It was essential to hold a balance between progress towards self-government in the political field and the recruitment of native-born administrators for the higher posts in the local Civil Service.

The Cabinet:—

Took note of C.P. (50) 171.

---

[1] See 356.

[2] See part 3 of this volume, 222.

358 CO 877/34/8 — 24–26 Oct 1950

[Africanisation of Kenya administrative service]: minutes by J B Williams[1] and Sir C Jeffries

The draft despatch on this file takes up with the Governor of Kenya a matter which was discussed by Mr. Cohen and Mr. Rogers[2] with Sir Philip Mitchell during his leave, namely the appointment of Africans to the Administrative Service in Kenya. That discussion is recorded in Mr. Newsam's[3] minute of 16th August.

The general situation with which we are faced is that there undoubtedly seems some reluctance on the part of the Kenya Government to appoint Africans to the Administrative Service, that the reasons for that reluctance are easily understandable when regard is had to the difficulties of posting, etc., but that it is clearly our duty to urge the Kenya Government to proceed as fast along the road as they can. Not only is it our duty but we know that even if we ourselves were disposed to be acquiescent in lack of progress the matter would certainly not be allowed to rest by the many persons and organisations in this country espousing African interests.

The object of the present exercise is therefore to send Kenya a despatch asking for a statement of their intentions in this matter. We know from the talk between Sir

---

[1] CO assistant under-secretary of state, responsible for Colonial Service and Welfare Depts.

[2] P Rogers, CO assistant secretary (establishment and organisation officer).

[3] R W Newsam, CO principal.

Philip Mitchell above referred to that he would find such a despatch helpful rather than the reverse.

After speaking to Mr. Rogers I have substituted a new draft for the one originally on this file because the latter gave me the impression (not intended I am sure by its draftsman) that we were putting this matter to the Kenya Government rather as a matter of form so that we could have an answer to critics. I am sure that it is essential to avoid giving any such impression and that we should make it quite clear that the Secretary of State regards this as a most important matter of policy. We shall be allowing Kenya to store up for themselves infinite trouble and bad relations in future if we do not do all within our power to make them realise that full scope must be given to the African inhabitants of the country as well as the Europeans, not merely in the legislative but also in the administrative side of Government. Otherwise the African intelligentsia in Kenya will be bound sooner or later to get it into their heads that all talk of advancement for their people is really a sham because we are not prepared to put them into positions in which they can exert real influence.

J.B.W.
24.10.50

I agree about the need to get this important question thrashed out.

There is much to be said for the view that our system of "district administration" is suited only to a phase in which a primitive society has to be organised and trained by experienced people who are not themselves members of that society. As educated local leaders emerge, it is questionable whether it is in the best interests of the people that these leaders should be absorbed into what is essentially an alien organisation. Yet to refuse to admit them arouses suspicion and misunderstanding. In West Africa we have been obliged, for political reasons, to admit Africans into the district administration; but the disadvantages of this course are to some extent offset by the probability that within the next few years district administration as we have known it will give place to local government. In East Africa such a development is doubtless much farther off, and the anomalous position of the occasional African district officer will present a more difficult problem.

C.J.J.
26.10.50

359 CAB 129/44, CP(51)51, annex 12 Feb 1951

'Immigration of British subjects into the United Kingdom: report by a Committee of Ministers', 6 Feb Cabinet memorandum circulated by the chairman, Mr Chuter Ede (Home Office)

At their meeting on 19th June, 1950 (C.M. (50) 37th Conclusions, Minute 2),[1] the Cabinet invited the Prime Minister to arrange for a review to be made of the further means which might be adopted to check the immigration into this country of coloured people from British Colonial territories, if legislation were passed limiting the right of British subjects, or of any class of British subjects, to enter and reside in

[1] See 355.

the United Kingdom, and of the issues of policy involved in making such a change in the existing law. To carry out this review the Prime Minister appointed an *ad hoc* Committee composed of the following Ministers:— Home Secretary (*in the Chair*), Minister of Labour, Minister of Health, Secretary of State for the Colonies, Secretary of State for Scotland, Secretary of State for Commonwealth Relations, Attorney-General.[2] Our report is as follows.

Extent

2. We first considered the extent of the problems presented by the immigration into this country of coloured people from British Colonial territories. For many years permanent communities of coloured persons of Colonial origin have lived in various parts of the United Kingdom. Most of them are either of West African or West Indian extraction, or Moslem people, mainly from Aden or Somaliland. In general, they look to this country as their home and have no intention of returning to their countries of origin. They are thought to number some 30,000, the larger groups being found in Merseyside, London, Cardiff and Tyneside.

3. Since 1945, at least 5,000 coloured immigrants from the Colonies, almost all West Africans or West Indians, have arrived here. They have come as stowaways, seafarers or fare-paying immigrant workers. Over the past four years the stowaways have arrived—and continue to arrive—at the rate of about 400 a year. It is not known how many have come as seafarers, but at present about 500 coloured men who are unemployed call themselves "seamen": there is no doubt that in the past many "one-trip seamen" have signed on in overseas ports for discharge in the United Kingdom in the vain hope of obtaining seafaring employment here. In the years following the war there were a number of notable shipments of fare-paying migrant workers. It is estimated that since 1945 about 2,000 migrant workers have arrived from the West Indies, many of them in large parties travelling in troopships at cheap rates. Since 1949 there have been no large parties, but there is reason to believe that the total number of workers arriving has not fallen off.

4. Unemployment and destitution among these coloured people of all types are not so widespread as to have any noticeable effect on our economy. On 24th July, 1950, the number of unemployed male Colonials (including the "seamen" mentioned above) in the main areas where coloured persons live was 1,102; the corresponding figure on 24th July, 1949, was 1,200. Many of these persons were only temporarily out of work. As regards reliance on national assistance, a sample check during one week in August 1950 showed that 572 coloured Colonials had applied for such assistance; 112 of them had come here as stowaways and 85 of these 112 had arrived during the last two years.

Possible legislation

5. We examined three possible methods involving legislation by which the entry of British subjects into the United Kingdom, or their residence here might be controlled. These are described in the following paragraphs and are: the application to British subjects of the controls now applied only to aliens; the deportation of British subjects coming within certain categories; and the return of British

[2] Labour—Mr H Marquand; Health—Mr A Bevan; Scotland—Mr H McNeil; Attorney-General—Sir H Shawcross.

stowaways to the territory from which they embarked or to which they belong.

6. *Application of aliens control to British subjects*. Powers might be taken similar to those now applied to aliens. An account of the law and practice relating to aliens is given in Appendix I.[3] Briefly, this method of control would mean that a British subject from a Colony or independent Commonwealth country would not be admitted to the United Kingdom unless the Immigration Officer were satisfied that he was a returning resident or genuine visitor, or was coming to take up employment authorised by the Ministry of Labour or for some approved purpose such as study. The primary object would be to ensure that British subjects who had no work in the United Kingdom did not settle here.

7. There would be no insuperable administrative difficulty in exercising the necessary control at the ports, though it would mean subjecting British subjects to some delays. The main burden of administration would, however, fall on the Ministry of Labour. The conditions for the grant of labour permits need not necessarily be identical with those applied to aliens but some check of the *bona fides* of the application would clearly be desirable. It would also be necessary to verify that wages and conditions of work were suitable even if there were no condition, such as that applied to aliens, that labour was not already available in this country. But in some industries and occupations the introduction of legislation to control the admission of citizens of the Commonwealth and Colonies might give rise to demands for safeguards of this type from competition by overseas labour.

8. The additional staff requirements needed to operate such an extension of the permit procedure would, of course, depend on the number of applications received but might be substantial. If the control were applied to persons from the Colonies and the independent Commonwealth countries, it would be difficult to justify the exemption of persons from the Irish Republic. On the basis of the number of applications for insurance cards it appears that some thirty or forty thousand persons come to Great Britain from the Irish Republic each year. The issuing of permits to all citizens of the Irish Republic who come for employment might, therefore, by itself, be almost as substantial a block of work as the present aliens permit administration, and it would be particularly unrewarding as there would be few, if any, Irish workers whom we should wish to exclude.

9. Such a system of control could not be effective without the interrogation of individuals and the imposition where necessary of landing conditions as in the case of aliens. A power to deport persons who broke their landing conditions would also probably be necessary.

10. *Deportation of British subjects*. The main problems in relation to the immigration of British subjects from Colonial territories arise because they are tempted to come to the United Kingdom by better prospects of employment and in the knowledge that if they fail to find work they will be supported by the social services at a higher standard of living than many of them had in the Colonies. A possible scheme would, therefore, be to leave the entry of British subjects into the United Kingdom unrestricted, but to empower the Home Secretary to deport any overseas British subject who had been resident in the United Kingdom for not more than two years (or perhaps a longer period) and who had (i) applied for national assistance; or (ii) been convicted of a serious offence; or (iii) attempted to create

[3] Appendixes I–III not printed.

industrial unrest. This last condition, which would be difficult to define in legislation, might operate only if a state of emergency had been declared. The Cabinet considered at their meeting on 27th July, 1949 (C.M. (49) 49th Conclusions, Minute 5) whether power should be taken to permit the deportation from the United Kingdom of British subjects who, not being United Kingdom citizens, engaged in subversive activities in this country, but no decision was reached.

11. A scheme on these lines would probably be administratively practicable, though we understand that it would involve certain difficulties for the National Assistance Board. There is also the point that in order to operate any system of deportation it is necessary to get some country overseas to receive the person deported. In the case of independent Commonwealth countries this should not give rise to serious difficulties since it could be established that the person was a citizen of the country concerned. But Colonials are citizens of the United Kingdom and Colonies, and it would be necessary to devise some means of determining to which Colony a particular person belonged; this would probably not be beyond solution in the majority of cases.

12. *Return of British stowaways*. A third possibility would be to confine any measures taken to British subjects who come to the United Kingdom as stowaways. This would deal with only part of the problem, but, nevertheless, a considerable improvement might be effected if power were taken to deal with this particularly difficult class of person. The existing practice in relation to alien stowaways is to refuse them leave to land. The master of the ship on which they came is under an obligation to take them back to the port from which they embarked and the owners or agents are under a contingent obligation to do so or to return them to the country of which they are nationals. In order to enable British stowaways to be dealt with similarly, it would be necessary to take power by legislation (i) to require the master, owners or agents of the ship to remove the stowaway to the territory from which he embarked for the United Kingdom or to the territory to which he belongs, (ii) to require the master to detain the stowaway on board until seen by the Immigration Officer, or, if the Immigration Officer so directs, to continue to detain him while the ship remains in port, and (iii) to place the stowaway temporarily on shore and to detain him there, either at the request of the master or on the instructions of the Immigration Officer. The powers relating to return of the stowaway and detention on shore would apply to stowaways found in the United Kingdom up to, say, two months from the date of arrival, and penalties would have to be prescribed not only for contraventions but for aiding and abetting contraventions. Corresponding powers would be necessary with regard to stowaways in aircraft. The new powers would be in addition to the existing powers in the Merchant Shipping Acts and the Air Navigation (Stowaways) Order; the existing powers would still be invoked in cases where it was thought necessary to prosecute a stowaway because his presence had endangered the craft. This general solution would not present administrative difficulties.

Issues of policy

13. The three possible courses outlined in paragraphs 6 to 12 above, all raise to a greater or less degree the following issues of policy:—

(i) The United Kingdom has a special status as the mother country, and freedom to enter and remain in the United Kingdom at will is one of the main practical benefits enjoyed by British subjects, as such. All the Colonies and independent Commonwealth countries (except, at present, India and Pakistan) impose restrictions on the entry into their territory of British subjects, though the extent of the restrictions varies. An account of the law and practice on this matter in the Colonies, independent Commonwealth countries and the Irish Republic is given in Appendix II.

(ii) The present concept of British nationality, as embodied in the British Nationality Act, 1948, is that British nationality is derived through citizenship of any one of the self-governing countries within the Commonwealth. For citizenship purposes, the United Kingdom together with the Colonies forms one unit and it would be contrary to the scheme to subdivide that unit. Furthermore, it would be difficult to justify restrictions on persons who are citizens of the United Kingdom and Colonies, if no comparable restrictions were imposed on persons who are citizens of other Commonwealth countries, or even, as in the case of citizens of the Irish Republic, are citizens of a country outside the Commonwealth. Yet on general grounds it is undesirable particularly at the present stage of Commonwealth development, that such restrictions should be imposed on citizens of the independent Commonwealth countries and it is agreed policy that in these matters the Irish Republic shall be treated on a similar basis to Commonwealth countries.

(iii) Any solution depending on an apparent or concealed colour test would be so invidious as to make it impossible of adoption. Nevertheless, the use of any powers taken to restrict the free entry of British subjects to this country would, as a general rule, be more or less confined to coloured persons. We consider that this fact provides an argument in favour of limiting any powers taken to the exclusion of specific and well defined categories of persons, such as those who become a charge on public funds or stowaways, whose continued presence here is clearly open to objection. Even so, coloured persons would be mainly concerned, and this might possibly give rise to resentment in India, Pakistan and Ceylon and in the more advanced Colonial territories.

14. It has been suggested to us that, if the scope of a Bill on stowaways on the lines indicated in paragraph 12 above were widened to cover both alien and British stowaways and were presented as a measure dealing with stowaways in general, it might thereby be made less controversial. But the existing powers of the Aliens Order are quite adequate to deal with alien stowaways, and it would be difficult to argue that they need to be duplicated. Moreover, if powers to deal with alien stowaways were included in the Bill, there would be a risk that through amendments made during its passage the existing powers would be weakened.

Conclusions

15. In view of the comparatively small scale of immigration into this country of coloured people from British Colonial territories (see paragraph 2 above) and the important and controversial issues of policy involved in legislation to control it, we consider that no such legislation should at present be introduced. Even the legislation on stowaways outlined in paragraph 12—the least far-reaching of the methods of control we have considered—would mean a break in the traditional policy of giving all British subjects the right to enter the United Kingdom and to

enjoy the same rights and privileges as are given to United Kingdom citizens. We are aware, however, that in the long-term social standards in the Colonies lower than those in the United Kingdom, may well result in considerable migration to this country and that the social services in the United Kingdom, particularly the rights of which any destitute person can avail himself under the National Assistance Act, must inevitably act as a considerable attraction. We recognise that a very large increase in such migration in the future might produce a situation in the United Kingdom rendering legislation for its control essential, despite the very strong opposing considerations which we have mentioned; but, for the present, we regard these opposing considerations as conclusive. The Secretary of State for the Colonies has undertaken to advise his colleagues if, at any time, there are indications of any large increase above the present scale of immigration from the Colonies, so that the question of introducing legislation may then again be considered.

Administrative measures to control stowaways

16. In view of our conclusion that legislation would not, under present circumstances, be justified, we thought it proper to review in some detail administrative measures for the control of stowaways and "one-trip seamen" from Colonial territories, not involving legislation. The Minister of Transport took part with us in this review. An account of these administrative controls is given in Appendix III. Their effect is limited, but we consider that if applied vigorously they should, under present conditions, prevent serious difficulty. We therefore recommend that these measures should continue and should be made as effective as possible.

Summary

In brief, our conclusions and recommendations are as follows:—

(i) At least 5,000 coloured immigrants from the Colonies have arrived in the United Kingdom since 1945. They have come as stowaways, "one-trip seamen" and fare-paying immigrant workers. Unemployment and destitution among coloured Colonials in this country is not so widespread as to have any noticeable effect on our economy (paragraphs 2 to 4).

(ii) Three possible methods of control would be: to apply to British subjects the controls now applied to aliens (paragraphs 6 to 9); to deport British subjects coming within certain categories (paragraphs 10 and 11); to return British stowaways to the territory from which they embarked or to which they belong (paragraph 12).

(iii) Each of these methods of control would be controversial and at variance with our traditional policy of giving all British subjects the right to enter and reside in the United Kingdom (paragraphs 13 and 14).

(iv) We consider that the introduction of legislation to control immigration from the Colonies would not at present be justified (paragraph 15).

(v) We recommend that the Departments concerned should continue to render as effective as possible administrative measures for the control of stowaways and "one-trip seamen" from Colonial territories (paragraph 16).

360 CO 967/143, no 2 8 May 1951

[Possible appointment of 'a coloured person to a colonial governorship']: letter from Sir T Lloyd to Sir G Seel

[In January 1949 Creech Jones told Seel there was a need to appoint 'a person of colour' to a colonial governorship. Seel agreed this was desirable and necessary; Norman Manley[1] had the necessary integrity and intellect, but led a political party, and colonial nationalism in West Africa would operate to prevent his appointment there. Sir C Jeffries pointed out that it was of paramount importance that the first experiment should be successful; he believed 'the likeliest colony for the first experiment in this field is the Gambia, and the likeliest candidate for that Governorship is Mr Korsah'.[2] Cohen agreed as to the value of having a coloured governor, the suitability of the Gambia and the excellent potential of Mr Korsah—provided Gambian opinion would accept the idea. Lord Listowel hoped the experiment would be made as soon as possible. Sir T Lloyd described it as a question of 'great interest and complexity'. Creech Jones found the survey of this question useful, but the situation revealed was not encouraging: 'I hope we shall, however, keep in mind the idea' (minutes, 28 Jan–16 Feb 1949). Lloyd raised the matter again in this letter. Nobody found it easy to suggest names. The consensus seemed to be that a non-political governor would carry more weight, and in any case after federation in the West Indies there would be a shortage of political leaders. Seel thought Dr P M Sherlock[3] had the right detachment and social acceptability, but according to Governor Foot he was not strong enough (minute, 27 June 1951).]

I am sorry to have been so long in replying to your letter of the 22nd of March about your talk with [Mr V] Bryan, Minister of Agriculture in Trinidad, about the appointment of West Indians to the highest offices. As you said that you had shown your letter to Luke[4] I kept it to talk over with him after his return from the Caribbean, and I have only now got round to it. I agree with all that you say about the importance of satisfying reasonable West Indian opinion on this issue. There are, as I see it, three main considerations. First, the Secretary of State must have complete confidence that the first person selected for what would be a most important experiment has all the qualities which should ensure its success; a failure at the outset, though it would make repetition difficult, would not be likely to deter vociferous demands from other Caribbean territories that they too should have a West Indian Governor. Secondly, the person selected for the experiment should be one who commands respect throughout the British Caribbean and who is acceptable to the territory he is sent to govern; for reasons given later I doubt whether at this stage it would be wise to make anyone Governor of his own territory. Thirdly, it must be recognised that it might be very difficult for even the best of West Indian politicians to make comfortably and successfully the sharp transition to the detachment of Governorship, and that it may therefore be necessary to look outside the political field.

It may help if, at this point, I recalled the conclusions reached in minutes here (to which you contributed) in 1949 and then accepted by the late Secretary of State. They are as follows:—

---

[1] N W Manley, KC, founder of the Jamaican People's National Party (1938); later chief minister (1955–1959) and prime minister (1959–1962) of Jamaica.

[2] K A Korsah, CBE, puisne judge of the Gold Coast since 1945.

[3] Dr P M Sherlock, historian, vice-principal and director of extra-mural studies, University College of the West Indies.

[4] S E V Luke, assistant under-secretary of state.

"(a) That [there] should be no question of appointing a coloured person to a Colonial Governorship otherwise than on strict merits, and every care must be taken to make as certain as is humanly possible that the first experiment of this kind is successful;
(b) That Mr. Grantley Adams[5] must be ruled out for reasons[6] given in the third paragraph of Mr. Seel's minute. The only other real possibilities from the West Indies are Mr. Manley (in the unlikely event of his being prepared thus to give up his political career) and Sir Harold Allan;[7]
(c) That neither Mr. Manley nor Sir Harold Allan could well be appointed to Jamaica, and West Indian parochialism and jealousy would be great handicaps to them if appointed elsewhere in the Caribbean; and
(d) That the Gambia is the most promising place for trying out the experiment of a coloured Governor and on present information and showing the likeliest candidates are the two West Indians already mentioned and Mr. Korsah."

By and large those conclusions to my mind still hold good. Also I am doubtful, as I have already said, whether any West Indian should yet be appointed to govern his own Colony. I have two reasons for that view. One is that anyone but a quite exceptional man would have difficulty in ridding himself of local prejudices and attachments and even more difficulty in convincing public opinion that he was in fact free of them. Secondly, a locally appointed Governor would presumably continue after retirement to reside in his native territory and his presence there might easily be an embarrassment to his successor.

I have not put your letter up to Ministers at this stage as I should like first to have your views about (a) possible candidates from the Caribbean for a small Governorship, and (b) which place in the Caribbean you would think most appropriate for the experiment in the case of any individuals whose claims you think worth consideration. There is, of course, no hurry about this if only because no Governorship likely to come into this picture is expected to be vacant this year. Two names which have come up in discussion here are Springer[8] and Sherlock, both now at the West Indian University, and when you do reply I shall be most interested to know whether either of them is in your view remotely "possible" for this particular purpose.

---

[5] Grantley H Adams, leader of House of Assembly and member of Executive Council in Trinidad.

[6] The letter was annotated at this point: 'i.e. that the appointment would be regarded as a reward for subservience to H.M.G.'s policy'.

[7] Sir H E Allan, minister of finance, Jamaica, 1945; a businessman.

[8] H W Springer, registrar (secretary), University College of the West Indies.

361 CO 554/134/12, p 35 7 Jan 1946

[Higher education in West Africa]: minute by Mr Creech Jones on the Elliot Commission's reports[1]

[Col Walter Elliot's Commission reported its findings early in 1945. The majority report recommended the establishment of three university colleges (Ibadan, Fourah Bay and Achimota); but there was a minority report (signed by Sir Geoffrey Evans, Sir H Channon, Creech Jones, Julian Huxley and Margaret Read)[2] recommending a comprehensive unitary British West African university college at Ibadan, for which three merely territorial colleges (Nigeria, Gold Coast, and Sierra Leone + Gambia) would act as 'feeders'. The powerful group who signed the minority report believed British West Africa could not sustain more than a single university of high quality; three institutions, they argued, would be under-staffed and under-used (CO 554/134/12, no 8). The 'minority' argument was persuasive on administrative grounds: it was in line with the conclusions of the Asquith Report[3]; it was strongly supported by governors Sir A Burns and Sir H Stevenson (of the Gold Coast and Sierra Leone respectively), by Sir C Cox (CO educational adviser), and Creech Jones claimed 'most competent people to judge here would agree' (CO 554/135/1). Accordingly, a despatch of 1 Oct 1945 declared the CO's preference for the minority report (CO 554/134/3). The political reaction had been seriously misjudged, however, and there was an outcry in the Gold Coast and Sierra Leone. Creech Jones worked hard to produce a persuasive White Paper and to find some compromise concession which would mollify Gold Coast opinion, such as allowing 'post-intermediate' studies in arts and sciences, though avoiding overlapping with Ibadan. The Gold Coasters refused to accept anything less than full degree courses. Sir A Dawe analysed (see 362) the dilemma facing the S of S; and on another file commented that 'the whole business contains an interesting political lesson for us' (CO 554/134/13, minute, 6 June 1946). In the end, Creech Jones backed down, and agreed to the establishment of a university college in the Gold Coast, since educational advance 'must have active public support' and the Gold Coast was willing to finance it. But he still did not believe Sierra Leone could finance its own university college (CO 554/144/2, despatch, 16 Aug 1947).]

If the Minority Report is strongly opposed & some other course has to be pursued, the *Majority proposals* are *not the alternative*.[4] It would be wrong (just to satisfy African clamour in a matter which is only dimly understood in the Gold Coast & which is a reaction from their own emphatic stand of 2 years ago) to repudiate the principles of the Asquith Report, to discard the experienced judgment of the Minority Commissioners & to jump into a position that involves no real solution of the higher education problem in the Gold Coast or West Africa. Meantime, we must wait the reports from the other 3 Governors & we must discuss the problem with the S. of S. before he goes to West Africa.

---

[1] *Report of the Commission on Higher Education in West Africa* (chairman, Col Walter Elliot), Cmd 6655, 1945.

[2] Geoffrey Evans was an economic botanist at the Royal Botanic Gardens, Kew; Henry Channon was a Conservative MP; Julian Huxley was a biologist and director-general of UNESCO, 1946–1948; Margaret Read was head of the Department of Education in Tropical Areas at the Institute of Education, University of London.

[3] *Report of the Commission on Higher Education in the Colonies*, Cmd 6647, 1945. The chairman, Sir Cyril Asquith, was judge of the High Court of Justice (King's Bench Division), 1938–1946.

[4] Emphasis in original.

362 CO 554/135/3, pp 7, 15–17 18 & 26 June 1946

[Higher education in West Africa]: minutes by Sir A Dawe on the Elliot Commission's reports [Extracts]

. . . I agree that the stage has been reached where it is desirable for the Secretary of State to bring the debate to issue and give a decision. But at the same time I feel that it would be most unfortunate for him to attempt to impose a decision which would not in the event be able to withstand any strong currents of local opinion running against it. In view of the way in which feeling on this subject has developed on the Coast, I do not feel confident that it will be possible as years go on to sustain the decision that there should only be one unitary university in West Africa situated in Nigeria. Is it not possible that, with the growing local patriotism of the Gold Coast and its rivalry with Nigeria, which will soon find a means of political expression in the new constitution, it will eventually be found that any unitary scheme which we attempt to impose on paper from Downing Street will be wrecked?
. . .

A.J.D.
18.6.46

. . . The new draft [despatch], in waiving any objections to the arts or science facilities [sic] at Achimota, should make the decision more palatable to the Gold Coast.

But I feel bound to say that the more I think about this question the more doubtful I become whether it is possible or desirable to impose the policy of a unitary university. Personally, I have always agreed with the Minority findings, and it seems to me that, on administrative and practical grounds, they are not open to serious question. But what the Secretary of State now has to consider is essentially a political problem, i.e. whether it is possible or wise for him to attempt to impose a policy which, however, sound administratively, does run up against some forces in the political field which are strong and seem bound to become stronger. Does it not seem likely that, whatever decision we may seek to impose on paper from here, the Gold Coast will, in fact, as time goes on, develop Achimota into a university of their own? The people there seem to have the desire to do this & the financial means: and they are increasingly acquiring the political power to do what they want. Is it advisable for us to appear to impose a decision on a situation where events, before long, may show only too clearly that we have no power to do so? These are the doubts which occur to me, and I can only hope, if the decision is taken, that they will be falsified by events.
. . .

A.J.D.
26.6.46

363 CO 859/89/8, no 31, EC/11/46 18 July 1946

'Education for citizenship': skeleton draft interim report[1] of the Sub-Committee of Advisory Committee on Education in the Colonies, by W E F Ward (chairman)

A. Definition of the problem as originally made by Mr. Creech Jones and adopted by the Sub-Committee:— "The problem, with a developing people, of building up a sense of public responsibility, tolerance and objectivity in discussion and practice, an understanding of social values and democratic practice, and an appreciation of political institutions, their evolution and progress". Importance of the problem at this stage in colonial development.

B. Aspects to be considered:—

(a) diversity of colonial conditions—culture, social background and institutions, economic structure, etc;
(b) need to take account of native culture and social organisation: education must be based partly on native culture, etc. if it is to make root and draw on (and contribute to) spiritual forces in native life;
(c) but education must also be based partly on best elements of Western culture—in this instance, political and social culture: the essence of democracy—not necessarily blindly copying details of British or American or Swiss institutions but inculcating the spirit which inspires them;
(d) present wide-spread evidence of maladjustment (see below), economic, psychological, etc: and problems arising from impact of Western materialistic economy on primitive organisations.

C. General view of present conditions:—

(a) widespread tension—Nigeria, W. Indies for example;
(b) incipient nationalism;
(c) press campaigns: irresponsible politicians: graft;
(d) gap between illiterate peasant and semi-literate townsman, between traditional elders and young "intellectuals": increasing futility of traditional native organisations;
(e) wide-spread illiteracy: narrow base of educational pyramid and inadequacy of Government contact with credulous and neglected masses;
(f) grievances openly put forward by native leaders:
 (i) economic exploitation by European business
 (ii) inadequate share of "educated" in administration of their own country etc., etc.

and remedies they propose—nationalisation etc.—how far are these consciously expressed grievances the real trouble, and how far merely symptoms of a deeper semi-conscious feeling of frustration? And consequently, how far can adoption of their suggested remedies help the situation?

What are the true causes of these disquieting symptoms? Analogy of adolescence: assertiveness and lack of self-confidence.

---

[1] Eventually the full report was published as Colonial No 216, 1948.

D. Need to decide general lines on which we wish colonies to develop politically:—

(a) democratic spirit: discussion of its essentials as seen in Britain or Switzerland, and democratic elements in spirit and form of native constitutions as in Gold Coast. Importance of preserving spirit and not killing spirit by too literal adherence to European forms.

(b) necessary foundations for democracy:

(i) straight thinking;

(ii) public spirit—unselfishness;

(iii) well-informed citizens—politically and technically;

(iv) communal solidarity—general confidence in fellow-citizens;

(v) feet on the ground: not abstract doctrinaire theorising, or pedantic tidy-minded bureaucracy aiming first at administrative convenience, but test of greatest practical good to greatest number;

(vi) belief in value of individual.

E. Education must aim at developing these qualities and providing the technical skills and information required:—

(a) what can and should be done in school?;

(b) what can and should be done outside school? (adult education).

(review methods now in use for both types of work—e.g. Bakhter Ruda,[2] and other evidence we have received.)

F. General agreement on certain principles:—

(a) citizenship is one of the things which can only be adequately learnt by practice—by one's own mistakes;

(b) therefore, advances in political responsibility cannot wait "until people are ready" for them;

(c) local government (properly run) is a school for national government;

(d) long-term work through the school and short-term work through adult education must both be made plainly useful by concurrent advances in self-government—cooperatives, education committees, municipalities, etc., tending towards complete self-government.

---

[2] An experimental institution in the Sudan. See footnote on p xxvii of Introduction, in part 1 of this volume.

364 CO 859/145/2, nos 18–25 9 July 1947

'Forced labour': despatch from Mr Creech Jones to the governments of various colonies[1]. *Annex*: 'Forced labour convention', memorandum by G StJ Orde Browne[2] (1 Nov 1946)

I have the honour . . . to refer to my despatch . . . dated the 4th March last transmitting . . . copies of a report, as communicated to the International Labour Office, on the operation of the International Convention concerning forced or compulsory labour during the year ending 30th September, 1946.

2. I have recently been giving special consideration to this Convention and in particular to the possibilities of reducing still further recourse to forced or compulsory labour in the territory under your administration.

3. As you are aware, the Convention, the provisions of which His Majesty's Government has applied without modification to non-self-governing British territories, lays down that forced labour, as defined, shall be suppressed in all its forms within the shortest possible period. It is recognised, however, by paragraph 2 of Article 1 that, with a view to this complete suppression, recourse to forced or compulsory labour may be had during the transitional period for public purposes only and as an exceptional measure, subject to certain conditions and guarantees.

4. Forced or compulsory labour, as defined by the Convention, is permitted by legislation and exacted in the Gold Coast, Kenya, Nigeria, Uganda, Nyasaland, Sierra Leone, Tanganyika Territory and North Borneo, and while in all these territories the conditions and guarantees laid down in the Convention are observed, the use of forced or compulsory labour is considerable for such services as porterage (Article 18), minor public works (Article 10) and for chiefs who exercise administrative functions (Article 7).

5. From reports submitted by the first seven territories enumerated in the preceding paragraph it seems however that there is a divergence of view on what is forced labour within the meaning of the Convention. Some of the activities reported as forced labour by these Governments are work or services which by Article 2 or Article 19 are excluded from the definition of "forced or compulsory labour" and should not be reported in the Annual Report for communication to the International Labour Office.

6. Accordingly in order to remove as far as possible any doubt that exists as to the exact meaning and application of the various articles of the Convention, I have consulted my Advisers and now enclose a memorandum prepared by my late Labour Adviser, Major Sir Granville Orde Browne, analysing the Conventional requirements. For ease of reference I also transmit copies of the Convention itself and Recommendations and of the Questionnaire issued in 1936 by the International Labour Office which provides for the form of Annual Report to be submitted by Members who have ratified the Convention.[3]

7. You will see from the Memorandum that I am advised that the exaction of work

---

[1] Sent to: Gold Coast, Nigeria, Sierra Leone, Kenya, Nyasaland, Tanganyika, Uganda, North Borneo. (See para 4.) Also sent, for information, to Northern Rhodesia, Gambia and Zanzibar.

[2] Sir Granville Orde Brown, CO labour adviser, 1938–1947 (died 12.5.47).

[3] Not printed.

or services for soil conservation and other similar measures essential for the life and welfare of the community can be fully justified under Article 2 or Article 19 either severally or in combination with each other. Such work, being permitted by Article 2 or 19 is not "forced labour" within the meaning of the Convention. I am further advised that the time is not yet ripe for the total abolition of forced labour exacted under Articles 7, 10 and 18.

8. I should be grateful if you would arrange for all officers concerned to be supplied with a copy of the Memorandum on the Convention. They will find in it not only a clear statement of the position but also valuable guidance as to the information to be furnished in the annual reports and the appropriate Article under which the information should be shown. Thus, particulars of work or services exacted for the purposes enumerated in Article 2(a)–(e) inclusive or under Article 19 should not be shown in the Annual Report or in the special report provided for by Article 22, but forced labour under Articles 7, 10 and 18 should be reported under those Articles respectively.

9. I now turn to the important question of the continued existence of forced labour in Colonial territories. The Convention was ratified in 1931 by His Majesty's Government who thereby undertook to suppress all forms of forced labour, as defined in the Convention, within the shortest possible period. The annual reports forwarded to me show that despite the considerable time that has since elapsed, forced labour is legally permitted and exacted in certain Colonial territories. I fully accept the position that certain forms of compulsory work or services are excluded by Articles 2 and 19 from the definition of "forced or compulsory labour", and I accept my late Labour Adviser's view that resort to compulsion for soil conservation measures such as terracing etc. can be justified under Article 2 or Article 19. Indeed such measures are the basis of the welfare and livelihood of rural communities and of future economic development. I am anxious that this may be clearly understood by all concerned. On the other hand I consider that any work or service exacted by compulsion, falling within the conventional definition of "forced labour", is undesirable except in cases of emergency, and that broadly such work or service ought to cease in all Colonial territories. I should prefer to see its total abolition by the repeal of legislation under which it is permitted; alternatively if such a course is not feasible administrative measures should be employed to bring about a progressive reduction in the purposes for which compulsory labour may be exacted and the number of cases in which it is in fact resorted to.

10. I should be glad if you would review the whole position so far as concerns the territory under your administration and inform me what are the possibilities of abolishing by legislation or alternatively by reducing, through administrative action, recourse to compulsion in respect of the services referred to in Articles 7, 10 and 18 of the Convention.

Annex to 364

Some doubt appears to exist as to the exact meaning and application of the various sections of the Forced Labour Convention, and in some colonies its provisions are apparently understood [sic]. The following analysis has therefore been prepared in order to indicate the principal features, and then to examine their application in specific instances; after consideration, and reference to the legal advisers, it may prove suitable as a basis for a circular despatch on the subject.

After an introductory passage, Article 2 (766 of the International Labour Code) defines "forced or compulsory labour" as all work [or] service which is exacted from any person under the menace of any penalty and for which the said person has not offered himself voluntarily. Section 2 then states that the term "forced or compulsory labour" does not include (a) military employment; (b) the normal civil obligations of the citizens of a fully self-governing country; (c) prison labour; (d) any work or service exacted in case of emergency, such as war or calamity in the form of fire, flood, famine, earthquake, disease, pests, and generally, anything that would endanger the existence or wellbeing of the population; (e) minor communal services performed in the interests of the community, provided that the members of the community are consulted in regard to the need.

The last two sections of the foregoing definitions may need some care in application to certain cases; for instance, under (d) the compulsion is obviously restricted to cases of real emergency of short duration; it is not intended to apply to measures taken to deal with prolonged requirements, however urgent these may be. (e) restricts the use of compulsion to the actual local needs of the community concerned, and requires their consultation as to the need. Thus the annual clearing of the paths around a village would come under this section, but the upkeep of a main motor road, or the construction of an aerodrome, would be outside it. This Article should be read in conjunction with Articles 9 and 19, dealt with below.

It will be observed that the foregoing paragraphs rule out the various forms of labour enumerated from the definition of forced labour; in other words, they are not to be regarded as such, and therefore can be included in a special section, for information, in the reports mentioned in Article 22 (789 of the Code) which are to contain full particulars about any resort to forced labour.

The Convention then goes on to deal with the circumstances of forced labour, the "competent authority" approving it being either the metropolitan country or the highest authority of the territory concerned. Articles 4 and 5 (768 and 769 of the Code) prohibit its use for private individuals or concessionaires, and Articles 6 and 7 prohibit officials and chiefs resorting to it. Article 8 allows of delegation by the highest authority to local authorities to enable them to resort to forced labour in certain cases.

Article 9 (773 of the Code) is important, as it details the circumstances in which forced labour may be justified. These are (a) that the work to be done is of important direct interest to the community concerned; (b) that it is of present or imminent necessity; (c) that voluntary labour is unobtainable for the purpose; and (d) that the labour will not lay too heavy a burden on the community concerned.

Some discrimination may be necessary to decide how far a particular requirement comes within the foregoing definitions of permissible resort to compulsion, or on the other hand, whether it may not come within the terms of Article 2, 2, (d) and (e). Analysing the conditions, (a) may be regarded as allowing compulsion for the construction of a bridge or road which is urgently needed for the supply of food to the local community which is famine stricken, but it cannot be considered as applying in the case of a bridge of general need to the public, but not of special labour importance. The difference between Article 2 and Article 9 might be illustrated by the case of a vitally important bridge which is threatened by a grass fire; clearly compulsion to save it is sanctioned by Article 2, 2, (d), which takes the labour out of the category of forced labour. But if the bridge has been burnt, and its repair is urgently needed to bring up supplies of food, it is no longer a case of emergency in the face of calamity, since the fire is out; but it is work of "present or imminent necessity" for the community, and is therefore sanctioned by Article 9 (b). It will in that case require inclusion in the list of occasions when forced labour has been employed. Article 9 (c) introduces a decisive factor in differentiation, by the stipulation that force is not justified if voluntary labour can be procured. In the foregoing instance of the bridge, therefore, the imminence of the necessity will form the criterion. If the repair of the bridge is immediately essential to save lives of starving people, compulsion is obviously justified; if however it is only required at an early date, or if in any case some delay must arise through waiting for the arrival of materials for construction, the necessary labour may well be procurable within a reasonable distance; the offer of better wages, or more probably improved conditions or rations, may serve to attract volunteers. Still less will it be possible to justify compulsion in the case of some major work such as an embankment, canal, etc., required to protect an area from flood. Such a work will probably continue for months or possibly years, and, although it may be of great importance to the local community, it can hardly be regarded as of "imminent necessity" to an extent that precludes the supply of labour from a distance. In such a case, the construction is probably of the type that might well be carried out by a contractor; clearly, the contractor would not expect to be supplied with forced labour, so a resort to this on the part of the Government would not be justified.

Article 10 (774 of the Code) deals with forced labour exacted as a tax, or by chiefs for the execution of public works, and states that this shall be "progressively abolished". Compulsory labour for chiefs may take one of two forms. I[t] may be a survival of the old custom whereby the chief was entitled to service from every member of the community, in order to maintain the communal resources for relief of necessity, exercise of hospitality, etc., or it may be the use of powers conferred on the chief for the execution of public works such as road construction. The first of these was originally well justified, but tends in modern conditions to become a perquisite for the chief, and a mere addition to his income, and is thus objectionable; the second is a crude method of carrying out public works which may be admissible in primitive circumstances but is increasingly liable to lead to corruption and inefficiency. Hence the stipulation that each of these forms of compulsion shall be progressively abolished; pending its disappearance, conditions governing its use are laid down, and will be found to be the same as those in Article 9, except that the work must not entail any moving of the population, and must accord with custom and also agricultural requirements.

Articles 11 to 15 (775 to 779 of the Code) detail the conditions to be observed in the management of forced labour. Limitations of age, period of employment, duration of working hours, weekly rest, wages and rights to workmens compensation are included. Article 16 (780 of the Code) reluctantly sanctions occasional transfer of forced labour to distant places where climatic conditions differ from those of the home area; in such cases, appropriate medical safeguards are detailed for observance. Article 17 elaborates these provisions and makes rules for the benefit of families, and for the journey and eventual repatriation.

Article 18 (782 of the Code) deals with forced labour for transport of persons or goods, "such as the labour of porters or boatmen"; this is to be abolished "within the shortest possible period". Porterage was formerly one of the main causes for resort to compulsion, since without it, much essential travelling and transport would have been impossible; with the extension of the road systems, and the increasing use of motor vehicles, however, the use of human carriage has rapidly dwindled. The duty of including figures for porterage in the annual returns of forced labour serves to ensure a constant revision of its use with a view to its reduction by further resort to mechanical means, and also by methodical planning of transport so as to utilise favourable seasons and weather. Human carriage is a wasteful, uneconomic and unpopular form of transport, to be eliminated as far as possible; nevertheless, there will for long remain certain remote areas where hilly or swampy country precludes the use of motor vehicles, and in such cases emergencies will still justify compulsory porterage, since it would be manifestly unreasonable to risk the spread of epidemic disease or other threat to the community, merely because of a meticulous reluctance to use compulsion for a brief period to enable the doctor or the administrative officer to reach the danger point. The Article goes on to define strictly the conditions to be observed in cases where this form of forced labour is used.

Article 19 (783 of the Code) authorises a resort to compulsion to ensure the cultivation necessary to safeguard the community against famine; this must always be on condition that the resultant food or produce remains the property of the community producing it. This therefore completely rules out compulsion for the production of a crop which is to be subsequently sold to a specified purchaser; it even precludes the compulsory sale to government of surplus to be used for the relief of less fortunate communities elsewhere; such a step however would hardly be required, since any surplus resulting from the compulsory cultivation would no doubt be readily sold by the growers. It would be observed that this resort to compulsion does not admit of the use of "educative forced labour" as advocated by certain colonial powers; i.e. insistence on the planting of a particular crop of special suitability, in order to enrich a certain area. A plausible case may be made out for this form of compulsion, and the British authorities formerly regarded it as legitimate; (the great Uganda cotton industry originated in compulsion). In practice, however, it has been found to lead so rapidly to restricted right of sale, price regulation, irksome insistence and supervision and other objectionable features, that it is excluded from the permissive clauses of the Convention, agricultural development and progress depending rather upon education and propaganda.

Paragraph 2 of Article 19 is of great importance, as it expressly maintains the obligation on members of a community to perform the work demanded by the community by virtue of law or custom. This covers the duties falling upon members of a tribe where a custom requires periodical communal effort; it also foresees the time when this tribal custom shall be superseded by the laws of a community evolved on democratic lines. It may in fact well be read in conjunction with the provisions of Article 2, (2), (e) referring to minor communal services in connection with which the members of the community have the right to be consulted. These two articles may be regarded as complementary, and borderline cases may be difficult to assign precisely to one or the other; this is however of little moment, since the employment is in any case authorised, and is not regarded as coming within the definition of Forced Labour.

These two articles provide for the highly important work involved in communal efforts against such threats as soil erosion, tsetse invasion, the locust menace, and similar dangers to a community. In many countries, sustained exertions are essential both for the due preservation of existing soil, and for the reclamation of areas already lost by past neglect. It is insufficient for the majority of people to take the necessary steps to cherish the tribal inheritance; the careless minority must if necessary be coerced into the essential co-operation, without which the enemy may penetrate the defences. Just as the neglectful English farmer can be forced to destroy the thistles that are contaminating his neighbours' land, so the careless African should be compelled to carry on his cultivation in such a manner as to conserve the soil and maintain the fertility of the area. Such duties are readily assumed by a self-governing community, and it would be manifestly preposterous to condemn a dependent territory to the prospect of steady deterioration of its main asset, merely because the responsible authority shrank from exacting the necessary compliance.

The degree to which compulsion is justifiable for such purposes may need some discrimination. Measures directed against soil erosion in particular may involve anything between the constant observance of contour cultivation and the prevention of formation of watercourses, up to the construction of very considerable undertakings such as canals and embankments involving major works and extending over a period of years. The distinction may be found in the spirit underlying the wording of Articles 2 and 19. Where the work consists of activity organised on tribal lines, under the supervision of the native authorities, or where it involves only the observation of certain recognised principles of agriculture, it can be regarded as a legitimate object for compulsion; as the community aquires powers of self-government, it may be expected to maintain such duties for its own benefit. If however the undertaking involves regular work of the kind usually performed by organised wage-earners, extending over a considerable period, or where its execution requires the supervision and control of skilled Europeans, it must be regarded as beyond the potentialities of a local community; it must be carried out by the resources of the country as a whole, either from its own revenue or with assistance from the metropolitan power.

Article 20 prohibits forced labour as a collective punishment, and Article 21 excludes it from any mining operations. Articles 23 and 24 deal with regulations and inspection, and Article 25 makes illegal exaction of forced labour a crime. Article 22 sets out the form and contents of the reports to be rendered regarding the extent of the resort to forced labour.

Recommendations follow relating to (I) indirect compulsion; (II) pressure exercised by means [of] taxes, pass laws, vagrancy acts, etc.; (III) non-interference with normal flow of labour; and also to (I) publications for general information; (II) forced labour as a threat to food supply; (III) the prohibition of forced labour for women or children; (IV) the reduction of porterage; and (V) the avoidance of alcoholic temptation for forced labourers.

365 CO 859/135/2, no 15 10 Nov 1948

[Mass education]: circular despatch from Mr Creech Jones to African governors and others [Extract]

It is now eighteen months since I addressed you in my despatch No. of the 25th April, 1947 on the subject of mass education. I now forward for your consideration a copy of a report[1] on this subject by a sub-committee of the Colonial Economic and Development Council, which has recently been considered and endorsed by the Council itself. This sub-committee, of which Mr. A.B. Cohen was chairman and Sir John Waddington[2] one of the members, was set up at the instance of the Council because it was suggested that insufficient provision for mass education had been made in the ten-year development programmes of the African Territories. I shall discuss some of the main conclusions of the sub-committee, with which I am in general agreement, in the later paragraphs of this despatch. The whole subject of mass education in all its aspects was discussed in detail at the African summer conference held at Cambridge in August,[3] which dealt with the subject under the headings of the content of mass education, education for citizenship, the part to be played by women, incentives to progress in African society, technique and organisation. As you know, the conference was attended by some 70 officers from the African Territories, many of them with long experience either in the administration or in departments. I am addressing you separately on the first four reports produced by the conference; I hope to send a further communication shortly regarding the report on technique, when I shall refer *inter alia* to the subject of broadcasting; the sixth report, on organisation, covers the same ground as the report of the sub-committee of the Colonial Economic and Development Council and I am forwarding a copy of it herewith. The members of the group which prepared this report had available during their discussions copies of the report of the sub-committee and it is these two documents which form the subject of this despatch.

2. The two documents are long and cover a great deal of ground. In spite of the many points dealt with in them I want to make this despatch as short as possible, because I entirely agree with the sub-committee when they say that "we believe that the time has come when the arguments about the merits of mass education must somehow be brought to a close. Debate by means of despatch and memorandum has gone on too long. The conception of mass education by community effort should now be accepted as settled policy and on this basis mass education along with the development of local government should be placed in the forefront of our development policy in Africa. The administration of provinces and districts must be planned so that officers can devote their energies to these two ends."

3. In most African Territories mass education has in my opinion so far made disappointing progress. I believe this to be due partly to misunderstanding of the nature of mass education and partly to the fact that the machinery of government is not normally so organised as to give the best chance for the successful planning and execution of mass education programmes. The sub-committee deal with these points in their report and I am in general agreement with their views. It is important for all concerned to realise that mass education is not an inferior substitute for education in

---

[1] Enclosures not printed. [2] Gov of Northern Rhodesia, 1941–1947. [3] See part 1 of this volume, 51.

the formal sense, as many Africans have believed, nor as some Government officers seem to have understood, an attempt to import into Africa a system of administration which is completely new. It is a movement to secure the active co-operation of the people of each community in programmes designed to raise standards of living and to promote development in all its forms. It is no new movement, but the intensification of past plans for development by means of new techniques; its main novel feature lies in the great emphasis which it places on the stimulation of popular initiative.

4. The purpose of this despatch is to make it clear beyond all doubt to the Governments of the African Territories that mass education is to be regarded as one of the central features of the African policy of His Majesty's Government. It was evident from the discussions at the Cambridge and London conferences that there is wide support for this policy both among officials and unofficials in Africa itself. I therefore ask all the Governments concerned to devote the most energetic efforts, in consultation with their Legislative Councils, to the planning and carrying into effect of programmes of mass education.

5. It is unnecessary for me to deal at length in this despatch with the points made quite clearly in the two papers forwarded with it. I wish, however, to refer as briefly as possible to certain recommendations which seem to me to be of particular importance. These relate to the definition of mass education, to questions of organisation, to finance and to training.

Definition

6. The summer conference, following the sub-committee of the Colonial Economic and Development Council, has defined mass education as follows:— "We understand the term 'mass education' to mean a movement designed to promote better living for the whole community, with the active participation and, if possible, on the initiative of the community, but if this initiative is not forthcoming spontaneously, by the use of techniques for arousing and stimulating it in order to secure its active and enthusiastic response to the movement. Mass education embraces all forms of betterment. It includes the whole range of development activities in the districts, whether these are undertaken by Government or unofficial bodies; in the field of agriculture by securing the adoption of better methods of soil conservation, better methods of farming and better care of livestock; in the field of health by promoting better sanitation and water supplies, proper measures of hygiene and infant and maternity welfare; and in the field of education by spreading literacy and adult education as well as by the extension and improvement of schools for children. Mass education must make use of the co-operative movement and must be put into effect in the closest association with local government bodies". I accept this definition, which should now be regarded as authoritative. I also accept the proposal of the Cambridge conference that as an alternative to the term "mass education" the term "community development" should be used. In accordance with the recommendation of the conference I am making arrangements for a small pamphlet to be prepared setting out in the simplest language possible the definition of mass education or community development and suitably amplifying this in the same simple language. I hope that this pamphlet will be useful to Governments, but action on this despatch should not of course await its receipt.

Organisation

7. Since it is accepted that mass education or community development covers all the development activities of government in the districts, if follows that the planning and execution of programmes must be the responsibility of teams consisting of all the administrative and technical officers working in the area concerned. In most territories I believe that the main operative unit for this purpose will be the provincial team under the chairmanship of the Resident or Provincial Commissioner; although in some territories, as for example in Kenya, it may be found that the district rather than the province is the most convenient unit of operation. Wherever possible the provincial team should include one officer specialising in mass education or community development, who should, again wherever possible, have been specially trained for the purpose. He should have the title of Community Development Officer and should form part of the Provincial Administration. It is important, as the report of the conference says in paragraph 27, that Community Development Officers with comparable qualifications to Administrative Officers should be eligible to rise to the top of the administrative service and should not be limited indefinitely to what may well appear at present as a small specialised section of that service.

8. I wish here to make the point that mass education or community development programmes ought not to be regarded as the responsibility of any one department of Government only, such as for example the Education Department or the Social Welfare Department, as has happened in certain territories. Adult education in the sense of organised classes and mass literacy are admittedly the special responsibility of the Education Department as far as Governments are concerned and the officers concerned should not be called Mass Education Officers; but these subjects only form part of the work of mass education or community development and where specialist advisers are required on them they would no doubt form part of the staff of the Education Department. Similarly the term Social Welfare Officer should be confined to officers dealing with social welfare activities in the technical sense, mainly in the urban areas. Where, as in most rural areas, Social Welfare Officers are in fact dealing with mass education or community development programmes, Community Development Officer would be a preferable title. The present differences in title lead to confusion and misunderstanding and should in my view be avoided.

9. Mass education programmes will have no chance of succeeding in their purpose unless the representatives of the local communities are in a position to take a full and constructive part in their planning and execution. For this purpose it is most important that the provincial teams, as well as the district teams, should work in the closest consultation with local opinion. The conference therefore recommended that provincial and district committees, and where appropriate committees covering smaller areas below them, should be established. The recommendations of the conference are set out at considerable length in paragraphs 13 and following of the report. This was, I have no doubt, done for the purpose of illustration, as there is no suggestion that a universal blueprint can be laid down. I am sure, however, that Governments will find the recommendations valuable for the purpose of their consideration of the subject and in asking that Governments should take steps to establish the missing machinery, in the form most suitable to local conditions, wherever it does not at present exist, I wish to emphasise the very particular importance which I attach to this aspect of the subject . . . .

366 CO 859/210/7, [no 46] [17 Nov 1948]

[Venereal disease in the colonies]: CO departmental memorandum[1] for the VD Sub-Committee,[2] summarising reports from colonial medical officers

In August 1947 a circular despatch was sent to all Colonies enclosing a memorandum prepared earlier in the year by the Sub-Committee on the Control of Venereal Disease in the United Kingdom. In this despatch it was stated that the Sub-Committee thought it might be helpful to Colonial Medical Officers to know how some aspects of the venereal disease problem had been dealt with in this country. There was general agreement that it would be impracticable at this stage to put forward proposals for the control of venereal disease which would be applicable to the Colonies but some of the measures described in the memorandum might be capable of adaptation for use overseas. It was suggested that this information should be brought to the notice of Administrative Officers, Social Welfare Officers and others whose co-operation is essential for the institution of effective control measures: in addition this offered a suitable opportunity for Colonial Governments to review their policy of control.

2. Replies have been received from many of the more important Colonies of which summaries on a regional basis follow. All Governments record that the memorandum has been received with great interest and in many places careful attention has clearly been given to the whole problem.

3. *East and Central Africa*

(a) *Kenya.* The Government of Kenya report that the mass of the native population is not likely to be influenced by an awareness of the social consequences of venereal infection. Additionally, the presence of large numbers of troops in this Colony during the war and the social problems of the urbanisation of the African are responsible for a state of society where prostitution has increased and moral deterioration has occurred. It is true that a nucleus of opinion among Africans is showing a greater interest in the moral side of the question and particularly in its socio-economic aspect but it is quite clear that a difficult and complex course lies ahead in educating the mass of people to a proper appreciation of the seriousness of the problem. Much, however, can be done by exploiting the wish of nearly all Africans for a numerous family. As the memorandum itself says, long and patient teaching, with the co-operation of all the influences which can be brought to bear upon opinion, is required.

As to methods of instruction the Government considers that propaganda suitable for the United Kingdom could not be used in Kenya at present. Propaganda, including posters, (a sample of which was enclosed with the despatch) prepared for use with African troops during the war, was not directly applicable to the civilian population and further consideration was being given to this aspect of the problem by the Medical Department and Information Officer.

On the question of treatment, it is considered that as full and adequate a service

---

[1] Prepared by M H Dorman, a seconded assistant secretary, 1948–1950; subsequently Sir Maurice Dorman, gov of Sierra Leone, 1956–1961.

[2] A Sub-Committee on the control of VD, an Advisory Committee set up in 1943.

should be provided as circumstances and the staff position permit. Such treatment is, in all cases, free of cost. There is, however, without doubt, room for considerable expansion but this is equally true of almost any field of medical service in East Africa. As suggested in the Report, the results of treatment are largely invalidated by the fact that many patients discontinue treatment at an early stage, often after the infective symptoms, of which the patient is physically aware, disappear. Perhaps the best hope of progress lies in developing an intensive short form of treatment. This question is being carefully studied and, if supplies of drugs could be guaranteed, would be widely introduced.

During the war defence regulations of similar effect to D.R.33(B) in this country were introduced. They lapsed last year and have not been re-enacted. Legislative measures regulating notification and treatment are not considered to be of great value in Kenya because their administration is so difficult. The regulation of prostitution is neither practicable nor desirable in Kenya although it is admitted that prostitutes are a common source of infection. Centres in urban areas managed by women health visitors or nursing sisters have gained the confidence of their patients and meet with considerable success. Clinic returns for 1946 in Nairobi alone showed a total annual attendance of almost 23,500. The Government hope to second an officer with specialist knowledge to study the whole question in the near future. They attach importance to the use of qualified women workers especially those with a bias towards social welfare work and they have considered the possibility of using travelling teams and propose to make provision in health centres to be established under the development plan for adequate treatment along these lines.

(b) *Uganda.* The Government report in similar terms to Kenya that there is little shame, guilt or criticism associated with an attack of venereal disease in the African population. The African adopts a happy-go-lucky attitude towards those diseases while a European regards them with shame. Both attitudes require correction and the Uganda Government concentrates primarily on propaganda. Elementary sex instruction is given in the top classes of full primary schools. It is the majority opinion that sex instruction should not be given at an earlier age, partly because there are few teachers competent to speak on the physiology of sex and partly because the technique of teaching such matters to African children of different tribes with varying customs needs careful study if its aim and purpose are not to be misinterpreted by adolescents. As regards the adult, Press advertisements, leaflets and posters convey knowledge to only a limited section of the community. There are few African wireless sets in Uganda and this method of propaganda among Africans must be discounted at present. Valuable work is being done by the Demonstration Teams of the Department of Public Relations and Social Welfare which frequently include sketches and plays about the ravages of venereal disease in their programmes. The emphasis given in these plays is generally that the infected persons are fools, not merely sinners, and the Governor is satisfied that in Uganda this must at present be the right approach. Propaganda films locally produced are under consideration and a Luganda Book on Sex Instruction has been commended for use in schools by the Church.

There has been much discussion in this territory on the merits of compulsory treatment in venereal disease. A Buganda Government Law (applying only to the Kingdom of Buganda) known as the "Law for preventing Venereal Disease" was promulgated in 1913 and is still theoretically valid. This law provides for the compulsory attendance and treatment of Africans subject to Buganda Lukiko[3] jurisdiction should they be discovered to be suffering from venereal disease in an infectious stage. This law has not been effective due to difficulties in determining the existence of an infection and the indifference of public opinion. The legislation introduced in 1944 under the Emergency Powers (Defence) Acts following the lines of the English Defence Regulations 33(B) was intended primarily to protect military personnel from the heavily infected prostitute population in townships. As infected askaris[4] could not or would not name the person from whom their infection was believed to be obtained, the persons could not be found or traced and again the legislation was not justified by the results obtained. Until public opinion has reached the stage when public co-operation can be expected, it is not considered that useful results will be produced by compulsion.

The Government propose to recruit an experienced Venereologist and to attach a Medical Officer to work with him, but until the shortage of accommodation has been relieved it is not possible to proceed with the appointment.

(c) *Tanganyika.* The Government reports that while there is no lack of interest on the part of the African public in the benefits to be gained from the specific forms of treatment available in the initial stages of the diseases, there is as yet little evidence of any strong desire to avoid the diseases or, having acquired them, to carry on the full courses of treatment. The African remains too easily impressed by the removal of signs and symptoms.

The staff position has made it impossible to divert medical officers to specialist duties in connection with venereal diseases, but a health unit system will assist in combating them and educating public opinion.

(d) *Northern Rhodesia.* The Government of Northern Rhodesia also reports that the African attaches little or no stigma to venereal disease. The argument which most appeals to him is that control of the disease promotes the successful termination [sic] of pregnancy and the production of healthy children. The matter is further complicated by the fact that it would be most undesirable at this stage to initiate throughout the Territory propaganda encouraging people to come forward for full treatment, when it is quite impossible for the treatment to be given.

Since July, 1946, a Venereal Disease Specialist has been conducting a campaign in the Namwala District. With the co-operation of the District Commissioner and the Native Authorities, he has been very successful in gaining the confidence of the population and large numbers of people have presented themselves for examination and full treatment. When he has completed his task in that area and his team has moved on to a new area, the supplementary "follow-up" work will have to be done through the medium of the ordinary medical staff of the district with the continued co-operation of the Native Authorities.

I am informed that, although contact tracing is possible in some cases, particularly through the examination of the consorts of infected people, nevertheless the habits of the Africans are such that it does not appear to offer any great hope as a preventive measure.

(e) *Nyasaland.* Under Colonial Development and Welfare Scheme No.D.505, a grant of £42,000 over a period of 5 years was made for the treatment of venereal diseases in Nyasaland. Since May, 1946, when an adequate supply of the requisite

[3] Parliament of Buganda.

[4] African policeman/soldier (Swahili).

drugs became available, all reporting cases of venereal disease have received free treatment at both Government and non-Government medical institutions; all Missions equipped with competently trained staff receive free issue of these drugs. When the transport provided for under the Medical Post War Development Scheme becomes available it is intended that intensive propaganda and treatment campaigns will be carried on throughout the Protectorate.

As regards propaganda, posters and pamphlets, one of which was addressed especially to women, have been printed and issued to all institutions carrying out the treatment of venereal diseases. These stress the consequences of these diseases and the importance of persevering with treatment until cure is effected, and emphasise that all treatment is free. The dangers of these diseases and the need for early treatment are also the subject of regular propaganda by Medical Officers when on tour and when lecturing in schools. A keen interest in the subject has been displayed by leading members of the African community, especially the members of the Northern Province African Provincial Council.

4. *West Africa.* The Nigerian Government explained that in September, 1946, Dr Freshwater, Government Dermatologist, after a tour of the country, drew up a scheme for a Venereal Disease Treatment Service with a view to treating only infectious cases until such time as they became non-infectious, on the assumption that a non-infectious case, though naturally of importance to the individual, is not a public health problem. When detailed costings for the scheme, which was based on a similar use of penicillin to that suggested in the Memorandum, was made, it was found that the cost for a single province, Abeokuta, was £42,500 for the first year, £10,648 for the second and a residual recurrent cost of £8,648 per annum. It is obvious that the revenues of Nigeria could not support such an expenditure over the whole country and the project had regretfully to be dropped.

Lack of necessary staff and buildings for the enforcement of compulsory treatment and the financial impracticability of the scheme mentioned above must mean that for the time being the treatment of venereal disease must remain the responsibility of the ordinary Medical Officer, and of the Epidemic Health Units (now entitled Medical Field Units) which are being set up under the Medical Development Plan. But in their attack on the disease the Medical staff will have, especially in urban areas, new allies in the staff who will implement the Social Welfare Policy. They, it is hoped, will be able to enlist the co-operation of the people, both individually and as a community, in the campaign to obliterate disease. One of the great difficulties experienced by doctors in the treatment of this disease is that patients will not take the treatment seriously and continue with it until cured. The best remedy for this lies in continued propaganda. Without this it is likely that any efforts on the part of the Medical Department will be doomed to failure.

5. *West Indies.* The Government of Trinidad report that the present V.D. Control Programme in this colony conforms very closely to British practice. All the major important measures advocated in the memorandum have been put into operation to a surprisingly effective extent in the face of considerable difficulty.

The provision of adequate facilities for the examination, diagnosis and treatment of the V.D. patient, which are both attractive and frequently available, has been regarded as the essential foundation on which to build a policy of control. The co-operation of other Departments and of voluntary agencies has been sought. The Caribbean Medical centre has seen between 26,000 to 30,000 persons a year and has treated about 10,000 cases of venereal disease a year. Thus not only did this large number of people receive the medical care they needed but also about 10,000 possible foci of infection were rendered non-infectious—a valuable measure for the protection of the health of the community. The Centre was fortunate in having penicillin available for the treatment of venereal diseases since April 1945, and it has been possible to offer patients a nine-day course of treatment for certain stages of syphilis and a four-hour treatment for gonorrhoea. Both schedules were apparently very effective. The rapidity of action and the apparent effectiveness of the newer forms of treatment offer the programme, for the first time, the prospect of reducing the incidence of these diseases by treatment alone provided it is afforded the opportunity of applying them on a sufficiently large scale and for a sufficiently long period of time.

No drive against prostitution *per se* has been made but special efforts have been made to educate this group in regard to venereal diseases and they have been offered special facilities for examination and treatment. The contact tracing section is the most recently developed one and much emphasis is being put on its activities. Legislation is being introduced which should be of assistance in dealing with a certain number of un-co-operative people suspected of being fruitful sources of infection.

5. *Far East*

(a) *Singapore.* The Medical Department Report for 1946 includes the following passage regarding venereal disease:

> Venereal Disease needs special consideration in view of the aftermath of the war and the advances which have been made in the treatment of the disease. A special hospital with treatment and follow-up concentrated in the most suitable areas of the town has led to unexpected and remarkable success in the present campaign. Better-class patients will, of course, continue to receive attention in the paying wards of the General Hospital. That confidence between patient and doctor which is an essential in such a condition will continue to be the key-note of work in this direction. There will be no coercive compulsion as far as the Civil Authority is concerned. An excellent beginning has been made in our new approach to this disease under very difficult and exacting conditions. The present building—an old Japanese hospital—is quite unsuitable in its present form as a medical institution. With proper up-to-date facilities I anticipate a most satisfactory expansion in the control of this most important of social evils.

Particular attention will be given to this subject in the report for 1947.

(b) *Malaya.* The Government report that the distribution of the populace into relatively small urban groups and extended kampong[5] and estate areas make it difficult to reach the people for teaching and propaganda, while the problem of providing treatment is insuperable at the present time. The Department of Public Relations is providing posters and giving preliminary talks from their travelling vans; but the low standard of literacy, the differing moral standards, regard for the marital tie and sexual relations, together with the multiplicity of languages, are factors that add to the difficulties in this country. It is hoped to be able to re-introduce some medical teaching in the schools. A start has been made in contact tracing in Kuala

---

[5] Kampong: a Malay village associated with subsistence farming and cash-cropping.

Lumpur with some success and it is being extended to other places as a part of the work of health nurses.

6. *Mediterranean*

(a) *Malta*. The problem of venereal diseases in these islands is not serious in view of the strong moral influence of the home.

(b) *Cyprus*. The Government report that there has been a steady annual decline in the incidence of venereal disease between 1939 and 1944. Since 1944 there has been a slight increase but at present this event does not form the problem in Cyprus that it would seem to be in certain other countries. The increase in incidence since 1944 does not give any cause for alarm.

7. *Conclusions*. Experience in Trinidad should be relevant to other parts of the West Indies, and if it has been possible to make a successful attack on the diseases there it should be practicable in other islands given the necessary finance. The most difficult problems arise in Africa and probably to a similar degree in Malaya. The replies to the Sub-Committee's memorandum all dwell on four main points.

(a) The difficulty of making any immediate progress based on propaganda campaigns. This was due primarily to the difficulty of reaching a sufficiently wide body of public opinion with the limited means available and of explaining concurrently a wide variety of complex problems of which venereal disease only formed a small part.

(b) The failure of contact tracing, drives against prostitution and compulsory measures based on legislative sanctions.

(c) Inability to give treatment on a sufficiently wide scale. From the replies received it appears to be partly a question of the supply of expensive drugs, partly of finance and partly of highly qualified venereologists.

(d) The possibility of controlling the disease given a sufficiently quick method of treatment available on a wide enough scale.

367 CAB 134/56, CA(49)2 9 Feb 1949

'Population problems in the West Indies': memorandum by Mr Creech Jones for Cabinet Commonwealth Affairs Committee. *Annex*: note

At the meeting of the Commonwealth Affairs Committee on the 29th October (C.A.(48) 8th Meeting, Minute 1),[1] reference was made to the population problem in the West Indies. The attached note is circulated for the information of my colleagues. It contains little that is new, for the subject was discussed by the West India Royal Commission (Cmd. 6607) and references to the problem are frequent in other Reports about the West Indies.

2. With the exception of Trinidad oil and the bauxite and (highly speculative) mineral prospects in British Guiana, there is no mineral wealth in the British colonies. The soil generally is poor and for the most part unsuited to crops which do not themselves provide means of re-fertilising the soil. Even the crops which are produced, such as sugar and bananas, are produced under conditions which would, on a straight competitive basis, not stand up to those in other parts of the world

[1] See part 3 of this volume, 252.

where similar crops are grown. Again with the exception of Trinidad, there is no ready and cheap source of power for industry. The Colonies are small and intensely parochial, and only now are we beginning to bring them together so that they can organise common services and speak as a more effective whole. Politically, they have inherited advanced forms of parliamentary representation without as yet any stable basis of democracy, and the traditional hostility to the executive Government which was inherited from the days of the planters has militated against the building up of any efficient Government machine. Added to this, whether as a further legacy from the days of slavery or not, there is little sense of personal or social responsibility. The population has increased beyond the bounds of what the resources of the area can maintain on a reasonable standard of living, and looks like going on increasing; so that it will be impossible not only to improve but even to maintain the present standard of living. In the last nine years, money has been provided by the British taxpayer for developing natural resources, building public works and utilities, extending social services, and teaching such civic lessons as the development of trade unionism, co-operation, local government, etc; but all this effort may later be engulfed in the menacing rise of the population.

3. This is a gloomy picture. Further scientific enquiries by economists and demographers would not be likely to do more than confirm what we already know in broad outline. The principal answers to the problem appear to lie in (a) improved social standards and birth control or, as it is sometimes now described, "family planning"; (b) outlets for population, as proposed in the Evans Report[2] on British Guiana and British Honduras, and temporary employment overseas; and (c) increasing human efficiency, developing economic activities, and improving the exploitation of such material resources as the area possesses.

4. I should add that, up and down the area, in addition to the work of the Governments, quite a few people are generally trying to improve methods of cultivation and develop new crops in the hope of providing employment for a greater number of people, although of course some of them are also moved by the hope of private profit to themselves. There are also the British companies which own sugar and other estates in the West Indies and who, whatever their record in the past, are now generally prepared to improve working conditions on their estates, although the legacy of the past and the erratic lines on which trade unionism is developing do not make it easy for them. All these people who are trying further to develop the natural resources are up against the same problem. New development, whether it means new machinery, taking new land into cultivation, or experimenting with new varieties, is an expensive matter in these times, and seems to them not worth while unless there is some form of guarantee for a reasonable period that the crops when produced will be saleable. It is this consideration which has led the citrus growers, the banana growers, and the sugar producers to demand as long-term an assurance as possible that His Majesty's Government will purchase their crops. They know that, without such a guarantee of market and price and, indeed, unless Great Britain buys from them, they are not likely to be able to sell their products in competition with other countries. Some good progress has been made to meet this point, thanks to the Treasury and the Ministry of Food.

---

[2] Commission for Settlement in British Guiana and British Honduras, 1947–1948 (chairman, Sir Geoffrey Evans).

5. The basic issue is, of course, birth control. The great difficulties here are alluded to in the attached note, but I propose to discuss the matter again with the West Indian Governors and also to seek their views on the possibility of an enquiry on broad lines into future population trends in relation to living standards and available material resources. I feel that such an enquiry might be helpful in bringing home the facts of the situation to the ordinary man and woman in the West Indies, on whose response to this social problem any improvement must ultimately depend.

Annex to 367

Introduction

1. Over-population is the principal problem in the West Indies. Coupled with it are the problems of unemployment and under-employment. Over-population is most acute in Jamaica, Barbados and Trinidad, and it is in these Colonies that unemployment is most serious. Broadly speaking, over-population and unemployment exists in varying degrees in all the Island Colonies. By contrast, British Honduras and the interior of British Guiana are under-populated and have no important unemployment problem (the 1000 or so unemployed in British Honduras are at present causing concern disproportionate to their numbers, since they are concentrated in Belize and a possible target for Guatemalan agitation).

Over-population

2. The problem of over-population is two-fold. There is the problem of absolute over-population; and there is the problem of the excessive rate of increase of population. In Barbados absolute over-population exists in an acute degree: the density of population there is about 1,200 to the square mile. The more serious problem, however, is that of the excessive rate of increase. Nearly all the Island Colonies suffer from this in some degree. The reason for the excessive rate of increase is that the birth rate remains high, while with the improvement in medical knowledge and practice over the last century the death rate has fallen, and is still falling. The natural increase of population is now in many Colonies at a rate that will cause the population to double in 25 or 30 years. The West India Royal Commission emphasized "the extreme and fundamental importance of the question of the growth of numbers"; and said that behind the various economic and social difficulties that they described in their Report "the rapid increase of population is to be found, sometimes as a major cause, and almost always as an aggravating factor".

Unemployment

3. The Royal Commission stated that "unemployment has taken the place of an unsatisfied demand for labour as the dominating fact throughout the Caribbean area". There are no accurate statistics of unemployment in the British Colonies, but the following figures (based on the most recent estimates from the Governments concerned) give an indication of the numbers involved:–

Colony	*Population* (1946 Census)	*Unemployed* (latest available information)	*Approx %*
Jamaica	1,308,000	64,000	4.9
Trinidad	558,000	15,000	2.7
Windward Islands Leeward Islands	361,000	7,500 2,400	2.75
Barbados	193,000	7,250	3.75
British Guiana	376,000	3,700	1.0
British Honduras	60,000	1,000	1.7

4. No figures of persons out of work could reveal the full nature of the unemployment and under-employment problem. The economies are agricultural, and there is much opportunity for part time occupation in work on estates combined with work on allotments or smallholdings. It is therefore only in the towns that the problem shows itself as a complete want of employment. The standard of living is probably more seriously depressed by the prevalence of under-employment, a condition in which the worker is totally unable to earn sufficient to maintain even the lowest standard of living, or to gain any self-respect from such spasmodic occupation as comes his way. This is widespread in most of the Islands, since they depend largely upon the sugar industry, in which under-employment can be expected even in normal years and may become severe in years of drought.

5. The growth of unemployment reflects the difference between the rate of increase of the population and the rate of expansion of economic opportunities. The West Indian colonies depend mainly upon agriculture, and most of them upon a very limited number of export crops. Of these, sugar is by far the most important, and the world market for sugar up to 1939 did not encourage expansion. The prospects for other crops have been damaged not only by market declines but also by diseases and hurricanes. Subsistence agriculture has not been able to absorb the increase of population, partly because arable land of good quality is not everywhere available, partly because the people themselves have been drifting to the towns. Industries other than agriculture, though they have made progress, have not provided employment on the scale required. Except for the petroleum industry in Trinidad, bauxite mining in British Guiana, and forestry (along with sawmills) in British Guiana and British Honduras, no industry other than agriculture operates on a scale that calls for workers in large numbers.

6. The closing of outlets for emigration, the return of former emigrants to their Colonies of origin and the difficulties of inter-Caribbean communication are contributory causes of unemployment. Mechanisation of agriculture, especially of sugar cultivation, is likely to result in a fall in the demand for labour on estates in colonies where the acreage under sugar-cane does not expand. The temporary relief at one time by recruitment for the services is no longer effective, and the demobilization of ex-Servicemen has caused special unemployment difficulties in some colonies. But in the main the problem can properly be called Malthusian.

Summary of problem and its causes

7. The economy of the British West Indies suffers from certain fundamental handicaps; the absence of mineral resources (except for oil in Trinidad and bauxite in British Guiana), and the comparative poverty of the soil. These handicaps are

aggravated by existing over-population, and all efforts to overcome them tend to be negatived by the excessive rate of growth of population. There are various contributory causes, principally the closing of emigration outlets, but the high birth rate is undoubtedly the greatest menace to the standard of living of both present and future generations.

Remedies

8. The main remedies appear to lie in the direction of:—

(i) a reduction in the birth rate;
(ii) emigration for settlement;
(iii) temporary employment overseas;
(iv) greater economic development;
(v) regional co-ordination.

(a) *Reduction in the birth rate*

The Royal Commission regarded a reduction in the birth rate as "in one sense the most pressing need of the West Indian Colonies". They observed, however, that this raised a problem which was far too difficult and complex to form the subject of concrete recommendations. They thought that higher wages and better housing conditions might help to secure a reduction in the number of children born; but experience did not suggest to them that any of these measures would be likely in practice to have the desired effect unless public opinion in the West Indies became widely and vividly convinced of the need for a limitation of the birth rate. They regarded an awakening of public opinion as the indispensable condition of a solution of the problem. They nevertheless realized that a reduction in the average size of the family could only come as a very gradual process, and they thought it was no less essential to find means of absorbing the existing West Indian population of working age into useful activity. No action to awaken public opinion on the necessity for a reduced birth rate has, in fact, been taken. Indeed any reference to this matter brings forth immediate evidence of the opposition which would be offered from many quarters, especially the leaders of certain religious denominations. Government policy has concentrated on developing the area, seeking overseas outlets and building up a structure for regional co-operation.

(b) *Emigration for settlement*

Efforts were made in 1946 and 1947 to find outlets for the settlement of surplus West Indian population in various South American countries. These efforts failed, mainly because the countries concerned had their own unemployment problem to contend with and had passed immigration laws which discriminated against immigrants of African stock. This antagonism to the admission of negroes is widespread on the South American continent. Cuba, Haiti and Santo Domingo, which after the first world war—during the period of the sugar boom—accepted large numbers of British West Indian immigrants to settle and work on the sugar estates, are now no longer willing to accept further immigrants. On the contrary they have passed legislation which discriminates against those of the earlier immigrants who are still there, and even against their local-born descendants. Even further back, many British West Indians went to Panama and settled there in connection with the Canal construction work. The Panamanian Government has not made things easy for them and their descendants. Organized emigration from the over-populated British West Indian Islands to the two British Mainland Colonies, on a limited scale, is looked for as a result of the Evans Commission recommendations. The Commission think that if their proposals are implemented about 100,000 persons (including 25,000 adult workers) might be absorbed over ten years and start a "chain reaction" of further development and emigration in the future.

(c) *Temporary employment overseas*
With the closing of opportunities for emigration and settlement overseas, West Indians have in recent years sought opportunities for temporary employment on contract in other countries. About 40,000 West Indian workers from Jamaica, Barbados and the Leeward Islands were employed in the United States during the war. After the war the number fell to 3,500 but it has risen to about 8,000 in recent months. This emigration, however, rests somewhat precariously on the goodwill of the United States administration and no substantial increase can be hoped for. The Colonial Governments concerned maintain a Central Labour Organization in Washington to supervise the welfare of workers. Efforts have been made to get work for British West Indian labourers in Dutch Guiana and the Dutch West Indies, and trial shipments of 50 families have recently been sent to Dutch Guiana from both Barbados and St. Lucia; but unfortunately the St. Lucia families have had to be repatriated. Enquiries have been made about the prospects of obtaining employment for West Indian labour in connection with the proposals of the United States Government for the reconstruction of the Panama Canal. The proposals have, however, been dropped by the United States Government for the time being. It has not proved possible to devise any official scheme for employing West Indian workers in the United Kingdom, even for seasonal work in agriculture.

(d) *Economic development*
Each Colony has prepared a ten-year programme of development, financed in part from Colonial Development and Welfare funds. Agricultural development figures largely in these plans. Provision is made for soil conservation, drainage and irrigation, improved methods of cultivation, better quality strains, pest control and the like. Improved marketing arrangements have also been made for many commodities. His Majesty's Government have agreed to take all the Colonial sugar and all Jamaica bananas produced up to the end of 1952. A ten-year contract for concentrated orange juice, with a price formula for the first five years, is being negotiated. The general aim is to increase and stabilise production and improve quality. Provision is made for industrial development in the various Colony programmes, and a survey of possible industrial development in the Caribbean Area has recently been made by the Caribbean Commission. The Colonial Development Corporation has established a West Indian Regional Board and is examining various developmental projects. Action has already been taken by the Corporation in a few cases.

(e) *Regional co-ordination*
Many of the Islands are too small to organise governmental business and social services on a large enough scale to make them economical and efficient. The need is

recognised for organised services on a regional basis. Britain co-operates with the United States, Netherlands and France in the Caribbean Commission which was intended, as one of its main functions, to co-ordinate research into problems common to the whole region. The results of this Commission are as yet not particularly impressive. As a result of the Montego Bay Conference, 1947,[3] a Standing Committee has been established to prepare a plan for federation of the British territories, which will in due course be submitted to the legislatures. The Montego Bay Conference passed a number of resolutions aimed at closer economic co-ordination, and action now being taken includes the preparation of a scheme for a Customs Union, the establishment of a Committee to study economic development in the Region, the setting up of a Central Body of Primary Producers and a British Caribbean Trade Commissioner Service in the United Kingdom. The Geological Survey of British Guiana will be built up in such a way that it can cater for and co-ordinate the geological needs of all the West Indian Colonies.

Further investigation

9. Consideration has been given to a recent suggestion that the time has come to appoint a group of economists and demographers to study the inter-relationship of potential population growth and available natural resources within the British Caribbean territories with a view to discovering whether they are likely to be able to support their expanding population 50 years from now. There has, it is true, been no authoritative and scientific examination of this problem; and it is doubtful whether such a study, by experts alone, would add much to our knowledge of the broad position as it is now, or of likely tendencies in the near future. On the other hand a study with a wider scope, of the future population trends in the West Indian Colonies, in relation to their standards of living and the natural resources available to support those standards, might give helpful results; particularly if there were associated with such an enquiry a few prominent West Indians known to be interested in social and economic problems.

10. There is room for an enquiry into human efficiency. Progress has been made in increasing the productivity of land, but the productivity of labour does not appear to have been so successfully tackled. It is true that better housing, education and social services generally are thought to have had beneficial results but it might be that much more could be done if effort was concentrated on certain essential lines. There is inadequate understanding of the nature of the problem. The West Indian is commonly regarded as indolent, but West Indian labourers who have been employed in the United States during the war and subsequently are understood to have worked well. There must be an explanation for this. A labour efficiency survey was undertaken on the Kenya–Uganda Railway and something of the sort might usefully be done in the West Indies.

11. The basic problem is birth control. It has been shirked owing to the great inherent difficulties. Facilities for family planning are provided in this country by many local authorities as well as by voluntary agencies. How to get some such development in the West Indies and how to circumvent religious susceptibilities present almost insurmountable problems. No such policy could succeed without an influential and substantial number of people in the West Indies approving and advocating the idea of family planning.

[3] On federation of the West Indies: see part 3 of this volume, 251.

368 CO 859/176/3, no 11 9 Sept 1950

[Educational policy in Africa]: CO circular despatch to African governors about proposed review [Extract]

[The preparatory work for this despatch was done by Sir C Cox, the CO educational adviser, but the strategy of a high-calibre inquiry was Cohen's idea, and he finalised the drafting of the despatch. The Conservative Party had been calling for a royal commission on colonial education, but Cohen and Cox regarded this as impracticable, if only because of regional variation in the problems. What they wanted was an inquiry controlled by the CO, restricted to Africa for the moment, with two panels of experts visiting and reporting on West Africa and on East and Central Africa. The governors who were sounded out were mostly in favour. Griffiths indicated that he warmly welcomed this proposal, which he recognised was 'of immense importance' (CO 859/176/3, no 3, and minutes, 22 July–9 Sept 1950).]

I am writing to you to say that I believe the time has come for a review of our educational policy in Africa and to tell you of the method which I propose should be adopted for this purpose.

2. Although education policy was discussed at the Governors' Conference in London in 1948 [sic] and at the Legislators' Conference in 1949 [sic], there has been no re-examination of policy for the last 25 years. During that period great developments have taken place in all the Territories, the attitude of the people has changed and our own approach to colonial problems has radically altered. Meanwhile the education services of the Territories have been greatly expanded and Education Departments, missionaries and others have been devoting themselves to improving its quality. But we have not at any time during the period had a general review of policy in the educational field to see whether it is adequate to the needs of the situation as it now is.

3. Our education practice in Africa has come under fire from various quarters. Not all the criticism is well-informed, but I believe it fair to say that there is a real and widespread anxiety on the subject among those best qualified to know in the African Territories themselves.

4. Broadly speaking the criticism takes three forms. There are those who say that the education we offer is too bookish, is not related to the environment of the country and does not pay sufficient attention to character training; that primary education ought to have an agricultural and rural bias; that secondary education turns out too many people with a desire for white collar employment at a desk and not enough technicians and professional men; in a word, that the machine takes in countrymen and turns out would-be townsmen with a contempt for manual labour.

5. Secondly there are those who are concerned with the rate of progress and the quality of the education we offer. They see material development going forward rapidly and educational facilities advancing too slowly, both in quantity and in quality, to produce a sufficient number of intelligent people ready to take their part in the political, administrative and economic life of the Territories. These critics, while anxious for a quantitative increase at the primary level, are particularly concerned with the need to raise quality through the development of a responsible teaching profession.

6. Thirdly there are Africans, particularly in West Africa, who are suspicious of any measure of adaptation of education to give it a particularly African bent; they feel

they are being passed an inferior article if it does not conform to the European pattern and is not crowned with the same paper symbols of success. They do not appreciate attempts to reorientate education and of course are also critical of the speed at which it is developing.

7. I know that some of this criticism is ill-informed and some of it exaggerated or too idealistic, but there remains a core of serious opinion that all is not right that we cannot ignore. Sir Christopher Cox has put this in a slightly different way in writing: "None the less our consciences as educators cannot be clear as long as there is so big a gap between the performance in so high a proportion of schools and the principles which all colonial educators who know their job share with educators in the United Kingdom."

8. There is one further point. United Kingdom educational policy has been completely re-examined both before, during and since the passage of the 1944 Act. The new ideas thrown up by this process have scarcely yet been considered in relation to colonial conditions and the parallel activity of re-examining our colonial policy has not yet begun. Educational policy requires re-examination from time to time, and this seems to me a good time to do so.

9. What seems to me to be required is an agreed re-statement of policy in a form and in terms which will lead to the improvements in practice which are recommended being actually carried into effect. Such a re-statement of policy need not necessarily be for publication, although I would not exclude that; it should be designed primarily for the guidance of all those who are engaged in educational work in the Territories. It might well have to be in a different form for East and West Africa. To my mind it is important that those who are working in the Territories should take a full part in the preparation of the re-statement of policy. For that reason I should be opposed to the appointment of a Royal Commission on Colonial Education such as was recommended in the Conservative statement on colonial policy. What I want to do is to associate leading experts from this country with those dealing with education in Africa in a thorough re-examination of the principles on which we are working.

10. I suggest that the review should be concerned with the following aspects of educational policy:—

(i) the relationship of the curriculum to the needs of society and the establishment of arrangements for the study of content and methods;
(ii) the supply and training of teachers;
(iii) the amount of primary and secondary education and the incidence of responsibility for cost and administration;
(iv) the education of women and girls;
(v) the relationship between formal and informal education;
(vi) the relationship between government and voluntary agencies;
(vii) the relationship of education to economic development.

I do not think that the review should cover higher education, since policy in this field has been largely settled by the work of the Inter-University Council. I have not included technical education in the list, in spite of its importance and present backwardness, because I think that that would have to be covered separately and would require to be examined by people with rather different experience. I suggest that the review should be confined to education for Africans. The needs of

Europeans, Indians and Arabs in East and Central Africa raise different problems which can I think be more effectively handled in a different way.

11. The method by which I suggest that the enquiry should be carried out is described in the attached note[1]. You will see that what is proposed is the appointment of two small groups of experts each consisting of three people, one of which would visit West Africa and the other East and Central Africa during 1951, followed by a conference to be held in this country during the summer of 1952 which would be attended by representative groups of educational experts from each Territory. The method should ensure that the conclusions finally reached are thoroughly practical and take into account the needs of the Territories . . . .

---

[1] Not printed.

369 CO 859/183/3, no 29 26 July 1951

'Problems of trade unionism': circular despatch from Mr Griffiths to governors. *Annex*: memorandum on colonial trade unionism, submitted by Colonial Labour Advisory Committee (24 May) [Extracts]

I have the honour to address you on the subject of the development of trade unionism. You will recall that in my circular despatch of the 25th April, 1951, in which I put forward a proposal for a Conference of Heads of Labour Departments to be held in the Colonial Office between September and October of this year, I mentioned that my Colonial Labour Advisory Committee had recently concluded an examination of the general problems of trade unionism as part of a comprehensive review of our work in the field of labour relations. I have now considered the Committee's conclusions with great care and I find myself in full agreement with them. I am therefore enclosing copies of the Committee's Report to myself, which I commend to your study in the light of the observations which follow.

2. The development of trade unionism in the Colonial Territories has been particularly rapid during the last ten years, and, while this development can be said to have been broadly successful, experience has revealed certain defects in organisation and practice which it is clear must be remedied if the movement is eventually to make the responsible contribution which it should to their economic and social life. It is natural that the problems arising from these defects should present themselves in different shapes in different Territories; but there is one generalisation that may properly be made—that such defects are largely attributable to the comparative immaturity of the unions which, lacking the hard won experience of the movement in this country, have for the most part not yet had time to build up their own local traditions. There is clearly still a great need for guidance and education in trade union principles and practice; but it is equally clear that a sound legislative framework for the activities of the trade unions is essential if this assistance is to be of value and if the future development of the movement is to be properly safeguarded.

3. In examining the general question of labour relations my Labour Advisory Committee have accordingly directed their attention in the first place to a review of trade union legislation. It is a natural result of the historical development of the

trade unions that this legislation should be largely based on that of the United Kingdom; but you will observe that the Committee, in making their recommendations for additional provisions, have recognised that conditions in the Territories may call for legislative and administrative action which might not be regarded as appropriate in this country. They have stressed that local problems must in the last event be solved in their local context and that local experience must largely determine the kind of amendment to the law which may be needed. Some provisions of United Kingdom legislation may well prove to be inappropriate to conditions in certain Territories, and an approach different from that in this country may on occasion by judged to be necessary and wise. While I endorse these conclusions, I must emphasise that our approach to these problems cannot now be entirely empirical. The form of trade unionism in the Territories, and such tradition and practice as has already been established, are based on the broad general principles of trade unionism as it has evolved in the United Kingdom. The effect of disturbance of this development, if radical changes were now to be contemplated, must obviously be carefully balanced against the possible gains that any such changes might bring. It will be clear that certain of the recommendations of the Colonial Labour Advisory Committee may be more readily applicable in those Territories where trade unionism has not yet developed to any appreciable extent, and indeed were framed with conditions in those Territories in mind . . . .

9. If the trade unions are eventually to take a responsible part in the affairs of the Territories, it is clear that a great deal must depend on the quality of trade union leadership. Signs have not been lacking, however, that the movement has, from time to time attracted to itself persons actuated by personal motives rather than by conviction, whose activities have either brought the movement into discredit or have created disillusionment among the members. While it is recognised that young unions may well require the help of officials drawn from outside the industry or trade concerned to build up their organisation and assist in managing their affairs and that a great deal of valuable and selfless service has been rendered by such men, I commend to your careful consideration the proposal, made in paragraphs 39 and 40, that the officials of trade unions should, with certain exceptions, be men whose livelihood depends on their work in the industry concerned. I consider that the stability and value of the trade union movement in the territories depends to a large extent upon the degree to which leadership is developed from within its own ranks.

10. The task of my Advisory Committee was to review trade union legislation, and their recommendations are, as you have seen, aimed at remedying those defects in trade union structure and organisation which experience has revealed. Nevertheless, they have emphasised that at present some ninety per cent of Colonial workers are untouched by union organisation, and I welcome their concern that, in any discussion of the problems of industrial relations in the Territories, the interests and claims of these workers should not be overlooked. It remains the policy of His Majesty's Government to ensure a steady improvement in the wages and conditions of employment of all workers in the territories, and where this has not as yet been adequately achieved by trade unions operating through the process of collective bargaining, I endorse the Committee's recommendation in paragraph 42 of the Report that there should be a substantially greater readiness to establish statutory wage fixing machinery. In doing so I would reiterate their comment that this in no way implies a lack of faith in the ultimate ability of the unions to achieve

improvements by voluntary methods of negotiation, but rather reflects the view that where trade unions are poorly organised it is a duty of government to ensure the payment of reasonable wages and the establishment of reasonable working conditions. I am confident in fact that the development of statutory wage-fixing machinery can provide valuable experience and training in the practice of negotiation and compromise to both employers' and workers' representatives; I should hope that such experience would often lead eventually to the growth of conditions in which voluntary negotiating machinery can replace the statutory arrangements; and I consider that the introduction of statutory machinery should be undertaken, wherever circumstances call for it, with this long-term objective in view.

11. You will observe from paragraph 54 of the Report that the Committee, in its deliberation of these questions, has not taken into consideration the detailed effect of the various provisions of the International Labour Conventions covering the field of trade unionism, but has re-examined trade union policy in the light of actual experience. While you will wish to examine the recommendations in the attached Report on their merits, it will, of course, be necessary to keep in mind our international obligations. It will be recalled that freedom of association of employers and workers is the subject of the International Labour Conventions Nos. 84 and 87. Convention No. 84, (although it has not yet attracted the second ratification required to bring it into force) has been ratified by His Majesty's Government and declarations have been made under which most Governments in the Territories have accepted the obligations of the Convention. Convention No. 87 has been similarly ratified and is in force for Great Britain, but a declaration stating the extent to which it has been applied in the non-metropolitan territories as required under Article 12 of the Convention, has not yet been made. It is clear from the replies received to my predecessor's circular despatch of the 29th October, 1948, that modified acceptance only is possible in many Territories, since *inter alia*, the following matters which appear in the legislation of certain territories must, I am advised, be regarded as modifications of the Convention: restrictions on persons who may be elected to trade union office, restrictions on the freedom of government employees to join associations of their own choosing, the exclusion of certain classes of workers from the scope of trade union legislation, restrictions on the amalgamation and federation of unions. As it is probable that the implementation by Colonial Governments of some of the recommendations in the enclosed Report would necessitate further modifications, it will be desirable to consider whether provision for the inclusion of such additional modifications can be made in the proposed declaration in regard to Convention No. 87. I propose to address you further on this matter shortly, and it is perhaps sufficient to say here that, while I should wish you to have regard for the Conventions I have mentioned, I have no objection to the adoption in the Territory under your administration of such additional trade union legislation on the lines recommended in the enclosed Report as you may deem to be desirable in the interests of proper trade union development.

12. Finally, I turn to the Committee's comments on the vital subject of education and training, contained in paragraphs 48–53. The importance to the future of the movement of informed and responsible officials and members, well grounded in trade union principles and practice, cannot to my mind be over-emphasised and I propose to address you separately on this most important question. I should, however, welcome your views on the proposal that a trade union handbook should be

produced. It is clear that any centrally prepared draft will need adaptation to meet the requirements of different areas, but it will be of the greatest advantage in producing the basic text and in deciding the best approach for each subject, if copies of booklets or pamphlets prepared in the light of local experience could be made available. I should be grateful, therefore, to be supplied with copies of any such documents that may have proved useful in your territory.

13. As I indicated in my despatch of the 25th April, to which I have already referred, there will be a full opportunity at the proposed Conference in September for discussion of the attached Report and for consideration of the extent to which its recommendations may usefully be applied in the various territories. It would clearly be an advantage, and add point to the discussion, if by the end of August at latest I could have your brief comments on any points in this Report, or in the Memorandum dealing with other aspects of industrial relations which will follow, on which you have particular views.

14. In conclusion, I wish to take this opportunity of paying tribute to the steady and patient work over the past years of all those officers who have been concerned with the development of the trade union movement in their territory. If, by its very nature, the attached Report reads more as an analysis of defects than an appreciation of achievement, it is not because the achievement is not recognised. There has been a remarkable development which could not have been attained without the experience, guidance and encouragement of sympathetic Departments. It would have been strange if this development had not been accompanied by problems and difficulties, and I trust that by tackling these realistically in the light of experience we can further assist the Colonial trade union movement to a future of full self-reliance and responsibility.

15. The Circular has not been addressed to the Governments of Brunei, Falkland Islands, Malta and St. Helena. It has been sent for information to the Comptroller, Development and Welfare in the West Indies, the Commissioner General, South East Asia, and to the Colonial Attaché, Washington. It has also been sent to the High Commissioner, Federation of Malaya under cover of a separate despatch.

Annex to 369

Introduction

We have been asked by the Secretary of State to carry out a review of Colonial trade union legislation in the light of the experience which has been gained during the past twenty years of trade union development in the Colonial territories. That review has now been completed and this Memorandum embodies the results of our deliberations. We have been materially assisted in our discussion of the sometimes controversial issues and the technical questions involved by the opportunity we have had to hear at first hand the opinions and experiences of Labour Commissioners from some of the more important territories.

Since the definition of a "trade union" in Colonial legislation includes organisations both of workers and of employers, it is necessary for us to make plain that our examination has been directed to the problems of *workers' organisations*, and that the phrases 'trade union' and 'trade unionism' are to be interpreted in that sense throughout our Memorandum, except where there is indication to the contrary. In suggesting legislative provisions, however, we have throughout borne in mind that such provisions would apply to employers' organisations as well as to workers' organisations and our recommendations in such respects are made on this understanding.

Our examination has not revealed any fundamental weaknesses in Colonial trade union legislation, but it is our view that existing legislation, which is largely based on that of the United Kingdom, requires strengthening in certain respects in the light of local experience, with a view to remedying defects which have appeared in trade union structure and organisation. Just as there are provisions in United Kingdom legislation and practice which are inappropriate to conditions in the various Colonial territories, in the same way conditions in these territories may call for legislative or administrative action which would not be appropriate in this country. In particular, we recommend that, in the interests of the trade unions themselves, there should be closer control over trade union finance than is customary, or would indeed be acceptable, in this country. We have also felt the need to make some comments on the problem of the education of the officials and rank and file of colonial trade unions, and these are embodied in our Memorandum.

We have been conscious of the wide variations in conditions between territories and our examination of the trade union problem has emphasized the importance of allowing local discretion in determining the need for and the nature of amendments in the law. Our recommendations give due weight to this need to have regard for local experience.

We regard our present report as presenting one aspect only of the general problem of industrial relations in the Colonial territories. A sound legislative basis for trade union activity is clearly essential but in our view it is equally important to promote the development of organised machinery, whether voluntary or statutory, through which workers and employers can co-operate. We would draw attention to our general recommendations regarding the wider use of statutory wage-fixing machinery.

We now propose to examine the arrangements which exist in the various territories for negotiating or fixing wages, and for conciliation and arbitration. This examination will necessarily bring into review the important aspect of the employers' position and responsibilities which is the necessary complement to our present report.

Trade unionism in the colonies

1. The central purpose of British Colonial policy is to guide the Colonial territories to responsible self-government within the Commonwealth in conditions that ensure to the people both a fair standard of living and freedom from aggression from any quarter. Inherent in this policy is the recognition of freedom of association, and the aim therefore has been to pass on to Colonial peoples the protection and experience gained by labour in this country over the past century. From the time of Lord Passfield's[1] despatch in 1930, emphasis has been laid upon the encouragement of the trade union movement. The rate of advance since then has been swift, and it is not surprising that many of the problems facing Colonial trade unionism today can be traced to the fact that the great increase in the number of unions and their

[1] S of S for colonies, Labour government, 1929–1931.

membership during recent years has not been matched by an equally effective growth in the understanding by members and officials of trade union principles and practice.

2. A great deal has been achieved by the movement, considering its youthfulness; but the quality of future progress depends upon the removal of those weaknesses which have manifested themselves. It was in an attempt to assess and find an answer to the problems facing Colonial trade unionism at the present time that we undertook an examination of the subject. Our conclusions are now submitted for the approval of the Secretary of State.

Is the policy of encouraging trade unionism in the colonies sound?

3. The people who ask whether trade unions are really necessary in some of the less developed Colonial territories, and who question whether the unsophisticated workers of those territories are ready for them, are in part answered by what is written above. The formation of workers' organisations is a natural accompaniment of the economic and political progress of each territory, and it is the aim of our labour policy overseas, by passing on all the experience we have gained, to guide this inevitable development into a sound and *responsible* movement, able to play its proper organic part in the democratic structure of the territory. But such criticism also implies that it is unrealistic to impose the pattern of orthodox British trade unionism on the Colonial worker, who cannot appreciate all that went to its making and finds some of its rigidity unsuited to his simple needs. This is, on the face of it, a reasonable argument and it would indeed be foolish to assume that experience in this country, although of great value, necessarily provides the ready-made and only answer to the various problems that arise in the vastly different conditions of the Colonies. Nevertheless, it has been shown that there are many features of British trade union organisation which are adaptable enough to provide a sound foundation from which the Colonial movement can develop its own traditions. Defects there are and the pace, accelerated by the last War, may have been too swift to give time for thorough absorption in the Colonies of the underlying principles and ideals of the movement; but it is significant that no effective alternative has been suggested by the critics. The difficulties which seemingly arise out of the trade union movement would certainly have arisen in a different and more acute form without the safety valve which it provides . . . .

370 CO 859/183/3, no 47 [Oct 1951]

[Labour relations]: report on conference of heads of colonial labour departments (CO, 24 Sept–5 Oct) [Extract]

Introduction

In a confidential circular despatch dated the 25th April, 1951, the Secretary of State suggested to Colonial Governments that, having regard to the advances made in recent years in the economic, social and political development of the Colonial territories, the time was opportune for a comprehensive review of work and progress in the field of labour relations, as a vitally important feature of Colonial policy in modern conditions. His proposal that a Conference should be held in London for this purpose, to be attended by Heads of Labour Departments and senior officers concerned with trade union work in the territories, was warmly received by Colonial Governments; and the Conference was convened between the 24th September and 5th October, 1951. It was attended by thirty-two officers from twenty-two different territories, whose names are shewn in the list at Annex I.[1] In order that these officers might be in a position to speak authoritatively, Colonial Governments were asked as far as possible to study the subjects for discussion in advance of the Conference: but it was not the intention that the officers present should be regarded as committing their Governments to any particular course of action.

2. In putting forward the proposal for a Conference, Mr. Griffiths explained that he had already taken the first step towards a review of Colonial labour policy by requesting the Colonial Labour Advisory Committee to examine the general problems of trade unionism in the territories. The Committee's detailed recommendations on this subject, endorsed by the Secretary of State, were subsequently communicated to Colonial Governments with his confidential circular despatch of the 26th July, 1951.[2] This despatch, while recognising the achievements attained in the trade union field largely through the wise and patient guidance of Colonial Labour Departments, drew attention to the problems and defects in trade union organisation and practice which experience had revealed: and recommended for the consideration of Governments the Advisory Committee's suggestions for modifications in legislation and administrative practice which might afford greater protection and guidance to the trade union movement while it remained comparatively immature and provide a sound framework within which it could develop and take its proper place as a responsible element in the economic and social life of the various territories. At the same time, the wide variety of conditions in the territories was fully recognised both by the Advisory Committee and by the Secretary of State, and it was emphasised that the application of the Committee's recommendations must in the last resort be a matter for determination in the local context and in the light of local experience.

3. Mr. Griffiths also pointed out that trade union development was only one aspect of the general problem of industrial relations and that he would wish the Conference to survey the whole field covered by that subject, with a view to the direction of future effort throughout the territories on the basis of a coordinated and positive line of policy. Before the Conference met, the Colonial Labour Advisory Committee was asked to examine the existing policies and methods which were designed to contribute to the promotion and maintenance of industrial harmony, as an essential element both in the economic development of the territories and in the movement towards the establishment of responsible democratic societies. The Committee's preliminary views on such subjects as the development of standing machinery for consultation and negotiation between employers and employed, the use of statutory wage-fixing methods, the possible improvement of conciliation and arbitration procedures, and the stimulation of organisation on both sides of industry and of cooperation between the two sides were taken into account in the preparation of a Colonial Office paper presented to the Conference as a basis for discussion.

4. The main emphasis of the Conference was thus laid upon reviewing the policies and practices which Colonial Governments had pursued and could pursue

---

[1] Annexes to this report not printed.

[2] See 369.

towards the objective of establishing good labour relations on a stable and permanent foundation. As one aspect of this subject, there was exposition and clarification of the general principles underlying the possible legislative and procedural changes recommended and endorsed by the Secretary of State in relation to trade union development, and discussion of the possible applicability of those recommendations in the various territories. In the wider field of industrial relations generally, the concern of the Conference was to attempt to educidate, in the light of experience, broad principles of policy that might prove acceptable and effective as a guide to future action under local conditions.

5. Particular features during discussion of the main theme of the Conference were (i) the emphasis laid upon trade union education and training, (ii) the views expressed upon the merits of Statutory Wages Boards on modern lines as a means both of ensuring adequate standards for Colonial workers and of promoting the habit of negotiation in industry and (iii) consideration of the principles previously communicated to Governments by the Secretary of State in his circular despatch of the 22nd August, 1951, on the treatment of strikes and lock-outs in essential services.

6. Although the primary aim of the Conference was to discuss industrial relations, it afforded a valuable opportunity for the discussion of a number of other common problems in the labour field: and the Agenda (a copy of which is attached as Annex II) was extended to cover discussion of the administrative and economic aspects of social insurance, workmens' compensation, technical training and the development of employment exchanges. The study of these subjects was inevitably cursory, but nevertheless a useful exchange of views resulted. In addition, the Conference was addressed by experts on the work of the International Labour Organisation, the problems of international trade unionism, and the "Cold War": and representatives from the Trade Union Congress took part in the discussion on trade union education and training. The opportunity was also taken to hold a number of useful meetings on a regional basis to discuss special problems outside the main work of the Conference.

Trade unionism in the colonies

7. The Conference had as a basis for its discussion Mr. Griffiths' despatch of the 26th July, 1951, and its accompanying Memorandum. It was recognised that, while the legislative changes proposed in these documents might in themselves seem to suggest a legalistic and restrictive spirit that was alien to proclaimed liberal ideas about freedom of association, these proposals implied no shift of policy: they must be viewed simply as a reappraisement of the measures of guidance and control which might be desirable to promote the growth of an independent, responsible and effective trade union movement. It was emphasised once more that the extent to which the proposed legislative changes might be applied must be conditioned by local circumstances. Indeed, Mr. Griffiths had made it clear that the changes recommended were more readily applicable in those territories where trade unionism had not as yet developed to any appreciable extent.

8. The Conference endorsed the principle that a sound and responsible trade union movement was essential to economic and political progress, but there was agreement that in no two Colonies were circumstances so alike as to enable such a movement to be fostered by exactly similar methods. More particularly was it

difficult in territories where trade unionism was already strongly developed to attempt by legislation to correct faults which might now have become apparent. In those cases, a more indirect approach was essential and influence and persuasion must be preferred to legal sanctions.

9. The duties and functions of Labour Officers in regard to the encouragement of trade union development were carefully examined and it was agreed that trade union organisation should be directly encouraged only when industrial relations would be strengthened and improved thereby. There should be no haphazard encouragement of the formation of trade unions for its own sake. No amount of encouragement could infuse life into unions which had no vigour in themselves. On the question whether the inevitable concentration on the problems of workers' organisations in the territories had not perhaps led to some neglect of employers' associations, it was generally agreed to be the duty of Labour Officers to help to create the conditions in which people who employ could meet those employed by them. There were, however, reservations in some quarters about the value of actively encouraging the formation of employers' associations; these reservations were largely attributable to the feeling that such initiative would not readily be understood by many Colonial workers. It might indeed undermine their confidence in the good faith of the Labour Departments. Similar considerations arose on the problem whether the important function of industrial conciliation might not be prejudiced by the close relations with trade unions maintained by Labour Departments and the positive action taken by Labour Officers in regard to trade union development. While there were differences of opinion and practice on the extent to which it was desirable to separate the two roles of conciliation and trade union development within a Labour Department by allocating them to different officers, there was agreement that the dual function was in general being satisfactorily fulfilled.

10. The registration of trade unions in the United Kingdom is voluntary; but from earliest days of Colonial trade unionism compulsory registration has been recommended and adopted on the grounds that sympathetic supervision and guidance are necessary for organisations of workers without previous experience of combination for industrial purposes. Northern Rhodesia is the only territory where trade union registration is voluntary. Subject to this exception, the Conference confirmed and supported the principle of compulsory registration. It was clear that the compulsory system involved the wise exercise of local discretion since the somewhat widely drawn definition of 'trade union' which had been adopted from United Kingdom legislation, if strictly applied, must entail the compulsory registration of even the smallest and most temporary of workers' combinations. The registration of trade unions on a probationary basis did not receive the same general support, although there were certain territories, particularly in East Africa, where this system was welcomed as providing an interim period during which trade unions could demonstrate their *bona fides* and their capacity, under help and guidance, to develop into a sound organisation; the system might also provide some protection against the growth of a multiplicity of unions. There had been many cases in the past of trade unions registering and then fading out of existence and being de-registered; it was hoped that, by introducing a probationary period during which the full privileges and protection afforded to registered unions would be enjoyed, it would come to be appreciated by the workers concerned that registration carried with it obligations essential to sound democratic development. It was also felt that in certain

territories it would be useful to make provision for a form of registration for certain kinds of small bodies such as works committees which would not involve them in the obligations of full trade union registration, though the latter would be necessary if such bodies wished to enjoy the privileges and protection that went with it.

11. The question of registration led to the problem of the powers of the Registrar of Trade Unions. It was the general feeling of the Conference that, so far as the registration of unions was concerned, the Registrar should operate on the basis of clearly laid down legal criteria with as few discretionary powers as possible. For this reason, even those territories which proposed to adopt a system of probationary registration saw difficulty in any requirement that a trade union should prove to the Registrar's satisfaction "a reasonable degree of organisation" before being finally registered. As regards other controls, it was agreed that laxness in financial matters had been a disturbing feature of trade union management in many territories. The proposal that there should be an extension of the Registrar's powers in relation to union accounts, including the power to sue defaulting officials, was the subject of a general measure of agreement, as were proposals aimed at improving the quality and frequency of auditing.

12. The extent to which trade unions might indulge in political activities had been a source of difficulty. The primary purpose of trade unions was industrial and it was clear that they would fail to carry out this primary purpose if an undue proportion of their energies was misdirected to political ends, particularly in the early stages of their development. The Conference accepted the principle that the control of union funds should belong to a union and its members but recognised that there might exist conditions where, while some degree of political activity was legitimate, some restriction on political expenditure was wise and justifiable. Where control was regarded as justifiable, care should be taken to ensure that a trade union was left free to undertake all normal and reasonable union activities.

13. However careful the supervision exercised by the Registrar, trade unions must in the last analysis depend on their own leaders. The lessons of the past and present showed the need for realism in recognizing that the control of a trade union offered a power and prestige irresistibly attractive to certain personalities. The choice of leadership must, it was realised, rest with the unions themselves, but there was a general acceptance of the principle underlying the views expressed by the Venn Commission to British Guiana in 1949 that trade union officials, with limited exceptions, should be men whose livelihood depended on their work in the industry concerned. The particular need for local discretion in applying legal restrictions to this and was [sic], however, emphasised: to ban "outsiders" completely might deprive unions of valuable leadership. It was similarly stressed that local circumstances must govern local application of the generally acceptable proposal that the more important decisions of a trade union should be taken by means of secret ballot.

Industrial relations

14. Trade unions cannot operate in a vacuum. Their primary purpose calls for bargaining and negotiation with employers preferably on the basis of established and recognised procedures and it is the duty of government in the general public interest to see that the necessary machinery of negotiation is built up and to ensure that services of conciliation and arbitration are available when agreement by voluntary negotiation cannot be reached. The field covered by the discussion at the Conference

can be broadly divided into three main parts: first of all, methods for regulating wages and conditions of employment; secondly, methods for reducing the incidence of disputes and for settling them when they arise; and thirdly, ways and means of achieving constructive co-operation between employer and worker. . . .

Trade union education and training

28. One of the major problems of Colonial trade unionism was the high rate of illiteracy among the members of unions and the prevailing lack of knowledge, not only of the element of idealism which underlay the principles of association, but also of the practical functions of a trade union and the comparatively simple mechanics by which a union was conducted. When many trade union leaders in the Colonies fell short of the standard that might be desired, it could be realised how much needed to be done among the ordinary trade union members. The ideal was that trade union training should be undertaken by the trade unions themselves, but the stage when this could be a practical possibility had not yet been reached in the majority of territories. Until it had been reached, the primary responsibility must rest with government as part of its acknowledged policy of fostering the growth of a sound trade union movement. At the moment, government was in the position of a guardian of the movement, but obviously its activities should always be exercised in such a way as to strengthen rather than weaken the independence of the movement. This was important, since in present conditions labour policy in the Colonies involved a far more direct interest in trade union activities, by way of guidance and help, than would be appropriate in the United Kingdom. It was this which underlay the appointment and functions, for example, of trade union labour officers.

29. Nevertheless, the desired results could not be achieved by government action alone: and the effectiveness of the training provided was likely to be enhanced by the association of other independent bodies with the work. The T.U.C. for example, had a close interest in Colonial trade union education and had already done a great deal of valuable work in this field. The I.C.F.T.U. was also entering the field and the British Council had made a useful contribution. The role of the Universities, particularly in regard to extra-mural work, was also an important one, although experience had perhaps shewn the need for some definition of the part which Universities might play in this field. It seemed important to draw a distinction between the teaching of industrial relations and trade union practice as a general subject, and courses expressly designed for trade union officials on the techniques of trade unionism from which other members of the community were excluded. The former role, designed to give the benefits of a dispassionate study of the problems of industrial relations to employers and workers alike, was clearly an appropriate one for the Universities. In the latter role of teaching the mechanics of trade unionism to trade union members, the Universities might also give valuable help: but just as the help which the independent university institutions in the United Kingdom give in this field is naturally applied in consultation with the trade union movement, so it was desirable in the Colonies that there should be consultation with Labour Departments as the guardian of the movement. The vital need in the territories for training of this kind called for the closest collaboration of all who were interested and could assist in the work, including of course Colonial trade unions themselves.

30. The direct association of the T.U.C. with Colonial training courses was a great advantage. Not only did it give an independent character to such courses, but also

provided an opportunity for strengthening the links between responsible trade union opinion in this country and the growing movement in the Colonies and so increasing the educative and moderating influence which the former could be expected to bring to bear. An informal agreement which existed between the T.U.C. and the I.C.F.T.U. made trade union educational work in the British Overseas Territories primarily a matter for the T.U.C.; and where local training projects were contemplated, it would be preferable for consultation to take place with the T.U.C. before the I.C.F.T.U. was associated with them. The T.U.C. for their part were intending to keep the Colonial Office fully informed of their plans in the field of trade union education. However, the work done by trade union labour officers was at this stage, at least, the most important element in the creation of a stable and responsible trade union movement. Great praise was due to the work which had already been done. A great variety of pamphlets and booklets had been produced in the territories by local initiative and the trade union labour officer had been able by his special position to reach the ordinary trade union member at his branch meetings and in the workshop.

31. It was important that trade union education should aim at spreading knowledge downwards and outwards through the movement to the individual member. There was too great a tendency for members to remain merely passive supporters and the collective will and interest was often lacking. The member could only be reached by work done in the territory; by the distribution of literature, by training in negotiation at a low level, and by lectures and informal talks in the branches. This was sufficient for the member but the trade union official needed more specialised training. It was agreed that in general, such training also could best be carried out in the territories themselves. This did however, raise a difficulty in some places since a course in the United Kingdom had a prestige value which made union leaders look askance at any scheme for local training. Moreover, in some small territories local facilities were altogether lacking. It was accepted, therefore, that there would be exceptions to the general rule, but that sparing and selective use should be made of training facilities in the United Kingdom. There was general endorsement of the view that, when trade unionists were brought to the United Kingdom, they should have an opportunity to participate in local branch activities (so far as that was practicable and acceptable to the United Kingdom trade unions concerned) and see something at first hand of the practical day-to-day working of a trade union's affairs. There was at present a tendency for too much time to be sepnt at head offices. There should, moreover, be the greatest care in selection; particular attention should be paid to the character and personality of the candidates. Too often men were chosen who were more concerned with their own advancement than the welfare of the union to which they belonged.

32. It had been thought for some time that there was a place in the Colonies for a well produced Trade Union Handbook which would be more than a mere reflection of United Kingdom trade union history, and which would place the elements of trade unionism in perspective against the background of Colonial problems. The idea was most strongly supported and several suggestions were made as to the general lines which should be followed in its preparation. The handbook should be written in simple direct language, avoiding unnecessary generalities and discussion on British trade union background, and dealing more with the practical every-day problems of trade union administration. It would be useful if it could give some outline of the duties of the various officers of a union, the keeping of accounts, the management of

meetings, the technique of negotiation and other practical matters in the day-to-day work of a union. It was also felt that the handbook, in addition to giving a general outline of industrial relations, should depict the economic and social position which trade unionism occupied in a democratic community. There were strong advantages in a first draft being prepared in London by collaboration between the T.U.C. and the Colonial Office which could then be submitted to Territories for their comments and suggestions for adaptation in the light of local conditions. There was no question but that such a handbook would have a greatly increased influence if it were to be issued as a T.U.C. document.

Labour administration

33. As the Conference had as its main objective a study of the problems of industrial relations and trade union development, which occupied the greater part of the time available, discussion upon other important activities of Colonial Labour Departments was necessarily curtailed. The other obligations which they carried, as their part of the general duty of Government to promote a higher standard of living in the territories, were not however overlooked. There was on the one hand the need to establish certain basic conditions for the assistance and protection of workers, particularly of women and children who entered employment; in this field were included, for example, regulation of hours of work, factory inspection to ensure that working conditions and safety measures came up to predetermined standards, and the provision of labour exchanges. There was also the call for development of those services which are now comprised under the general heading of "social security".

34. It was clear to the Conference that the highly developed structure of social security which had been achieved in the United Kingdom could not be regarded as a measure of what the Colonial territories might hope to achieve in the near future. In many places, the provision of social security in its broadest sense still largely remained a problem of fundamental economic and social development: there was still a great need for the expansion of basic social services such as health and education and for the economic development of local resources to support such services. The introduction therefore of measures of security in the more advanced sense against such vicissitudes as unemployment, sickness, old age and the death of the family bread-winner (however desirable such measures might be) must inevitably be conditioned by the financial, economic and social circumstances in each territory: and careful assessment of practical possibilities and priorities was involved. . . .

40. Turning from social security to other problems of labour administration, it was recognised that there was an urgent need everywhere for the training of native skilled craftsmen, more particularly in Africa. Development projects were increasingly hampered through the lack of skilled artisans capable of adapting themselves to changing situations and capable of accepting responsibility. Frequently, the employer in the Colonies was not equipped to give proper apprenticeship training and the difficulty could probably only be met by government training, e.g., in trade schools, followed by training on the job in industry. Apprenticeship training was a long-term measure for raising the degree of industrial skill and, however successful, it would be some years before appreciable results were achieved, particularly where stable communities in urban industrial areas had not yet become established. In the interim, the best use had to be made of existing sources of skilled or semi-skilled labour and systems of trade testing by properly qualified persons could provide

evidence of ability, as a substitute for the apprenticeship certificate of the future, which might do much to give a cash value, to the degree of skill attained and provide an incentive to the acquisition of higher skill qualifying for higher pay.

41. Development projects in many territories were also often faced with a lack of reliable data regarding the availability of labour. This need might to some extent be met by the development of employment exchange services, although anything in the nature of a comprehensive exchange system on the United Kingdom model was probably beyond expectation in most territories at present. There appeared however to be scope for such services both where there was a shortage of manpower, as in Africa, and where there was a surplus, as in the West Indies. Local difficulties were nevertheless stressed. In some places, traditional methods of recruiting labour, coupled with the existence of a labour surplus, militated against the use of employment exchanges. In other territories, there was a fear that the existence of exchanges in rural areas might help to disturb the social pattern. There were also practical difficulties in recruiting men at a distance from remote exchanges. Again where labour was easily obtainable, it was to be expected that only [the] poorer type of worker would have recourse to the exchange, which could not therefore be expected to gain estimation in the eyes of the employer: Governments could however help to overcome this by notifying all their own labour requirements to the exchange. Resistance from employers was marked in places, though in some territories they were coming to appreciate the advantages of the services of careful sifting and selection which a labour exchange could provide. There were also examples of the workers sense of dignity being opposed to use of labour exchanges. The problem of identification also arose in this context, but it was felt that it need not interfere to any material extent with the development of machinery for registration and placement of workers. Time was not however available for detailed examination of these problems, and the Conference could not go farther than this cursory survey. Registration had fulfilled a particularly useful function in the case of port schemes for the decasualisation of labour. While accurate assessment of the state of employment in any territory probably called for proper statistical investigation, an employment exchange service might assist materially in providing information about employment trends and useful data in connection with migration or immigration problems.

International Labour Organisation

42. The activities of the I.L.O. have tended in recent years to throw an increasing burden of work on Colonial Labour Departments, and the doubts often expressed as to the value of such activities were fully ventilated and countered in a stimulating discussion opened by a representative of the Ministry of Labour and National Service. There was, he said, a tendency to apply to the work of an international organisation the same criteria as would apply to a national administration; a tendency to judge each activity strictly on its individual merits and to expect the same nice adjustment of means to ends. But the activities of an international organisation could not be judged purely in relation to the particular situation or particular problems of an individual territory. The policies of a world wide organisation had to take account of many diverse needs and necessarily reflected the efforts of compromise between governments and, in the case of the I.L.O. between governments, employers and workers. The real achievements must be assessed over a period and not only on the

basis of concrete results, however notable, but also on the less tangible influence which it had exerted on the minds and actions of those who had participated in it. The concrete results were nevertheless formidable. The effective establishment of the now familiar idea of world standards on labour matters, and the way those standards had guided and assisted many countries all over the world in the framing of their social policies were matters of history. The basic strength of the organisation rested upon the common social consciousness which it created. It was the only international organisation where employers and workers could put their views and vote in their own right along with government representatives.

43. As regards the much debated 'Colonial application clause' in the Constitution of the I.L.O. (Article 35), it was to the advantage of Colonial Governments to show that these constitutional provisions did, in fact, encourage the progressive application of the provisions of Conventions in non-metropolitan territories. In the I.L.O., as nowhere else, His Majesty's Government were presented with the opportunity for removing misconceptions about labour conditions in the Colonies, of expounding the facts as they existed, and explaining their policies and practice.

International trade unionism

44. The Head of the International Department of the T.U.C. addressed the Conference on the problems of international trade unionism. Tracing the circumstances which had led up to the formation of the International Confederation of Trade Unions (I.C.F.T.U.) in 1949, he emphasised that the withdrawal of the T.U.C. from the World Federation of Trade Unions (W.F.T.U.) had been caused by the determination of certain elements within the organisation to use it as a political instrument for the furthering of Communism. The aim of the I.C.F.T.U. was not however merely to fight the W.F.T.U.; something more constructive was needed, if the policy of the new organisation was to appeal to trade unionists everywhere. The primary purpose of the organisation was the establishment of a powerful and effective international organisation, composed of free trade unions independent of any external domination and pledged to the task of promoting the interests of working people throughout the world. Another important aim was to assist the establishment, maintenance and development of trade union organisation, particularly in economically and socially under-developed territories. In the short period of its existence the I.C.F.T.U. had gone a long way to overcome the basic defect of previous "internationals"—their fundamentally European character—by adopting a regional structure. It was intended that regional organisations should exist for Europe, the Americas, (with a sub-section in the Caribbean), Asia and Africa; and that each region would have responsibility for discussing its own problems and correlating its own policies, although new policy decisions would be subject to the approval of the Executive Board of the I.C.F.T.U. The operations of the I.C.F.T.U. were also being greatly assisted by the co-operation of the long-established International Trade Secretariats. International policy was to be built up in the light of the knowledge and advice of the local trade unions in the various parts of the world.

45. In British Colonial territories, the work of the T.U.C. and the I.C.F.T.U. would be complementary; indeed, in all probability the implementation of I.C.F.T.U. policy in these areas would be achieved largely through the agency of the T.U.C. While for obvious reasons the I.C.F.T.U. and the T.U.C. had to avoid the impression

of being too closely associated with Governments, it was the intention that in all this work proper liaison should be maintained with Colonial Labour Departments.

A further talk from a Foreign Office representative placed this account of the opposing forces of international trade unionism in perspective against the background of the "Cold War".

Conclusion

46. A review of the tangible and intangible elements which go to make up a system of industrial relations must necessarily be somewhat imprecise in its conclusions. The reactions of people of widely varying temperament and race, living under diverse conditions, to ideas which are for the main part new and foreign to them, must obviously reveal great variations; and the Conference, in emphasising this aspect of Colonial administration, underlined the importance of a flexible and non-doctrinaire approach to the problems of labour relations.

47. There was nevertheless a wide field of general agreement and such differences of view as the Conference revealed were largely over questions of method and timing rather than policy. Opinion was unanimous that, within the agreed framework of general principles, the choice of method, the pace and the timing must be left to local judgement. Mr. Griffiths' despatch of the 26th July, 1951, on "Trade Unionism" clearly implied that the various proposals contained therein were to be regarded as providing general guidance within which local judgement might operate, rather than a set of precise directions to be applied uniformly everywhere; the same considerations must necessarily apply in the related field of industrial relations. Nevertheless, the need for local judgement to be stimulated by a sense of urgency was emphasised. That did not mean that imminent crises were to be expected in the field of trade unionism or industrial relations: it meant only that, in this as in other aspects of our Colonial work, "time was not on our side". The tide of events was moving rapidly, and might well not allow scope for the organisations and structures which we wished to see develop in Colonial societies to grow up by the slow and sure processes of natural evolution and "learning by experience". In setting our aims and deciding upon methods, the object must be to achieve tangible and lasting results within the time likely to be at our disposal.

48. While therefore it was unanimously agreed that the basic aim of labour policy in our territories must be the fostering, as a spontaneous and soundly-rooted growth, of those voluntary principles of association, consultation and cooperation which have inspired labour relations in the United Kingdom, the practical limitations and the time factor could not be disregarded. The natural development of trade union organisation in the Colonies is hampered by formidable difficulties. Poor communications, long distances, the scattered nature of industrial occupations, are practical obstacles, to which must be added the high degree of illiteracy among workers, the tendency to distort trade union organisation for political purposes (in part because of the absence of organised political parties), and other weaknesses. Moreover, trade union education involves a transfer of ideas and ideals that may not be readily assimilable. However active the help and guidance of Labour Departments, the British T.U.C. and other sympathetic bodies, it is hardly to be expected that the area of effective trade union organisation can be appreciably extended in some territories for many years to come: and the development of sound leadership may be an equally long process.

49. The case put forward at the Conference for examining the need for statutory wage-fixing machinery rested as much on these practicalities, as upon the weakness and even danger of leaving the wages of the vast majority of Colonial workers completely unregulated while the slow process of developing systems of collective bargaining took place. The possible link between better wages and higher productivity was also recognised: the tendency is for cheap labour to be carelessly used, and increased wage levels might result in more sustained efforts by employers to obtain, by improved supervision and other means, a more reasonable level of effort and production.

50. Great appreciation was expressed of the opportunity presented by the Conference not only to review the wider issues of policy involved in the main items of the agenda, but also to discuss the administrative and other problems associated with the day to day work of labour Departments. The value of the interchange of ideas and information specialists engaged in similar fields of work in different territories was demonstrated throughout the proceedings, and emphasised the usefulness of periodic meetings of this kind. The varying pace of development means that yesterday's problems in one territory are tomorrow's problems elsewhere: and the hope was generally voiced that further conferences on labour administration could be arranged, so that there might be a regular opportunity for the exchange of views and experiences which was so valuable an aide [sic] in the evolution of policies and the conduct of administration.

371 CO 927/1/2 12 Feb 1946

[Role of the Treasury in funding research schemes]: minute by C Y Carstairs[1]

Mr. Serpell[2] of the Treasury called this morning in order to have a discussion regarding the respective parts which the Treasury and the Colonial Office must play in dealing with proposals for research schemes. I gained the impression that what was chiefly exercising his mind was the same point as regards the much more difficult and bigger job of dealing with development proposals, and he did not have any particular criticisms to make regarding the method in which research schemes are at present put up. I assured him, however, that we would in no way take it amiss if the Treasury raised what appeared to be comparatively minor points since to reduce Treasury concurrence to a formality would not be consistent with the purposes of the Act, and it is always possible that the Treasury, coming to our schemes with a fresh mind, may be able to spot points which have been overlooked here. I tried, however, to lead his mind in the direction of working towards a policy of broad allocations of research funds, linked to a broad definition of the respective programmes of work to be undertaken under the various branches of research, with the idea that when this result had been achieved the Treasury would not need to trouble themselves very much about the details of schemes submitted as falling within the scope of policy and allocations so defined. Indeed, I think that with some pressure from the Treasury to enable us to press our various Research Committees

---

[1] Head of the CO Research Dept; subsequently director of CO information services, 1951–1953.

[2] (Sir) D R Serpell, principal; subsequently under-secretary, Treasury, 1954–1960.

for outline programmes of this kind this would not be unwelcome, since it is a long term task which busy people find it easy to postpone. We shall, however, I hope make much more rapid progress in this regard when we have completed our team of scientific secretaries of Research Committees. . . .

372 CO 927/1/2, no 1 11 Apr 1946

'Colonial Development and Welfare plans': minute by J B Williams. *Annex*: Research Dept record of discussion with Treasury, 14 Feb 1946

I circulate to other Departments likely to be interested the attached record of a discussion with the Treasury on certain general points raised by them in connection with colonial development and welfare plans. I think it may be helpful to other Departments to see this indication of Treasury views on the various points.

It will be seen that the four principal points made by the Treasury were the following:—

(a) The Treasury would like to receive at an early stage a copy of the comprehensive development plan of each Colony.

(b) They would like to be sure that full advantage is taken by Colonies of experience gained by the Colonial Office itself, particularly through research and other central schemes.

(c) They expect to see adequate provision in all plans for economic schemes.

(d) They expect the Colonial Office, when submitting applications for grants, to draw attention themselves to points which seem doubtful or open to possible objection.

Compliance with the last mentioned condition is clearly in our own long run interests, as otherwise the Treasury will be bound to scrutinise all applications more critically than they do at present, and thus cause additional delay.

Annex to 372

Mr. Serpell referred to Mr. Winnifrith's[1] letter of 8th December to Mr. J.B. Williams, in which was emphasised the importance attached by the Treasury to the ensuring that an adequate proportion of each colony's Colonial Development and Welfare allocation should be devoted to projects which would directly develop the economic potentialities of the territory. Suitable development of this kind was all the more important if the colony was to be able in due course to meet the recurrent expenditure on Welfare schemes, such as medical and educational services.

Mr. J.B. Williams said that the Colonial Office fully agreed with the importance of this consideration and pointed out that it was in fact always in their minds when dealing with development programmes.

Mr. Serpell said that, both in formulating and carrying out their development programmes, colonies should take advantage, to the maximum possible extent, of

---

[1] A J D Winnifrith, under-secretary; subsequently Sir John Winnifrith, third secretary, Treasury, 1951–1959.

the guidance to be obtained through the Colonial Office itself, more particularly from the various central and research schemes under the Colonial Development and Welfare Acts. It was important therefore that there should be a certain elasticity in colonies' programmes and even in individual schemes.

Whilst agreeing with this policy in theory, Mr. J.B. Williams pointed out that in practice two difficulties arose:—

(1) Political considerations could not be ignored and these in many cases made it necessary to consider allotting a larger proportion of funds to schemes of a social and welfare character than would be done if the problem could be approached purely objectively.

(2) The £120 million vote lapses at the end of 10 years and, apart from the undesirability of allowing expenditure to be concentrated into the last few years of that period (thereby making the burden of recurrent expenditure more difficult to bear, when the Colonial Development and Welfare assistance ceased) a yearly maximum had been fixed by the Act. It was necessary, therefore, to encourage the colonies to get their Development Programmes started as soon as possible.

One difficulty, which Mr. Serpell thought might arise was in the fact that materials were likely to be scarce for a number of years, and the projects most likely to be immediately practicable were those which required labour more than material and very often these were the "Charitable Works" mentioned above, and this might be to the prejudice of Development Works. He suggested that the Colonial Office should strive to ensure over the 10 year period the right balance between Development and Welfare despite any initial tendency to concentrate on Welfare.

Referring to his opening remarks, Mr. Serpell said that the Treasury would like to see the individual Colony Sketch Plans, when they became available, so that the complete picture could be seen and the Plans reviewed in the light of the policy outlined by him. Mr. J.B. Williams said that this would be done.

Mr. Serpell concluded by asking that the Colonial Office, when submitting applications for grants, should call attention to any points about which they themselves were doubtful, and on which they thought the Treasury would probably want to comment. Mr. J.B. Williams said that the Colonial Office would keep this request in mind and do their best to comply with it.

373 CO 927/1/3, no 12 17 Oct 1946

[Planning]: address by Mr Morrison (lord president) to the Institute of Public Administration.[1] *Minutes* by C Y Carstairs and Sir S Caine

We talk a good deal in these days about planning, but planning is a very large and complicated business and Britain is the first great nation to attempt to combine large scale economic and social planning with a full measure of individual rights and liberties. So far we are still at the experimental stage—indeed planning must never be rigid—but I will try to give you some idea how this experiment is shaping.

[1] The Institute was an association of central and local government officers and others interested in the study of public administration. Mr Morrison had been a member for some years.

I will first try to outline what is meant by planning as we in Britain understand it. Then I will review the machinery and methods of planning, and finally I will say something about the current and future problems to which planning must find the answer.

Planning's five stages

Planning can be divided logically into five stages:—

The first, without which none of the others can happen, is making up one's mind to plan and grasping what planning means.

The second is assembling the necessary facts and forecasts to make sure that the plan can be put on a sound practical basis.

The third stage is actually devising alternative plans and seeing what they each offer and what they each cost in terms of resources and disadvantages.

The fourth is the taking of decisions between alternative plans, including the decision what is to be planned and what is to be left unplanned.

The fifth, and by far the most extensive stage, is carrying out the plans in practice. This includes explaining them, adjusting them and devising all the necessary ways and means of ensuring that what was planned on paper does in fact happen at the right times and in the right places and in the right way.

I suggest that the first and vital stage was when the British people made up their minds to plan.

We sometimes need to remind ourselves that planning in the sense of deliberately using the main available national resources, in the endeavour to secure the good of the nation as a whole, is a very new thing. Until very recently the dominant idea was that it was unnecessary for the nation to know what its resources were and best not to attempt to control their use. That is still the view of a minority. Obviously while that view prevailed the necessary conditions for planning could not exist. Using a wartime parallel, the modern nation which is not prepared to plan is like a country which expects to win a war without mobilising for it.

Well, it is no less impossible to achieve social and economic well-being without planning and working for it. That really is obvious and it is time the obvious was accepted, even by people who prefer abstract dogma to the facing of plain facts. Unemployment and destitution were, in the main, the products of letting things drift—the muddled outcome of muddle. All our machinery and methods of planning are based on the express willingness of Parliament and of very large numbers of citizens in all areas and activities, to support and participate in social and economic planning, and to censure Ministers and public authorities if they plan wrongly or fail to plan when they ought. And let not the individual citizen forget that he has his responsibilities in planning no less than Ministers.

Assembling the facts

Given the will to plan the next stage has been to ascertain and assemble facts. This process of fact finding is immensely complicated. In the past government has made the worst of both worlds by demanding a mass of information which was only useful for limited purposes and did not fit together. The need now is for facts and figures to give all concerned—not only government—a clear up-to-date picture of what is happening with the minimum of effort. Before planning decisions can be taken we have to know what millions of business men, farmers, workers and others are making or growing or distributing. Statisticians have to ascertain how many people there are in the country, where they are, where they live, how many of them are of working age, how many of them are employed, in what occupations and industries and grades and so forth. In the same way information has to be compiled on the amount of fuel and raw material used in industry and the value of the products made and sold, together with the resulting earnings and profit. For many purposes the survey must be widened out to cover not only Britain but the world background. All this information has to be available promptly and adequately, so that any changes can be picked out without delay. On this basis forecasts are prepared of what will happen to production, to incomes, to employment and so forth if current trends continue.

All this correspondents [sic] to the work of Intelligence in the Armed Forces. In the peace-time machinery these facts are collected by Government Departments, public boards, local authorities, trade associations, trade unions and many other bodies and most of the key material is eventually funnelled into the Central Statistical Office, which is a part of the Cabinet Office, created during the war to produce a systematic picture of what is taking place. The outline of this picture, so far as it relates to the past, can be seen by anyone who takes the trouble to get a copy of the Monthly Digest of Statistics, compiled by the Central Statistical Office and published by the Stationery Office about the end of each month. Much more detailed material is of course given in the Board of Trade Journal, the Ministry of Labour Gazette and other well known sources. The wartime "Statistical blackout" is a thing of the past; indeed we can claim to be well launched on a campaign for statistical floodlighting. I recommend these publications to you all, and to the careful study of the B.B.C. and of all newspaper offices.

Examining the facts

Given the will to plan, and the necessary facts and forecasts, the process of planning in the strict sense can begin. This process consists of looking at the facts and forecasts and examining what are the possibilities of changing socially undesirable trends. So far we have been forced to concentrate so largely on pressing short-term problems that we have hardly begun to get the benefit of the scope which long-term planning will give for broad adjustments decided in advance.

As an example of short-range planning the forecasts of coal production may indicate—I do not say they do—that if the number of miners we expect to have produce the amount of coal we expect them to produce, there will not be enough coal to go round and factories will have to shut down and houses will have to go unheated. In such cases obviously the plan must not merely consist of rubber-stamping the forecast—either more men must be found or the output from the existing manpower must be stepped up, or means must be found of economising the use of coal.

In other cases forecasts may show that an industry is likely to export more or less of its product than is considered desirable, after weighing the need for more exports to pay for our imports, as against the urgent, natural and legitimate desire of consumers for more British goods, of the most urgently wanted sorts, to be kept in our own shops instead of being sent overseas. Given that we have to export enough to earn a certain amount of foreign exchange, we may have the choice of earning more by exporting turbo-generators and keeping all the shirts we make at home, or alternatively of pushing exports of shirts and re-equipping our power stations with turbo-generators. The method we use here is for Departments representing all the main demands upon resources to put in their claims and see to what extent the claims conflict with one another. Where there is a direct conflict one or other claim has to give way.

The stage of decision

Here we come on to the fourth stage, that of taking decisions. Just as in war the military planners would, on instructions from the Chiefs of Staff, submit proposals for invading various enemy-held territories and the Chiefs of Staff would then advise Governments what was the most promising objective to go for first in view of the manpower, shipping and equipment available, so in the economic and social field, the staffs engaged on planning work out in consultation the various possibilities and try to point out the snags and advantages of each. On this basis Ministers decide on the strategy of the use of our national resources. For example, what size of Army, Navy and Air Force can we afford to or must we keep, what level must our exports reach and what claims must be cut down or postponed in order to keep the total demand on our resources within the limits of the resources available.

Here follows the most important and far-reaching stage of all, when Ministers, having made decisions for which they are prepared to take responsibility, come before Parliament and the nation and set in hand the task of carrying those decisions out.

Execution of the plan

The carrying out of economic plans is a job not simply for Government agencies, but for the whole nation. By informing the public of the trend of the economic situation, by making known the Government policies as to the best allocation of available resources, by promoting discussion of these matters and by revising estimates and forecasts from time to time, the Government can do much to shape the future course of economic affairs by ensuring that industry and agriculture shall be able to look further ahead with confidence and to form their expectations on explicit assumptions which can be tested and criticised, instead of on a vague hunch. Then the prospect of realizing the Government's plans will be seen to depend on a number of factors such as Chancellor's annual budget, his control of credit policy through the nationalised Bank of England and his control of investment policy through the Capital Issues Committee and other channels. The extent to which Government Departments and nationalised boards can speed up or retard development plans is another very important factor in resisting tendencies towards inflation on the one hand or trade recession on the other.

To give another example, the control of industrial location exercised by the President of the Board of Trade through the Distribution of Industry Act and through Town and Country Planning enables the government to prevent industry from flocking to certain areas, with adverse social and economic effects, while masses of citizens in other areas are unemployed.

National co-operation for public well-being

But when full account has been taken of all the instruments at the disposal of government the fulfilment or otherwise of the major part of economic plans is dependent on the actions of employers and workers generally. For that reason alone it would not be enough for the control by blind forces to be replaced by control by a few people sitting in Whitehall. Everyone must be encouraged and assisted to understand at least in outline the economic position of the nation, the aims of economic plans and the part which every citizen should play both in criticising those plans before they become operative and in carrying them through afterwards. In this way only can we ensure that we are developing a system of planning from the consumer end—and planning must be inspired from the consumer end if it is not to be bureaucratic and inefficient.

As we believe in a free society we must have the courage of our convictions and trust the people to achieve more by understanding and backing an agreed plan than other nations might achieve by carrying out under orders a plan dictated to them by their rulers. Do not let us be discouraged or confused by attempts to represent planning as the opposite of freedom. We in Britain stand for free planning and for planning as a means to fuller freedom. I am convinced that we shall get it.

Machinery of planning

This brings me to the machinery and methods of planning. I obviously cannot deal with these here in detail, but I will try to summarise them as well as I can. The central piece of machinery to assist the Cabinet in planning is the Official Steering Committee representing the key economic Departments together with the Economic Section of the Cabinet Office, the Central Statistical Office and my own Office. This Steering Committee forms the central economic team responsible for gathering and assessing economic intelligence, preparing forecasts, framing economic plans, advising Ministers on the advantages and disadvantages of these plans, and keeping under review the execution of plans when authorised and put into operation.

For this purpose the Steering Committee is assisted by a number of working parties. For instance one makes estimates of the total manpower available and of the forward distribution of manpower on various assumptions. Another assesses the forward demand for expenditure in the investment field and devises means, in times like these, of holding back investment which is inessential or can be deferred, while at the same time ensuring that a reserve of non-urgent investment projects is built up for rapid execution as opportunity arises—for example if and when tendencies towards trade recession and unemployment should become significant in the world. Another working party watches over our import needs and the methods of paying our way by visible and invisible exports. Material produced by these working parties is put together in the form of trial balance sheets of manpower, national income and expenditure, and overseas payments and receipts.

The balance sheet of manpower shows the available supply of manpower in comparison with the sum of all the various demands for manpower which would result from the current departmental programmes and policies in the various economic fields. Similarly, the national income and expenditure balance sheet shows, in pounds, shillings and pence, the value of the available national product, and, again in pounds, shillings and pence, the sum of the various demands which current departmental programmes and policies would make on that product.

Trial balance sheets

These trial balance sheets naturally show a gap between demands and available resources. One of the greatest differences between planning and *laisser faire*, is that under *laisser faire* it is no one's business to forecast this gap which is left to close itself under the uncontrolled interplay of economic forces. Whereas planning throws a spotlight on the gap and then arranges to close it in the way most advantageous to the national interest by measures taken by the Government or on Government initiative. The decisions relating to the closing of this gap are perhaps the most important immediate decisions which have to be made. For example, the manpower gap for 1946 had to be closed to a large extent by cuts in the Services and in industries working on their supplies.

The manpower gap is of course not an isolated problem but an expression in terms of manpower of much the same gap which shows itself in the national income and expenditure balance sheet as an excess of the value of anticipated demands of all kinds over the value of the prospective national product. Therefore if we cut the number of men serving in or working for the Forces we automatically reduce the expenditure on these sectors and release manpower to expand civil production, thus narrowing the gap between demands and resources both in terms of manpower and of the value of the national product; but do not forget that the state of the world might make it vital to step up provision for the Forces, in which case the necessary economic adjustment would have to be made. Similarly, if we cut investment, say in public works construction, we automatically reduce the manpower demand as well as the money demand for resources in that sector, and thus help to close the manpower gap as well as the gap between the value of the available national product and the various demands which are programmed to be made upon that product.

The difficulties are often emphasized of planning effectively while sweeping away controls over labour and reducing or eliminating many of the war-time controls over industry. These difficulties are of course much more acute in a time like the present when we have inherited both from the war and pre-war periods serious maldistributions of manpower which could only be quickly corrected by more drastic measures than the citizen should be asked to tolerate in time of peace. As we get through the reconversion and transition stage the number and scale of these problems can be expected to diminish. Often, moreover, there are several alternative ways of achieving the desired result. There are well-tried instruments of government whose use can be adjusted to assist fulfilment of the plan. The art of government is to achieve the result by the most economical, efficient and acceptable means.

The Steering Committee having assembled its balance sheets, with a mass of supporting material in every field, reports to Ministers—for it is they who are responsible for policy—who study the economic tendencies and forecasts and take decisions on plans to be adopted. To a large extent the actual execution of these decisions is a matter for individual Ministers dealing with a particular branch of the economy, such as coal, building and housing, transport, or agriculture.

Consultation with employers and workers

There are, however, some difficult and rather intangible problems which range over a wide field. For example, there is the problem of manning-up the under-manned industries, and of levels of wages in conditions of full employment. The Government is therefore developing machinery for tripartite contacts between itself, organised employers and organised workers through the National Joint Advisory Council, which is convened by the Minister of Labour and will serve as a standing national industrial conference on matters affecting manpower in industry. The Government is also arranging for widespread publicity on the objectives and problems of economic planning, and particularly the inescapable fact that all the collective and individual elements in the British standard of living ultimately depend on productivity. The more productivity increases the more prosperous the nation will be and, from a planning point of view, the fewer difficult priority problems will arise and the more latitude can be left to the individual and to industry. No less is it true that if production falls or stagnates the cheques which the nation has already drawn on the future in the form of increased wages and salaries, reduced hours, increased social services and a higher school-leaving age, cannot be met. We need higher productivity even to make good our losses and to cover commitments already made. It will have to be higher still before additional commitments can safely be assumed.

In the cock-eyed economy of the 'thirties people used to imagine that the great problem was how to abolish unemployment; in the clearer light of the middle of the century we know that even full employment will not be enough—we must also secure a greater output of goods and services all round if we are going to have a decent standard of life and fair shares for all, coupled with adequate incentives for effort.

I would put this problem of increased productivity first among the current economic problems to which planning must help to find the answer. I think there is an answer although this is not the place to elaborate it. A second problem which I look to planning to solve is the organised extension of our national vision several years further ahead than we have been accustomed to look. You really cannot run a complicated modern civilisation on a basis where the whole machine is crazily accelerated for a few months and then has to swerve violently or be braked almost to a standstill because some perfectly foreseeable snag or fluctuation has not been foreseen and tackled in time.

Estimating ahead

We know approximately how many people there are going to be in this country at least five years ahead, and we can estimate within wider margins of error how many houses they are going to need at a given housing standard, how much clothing they are going to need as a decent minimum and how much food they are going to need if they are to be properly nourished. It would be foolish to suggest that we can forecast actual demand and supply, or to forget that knowing just what we don't know is itself a useful and important piece of knowledge.

On the other hand for some purposes useful decisions can be made on estimates which are known to be subject to a 30 or 50 per cent variation in the out-turn, and in these cases it would be unjustifiable to refuse to make up our minds until we have everything worked out to 2 places of decimals. You may remember about the American officer before D-Day who could not restrain himself from telling a meeting "Well, gentlemen, we may lose this war, but if we do we shall lose it statistically perfect!" Our job in winning the peace is to see that we make the figures tell us all they can as early as they can, and yet not to put more weight on each figure or forecast than it will bear.

How many people have considered just how much difference every improvement in forecasting and planning will make to business and to employment? Security of employment in modern business depends on successful forecasting of markets, profits depend very largely on increased turnover, which in turn depends on reduced costs, which in turn depend on the placing of large orders for long runs of standard products, instead of constantly chopping and changing with every economic breeze that blows.

I suggest to you that in a few years' time people looking back will be amazed to see how much was written about the restrictive and bureaucratic dangers of planning, and how little was understood about the part which planning could play in freeing employers and workers and farmers from the horrors of uncontrolled and unforeseen fluctuations, which might bankrupt honest men in all directions and leave workers lining the streets with despair in their hearts.

Avoiding mass unemployment

Closely related to this problem of pushing the horizon further ahead of us and giving us more time and elbow room to work in, is the problem of maintaining a reserve of orders for industry and of work for the workers, to free the nation of fears of uncontrollable recession. At present, there is a considerable excess of demand over available resources and the machinery which we are building up for looking ahead to see how the total demands match with the total resources is at present used as a means for achieving a more rational pruning of the demands, all of which cannot be met in total. But when the present period of acute shortage is over, we may be threatened again with a general decline in the total demands for goods and services, which, if uncontrolled, would bring with it again the evils of depression and mass unemployment. The same technique of looking ahead at the total available resources and the total demands which are likely to be made upon them should enable us to foresee the threat of such a general decline in demand in sufficient time to take adequate steps to offset it, at least in great measure.

We should have, and we will have soon, a long list of projects—buildings, roads, railways, afforestation schemes, ports, airfields, industrial plants, national parks, public buildings and so forth—all blue-printed and prepared, waiting for investment and manpower resources to be made available to carry them out. We are also preparing our plans for methods whereby the ordinary consumers' demands for goods and services can be stimulated in times when there is a general slackening off of demand and a consequent threat of unemployment.

It is the intention of the Government to ensure that, in times when our resources of men and capital would otherwise be idle or under-employed, a useful demand for their services is in fact found. The knowledge that there is a queue of deferred capital projects, and that there are devices at hand for maintaining or, if necessary, stimulating the ordinary citizen's demand for goods and services will, I think, have a marvellously heartening effect on industry. By failing to get future demands sorted out into definite projects and to take measures to maintain the general demand for goods and services, we have in the past imposed an enormous economic waste and an enormous burden of insecurity upon industry which can be removed.

A constructive and peaceful revolution

I have no time to give further examples of the problems in front of planning, and indeed many of them will be familiar to you. I would simply like to emphasize that planning as it is taking shape in this country under our eyes is something new and constructively revolutionary which will, I think, be regarded in times to come as a contribution to civilisation as vital and as distinctively British as parliamentary democracy and the rule of law. Some people dogmatize about planning and say that planning is this and planning prevents that; my own view is that planning informed by the British political sense and the British resourcefulness will be something very different from what many of these writers and speakers have dreamed of. It will be something to which all of us can contribute and something from which we will all draw benefits.

After all, planning, though big and complicated, is not much more than applied common-sense.

Minutes to 373

This address is of considerable general interest from the point of view of this Dept., especially when it is borne in mind that we cover Surveys and Statistics as well as Research properly so called. The five-stage analysis of planning is most useful; as I see it we come in principally in Stages 2 and 5. Stage 2—fact-assembling—is principally, I think, a statistical matter in the broadest sense, and heaven knows that Colonial statistics are in sad need of [?] amelioration. We have in the last few months issued broadsides about census data, and about agricultural statistics, which may, one hopes, point the way to better things.

Stage 5 is that at which there is a need, not so much for research as for the *results* of research; and an important problem facing us, in all spheres of research, is to know far enough ahead which researches are going to be most valuable at this stage of execution. Previous minutes and papers on this file give some indication of the thought that has been given to this problem, which should become more tractable now that Development Plans are beginning to come in. It is most important that these plans should be carefully scrutinised by Research Dept—not only in respect of the actual research proposals which they contain, but also in regard to the light they throw on the problems facing Col. Govts which would benefit from timely research.

The matter is now open for general discussion and comment.

C.Y.C.
21.11.46

Mr. Caine

You will remember that at one of our Friday meetings before Christmas, there was some discussion of the desirability of evolving some kind of doctrine or statement of method in considering as a whole the problems involved in the efficient laying out of the funds provided under the Colonial Development and Welfare Act, and there was some discussion of the proposition that the matter might be explored by the Finance and Research Departments in conjunction with representation of other points of view in the office, those of members of the Colonial Service now working here being mentioned in particular. It was suggested that, while Colonies have clear instructions on what might be described as the mechanics of development planning—submission of schemes, accountancy and the like—there is not at present at any rate an equal body of doctrine on the fundamentally much more important problem of how to make sure in so far as one can that the funds are spent to the best long-term advantage.

The Lord President's address at (12) constitutes to my mind in many respects a very useful basis for discussion, in the light particularly of the analysis of the problem under five stages. The matter bristles with complexity and also with interest in that I think there is involved also some consideration of the respective places in the whole process of the Colonial Office (not to speak of the Treasury) on the one hand and Colonial Governments on the other. It is a truism to say that Colonial development cannot be planned in detail from the centre, but I think it is worth trying to specify what the functions of the centre are, apart from the relatively passive ones of receiving and vetting plans and individual schemes. As I see it, an important positive function of the centre is precisely to do what I have suggested above, namely to evolve some sort of guidance on doctrine and method.

I think that this is the more important in that in so far as I have seen them to date, development plans do rather tend to consist of an agglomeration of bigger and better Departmental plans, without any very fundamental examination of where they are all tending in the aggregate. An outstanding exception is I think . . . [the] revision of the Uganda plan which, although we only have it so far in tentative and not in a final condition, does show the beneficial results of what might be called the analytical and scientific approach.

In all the above, I am conscious that I have been trespassing on the Development side, but for this my excuse must be that I do not feel that the research effort can realise anything like its true beneficial potentialities unless it is fitted into and indeed forms a part of a thoroughly integrated approach to the whole problem with which we are confronted.

C.Y.C.
3.1.47

I think it would be useful if we had some further discussion on this general problem. I agree that there is a very serious lack in the approach to nearly all the development plans we have had so far, although I should describe it as lack of general constructive imagination rather than lack of the scientific approach. Ideas have been stirring in the minds of some of the members of Finance Department also on these matters, and I have, therefore, proposed to Mr. Williams that we should have a general discussion of the two Departments . . . .

S.C.
4.1.47

374 CO 123/398/66969/47 2 Sept–11 Oct 1947

[British Honduras]: minutes by S J E Southgate[1] and Sir S Caine on Prof Beasley's report on the financial and economic position (12 Apr 1947)

Professor Beasley's[2] Report on the financial and economic position of British Honduras has now been received. It is adverse, and as the Evans Commission[3] will

[1] Principal, CO West Indian Dept.

[2] C G Beasley, economic adviser, CD & W organisation, British West Indies, 1946; formerly professor of geography and geology, University of Rangoon.

[3] See p 69, n 2.

cover much of the same ground, the Comptroller suggests that it should be treated in British Honduras as a confidential document.

The report is not long and is clear, but a brief summary may be useful.

1. The tendency is to disregard long-term trends in the economy of the Colony, and to pay too much attention to present inflated revenue and prices. But without major reconstruction, particularly to overcome the remaining effects of the 1930 hurricane, government revenues and taxable capacity will not maintain the existing level.

2. A generation ago greater quantities of important primary goods were being produced for export: mahogany, chicle,[4] bananas and coconuts come within this category. The impression of improvement in the trading position is due to inflated war time prices.

3. In general terms, from 1919 to 1939 true revenue averaged $1,000,000 and during the latter years of the last war $2,000,000. Government expenditure year by year tended to outstrip realised revenue. Increases in Government expenditure are due largely to the increasing cost of personal emoluments of Government Servants (ignoring any increases as a result of the Sandford Report)[5]. It is at present difficult to assess satisfactorily the financial position of the Colony because the large sums associated with the trading activities of Import Control were not accounted for on a commercial basis, and transactions were not audited. It is estimated that in the next few years revenue can hardly be maintained above $1,750,000. At this level almost 60% of revenue will be absorbed in payment of personnel. Those recommendations of the Fiscal Revision Committee which relate to the collection of income tax deserve full consideration, but those which suggest additional rates of import duty and absorption of war time surcharges in permanent rates should be treated with great caution.

4. The cost of living has undoubtedly risen sharply and is causing serious concern. It is considered that the situation was made worse by measures allowing merchants excessive "mark-ups" without regard either to rate of turnover or the absence of risk of holding reserve stock. The cost of living Index is regarded as statistically useless and misleading. (There is a detailed analysis in paragraph 13).

5. Subject to an element of inaccuracy introduced by the consideration of 8,000 small cultivators, whose activities are imperfectly related to a monetary economy, it is calculated that the national income for the year 1945 is approximately $5,800,000 (B.H.) i.e. rather less than $100 per head. There is, therefore, little chance of maintaining indirect taxation at the present very high level.

6. The present development plans do not provide for the short term increased production commensurate with the decline of forest products and inadequate production of food. Professor Beasley's view is that a scheme is required involving large capital expenditure and the immigration of many West Indians, and probably trained artisans from elsewhere. It is necessary to provide services for a population at present too scattered to develop the agriculture of the more fertile areas, and to organise modern exploitation of forest products. Such a plan would require adjustment in Government Departments, and it is suggested that it can only be achieved by a Development Commission or by ad hoc Corporations with very wide

---

[4] The basic ingredient in chewing-gum.

[5] (Sir) George Sandford, chief secretary, East African Governors' Conference, 1946, and first administrator of East Africa High Commission.

powers and large resources both of capital and trained technical personnel. The lack of agricultural production is admitted, but remedies suggested too often encourage small scale peasant cultivation in difficult conditions. West Indians prefer to work in organisations and the best opportunity for real development lies with corporations in agriculture aiming in the long run at co-operative management but primarily dependent upon planning and outside direction.

7. Professor Beasley states that the Comptroller of Imports (Mr. Thomas) was endeavouring to straighten out the trading accounts of the import control, and that he had done a great deal, under the face of opposition, to eliminate the effect of excessive margins of profit on the cost of living. Professor Beasley hopes to re-visit the Colony in November.

8. I may add that my general impression of conversations with Mr. Thomas agrees very well with most of the points made in this Report, although Mr. Thomas is less pessimistic.

S.J.E.S.
2.9.47

This is certainly a rather depressing report. It rubs in again the lesson that no amount of external planning is an adequate substitute for initiative and energy on the spot. If we could pour in unlimited sums of money we might increase the immediate well-being, if not the productivity, of British Honduras, but it can be taken as certain that in present conditions that solution is not open to us. We have, therefore, to look for some source of enterprise and industry in British Honduras itself and if, as seems only too probable, there is no such source among the inhabitants of the Colony, we may be forced, as Professor Beasley suggests, to arrange for its importation on a commercial basis. If, however, we are to go on that policy, it is no use closing our eyes to the fact that it would only succeed if we give any such imported enterprise a chance of earning substantial profits. In other words, Professor Beasley's conclusions point to a very substantial reorientation of the whole trend of policy over the last generation.

I agree that no action need be taken on the report. We can await the conclusions of the Evans Commission. Meanwhile, Mr. Seel should see on return.

S.C.
11.10.47

375 CO 927/88/5, no 23 3 Dec 1947

Recommendations for the organization of colonial research in agriculture, animal health and forestry **(Report by the Colonial Agricultural Research Committee: Colonial no 219, 1948)**

[This report, drafted by Dr H H Storey, FRS, the Committee's secretary, was welcomed by officials as constructive and valuable in itself and useful as showing sceptics the considerable progress which could be made in organising research, despite the difficulties in dealing with very complex problems in a quite novel way over a very extensive field of scientific activity. In particular it would show the Colonial Medical Research Committee 'what an efficient committee can do'. Creech Jones agreed, while Mr Rees-Williams minuted (19 Dec 1947): 'I agree. I consider it a fine, comprehensive Report'. It recommended that research should be regionally organised wherever possible.]

1. *Introduction*

The Committee for Colonial Agricultural, Animal Health and Forestry Research was established by the Secretary of State for the Colonies for the purposes, among others, of advising on the general policy for research within the fields covered by its title, on the provision required for such research, and on the scope and functions of regional and other research institutions in the Colonial Empire. We have, therefore, considered it appropriate that we should state the policy upon which our recommendations will be based.

2. As recently as 1945 the subject of this memorandum was reviewed by a Sub-Committee of the Colonial Advisory Council for Agriculture, Animal Health and Forestry[1]. We traverse much the same ground; and we could have simplified our task of writing by endorsing large sections of this report. But we have considered it desirable to present a self-contained document avoiding cross-references tiresome to the reader.

3. Two recommendations of the Sub-Committee's report—in addition to that which led to our establishment—have been accepted in principle by the Secretary of State: namely, that a Colonial Research Service should be set up, and secondly, that agricultural research in the Colonies should be organized as far as possible on a regional basis. The memorandum is mainly concerned with planning the measures to carry out the second of these two points of policy.

4. We are well aware that agricultural research is no new thing in the Colonial Dependencies. "What we have to propose does not represent any fundamental change in existing arrangements; it is merely a step in the logical evolution of a process, of which the foundations were laid by the first Lovat Committee in 1926, and which was elaborated at the Imperial Agricultural Research Conference in 1927 and by the second Lovat Committee of 1928."[2] But a re-examination of the position is now overdue; and post-war planning for Colonial development has emphasized the need for expansion of research services that had, in any case, inevitably become attenuated during the war period. Furthermore, the provision of funds for research by His Majesty's Government, under the Colonial Development and Welfare Acts, will greatly assist the expansion that we advocate; although it is evident that these funds can serve only to augment provisions that will need to be made by the Colonial Governments, and not to replace them.

5. For conciseness, we shall use the word "Agriculture" to cover not only agriculture in the narrow sense, but also animal health and forestry, unless the context requires a limited connotation. The word "Colonies" includes the Colonies, Protectorates and Mandated Territories that make up the Colonial Empire; "Departmental Director" includes the Directors of Colonial Departments of Agriculture, Veterinary Services and Forestry.

2. *General principles in organizing colonial agricultural research*

6. "The progress and development of Colonial Agriculture depends on two forms

[1] Report of the Sub-Committee of the Colonial Advisory Council of Agriculture, Animal Health and Forestry on "The Organization of Agricultural, Animal Health and Forestry Research in the Colonial Dependencies." C.M. No. 12, 1945.

[2] Loc. cit.

of activity, the constant accumulation of new knowledge and its wise application."[3] While it is our main function to advise on the manner of re-organizing and co-ordinating the former of these two activities throughout the Colonial Empire we are fully conscious of the truth that, unless the new knowledge is applied to the practice of agriculture, the efforts devoted to research are sterile. Further, there is no finality in research, and the acquisition of knowledge must be a continuing process. The purpose should be, not solely to solve a range of scientific problems, but to build an organization for agricultural research that will endure as an integral part of the Government activities of each Colonial region.

7. We consider, therefore, that three principles should guide us in recommending measures for the future organization of agricultural research in the Colonies:

I.—That agricultural research shall be so organized and so maintained that it shall play its full part in providing the knowledge upon which agricultural improvement can be based;

II.—That the organization of agricultural research shall be such that the resulting knowledge obtained flows freely to those who will apply it to practice or will convey it effectively to those who will apply it; and

III.—That agricultural research shall be so organized that it is accepted as an essential and continuing activity in Colonial communities.

8. The first of these principles will be met only if two conditions are satisfied:

(a) That the tasks undertaken by the agricultural research service are so chosen that the knowledge gained will contribute in the fullest possible measure to agricultural improvement; and

(b) That the research service is fully efficient to perform these tasks.

We deal with these in Sections 3 and 4 below.

9. In order that the second principle shall be met, it is essential that there shall be complete understanding and co-operation at all levels, between the research service and Colonial Departments. As users of research results, the Departments should not only play their part in pointing out the gaps in knowledge to be filled by research, but there should be constant collaboration to develop research results into terms of agricultural practices. To meet this need at the highest level we recommend the establishment of regional Agricultural Councils; but we believe that it may be one of the most important functions of such Councils to ensure that there is no barrier to collaboration between workers at all levels in the research and departmental services.

10. In order to ensure the continuity that is the purpose of our third principle, we consider it important that no impression be created that the planning and execution of agricultural research are not the intimate concern of the Colonial authorities. Mainly for this reason we advise against any proposal that funds made available by His Majesty's Government should be used primarily to set up a central establishment carrying out agricultural research in and for the Colonies, but administered and directed from London. This arrangement would tend to give to research the appearance of an alien activity imposed from outside. We believe it essential, on the contrary, that the responsibility of the Governments and the people of a Colonial region for establishing and maintaining research organizations be clearly recog-

[3] Loc. cit.

nized. The Committee for Colonial Agricultural, Animal Health and Forestry Research has an important part to play in assisting development along the best lines; it has functions of initiating and inspiring new research, of advising upon and criticising research programmes and of ensuring co-ordination; and, furthermore, of assisting in the selection of research workers, watching over their interests and keeping them in touch with developments in the scientific world. But it should not attempt to direct research in detail or to control research workers, which are functions that must be exerted by authorities on the spot.

3. *The nature of colonial agricultural research*

11. The tasks confronting an agricultural research service in the Colonies may be classed under three heads:

(a) Basic surveys, aiming at the better identification of the problems for detailed research and contributing to the proper assessment of the agricultural resources and potentialities of the Colonies.
(b) The solution of the problems of agriculture that come under examination by the research worker as being *prima facie* amenable to scientific investigation.
(c) "Research directed to the maintenance of steady advance in those fields of application of science which are primarily related to agriculture, so that agricultural science may continually strengthen itself to deal with recognised problems of the industry, so that advantage may be taken of all fresh developments in pure science, and so that new ideas in agriculture may be stimulated."[4]

12. With regard to (a), basic surveys are of great general importance as contributing knowledge essential to the proper planning of both research and development. These surveys may be considered to fall into several broad categories; e.g., surveys of inanimate resources, such as soils, water supplies, fertilizer resources, climate; of biological resources, such as plants and animals and their interactions; and socio-economic studies, such as studies of systems of peasant agriculture and of agricultural populations in relation to physical resources. We realise that many of these studies, and particularly the socio-economic studies, are the primary concern of others rather than the agricultural research worker. In the case of some, e.g., meteorology, it may suffice simply to bring the requirements of agriculture to the notice of those responsible for the collection of data. But we are convinced that an agricultural research organization must be deeply concerned in the conduct of some and in the results of all these surveys, which should form the solid basis of its research work.

13. The tasks considered under (b) and (c) cover a wide variety of research activities in the laboratory and in the field, ranging from straight-forward applied or "technological" research through what has been termed "basic" research, occasionally to truly fundamental research. No exact division on this basis is, however, possible; and most problems will call for each kind of research for its complete solution.

14. We have intentionally placed (b), implying an emphasis on applied research, in the prior position. We are conscious that in many Colonies agricultural improvement is held up by problems for the solution of which the basic knowledge

[4] Loc. cit.

already exists. Thus great immediate benefit may be expected to accrue from applied research; and we consider that it should be a primary duty of the agricultural research organizations to undertake this work.

15. In thus recommending a concentration on programmes tending towards the applied side of research, we realise that we are deviating from the policy laid down by the Imperial Agricultural Conference of 1927 for regional research. We believe that the ruling then made, that a regional organization should devote itself to "long-range" and "wide-range" research, tended in the event to dissociate the organization from close contact with the agriculture of the region.

16. It would be a mistake, however, to go to the other extreme and to insist that the research organizations should concentrate solely on applied work. The scientific health of an organization requires a proper balance between applied, and basic and fundamental research. The denial to the competent research worker of any opportunity to embark on original lines of research would cause discontent and make the service unattractive; and a failure of the flow of new knowledge from basic research would ultimately impoverish the applied research and reduce it to an uninspired routine.

17. We are confident, however, that, provided suitable encouragement is given to initiative in the workers, a balance will be reached naturally between applied and basic research. The occasion for deviations from a strictly applied programme will emerge as work progresses; and it is important that those in charge of research recognise these occasions and be ready to exploit them. They should be given discretion in framing their programmes to include reasonably wide research projects that, with a liberal interpretation, are relevant to the objectives of the organization.

18. Thus the advancement of knowledge that constitutes item (c) will come from researches that have emerged from a programme of work correlated closely with the agriculture of the region; and the fact that it has emerged in response to recognised needs will ensure that it is not too remote from practical needs. It will often be found that the more fundamental type of work can best be done at universities or research institutions outside the Colonies, where the workers will have the advantage of special apparatus and contacts with workers in many fields of science. But, on the other hand, there will be fundamental work that cannot be done outside the Colonial environment, and there will be need to provide for this in planning both the staff and equipment of regional organizations, and by arrangements for collaboration with Colonial universities or university colleges. There should, furthermore, be every encouragement to visiting workers who may wish to spend long or short periods in the region; even though the line of research that they may wish to follow may be remote from the immediate problems of agriculture, the presence of such workers is worth while for the mental stimulus that it can provide to members of an institution relatively isolated from contact with fellow scientists. We should, furthermore, welcome arrangements whereby Commonwealth universities recognised Colonial Research Organizations as places where a student for the Ph.D. degree might spend a part of his course.

4. *The conditions for efficient research*

19. Scientific research is a product of orginal thought and skill in experiment by

the individual. It cannot be too strongly emphasized that organization can be no substitute for ability in the individual worker. The suitability of any form of organization for research will depend upon its capacity to provide conditions under which the individual will be willing and able to work at maximum efficiency. It will also depend on its capacity to recruit a fair share of workers of the highest calibre; but recruitment will itself depend upon convincing the candidate for a research post, and those who advise him, that he will find in the Colonies the conditions necessary for efficient research.

20. We, therefore, set out below our views on the conditions that should be met by an organization for Colonial research.

(1) *Satisfactory terms of service*

21. The Secretary of State for the Colonies has under consideration plans to establish a Colonial Research Service. The terms for this Service, concerning which we have made independent recommendations, will aim at a basic uniformity of salaries with the United Kingdom Scientific Civil Service, with provision to bring the officer's emoluments to substantial equality with those of officers of similar status serving Colonial Governments. With this will be combined a transferable superannuation scheme, permitting movement into or out of the Service at any stage, without loss of rights to benefit. The intention is to recruit a part of the Service from among those wishing to make a career in the Colonies, and a part from among those of more mature experience who are prepared to serve for limited periods overseas. It is also hoped that officers already serving in Colonial appointments, who have shown an inclination for research, may be considered for transfer into the Colonial Research Service.

(2) *Minimising scientific isolation*

22. We believe that the isolation in which many Colonial research workers have found themselves in the past has been a serious bar to efficiency. Some loss of scientific inspiration is inevitable when the individual moves from, perhaps, a British university to a Colonial environment. This drawback can be minimised by grouping research workers into regional Organizations, in place of scattering them, one or a few, at many territorial stations. A close association with Colonial universities and university colleges will also play a part. Opportunities for keeping abreast of modern scientific developments can be provided by maintaining and expanding a system of generous vacation and study leaves. Finally, through the existence of the Committee for Colonial Agricultural, Animal Health and Forestry Research, Colonial research workers will be assured that their work is not overlooked by the leaders of scientific thought in the United Kingdom.

(3) *Reasonable freedom in research*

23. There are some who hold that organization and research are incompatible: that the research worker who is organized ceases to be more than a routine investigator, and that, with the loss of intellectual freedom, original thought tends to disappear. This may result from organization in research, but need not; and we believe that a form of organization can be devised under which research workers can give willing and efficient service. That is to say, a compromise is possible between complete freedom in research and research in which major objectives are proposed

and accepted. Freedom in research requires that the research worker shall not be debarred from the pursuance of lines of work of his own choice. To grant such freedom might be held to risk losing sight of the main objectives. But, in fact, it is comparatively seldom that the occasion for any major deviation from an agreed line of research arises; and the majority of research workers are not unwilling to accept guidance in respect of the objectives of their research. Nor is initiative stifled, even though it be guided to a particular end. Where, exceptionally, a competent research worker is led to a major deviation from the agreed programme, it is seldom unprofitable to allow him to follow it.

(4) *Confidence in the direction of research*

24. One essential feature of the form of organization that, in our opinion, will meet the needs of research is that the Director in charge shall be a man of science, who from his own experience in research, knows the possibilities and methods of research, the ways of research workers and their difficulties. We doubt whether anyone who has not been an active research worker for a part of his life can effectively lead a research team with the understanding and appreciation that will bring out the best of which the members are capable. It is important also that the Director's standing as a scientist should command the respect of those who serve under him. (He must also have other qualities to which we shall refer later.)

(5) *An assurance of reasonable continuity in research*

25. The efficient research worker should be assured that, within reason, he will be permitted to prosecute a line of research to its conclusion.

(6) *Responsibility in the framing of research programmes*

26. Since the formulation, equally with the execution, of programmes of research is a matter requiring scientific knowledge and experience in research, the main authority for planning research should be in the hands of research workers. Although we recommend elsewhere that others be given the opportunity of advising in the selection of problems for research and in the allocation of priorities, the possibilities of each line of research and the manner in which it should proceed are matters on which the experienced research worker can alone form an adequate judgement. The research staff of an organization should be in a position to feel that they have contributed to the planning of the programme they are asked to execute.

(7) *Freedom to publish*

27. We believe that freedom to publish is as indispensable in applied scientific research as in pure scholarship. This freedom is highly valued by the research worker, whose scientific reputation largely rests on his published papers. We recommend that all research workers should be free to contribute to journals of international circulation papers under their own names dealing with their scientific research, if accepted by the Director as of suitable merit.

(8) *A satisfactory physical environment*

28. On this question we need only refer to the obvious necessity of full facilities for the economical and efficient prosecution of research—adequately equipped laboratories and field stations dispersed through the main ecological zones—and of

satisfactory provision for the housing, health and recreation of the staff. Full consideration should be given to modern developments in the design and air-conditioning of houses in the tropics, whereby the comfort and consequently the efficiency of the staff may be enhanced.

5. *Regional organization of agricultural research*

29. The Colonial Empire consists of some thirty Dependencies, varying widely in their degree of social and agricultural development, and in their needs for, and ability to use the results of agricultural research. "Some Dependencies lie together and in their inherent circumstances and agricultural development constitute what can be treated as 'regions' in considering the needs of agricultural research; others, however, are remote and at present completely isolated from the research point of view."[5] We have to consider how best these varying needs can be met.

30. We are impressed by the advantages of organizing agricultural research in regions wherever this is possible. Relative to the area of the Colonies the number of research workers must always be small; but the scientific isolation that is to some extent inevitable can be minimised by grouping the workers into regional Organizations covering as wide an area as is practicable. Although the workers must still remain to come extent dispersed to the points where their research can most suitably be done, membership of a large Organization would give them ties with their specialist colleagues and the advantage of assistance from experienced seniors. Regional organization would provide for a larger and more varied body of specialists than it would be economical to employ in a single Colony. Furthermore, since many of the problems of adjacent countries are identical, they can best be solved by the concerted attack of teams regionally co-ordinated, rather than by individual officers or local teams not fully co-ordinated with others in adjacent countries.

31. The building up of a series of regional Research Organizations to serve the major Colonial regions cannot be other than a gradual process. There is at present a marked shortage of workers in all the sciences, and any hasty establishment of regional Research Organizations might be at the expense of quality in their staff. We consider, therefore, that any attempt to force the pace would not be in the best interest.

32. In East Africa agricultural research has, since 1927, been in progress on a regional basis at Amani; and since 1941, as a result of recommendations by the East African Standing Veterinary Research Committee, there have been similar steps towards organizing regional veterinary research. The foundations for expansion and re-organization on the lines proposed in this memorandum were laid at two Conferences in 1946[6] and 1947.[7] The region covered will be primarily Kenya, Uganda, Tanganyika Territory and Zanzibar; but it is expected that a close liaison will be established with research workers in Northern Rhodesia and Nyasaland, within a framework of research now being worked out by the Central African Council. It is expected that Colonial Departments in British Somaliland, Mauritius and the Seychelles will look to East Africa for specialist help.

[5] Loc. cit.

[6] "East African Research: Agriculture, Animal Health and Forestry." Proceedings of a Conference held in Nairobi on the 21st and 22nd March, 1946.

[7] "Agriculture and Forestry Research Conference." Proceedings of a Conference held in Nairobi on the 29th, 30th and 31st July, 1947.

33. In the West Indies a number of separate research schemes, each of regional implications, have been centred on the Imperial College of Tropical Agriculture, Trinidad. It is possible that, from this beginning, a general regional Organization may emerge, serving the West Indian Islands and adjacent mainland Colonies in the Caribbean.

34. Other possible regional groupings for future consideration are the West African Colonies; and Malaya, Sarawak and North Borneo. Until regional Organizations are established, and in such Colonies as do not fit into any regional grouping, we recommend that the research needs continue to be met through research branches of the individual Colonial Departments; or, where suitable, by visits of research specialists or teams, either from appropriate regional Organizations, or specially appointed for the particular purpose.

35. We have given much thought to the question whether there should be a single Organization embracing research in agriculture, animal health and forestry, or separate Organizations for each of these subjects. We are in no doubt that the objective should be to ensure that research in the several facets of land use should proceed as a fully co-ordinated activity; and we recognise that to this end if will often be necessary that research workers in all three subjects collaborate as a team. The consolidation of all the sciences within a single Organization would ensure collaboration at all levels; and, in the view of the majority of us, this is the desirable aim. We recognise, however, that there are other factors to be considered; and consolidation may, in practice, be impossible. The objective we have stated above should be possible of achievement provided there is close collaboration between separate Organizations functioning as individual units. Where, however, separate Organizations are set up, it will be of the utmost importance to ensure that no barrier arises to hinder collaboration between the Directors and staffs of the several Organizations. An important means to the desired collaboration would be the siting of the headquarters and main laboratories of the Organizations in the closest possible proximity, so that personal consultation between all research workers, and mutual understanding and appreciation, may be facilitated.

6. *Regional consultative machinery*

36. In paragraph 42 we state our view that the special circumstances of a research organization require that it shall have a certain measure of independence; but it is equally essential that those in charge of research organizations shall consult those who administer or practise agriculture. We recommend that this need should be met by establishing a standing Advisory Council for Agriculture, Animal Health and Forestry in each region.

37. This Council should contain representation of the Agricultural, Veterinary and Forestry Departments of the Colonies forming the region, and of agricultural producers; and, on the research side, it should contain the Directors of Research Organizations and of important Commodity Research Stations, and a number of senior research officers. The exact pattern would be dictated by the circumstances of the region; and the only point that we consider it necessary to emphasize is that the representation of the several interests should be adequate to ensure that each has a full hearing.

38. The functions of the Council would be generally to discuss and advise on

agricultural policy in the region, on the needs for research arising therefrom, and the priorities to be accorded; to examine and comment on research programmes presented by the Directors of Research; to receive reports of research completed and to advise on the means for ensuring that the results of research are applied to the practice of agriculture. The Council should be entitled to invite the attention of the Secretary of State to any matters that it might consider appropriate. It should be kept fully informed of the activities of any similar Councils that might be set up for medical, social or other sciences, and for higher education, thereby ensuring that no conflict arose in the policies advocated by each separate Council.

39. The Agricultural Council should not itself be responsible for framing actual programmes of research. This duty should be the responsibility of each Director of Research. We have already expressed our view, however, that the Director of Research should always consult his research staff in preparing programmes of research, and that his staff should be in no doubt that they will be called upon to contribute to their preparation. This need will usually best be met by establishing Research Committees, under the Chairmanship of the Director, within the Research Organization.

7. *The form and constitution of a regional research organization*

40. We consider that the Research Organization should normally form a constituent unit in the group of common services where agreement has been reached to administer these through a single regional authority. We recognise, however, that in some regions circumstances may require a deviation to a somewhat different form. We do not consider this undesirable, provided the pattern meets the condition that we regard as essential; namely, that the Organization shall be established, administered and directed from within the region.

41. The post of regional Director is of cardinal importance. It calls for a man of exceptional attainments if the system is to work. As we have already stated, he should be a research worker of proved ability in his science; in addition, he should possess a sound agricultural background to enable him to appreciate the problems that arise in agricultural development. He should have considerable administrative gifts, be able to delegate responsibility and to bring the best out of his staff. Finally, he should be able to win the confidence of Colonial departments and unofficials with whom the regional Organization will have contacts. Such men will not be easy to find and in framing terms of service this point should be borne in mind.

42. The Director should have independent charge of the regional Organization and should be directly responsible to the appropriate authority in the region, not only for the execution of the research programme but also for the proper administration of the Organization, the expenditure of its funds in accordance with its estimates, the discipline and posting of its staff and the construction and maintenance of its buildings and stations. In addition, we consider it important that he should be free to correspond directly with the Secretary to the Committee for Colonial Agricultural, Animal Health and Forestry Research, and through him bring to the notice of the Committee any matters affecting the research work of the Organization. This arrangement would in no way diminish the Director's responsibility to the regional authority for the research and administration of the Organization; but we regard it as most desirable that a direct channel should exist for

consultation on scientific matters between the Director and leaders of research in the United Kingdom.

43. We recommend that important decisions on research policy in respect of individual regions should not be taken in advance of the appointment of the Directors, on whom will principally rest the responsibility for implementing the policy and who should, consequently, have a voice in its formulation. The general research programme of a regional Organization must be strongly influenced by the circumstances, needs and opportunities of the region in which it is situated; and only after a Director has taken up his post in the region can he assess these factors and prepare a satisfactory programme. The Director should normally be the first appointment to a regional Organization; and research staff should only be appointed when he has had time to decide on the nature of the staff required to implement his programme and to prepare the laboratories, houses, etc., to receive them.

44. The regional Research Organization should be constituted basically of a Headquarters Division and a number of "branch of science" Divisions. The Headquarters Division would provide for administrative, library, editorial, statistical and engineering and workshop services. The Science Divisions would represent those sciences that the particular needs of the region required; thus within a purely agricultural Organization there would be Divisions selected from the sciences of Genetics, Entomology, Plant Pathology, Plant Physiology, Ecology, Soil Science, Biochemistry, and so on. Similarly in animal health there would be Divisions of Pathology, Animal Physiology, etc. In forestry the sciences to be covered largely parallel those in agriculture, but the great complexity of problems arising in the forest call for special forestry training in the staff concerned. Each important Division should contain at least two senior research officers and the necessary complement of juniors.

45. It is important, however, that these Divisions should not work in any kind of isolation from one another. On the contrary, we consider that there would often need to be a parallel sub-division of the staff into teams on a "project" basis. For example, pasture research is a subject that may need to be handled by a team consisting of ecologists, plant breeders, plant and animal physiologists, soil scientists, biochemists and, perhaps, entomologists and plant pathologists. The leader of such a team might be a senior officer of one of the Science Divisions, or he might be a specially appointed officer experienced in pasture research. Each member of the team would be primarily a member of a Science Division and, therefore, responsible in technical matters to the head of his Division, and, if at headquarters, working in the Division's laboratory; but at the same time he would have a second responsibility to the team leader for directing his work along lines conforming with the team's programme. Where separate Organizations exist to cover the plant and animal sciences, a single project team will often contain workers from both Organizations.

46. It may be thought that this form of dual responsibility will lead to difficulties and prove unworkable. Provided that there is close consultation between the Directors, the heads of Divisions and the team leaders, we consider the difficulties should not arise. We can see no alternative that will ensure the best results. Thus, for instance, the Soil Chemist in a pasture research team must work in a soils laboratory; if supervised at all, his soils work must be supervised by a Soils Chemist and he must have the constant advice of his specialist senior in all his problems. But the team leader, who cannot be in a position to supervise the technique of each

member of his team, must, nevertheless, be responsible for ensuring that the work of each member of his team proceeds along the general lines required by his programme. Often an individual officer will be a member of two or more teams, when the work of one team does not occupy his full time.

47. Of outstanding importance among "team" activities is that covered by the title of Crop and Animal Husbandry. It will call for integration of the research by plant and animal workers; and since its activities will be mainly on experimental stations of Departments, it will require the closest collaboration with Departmental officers. For the important post of head of this team it will be necessary to have a man who is not only a master of his subject, but has also personal qualities that will win the confidence of those with whom he must collaborate.

48. The physical establishment of a regional Organization should consist of a Headquarters with offices, main laboratories for each science Division, experimental grounds, and staff housing; and branch establishments as required in a range of ecological zones equipped with the laboratories, houses, etc., needed for the work undertaken and the staff employed. We assume that these secondary stations will usually be established at suitable Departmental Experimental Stations, by agreement with the Director of the Colonial Department, or at Commodity Research Stations. While, as we have already suggested, the field work of such teams detached from Headquarters will be in collaboration with the Departmental Officers, we consider that it will often be advisable to allow research officers the sole control of relatively small areas of land for special work that cannot well be done on a co-operative basis. In cases where the Departmental Stations are unable to provide the facilities required, it may be necessary for the Research Organization to establish sub-stations under its own control.

8. *The relation of the regional research organization to colonial departments of agriculture, animal health and forestry*

49. We have already emphasized in paragraph 9 the paramount necessity of co-operation between Research Organizations and Colonial Departments in the region. Each has an essential part to play in a partnership working to the single end of agricultural advancement. An effective partnership requires that each partner shall understand the other's part and shall have confidence that he will play his part.

50. The keys, therefore, to successful agricultural advance are mutual appreciation and confidence. One important means to this is consultation. The regional Agricultural Council that we recommend will do much to remove the barriers to free consultation that tend to arise. Much will depend, however, on a good personal understanding between the Directors concerned; and, through their influence, on a similar understanding between all members of the services they control.

51. A second means to confidence is a clear definition of responsibilities. The establishment of a separate organization for research, where, as in many Colonies, research and administration have hitherto been under a single control, will require some adjustments of authority. These should be recognised in advance and freely accepted.

52. The primary functions of a Colonial Department—the implementation of agricultural policy in its many aspects—are well understood, and the responsibility of the Departmental Director is not in doubt. But in the field of research, in its widest

sense, there is an overlap of functions between a Research Organization and a Department; and it is here that a definition of responsibilities is needed if misunderstandings are not to arise.

53. In the first place we should say that it is implicit in our proposals that the main responsibility for the planning and execution of agricultural research should devolve on the regional Research Organizations. We feel that the principle cannot be questioned that research will proceed with the greatest economy and efficiency if it is carried out or supervised by research workers, free to devote their whole time to research, and under the direction of a man experienced in the control of research. But we are fully aware that the Departments are staffed not only with a number of specialists but with trained agriculturists, veterinarians, etc., who are qualified to contribute much to the advance of research in a variety of ways, and are often able to do so in the course of, or incidentally to, their primary departmental duties. Furthermore, the research worker will often be dependent on the departmental officer for the provision of the material for his research.

54. In the choice of objectives for research, the Departments have an essential part to play. In consequence of their close association with the practice of agriculture and with the producers, they will generally be the first to recognise the outstanding problems and the best equipped to judge the relative urgency of their solution. On the Departments, therefore, should rest a responsibility to ensure that the Research Organization is fully aware of these problems, and, in the light of their special knowledge, to advise on the Organization's research programmes. Conversely, and more particularly if, as we propose, the specialist officers hitherto available to the Departments for research are partly transferred into the regional Research Organization, a responsibility must rest on the Research Organization to ensure that the problems in agricultural development which the Departments bring to light are given the fullest consideration in the research programme. The Departments would not concern themselves with the detailed planning of research, which is a matter that should rest with the Director of Research and his staff. But they should have the right, and the duty, to advise on objectives and priorities. The proposed Agricultural Councils will provide the opportunity, at an official level, for full consideration of these points.

55. The process of developing a typical research project passes through a number of stages. The early stages will usually constitute work that can be done only by, or under the supervision of, workers possessing specialised qualifications. A stage will ultimately be reached, however, when this no longer applies; and the project then becomes one for "technological research", generally at an experiment station. A third stage is reached when the project becomes one for demonstration and advice to producers. Whereas the first stage is the responsibility of the Director of Research and the officers of the Research Organization, the last stage is the responsibility of the Departmental Director and his staff. The intermediate stage is essentially one for collaboration between the two authorities; and responsibility should rest with the two Directors in consultation.

56. A particular case of technological research, where the Research Organization and the Colonial Department are equally concerned, is that of the long-term experiment in husbandry, on agricultural systems, the use of fertilizers, the management of animals and grassland and the like. Since these experiments must usually be done on Departmental Stations, executive authority over them should rest

with the Director of the Department; but we consider that he should accept an especially close form of collaboration with the Research Organization in the planning, recording and interpreting of the experiments. To give the Research Organization such a form of limited responsibility for these experiments (while retaining the Departmental Director's executive authority) would ensure a continuity that a Department may often find difficult to maintain in view of the numerous other calls on its staff.

57. In contrast with what we have termed the "research project", which implies a search for knowledge of a somewhat wider and more general nature, there is a type of "investigation", which for reasons of limited, and often local, significance, and for lack of research staff, it is impossible to include in the Research Organization's programme. Such investigations will embrace agricultural and socio-economic surveys, short-term experiments in crop and animal husbandry, variety trials, the mass selection of crops (which, of necessity, will have a strictly limited and local value), and similar matters. These do not call for the direct service of the specialist research worker. They should remain the responsibility of the Departmental Director, whose freedom to embark on such work should in no way be restricted. We recommend, however, that it should be the policy of Departmental Directors to advise the Research Director of any investigations that they propose to initiate, to seek his advice on the conduct of such investigations and, perhaps most important of all, to keep him fully informed of the progress and results. For whilst we do not wish to stress unduly the need to avoid duplication of work on common problems, we feel that the Research Organization should, amongst its other functions, act as a repository for information on all research and investigations carried out in the region.

58. The re-organization that we propose may involve some redistribution of specialist staff. The Colonial Departments will continue to require a number of specialists on their establishments—such as entomologists, plant pathologists, etc.—for the technical work of administering control legislation, and to provide analytical, diagnostic and advisory services. It is essential that the Department should remain adequately staffed to perform these functions. But a number of Colonial Departments have, in the past, built up a cadre of research staff with the object of prosecuting research of the type that will now fall within the sphere of the regional Organization. We recommend that the Departments should agree not only to resign this research to the new Organization, but also transfer to it such specialist staff as are not an essential part of the Departmental machine.

59. The existence of a body of specialists in a Research Organization will lead to calls for advice on scientific matters outside the specific programme of research. We consider that these calls should be met to the best ability of the Organization. But it should not be overlooked that the Colonial Departments exist to give advice to agricultural producers and, while the Organization should be ready to assist when requested to do so by a Department, it should take care not to advise producers directly except by agreement with the Department concerned. Industries served by Commodity Research Stations will naturally look to these Stations for advice on their problems.

9. *The relation of regional organizations to commodity research stations*

60. In many Colonies there have developed Commodity Research Stations under auspices that place them to varying degrees outside the Government machine. Examples are one-crop Stations, as for cotton, rubber, or cocoa, where finances are provided, wholly or in part, by producing or consuming industries.

61. Such Stations are usually under the control of Governing Bodies whose authority to determine policy is not in question. We commend to their consideration, however, the advantages likely to accrue from a close liaison with the Agricultural Research Organization, if one has been established in the region. We have already recommended that the Directors of major Commodity Stations should be invited to serve on the regional Advisory Council; and, conversely, we suggest that the Stations might benefit by co-opting the regional Director of Research on to their Governing Bodies. Furthermore, we believe that the Commodity Station might often find it convenient to come to an arrangement for the Research Organization to second to it research staff for prosecuting particular enquiries. We should welcome developments that led to a free movement of officers from the Research Organization into and out of the Commodity Station, as the problems requiring attention changed in their nature and emphasis.

62. The work of the Commodity Station, which must necessarily be of an applied character, will often reveal problems requiring basic research for their solution. We should welcome requests from the authorities of the Station for such work to be undertaken by the Organization, if, as will often happen, its equipment and more varied staff place it in a better position to prosecute efficiently the required research.

10. *Relation between regional research organizations and colonial institutions for higher education*

63. We consider it to be important that satisfactory relations should be established between Research Organizations and Colonial universities and university colleges. On this matter we endorse fully the views expressed by the Commission on Higher Education in the Colonies in Chapter VI of their Report.[8] It is there emphasized that the new Colonial universities should be recognised "not only as agencies for instruction, but as centres of research". It is especially important that a Director of Research should constantly bear this in mind and should assist in any way possible in the establishment in the developing universities of strong research schools in the sciences bearing on agriculture. We should deplore the appearance of any spirit of rivalry.

64. The Research Organization and the university can be complementary to one another. As is emphasized in the Commission's Report, "it is fundamental research which is proper to a university." On the other hand, much of the work of the Organization, which is on the applied side, is of a type that cannot suitably be delegated. We believe that the university will often welcome the opportunity to study fundamental problems bearing on agriculture; and the Organization should not neglect to bring to the notice of the university problems requiring fundamental research that may emerge in the course of its agricultural work.

[8] *Report of the Commission on Higher Education in the Colonies*, Cmd 6647, 1945.

65. The Research Organization can derive much from a close association with a university; and where other circumstances allow, we recommend that research establishments be located close to universities. Contact with other scientific workers, sharing general interests but with somewhat different outlook, can be a valuable stimulus to a research team. We consider that every opportunity should be taken to organize meetings for the interchange of information and opinions between Government and university research workers.

66. While we regard teaching as a function outside the normal work of a Research Organization, we recognise that it may be desirable for research staff to give occasional lectures on the subject of their own research work and sometimes, for special reasons, to undertake the advanced training of specialist students. This latter arrangement may often be a temporary one, as, for instance, filling a gap during the phase of building up the university's full structure. We see no reason to oppose a proposal on these lines, provided that the effective prosecution of research by the Organization does not suffer by the calls on its staff for teaching duties.

67. A Research Organization should offer every possible facility for post-graduate students to work in its laboratories on research projects for higher degrees.

376 CO 859/155/1, no 12 [Sept 1948]

'Medical policy': African Conference report (AC(48)4)

Medical policy and development

The development of medical and health services must figure prominently in any scheme of colonial development. Apart from their importance in promoting individual well-being and improved social standards, these services are very closely connected with economic development. The prevention and cure of disease and the improvement of physical standards have a direct effect on work and output and on the general capacity of a population to pursue its daily work or to undertake special development schemes with enthusiasm and energy. A disease-ridden, under-nourished community cannot hope to achieve the same results as one which is adequately fed and reasonably free from disease. This fact must be borne clearly in mind in assigning a place to medical and health programmes in any general plan of colonial development and in allotting to it a proper proportion of the resources available.

2. *The various aspects of medical policy.* There are two principal aspects of a fully developed and balanced medical programme, curative medicine on the one hand and preventive and social medicine on the other. Curative medicine includes the general medical service and the system of hospitals and dispensaries and is concerned with the treatment and cure of disease in individuals. Preventive and social medicine includes all public health work, better nutrition and the general eradication of disease from a community as opposed to the treatment and cure of individual sufferers. This side of medicine involves the provision and use of clinics, the work of health officers and visitors and services concerned with the prevention of disease. These are the two aspects of policy with which this paper is principally concerned, but there are other branches of medical work which are essential to the full development of a balanced policy. Both curative and preventive work require a solid background of research. This should include investigation into basic health problems

as well as into specific diseases and treatments; it will also be concerned with the collection and examination of vital and other statistics. Its function is to extend the scientific knowledge on which medical practice depends. Another important aspect of policy is the recruitment and training of personnel for medical and health work both locally and overseas. The medical and health services require very large numbers of locally recruited and locally trained personnel together with numbers of more highly trained experts who for the time being must necessarily to a large extent be recruited and trained outside the African territories, until local personnel is available in sufficient quantities and local facilities for training are adequately developed. The expansion of local training facilities is a major aim of policy in Africa.

3. *The conclusions of the Governors' Conference.* The general lines of a long-term medical and health policy for Africa were discussed by the Governors of the African Territories during the London Conference of November, 1947. A paper prepared by the late Dr. W.H. Kauntze then Medical Adviser to the Secretary of State, which had the approval of the Colonial Advisory Medical Council, was laid before the Governors. They endorsed this paper as a general statement of the long-term principles on which sound colonial medical policy should be based. The Governors recognized that the actual implementation of the principles and objectives laid down in the paper would necessarily vary from territory to territory in the light of local conditions and financial and other resources. The substance of the paper laid before the Governors is contained in the following paragraphs. The paper was mainly concerned with the consideration of the relative importance of preventive and curative medicine under colonial conditions. For various reasons connected partly with the lack of men and resources, the African territories have not in the past achieved fully developed and balanced medical policies. There has in general inevitably been a special concentration of resources on the construction of hospitals and dispensaries and a disproportionate development of the curative side of medicine. This has apparently been largely due to the basing of policy on the satisfaction of the most obvious demands on medical staff.

4. *Community diseases due to* (a) *poor and backward people.* The problem of disease in most tropical territories requires to be dealt with on different lines from the problem in more highly developed countries. Diseases in African territories can be divided into two groups, those which often attack whole communities and those which affect only a few individuals at any one time. In developed countries like the United Kingdom, community-wide diseases have almost disappeared apart from a few infectious diseases. The Colonial territories have not as yet reached this stage and community-wide diseases constitute the most important immediate problem, for they sap the vitality of the whole population. They are often carried by tropical or sub-tropical insects; they often have a nutritional deficiency background; and they can as a rule only be dealt with on a community basis. Most of the sufferers from these diseases are dealt with piecemeal at dispensaries or hospitals where more often than not treatment is discontinuous, since the sick cannot walk long distances daily or even weekly. Most cases however require continuous treatment and would be better dealt with in their homes. At the same time preventive measures against these community-wide diseases can be instituted since in these days our knowledge of their causes is greater and there are many new drugs and insecticides to guard against and stamp out insects which carry them. The solution of the medical problem in Colonial territories is further complicated by the illiteracy of most

communities, with the consequent difficulties of giving training in health matters, and by the fact that in the country people live in huts which are usually badly lit and ventilated, and tend to be overcrowded. It is, however, in the urban areas that the overcrowding problem is at its worst. In rural areas the family can usually manage to build for themselves accommodation of sorts sufficiently commodious for their needs. In the town this is impossible, and the countryman with his family who has come there to find work must accept whatever lodging he can get and often share a room with other families.

5. (b) *Bad water supplies and sanitation.* Water supply and sanitation provide further problems. Except in large towns where there is a pipe-borne supply, the people are dependent upon rivers, springs and wells for their water, none of which is purified although in most cases it is heavily contaminated. Moreover it has often to be carried by hand for long distances, particularly in those places where the people do not live in villages but on small holdings. In such circumstances bathing and laundering are usually carried out at the river or well side, a potent cause of pollution. Sanitation is also primitive, if indeed it exists at all.

6. (c) *Diet.* The most important contribution of all to the ill health of people in Colonial territories is an insufficient and ill-balanced diet. Too frequently the diet is over starchy and methods of cooking unsatisfactory. Although to a casual glance the African may look well nourished, a closer examination often reveals signs of nutritional deficiency.

7. *Results of community diseases.* These conditions of living must inevitably be damaging to health and must constitute a formidable problem for all concerned. Account must also be taken of the many community-wide diseases which reduce the vitality of the people where they attack and make them less resistant to other diseases. As a result many Colonial territories have high infant and maternal mortality rates. Furthermore a legacy of deformity or chronic diseases is frequently left, so that the population is more susceptible to the diseases usually confined to individuals and which form the greater part of the sick population in this country.

8. *Difficulties in way of eliminating community disease.* There are many reasons why it has not been possible in the past to do more to eliminate these community-wide diseases. The financial resources and the number of trained men available have been inadequate. In the earlier years of development emphasis was inevitably laid on curative work although much valuable sanitary and health work was carried out. There has however for some years been a steady increase in the emphasis on preventive measures which has been greatly assisted by the rapid extension during the present century of the knowledge of tropical diseases and their causes. This growing emphasis on the preventive side has followed the trend in this country where it is no longer sufficient to attempt to make the sick well but where the aim is now to create healthy living conditions and eliminate preventable disease. A standard no less high must be the aim in Colonial territories, where in the light of modern knowledge much of the community-wide disease is preventable. But this can only be done if adequate staff is provided and adequate funds given to carry out the measures, many of them expensive, which are needed.

9. *Attitude of the people.* Another very important factor is the reaction of the people themselves who are sometimes suspicious of new ideas. If however community disease is to be tackled, the confidence of the people must first be secured and their whole-hearted cooperation in the measures for their welfare enlisted, because it

is only when they realise that they are responsible for their own health that measures taken to eliminate disease can ever have any permanent effect.

10. *Previous attempts to eliminate community diseases.* In the past attempts to eliminate community-disease have been made in various ways and experience gained in the methods adopted have suggested that a new approach is necessary. In some cases a campaign has been undertaken designed to stamp out a particular disease only. This method has not had conspicuous success when the people have merely been passive agents of the campaign, not having it properly explained to them what it was about and perhaps a little resentful at the work which they were being forced to do for their own good. Moreover an attempt to eliminate one disease may have left many other diseases and other factors untouched.

Arrangements have not always been made in the past to continue the work done in particular campaigns of this sort. There may have been no adequate follow up and consequently no permanent effect on the lives of the inhabitants in spite of the fact that many individuals may have been cured. Another method adopted has been for the regular medical staff in an area to undertake a health drive on preventable disease. Unfortunately the size of the local staff has often been too small to achieve much or to maintain the campaign for very long.

11. *The special team method.* It is clear therefore that what is required is a general health campaign and mass attack on all forms of preventable disease. Staff and resources are not sufficient for this to be undertaken all over a Colonial territory at the same time and the right course may therefore be for a special team of doctors and assistants to be sent to a selected rural area to clean it up from the health point of view. The team would absorb, for the time being, all the regular medical staff of the area in which it was working. It would attack all preventable disease and at the same time train the local medical staff in the way in which disease could be excluded for the future. When the area had been cleaned up, the team would move on to a new area, leaving behind the local district staff, now trained in the new methods, to maintain what had been done and to cope with those diseases which attack individuals rather than the community. The success of this method lies in making a good start. Once an area has been cleaned up successfully, there will inevitably come a call from the people in surrounding districts demanding similar action in their own neighbourhood; an example of this is the demand for D.D.T. in the neighbourhood of places where experimental insecticide teams are working. The most important feature of this method is to secure the active cooperation of the inhabitants of the area in which the team is working. It is it therefore essential to choose for the initial venture an area where there are leading citizens genuinely anxious to improve their own condition and that of their neighbours.

12. *The need to associate the local people with the work.* Before the actual work begins, the possibilities of disease control must be explained to these men in such a way that they not only grasp the plan of the work, but become urgent in demanding that a start should be made in controlling disease in and about their own homes. The idea of individual responsibility for health must be driven home and the active cooperation of the people in carrying out and maintaining the measures required for disease control obtained. Each man, woman and child in the village must feel himself, or herself, personally responsible for taking an active part in the undertaking and for the maintenance of control measures after the team has left. This will be made easier if, from the start, the assistance of a village health committee, elected by

the people, is secured. In this connection full use should be made of the existing local government machinery. It will be seen that a health campaign is essentially a venture of community betterment [or] mass education. It can be best handled as part of a general scheme to improve conditions in a particular area.

13. *The work of special team.* The actual work which will be required in a campaign of this sort will vary from area to area, but generally speaking the measures to be undertaken will be the provision and protection of water supplies; adequate provision for refuse disposal; measures against disease-carrying insects; improvement of houses and prevention of overcrowding; improved agricultural methods; cultivation of the right food crops; provision of adequate infant and child welfare clinics and ante-natal clinics; adequate provision for regular home visitors, and so on. In the campaign against preventable disease, the team will have to keep clearly in mind what it has to do if it is to complete its task within a reasonable period; there are certain diseases, for example yaws,[1] in which sufferers can be made non-infective to others in a comparatively short period of time, yet to free them completely from the disease may require treatment over many years. The rendering of such patients non-infective is sufficient for the purposes of the team; the treatment to complete the cure of individual cases must be left to the local district staff. To the medical man brought up to think of the treatment of individual patients, this system may at first be difficult to accept, but when the first aim must be to rid the coming generation of the risks its fathers had to meet, medical effort must be expended in the way which will most benefit the community and not the individual. That it is possible to work on these lines is indicated by experience in one Colonial territory, where in the early twenties, a certain clinic dealt with over a thousand cases of yaws a week. To-day it is extremely difficult to find a case anywhere in that district, yet no-one pretends that the cases treated originally in the clinic were completely cured. They were merely rendered non-infective.

14. *The part to be played by the existing local medical staff.* It will be the task of the present local medical staff both to follow up the work of the special team and to tackle individual diseases. For the detection of these diseases in the early stages the skilled eye of a doctor or nurse is needed. Doctors are scarce, so reliance must be placed on nurses, who to fulfil this function must have special training. Such a nurse might be called "community nurse". She should wherever possible be under the supervision of a medical officer.

15. *Preventive health services.* But the district staff of community nurses and medical practitioner can do more than detect the early onset of disease. They can prepare the ground for and follow the work of the special team in taking steps to prevent disease. They can teach the value of prophylactic inoculation for smallpox, yellow fever and diphtheria. They can educate the people in the measures to be taken against insect-borne disease. Even more important can be the measures they take to maintain the health of those who are well. Experience in Colonial territories has proved it best to start these preventive services by the establishment of ante-natal clinics at suitable places so as to give the unborn infant the best chance in life. These would be held by the community nurse and the midwife and attended at regular intervals by the doctor. Then provision should be made for maternity services, followed by the institution of infant welfare clinics, nursery school clinics, school

[1] A tropical skin-disease causing raspberry-like swellings.

clinics and industrial clinics, so that all through life the individual would be cared for and advised how to maintain health. In their visits to homes, the community nurse and medical practitioner must carry on propaganda directed against any conditions in the home which are damaging to health. Their advice is the more likely to be accepted, because, being the two members of the medical services who come into close contact with the people in their homes, both in health and sickness, they will be looked upon as friends.

16. *Local medical services and follow up of special team work.* The essential factors in the attack on preventable disease in Colonial territories are thus the local doctor and the community nurse. During the period when the special team is cleaning up community-wide disease, it is their influence which will be largely instrumental in explaining what is being done and in enlisting the support of the local government and the general population in health measures. After the special team has left the area, it will be upon the shoulders of the community nurse and the doctor that the maintenance of health in the community will depend.

17. *The necessity of deciding the aspect of medical policy to be emphasized.* This paper has so far been concerned with the need to lay greater emphasis in medical policy on preventive as opposed to curative work. This does not mean that the importance of curative work is underestimated, but it is suggested that the health of the community as a whole is of greater importance than the curing of sick individuals. The complete control of disease and especially the provision of treatment for those affected is a very expensive matter, and probably beyond the financial resources of most Territories. There is moreover a limit to the number of doctors, nurses and other subordinate staff who can be obtained or trained. In most territories a choice will have to be made between extensive attack on community-wide disease with reliance on simple accommodation for the treatment of the sick and the spending of money freely on large well-equipped hospitals and expensive specialist staff. As regards hospitals it does not matter how large or how many they are, they will never be able to cope with all the patients who seek to use them unless at the same time disease is being prevented in the home. Moreover since the number of doctors is limited by costs and recruitment, the larger hospitals grow, the more will medical staff be tied to them and the fewer men will be available for preventive work.

18. *The general lines of a policy of preventive medicine.* If the Conference accepts the proposition that, while not neglecting adequate provision for curative treatment, the most important object of medical and health policy should be preventive, it is necessary to consider the general lines upon which such a policy might be developed. It is suggested that the steps to be taken in establishing such a policy should be as follows:—

(a) a survey of the health needs, including the prevention and cure of disease, of the whole country, with a statement of hospitals, clinics, organisations, such as mission medical activities, voluntary society activities etc., already serving those needs;

(b) the settling of the relative priorities of the various health needs, their cost and the rate at which they can be financed;

(c) the organisation of the medical department to meet the health needs in order of priority;

(d) the establishment of training schools to provide the increased staff required;
(e) the establishment of full cooperation with local government bodies and if necessary the setting up of such additional committees as may be required to bring the people who are being served into relation with the control of health measures.

19. *Methods of examination.* If such a policy is acceptable it will inevitably take time to build up the local medical organisation and to train the necessary staff. A start has of course been made in all territories in introducing health measures, particularly in the urban areas, and much is already being done in various ways to teach personal and community hygiene particularly in the schools. A great deal remains to be done and it will be necessary to obtain the fullest cooperation of all persons and bodies interested in improving health. The various departments of Government will have to work together and the active cooperation of native administrations, town councils and other local government bodies will be essential to the success of any policy of preventive and social medicine. The Education Department and the schools together with those bodies and persons concerned with mass education will of course have a most important and direct contribution to make in securing the cooperation of the people in such a health policy.

20. *The needs of non-African communities.* It is not possible in this paper to make a complete review of medical policy and certain main aspects of policy have either received very brief mention or are not mentioned at all. No reference is made, for example, to the special medical needs of the non-African communities which arise from their lack of natural immunity to local disease and from the care necessary to maintain health in the African climate, particularly in the case of people from temperate climates. Although it has not been possible to deal with this special problem in the paper, its great importance is fully recognised.

21. *Emphasis on rural problems.* The policy discussed in this paper is primarily concerned with the prevention of illness and the improvement in the health of the African population in the rural areas. In the towns much progress has already been made in sanitation, the teaching and adoption of hygienic measures, the exclusion of infected people from public places, inoculation and the provision of welfare clinics, dispensaries and similar services. In the rural areas on the other hand the problem is bigger and more difficult and progress has been much slower owing to primitive conditions, the wide spread of population and the conservatism of most rural people. These areas are reservoirs of endemic diseases, the elimination of which is necessary for the protection of the health of all sections of the community. The policy recommended in this paper is designed to raise health standards in the rural areas, thus making a most important contribution not only to the health but also to the economy of the community.

22. *Resources available.* The resources available for carrying into effect the policy advocated in this paper must be considered. It has already been pointed out that the resources of individual Territories are strictly limited and that it will not be possible to provide completely all the facilities and services desirable. The supply of trained doctors is short and recruitment is difficult. The training of local people both as doctors and as subordinate staff in the numbers required will take time, particularly as the number of candidates with the necessary standard of general education is still relatively small. Material resources for building and other work are limited. As a result the medical plan must inevitably move slowly, and this makes it all the more

necessary for policy to be selective in order that the most may be made of the men and other resources available. It is for this reason that the paper suggests that these resources should not be used to build and staff elaborate hospitals where more modest accommodation would be adequate. It is not suggested that hospital and other facilities for the treatment of disease should be neglected, but that the introduction of measures to prevent community-wide diseases should receive high priority in the allocation of funds. As regards finance there are in addition to territorial financial resources, sums being made available under the Colonial Development and Welfare Act. But the problem at present is not so much one of financial [sic] as a problem arising from the shortage of material and particularly of human resources.

23. *Conclusion.* As to the future success of the proposed Medical Policy much will depend on the people of the individual Territories. They alone can make the necessary effort and improvement in standards of personal and community hygiene which will be required if real progress is to be made. Progress in health and preventive medicine is closely connected with general social progress which is the object of the mass education or better living campaigns now being carried on in the various territories. The improvement of educational standards and the spread of knowledge, apart from their direct influence in improving social conditions, will greatly help medical workers in their task of teaching health measures to the community. Finally, just as economic development will be affected by the level of health in the community, equally a successful health policy will depend on the enthusiasm and hard work of the people and the extent to which their efforts in the economic field earn the means to maintain a high level of social services.

24. The following is a brief summary of the main points raised in this paper:—

(1) The main aspects of a fully developed and balanced medical policy, including curative medicine, preventive medicine, research and recruitment. (Paragraph 2).

(2) The endorsement by the Governors' Conference of the paper on medical policy by the late Dr. W.H. Kauntze, the substance of which is set out in the succeeding paragraphs. (Paragraph 3).

(3) The problems of community diseases arising from (a) poor and backward people, (b) bad water supplies and sanitation and (c) diet. (Paragraphs 4–6).

(4) The results of community diseases. (Paragraph 7).

(5) The difficulties, such as inadequacy of financial resources and trained personnel, in the way of eliminating community diseases. (Paragraph 8).

(6) The reaction of the people and the importance of obtaining their co-operation. (Paragraph 9).

(7) Measures taken in the past to combat community diseases. (Paragraph 10).

(8) The necessity for a general health campaign and mass attack on all forms of preventable disease to be undertaken by a special team of doctors and assistants. (Paragraph 11).

(9) The need to associate the local people with the work and to drive home the idea of individual responsibility for health. (Paragraph 12).

(10) The general measures to be taken by the special team. (Paragraph 13).

(11) The part to be played by the existing local medical staff. (Paragraph 14).

(12) The value of starting preventive health services by setting up ante-natal clinics. (Paragraph 15).

(13) The influence of the local doctor and the community nurse. (Paragraph 16).

(14) The necessity of deciding the aspect of medical policy to be emphasized. (Paragraph 17).
(15) The general lines of a policy of preventive medicine. (Paragraph 18).
(16) The need for the active cooperation of Government Departments, native administrations, town councils and other local government bodies. (Paragraph 19).
(17) The special medical needs of the non-African communities. (Paragraph 20).
(18) The reason for the emphasis on the prevention of illness and the improvement of health of the African population in the rural areas. (Paragraph 21).
(19) The resources available for putting the policy into effect. (Paragraph 22).

377 CO 927/61/7, no 20 29 Nov 1948

[Promotion of social science research in the colonies]: CO Research Dept 'outline of note for presentation to the Colonial Social Science Research Council'

Consideration has recently been given in the Colonial Office to what can be done to stimulate the promotion of social science research in the Colonies and to facilitate the work of the Colonial Social Science Research Council.

2. As regards the Colonies, it is clear that researches undertaken by workers sent out from this country will be severely handicapped so long as there is no institute in the area specialising in social and economic research to which they can be attached, and so long as Colonial Governments have no specialist in this field of research on their own staffs.

3. The Colonial Office accordingly propose (a) to proceed with all possible speed with the staffing of the socio-economic research institutes or departments which it is proposed to set up in West and East Africa and in the West Indies; (b) to explore the possibility of social science specialists being attached to appropriate departments in Colonial Administrations, such as Native Affairs Departments.

4. As regards the work of the Colonial Social Science Research Council, it appears to the Colonial Office that there are two matters requiring action.

5. The first is the obvious desirability of associating the work of the African Studies Branch of the Colonial Office with the Council. The African Studies Branch was created about a year ago in order that long-term administrative problems in Africa, especially questions of local government, native law, land tenure and contemporary history, could be studied at greater leisure than was possible by Geographical Departments burdened with heavy day to day business. The Branch acts as a sort of "Intelligence" Branch for the three African Geographical Departments. It works in close association with, and provides the Secretariat for, the Colonial Native Law and Land Tenure Panels which have been instituted. It is at present staffed by a Colonial Administrative Service Officer (Mr. G.B. Cartland), a Research Officer (Mr. R.E. Robinson), and a Research Assistant (Mr. L. Branney).

6. The second matter in regard to which the Colonial Office suggests that a change is necessary concerns the volume of work with which the Colonial Social Science Research Council is at present called upon to deal. The Colonial Office have noted that, although the Council meets as frequently as every four weeks, the volume

of business on the agenda of each meeting shows no sign of diminishing, and that much of this business concerns matters of relatively minor importance with which it is felt the Council as a whole ought not to be burdened. The Colonial Office would accordingly suggest that the Council's Geographical Sub-Committees, i.e. the West African, East and Central African, West Indian and Far Eastern Sub-Committees, should be abolished, and that in their place should be substituted five Panels comprising respectively Sociology and Anthropology, Administration and Contemporary History, Linguistics and the Native Law and Land Tenure Panels mentioned above. To these should be added a sixth body in the form of a Personnel Panel or Sub-Committee which should have as Chairman a member of the Council selected for this purpose with ad hoc membership according to the nature of the appointments for which applications by candidates are to be considered.

7. The adoption of this proposal would necessitate some re-organisation of the membership of the Council, and the Colonial Office would suggest that the Council should consist of a Chairman, the chairman of the six Panels mentioned above and such other persons whom the Secretary of State considers it desirable to appoint. The Colonial Office hopes that it may be possible to retain the valuable assistance which can still be given by such of the present members of the Council who may not be required to become members of the new Council, by enlisting their services as members of one or other of the Panels.

8. It is thought by the Colonial Office that these arrangements will relieve the Council of a great deal of work, since the re-organisation of the subsidiary bodies of the Council on a subject instead of a geographical basis will enable matters which hitherto have had to be considered by the full Council to devolve upon the Panels. The Colonial Office would propose normally to accept the recommendations of the Panels and act upon them, without awaiting the formal confirmation by the Council of the Panels' recommendations, but it would at the same time reserve the right to refer a recommendation by a Panel to the full Council, if it considers this desirable. Cases may well arise in which the Panel itself would feel unable to take the responsibility for a definite recommendation to the Colonial Office and would itself wish to discuss the matter jointly with the members of other Panels or refer it to the full Council.

9. If effect is given to the above proposals, it will necessitate some re-organisation of staff and duties in the Colonial Office. The Colonial Office would propose that the concurrence of the Treasury should be sought in the appointment of an Administrative officer of Principal rank to act as Secretary to the Council and as Secretary of all its Panels, and in the appointment of a Research Assistant who would be associated with the Secretary of the Council and be concerned with all non-African [social] science research questions and projects. The African Studies Branch would be responsible not only for the work described in paragraph 5 of this memorandum, but for the handling within the Colonial Office of all social science schemes envisaged for the West, East and Central African territories. It may well be that it may later be possible for the Colonial Office to envisage setting up Studies Branches for other areas in the Colonial Empire, but at the present time the staff position does not permit of this.

10. The Research Department will continue to be responsible for the submission of all social science research schemes to the Treasury.

378 CO 927/175/1, no 26 24 July 1950

'Organisation of medical research for the colonies': note by the S of S on recommendations of the Colonial Medical Research Committee

I have now given very careful consideration to the views expressed on the above subject in the memorandum prepared by the Colonial Medical Research Committee, and I have also discussed it with the Chairman.

2. The Committee in their memorandum differentiate between 'general research', which is defined as meaning research directed to obtaining knowledge capable of general application, and 'local research', which is defined as meaning investigations aimed at applying the results of general research to particular or local circumstances.

3. It would appear that the Committee consider that the planning, administration and execution of general research in medicine for the benefit of the Colonial territories should be the responsibility of a separate organisation outside the Colonial Office consisting solely of scientific specialists of highstanding, and that such an organisation could appropriately be the Medical Research Council. The memorandum also suggests, as an alternative (paragraph 26) that there might be an organisation of this kind directly responsible to myself. As regards local research, the Committee again stress the desirability of the workers engaged on this being distinct and segregated from medical officers in the Colonial Medical Service, and the desirability of any such activities being suitably associated with the organisation for general medical research.

4. Before commenting in detail on these proposals, I feel it desirable to make clear the constitutional position, since that must necessarily govern all proposals for any alteration in the existing machinery. The memorandum of the Committee would suggest that considerable misapprehension exists both as regards the relations between the Secretary of State and the Colonies and also as regards the relations between the Secretary of State and Parliament.

5. As regards the former, it will be common ground that any research directed to obtaining knowledge capable of general application is bound to have a projection into the Colonial territories which it is designed to assist, and sooner or later will lead to the sending of investigators to one or more of the Colonies. It will also be common ground that, in order to achieve the maximum of success, any investigation conducted in a Colony must have the good will and co-operation of the Colonial administration concerned. The Secretary of State is not in a position to order any particular investigation to be carried out in any particular territory. The Government of the territory has to be asked in the first place whether it agrees to the investigation being carried out and how soon. Colonial Governments have a steadily increasing degree of independence. Some are well on the way to Dominion status and in a great many of them the majority of the members of the Legislature are local residents, either indigenous or European. In such cases there is no official control over its decisions. In several Colonies there is the beginning of Cabinet Government, i.e. the placing of the actual administration in the hands of local people.

6. Nor, even if it were practicable, would it be desirable for Colonial Governments to have no concern with medical research in the Colonies. We must look forward to a time when many Colonies will have much more independence than they have to-day.

It is part of the process of education for self-government that they should appreciate the value of research and they will not appreciate something in which they have had no share. For this reason, as well as for purely financial reasons, it is desirable that they should make some contribution towards medical research and it would not be appropriate that that contribution should only be given to a remote body in England; it must generally be to some specific object of local significance. One must also look forward to the time when there will be local people able to undertake research themselves. In some parts of the Colonial Empire and for some subjects they exist already.

7. Turning now to the relationship of the Secretary of State with Parliament, this very materially affects administration and finance. The Secretary of State alone is responsible to Parliament for all matters affecting the Colonies and for all matters arising in connection with the expenditure of the funds provided by Parliament under the Colonial Development and Welfare Act, which is the sole source of supply at his disposal for Colonial research. The Act opens with the words:—

> "The Secretary of State, with the concurrence of the Treasury, may make schemes for any purpose likely to promote the development of the resources of any Colony or the welfare of its people . . .".

Under this provision it is the practice to regard as a scheme, for the purposes of the Act, any single definable project whether it relates to a particular piece of research by an individual or to the setting up of a research institute. But I fear it would be inadmissible to make a scheme for the handing over of a block sum of money to a separate body to be spent on "medical research" generally, without further definition or question. To do so would be to abrogate the functions of the Secretary of State and the Treasury under the Act. If the separate body in question were the Medical Research Council, there would be the added complication that another Minister, the Lord President, and not the Secretary of State is responsible to Parliament for its activities. But even if it were the Colonial Medical Research Committee the main objection would remain. The Secretary of State must retain the ultimate final responsibility and he could not, for constitutional reasons, make an unconditional block grant even to the Colonial Medical Research Committee.

8. Apart from this constitutional reason, I should not, for the practical and political reasons set out in paragraphs 5 and 6 consider it wise to place sole control over medical research in the hands of a body with whose activities I had no concern. While I am most anxious that the scientific direction of medical research should be in scientific hands, it cannot be denied that, on almost every proposition for research in the Colonies, there are political and other non-scientific considerations to be taken into account. I should feel it necessary to have the advice and assistance of my usual officials in the Colonial Office and the opportunity if necessary to consult Colonial Governments. (See also paragraphs 14–16 below).

9. What I have said above does not preclude the drawing up of plans whereby, by agreement, the Medical Research Council, or any other body, undertakes to carry out particular pieces of research. Thus the Medical Research Council, with assistance from Colonial Development and Welfare funds, has set up the Human Nutrition Research Unit. Again, the Lister Institute is responsible for the work which Dr. Weitz is doing; and so forth. Arrangements of [t]his kind are most valuable and it is much to be hoped that more of them will be made in the future.

10. I fully realise that apprehensions may be felt by members of the Colonial Medical Research Committee lest sufficient funds may not be available to finance Colonial medical research schemes which they may recommend. There are strong practical arguments against allocating far in advance too much of the limited funds available for Colonial development to specific fields of research, but I should be very ready to arrange for my officials to agree with the Committee upon a figure to be earmarked during the next five years as the sum available, if required, to assist medical research in the Colonies. This sum would of course be over and above the moneys already allotted under the Acts for medical research schemes but not yet spent.

11. It will now be convenient to consider the Committee's memorandum paragraph by paragraph.

12. The opening paragraph states that "the arrangements for the organisation of medical research for the Colonies, both existing and proposed, do not fulfil the requirements for satisfactory conduct of research and cannot be effective." I am distressed that this should be the opinion of the Committee. If the reference is to the organisation within the Colonial Office itself, that is a matter to which I am giving special attention. I discuss it further below. If the reference is to organisation overseas, I find it difficult to reconcile with the facts as given to me by my advisers—for instance with the large number of medical papers, accepted for publication . . . . . . by scientific journals, that are enumerated in the Colonial Office pamphlet, "Miscellaneous No. 515" entitled: "A note on some of the Scientific Studies undertaken by members of the Colonial Medical Service during the period 1930–47"; or, to cite a few instances in more detail, with the pioneer work of Dr. H. Fraser and the late Sir Thomas Stanton on beri-beri; the brilliant researches of the late Dr. William Fletcher on the typhus-like fevers, the benefits of which we are still reaping; the work of Dr. J.W. Field on the suppression of clinical malaria by atebrin, which was of such tremendous consequence to the maintenance of our armies in the field in the recent war, and which won for him the award of the Chalmers Medal; the work of Dr. P.C.C. Garnham and Dr. Bagster Wilson in East Africa, or of Mr. B.A.R. Gater in Malaya. No doubt the organisation left room for improvement in the past, and no doubt there is still room for further improvement. But the impressive results obtained by these investigators in Colonial territories should surely render it immune from a charge that it cannot be effective.

13. With regard to paragraph 1 of the memorandum, the Committee would seem to consider that a broad dividing line can be drawn between general research and local research, as defined therein. Experience however has shown that these two types of research shade into one another. It would, I suggest, be a mistake to draw too sharp a distinction between the two, or to underestimate the importance of local research, that is to say work in Colonial territories where the challenge of disease originates.

14. As regards personnel, I entirely agree with the principles outlined in paragraphs 2 and 3 of the memorandum. I also accept many of the arguments advanced in paragraphs 4–6. In particular I realise that it is the general experience that administration of a research organisation can usually best be carried out by men who are themselves qualified in research. At the same time, for the reasons given in earlier paragraphs of this memorandum, the ultimate direction of scientific policy in the Colonies must rest with the Secretary of State and it has at some stage, which

must necessarily be a good deal lower down in the hierarchy, to be married with other aspects of policy and with the practical requirements of the changing situation in the Colonies. It seems that here lies the root of the difficulties which the Committee feel.

15. It has been the object of the Colonial Office over the past five years or so to build up a system which will reconcile these two desiderata. Under it virtually the complete scientific control of research in the Colonial Empire is in the hands of scientists, i.e. it lies with the members of the various Committees attached to the Research Department and (in the case of medical research) with the Director of Colonial Medical Research. At the same time the administrative civil servants in the Research Department are associated with the scientists in the implementation of scientific policy.

16. The present system has been carefully thought out and elaborated in the light of experience and, in other fields of research, it is believed to be working well and to the general satisfaction of those engaged on research in the Colonies. In agriculture, for instance, both the Colonial Agricultural Research Committee and leading scientists employed in the Colonies are understood to be well content with it. The same would be true of the social sciences. It may of course be dangerous to apply to one branch of science lessons drawn from another, and it may well be that present arrangements at the Colonial Office are capable of improvement. The Colonial Research Council recently suggested, for instance, that there should be on the administrative side of the Research Department men with first-hand scientific knowledge and training. I think this would be useful. There is already one such officer in the Department and I intend to see whether it cannot be arranged that there should be more. I shall be very ready to consider any other practical suggestions.

17. There seems to be a very considerable misapprehension on the part of the Committee regarding the Colonial Research Service. Up to the present time the Colonial Office had gladly availed itself of the very great assistance which has been afforded in recent years by the Medical Research Council and the Colonial Medical Research Committee in providing scientists from this country to undertake research of major importance both in this country and in the Colonies. I should like to express unreservedly our sincere gratitude to the scientists, whose help has been ungrudgingly and usefully given, and we have every desire to avail ourselves of this assistance in the future. The concluding part of paragraph 6 of the memorandum would, however, seem to convey that its authors are under the impression that the institution of the Colonial Research Service will in some way or other make this impossible. I am at a loss to understand why this impression should have arisen. The Colonial Research Service will merely be an extremely flexible piece of machinery designed to regularise the terms of service on which research workers are employed in the Colonial Empire; to give them a recognised status of their own; to enable them to move from one Colony to another or to this country as their work dictates; and to enable scientists working in this country to work for brief periods in the Colonies, without suffering any disadvantage in the careers which they are making for themselves. For this reason, the Service should greatly assist the mobility which is rightly emphasised by the Committee in paragraphs 7 and 8 of their memorandum and provide an attraction and not a deterrent to the acquisition of young scientists who wish to augment their knowledge by first-hand experience overseas.

18. The following cases illustrate the manner in which mobility of scientific personnel, both for work and study, has been encouraged in different territories of the Colonial Empire in accordance with the needs of the moment. Dr. Muirhead Thomson has moved from the Gambia to East Africa, and now to Jamaica. Dr. John MacArthur is, in due course, to extend his malaria investigations from Borneo to Sarawak. Dr. F.S. Airey, after preliminary study of specialised techniques at Oxford and London, has provision in his scheme to proceed from Malaya to India to discuss leprosy problems with Dr. Cochrane. Every facility has been given to ensure that members of Professor Gordon's group of workers may undertake periodic visits to their field work in the British Cameroons; and for Dr. Bernard Weitz, in his studies on precipitin sera, to correlate the two phases of his work in East Africa and London respectively. Dr. R.C. Burgess, Senior Nutrition Officer at the Institute for Medical Research in Malaya, recently spent many weeks in the Gambia studying nutrition problems and counter-measures with Professor B.S. Platt.

19. Concerning paragraph 9, the need for a wide range of apparatus is fully realised. For this reason it may well be that certain branches of research can best be undertaken in this country and if the Committee so advises practical plans for this can be drawn up. As stated in paragraph 9 of this memorandum, arrangements can easily be made for research in particular subjects to be carried out by bodies like the Medical Research Council or the Lister Institute with, if need be, 100% assistance from Colonial Research funds. However, the leading Colonial research institutions are themselves finely equipped; and in the instances where a piece of research demands the use of special apparatus available only in laboratories in Britain, or consultations with other scientists, every facility in the way of study leave would be afforded.

20. I accept the principle of scientific independence enunciated in paragraph 10, and this principle is being upheld in a case which has recently arisen (Dr. MacArthur). In Malaya it is safeguarded by printed regulation, a procedure that will, I hope, be copied elsewhere. There are also other devices for securing it.

21. I entirely agree with the views expressed in paragraph 11 regarding the need for central scientific direction, subject to what is said in earlier paragraphs as regards the necessity for the integration of scientific with general policy.

22. As regards paragraph 12, I want to make it clear that, although it has been thought best to establish one Colonial Research Service covering all scientific research, the affairs of each branch of science will continue to be conducted with the closest regard to the needs of that branch. Thus the Director of Colonial Medical Research and the Colonial Medical Research Committee will be closely associated with the selection and supervision of all those engaged on medical research.

23. Comment made in earlier paragraphs of this note covers the matters raised in paragraphs 13 and 14 of the memorandum.

24. As regards local research, subject to what I have said in paragraph 12, I agree generally with the views postulated in paragraphs 15 and 18 of the memorandum, which largely constitute existing practice.

25. With reference to the summary of Conclusions and Recommendations at the end of the memorandum, I would only say that while I cannot accept certain of the views expressed, notably those in paragraph[s] 20, 25 and 26, I hope that what I have written will make it clear that there are good reasons why this must be so. I hope this memorandum will also show that I have given much thought to the Committee's

representations and that I am most anxious to do anything I properly can to enable them to carry on as efficiently as possible the good work they are doing for the Colonies.

379 CO 927/116/3, no 25 21 Nov 1950

'Provision of funds to finance Colonial Development and Welfare research schemes': CO memorandum for Colonial Research Council (CRC(50)16). *Appendix*: allocation of funds under the CDW Act, 1945

1. The Secretary of State desires the Council to consider the above matter in the light of the following information.

2. The Colonial Development and Welfare Act, 1940, provided for the disbursement of not exceeding £500,000 in any financial year for the purpose of schemes for promoting research or inquiry calculated to assist the development of the resources of any of the non-self-governing Colonial Dependencies or the welfare of their peoples. The Act also provided for the disbursement of not more than £5,000,000 in any financial year for other schemes made for the above purposes.

3. It was of course impossible to make many schemes of this nature in the first few years on account of the war, and up to the 31st March, 1945, only 51 research schemes had been made under the Act, involving grants totalling £414,128. The money disbursed on these schemes up to the 31st March, 1945, amounted to only about £150,000.

4. In April, 1945, the Colonial Development and Welfare Act, 1945, was passed. This laid down that the sums which could be disbursed for the purposes of all schemes made for promoting development and welfare in the Colonies should not in the aggregate exceed £17,500,000 in any financial year, and should not exceed £120,000,000 in the period of ten years ending 31st March, 1956. Further, that the sums paid for research schemes should not in the aggregate exceed £1,000,000 in any financial year.

5. It was for the Colonial Office to decide within these limits how the £120,000,000 should be allocated. Details of the allocation decided upon are given in the Appendix. As will be seen, most of the money was allocated to individual Governments for their development plans, some was kept for various "central" development schemes, and £8,500,000 was allocated to research, including geological surveys. This last allocation was intended to provide sufficient for the full expenditure on research that would be practicable within the limit of £1,000,000 a year for ten years laid down by Parliament; owing to the need to build the research organisation from the foundations and the shortage of staff and supplies, it was clearly going to be a year or two before expenditure could reach anything like £1,000,000 a year.

6. In 1947, it was decided that the geological survey, for which £1,000,000 had been set aside within the £8,500,000, could be regarded more appropriately as "Development" rather than "Research", and the allocation for research schemes accordingly became *£7,500,000*. This was the figure obtaining up to the beginning of 1950.

7. The passage of the 1945 Act, making greatly increased sums available,

combined with the ending of the war, the gradual return to normality, increasing development of the Colonial Office machinery for dealing with these matters* and the gradually increasing interest of Colonial Governments, has led to a great expansion of research work in and for the Colonial Empire over the last five years. The number of schemes made increased from 51 at the end of March, 1945, to 107 in March, 1946, to 174 in March, 1947, to 234 in March, 1948, to 317 in March, 1949, and to 395 in March, 1950. At the 30th September, 1950, 426 schemes had been made. Of these 104 were for agricultural, veterinary or forestry research, 32 for fisheries research, 28 for insecticides research, 9 for anti-locust research, 78 for medical research, 6 for research sponsored by the Colonial Products Research Council, 14 for tsetse and trypanosomiasis research, 119 for social science and economic research and 36 for miscellaneous research, including engineering research of various kinds.

8. The making of these many new schemes was noticeably reflected in the annual disbursements, as the following figures show:—

Financial Year	*Issues* £
1940–41	Nil
1941–42	6,670
1942–43	13,793
1943–44	30,450
1944–45	58,345
1945–46	93,307
1946–47	169,388
1947–48	425,761
1948–49	763,300

9. Early in 1949 it became evident that the disbursement limit of £1,000,000 per annum was likely to be exceeded during the financial year 1949/50. Accordingly proposals were put to Parliament for an amendment of the 1945 Act whereby the annual disbursement limit for research schemes should be raised to £2,500,000. The Colonial Development and Welfare Act, 1949, gave effect to this change. The actual disbursement figure for the year 1949/50 was £1,284,311.

10. The 1949 Act did not increase the overall total of £120,000,000 for development and welfare including research. Nor of course did it affect the internal allocation by the Colonial Office within this total of funds for research schemes. This still therefore remained at £7,500,000. Early in 1950, however, it became clear that further funds would have to be found for research if adequate effect was to be given to schemes already made and schemes of importance that might be projected. It at the

* Up to the time of the passing of the 1945 Act, the Colonial Office had had available for advice on research schemes the Colonial Research Committee, which had been established in 1942, the Colonial Products Research Council (1941), the Colonial Fisheries Advisory Committee (1943), the Colonial Social Science Research Council (1944), the Tsetse and Trypanosomiasis Committee (1944) and the Anti-Locust Research Centre (1929). To these bodies were added the Colonial Medical Research Committee (1945), the Committee for Colonial Agricultural, Animal Health and Forestry Research (1945), the Colonial Insecticides Committee (1947) and the Colonial Economic Research Committee (1947). Full-time scientists have been appointed as Director of Colonial Medical Research and Secretary for Colonial Agricultural Research, while the administrative machinery of the Colonial Office has been greatly strengthened.

same time became apparent that the overall figure of £120,000,000 would have to be increased to provide not only for further research but for further development schemes, including geological and geodetic surveys. The position was discussed by the Colonial Office with the Treasury and temporary arrangements were made for the sum of £7,500,000 to be exceeded pending the provision of further funds by Parliament.

11. The cumulative allocations of research monies in fact rose from £57,158 at the 31st October, 1942, to £7,727,979 at the 31st March, 1950, and at the 30th September, 1950, the gross figure was £9,261,279. From this figure has to be deducted £202,565 disbursed under the 1940 Act and some £750,000 arising from unspent balances on completed schemes, revision of schemes, etc., so that the net total commitment and expenditure at the 30th September, 1950, was about *£8,300,000*.

12. A Bill has now been presented to Parliament proposing that the overall figure of £120,000,000 provided by the 1945 Act should be increased to £140,000,000. The Secretary of State has decided that, if the Bill becomes law, out of the additional provision of £20,000,000, no less than £5,500,000 shall be allocated for research schemes, making with the original £7,500,000 a total sum allotted for research schemes of *£13,000,000*. Against this there is the commitment of £8,300,000 mentioned above.

13. *This leaves a sum of £4,700,000 no less and no more, available for all purposes up to the 31st March, 1956 including the provision necessary for renewing important schemes, the currency of which may expire between now and that date.*

14. The sum of £9,261,279 (see paragraph 11) has been allotted to the various fields of research as follows:—

	£	*Percentage of total*
Agriculture, Animal Health and Forestry	3,109,423	33.57
Work sponsored by the Colonial Products Research Council	387,234	4.18
Fisheries	1,095,826	11.83
Insecticides	530,167	5.73
Anti-Locust Research	293,534	3.17
Tsetse and Trypanosomiasis	1,026,928	11.09
Medical	1,392,348	15.03
Social Science and Economic Research*	816,242	8.81
Miscellaneous (including industrial and engineering research)	609,577	6.59
	£9,261,279	100.00

(* the proportion of Economic Research in this figure is fractional)

15. In order to enable the Secretary of State to determine the total maximum amount which it would be possible to allot to research schemes, the Research Department of the Colonial Office prepared a list showing, as far as was known, the schemes involving new money which the various advisory committees or Colonial Governments were likely to put forward between now and the 31st March, 1956. The list, a copy of which is annexed[1], was based on material provided by the secretaries of the various specialist advisory research committees, and is divided into (a) Essential

[1] Not printed here; the list is reproduced in part 1 of this volume, enclosure 2 to 76.

or Important Schemes and (b) Other Schemes. The division between "essential" and "other" is obviously rather arbitrary. Some of the schemes in the "essential" category are really essential; for others the term is too strong; what it means is that there is a strong case for undertaking them and that, while modifications or economies may be practicable, they could not be dropped altogether without serious disadvantages. Schemes in the "other" category are simply the rest that can at present be foreseen, some of which may of course not materialize.

16. The totals for each field of research and for each division are as follows:—

Field of Research	*Essential Projects* £	*Other Projects* £
Agriculture, Animal Health and Forestry	1,097,350	128,500
Colonial Products Research Council, including Colonial Micro-biological Research Institute and sugar technology research at Imperial College of Tropical Agriculture	200,000	30,000
Anti-Locust Research	88,900	–
Insecticides	529,000	130,000
Tsetse and Trypanosomiasis	211,000	293,500
Fisheries	258,470	311,625
Medical	344,850	350,000
Social Science	219,500	175,000
Economic Research	48,750	3,250
Miscellaneous	114,900	150,000
	£3,112,720	£1,571,875

or approximately £4.7 millions in all.

Thus, if all these schemes were proceeded with on the above basis, they would completely absorb the whole of the remaining available funds. But it is obvious that schemes of considerable importance which cannot now be foreseen are likely to arise in the next five years and clearly there must be some provision for these. Consequently, the £4,700,000 available must be very carefully and sparingly administered if it is going to be used to the best advantage.

17. The Secretary of State would welcome the advice of the Colonial Research Council on the best way of dealing with the situation. The following suggestions are put forward for their consideration:—

(a) The Secretary of State considers it essential that there should be a fairly substantial general reserve. It is suggested that this might be put at a minimum of £450,000.

(b) This would leave £4,250,000 available to cover all further schemes *including provision for the renewal of existing schemes*. It is suggested that this should be allocated between the various fields of research, leaving to the Committee dealing with those fields the administration and division of the sums so allocated. The suggested allocation is as follows:—

	Maximum allocation £
Agriculture, Animal Health and Forestry	1,300,000
Work sponsored by Colonial Products Research Council	200,000
Anti-Locust Research	100,000
Insecticides	550,000
Tsetse and Trypanosomiasis	425,000
Fisheries	475,000
Medical	600,000
Social Science	325,000
Economic Research	50,000
Miscellaneous (including industrial and engineering research)	225,000
	£4,250,000

In framing this suggested allocation the Colonial Office have taken into account the likelihood of the schemes listed in the annexure to this memorandum coming to fruition. The last page of the annexure indicates the kind of subjects covered under the heading "Miscellaneous".

(c) Each Committee should be informed of the allocation made for its subject and told that, so far as can be seen at present, no further funds are likely to be available between now and the 31st March, 1956. They would each be recommended to earmark a substantial percentage of their funds, which might be at least 15%, as a reserve against unforeseen contingencies. This would be, as it were, a first line of defence to provide for the unforeseen, the general reserve of £450,000 being the second line of defence. The two would provide a total reserve of over £1,100,000.

18. The Secretary of State fears that the limitation of the funds available, even though the considerable figure of £4,700,000 still remains, will inevitably limit to some extent the activities of the Council and the various specialist committees. He much regrets this. There are, however, heavy demands on the Exchequer at the present time for services of great national urgency, and he must make it quite clear that there is no chance of further monies being made available in the foreseeable future. Every endeavour will be made to obtain contributions from Colonial Governments towards the cost of new schemes, but it must be borne in mind that the large majority of the smaller territories are not in a position to assist, and that several of the larger territories have already contributed substantial sums to existing schemes and their legislatures are not favourably disposed to incurring additional liabilities.

19. The Council and the specialist Committees will, however, have the satisfaction of knowing that, largely owing to their interest and assistance, research has definitely been put on the map of the Colonial Empire. The hard spade work put in during the last five years has prepared the ground for the building up of many most important regional and other research activities, and a large number of really important projects have been initiated. We can, it is suggested, usefully make it our primary objective during the next few years to consolidate the ground gained and complete the building up of the work begun. Fortunately, in addition, it should still be possible to assist new projects of clear importance to the Colonial Empire.

Appendix to 379: Allocation of CDW funds

Summary

	£
Central Schemes, including Research	23,500,000
Allocations to Colonial territories	85,500,000
General Reserve for supplementary allocations	11,000,000
	£120,000,000

Allocations

I. *Central schemes*

	£	£
(i) Research (including Geological Survey)	10,000,000	
less amount estimated to be unspent during period 1946–56	1,500,000	8,500,000
(ii) Centrally administered schemes		
(a) Higher Education		4,500,000
(b) Training Schemes for the Colonial Service		2,500,000
(c) Geodetic and Topographical Surveys		2,000,000
(d) Aeronautical Wireless Communications		1,000,000
(e) Meteorological Services		1,000,000
(f) Other Central Schemes, such as the Central Nutrition Unit, Contributions to the Imperial Forestry Institute, Higher Training in Social Sciences, etc.		1,000,000
		£20,500,000
(iii) Margin for Supplementary Allocations to Central Schemes		3,000,000
		£23,500,000

II. *Allocations to colonial territories*

West Indies	
Barbados	800,000
British Guiana	2,500,000
British Honduras	600,000
Jamaica	6,500,000
Leeward Islands	1,200,000
Trinidad	1,200,000
Windward Islands	1,850,000
West Indies—General	850,000
	£15,500,000
South Atlantic	
Falklands	150,000
St. Helena and Ascension	200,000
	£350,000
Fiji and Western Pacific	
Fiji	1,000,000
Western Pacific	800,000
	£1,800,000

	£
Far East	
Hong Kong	1,000,000
Borneo and Sarawak	1,500,000
Malaya	5,000,000
	£7,500,000
Indian Ocean	
Ceylon	—
Mauritius	1,750,000
Seychelles	250,000
	£2,000,000
Middle East	
Aden and Protectorate	800,000
Palestine and Transjordan	1,000,000
	£1,800,000
Mediterranean	
Cyprus	1,750,000
Malta	50,000
Gibraltar	100,000
	£1,900,000
West Africa	
Gambia	1,300,000
Sierra Leone	2,600,000
Gold Coast	3,500,000
Nigeria	23,000,000
	£30,400,000
East Africa	
Somaliland	750,000
Kenya	3,500,000
Uganda	2,500,000
Tanganyika	5,250,000
Zanzibar	750,000
East Africa—General	3,500,000
	£16,250,000
Central Africa	
Nyasaland	2,000,000
Northern Rhodesia	2,500,000
Central Africa—General	1,000,000
	£5,500,000
South Africa	
High Commission Territories	2,500,000
Total	£85,500,000

CHAPTER 8

The Commonwealth

Document numbers 380–444

---

380 CAB 128/6, CM 80(46)5 9 Sept 1946

'British nationality law': Cabinet conclusions on policy arising from the Canadian Citizenship Act, 1946

[Canada, without prior Commonwealth consultation, proposed to enact a citizenship bill inconsistent with the prevailing principle of a single common code of British nationality applicable throughout the Commonwealth (except Eire since 1935), under which all member states had identical statutes on the subject. The Canadian Act proceeded on the fundamentally different principle that each of the self-governing parts of the Commonwealth (except Eire) would have its own local separate citizenship, and all persons possessing it should be recognised as British subjects throughout the Commonwealth. At a Cabinet meeting on 22 Nov 1945 it was accepted that there were advantages in the new Canadian system, but it was not something which should be adopted unilaterally but by Commonwealth agreement, and there ought to be a conference of experts to review nationality law and the Canadian proposals (CAB 128/2, CM 55(45)5). A Prime Ministers' Meeting in May 1946 sanctioned this, and a committee of officials chaired by Sir A Maxwell (Home Office) quickly reported favourably on the Canadian idea, calling for a further conference of experts from the self-governing countries (DO 35/2203). As this document shows, the Cabinet authorised this procedure in September 1946. The conference was held in London in February 1947, again chaired by Sir A Maxwell. It was attended by officials from the UK, Canada, Australia, New Zealand, South Africa, Eire, Newfoundland, Southern Rhodesia, Burma and Ceylon, with the Indian high commissioner attending as an observer. A draft scheme (legislative model), prepared by the British delegates, was used as the basis for discussion. The experts concluded it *would* be desirable to combine citizenship with nationality, the common status of British subjects throughout the Commonwealth, each country determining by legislation who were its citizens. The basic conception was that the combined total of the citizens of the various Commonwealth countries would form the general body of 'British subjects'; the citizens of Eire should not have the status of aliens (DO 35/3535, no 1, conference report, 26 Feb 1947). It was a friendly and harmonious conference, 'an excellent example of Commonwealth co-operation', and the British felt it was successful in achieving its objects, not least that of recapturing the initiative from the Canadians (DO 35/3530, minutes by Sir C Dixon and Sir E Machtig, 28 Feb 1947). The ensuing British Nationality Bill provided that all persons who were citizens of any Commonwealth country except Eire should, by virtue of their respective citizenships, be British subjects; and that citizens of Eire, though not British subjects, should in the UK and colonies be in a position equivalent to that of British subjects. Although some politicians, especially the Conservative Opposition, had misgivings about this change, the Act really did no more than recognise the *de facto* position that each separate independent Commonwealth member was an individual entity with its own national identity, but united in a common association as British subjects. The government agreed to meet the Indian objection to the term 'British subject' by providing the alternative designation 'Commonwealth citizen' (DO 35/3532, no 308). Moreover, a long-standing difference with Eire was settled in a satisfactory compromise. The government thus believed that the cause of Commonwealth unity had been substantially advanced by the new law (CAB 128/12, CM 31(48)8, 6 May 1948).]

The Cabinet considered a memorandum by the Home Secretary (C.P. (46) 331) submitting the recommendations of a Committee which they had appointed on the 1st August to report on certain questions of policy arising from the passage of the Canadian Citizenship Act, 1946.

The Committee recommended that arrangements should now be completed for the holding of a conference of experts from the United Kingdom and the Dominions to discuss the position arising from the passage of this Canadian Act, and that the instructions to the United Kingdom representatives at this conference should be based on the following principles:—

(i) that the United Kingdom should participate in the new citizenship system;
(ii) that this should be done by the creation in United Kingdom legislation of a combined citizenship of the United Kingdom and Colonies which would be the gateway through which the common status of British subject should be conferred upon the inhabitants of both the United Kingdom and the Colonies;
(iii) that India (if she remained within the Commonwealth), Burma, Newfoundland and Southern Rhodesia should be brought within the framework of the new system as countries having the right to enact their own citizenship legislation;
(iv) that India, Burma, Newfoundland and Southern Rhodesia should be invited to send representatives to the experts conference;
(v) that in the United Kingdom citizenship legislation the status of British subject should not be automatically conferred upon Eire citizens against the wishes of the Eire Government, but that in order to avoid the hardship which would otherwise result from this new situation under which Eire citizens would no longer be British subjects under United Kingdom law, the experts conference should work out detailed provisions for insertion in the new legislation on the following lines:—
(a) a saving clause to preserve the status as British subjects under United Kingdom law of Eire citizens born before the new legislation came into force;
(b) a provision to enable Eire citizens in the service of the Crown or resident in the United Kingdom or the Colonies when the new legislation came into force to acquire citizenship of the United Kingdom and Colonies without undue formality;
(c) a provision (on condition of reciprocity) which would give Eire citizens born after the new legislation came into force all the rights of British subjects while they were in the United Kingdom or the Colonies.

In discussion the following points were made:—

(a) *The Civil Lord of the Admiralty*[1] said that these proposed changes in British nationality law might affect service in the Royal Navy, as regards both the colour bar and the recruitment of Eire citizens. He suggested that arrangements should be made to keep the Service Departments informed of the progress of the discussions at the conference of experts, so that the United Kingdom Delegation might be made aware of the effect which possible changes in British nationality law might have on conditions in the Fighting Services. This was agreed to.

(b) Would it be wise formally to invite India, Burma, Newfoundland and Southern Rhodesia to send representatives to the conference of experts before it was known

[1] Mr W J Edwards.

whether the Governments of those countries would wish to participate in the conference? It would be embarrassing if formal invitations were declined.

The Home Secretary[2] said that preliminary soundings would be taken before formal invitations were issued to those Governments.

(c) *The Home Secretary* said that the experts' discussions would probably be protracted, and it was unlikely that legislation based on their findings would be ready for introduction during the course of the forthcoming Session.

The Cabinet:—

(1) Approved the recommendations made in C.P. (46) 331 as set out in (i)–(v) above.
(2) Invited the Home Secretary and the Secretary of State for Dominion Affairs to proceed with the arrangements for holding a Commonwealth conference of experts on British nationality law, and to settle the instructions to the United Kingdom representatives on the basis of the principles set out in (i)–(v) above.
(3) Agreed that the Service Departments should be associated with the United Kingdom Delegation to the conference, as suggested in paragraph (a) above.

---

[2] Mr J Chuter Ede.

381 CAB 129/13, CP(46)391 18 Oct 1946

'Eire and Northern Ireland': Cabinet memorandum by Lord Addison (DO)

I have read with very great interest the memorandum by the Lord President circulated as C.P. (46) 381. I should like to congratulate him both on the very clear and interesting account which he has given of the position and also on his handling of what cannot have been an easy interview with Mr. de Valera.[1]

I am glad to take this opportunity to express to my colleagues my views as to our policy in regard to the question of Partition. For my part I find myself entirely in agreement with the line which the Lord President took in his conversation with Mr. de Valera and would only wish to offer a few comments.

It is clear that Mr. de Valera and the present Eire Government intend to maintain on all public and other occasions their agitation in favour of ending of Partition. There are, indeed, many evidences of a plan to intensify this agitation in all possible directions and in a manner which seems calculated to excite the Catholic Nationalists in the North to outbreaks of violence. We must, therefore, be quite clear as to the line which we should take.

To my mind there are two essential considerations. First, the attitude of the majority of the inhabitants of the six counties of Northern Ireland. It is clear that they are determined to oppose any form of union with Eire. The roots of this feeling go deep. Religion, loyalty to the Crown and the British connection, and material interests are all factors which govern their attitude. They have been strengthened in their view by the events of the war and, in particular, by the Eire Government's

---

[1] Eamon de Valera, Irish taoiseach (1932–1948, 1951–1954, 1957–1959), president, 1959–1973.

attitude of neutrality. It is unthinkable that we could or should persuade or force them against their will.

But in our own interests also it seems to me that on strategic grounds we must bear in mind the lessons of the war. The retention of a base in Northern Ireland for the protection of shipping was one of the principal factors which enabled us to carry on. Without such a base the task of keeping open the shipping routes (including the transport to this country of the American forces for the invasion of Europe) would have been infinitely more difficult if not impossible. In the light of this it would be folly on our part to throw away the safeguard of our security provided by our present position in Northern Ireland unless on terms which will secure its continued availability and the availability of bases also in Eire. It must never be forgotten that, when at the time of the fall of France in 1940 Mr. de Valera was invited by us to join with us in the war on the understanding that we would do our best to bring about union with Northern Ireland, he replied that he could only contemplate a united Ireland on the basis of the whole being neutral in the war.

Whilst it is right to remind ourselves of these facts it is important that we should do all we properly can to promote friendly relations between Eire and ourselves, and I have no desire that we on this side should discourage the North and South of Ireland in any move that they may make with the object of getting together. As a long-term policy it is no doubt right and indeed inevitable that Northern Ireland and Eire should enter into some kind of closer relation. But, as the Lord President says, it is for Eire to give as well as to take, a necessity which as shown by the instance quoted above (and indeed on every occasion when we have made an "arrangement" with him) Mr. de Valera has so far shown no inclination to recognise. I am sure therefore that for the present our only safe course is to maintain silence so far as possible and not allow ourselves to be provoked into controversy. As the Lord President said to Mr. de Valera the wisest course on all sides is not to hurry this issue. Any pronouncement on our part or any suggestion that we are prepared to give the matter consideration, is, in view of the strong feelings existing on both sides, certain to lead to serious trouble. We must be careful not to find ourselves on a slippery slope.

I emphasise this in view of the activities of the "Friends of Ireland" group of Labour members in the House of Commons who, as one of the planks in their programme, are advocating that we should send a Cabinet Mission to Ireland to investigate Partition. This, I am sure, would at once plunge us into the difficulties to which I have referred above. Generally, I am sure that we ought to continue the policy which I and my predecessors at the Dominions Office have followed, and decline to be drawn on this matter of Partition.

382 FO 800/444, ff 20–23 14 May 1947

[Reconsideration of Commonwealth relationships]: minute by Mr Attlee to Mr Bevin and other ministers[1]

The progress of events in recent years in various parts of the British Commonwealth

---

[1] Mr Morrison (lord president), Sir S Cripps (Trade), Mr A V Alexander (Defence), Lord Jowitt (lord chancellor), Lord Addison (DO) and Mr Creech Jones.

and Empire appear to me to call for a review of the existing status and inter-relationship of its constituent entities. Theoretically there is a broad division between the self governing states Great Britain and the Dominions on the one side and the Colonial Empire on the other, the former group having their equality of status defined by the Statute of Westminster. This Dominion status is regarded as the final stage of evolution already reached by some and to be reached ultimately by others of the constituent parts of the Empire. In fact, however, this pattern has already been broken. Eire is in an anomalous position as an independent republic. The Dominions, notably South Africa and Canada, dislike the term "Dominion status". India, which only twenty years ago clamoured for Dominion status, now demands independence. Ceylon and Burma both ask for independence either within or without the Commonwealth. It is, I think, clear that, while there is strong evidence of the reluctance of many leaders of political opinion in the Asiatic countries to leave the Commonwealth, the phrase if not the content of "Dominion status" is not now attractive.

2. Further, Dominion status produces some curious anomalies. Thus, the Dominions, which are now fully recognised on the international stage as Sovereign States with Ambassadors in foreign capitals, are represented in Britain by High Commissioners who rank after the representatives of Liberia or Guatemala, although India is now seeking to send an Ambassador to China.

3. There is, therefore, need for reconsideration of the present position. The critical position in India, Burma and Ceylon makes this an urgent need. There is no time for a lengthy examination by constitutional lawyers. What is required is a political decision. This needs to be taken here by the Cabinet with a view to seeking the opinion of the Dominions and if possible getting a decision without the lengthy formalities of an Imperial Conference.

4. What I think is required is the finding of a formula which will enable the greatest number of independent units to adhere to the Commonwealth without excessive uniformity in their internal constitutions or in their relationship to Great Britain, the Commonwealth and one another. Some such phrase for instance as "The Associated States of the Commonwealth" might provide an umbrella under which a number of independent States might be brought together—Britain, Eire, the existing Dominions, Rhodesia, India (whether single or multiple), Burma and Ceylon. Other colonies and dependencies such as Malta and Gibraltar which for military reasons cannot have exactly the same degree of freedom as a Dominion might also be brought in.

5. I think that the problem should be considered first by a small Committee of Ministers who should be assisted by a few experts. It might be useful to bring in some of the type of R. Coupland[2] as the matter is really rather outside the range of departmental officials, though their expert advice will be required.

6. I should be glad if you would give this matter your consideration with a view to an early meeting to discuss the broad principle involved.

---

[2] Sir Reginald Coupland, Beit professor of the history of the British empire at the University of Oxford, 1920–1948.

383 FO 371/70198, nos 987, 3459, 4700, 6848 & 7550

2 Feb–24 Nov 1948

[India's future relations with the Commonwealth]: FO minutes and briefs by Mr McNeil, Mr Bevin, Sir O Sargent and G W Furlonge,[1] including comments on a paper by P J H Stent [Extracts]

Secretary of State

Here is a rather long paper from Stent. You will see that it is a proposal to make preparation for an associate Commonwealth membership for India, Pakistan, Burma, Ceylon, and eventually, no doubt, the units of the Malay Federation. Their status would be rather like the status of Eire.

This, Mr. Stent thinks, would be a ruse acceptable to many of the more responsible Asiatic leaders because it is true that one of the most difficult arguments with which they have to contend in pleading with their constituents to remain a member of the Commonwealth is that the Asiatic people cannot reconcile independence with acknowledgement of a white King as their sovereign.

For my part, I still think that there is a lively chance of retaining India and Pakistan in full membership of the Commonwealth. Mr. Stent concedes that in these circumstances his case does not arise. Nevertheless, there would be much to be said for our legal boys making a study of Mr. Stent's case so that we could be prepared for the worst contingency.

Perhaps, if you agree with me, you will so direct. Naturally the Commonwealth Relations Office should be associated with any study or enquiry.

H.McN.
2.2.48

I have no objection to study but is it not a matter for the Commonwealth & Col. Offices as well [?]

They should be asked their opinion before we proceed with the study.

Who is Stent?[2]

E.B.
[nd]

In reading the scheme as set out in paragraph 8 of Sir Noel Charles'[3] minute for diluting the Commonwealth so as to induce the three Indian Dominions to remain within it, I am reminded of the decision that H.M.G. took in 1920 to dilute the Anglo-Japanese Treaty in order to placate the U.S.A. The dilution took the form of converting the Alliance between the two countries into a Treaty between the four countries interested in the Far East. The result was deplorable. We might have restrained and guided the Japanese in the right direction if the Alliance of which they were proud had remained intact. As it was they felt alienated and humiliated and considered the four Power Treaty a sham, which indeed it was. As a result they drifted away from us and soon afterwards embarked upon a policy of adventure and

---

[1] G W Furlonge, FO foreign service officer.

[2] P J H Stent was an ex-Indian civil servant, temporarily employed by the FO, chief British delegate to the Economic Commission for Asia and the Far East.

[3] Sir N Charles, formerly high commissioner in Italy (1944–1947), working in FO, 1947–1949.

aggression which ended to our cost in the disaster of 1941. As to the four Power Treaty, it was never heard of again after it had been signed.

Although there is of course no analogy between the Anglo-Japanese Alliance and the British Commonwealth, nevertheless I cannot help feeling that if we begin to tinker with the latter in order to propitiate the Indians and Sinhalese we may be doing irreparable harm to an institution which has grown to what it is as a result of natural evolution and not of political planning.

The bonds which hold the Commonwealth together are intangible and indefinable. They have grown out of the common heritage of peoples who have had the same upbringing and traditions, the same outlook on life and the same standards of conduct and these bonds are symbolised by describing the Commonwealth as *British* and by the acceptance of the common crown. If both these features are now eliminated, as I see is proposed in the scheme in paragraph 8, what will remain? A common interest in economic affairs as represented by imperial preferences? A common foreign policy in periods of emergency? I am afraid that these common interests while sufficient to bring countries occasionally into temporary alliances with one another, are not the kind of cement which will hold the British Commonwealth together for any length of time. The fact is that the British Commonwealth has never relied on such material interests to bind it together. They are no substitutes for the bond of sentiment as typified by the Crown and the bond of tradition as typified by the word "British" and once these sentimental bonds were severed I wonder if they could ever be restored.

I cannot help feeling that there is very real danger that in our efforts to make the Commonwealth comfortable and agreeable to India and Ceylon we shall so weaken the unity of the real and original Commonwealth that it will disintegrate gradually and that we shall lose the Old Dominions without retaining the New.

These considerations do not apply to Mr. Stent's proposal which contemplates the maintenance intact of the Commonwealth based on the *British* Dominions and the association with it of certain non-British countries such as India, Pakistan and Ceylon. This association would not be based on sentiment and tradition, but on material convenience and would therefore be represented not by the common Crown or common nationality, but by treaties which would define the nature, extent and duration of the association. On such a basis the Asiatic "Dominions" might be kept within the British orbit without any weakening of the British Commonwealth as it exists today. But to go any further than this would surely be a risk which we ought not to run.

O.G.S.
2.6.48

Secretary of State
I think you should know the latest developments arising out of the last meeting of the Cabinet Committee on Commonwealth Relations (C.R.(48) 3rd meeting).

At that meeting it was decided that an approach should be made to the Prime Minister [sic] of Canada, Australia and New Zealand on the basis of C.R. 48(2), which sought to "redefine" the existing Commonwealth relationship and lay down the minimum formal ties which must be accepted by a state member of the Commonwealth.

I now learn that the Commonwealth Relations Office ran into drafting difficulties when an attempt was made to put our views to Commonwealth Governments by telegram, and that it was therefore decided by the P.M. and Mr. Noel-Baker that the question could best be handled by a less formal, oral approach. Sir N. Brook accordingly departed for the 3 capitals concerned on August 7th to discuss, without commitment by H.M.G., the problem of the future constitution of the Commonwealth on the basis suggested in C.R.(48)2. His object, as given in a warning telegram to the U.K. High Commissioners concerned, is to give Commonwealth P.M.s an opportunity "of turning these matters over in their minds" before the October meeting.

We had previously been promised an opportunity to comment on the telegram which it was assumed would be sent off as a result of the last meeting of Ministers, but owing to the change of plan we have no precise knowledge of the line Sir N. Brook is taking, nor can we get clarification from anybody now in London except Mr. Noel-Baker. In view of your great interest in the problem, it seems to me it would have been preferable if you had been informed in advance of these arrangements—I understand you do not know of them: but all we can now do is to await Sir N. Brook's report.

O.G.S.
20.8.48

This is astonishing. The PM have [sic] had me in on all the discussions & now leaves me in the dark.

E.B.
22.8.48

Brief for S of S

. . . The relative advantages and disadvantages of India being permitted to remain in the Commonwealth on the somewhat vague basis proposed are discussed below.

Advantages

(i) India is so new to independence, as Pandit Nehru at least has admitted, that she has not yet achieved a policy in world affairs nor determined her objectives. Considering the immense potential force and wealth of this sub-continent, there is clearly much to be said for retaining any ties, however tenuous, which might enable us to influence her course.

(ii) Pandit Nehru, at least, would genuinely like India to remain in the Commonwealth, as he fears that, if she severs all her connexions with it, conflicting forces within her will prove beyond his powers to control. He is doubtless not unmindful of what has occurred in Burma. He was outstanding amongst the Commonwealth Statesmen at the recent meeting of them and might well cast himself for the role of a Smuts in a new Commonwealth, based on his proposals.

Disadvantages On the other hand,

(i) Acceptance of the Nehru proposals would inevitably result in a weakening of the Commonwealth structure and the encouragement of the idea that membership of the Commonwealth involves virtually no obligations, as regards the acceptance of either minimum legal forms or a common standard of behaviour. This in turn would have the effect of encouraging the isolationist or separatist tendencies already manifest in Canada and South Africa. It might seriously affect the most vital question, hitherto always answered affirmatively (except by Eire) namely, "Shall the Commonwealth stand together in the event of war?"

(ii) Furthermore, India having secured all the advantages of membership with virtually none of the obligations (except those which it may suit her to undertake from time to time) will no doubt seek to use the Commonwealth for her own advantage whilst contributing as little as she may for the benefit of the Association as a whole. She may, for example, seek to involve the Commonwealth in her schemes in South-East Asia and the Far East, some of which may be doubtful and all of which may ultimately mean the extinction of United Kingdom influence in Asia. It is to be noted that Pandit Nehru has just stated in Paris that Colonies must be abolished.

(iii) Again, the proposals appear to be personal ideas of Pandit Nehru and would therefore depend largely for their execution on his personality; and Pandit Nehru, for all his great qualities, is hardly likely to rise above his background as Field-Marshal Smuts did above his. It is therefore surely unwise to place the future of the Commonwealth in his hands, which is what in fact acceptance of his proposals would involve.

(iv) Finally, the real tests of the Commonwealth must surely be first, whether and to what extent the members trust each other, e.g. for the purposes of supplying each other with confidential information, and, secondly, whether they are like-minded on fundamental issues. It is suggested that, in the case of India at least, these conditions do not exist; and in their absence no form of association can be devised which will be a reality.

G.W.F.
11.11.48

. . . from the Foreign Office angle, the disadvantages attaching to India's secession from the Commonwealth may be expected, on balance, to be less serious than those attaching to her retention either (a) in a relationship similar to that in which Eire stands at present or (b) as a full member of a Commonwealth of which the ties and obligations on members have been deliberately weakened so as to permit that retention. In other words (if Mr. Grey[4] will allow me to quote a remark of his which I think epitomizes the position), the policy at present envisaged appears to involve us, in the international field, in the risk of "selling our birthright for a mess of curry".

4. One other alternative to the solutions referred to above is suggested by that now apparently in process of adoption in Eire. This is that India, if she adopts a republican constitution and thereafter declines to accept the minimum obligations of Commonwealth membership, should be informed that while we can no longer regard her as an orthodox member, nor consider modifying the Commonwealth creed in her favour, we do not propose formally to excommunicate her unless and until she openly declares (as Eire has now done) that she wishes to renounce her membership; and that we should thereafter treat her as suited our interests best in such matters as the grant of privileges and the exchange of information.

5. Such a solution would, however, be unlikely to last; and the objection to it is that while it lasted we might in practice find ourselves in the position of according

---

[4] P F Grey, head of FO South-East Asia Dept.

India many of the privileges of membership of the Commonwealth while she accepted even less of the obligations than she appears to do at present.

6. In fact, as the experience of Eire has shown, the test of the Commonwealth relationship must lie, not in the formal ties which do, or do not, exist between the members, but in the existence or absence of that common-mindedness and mutual trust without which the relationship can have no real meaning.

G.W.F.
24.11.48

384 PREM 8/735, CR(0)(48)2 [9 Mar 1948]

[P J H Stent's paper, 'The British Commonwealth and Asia']: minute by Mr Attlee for Official Committee on Commonwealth Relations[1]

I have read the paper entitled the British Commonwealth and Asia with interest, but I am not clear how the proposals therein differ from an ordinary alliance by treaty. None of the advantages suggested are beyond the scope of an ordinary alliance. In fact they are already conceded in some respects to Burma and even as in the matter of admission to the Imperial Defence College to Americans.

The treatment of Indians in British Colonies and in the Dominions is one of the thorniest subjects arising from relations between different parts of the Commonwealth. The real difficulty which arose in the case of Burma and may arise in the case of India is that of theoretical republicanism. It is also latent in our relations with Eire and South Africa. I say theoretical because there is really no practical issue. Eire has travelled furthest on this road and is in practice a republic only retaining the connection with the Crown for the formal purpose of accrediting ambassadors to Foreign Powers. But in actual fact all the Dominions are as free from control by Great Britain as a republic entirely separate would be. The difficulty arises over theoretical republicanism as preached by Dutch in South Africa, Irish in Eire and Congress in India. This was too, I think, the only reason which caused the Burmese to leave the Commonwealth.

Actually common allegiance to the Crown is, as Laski[2] points out, the only real link connecting the parts of the Commonwealth. It is a very strong link in the cases of Canada, Australia and New Zealand. In these countries there would be strong resentment at any attempt to remove it. It is strong also in the Colonies. I think that the section in South Africa that approves of it has been much strengthened by the recent Royal visit. There is probably a great deal of latent loyalty to the Crown in India, especially among the less vocal classes, for republicanism is not indigenous in India but is an exotic cultivated only by the intelligentzia. There is no doubt that Mountbatten's connection with the Royal House helped him very much in India.

I am inclined to think that in India and Burma if some face saving device could be adopted there would be not only willingness, but eagerness to remain within the Commonwealth.

For instance, if the President of Burma were also to be the King's representative,

---

[1] Stent's paper was considered by the Committee at their meeting on 9 Mar 1948.

[2] Prof H J Laski, professor of political science, University of London.

he could be the nominee of the Prime Minister of Burma just as McKell[3] is the nominee of Curtin.[4] He might even be elected by the popular vote and yet be formally appointed by the King. His powers in respect to the affairs of Burma being those laid down in the constitution, the King would have no more control over him than he has over Mr. Jinnah. To try to substitute some other link would, I think, be apt to raise all kinds of difficulties. It would involve definition and some form of written constitution whereas the relationship today is operated successfully by convention.

The Dutch are today working out a relationship between the Kingdom of Holland and the republics in Indonesia. In the first German Reich the republics of Hamburg, Lubeck and Bremen were parts of the German Empire. There is, therefore, nothing inherently impossible in a republic forming part of a monarchy.

There should be no serious difficulty in altering the title of the British Commonwealth. I suggest the Commonwealth of British and Associated Peoples.

---

[3] J W McKell, premier and treasurer, New South Wales, 1941–1947.

[4] J Curtin, prime minister of Australia, 1941–1945.

385 PREM 8/820, pp 29–37 11 Mar 1948

[Relationship between India and the British Commonwealth]: personal letter from Mr Attlee to Pandit Nehru

My dear Nehru,

I have observed that the Indian Constituent Assembly has made great progress in formulating a constitution for India. The question will naturally arise as to the relationship between India and the British Commonwealth. I believe that the association of a number of Nations in the Commonwealth is not only a great advantage to every one of the constituent States, but is an important factor in building up a peaceful world. It conflicts in no way with the principle of world co-operation for peace and prosperity which is expressed in the United Nations.

The British Commonwealth as we know it today has evolved not by design or by the application of theories of the interrelation of States, but from the application of democratic principles of self-government and from the practical needs of the age.

The four Dominions have their own historic evolutions, no one of them exactly the same. Their status within the Commonwealth developed by practice rather than theory and the Statute of Westminster, which established the complete equality of the Dominions and Great Britain, was really a formal recognition of an existing position rather than the enactment of something new.

The course of Irish history resulted in the establishment within the Commonwealth of a republic which is, however, linked to the other States by the Crown. It is, as so many things British are, illogical, but it works. Even during the world war the ambassadors of Eire to countries with which we were at war received their authority from the Crown.

We have now reached another stage in the development of the Commonwealth. Hitherto the Dominions, although in South Africa the majority of the population are Dutch and in Canada a large percentage French, have been countries whose population has had a large element of United Kingdom stock. The attainment of full stature by countries such as India and Ceylon opens a new era. I have myself always regarded the Commonwealth and Empire as a collection of nations all moving to a common goal of self-government and equal status, though necessarily at a different rate in accordance with their individual histories and internal conditions. It has been a matter of pride to me that during my Premiership in Great Britain the family circle should have been enlarged by the coming of age, so to speak, of the nations in Asia. The British Commonwealth of Nations is now in effect the Commonwealth of British and Asiatic nations. It may well be that the title should be changed, but it is my hope that the reality may remain.

I am, however, far from under-rating the importance of names. For instance the term Dominion status has offended some people because Dominion was held to imply domination. In fact I believe that it was adopted because Canada called itself a Dominion having taken the term from some phrase in the Bible. The change of title from Secretary of State for the Dominions to Secretary of State for Commonwealth Relations was a recognition of this objection and an attempt to express more clearly what was the true function of the Minister. We are in this country rather insensitive to the content of names and cheerfully keep on titles that have come down to us from the past, although the functions exercised by the holder are now quite different from those exercised by earlier holders. This applies among other things to the title of King. The functions of our King are very different from those of King Ibn Saud,[1] but their titles are the same. The same incidentally applies to the term republic. The actual position in Australia and New Zealand gives far more real freedom and democracy than the position in some of the South American republics.

But still one has to reckon with the power of words. I think that many, probably a majority, of the Burmese would have liked to have remained in the Commonwealth, but they had tied themselves to the word republic. There was, I think, also a certain feeling that they were being kept under foreign domination owing to the King being of a different race. Here again we in England, who have had Scotch, Dutch and German Kings, are apt to underestimate this feeling. I have examined the question of what are the links which bind together the various peoples of the Commonwealth. They are mostly intangible. In some instances a common racial background, in others historical association, in others common economic interests, but more generally they are, I think, rather moral than economic. Adherence to certain absolute values, faith in democratic institutions, belief in the rule of law and acceptance of the need for toleration. All these things make up together a 'way of life' which with many local differences yet give a general sense of community.

But apart from these intangibles there is only one link, the Crown. The common allegiance to the Crown is the link within which all kinds of association for mutual advantage are possible; without it they are more difficult to establish. If one seeks to go beyond this and to draft any form of constitutional relationship one finds oneself in very great difficulties.

The point, therefore, which I would like you to consider is whether there is any real objection to the continuance of India in the British Commonwealth owing to the common allegiance to the Crown.

You are, of course, aware that in practice now the King's representative, the Governor General, is appointed on the recommendation of the Prime Minister of the

---

[1] Of Saudi Arabia.

Dominion concerned and that the whole matter is right outside the sphere of the Prime Minister and the Government of the United Kingdom. If, for instance, it were desired that the Governor General should be appointed by the King on the recommendation of the Prime Minister after a vote in the Parliament or even after a vote by the electorate of a Dominion, I do not see that there need be any difficulty. As far as the content of a republic constitution is concerned there is no real change in the position unless it is desired to give the President more extensive powers than those possessed by a Governor General. In my own view it is better to have the King or the Governor General as someone above the political battle rather than a protagonist. There is also much to be said for having a personage who is a symbol of the State more readily understood by all sorts and conditions of men than an abstraction. For instance, in the British Commonwealth and Empire are many simple people who can understand a king better than they can apprehend a formula.

In India, I think, there is no native tradition of republicanism. It is really an importation from the West. There is a good deal to be said for having as the ultimate head of the State someone who does not belong to any section of the community and therefore has no special affinity to any one of them. This has shown itself in practice. When for instance the King and Queen visited Canada they got an equally cordial reception from French and English speaking Canadians and in South Africa it was the same in regard to British and Dutch, Europeans, Indians and Africans.[2]

I know how much you have at heart the unity of India. It will, I think, be of very material assistance in promoting this unity if India and Pakistan are both within the Commonwealth, and it will also help relations with Ceylon and Malaya, for in my view it is right and natural that India should increasingly take a leading part among the nations of Asia.

I should very much like to have your views on these high matters, for I know that you have in mind not only the affairs of India but also of the world. I think you would agree that what we need today is more unity in the world and that unnecessary fragmentation is to be deprecated. In my view the British Commonwealth is a unique experiment, in that we have there close association with complete freedom on the part of its constituent parts and a remarkable degree of flexibility owing to the absence of any constitution. The exact relationship of any component part to the whole or to other parts can vary not only from that of others, but also from time to time. This is shown in the case of the Dominions and more recently in the case of Ceylon. This flexibility gives an advantage not only over the provisions of a written constitution but also over the provisions of a treaty.

If it were possible I should welcome a visit from you which would give opportunity for a talk on these matters.

Yours sincerely
C.R.A.

---

[2] King George VI visited Canada, May–June 1939, and South Africa, Feb–Apr 1947.

386 PREM 8/820, pp 13–15 18 Apr 1948

[India's association with the Commonwealth]: personal letter (reply) from Mr Nehru to Mr Attlee

My dear Attlee,

I must apologise to you for the delay in acknowledging your personal letter of the 11th March which was sent on to me by the office of the High Commissioner for the United Kingdom in New Delhi. Before answering it I wanted to give it full consideration. As a matter of fact it is not easy for me to answer adequately at this stage. The question you have raised is important and vital for the future of India and will have to be decided ultimately by the Constituent Assembly.

2. I am, therefore, not attempting an answer at this stage. You will appreciate that strong views are held by various groups and individuals on this subject. For my part I have deliberately tried to delay any decision so that we might be able to consider the question as dispassionately as possible and without the heavy legacy of the past.

3. I agree with you in much that you say and I can assure you that it is my desire and the desire of many of my colleagues that the association of India with the United Kingdom and the British Commonwealth of Nations be close and intimate. I am more interested in real friendship and cooperation between these countries than merely in a formal link which does not carry with it that friendly cooperation. The problem before us, therefore, is this close psychological as well as other relationships. I am myself not clear in my own mind what the best way would be to ensure this. I have been hoping that the course of events would help in clearing the atmosphere to enable us to decide the question dispassionately and objectively.

4. If anyone had asked this question of us about a year ago, I have little doubt what the answer would have been, and this answer would have been almost unanimous. The mere fact that another opinion is held now by many persons indicates the change that has come over the situation. This change has undoubtedly been due to the change in British policy in regard to India and more particularly to the presence and activities of our present Governor-General. Indeed it is remarkable what Lord Mountbatten, and may I add Lady Mountbatten also, have done to remove many of the old causes of distrust and bitterness between India and England. I have often wondered what the history of India would have been if they had come a year earlier. I imagine it would have been very different and that we might well have avoided many of the perils and disasters that we have had to face. It is with exceeding regret that we shall part with Lord and Lady Mountbatten when they go away in June next.

5. You are aware that the Constituent Assembly of India has been drafting a constitution and has now reached a stage when the final draft will be considered. Right at the beginning of its existence the Constituent Assembly laid down certain objectives. It stated that the constitution was going to be for an Independent Sovereign Republic. Whether we use those exact words or not will be decided later; but in any event the constitution as drafted had to follow this direction. Even then, however, we made it clear that the question of India's relation with the United Kingdom and the British Commonwealth will be considered separately. We were anxious not to come to any hurried decision and we hoped that the lapse of time

would make it easier to decide. That decision was bound to be influenced by the events which preceded it.

6. You refer to the power of words, and I entirely agree with you that words have an inherent force and power of their own. Behind the words, of course, lies a complex of thoughts and memories, both conscious and sub-conscious, which exert a powerful influence on the minds of a people.

7. I might mention that our formal constitution will probably be finally drafted in the Hindi language, though of course there will be an official English translation of it. The words used in Hindi will not have the same historical background and associations which English words might have, although outwardly they may mean much the same.

8. I shall not say much more at this stage except to repeat the hope that India and England will be closely associated to their mutual advantage. In a world full of conflict and difficulty this is even more necessary than it might have been at any other time.

9. I am very grateful to you for your invitation to me to visit England. Even without that invitation I have wanted to come to England, and your invitation has strengthened that wish. But the Fates have been hard on us and it has been very difficult for me even to leave Delhi for any length of time. The recent illness of my colleague, Sardar Vallabhbhai Patel, the Deputy Prime Minister, has added to the difficulty of my leaving India. But I still hope to visit England perhaps some time in the late summer or early autumn.

Yours sincerely
Jawaharlal Nehru

387 CAB 129/30, CP(48)244 26 Oct 1948

'The Commonwealth relationship': Cabinet memorandum by Mr Attlee. *Appendix*: draft statement of general principles for discussion

For some time past we have been aware that the new Indian Constitution might emerge from the Constituent Assembly in a form not fully consonant with the preamble to the Statute of Westminster, which describes the members of the Commonwealth as "united by a common allegiance to the Crown." I therefore thought it advisable to set up, in the summer of last year, a small informal Committee of Ministers to re-examine the nature of the Commonwealth relationship and to consider on what constitutional basis India might remain within the Commonwealth if in the event she were unable to accept the Crown as "the symbol of free association" in the Commonwealth. I apprehended that, if this situation arose, we might have to reach a quick decision; and I was anxious that, so far as possible, these difficult issues should have been fully examined and sifted in advance.

This Ministerial Committee was assisted by a small group of officials. Two of the reports prepared by this group are attached to this memorandum (Annexes I and II).[1] The broad conclusions reached in these reports were endorsed in the summer of this year by the Ministerial Committee, who invited me to communicate their provisional

---

[1] Annexes I–III not printed.

views to the Prime Ministers of Canada, Australia and New Zealand as a basis for the informal discussions which I hoped to have with them at the time of the meeting of Commonwealth Prime Ministers. I therefore asked the Secretary of the Cabinet to visit those countries on my behalf in August and explain the position to Mr. Mackenzie King, Mr. Chifley and Mr. Fraser. His report of these conversations is also attached (Annex III).

The Ministerial Committee approved the draft statement of general principles set out in the Appendix to that report as a basis for the informal conversations which I proposed to hold with other Prime Ministers during the course of that meeting; and there then seemed to be at least a reasonable chance that these principles would be endorsed by the representatives of Canada, Australia and New Zealand. As will be seen, the basic assumption was that, for continuing membership of the Commonwealth, the minimum constitutional link should be some recognition of the Crown; but that, if some Commonwealth countries were unable to accept the jurisdiction of the Crown for internal purposes, it would suffice that they should accept the King's jurisdiction in their external relations.

2. In the informal conversations held since the opening of the Conference of Commonwealth Prime Ministers, two major developments have taken place. First, it has been made clear that the present Government of Eire are determined to repeal their External Relations Act and unwilling to put in its place any other constitutional link involving any recognition of the Crown. Secondly, it is now known that the new Indian Constitution will provide for the establishment of India as a "sovereign independent republic" and it seems likely that India will not be willing to accept the King's jurisdiction even for the purpose of her external relations.

3. The Eire Executive Authority (External Relations) Act, 1936, is the last constitutional link binding Eire to the Commonwealth. Within the last few months Eire Ministers have publicly stated that Eire has ceased to be a member of the Commonwealth; and, when they have carried out their declared intention of repealing their External Relations Act, it will no longer be practicable for other Commonwealth countries to continue to maintain that she is a member of the Commonwealth. It is conceivable that, once she had repealed the External Relations Act and severed the last link with the Crown, Eire might, after an interval, be willing to re-enter the Commonwealth on some new basis not involving any relation to the Crown.

4. Indian Ministers, on the other hand, are anxious that India should remain within the Commonwealth, if they can find a constitutional basis which will be acceptable to their Constituent Assembly. During the past two weeks I and some of my colleagues have been discussing with Pandit Nehru the possibility of devising some satisfactory constitutional link, preferably through the Crown, which would be acceptable to public opinion in India.

5. I will explain orally to the Cabinet, when this issue comes before them on 28th October, the latest developments in these conversations, both with Eire Ministers and with the Prime Minister of India. But I thought it would be useful to those Ministers who have not taken part in our preliminary discussion of these constitutional issues over the past twelve months if I circulated in advance some of the documents on which our earlier consideration of these issues was based, and also this brief indication of the developments which have taken place in the last few weeks.

Appendix to 387: Commonwealth relations: draft statement of general principles for discussion at October meeting of Commonwealth prime ministers

1. Commonwealth policy should be directed towards maintaining the existing membership of the Commonwealth, even though some Commonwealth countries (i.e., Eire, India, Pakistan and possibly South Africa) may be unable to accept the precise form of constitutional relationship which is preferred by the other members.

2. Asiatic and African peoples, in particular, on attaining their independence may find difficulty in accepting the full implications of the common allegiance to the Crown. But the policy of educating dependent peoples to the point of attaining "independence *within the Commonwealth*" will be frustrated unless the way is smoothed for these peoples to remain within the Commonwealth when they have become fit for independence.

3. There should therefore be room within the Commonwealth for some independent peoples who cannot formally accept the full constitutional ties implied by the preamble to the Statute of Westminster.

4. At the same time it is important that nothing should be done to impair or disturb the constitutional relations of those Commonwealth countries which accept and value the existing relationship which is symbolised and expressed by the common allegiance to the Crown. There can, therefore, be no question of diluting the nature and quality of the Commonwealth relationship to a point at which it could be accepted by all.

Nor is it desirable that the independent peoples of the Commonwealth should be formally divided into two classes, according to the extent to which they accept the full constitutional implications of the preamble to the Statute of Westminster. The conception of a "Commonwealth of British and Associated Nations" must be rejected.

5. The objective of Commonwealth policy must therefore be to retain the independent members within a single group even though their constitutional relations *inter se* may not all follow precisely the same pattern. It is not necessary to change the constitutional relations of all the independent members of the Commonwealth merely because one or two of them insist upon a form of relationship which is rather less close than that preferred by the majority. There can be scope for some variety in the relations between the different parts of the Commonwealth.

6. On this basis the practical question will be—how far can a Commonwealth country deviate from the "normal" form of constitutional relationship and still be regarded as a member of the Commonwealth? There must be evidence of a continuing desire to share in the practical aspects of Commonwealth collaboration; and also an acceptance of the link of common citizenship within the scheme of the British Nationality Act recently passed by the Parliament at Westminster. But, if those conditions are satisfied, what is to be the minimum constitutional link? Since the Crown is the symbol of the Commonwealth association, there must be some recognition of the Crown. If, however, some Commonwealth countries are unable to accept the jurisdiction of the Crown for internal purposes, it would suffice that they should accept the King's jurisdiction in their external relations.

7. This recognition of the Crown for external purposes only must be regarded as the minimum constitutional link; and it must be accepted that a country which cannot profess even this limited allegiance to the Crown cannot be treated as a member of the Commonwealth.

Thus, if the Government of Eire fulfil their declared intention to repeal the Eire Executive Authority (External Relations) Act, 1936, they must be regarded as having severed the last constitutional link connecting Eire with the Commonwealth, and Eire must be treated as having ceased to be a member of the Commonwealth.

8. It is not essential that the King's representative should in every Commonwealth country bear the title 'Governor-General." Each of the independent Governments of the Commonwealth should be free to confer on the King's representative whatever title they prefer.

9. If a Commonwealth country should adopt a "republican" form of constitution, providing for a President as the Head of the State, this need not be regarded as inconsistent with continuing membership of the Commonwealth so long as it is accepted that the President will act as the King's representative, at least for purposes of external relations. In such an event, it would be preferable that the President should be nominated by the local Government for appointment by the King. But even if the constitution provided for the election of a President, this system could be accepted if it involved no serious departure from the normal status of the King's representative.

10. If India or Pakistan or any other Commonwealth country should elect to remain within the Commonwealth on the limited basis of "external relationship," the United Kingdom Government would publicly declare that this development involved no change in the constitutional relations between the other members of the Commonwealth. Similar assurances might be given at the same time by other Commonwealth Governments.

11. A country which is unwilling to accept the jurisdiction of the Crown even in respect of her external affairs cannot be regarded as a member of the Commonwealth. If Eire repeals her External Relations Act, or if India is unwilling to recognise the King's jurisdiction for any purposes, they will cease to be members of the Commonwealth and for all constitutional purposes will become foreign States. If in that event either of these countries wishes to state that she continues to be "associated" with the nations of the British Commonwealth, there is no reason why this special association should not be acknowledged. This need not, however, imply any new kind of formal union of "British and Associated Nations." Countries which cannot accept any form of constitutional link must be regarded as foreign States; and it would be inexpedient to attempt to define what is meant by their "association" with the British Commonwealth. Some definable aspects of that new "association" may emerge as time goes on; but it will be preferable to wait and recognise subsequently links which have developed in practice rather than seek to devise in advance a formula of "association" with which such States would be required to comply.

12. The existing relationship between Commonwealth countries would be more accurately reflected if certain terms and phrases which are now out of date were allowed to pass out of official use. Thus:—

(a) The terms "Dominion" and "Dominion Government" should be avoided; such expressions as "Commonwealth country" or "member of the Commonwealth" should be used instead in all official publications and correspondence. This would carry to its logical conclusion the change which was made when a "Commonwealth Relations Office" took the place of the "Dominions Office."

(b) The use of the term "Dominion status" should similarly be abandoned, in favour of such expressions as "become a fully independent member of the Commonwealth" or "attain independence within the Commonwealth."

(c) No opportunity should be lost of using language which stresses the fact that all the fully self-governing countries of the Commonwealth are of equal status. Thus, the term "Commonwealth Prime Ministers" should in future be used to describe the Prime Ministers of all Commonwealth countries, including the United Kingdom.

(d) Though no formal change is recommended, it may be useful to establish a practice by which the Commonwealth would commonly be described as "the Commonwealth of Nations," instead of "the British Commonwealth of Nations."

388 CAB 128/13, CM 67(48)3 & 4 28 Oct 1948

'Commonwealth relations: constitutional developments in India and Eire; title of the Commonwealth': Cabinet conclusions

[As a result of the passing by the Irish government of a somewhat ambiguous External Relations Act in 1936, and the enactment of the Irish Constitution of 1937, the association of Eire (as the Irish Free State was now commonly known) to the Commonwealth was decidedly ambivalent. Was she or was she not a 'member state' or only 'externally associated'? The British and Commonwealth governments chose to regard the changes as less than a fundamental alteration of the relationship, but this implied a continuing degree of Irish allegiance to the Crown. Irish dissatisfaction over this came to a head with the formation of Mr J A Costello's[1] government in 1948, since he had from the first been a critic of the External Relations Act, and now only held office with Labour and republican support. The new government thus decided in the summer of 1948 in principle to repeal the Act and to designate the state formally as a republic. The Republic of Ireland Bill was introduced in the Dáil on 24 Nov 1948. The Republic was proclaimed on Easter Day 1949, and Ireland seceded from the Commonwealth. These measures were not designed or conceived in hostility to the British people or the Crown; recognising this, the British government tried to deal amicably with the various practical questions necessarily arising (see 397 below).]

3. The Cabinet considered a memorandum by the Prime Minister (C.P. (48) 244)[2] on the nature of the constitutional relation between the various countries of the Commonwealth and the probable course of future constitutional changes in India and Eire.

The Cabinet's discussion regarding India, and the conclusions reached, are recorded in the Secretary's Standard File of Cabinet Conclusions.[3]

Regarding Eire, it was pointed out that the Eire Government had publicly stated that their country had already ceased to be a member of the Commonwealth and the object of their proposal to repeal the External Relations Act was largely to put this issue beyond dispute. During the recent discussions the representatives of Canada, Australia and New Zealand had, however, impressed on United Kingdom Ministers the need for handling the negotiations with the Eire Government in a spirit which would not create such bitterness between the two countries as might diminish the chances of Eire's ultimate return to the Commonwealth. During the discussions which had taken place at Chequers on 17th October, the practical consequences of the repeal of the External Relations Act had been frankly explained to Eire Ministers;

[1] Taoiseach, 1948–1951. [2] See 387. [3] See 389.

but it was clear that they were now too far committed to be able to abandon their declared intention to repeal the Act. It must, therefore, be expected that legislation for its repeal would be introduced in the Dail at an early date. Once the Act had been repealed, it would no longer be practicable for other Commonwealth countries to continue to maintan [sic] that Eire was a member of the Commonwealth.

The suggestion was made that, in view of the serious and far-reaching consequences of Eire's secession from the Commonwealth, a further effort ought to be made to persuade the Eire Government at least to postpone the introduction of legislation to repeal the External Relations Act. In the discussions with the Eire Ministers emphasis had been laid on the practical consequences of repeal in the field of personal status and trade preferences. Every effort would no doubt be made to mitigate these consequences to the maximum extent compatible with the United Kingdom's international obligations. But behind the immediate issue lay the Eire Government's determination to end partition, and there was little doubt that they recognised that they would be in a better position to put pressure on the United Kingdom Government once Eire had become a foreign country. For it could be assumed that no further obstacles would be placed in the way of Eire's admission to the United Nations; and it would then be open to her to raise the question of partition in the General Assembly with the assurance of substantial support. The United Kingdom Government had hitherto maintained the attitude that partition was an issue for settlement by the Irish themselves. But Eire's secession from the Commonwealth would raise acutely the issue whether, for defence reasons, it was possible any longer to maintain that attitude; and it would certainly be embarrassing for the United Kingdom Government to be put in the position of having to support the continuance of partition. The Government and people of Northern Ireland would undoubtedly regard Eire's secession from the Commonwealth as a serious threat to them; and, whatever mitigation of the practical consequences of secession might be acceptable to the United Kingdom Government, it was likely that the Government of Northern Ireland would feel bound to adopt rigorous measures in protection of their interests. This was a further reason for pressing the Eire Government to postpone action for a few months. By then it might have been possible to devise a constitutional status for India which might be also acceptable to Eire as the basis for her continued membership of the Commonwealth.

The general view of Ministers was, however, that further efforts to persuade the Eire Government to postpone the introduction of legislation to repeal the External Relations Act were likely to be ineffective. The arguments for delay had been put before their representatives in the conversations at Chequers, but they clearly felt themselves committed to immediate action. Moreover, it was not clear that delay would produce the advantages desired. The Eire Government were determined that Eire should cease to be a member of the Commonwealth, and no constitutional status which involved continued membership of the Commonwealth would be acceptable to them. It was, however, agreed that the practical consequences of the repeal of the External Relations Act might be brought more formally to the notice of the Eire Government. No written communication on this point had yet been sent to them, and they were still inclined to think that the practical difficulties were all susceptible of easy solution if there was goodwill on both sides. While it was important to avoid the impression of attempting to coerce them, would it not be fairer to ensure that they were fully aware of the practical consequences of their policy? It had been agreed, at the end of the discussion at Chequers, that both sides should explore possible solutions of these difficulties, and an aide-mémoire had subsequently been received from the Eire Government. It would, therefore, be quite appropriate to send a formal statement of the position in reply to that communication. But, before any such statement was sent, Ministers should themselves be clear how far they were prepared to go towards mitigating the practical consequences of Eire's secession from the Commonwealth. It would be most inadvisable to give the Eire Government the impression that they were being threatened with measures which the United Kingdom Government were not in fact intending to enforce. And the Government would no doubt be pressed in Parliament to make their attitude clear once the External Relations Act had been repealed.

The Cabinet:—

(1) Invited the Secretary of State for Commonwealth Relations to submit a memorandum setting out—

(i) the terms of a written communication which might be sent to the Eire Government on the practical consequences of the repeal of the Eire Executive Authority (External Relations), Act, 1936; and

(ii) the measures which might be taken to mitigate the consequences of such repeal so far as concerned the United Kingdom and other Commonwealth countries.

(2) Invited the Lord Chancellor, in consultation with the Attorney-General and the Solicitor-General, to consider and report whether, after the repeal of the Eire Executive Authority (External Relations) Act, special privileges accorded to Eire and her citizens in such matters as trade preferences and freedom from aliens' restrictions could be defended against challenge by foreign Governments based on "most-favoured-nation" clauses in Commercial Treaties; and, in particular, whether the grant of trade preferences to Eire would be safeguarded by the Geneva General Agreement on Trade and Tariffs [sic].

4. *The Secretary of State for Commonwealth Relations* said that in several Commonwealth countries there had been public comment on the fact that, in the final communiqué issued to the Press at the conclusion of the recent meeting of Commonwealth Prime Ministers, the word "British" had not been used in the various references to Commonwealth countries, Commonwealth Governments and members of the Commonwealth. Although this had not in fact been a deliberate omission, it was true that, in informal conversations with several Commonwealth Prime Ministers, the suggestion had been put forward that it might be useful to establish, without any formal change, the convention of describing the Commonwealth as "the Commonwealth of Nations" instead of "the British Commonwealth of Nations." The object of this informal change would be to foster the impression that the Commonwealth was wide enough to include nations which, by reason of their race and history, could not feel that they were "British" nations. The Prime Minister of New Zealand, who had been asked to reply publicly to comment in the New Zealand Press, had proposed to indicate that this was the purpose of the change; and, after consulting the Prime Minister, the Secretary of State had told him that we should have no objection to his giving this explanation. There were some grounds for believing that in the Parliament at Westminster the official Opposition would not raise objection to the informal adoption of this convention.

The Cabinet:—

Agreed that it would be useful to establish, without any formal change, a convention of describing the Commonwealth as "the Commonwealth of Nations" instead of "the British Commonwealth of Nations"; and took note that this informal change should be defended on the basis that it was an object of policy to make it possible for nations to remain within the Commonwealth after they had attained their independence, even though they felt that, by reason of their race and history, they could not properly be described as "British" nations.

389 CAB 128/14, CM 67(48)3, annex 28 Oct 1948

'Commonwealth relations; constitutional developments in India and Eire': Cabinet conclusions (confidential annex on India)

The Cabinet had before them a memorandum by the Prime Minister (C.P. (48) 244)[1] on the nature of the constitutional relation between the various countries of the Commonwealth and the probable course of future constitutional changes in India and Eire.

The Prime Minister said that it had been clear for some time that the new Indian constitution might emerge from the Constituent Assembly in a form not fully consonant with the preamble to the Statute of Westminster, which described the members of the Commonwealth as "united by a common allegiance to the Crown". He had therefore set up a small Committee of Ministers to re-examine the nature of the Commonwealth relationship and to consider on what constitutional basis India might remain within the Commonwealth, if in the event she were unable to accept the Crown as "a symbol of free association" in the Commonwealth. Certain papers which had been considered by this Committee were annexed to C.P.(48)244. The Ministerial Committee had approved the draft statement of general principles set out in the Appendix to Annex III, as a basis for the informal conversation which he had proposed to hold with other Commonwealth Prime Ministers while they were in London for the recent conference. In the meantime, two major developments had taken place: first, the Eire Government had announced their intention to repeal the Eire Executive Authority (External Relations) Act, 1936, and discussions had shown that they were unwilling to put in its place any other constitutional link involving any recognition of the Crown. Secondly, it had become clear that the new Indian Constitution would provide for the establishment of India as a "sovereign independent republic", and that India would not be willing to accept The King's jurisdiction, even for the purpose of her external relations. In his discussions he had been much assisted by the helpful attitude adopted by the representatives of Canada, Australia and New Zealand, who had shown themselves greatly concerned to secure that India should remain within the Commonwealth. Any proposals for a new form of constitutional link must be considered in relation, not only to its acceptability to the country concerned, but also to its effect on other members of the Commonwealth; and, in any further discussions, it would be essential to maintain the closest touch with the Governments of Canada, Australia and New Zealand.

---

[1] See 387.

The Cabinet were informed that the Prime Minister of India had made it clear, during recent discussions in London, that he was anxious to keep India within the Commonwealth, if a constitutional basis could be found which would be acceptable to the Constituent Assembly; and, as was shown by a report from India published in the "Times" that morning, public opinion in India on this issue had radically changed in recent months. During discussions which Ministers had had with Pandit Nehru, various suggestions had been made which, taken together, might constitute an adequate basis for India's continued membership of the Commonwealth in a form acceptable to Indian opinion generally. The precise form of these suggestions was now being further studied by Pandit Nehru, but their general effect was as follows. The King's sovereignty in India should be regarded as dormant, but not extinguished; no United Kingdom legislation should be enacted to terminate The King's sovereignty over India, and this could therefore be revived by a unilateral act on the part of India at any time. In statements to the Parliaments of the United Kingdom and India, an identical formula would be used to the effect that, under the new Indian constitution, His Majesty would not exercise any of the functions of sovereignty. An historical link with the Crown would be preserved by the enactment, as Indian law, of Sections 1, 2 and 7 of the United Kingdom Indian Independence Act, 1947. India would adopt the provisions of the British Nationality Act, 1948, in so far as they related to India. The King would conclude with the new President of India an agreement by which he would act as the President's representative for the protection of Indian citizens in the United Kingdom, and the President would act as The King's representative for the protection in India of Commonwealth citizens other than citizens of India. In countries where India maintained no separate diplomatic representation, the diplomatic protection of Indian citizens would be undertaken by the diplomatic representatives of other Commonwealth countries. The King would be regarded as the fountain of Honour for the Commonwealth, and a new Commonwealth Order might be instituted, for which citizens of all Commonwealth countries, including India, would be equally eligible. In all future legislation in India, care would be taken to treat Commonwealth countries as a class apart from all foreign countries.

After further consideration, Pandit Nehru would inform the Prime Minister of the exact proposals on these lines which he was prepared to put to his Government. Although there would be no desire to approach this question in a purely legalistic spirit, it was clearly desirable that, as a first step, Ministers should be advised whether these proposals would together constitute an adequate legal basis for India's continued membership of the Commonwealth and, in particular, whether they would afford a basis which would enable foreign Governments to claim most-favoured-nation treatment in respect of any privileges granted to Indian citizens in other parts of the Commonwealth.

The Cabinet:—

Invited the Lord Chancellor, in consultation with the Attorney-General and the Solicitor-General, to consider whether the constitutional proposals discussed with the Prime Minister of India would—

(i) constitute an adequate legal basis for India's continued membership of the Commonwealth;

(ii) provide an adequate basis for resisting claims by foreign countries under the most-favoured-nation provisions of existing treaties.

390 CAB 128/13, CM 71(48)2 12 Nov 1948

'Commonwealth relations: Constitutional developments in India and Eire': Cabinet conclusions on Eire[1]

The Cabinet had before them the following memoranda:—

C.P. (48) 258: by the Prime Minister, covering an account of the meeting held with Eire Ministers at Chequers on 17th October;

C.P. (48) 253: by the Secretary of State for Commonwealth Relations, covering a note by the United Kingdom representative in Dublin on the repeal of the Eire Executive Authority (External Relations) Act, 1936;

C.P. (48) 262: by the Secretary of State for Commonwealth Relations, covering the draft of a reply to the aide-mémoire of 20th October from the Eire Government;

C.P. (48) 263: by the Secretary of State for Commonwealth Relations, covering a memorandum on the measures which might be taken to mitigate the practical effects on the United Kingdom of Eire's repeal of the External Relations Act;

C.P. (48) 264: by the Lord Chancellor, covering a Legal Opinion discussing the effect of that repeal on the special privileges granted to Eire and her citizens in such matters as trade preferences and freedom from aliens restrictions;

C.P. (48) 254: by the Prime Minister, covering (i) a note of the constitutional proposals discussed with the Prime Minister of India during his recent visit to London, and (ii) an Opinion prepared by the Lord Chancellor and the Law Officers on the question whether those proposals would constitute an adequate basis for enabling India to remain within the Commonwealth and for resisting claims by foreign countries under "most-favoured-nation" provisions in existing treaties.

The Cabinet first discussed the effect of the proposed repeal of the Eire Executive Authority (External Relations) Act. It was clear that the Eire Government were determined to carry through their declared intention of repealing that Act; and, further, that they were resolved that Eire should cease to be a member of the Commonwealth. What they desired was that Eire, while ceasing to be a member of the Commonwealth, should continue to enjoy many of the advantages of membership through a factual association based, not only on her historical relations with Commonwealth countries, but on a reciprocal exchange of trade preferences and citizenship rights. They evidently envisaged an intermediate position in which Eire would be neither a British nation nor a foreign State. Was it conceivable that such an intermediate position would be recognised in international law?

The Lord Chancellor[2] and *the Attorney-General*[3] said that they had considered this question with great care, but had reached the conclusion that there was no device by which they could hope to satisfy an international court that a country which was not a member of the Commonwealth was not a foreign State. If Eire repealed the External Relations Act she would, in the contemplation of international law, become a foreign State in relation to the United Kingdom and other Commonwealth countries. Some of the practical consequences might be mitigated

---

[1] Previous reference: see 388.

[2] Lord Jowitt.

[3] Sir Hartley Shawcross.

by United Kingdom legislation. The Parliament at Westminster could enact that Eire should be treated for some specific purposes as though she was within His Majesty's dominions. But such domestic legislation could not affect the position under international law. And it followed that we could not accord to Eire or her citizens any special privileges which we were not willing to accord to other foreign countries to whom we had contracted to give "most-favoured-nation" treatment. As was explained in the memorandum annexed to C.P. (48) 264, our position would not be secure even in respect of countries which had signed the General Agreement on Tariffs and Trade and the Havana Charter. For other countries not signatories to that Agreement and Charter could claim that the United Kingdom should accord to them the same trade advantages as she accorded to Eire; and, if that claim were conceded or upheld by the International Court, the countries which were parties to the Agreement and the Charter could then claim that they were entitled to the same privileges under article 1 of the Agreement and article 16 of the Charter. Full consideration had been given to the possibility that common citizenship might afford a constitutional link on which to found an adequate defence against a challenge made by third parties on "most-favoured-nation" grounds. But this had been found, on examination, to be inadequate even for India, which was prepared to declare that she remained a member of the Commonwealth. For a true common citizenship must confer on the citizen a right to enter any part of the territory of which he was a citizen and a right to share in its government; and the possession of Commonwealth citizenship would not confer those rights throughout all the territories of the Commonwealth. Even for India, therefore, the Commonwealth citizenship would not in itself afford a sufficient constitutional link; and it would be even less effective in respect of Eire, since her Government were determined to declare that she had ceased to be a member of the Commonwealth. If, therefore, Eire repealed the External Relations Act, there seemed no room for doubt that in international law she would become a foreign State and that, by reason of the treaty obligations which they had undertaken in "most-favoured-nation" clauses, the United Kingdom Government would have no alternative but to treat her as a foreign State and her citizens as aliens.

In discussion some Ministers stressed the disadvantages of Eire's becoming a foreign State. The Home Office would be confronted with the most formidable administrative difficulties if all Eire citizens had to be treated in this country as aliens. If Eire became a member of the United Nations and raised the Partition issue there, the United Kingdom Government would find it highly embarrassing to be forced to give positive support for the continuance of Partition—as they would probably find themselves compelled to do for strategic reasons alone, apart from any consideration for the feelings of the people of Northern Ireland. Account must also be taken of the unfavourable reactions on public opinion, both in the United Kingdom and in other Commonwealth countries, of Eire's secession from the Commonwealth. Were not all these good reasons for looking at the spirit, rather than the letter, of the aide-mémoire from the Eire Government? This had recognised the existence of a specially close relationship between Eire and Commonwealth countries "arising, not only from ties of blood and kinship, but from traditional and long-established economic and social trade arrangements based on common interest"; and had urged that this relationship "should be maintained on the basis that the rights and privileges involved . . . were dependent upon long-established custom and tradition." Was it not clear that Eire Ministers had been led by considerations of domestic politics to commit themselves too hastily to the repeal of the External Relations Act; and could not some means be found of helping them to extricate themselves from their difficulties? Might not a solution be found along the lines of persuading the Eire Government to make a public declaration that they did not regard Eire as foreign to the countries of the Commonwealth in certain specific respects?

In reply, it was pointed out that the difficulties in international law could not be evaded by a unilateral declaration made by one Government or even by domestic legislation enacted by one Government. Due consideration must also be given to the risk that, if Eire were allowed to secede from the Commonwealth and still retain many of the advantages of membership, other Commonwealth countries might ask what they stood to gain by their continuing membership. Further, if trade preferences and other privileges were accorded to Eire solely on the basis of the factual association which she advocated, how could we continue to maintain that our "most-favoured-nation" rights would be infringed by a similar relationship between the South American countries or the States of the Arab League, who could allege a similar historical association and similar ties through language, religion and political co-operation?

After further discussion Ministers agreed that we should at least put clearly on record the legal implications, as we saw them, of Eire's repeal of the External Relations Act and the difficulties to which this repeal would give rise. We should also make it clear that these were consequences which would inevitably follow, as a matter of international law, as a result of the action of the Eire Government in repealing the Act. It was important that it should, if possible, be brought home to public opinion in Eire that these were the inevitable consequences of the action taken by their own Government, and not measures applied by the United Kingdom Government, at their discretion, in retaliation against Eire's secession from the Commonwealth. It was therefore desirable that a formal communication should be sent without delay to the Eire Government and that full publicity should be given to its contents. The Cabinet recognised that there was little prospect that, as a result of such a communication, the Eire Government would delay the introduction of legislation to repeal the External Relations Act. They were, however, informed that this legislation was to include provision for its being brought into operation at a date to be determined by Order; and it might at least be urged that the date to be fixed for the commencement of the Act should be such as to allow ample opportunity for full discussion of all its legal implications and the practical difficulties to which it would give rise. It was also agreed that the communication might end with the suggestion that if the Eire Government had any doubt about our view of the legal implications of their action, they might appoint legal experts to discuss with ours the legal and constitutional issues which were involved. It was most desirable that our communication should be published before the proposed legislation was introduced into the Dail; and the text of the communication should be carefully worded with publication in view.

Representatives of the Governments of Canada, Australia and New Zealand had taken part in the conversations with Eire Ministers at Chequers on 17th October; and it was therefore desirable that they should at least be aware of the contents of the communication which we proposed to send to the Eire Government before it was despatched. After discussion, it was agreed that the Attorney-General, who was going to Paris on other business that afternoon, should take the opportunity of discussing the text of the proposed communication in Paris with the Prime Minister of New Zealand, the Deputy Prime Minister of Australia and the Canadian Secretary of State for External Affairs. Subject to their comments, the communication should be despatched to the Eire Government that evening; and, as soon as it had been delivered, it and the aide-mémoire of 20th October from the Eire Government should be communicated to the Press.

The Cabinet:—

(1) Agreed that the draft reply to the Eire Government annexed to C.P. (48) 262 should be revised on the lines indicated in the course of the Cabinet's discussion.

(2) Invited the Attorney-General to show the text of the revised communication to the Prime Minister of New Zealand, the Deputy Prime Minister of Australia and the Canadian Secretary of State for External Affairs in Paris that afternoon.

(3) Subject to any comments received as a result of the action to be taken under Conclusion (2) above, invited the Secretary of State for Commonwealth Relations to despatch a communication to the Eire Government in the terms of the revised draft and to make arrangements to ensure that it and the aide-mémoire of 20th October from the Eire Government should receive full publicity at the earliest possible date.

The Cabinet then discussed the issues raised in C.P. (48) 254 regarding India's future relations with the Commonwealth.

The Cabinet's discussion and the conclusions reached are recorded in the Secretary's Standard File of Cabinet Conclusions.[4]

---

[4] See 391.

391 CAB 128/14, CM 71(48)2, annex — 12 Nov 1948

'India': Cabinet conclusions on India's future relations with the Commonwealth[1]

The Cabinet discussed the issues raised in C.P. (48) 254 regarding India's future relations with the Commonwealth.

At their meeting on 28th October they had invited the Lord Chancellor, in consultation with the Attorney-General and the Solicitor-General, to consider whether the constitutional proposals which had been discussed with the Prime Minister of India during his recent visit in this country would (i) constitute an adequate legal basis for India's continued membership of the Commonwealth; and (ii) provide an adequate basis for resisting claims by [? non-] Commonwealth countries under the most-favoured-nation provisions of existing treaties. They now had before them a note by the Prime Minister (C.P. (48) 254) covering a summary of these proposals in the form in which they had finally been put forward by the Prime Minister of India, together with an Opinion which the Lord Chancellor had prepared, in consultation with the Law Officers, on the two questions remitted to him.

The Lord Chancellor said that he had reached the conclusion that, if the Indian

---

[1] Previous reference: see 389.

Constituent Assembly adopted a constitution establishing India as a "sovereign democratic republic" on the lines at present contemplated, the effect would be to extinguish His Majesty's sovereignty in India, which would no longer be a part of His Majesty's dominions either under Indian law or under United Kindom law. If it were thereafter desired to continue to treat India for all purposes as a member of the Commonwealth, claims by foreign countries under the most-favoured-nation clauses of existing commercial treaties could only be resisted before an international court with any hope of success if it was possible to point to a continuous and substantial tie between members of the Commonwealth after, as well as before, the repudiation of allegiance to The King. In his view, the only matters of substance capable of creating such a tie were a *de facto* general acceptance by all civilised nations of the existence of the Commonwealth as a unit composed of nations bound together by a factual association of long standing, based up till now on the common sovereignty of the Crown and still continuing; and declarations by Commonwealth Governments that they wished to be regarded thus as "still bound in a special form of association". These ties would not, however, be sufficient in themselves unless they were reinforced by a true common citizenship throughout the Commonwealth; and, on examination of the actual position, it was clear that this condition was not satisfied. He therefore thought that, on a strictly legal view, it would not be safe to say more than that, if preferential treatment were continued to India after the enactment of a constitution on the lines at present contemplated, more or less plausible arguments could be put forward in opposition to a claim by some foreign country that it was entitled to the same treatment under a most-favoured-nation clause. *The Attorney-General* was in general agreement with this Opinion, though he was more doubtful whether even a plausible case could be put forward. It was, however, difficult to estimate what view would be taken by an international court in considering a wholly new set of constitutional issues.

In discussion, emphasis was laid on the fundamental difference between the attitude of India and Eire respectively towards their future relationship with the Commonwealth. Eire Ministers were determined to put Eire's secession from the Commonwealth beyond question; the Government of India, on the other hand, were anxious to devise means, compatible with the form of her constitution, by which India could continue to be a member of the Commonwealth, and paragraph 10 of Annex A of C.P. (48) 254 gave hope that in time a closer form of association could be achieved. The problem was how to secure the recognition, under international law, of a Commonwealth group which might include States no longer subject to The King's sovereignty. The difficulty arose from the fact that, at present, international law recognised only "His Majesty's dominions" or "foreign countries", and the question therefore was whether the International Court could be brought to admit the existence of a third form of association intermediate between these. If the Indian constitution was enacted in its present form, it would no longer be possible to support the case for India's continued membership of the Commonwealth by reference to The King's sovereignty; a solution would have to be sought by creating and establishing a conception of customary association which would recognisably distinguish her from a foreign State. The Commonwealth was not a clearly defined international entity; and it might be possible in this way to persuade the International Court to accept the idea of its changed constitutional structure. As a practical issue, the United Kingdom Government would be faced in due course with the necessity of deciding whether to take the risk of continuing to treat India as a member of the Commonwealth: some time would no doubt elapse before any foreign country pressed a claim for most-favoured-nation treatment before the International Court, and there would be time to elaborate the conception of a new form of constitutional relationship.

The point was made that, before any final decisions were reached on this question, it would be necessary to consider carefully their possible repercussions within the Commonwealth. A decision to continue to treat India as a Commonwealth country, after her repudiation of allegiance to the Crown, would no doubt be strongly criticised both here and in other Commonwealth countries, and there was some risk that India's example might be followed elsewhere in the Commonwealth. Before any decision was taken, therefore, it would be necessary to consult other Commonwealth Governments and to discuss the whole question with the Opposition. The immediate question was whether anything further ought to be said to the Prime Minister of India at this stage. While no advantage would be gained by legal controversy with Indian lawyers on this issue, the wording of paragraph 10 of Annex A of C.P. (48) 254 suggested that Pandit Nehru should in fairness be informed of the legal advice which the United Kingdom Government had received in this matter. It was agreed, therefore, that the Lord Chancellor's Opinion should be sent to the United Kingdom High Commissioner in India, who should be instructed to convey its substance personally to Pandit Nehru. General Nye[2] should make it plain that this Opinion dealt solely with the legal issues involved, and that the United Kingdom Government had reached no conclusions on the wider issues involved. He should take the opportunity of emphasising the United Kingdom Government's desire to find a mutually satisfactory solution of this problem.

The Cabinet:—

(1) Invited the Secretary of State for Commonwealth Relations to instruct the United Kingdom High Commissioner in India to convey to the Prime Minister of India the substance of the Opinion annexed to C.P. (48) 254.

(2) Invited the Secretary of State for Commonwealth Relations to arrange for the documents annexed to C.P. (48) 254 to be communicated to the Prime Ministers of Canada, Australia and New Zealand, drawing special attention to the fact that the Lord Chancellor's Opinion related solely to the legal issues involved.

---

[2] Lt-Gen Sir Archibald Edward Nye, UK high commissioner in India, 1947–1952.

392 CAB 128/13, CM 72(48) 13 Nov 1948

'Commonwealth relations: constitutional developments in Eire': Cabinet conclusions[1]

On 12th November the Cabinet had agreed on amendments to the draft note to the Eire Government annexed to C.P. (48) 262, and had invited the Attorney-General to show the text of the revised communication to the Prime Minister of New Zealand (Mr. Fraser), the Deputy Prime Minister of Australia (Dr. Evatt) and the Canadian

---

[1] Previous reference: see 390.

Secretary of State for External Affairs (Mr. Pearson) in Paris that afternoon. They now had before them a note by the Secretary (subsequently circulated as C.P. (48) 268) covering the revised draft of the note, together with two telegrams, Nos. 390 and 391, of 12th November from the Attorney-General reporting the outcome of his talks with Mr. Fraser, Dr. Evatt and Mr. Pearson.

Both Dr. Evatt and Mr. Pearson had expressed concern at the proposal to send a note to the Eire Government in these terms. Dr. Evatt had recalled his earlier opinion that emphasis on the practical difficulties which would arise from the repeal of the Eire Executive Authority (External Relations) Act would prejudice the prospect of reaching a satisfactory settlement of the problem. He himself was not satisfied that the consequences described in the draft note need follow upon the repeal. They would follow if the United Kingdom Government repealed section 3 of the British Nationality Act, 1948, but he was not sure that this section need be repealed. Even if the views expressed in the draft note were correct, it was in his opinion inopportune to put them forward at this stage, and he could not associate himself with them. Mr. Pearson had said that he would have to consult his Government before expressing any firm views. Mr. Fraser had raised no objection to the despatch of the note, but had emphasised that the New Zealand Government could not be associated in any way with it. He had expressed anxiety about the development of events.

Ministers first discussed whether it would be advisable, having regard to these views, to proceed with their original intention of communicating the proposed note to the Eire Government immediately, so that it and the Eire aide-mémoire of 20th October might receive full publicity before the Bill to repeal the External Relations Act was introduced into the Dail on 18th November. The publication of these documents would bring home to the people of Eire the practical consequences of the repeal; and, if Eire Ministers felt less confident of public support, they might at least be prepared to adopt a more reasonable attitude in determining the date from which the new Act would take effect. Furthermore, no formal communication had so far been sent to the Eire Government on the consequences of the repeal of the External Relations Act, and the United Kingdom Government might subsequently be criticised for having failed to warn Eire Ministers in detail of what these consequences were likely to be. The Commonwealth Ministers in Paris were looking at this problem from the point of view of their own countries, none of which had interests in world trade comparable with those of the United Kingdom.

Against this, it was argued that a further effort ought to be made to reach agreement with the Commonwealth Ministers on the legal issues before any formal communication on the lines suggested was made to the Eire Government and, in particular, before further publicity was given to the United Kingdom Government's attitude on these questions. While it was true that the practical consequences of the repeal of the External Relations Act would be more embarrassing to the United Kingdom than to the other Commonwealth countries, the fact remained that there were substantial Irish communities in some of those countries and the Commonwealth Governments concerned were, therefore, naturally anxious that Eire should not secede from the Commonwealth in circumstances which left her with an enduring sense of grievance against the United Kingdom and the other Commonwealth countries. Moreover, it was clear that any action which could be taken at this stage would be unlikely to affect the Eire Government's intention to introduce this legislation during the following week. Wide publicity had been given, after the

Chequers talks, to the probable consequences of the legislation, and the publication of the two notes would not be likely to have any greater effect in deterring Eire Ministers at this stage. The important point was to ensure that the Act was not brought into force until there had been a sufficient interval to enable its implications to be fully discussed. When the Cabinet had considered this matter on the previous day, Ministers had been under the impression that the date of commencement was to be stated in the Bill itself, but it now appeared that the intention was to provide merely that the Act should come into operation on a date to be appointed by order. The aim should be, therefore, to persuade Eire Ministers to allow a reasonable time for discussions before the Act was brought into operation.

It was suggested that it might be advisable to communicate the text of the Legal Opinion annexed to C.P. (48) 264 to the Eire Government in confidence. It was, however, pointed out that this Opinion had not been drafted in terms suitable for communication to the Eire Government. Some communication should, however, be sent to the Eire Government before the proposed Bill was introduced into the Dail, in reply to their aide-mémoire of 20th October. It was agreed that an interim reply should be sent to the effect that the United Kingdom Government had been giving careful consideration to this aide-mémoire, but were still unable to find any way of overcoming the difficulties which had been fully explained to Eire Ministers; and suggesting that, if it was impossible for the Eire Government to postpone the introduction of the Bill, the date to be fixed for the commencement of the Act should be such as to provide a sufficient interval to enable the full implications to be further discussed.

It was further agreed that the next step would be to hold further discussions with the Commonwealth Ministers in Paris with a view, if possible, to reaching agreed views on the legal issues involved, and the Cabinet invited the Lord Chancellor and the Secretary of State for Commonwealth Relations to proceed at once to Paris for this purpose. They would doubtless bear in mind the possibility of obtaining early agreement to the despatch of a message to the Eire Government inviting them to join in further discussion of these problems; and would also consider whether the other Commonwealth Governments could be persuaded to represent to the Eire Government the advantage of allowing a reasonable interval to elapse before the proposed legislation was brought into operation. This opportunity should also be taken to hold a preliminary discussion with the Commonwealth Ministers on the question of India's future relations with the Commonwealth on the basis of the documents annexed to C.P. (48) 254; and attention should be drawn to the possible effects on India and other Commonwealth countries of the policy adopted in relation to Eire.

The Cabinet:—

(1) Invited the Secretary of State for Commonwealth Relations to send an interim reply, on the lines agreed in the discussion, to the aide-mémoire of 20th October from the Eire Government.

(2) Invited the Lord Chancellor and the Secretary of State for Commonwealth Relations to proceed to Paris for discussions with the Prime Minister of New Zealand, the Deputy Prime Minister of Australia and the Canadian Secretary of State for External Affairs on the legal issues raised by the Eire Government's declared intention to repeal the Executive Authority (External Relations) Act, 1936, and on India's future relations with the Commonwealth.

393 CAB 128/13, CM 74(48)6 18 Nov 1948
'Commonwealth relations: constitutional developments in Eire and India': Cabinet conclusions

The Cabinet considered a memorandum (C.P. (48) 272) by the Lord Chancellor and the Secretary of State for Commonwealth Relations reporting the result of the meetings held in Paris on 15th and 16th November to discuss with representatives of the Eire Government the consequences of the forthcoming repeal of the Eire Executive Authority (External Relations) Act, 1936.

The Lord Chancellor said that at an early stage in these discussions it became clear that, despite the strong appeals made to them on behalf of the other Commonwealth Governments, the Eire Government were resolved that the External Relations Act should be repealed and that Eire should not be or become a member of the Commonwealth. The only question then remaining for discussion was how the Commonwealth countries were to react to these irrevocable decisions of the Eire Government. The Eire Ministers had said that they were most anxious to preserve a close practical association with the Commonwealth countries and would not wish, despite the action which they were about to take, to regard those countries as "foreign." The representatives of Canada, Australia and New Zealand had welcomed this approach to the problem, as being fully in accordance with the facts of the situation; and it had become clear to the United Kingdom representatives that, if they persisted in the view that Eire must be regarded as a foreign country once the External Relations Act was repealed, they would find themselves alone in maintaining that view. They had therefore pressed the argument that, if Eire and the Commonwealth countries were not to be regarded as "foreign" to one another, the citizenship law of Eire must be amended so as to accord positive rights of citizenship in Eire to the citizens of all Commonwealth countries which accorded those rights to Eire citizens. The Eire Ministers had in the end accepted the understandings set out in paragraph 8 of C.P. (48) 272, which contemplated an effective reciprocal exchange of citizenship rights between Eire and the countries of the Commonwealth. The Lord Chancellor said that he had been careful to avoid committing the United Kingdom Government in any way to the provisional conclusions reached at these meetings; but he himself believed that, in the circumstances as they had disclosed themselves in the course of the discussions, there was no practical alternative to the solution outlined in paragraph 8 of C.P. (48) 272.

The Secretary of State for Commonwealth Relations said that it was admitted that a self-governing member of the Commonwealth had the right to secede from the Commonwealth; and, now that it was clear that all appeals to the Eire Government to remain within the Commonwealth were unavailing, the wise course was to seek means of mitigating the effect of the breach. The United Kingdom representatives in the recent discussions could not have presented the practical consequences of the repeal as measures of retaliation for Eire's secession from the Commonwealth: even if they had wished to take this line, the other Commonwealth Governments would have dissociated themselves from it. They had been compelled, therefore, to confine themselves to explaining the difficulties which might arise in international law, by reason of the most-favoured-nation provisions in commercial treaties; and the Eire Ministers had offered, as a means of overcoming those difficulties, to develop the reciprocal exchange of citizenship rights. By this means we might be able to avert any challenge by a third party, on most-favoured-nation grounds, of our treatment of Eire citizens. We could not be equally confident of defeating a challenge directed against the continuance of the trade preferences to Eire; but some of the other Commonwealth representatives had been doubtful whether such a challenge would, in fact, be made for some time to come, and the Eire Ministers had recognised that, if such a challenge were sustained in the International Court, the trade preferences would have to be discontinued. The Secretary of State said that he could see no alternative to the course proposed in C.P. (48) 272: he believed that it could be defended in law and that, from the political point of view, there was much to commend it.

In discussion the following particular points were raised:—

(a) If Eire were allowed to retain all her existing advantages on the basis of a reciprocal exchange of citizenship rights, was there not a grave risk that India and some of the other Commonwealth countries would demand the same treatment? By making this arrangement in respect of Eire, should we not be moving towards the conception, which had hitherto been rejected, of an inner ring of Commonwealth countries and an outer ring of associated States?

In reply it was pointed out that it was not here suggested that an exchange of citizenship rights should be accepted as a basis for membership of the Commonwealth: Eire was not to remain within the Commonwealth. Moreover, the argument that Eire was not "foreign" to the Commonwealth countries would be based, not merely on the statutory exchange of citizenship rights, but also on the many ties of blood, history and intermingling of peoples which bound Eire to the older countries of the Commonwealth. These latter arguments could not be used in support of a claim that an Asiatic country could still be regarded as not being "foreign" to Commonwealth countries after it had ceased to be a member of the Commonwealth.

(b) If the policy outlined in C.P. (48) 272 were approved, it would not be necessary to make any change in the domestic law of the United Kingdom, unless a claim by a third party on "most-favoured-nation" grounds were upheld by the International Court. We should, however, be seeking to create in international law a new conception of an intermediate position between that of a Commonwealth country and of a foreign country. From this point of view, it was important that an early declaration should be made to the effect that, despite the repeal of the External Relations Act, the Governments of the Commonwealth countries would not regard Eire as a foreign State. This declaration should not be deferred until the position in international law seemed likely to be challenged. It should be made as soon as possible after the Second Reading of the Bill for the repeal of the External Relations Act. If possible it should be made in similar terms by the Governments of all Commonwealth countries.

(c) The Government of Northern Ireland should be informed at once of the course of the recent discussions with Eire Ministers. It was possible that the policy outlined in C.P. (48) 272 might embitter relations between the Government of Northern Ireland and the Eire Government, and it might even prejudice the good relations between the Government of Northern Ireland and the United Kingdom Government. The British Nationality Act extended to Northern Ireland; but there were local powers under which restrictions could be imposed on Eire citizens in Northern

Ireland. Thus, we had no power to require the Government of Northern Ireland to extend their local franchise to Eire citizens.

(d) The Opposition Leaders should also be informed of the course of the recent discussions with Eire Ministers.

(e) Eire Ministers had indicated that the Act repealing the External Relations Act would not be brought into operation before 1st January. To avoid any doubts about the effect of section 3 (2) of the British Nationality Act, 1948, it was desirable that the date of commencement of the new Eire Act should not in any event be earlier than 2nd January, 1949.

The general conclusion of the Cabinet was that, subject to any views which might be expressed on behalf of the Government of Northern Ireland, the policy outlined in C.P.(48)272 should be adopted. Ministers reached this conclusion with reluctance, as they felt that Eire would thereby succeed in retaining many of the practical advantages of Commonwealth membership while renouncing its obligations. They recognised, however, that, if they insisted on treating Eire as a foreign State after the repeal of the External Relations Act, the practical difficulties would be greater for the United Kingdom than for Eire; and, furthermore, that they would thereby forfeit the sympathy and support of Canada, Australia and New Zealand. From the practical point of view, there was some reason to believe that, although Eire Ministers were insisting on this political gesture of severing the last constitutional link with the Commonwealth, the people of Eire were moving towards a closer and friendlier association with the United Kingdom and other Commonwealth countries; and it was possible that, as the Eire Ministers claimed, a better relationship with Eire might be built up over the coming years on the basis of the factual association now proposed.

The Cabinet:—

(1) Took note that the Prime Minister would at once inform the Prime Minister of Northern Ireland of the course of the recent discussions with Eire Ministers and of the policy outlined in C.P. (48) 272.

(2) Subject to the results of the consultation to be undertaken in pursuance of Conclusion (1), agreed that the Eire Government should be informed, in advance of the forthcoming debate in the Dail on the Bill for the repeal of the External Relations Act, that the United Kingdom Government were prepared to proceed on the basis indicated in paragraph 8 of C.P. (48) 272.

(3) Subject also to Conclusion (1), authorised the Secretary of State for Commonwealth Relations to consult other Commonwealth Governments on the terms of a declaration, to be made as soon as possible after the Second Reading of the Bill for the repeal of the External Relations Act on 24th November, to the effect that despite the repeal of that Act Commonwealth Governments would not regard Eire as a foreign country.

(4) Invited the Prime Minister to inform the Opposition Leaders, before 24th November, of the course which the Eire Government had decided to take and of the policy which Commonwealth Governments proposed to follow in respect of Eire's future relations with the Commonwealth.

India

The Cabinet were informed that the Lord Chancellor and the Secretary of State for Commonwealth Relations had on 17th November held a further discussion with the

Prime Minister of New Zealand, the Deputy Prime Minister of Australia and the Canadian Secretary of State for External Affairs on the constitutional proposals put forward by the Prime Minister of India and the Law Officers' Opinion on those proposals (C.P. (48) 254). The representatives of the other Commonwealth countries had not regarded those proposals as satisfactory; and had suggested that they should join with the Secretary of State for Commonwealth Relations in discussing them with the Secretary-General of the Indian Ministry of External Affairs and Commonwealth Relations (Sir Girja Bagpai) who was then in Paris. The Prime Minister had agreed that this meeting should take place, and it was held in Paris later on 17th November. It had then been represented to Sir Girja Bagpai, on behalf of the four Commonwealth Governments, that India's authority to appoint diplomatic representatives abroad should derive from the Crown, possibly through The King's delegation of the power of appointment to the President of the Indian Republic. Sir Girja Bagpai had undertaken to transmit the views of the four Commonwealth Governments to Pandit Nehru.

The Cabinet:—

(5) Took note of the representations which had been sent to Pandit Nehru through Sir Girja Bagpai, on behalf of the Governments of the United Kingdom, Canada, Australia and New Zealand.

394 PREM 8/1008, pp 116–118 16 Dec 1948

[India's relation to the Commonwealth]: note by Mr Attlee on a meeting with Opposition leaders

This afternoon, in company with the Lord Chancellor, the Chancellor of the Exchequer and the Secretary of State for Commonwealth Relations, I saw the Leaders of the Opposition on the subject of India and the Commonwealth. Mr. Churchill, Mr. Eden, Lord Salisbury, Mr. Stanley and Sir David Maxwell Fyfe were present. I outlined the position and gave them the substance of our talks last night with the three Commonwealth representatives, and the conclusion at which we had arrived, to the effect that while India did not fulfil the conditions for membership of the Commonwealth, the possibility of some form of association should be explored and that we were all of the opinion that it would be a disastrous step to meet India's desire for continued association with a blank negative. Mr. Churchill in response at once went off the deep end with his usual attitude on Indian matters, and suggested that India should now be a foreign power: if we wanted anything from them we could make a treaty, and poured scorn on any suggestion of an association.

I did not think that this expressed the opinions of his colleagues. I accordingly took him up on the matter and went into the whole question in considerable detail. There was a good deal of discussion to and fro. The Lord Chancellor and the Chancellor of the Exchequer had had to leave before the discussion had got under way.

The Opposition raised the difficulty of getting any form of association which would be sufficient to defeat the operation of the most-favoured-nation clause. Mr. Oliver Stanley argued that, if India was no longer a member of the Commonwealth, they would become a foreign power, and we should do better to treat them as foreign and to make a comprehensive treaty of the kind which we had negotiated with Burma. This seemed to him to be more defensible in an international court, and sounder politically. Lord Salisbury argued that the machinery of the Commonwealth could only work if the Governments of its Members had a common outlook; recent speeches by Pandit Nehru had made him doubt whether such a common outlook with India now existed. In reply I gave instances of the value leading Indians gave to their participating in Western European ideas. I pointed out that there was a tendency, which we were encouraging, for the emergence in the world of larger groups, and suggested that international law was not static and that present international law had been framed on the conception of independent sovereign states. Sir David Maxwell Fyfe agreed with me that international law was still in the making. By this time Mr. Churchill had considerably calmed down and eventually he agreed, with the concurrence of his colleagues, that the right thing was to explore the possibilities of some form of association.

He subsequently raised the question of defence, indicating that the Opposition were anxious as to the state of our defence forces, and that he would probably in the new year ask me to receive a deputation from the Opposition on this subject.

395 CAB 129/31, CP(48)307 30 Dec 1948

'Commonwealth nomenclature': Cabinet memorandum by Mr Attlee

Some confusion has been caused and wrong deductions drawn from the form of the final communiqué issued at the end of the recent Meeting of Commonwealth Prime Ministers. It has been suggested that the word "British" was deliberately omitted before the word "Commonwealth" and that this represented a significant change of policy. In fact, this is not so. There was no occasion in that document to refer to the Commonwealth by title and the title was not in fact mentioned either as "the Commonwealth of Nations" or as "the British Commonwealth of Nations." What was unusual in that communiqué was the frequent use of such expressions as "Commonwealth countries," "Commonwealth Governments," and "Members of the Commonwealth." This, however, was due, not to any conscious desire to omit the term "British," but to the avoidance of the word "Dominion."

2. As these misunderstandings are apt to arise, I think it is important that we should all be clear in our own minds about the ideas underlying these points of nomenclature.

The main principle is that all the fully self-governing countries of the Commonwealth are independent peoples and that the United Kingdom, though doubtless *primus inter pares*, has constitutionally no more than an equal status with the others. It is important, therefore, to avoid all phrases which might be taken to imply that the other fully self-governing countries of the Commonwealth are in any way subordinated to the Government or people of the United Kingdom. Thus:—

(a) The term "Dominion" and "Dominion Government" should be avoided; such expressions as "Commonwealth country," "Commonwealth Government" or "Member of the Commonwealth" should be used instead in all official publications and correspondence. This carries to its logical conclusion the change which was made when a "Commonwealth Relations Office" took the place of the "Dominions Office."

(b) The use of the term "Dominion status" should simply be abandoned, in favour of such expressions as "become a fully independent Member of the Commonwealth" or "attain independence within the Commonwealth."

(c) No other opportunity should be lost of using language which stresses the fact that all the fully self-governing countries of the Commonwealth are of equal status. Thus, the term "Commonwealth Prime Ministers" should in future be used to describe the Prime Ministers of all Commonwealth countries, including the United Kingdom.[1]

3. It should not, however, be overlooked that the Commonwealth includes the Colonies and other dependent territories, some of which are under the administration of Australia, New Zealand and South Africa. The expression "Commonwealth countries" therefore includes the Colonies and those other territories. The phrase "Commonwealth and Empire," which conveniently implies a distinction between the self-governing and dependent parts of the whole, has no constitutional authority and is permissible only in colloquial use. In all formal documents, therefore, when it is intended to exclude dependent territories it will be necessary to use the terms, "fully self-governing countries of the Commonwealth" or, more simply, "Members of the Commonwealth." (A dependent territory is not a *Member* of the Commonwealth.)

4. On the use of the term "British" it is not possible to be so specific. The phrase "British Commonwealth of Nations" was, I think, first invented by Field-Marshal Smuts and was brought into more general use by those who sought a title for the British Empire which seemed more nearly in accord with modern ideas and constitutional practice. When it received statutory recognition in the Statute of Westminster, it was natural that in a formal instrument of that kind it should take the form "British Commonwealth of Nations." But for less formal purposes there has for a long time past been a tendency to use the simpler form "Commonwealth of Nations," which is fully appropriate for most ordinary occasions and in addition has a special attraction for those who, for one reason or another, are anxious to avoid emphasising the "British" aspect of the association. This tendency has increased in recent times. While Australia and New Zealand attach great importance to the term "British," other parts of the Commonwealth, e.g. South Africa and India, have their own reasons for wishing to avoid it. It is natural that Asiatic peoples, in particular, should feel that the application of the term to them implies some degree of subordination to the "British" peoples. Either description—"British Commonwealth of Nations" or "Commonwealth of Nations"—can properly be used as a description of the whole body of sovereign independent communities with their dependent territories. The choice between the two has turned sometimes on the context, sometimes on the individual tastes of the user.

5. At their meeting on 28th October (C.M. (48) 67th Conclusions, Minute 4),[2] the Cabinet agreed that it would be useful to establish, without any formal change, a convention of describing the Commonwealth as "Commonwealth of Nations," and that this change should be defended, if necessary, on the basis that it was an object of our policy to make it possible for nations to remain within the Commonwealth after

---

[1] See 387, appendix.

[2] See 388.

they had attained their independence, even though they felt that, by reason of their race and history, they could not properly be described as "British" nations. I do not now suggest that this decision should be modified; for it does not follow from it that we should not make even occasional use of the full phrase "the British Commonwealth of Nations." Shortly after we had referred in the communiqué to "countries of the Commonwealth," I myself, in my speech at the Mansion House, referred to "the British Commonwealth of Nations." In formal documents (e.g. communications to foreign Powers) it will often be necessary to use the full title. Nor is there any reason, as I have said, why we should not use it from time to time, according to context, in speeches or in written documents. But where there is doubt we can and should prefer the shorter title, "the Commonwealth of Nations."

6. I should be glad if my colleagues would issue suitable instructions, based on this paper, to all members of their Departments (whether at home or overseas) who deal with matters on which it would be useful to them to have this guidance.

396 CAB 134/119, CR 1(49) 7 Jan 1949

[India]: minutes of Cabinet Committee on Commonwealth Relations on India's future relations with the Commonwealth

[In his diary, Gordon Walker described this as a most important meeting, continuing: 'Bevin began by saying in effect the Commonwealth should be dissolved: his officials had been at him. . . . At the bottom of their hearts they think they could run foreign policy better than we can run Commonwealth relations: they want ambassadors under direct instructions. But people attacked him & NB [Noel-Baker] gave a child's lecture on the Commonwealth, when Bevin warmed up & began to help. The crown link is out. Let's fit India in as a Republic, based on the reality of a common act of will:— we can add embellishments, though not constitute them as the link. Shawcross attacked this as not standing up under international law. Cripps & PM in effect said law must be made for people & international law must adjust itself' (GNWR 1/7, 7 Jan 1949).]

The Committee had before them a note by the Secretary of the Cabinet (C.R. (49) 1) covering papers relating to India's future relations with the Commonwealth.

The Prime Minister recalled that, after discussion with Commonwealth representatives, he had informed Pandit Nehru on 16th December that the Eight Points set out in his memorandum of 11th December (circulated to the Cabinet under C.P. (48) 309) would not afford a satisfactory basis for India's continuing membership of the Commonwealth through the nexus of the Crown. He had, however, suggested to Pandit Nehru that, if he was unable to alter his position in this matter, it might still be possible for India to remain in a special association with the Commonwealth. No further communication had been received from Pandit Nehru, but there had been some informal discussions with the High Commissioner for India, who had made it clear that Pandit Nehru was unlikely to reconsider his attitude towards the Crown as revealed by his memorandum of 11th December or to be content with any form of "association" short of full membership of the Commonwealth. In these discussions, Mr. Krishna Menon[1] had himself made certain suggestions for maintaining some formal link through the Crown: he had, for instance, suggested that if the Indian

[1] V K Krishna Menon, high commissioner for India in the UK, 1947–1952.

Constitution defined Commonwealth citizenship in terms of the British Nationality Act, 1948, this might be sufficient to imply that Indians, as Commonwealth citizens or British subjects, owed some allegiance to the Crown, and that the King's title might be so amended as to indicate that India, though not subject to His sovereignty, was a member of the Commonwealth. There was still a possibility, too, that the Government of India might be prepared to recognise the Crown as the fountain of honour for the Commonwealth generally.

There was general agreement that it had been right to make every effort to persuade Pandit Nehru to accept a solution of India's future relations with the Commonwealth on the basis of a substantial link with the Crown. Any solution resulting in the weakening or abandonment of this link would involve formidable political complications, and the representatives of other Commonwealth countries with whom the matter had so far been discussed had emphasised the embarrassing position in which their Governments would be placed in defending any proposals which might be interpreted as having such an effect. Moreover, it was hard to foresee what might be the consequences of concessions to the Indian point of view: in particular, the Government of South Africa might be quick to take advantage of any arrangement which would enable a country which had severed its effective connection with the Crown to enjoy the full advantages of normal membership of the Commonwealth. But there now seemed little prospect that Pandit Nehru would be able to secure the acceptance of any arrangement involving the continuance of a substantial link with the Crown. Mr. Krishna Menon had emphasised the dangers of allowing this question of adherence to the Commonwealth to become an issue between the political parties in India; and it was also arguable that, by stressing allegiance to the Crown as the fundamental feature of Commonwealth membership, we might encourage those in other Commonwealth countries who were disposed to make the Crown an issue in local political controversy. It was necessary, therefore, to be prepared to find that Pandit Nehru would ultimately be unable to go beyond the Eight Points set out in his memorandum of 11th December. In that event there seemed to be three possible courses: (i) India might enter into a special form of "association" with the Commonwealth; (ii) she might become a foreign country in close treaty relationship; or (iii) the structure of the Commonwealth might be modified to permit the continued membership of a republic. From the discussions with Mr. Krishna Menon there seemed little prospect that India would be ready to accept any form of "association", for she was unlikely to accept any position which appeared to place her in a less favourable position than Pakistan. In practice, therefore, the choice seemed to lie between the second and third courses.

It was arguable that there might be advantages in allowing India to become a foreign state in close and friendly treaty relationship with the United Kingdom and the other members of the Commonwealth. In the field of foreign affairs, the United Kingdom Government were likely to find themselves embarrassed by the attitude of an independent India which was a member of the Commonwealth, and by the efforts which she would make to influence United Kingdom policy in her own narrower interests. It was an accepted assumption in the Commonwealth that the United Kingdom would automatically go to the defence of any Commonwealth country, but all Commonwealth countries expected to be allowed complete freedom to decide whether or not to remain neutral in the event of the United Kingdom itself becoming involved in war. This was an embarrassment to the United Kingdom, in the field of foreign policy and defence, even in the case of the older Commonwealth countries whose loyalty in time of grave crisis had been proved; but the same reliance could not be placed on India and she might become a grave and embarrassing liability. Against this, it was pointed out that there was a risk that too much emphasis might be laid on temporary disagreements that were apt to arise between Commonwealth Governments in peace-time on specific issues such as the Indonesian question. Experience over forty years had shown that Commonwealth Governments, while jealous of their right of independent action, could be trusted to support loyally a policy based on the principles of collective security and, in the last resort, to act together in war. It should be remembered that, while their tendency to independent action might prove embarrassing to the United Kingdom Government from time to time, it had been a matter for constant complaint with them that the United Kingdom Government had in the past failed to take them adequately into consultation before taking decisions which might have the most far-reaching consequences. The difficulties in the sphere of foreign affairs and defence to which attention had been drawn certainly constituted an argument for closer and more intimate co-operation and consultation between the United Kingdom and the other Commonwealth Governments, but it could not be regarded as a decisive argument for acquiescing in India's departure from the Commonwealth. Such a development would be a disastrous blow to the prestige and influence of the Commonwealth and would gravely affect the economic position of the United Kingdom and the sterling area generally. These were not the views of United Kingdom Ministers alone; the discussions had shown that there was a unanimous desire among Commonwealth Governments to find some solution which would enable India to remain within the Commonwealth. It was important also to remember that a number of Colonial peoples would be gravely affected by the failure of the Commonwealth to adjust itself to meet the susceptibilities of a non-European people. Very careful consideration ought therefore to be given at this stage to the question whether it was possible to admit a country with a republican constitution into full membership of the Commonwealth.

It was pointed out that the existing Commonwealth relationship, based on allegiance to a common Crown, carried with it certain definite rights and obligations which differentiated it clearly from the relationship created by an international treaty or agreement. A new form of Commonwealth relationship might be created based on the common will to maintain the existing membership; but, unless this was reinforced by a real Commonwealth citizenship, there seemed little prospect that it would be accepted in international law that Commonwealth countries not united by common sovereignty could be regarded as not foreign to each other. The basic feature of a real Commonwealth citizenship should be the right of Commonwealth citizens to enter and to share in the Government of all the countries of the Commonwealth; and it was clear that there was no prospect of securing acceptance of Commonwealth citizenship in this form. Admittedly, Commonwealth citizenship in this sense had existed only imperfectly in the past; but, so long as there was a common allegiance to the Crown, it had not been necessary to rely on the conception of common citizenship as a constitutional link between the members of the Commonwealth. In the absence of any substantial link through the Crown, and of a Commonwealth citizenship which carried with it at least the basic rights of common nationality, it seemed difficult to maintain that in international law there would be any such content in Commonwealth membership as would justify the claim that

Commonwealth countries were not foreign to each other. On the other hand, it was argued that this view gave insufficient weight to the extensive measure of reciprocal nationality rights and obligations already existing throughout the Commonwealth: in so far as these were defective, there were no obstacles to a close relationship based on reciprocal nationality rights between the United Kingdom and each of the other Commonwealth countries. But the crux of the matter was that it was impossible to isolate specific aspects of the Commonwealth relationship: there were other equally important features of the relationship such as common consultation and the absence of formal definitions. The basic reality of the situation was that India and the other members of the Commonwealth were determined to maintain a long-standing association: the cardinal facts of their relationship were their common history and their common will to remain in association with each other.

Some Ministers thought it would be premature to attempt to create, for the benefit of countries adopting a republican form of constitution, a new form of Commonwealth relationship based simply on the common will to continue in association. That might be the ultimate objective, but the transition should be eased by maintaining some part of the traditional ties, however tenuous in form. Individually, such ties might be insignificant, but in aggregate they might have considerable sentimental and legal importance, and their existence would be likely to diminish greatly political opposition, here and in other Commonwealth countries, to a new conception of the Commonwealth relationship. On this view it would be right to try to persuade India to go as far as possible in accepting some form of relationship with the Crown. Against this, it was argued that it would be preferable to admit frankly from the outset that the aim was to create a wholly new form of relationship. No advantage would ultimately be gained by building a facade of insubstantial forms designed to hide the real nature of the constitutional changes which the Commonwealth was undergoing, and there was risk that preoccupation with the problem of diluting existing ties in deference to Indian sensibilities might jeopardise the successful fulfilment of the main purposes of the policy.

After further discussion, the suggestion was made that a solution might be sought along lines suggested by the machinery established to give effect to the policy of Western Union. Under this proposal, a Commonwealth Conference might be established which would be open to all existing members of the Commonwealth irrespective of their constitutional status. This Conference would have no corporate powers, and it would be desirable that it should have as few rules as possible. The King might be President of the Conference, and might himself issue the invitations to the meeting. There was general agreement that this suggestion should be examined and a detailed scheme prepared for consideration at a subsequent meeting of the Committee. The point was made that, in working out concrete proposals, it would be necessary to bear in mind the importance of ensuring that any proposals finally put forward should do as little violence as possible to the very strong sentiment of devotion to the Crown which existed in many parts of the Commonwealth.

The Committee:—

Agreed that the official Committee on Commonwealth Relations should submit detailed proposals on the basis of the suggestions thrown out in the discussion.

397 CAB 128/15, CM 1(49)2 12 Jan 1949

[Eire]: Action consequent upon Eire's ceasing to be a member of the Commonwealth: Cabinet conclusions on draft Ireland Bill

[The issues discussed at this Cabinet meeting were: constitutional safeguards, the defence of Northern Ireland, titles, the boundary of Northern Ireland, the Irish Lights Commission, extra territorial powers, the Westminster franchise, membership of Northern Ireland parliament, and Commonwealth committees.]

The Cabinet had before them a memorandum by the Prime Minister (C.P. (49) 4) covering the report of an official working party on the action to be taken by the United Kingdom Government as a result of Eire's ceasing to be a member of the Commonwealth; and a later memorandum by the Prime Minister (C.P. (49) 5) modifying certain recommendations of the working party in consequence of discussions with Northern Ireland Ministers and annexing a revised draft of an Ireland Bill.

Constitutional safeguards

The Prime Minister said that in the Statute Book other countries were treated as either British or foreign, and legislation was therefore unavoidable if, as the Cabinet had decided, Eire was not in future to be regarded as a foreign country even though she ceased to be part of His Majesty's dominions. Since legislation was necessary, the Northern Ireland Government had pressed that statutory force should be given to the undertaking that the constitutional status of Northern Ireland would not be altered without Northern Ireland's agreement. When he had given this undertaking in the House of Commons, no disagreement had been expressed and he believed that a statutory declaration to this effect would meet with general acceptance.

The Minister of Civil Aviation[1] said that he thought it would be a mistake to give any guarantee of the territorial integrity of Northern Ireland. In two Northern counties there was a majority in favour of an ending of partition and, if the issue of partition ever came before an international court, the view might be expressed that these counties should be transferred to Eire. He believed that the right solution lay in the political unity of Ireland and the strategical unity of Ireland and the United Kingdom.

The general feeling of the Cabinet was, however, in favour of a statutory declaration in the form of Clause 1 (1) (b) of the draft Bill annexed to C.P. (49) 5. It was by no means certain that an international tribunal, if the issue were brought before it, would consider that the two counties of Tyrone and Fermanagh should be transferred to Eire: recent discussions on the partition of India and Palestine provided examples of the arguments which might be used in favour of treating these counties as essential to the viability of Northern Ireland. Unless the people of Northern Ireland felt reasonably assured of the support of the people of this country, there might be a revival of the Ulster Volunteers and of other bodies intending to meet any threat of force by force; and this would bring nearer the danger of an outbreak of violence in Ireland. From the point of view of Great Britain, experience in the last war had amply proved that Northern Ireland's continued adhesion to the

---

[1] Lord Pakenham.

United Kingdom was essential for her defence. There was nothing in past experience to give any reasonable assurance to Great Britain that Eire would not be neutral in a future war. In 1940 Eire had jeopardised her chances of ending partition by remaining neutral, and her recent legislation had shown that she laid more store on formal independence than on the union of Ireland.

Defence of Northern Ireland

The Prime Minister said that, in view of the anti-partition campaign which was being fostered by the Eire Government, he might be asked whether British troops would be used to defend Northern Ireland against aggression. The Cabinet agreed that it would be inexpedient for the Prime Minister to take the initiative in offering an assurance on the lines suggested in paragraph 3 of C.P. (49) 5. If, however, he was questioned on this point, he would have no alternative but to say that Northern Ireland would be defended against aggression just like any other part of the United Kingdom—though, even then, it would be wise to preface such a statement by expressing the hope that the differences between the North and the South would never give rise to the use of force. This reply might provoke enquiries about the application of National Service in Northern Ireland. On practical grounds, however, it was desirable to maintain the present arrangement by which the National Service Acts did not extend to Northern Ireland.

Titles

The majority of the working party had recommended that Northern Ireland should be known as "Ulster" and that Eire should be known formally as "the Republic of Ireland" and colloquially as "the Irish Republic." *The Prime Minister* pointed out, however, that the use of the title "Ulster" might provoke controversy among Irishmen in other parts of the Commonwealth, since the province of Ulster had included counties now within Eire, and it had also been ascertained that the Northern Ireland Government did not attach great importance to the use of the term "Ulster." He had just heard that the Northern Ireland Government still favoured the use of the term "Irish Republic," even in statutes, as a description of the South. The "Republic of Ireland" was, however, the term adopted by Eire in the recent Republic of Ireland Act and it would be difficult for us to avoid using that term as a statutory description.

The Cabinet agreed that the North should continue to be described as "Northern Ireland," and that the South should be described by statute as "the Republic of Ireland" but in official usage as "the Irish Republic."

Boundary of Northern Ireland

There was general agreement that it would be inexpedient to raise with the Eire Government at this stage any questions which might provoke legal argument about the boundary between the North and the South.

Irish Lights Commission

It was agreed that the Secretary of State for Commonwealth Relations, after consultation with the First Lord of the Admiralty and the Minister of Transport, should submit to the Eire authorities proposals for securing representation of United Kingdom interests on the Irish Lights Commission.

Extra territorial powers
The Home Secretary said that, subject to the concurrence of the First Lord of the Admiralty and the Minister of Transport, he would like to include the regulation of harbours among the matters which, under Clause 6 of the draft Bill, the Parliament and the Government of Northern Ireland could handle in concert with the Eire Government.

There was general agreement that the Home Secretary's proposal, if acceptable to the other Ministers concerned, should be adopted, and that a provision on the lines of Clause 6 of the draft Bill should be included in any legislation. Attention was, however, drawn to the undesirability on general grounds of adding substantially to the powers of the Northern Ireland Parliament in matters which might more properly be dealt with by the United Kingdom Parliament. It was also desirable that, in matters affecting Northern Ireland and Eire, the Commonwealth Relations Office should continue to communicate with Northern Ireland through the Home Office.

Westminster franchise
The Prime Minister said that the Northern Ireland Ministers were seriously concerned about the effect in Northern Ireland of the provision in the Representation of the People Act, 1948, by which the qualification for the Westminster franchise, both in Great Britain and in Northern Ireland, was simply residence on a qualifying date. They believed that Eire citizens might get their name on the electoral register by paying a short visit to Northern Ireland around the qualifying date, and that this strategem might be used on a scale which would falsify the representation of Northern Ireland at Westminster. The Northern Ireland Ministers had pressed for a six-months' residence qualification, and it had been suggested to them that the United Kingdom Government might see its way to propose a three-months' residence qualification, provided that the residence qualification for the franchise for the Northern Ireland Parliament was reduced from seven to, say, three years. He had, however, just heard that the Northern Ireland Government, on consideration, did not see their way to reduce the residence qualification for the Northern Ireland franchise.

In discussion, it was pointed out that the proposal to retain a residence qualification in Northern Ireland for the United Kingdom franchise had been put forward when the Representation of the People Act, 1948, was passing through Parliament, and had then been rejected without a division. If it were now proposed to impose a three-months' residence qualification without any concession by the Northern Ireland Ministers in respect of the Northern Ireland franchise, there would be much criticism in Parliament about the manner in which Northern Ireland elections were said to be conducted.

In support of a residence qualification in Northern Ireland, it was argued that before the Act of 1948 there had been a difference between the law in Northern Ireland and Great Britain on this point. In the Commonwealth generally the franchise was normally confined to British subjects, and there was usually a substantial residential qualification. The control on immigration into Great Britain and the fairly long sea-route from Ireland meant that in practice there was no danger of the register in Great Britain being flooded by foreigners and citizens of Eire, but the position in Northern Ireland with a long land frontier was very different. Moreover, the situation had altered since the Act of 1948 was passed, since Eire was now leaving the Commonwealth. It was understood that Eire was unlikely to give reciprocal rights to British subjects to vote in Eire elections.

While it was recognised that the Northern Ireland Ministers might not regard the time as propitious for lowering the Northern Ireland residential qualification, the general feeling of the Cabinet was that the Prime Minister should make a further attempt to persuade the Northern Ireland Government to reduce the residential qualification for the Northern Ireland franchise from seven to, say, five years, before a final decision was taken whether to propose a three-months' residential qualification in Northern Ireland for the Westminster franchise.

Membership of Northern Ireland parliament

There was general agreement that it was undesirable to deal in the Ireland Bill with certain minor points regarding the membership of the Northern Ireland Parliament which had been raised by the Northern Ireland Government, and that accordingly Clause 7 should be omitted from the draft Bill.

Commonwealth committees

With reference to paragraph 33 of C.P. (49) 4, *The Chancellor of the Exchequer* said that he was anxious that Eire should remain a member of the Sterling Area Statistical Committee. Although none of the foreign countries included in the sterling area was in fact represented on it, this was not in form a Commonwealth Committee; and it was to the advantage of this country that Eire should continue to be represented on it.

The Cabinet:—

(1) Approved in principle the introduction of legislation on the lines of the draft Bill annexed to C.P. (49) 5, subject to further consideration of Clause 5, to the possible amendment of Clause 6 mentioned in discussion and to the omission of Clause 7.

(2) Invited the Prime Minister to make a further attempt to persuade the Prime Minister of Northern Ireland to reduce the residential qualification for the Northern Ireland franchise, e.g., from seven to five years, in return for the introduction of a residential qualification of three months for the exercise in Northern Ireland of the Westminster franchise.

(3) Approved the other proposals put forward in C.P. (49) 5 as noted above.

(4) Approved the recommendations made by the working party in paragraphs 3–9, 12–13, and 32–37 of C.P. (49) 4, subject to the point noted above regarding Eire's membership of the Sterling Area Statistical Committee.

398 CAB 134/119, CR 2(49)2 8 Feb 1949

'India's future relations with the Commonwealth': minutes of Cabinet Committee on Commonwealth Relations

The Committee considered a Fifth Report by the Official Committee (C.R. (49) 2) on the question of India's future relations with the Commonwealth. They also had before them a note by the Secretary (C.R. (49) 3) covering a telegram addressed to the Prime Minister by the Prime Minister of Pakistan on certain aspects of the constitutional structure of the Commonwealth.

At their meeting on 7th January[1], Ministers had suggested that a new constitutional basis for the Commonwealth might be founded on the conception of membership of a Commonwealth Conference. The Official Committee had, however, reached the conclusion that it would not be practicable to develop this conception to a point at which it could be regarded as the central constitutional link between the countries of the Commonwealth. Any suggestions for formalising the procedure of Commonwealth meetings would be inconsistent with the development of opinion on this subject in recent years; and it would be difficult to secure general agreement among Commonwealth Governments to formal rules of procedure for a Commonwealth Conference, or to a definition of its powers and functions, to the extent necessary to elevate it into an important piece of constitutional machinery. The Official Committee had also pointed out that there was nothing in the conception of a Commonwealth Conference which would differentiate the Commonwealth relationship from that of an association of foreign states.

Ministers endorsed generally the Official Committee's conclusions on this point and proceeded to consider the re-definition of the Commonwealth relationship suggested in paragraph 4 of C.R. (49) 2.

The Lord Chancellor suggested that it might be convenient, in the first instance, to consider whether the formula proposed by the Official Committee would be an effective defence for the continuance of preferential treatment for trade or nationals between the republican members and the other members of the Commonwealth, if these should be challenged in an international court as inconsistent with the most-favoured-nation clauses in a commercial treaty. After consultation with the Attorney-General, he had reached the conclusion that that part of the proposed formula which stated that "the Members of the British Commonwealth of Nations are . . . not foreign in relation one to another" would not be accepted by an international court. Broadly speaking, the most-favoured-nation clauses in our commercial treaties fell into four categories; (i) those which contained no definition of the term "foreign countries"; (ii) those which defined "foreign" countries as territories "not being part of the British Commonwealth"; (iii) those which defined "foreign" countries as territories "not under the sovereignty of The King"; and (iv) those which excluded "foreign" countries from privileges extended to each other by territories "under the sovereignty of The King". Under the formula proposed in paragraph 4 of C.R. (49) 2, an international court would hold that India was a "foreign country" for the purposes of clauses in the third and fourth of these categories, and this would probably apply to the second category also. The Geneva General Agreement on Tariffs and Trade would not provide a solution for this difficulty, since certain important countries, such as Argentina, were not signatories to it. In so far as a claim to preferential treatment by such a country might be upheld by an international court, the signatories to the Agreement would be able to claim similar treatment.

In discussion, the general view of Ministers was that the aspects of the problem to which the Lord Chancellor had drawn attention were subordinate in importance to the far-reaching political issues raised by the proposal for a re-definition of the Commonwealth relationship on the lines discussed in C.R. (49) 2. The United

[1] See 396.

Kingdom Government had been faced with the same problems in the case of Eire, and they had, for political reasons, felt that there was no alternative but to accept the risks of consequential difficulties arising as a result of the terms of the most-favoured-nation clauses of commercial treaties. Nor was it any easier on this occasion to estimate the extent or nature of these risks. It could not be regarded as certain, for instance, that Argentina would maintain her refusal to join the International Trade Organisation or that she, or other countries, would wish to challenge the continued grant of preferential concessions to a republican India; and Ministers would need a comprehensive appreciation of these risks before forming a final view on the practical effects of a successful appeal to the international court. In any event, it must be presumed that international law was itself capable of modification and development in response to changes in external political relationships; and that foreign countries might, in any event, be ready to look at their legal rights under most-favoured-nation clauses in the light of the substantial mutual benefits derived from the Treaties as a whole.

Discussion turned next on the question whether it was desirable to attempt to devise a new form of constitutional relationship which would permit India to remain within the Commonwealth in spite of her repudiation of the link through the Crown. On the one hand, it was argued that the very fact of India's refusal to accept the central feature of the Commonwealth relationship implied that she did not share those intangible sentiments and emotions which, in the absence of any written constitution, were the cohesive power in the Commonwealth relationship. Would it not be preferable to recognise this fact and to substitute for the indeterminate Commonwealth association a form of treaty relationship with India which would specifically define the obligations assumed by both parties? As things were, the Government of India seemed likely to pursue in international affairs policies based solely on considerations of India's interests, and there was a serious risk that, so long as India was a member of the Commonwealth, the United Kingdom might become involved in embarrassments and dangers resulting from independent action taken by India. Was it reasonable to expect that the United Kingdom should continue to bear the moral obligation to assist India in times of trouble, while India was not prepared to accept a similar obligation towards this country? Moreover, the growth of nationalism in South-East Asia meant that India would be increasingly preoccupied with the problems of that region and with the responsibilities associated with her position as the leading Asian Power; and this might mean that she would be correspondingly less concerned to take a constructive and co-operative part in Commonwealth affairs. Finally, was it not probable that the re-definition of the Commonwealth relationship suggested in paragraph 4 of C.R. (49) 2 would weaken the cohesion of the Commonwealth and create, in fact, if not in constitutional terms, two forms of Commonwealth relationship? The influence in international affairs of the Commonwealth generally, and of the United Kingdom in particular, sprang largely from the world-wide recognition of the ultimate unity of aim and outlook shared by the members of the Commonwealth, and of their readiness to act together in times of grave crisis. Acceptance of the new form of relationship might create the impression that a fundamental change had taken place in the cohesion of the Commonwealth, and its prestige and influence in international affairs would then be sensibly diminished.

On the other hand, it was argued that excessive emphasis had been laid on India's tendency to pursue an independent policy in international affairs; in this respect, she did not differ substantially from the older Commonwealth countries, whose attachment to the right of independent action had been, indeed, so great that in their case no one would suggest that it would be practicable to devise a treaty relationship on the lines now contemplated for India. Nevertheless, experience had shown that, in the last resort, there existed a unity of aim and outlook, and emotional and sentimental bonds, strong enough to ensure that the Commonwealth would act together in a major crisis. Nor was it correct to suggest that the obligations implicit in the Commonwealth relationship were wholly one-sided. There was no reason to assume that the United Kingdom would feel bound, in all circumstances, to go to the help of a Commonwealth country; her policy would necessarily be determined by the facts of the situation, and it would be open to her, in certain circumstances, to dissociate herself from action taken by a Commonwealth Government, in the same way that Commonwealth Governments had declined to respond to the United Kingdom Prime Minister's appeal for joint action against Turkey in 1922. In the past, Commonwealth Governments had come spontaneously to the aid of the United Kingdom when she was gravely threatened by German aggression, and it should not be assumed that, if a major threat of this nature should occur again, India would remain indifferent or refuse active help. In the last war, when India had no freedom of action, and despite the opposition of her political leaders, some two million Indians had volunteered for the Fighting Services, and there was no reason why the sentiments of friendship with the rest of the Commonwealth which had prompted this response should disappear in the new circumstances. On the contrary, there were grounds for hope that, if a solution of the immediate problems could be found in a form acceptable to political opinion in India, the relationship between the United Kingdom and India would grow steadily closer in course of time. The strength of the intellectual and spiritual ties between India and this country should not be under-estimated. For many generations, educated Indians had been familiar with the main fields of English thought, and Indian political, legal and administrative ideas were largely English in inspiration. The strength of the feeling in India for this country had been vividly illustrated by the steady growth, since 1947, in the numbers of those political leaders who favoured India's continuance as a member of the Commonwealth. And this, indeed, was the crucial point. Whatever constitutional and practical difficulties might be involved, the central fact remained that India had expressed the wish to remain within the Commonwealth, and the majority of Commonwealth Governments were very anxious that some means should be found to enable her to do so. In these circumstances, a decision to insist on terms which made it impossible for India to remain within the Commonwealth would not only be a grave failure of statesmanship; it might in itself set in train forces which would have a corroding and disintegrating effect upon the cohesion of the remaining members of the Commonwealth. While full weight must be given to the considerations mentioned in paragraph 15 of C.R. (49) 2, it would also be necessary to take into account the practical disadvantages which would flow, both immediately and in the long run, from India's departure from the Commonwealth. Such a development would undoubtedly diminish gravely the influence and prestige of the Commonwealth in international affairs, and it would be widely assumed that the forces opposed to Communist aggression had suffered a further major setback. While it might be hoped that a close and friendly treaty relationship could be established with

India, there was a risk that her exclusion from the Commonwealth against her own wishes might encourage her to concentrate her attention on the creation of an Asiatic bloc isolated from, and possibly hostile to, the Western Powers. The problem of maintaining friendly relations with an independent India would undoubtedly present problems of great difficulty in this country so long as Pakistan remained within the Commonwealth, since in that event the United Kingdom Government would be under some moral obligation to aid and support Pakistan in her relations with India. In general, it was a matter of major importance that the leading Power in South-East Asia should remain a member of the Commonwealth, since this would enable the Commonwealth to maintain closer links with South-East Asia than would otherwise be possible; and it would offer the best hope of ensuring that South-East Asian nationalism developed on lines friendly to the Western Powers. These were considerations with which the Governments of Australia and New Zealand were increasingly concerned.

In further discussion, the following points were made—

(a) Attention was drawn to the Official Committee's discussion, in paragraph 12 of their report, of the question whether India should be urged to adopt any such "tenuous" links with the Crown as she might be willing to accept. While there was general agreement with the Official Committee's view that it would be a mistake to argue that such links were an essential feature of the new form of Commonwealth relationship described in their report, some Ministers thought that greater emphasis might have been placed on the value of such links as embellishments of that relationship. They recognised that Pandit Nehru, in his Eight Point Memorandum of 11th December, 1948, had not in fact placed any weight on the importance of "tenuous" links with the Crown, and they agreed that his one point that could be regarded as constituting any kind of link with the Crown was open to the criticisms made in paragraph 9 of C.R. (49) 2. They still thought, however, that it would be advisable to try to persuade the Government of India to acquiesce in the retention of any such tenuous links that might serve to strengthen the new relationship. In this connection, it was pointed out that the present attitude of the Indian Government on the question of allegiance obscured the very genuine sentiments of loyalty to the Crown which had inspired many Indians in the past.

(b) Attention was drawn to the possible effects of the formula in paragraph 4 of C.R. (49) 2 on the position of Indians in certain Colonial territories. The majority of these Indians had made their permanent homes in the Colonies, and had been encouraged to do so by Pandit Nehru. But many still had close ties with India; and an embarrassing, and possibly dangerous, situation would arise if some continued to acknowledge allegiance to the Crown and others were permitted to opt for Indian citizenship which carried no such obligation. The Colonial Office would wish, therefore, to have an opportunity of considering further whether paragraph (iv) of the suggested formula could be modified to prevent such a situation from arising.

Ministers recognised that it would not be possible to reach any final decision on the issues raised in C.R.(49)2 without full consultation with other Commonwealth Governments. But this raised practical problems of considerable difficulty. It was understood that the new Indian Constitution would probably be enacted by the Constituent Assembly in July next and brought into operation on 15th August. There was, therefore, little time for negotiations which were bound to prove both delicate and difficult. Issues of such importance ought to be discussed at a meeting of

Commonwealth Prime Ministers, but there would be great difficulty in arranging such a meeting before July next, having regard to the Parliamentary time-tables in the various Commonwealth countries. If such a meeting was to be arranged, it seemed likely that the best time might prove to be the latter part of April, when only the Parliaments of Canada and South Africa would be in session. But it would in any event be desirable to have preliminary consultations with the Prime Ministers of Canada, Australia and New Zealand.

The view was expressed that there would be very great advantages if some interim arrangements could be arrived at which would make it unnecessary to take any definite steps in this matter for a period of two or three years. This would give time for the situation to shape itself and for public opinion in the various Commonwealth countries to adjust itself to the new developments in Commonwealth relationships before a final decision was taken. Was there any possibility that Pandit Nehru might be induced to arrange that the Indian Constitution in its full republican form should be passed but not brought into operation as a whole in 1949? For the present, the provisions necessary for the holding of new elections need alone be brought into operation, and these elections could be held while the existing relations to the Crown subsisted. One important consideration in favour of this suggestion was that if any final decisions should be taken this year, the position of the Crown might become an issue in the United Kingdom General Election in 1950. On the other hand, it was pointed out that, if this suggestion were adopted, India's future relationship with the Commonwealth would become an issue at the Indian elections, and that it was for this reason that Pandit Nehru was anxious that a final decision should be taken before the elections were held. Further, the risks of bringing the Crown into party politics would be increased if no decision had been reached before the general elections pending in this and other Commonwealth countries, and it might therefore prove that no substantial advantage had been secured by postponement of a decision.

The Committee:—

Agreed to resume their discussion on the following day.

399 CAB 134/119, CR 3(49) 9 Feb 1949

[India]: minutes of Cabinet Committee on Commonwealth Relations on India's future relations with the Commonwealth[1]

[With reference to this meeting, Gordon Walker's diary entry for 10 Feb 1949 reads: 'N. Brook, Liesching & I agree to try to fit India in openly as a Republic. N-B [Noel-Baker] played very little part in discussion. Bevin was extremely defeatist. Under Orme Sargent's influence he argued repeatedly that it was not worth keeping India in: it wasn't going to be morally committed to us, but we to it, it would pursue its own foreign policy, etc. All such arguments would lead to the breakdown even of the old Commonwealth—& this Bevin once or twice said. From time to time he warmed up & made positive suggestions—not very good ones ("a commonwealth" for "the commonwealth"). But his role was almost wholly negative. Jowitt wobbled: Addison held clearly in mind the need to help India in: but did not clearly grasp the real problems. Shawcross was good. He overpressed the legal arguments but advised their subordination to political ones . . . . The PM was most impressive. He fully realises the difficulties of the King, opposition,

[1] Previous reference: see 398.

other Commonwealth countries: he does not rush. But he drove the argument steadily forward (in fact allowing it to repeat itself too much). He wants India in: realises the value of time: but also the need to press forward now .... The value, even of stupid & repetitious discussion is clear. It allows a gradual shaping of policy' (GNWR 1/7).]

The Committee resumed their consideration of the Fifth Report by the Official Committee (C.R. (49) 2) on the question of India's future relations with the Commonwealth.

Discussion turned first on the suggestion, put forward at their previous meeting, that India might be persuaded to enact her new Constitution in a form which would permit a final decision on her future relationship with the Commonwealth to be deferred for, say, two years. It was suggested that such a postponement might be secured by a declaration by the Government of India to the following effect:—

"That in declaring India to be a Sovereign (Independent) Republic the Government of India expresses its desire to continue in full association with (membership of) the British Commonwealth of Nations and in doing so recognises that this change calls for close consultation with the other members of the Commonwealth and declares its desire to enter into such consultation as soon as may be conveniently arranged, with a view to the determination of the different issues (questions) that may be involved."

The general view of Ministers was, however, that it was very unlikely that the Government of India would be prepared to agree to a proposal on these lines and that, in any event, the practical disadvantages of postponement would be very serious. Once the new Indian Constitution had been enacted by the Constituent Assembly, the question would be asked whether India was still a member of the Commonwealth, and it would not be possible to postpone an answer while the proposed consultations between Commonwealth Governments were taking place. An even more serious consequence of postponement would be that the question of India's future relationship with the Commonwealth would become a party issue, not only in the Elections under the new Constitution to be held in India early in 1950, but also the forthcoming Elections in the United Kingdom and other Commonwealth countries. The only way in which it was possible to prevent this question from becoming an electoral issue throughout the Commonwealth was to reach a decision in advance of the enactment of the new Indian Constitution; and, if the United Kingdom Government failed to take the initiative in calling for Commonwealth consultations on the subject at this stage, it was possible that the Australian Government would do so.

In further discussion of the general issues raised by C.R. (49) 2, the following points were made:—

(a) There was a risk that, by taking the initiative in devising a new form of Commonwealth relationship designed to enable India to remain a member despite her repudiation of the allegiance to the Crown, we might gravely jeopardise both the position of the Crown and the strength and cohesion of the Commonwealth as a whole. Would it not be better to leave India to secede from the Commonwealth and herself to take the initiative in negotiating the basis for her future association with the United Kingdom and the Commonwealth generally? Against this, it was pointed out that the present willingness of Indian leaders and the Congress Party to remain within the Commonwealth represented a notable change of outlook on the part of Indian opinion. If India had now to leave the Commonwealth against her own wishes, two serious consequences would follow. It would be necessary to explain that India's secession was due to our insistence on allegiance to the Crown as the essential feature of the Commonwealth relationship, and in that case the Crown might itself become an issue in party controversy throughout the Commonwealth. Secondly, India might leave the Commonwealth in a mood of resentment which might lead her to concentrate on the creation of an Asiatic bloc pursuing policies independent of, and possibly hostile to, the Commonwealth. While it might be argued that the recent Delhi Conference on Indonesia had illustrated the existing tendency of the Government of India to pursue a wholly independent line in international affairs, it was fair to note that they had had good reasons for not inviting this country to participate in the Conference, and that the discussions and conclusions of the Conference had been studiously moderate.

(b) The Congress resolution in favour of India's continued association with the Commonwealth suggested that there might be some advantage in attempting to devise a form of relationship somewhat different from normal membership. Subsequent discussions with Pandit Nehru had, however, revealed that anything less than full membership would not be acceptable to Indian opinion. In any event, it would be difficult to devise a form of associate membership which could be effectively distinguished from full membership.

(c) It was suggested that it might be possible to expand the formula in paragraph 4 of C.R. (49) 2 to embody the conception of allegiance to a community sharing common ideals and purposes. It was pointed out, however, that any proposal for the inclusion of a positive statement of purpose in the suggested formula was open to the objection that each Commonwealth country necessarily had its own point of view on these matters, and that great difficulty would therefore be found in securing general agreement to any effective definition of the basic principles of the Commonwealth. For that reason the preponderant emphasis in the formula of paragraph 4 of C.R. (49) 2 was on the conception of historical development and continuity.

(d) It was suggested that sub-paragraph (iv) of the re-definition of the Commonwealth relationship in paragraph 4 of C.R. (49) 2 might be modified to read: "freely associated as members of *a* Commonwealth and united . . .". It was pointed out, however, that this would imply a breach in the historical continuity of the Commonwealth and acceptance of the idea of a wholly new and different Commonwealth. Such a Commonwealth would moreover be a very nebulous conception; and it would certainly not be acceptable, for instance, to Australian opinion.

(e) A decision must now be reached whether the future Commonwealth should be large and loosely knit, or smaller and more closely knit; and the choice would have to depend on the consensus of opinion in the English-speaking Commonwealth countries. But a decision in favour of the larger Commonwealth might result in the development of two forms of Commonwealth association: those countries which still owed allegiance to the Crown might maintain a closer and more intimate relationship with each other than with those which had repudiated the Crown. Against this, it was argued that insistence on allegiance to the Crown as the essential and central feature of the Commonwealth relationship might result in so drastic a contraction of the Commonwealth as fatally to weaken its influence and standing in international affairs.

(f) The United Kingdom Government had never subscribed to the doctrine of the divisible Crown; and it was hard to see how this theory could be reconciled with the conception of common allegiance. Even as late as the Toronto Conference of 1933, the view expressed on behalf of the United Kingdom was that, in international affairs, the Commonwealth must be regarded as a single unit. On the other hand, it was pointed out that, whatever the theoretical basis for their attitude, Commonwealth Governments had long maintained that they had the right to choose neutrality in the event of war, whether or not the United Kingdom or any other part of the Commonwealth was engaged in it; and they would certainly not now accept the idea that the Commonwealth should be regarded as a single unit in relation to foreign States.

The general conclusion reached by Ministers was that it was necessary to explore, in consultation with other Commonwealth Governments, the possibility of enabling republican countries to remain within the Commonwealth on the lines discussed in C.R. (49) 2. It was not necessary, or possible, to reach final decisions at that stage; and discussion turned next on the procedure and time-table for such consultations. It had already been agreed that issues of such importance ought to be discussed at a full Conference of Commonwealth Governments; and, on the assumption that the most convenient time for such a Conference would be the latter part of April or early May, very little time remained to complete the detailed examination of the various aspects of the problem and to hold the necessary preliminary consultations, both in this country and with Commonwealth Governments. The Prime Minister undertook to consider at what stage it would be appropriate to consult The King and the leaders of other political parties at Westminster. The arrangements to be made for preliminary discussions with Commonwealth Governments would need careful consideration. The difficult and delicate nature of the issues involved rendered it difficult, and even dangerous, to conduct these preliminary consultations by correspondence, and Ministers thought that the best procedure might be for the Prime Minister to send personal emissaries to explain the problem in detail to the Prime Ministers concerned. It was suggested that, as in the case of Eire, such consultations should in the first instance be restricted to the Governments of Canada, Australia and New Zealand, but it was pointed out that the adoption of this procedure might give serious offence to South Africa. South Africa possessed, not only a large Indian population, but a large loyalist population, closely interested in this problem; and a very unfortunate impression would be created if she learned of her exclusion from the initial consultations, particularly if this implied that she was to be accorded the same treatment as Pakistan and Ceylon. It was agreed that officials should examine further the question of the procedure and time-table for the preliminary consultations with Commonwealth Governments, and should submit detailed proposals to the Prime Minister.

The Prime Minister recalled that, at their meeting on the previous day, the Committee had been advised that, if India were allowed to remain within the Commonwealth after severing her allegiance to the Crown, it would not be possible to maintain against a challenge in an international court the theory that India was not "foreign" to the other Commonwealth countries. He thought that it would be convenient if the Lord Chancellor and the Law Officers, in consultation with the President of the Board of Trade, could circulate a paper:—

(i) showing by which countries such a claim might be made, under the

most-favoured-nation clause of a commercial treaty, and what were the chances that any of those countries would take the matter to the International Court;
(ii) indicating whether such a challenge could be averted (e.g. by re-negotiating the commercial treaties involved) and, if so, at what probable cost;
(iii) assessing the value of the arguments which might be used in resisting such a challenge if it were made; and
(iv) stating the consequences which would follow if such a challenge were successfully made.

He considered that it would also be convenient to provide those who were to undertake preliminary consultations with Commonwealth Governments with a document summarising the arguments for and against a development of the Commonwealth connection on the lines discussed in C.R. (49) 2, and he suggested that the Official Committee should be asked to draw up such a document. It was agreed that this document should include an appreciation of the probable effects of such a development on the dependent Colonial territories. Finally, he suggested that it would be advisable to appoint a special working party to prepare, for the use of Ministers in the forthcoming discussions with representatives of other Commonwealth Governments, an objective appreciation of the implications of India's remaining in, or going out of the Commonwealth; and he proposed that the terms of reference of the working party should be as follows:—

"to prepare, for the use of Ministers in forthcoming discussions with representatives of other Commonwealth Governments, an objective appreciation of the political, economic, financial and military implications involved in the assumptions (i) that India remained a member of the Commonwealth, though owing no allegiance to the Crown; or (ii) that India became a foreign State in a specially close treaty relationship with the United Kingdom and other Commonwealth countries; or (iii) that India became a foreign State with no such close treaty relationship."

The Committee:—
(1) Took note that the Prime Minister would consider further the arrangements to be made for preliminary consultations, both in this country and with Commonwealth Governments, on the question whether a republican country should be permitted to remain within the Commonwealth.
(2) Invited the Lord Chancellor and the Law Officers, in consultation with the President of the Board of Trade, to circulate a paper examining, on the lines suggested in discussion, the probable implication, under the most-favoured-nation clauses of United Kingdom commercial treaties, of a decision to allow India to remain in the Commonwealth after severing her allegiance to the Crown.
(3) Invited the Official Committee to prepare, in a form suitable for communication to Commonwealth Governments, a statement of the arguments for and against a development of the Commonwealth connection on the lines discussed in C.R. (49) 2.
(4) Took note that the Prime Minister would arrange for a working party of officials to prepare, for the use of Ministers in the forthcoming discussions with Commonwealth Governments, an objective appreciation of the political, economic, financial and military implications of India's remaining in, or leaving, the Commonwealth.

400 DEFE 4/20, COS 31(49)1 21 Feb 1949

'Military implications of India's possible future status': COS Committee minutes. *Annex*: report by JPS, 17 Feb (JP(49)17)

The Committee considered a report by the Joint Planning Staff examining the military implications of possible future relationships between India and the United Kingdom and Commonwealth as set out in the Terms of Reference for a Working Party appointed by the Ministerial Committee on Commonwealth Relationship.

Sir Norman Brook said that although great efforts had been made during the past eighteen months to persuade India to remain within the Commonwealth, it now seemed possible that she was unlikely to do so if it required her to continue allegiance to the Crown. Her desire to remain in the Commonwealth, without this link however, seemed to have become stronger than was at one time thought possible. It was probable, therefore, that the Commonwealth would shortly have to face a difficult political decision on whether India as a republic could remain within the Commonwealth.

It was likely that India would make a final decision on her future status in July, 1949 and time was therefore short. It was being proposed, therefore, that a Commonwealth Conference should be held sometime in May to examine the whole problem. A Working Party had accordingly been set up by the Ministerial Committee on Commonwealth Relationship to prepare a paper on the implications to the Commonwealth of the three alternate [sic] hypotheses.

It was proposed that the military Appreciation, when approved by the Chiefs of Staff, should be attached at Annex to the paper to be submitted to Ministers. This paper was being prepared in a form suitable for presentation to the four old Dominions, and it appeared unlikely that whatever its form it would be suitable for Pakistan or Ceylon.

Sir John Edelsten[1] said that from the strategic point of view the status of India, provided she was friendly to the United Kingdom and to Pakistan, was of little concern. If India was unfriendly to the United Kingdom or to Pakistan, then the strategic position would become difficult. In his opinion, however, since India was economically dependent on the United Kingdom at the present time, he could not see how she could afford to become unfriendly towards us. He could not see, moreover, how if India turned against the Western Powers, she could expect to obtain either economic or military assistance from Russia.

The idea of an Asiatic Pact in which India would take a leading part would be advantageous to us from the military point of view, provided she was friendly to us. If, as was stated, India aimed at being the leading nation in South East Asia, then it was only reasonable to suppose that she would endeavour to maintain her friendly relations with the Commonwealth. In this event he thought that the possibility of India turning to Russia was over-emphasised in paragraph 13 (d). He suggested that the last sentence of this sub-paragraph should read "In fact there is a possibility that India might drift towards Russia".

General Scoones[2] said that if India left the Commonwealth and was not in close

---

[1] Vice-chief of naval staff (chairman of this meeting).

[2] Gen Sir Geoffrey Allen Percival Scoones, principal staff officer, India Office, 1947, CRO, 1948–1953.

treaty relationship with us, and Pakistan remained in, relations with Pakistan might worsen. Pakistan might then become a commitment.

It was visualised in the report by the Joint Planning Staff that India and Pakistan would co-operate with each other and that this co-operation was essential to the defence of the Indian Sub-Continent. This assumption might be unreal except as a long term policy. The Kashmir problem, apart from other problems, remained unsolved, and he believed that even if faced with aggression at the present time, the two countries might not collaborate.

He drew attention to paragraph 7 of the report in which it was stated that India might well, until such time as she could defend herself, adopt an attitude unlikely to provoke Russia into attacking her. If this was so, then he could not see that the requirements set out in paragraph 8 (a) would be available to us since these requirements might well lead to provocation.

In discussion it was generally agreed that the report under consideration, as amended by the Vice Chief of the Naval Staff, presented a sound appreciation of the military implications of India's possible future political status. In particular, the importance of India's influence in South East Asia as a bulwark against Communism, as set out in paragraph 9 should be emphasised.

The Committee:—

Approved the report by the Joint Planning Staff, as amended, and instructed the Secretary of circulate it over their signatures for use by the Working Party on Commonwealth Relations.

Annex to 400

We examine below the military implications of three possibilities regarding the future status of India. These are:—

(a) that India remains a member of the Commonwealth, though owing no allegiance to the Crown: or

(b) that India becomes a foreign state in a specially close treaty relationship with the United Kingdom and other Commonwealth countries: or

(c) that India becomes a foreign state with no such close treaty relationship.

2. From the military point of view the prime necessity is that we should have the friendly co-operation of India in both peace and war. This is obviously more likely to be the case under alternatives (a) and (b) above than under (c).

Pakistan

3. Militarily it is necessary that India and Pakistan should have a common policy for defence against external aggression. The relationship between India and the United Kingdom cannot therefore be considered in isolation. We believe that, irrespective of the policy pursued by India, Pakistan will continue as a member of the Commonwealth, and we have based our paper on this assumption.

Strategic importance of India in war

4. The strategic value of India and Pakistan taken together is:—

(a) India possesses large potential resources of all kinds including manpower and industry, and is thus the only area in South-East Asia capable of supporting a major military effort.

(b) Bases in India and Pakistan dominate sea and air communications in the Indian Ocean.

(c) Pakistan and India could provide strategic air bases for attacking Russia.

Even if India and Pakistan are both friendly to us, we cannot hope to make full use of the above unless they are prepared to afford each other mutual support.

Role in war

5. Should the Soviet Union attack India or Pakistan, the attack would be of purely preventive nature. Such an attack would therefore be unlikely unless the Soviet Union were convinced of the Anglo-American intentions of using air bases in India or Pakistan. Owing to the logistic difficulties of land attack every form of pressure will be used to prevent the use of bases there by the Anglo-American powers. Should these measures prove unsuccessful, military attacks on India or Pakistan would probably be limited to air attacks. These attacks would necessarily have to be delivered by the Soviet long-range air force at the expense of high priority air operations in other campaigns. Both India and Pakistan would need considerable assistance to meet this threat.

6. It is obvious that the Allies' requirements would best be met by a strong India in full co-operation with Pakistan as an active ally providing not only the necessary forces for her own defence but making a contribution outside India. Under these conditions we could make use of the Pakistan and Indian air bases for our strategic air offensive.

7. We do not believe, however, that the Allies will, even by 1957, be able to make any significant contribution to help India in her defence. This fact is certain profoundly to affect India's defence policy, and may well—until such time as she herself raises adequate forces to meet the external threat—cause her to adopt an attitude in war which she appreciates is unlikely to provoke Russia into attacking her. For instance, under present circumstances we believe it unrealistic to assume that she will permit us to use bases for the strategic air offensive, as this must inevitably force the Russians to take preventive action, nor would she contribute any forces outside India. We believe, however, that she may grant us the facilities set out below.

Our requirements in war

8. Our requirements are that India should grant us the following facilities even though she is not actively engaged in hostilities against Russia:—

(a) She should make available to our war economy her resources in manpower, industry and raw materials.

(b) She should grant us air transit facilities for military aircraft and the right to operate maritime aircraft from the Andamans, Nicobars and Laccadives.

(c) She should grant us fuelling and repair facilities for warships.

(d) She should allow us transit facilities for Gurkhas.

Our requirements in peace

9. Since India is the most powerful nation in South-East Asia, her effective

resistance to the spread of communism in her own territory and the lead she can give to other countries in South-East Asia will be a major factor in resisting the spread of communism, following on recent developments in China.

We should also afford India such military assistance as we can to sustain her resistance to communism.

10. Further requirements in peace are:—

(a) India, in co-operation with Pakistan, should develop her defences, particularly her air forces, so as to ensure the integrity of the Indian sub-continent.
(b) We wish to retain our transit rights and staging facilities for military aircraft.
(c) India should develop and maintain to the greatest possible extent her industrial capacity, port, transport, airfield and communication facilities.

Military implications of future possible relationships with India

11. Our requirements can only be obtained if India will co-operate in peace and in war with the Commonwealth, especially Pakistan. This co-operation is most likely to be attained if India remains in the Commonwealth, or is bound to us by a satisfactory treaty.

12. The position of India as a foreign country without close treaty relationship with the Commonwealth suggests that India would consider that her interests were not in harmony with those of the Commonwealth, or indeed with those of the Western Powers. India cannot develop or maintain her present industrial and war potential without external assistance. It would, therefore, be difficult for her to maintain an independent neutrality and she might tend to align herself with Russia and Russian satellites.

If this premise is correct the implications would be:—

(a) We should obtain none of our strategic requirements in India in either peace or war.
(b) India's relations with Pakistan, assuming the latter remains within the Commonwealth, might well worsen, thus weakening the combined defence of the sub-continent. Pakistan's position as a member of the Commonwealth would therefore be gravely threatened.

Conclusions

13. We conclude that:—

(a) Our strategic requirements in India cannot be considered in isolation from those in Pakistan. They remain the same whatever the final relationship between India and the Commonwealth may be and are as set out in paragraphs 8, 9 and 10 above.
(b) Our strategic requirements cannot be met unless India is friendly both to the Commonwealth as a whole and to Pakistan.
(c) The best way of ensuring this is for India to remain a member of the Commonwealth; failing this she must enter into close treaty relations with the United Kingdom and other Commonwealth countries.
(d) It is unlikely that our requirements would be met if India became a foreign state with no close treaty relationship. In fact there is a danger that India might drift towards Russia.[3]

[3] Report signed by: G P D Blacker, D Macfadyen, A R Pedder.

401 CAB 128/15, CM 17(49)2 3 Mar 1949

'Commonwealth relations: constitutional developments in India': Cabinet conclusions on policy regarding future relationship[1]

The Prime Minister made a report to the Cabinet on the recent course of the discussions on India's future relations with the Commonwealth.

When the Cabinet had last discussed this matter on 12th November, 1948,[1] the position had been reached that Pandit Nehru's "Ten-Point" memorandum had been found by the Law Officers to afford, from the strictly legal point of view, an insufficient basis for India's continued membership of the Commonwealth, and the Cabinet had agreed that the substance of the Law Officers' Opinion should be communicated to Pandit Nehru and to the Prime Ministers of Canada, Australia and New Zealand. Since then Pandit Nehru had sent a further "Eight-Point" memorandum, which provided, if anything, even less in the way of a connection with the Crown; and talks with Ministerial representatives of Canada, Australia and New Zealand had shown that there was general agreement that this memorandum could not be regarded as a sufficient basis for India's full membership of the Commonwealth. Pandit Nehru was so informed, but was told that the United Kingdom and other Commonwealth Governments welcomed India's desire to remain in association with the Commonwealth and were considering what form of special association could be devised. Opposition leaders were informed at that stage of the position which the negotiations had reached.[2]

Since then there had been no direct reply from Pandit Nehru, but indirectly it had been learned that India would not be satisfied with any form of association which implied a two-tier Commonwealth and fell short of full membership. India desired either to be in the Commonwealth or out of it, and was not prepared to accept any intermediate position in which her constitutional status would be inferior to that of Pakistan or Ceylon.

It thus appeared that India was not likely to be willing to accept any substantial link through the Crown, but would still desire to remain within the Commonwealth. If that situation arose, Commonwealth Governments would be faced with the question whether the constitutional basis of the Commonwealth connection should be so adapted as to enable the Commonwealth to include a republican country which owed no allegiance to the Crown. This was not a question which could be decided by the United Kingdom Government alone. It was clearly one on which all the Commonwealth Governments must, if possible, reach a common view. It was, therefore, proposed that a special meeting of Commonwealth Prime Ministers should be held at the end of April or the beginning of May to discuss the situation. It was not an easy time to arrange a conference, since General Elections were impending in Canada, Australia and New Zealand, but present indications were that it would be practicable to hold a meeting in London then, at which all the Commonwealth Governments would be represented and most of them would be represented by their Prime Ministers. In preparation for that meeting personal emissaries were being sent in the following week to the Commonwealth capitals to explain to the other Prime

---

[1] Previous reference: see 391.

[2] See 394.

Ministers the position reached in the discussions here and the various considerations which, in the opinion of United Kingdom Ministers, must be taken into account in reaching a decision. Lord Listowel was going to Australia and New Zealand; Mr. Gordon Walker to Pakistan and Ceylon and subsequently to India; Sir Percivale Liesching to South Africa and Sir Norman Brook to Canada.

The Cabinet need not at this stage take any final decision on the question whether the constitutional nature of the Commonwealth should be so adapted as to enable it to include a republican India. United Kingdom Ministers should reserve their final view on this until they had heard the opinions which would be expressed by other Commonwealth Prime Ministers at the forthcoming conference, including their views on the probable reaction of public opinion in the various Commonwealth countries. He would, however, be glad if he could have the general endorsement of his colleagues to the view that the political advantages of retaining India within the Commonwealth were so great that Commonwealth countries would, if it proved necessary for that purpose, be justified in making some concessions from their traditional point of view about the Commonwealth connection, and taking some risks, with a view to keeping India with them. The threat of Communist encroachment in South-East Asia was very real and, from the political angle as well as from the strategic and economic angles, there were very great advantages in retaining India within the Commonwealth. At the same time, he did not wish to underestimate the difficulty of devising an adequate link if India ceased to owe allegiance to the Crown. Wise statesmanship would be required if a satisfactory solution was to be found.

The King had been fully informed of the progress of the discussions and of the steps which were now proposed. The Opposition leaders had also been informed in confidence.

In discussion there was full support for the policy which the Prime Minister had outlined. It was recognised that on political, strategic and economic grounds it was important that India should be retained within the Commonwealth. There was general agreement that if in the last resort the choice were found to be between allowing India to leave the Commonwealth or adapting the constitutional basis of the Commonwealth in such a way as to enable a republican India to remain within it, every endeavour should be made to devise a satisfactory link which would retain India within the Commonwealth. Although the Crown had been the bond of unity in the Commonwealth, it would be a disservice to the Crown if Commonwealth Ministers allowed a position to develop in which the Crown was made to appear a stumbling-block to the continued cohesion of the Commonwealth. At the same time Ministers were impressed by the advantages of India's preserving some links with the other Commonwealth countries through the Crown. The development of the Communist threat in South-East Asia, the lesson of Burma, the general world situation and a growing feeling of goodwill towards this country were all factors which might operate to induce India to make some concessions for the sake of continued association in the Commonwealth. If, as seemed possible, the association of India with other Commonwealth countries grew closer as time went on, links with the Crown which might seem tenuous in present circumstances would grow stronger with the passage of time and with a growing desire to stress the bonds of unity. It was suggested in this connection that Commonwealth countries might be prepared to allow the Judicial Committee of the Privy Council to continue as the supreme court of appeal in certain classes of case.

The Cabinet:—

Endorsed the policy outlined by the Prime Minister for handling the question of India's future relations with the Commonwealth.

402 CAB 128/15, CM 18(49)3 8 Mar 1949

'Ireland: Ireland Bill': Cabinet conclusions, including discussion about partition[1]

The Cabinet considered a memorandum by the Prime Minister (C.P. (49) 47) on four points outstanding in connection with the Ireland Bill.

The Prime Minister said that, when the Cabinet had considered a provisional draft of this Bill on 12th January,[1] it had been assumed that the Republic of Ireland Act would be brought into operation on 21st January and that our consequential legislation would be introduced and passed, as a matter of urgency, as soon as Parliament reassembled after the Christmas Recess. In the event, however, the Eire Government had decided that their Act should not be brought into operation until Easter Monday, 18th April. It was important that no one should be given any pretext for representing that the United Kingdom Government had taken any initiative in the direction of thrusting Eire out of the Commonwealth; and he therefore proposed that the Ireland Bill should not be introduced until the Republic of Ireland Act had come into operation.

Since the Cabinet's discussion on 12th January other Commonwealth Governments had been consulted on the proposal that the Ireland Bill should include provision for changing the Royal Style and Titles by substituting "Northern Ireland" for "Ireland." All save Canada and Pakistan had concurred in this proposal and were prepared to promote corresponding legislation in their Parliaments. Both Canada and Pakistan had, however, raised difficulties; and, although they had been pressed to come into line with the other Governments, it was clear that neither would be prepared to promote legislation enabling this change to be made. In these circumstances, the Prime Minister recommended that no provision should be included in the Ireland Bill for a change in The King's title.

In pursuance of the Cabinet's decision of 12th January the Prime Minister had made a further attempt to persuade the Prime Minister of Northern Ireland to reduce the residential qualification for the Northern Ireland franchise, e.g., from seven to five years. The Northern Ireland Government were, however, satisfied that, for the reasons indicated in paragraph 8 of C.P. (49) 47, it would be politically impossible for them to put this proposal before their Parliament at the present time. There was a strong case on the merits for imposing a three months' residence qualification for the exercise of the Westminster franchise in Northern Ireland; and the Prime Minister proposed that provision should be made for this in the Ireland Bill, even though the Northern Ireland Government were unable to promise any reduction in the period of the residence qualification for the franchise for the Northern Ireland Parliament.

---

[1] See 397.

Finally, the Prime Minister said that the Northern Ireland Government had strongly urged that Eire should be described in the Ireland Bill as "the Irish Republic," rather than "the Republic of Ireland." The Prime Minister said that it did not seem possible to meet the wishes of the Northern Ireland Government on this point. He proposed that the Bill should formally recognise the title "Republic of Ireland" as the description which the Eire Government had themselves chosen; but the Bill could describe the 26 counties as "the part of Ireland hitherto known as Eire" and, in addition, an assurance could be given that in official usage the description "Irish Republic" would also be employed.

The Home Secretary and *the Secretary of State for Commonwealth Relations* endorsed the proposals put forward by the Prime Minister.

The Cabinet:—

(1) Agreed that the Ireland Bill should not be introduced until after the Easter Recess.

(2) Agreed that the Bill should not include any provision for a change in The King's title.

(3) Approved the proposal that the Bill should provide for a three months' residence qualification for the exercise of the Westminster franchise in Northern Ireland.

(4) Agreed that the Bill should formally recognise the title "Republic of Ireland" as the description of that part of Ireland hitherto known as Eire, although in official usage the description "Irish Republic" would also be employed.

Partition. The Cabinet next considered a memorandum by the Secretary of State for Commonwealth Relations (C.P. (49) 45) on the anti-partition campaign which was being fostered by the Eire Government, and a memorandum by the Home Secretary and the Secretary of State for Commonwealth Relations (C.P. (49) 48) on a suggestion made by the Prime Minister of Northern Ireland that the United Kingdom Government should lodge a protest against this campaign with the Eire Government and should make a public declaration condemning Eire's interference in the affairs of Northern Ireland.

The Home Secretary said that he doubted whether any useful purpose would be served by making a protest to the Eire Government about their anti-partition propaganda. The publication of the Ireland Bill and the statements which Ministers would make in support of it should be sufficient to reassure the people of Northern Ireland. He thought it would be inexpedient for the United Kingdom Government to seek to bring together at this stage representatives of the Governments of Northern Ireland and the Eire. *The Secretary of State for Commonwealth Relations* endorsed these views.

In discussion, there was general agreement that, in the debates on the Ireland Bill, the Government should take a clear and firm line in support of partition. Unless a firm line were taken, there was a serious danger than an effort would be made to embroil political parties in Great Britain in the partition issue. The conduct of the Eire Government was far from satisfactory, and it was right that the justifiable anxieties of the people of Northern Ireland should be allayed.

The Cabinet:—

(5) Agreed that the Government's attitude towards the anti-partition campaign of the Eire Government should be on the lines proposed in C.P. (49) 48.

403 CAB 128/15, CM 29(49)1 27 Apr 1949

'Commonwealth relations: constitutional developments in India': Cabinet conclusions on India's future relationship and recognition of the King as Head of the Commonwealth[1]

The Prime Minister made a report to the Cabinet on the course of the discussions at the Meeting of Commonwealth Prime Ministers which had been considering India's future relations with the Commonwealth. The discussions had shown that there was a general desire to find an acceptable basis for India's continuing association with the Commonwealth; but it had not been easy to secure common agreement on the constitutional issues involved. The representatives of all the Commonwealth Governments had in the end agreed to adopt the following declaration:—

> "The Governments of the United Kingdom, Canada, Australia, New Zealand, South Africa, India, Pakistan and Ceylon, whose countries are united as Members of the British Commonwealth of Nations and owe a common allegiance to the Crown, which is also the symbol of their free association, have considered the impending constitutional changes in India.
>
> "The Government of India have informed the other Governments of the Commonwealth of the intention of the Indian people that, under the new Constitution which is about to be adopted, India shall become a sovereign independent republic. The Government of India have, however, declared and affirmed India's desire to continue her full membership of the Commonwealth of Nations and her acceptance of The King as the symbol of the free association of its independent member nations and as such the Head of the Commonwealth.
>
> "The Governments of the other countries of the Commonwealth, the basis of whose membership of the Commonwealth is not hereby changed, accept and recognise India's continuing membership in accordance with the terms of this declaration.
>
> "Accordingly the United Kingdom, Canada, Australia, New Zealand, South Africa, India, Pakistan and Ceylon hereby declare that they remain united as free and equal members of the Commonwealth of Nations, freely co-operating in the pursuit of peace, liberty and progress."

The Prime Minister of South Africa had found difficulty in accepting the description of The King as "Head of the Commonwealth," since he feared that this might be misinterpreted as implying the existence of some sort of super-State. He had, however, subscribed to the declaration on condition that it was placed on record, in the minutes of the Meeting, that the designation of The King as "Head of the Commonwealth" did not connote any change in the constitutional relations existing between the members of the Commonwealth and, in particular, did not imply that The King discharged any constitutional function by virtue of that Headship.

The Prime Minister of Pakistan had at first hesitated to subscribe to that part of the declaration which affirmed that the basis of membership of countries other than India was not changed by this declaration. He had made it a condition of his

---

[1] Previous reference: see 401.

agreement that it should be placed on record, in the minutes of the Meeting, that if another member of the Commonwealth wished to continue her membership under conditions identical with those which had been accepted in respect of India, it could be logically assumed (though it was not possible to bind future Meetings or Governments) that a future Meeting would accord the same treatment to any other member as had been accorded to India by the present Meeting. It had at one time been feared that, if India were allowed to remain within the Commonwealth as a republic, Pakistan would also adopt a republican form of constitution. It now seemed possible that it would be sufficient for the Pakistan Government to be able to say that it was open to Pakistan, if she wished, to become a republic and remain within the Commonwealth. If they could say that, it might not be necessary for them to take any steps towards adopting a republican form of government.

In addition to the public declaration which was to be made, the Meeting had also agreed to place it on record that (i) all Commonwealth countries would continue to regard themselves as not foreign in relation to one another; and (ii) each Commonwealth Government would take any necessary steps, whether by legislation or otherwise, to enable it to maintain the right to accord preferential treatment to the citizens and trade of other Commonwealth countries, though each Government would remain free to determine the extent of that preferential treatment and the precise method of according it.

In discussion the following were raised:—

(a) It was unfortunate that the declaration made no reference to the important question whether India would stand at the side of other Commonwealth countries in peace and in war. The concluding words of the declaration might even be thought to throw some doubt on the question of India's co-operation in time of war.

In reply it was pointed out that these words were taken from the report of the Balfour Committee which formed part of the report of the proceedings of the Imperial Conference of 1926. There was no reason to doubt the sincerity of India's desire to co-operate with other Commonwealth countries. It would not have been possible, however, to ask her to enter into formal commitments for mutual co-operation in defence of a kind which none of the older Commonwealth countries had ever been willing to accept.

(b) India would, however, continue to be included within the scheme for Commonwealth co-operation in defence, as described in Part V of the White Paper on the Central Organisation for Defence (Cmd. 6923 of 1946). This contemplated regional or bilateral arrangements between Commonwealth Governments on defence questions. It would be necessary that bilateral negotiations should take place between the United Kingdom Government and the Government of India. The agreement now reached on the constitutional issue would, however, create a favourable atmosphere for the conduct of those negotiations.

(c) In view of India's recognition of The King as Head of the Commonwealth, would The King have any functions in relation to India? In reply, it was stated that The King would not be Head of the Indian Republic. India would, however, recognise The King as the symbol of the Commonwealth association, to which she adhered. For the present, the King would have no constitutional functions as Head of the Commonwealth. But it might well be that, by the process of evolution which had characterised the development of the Commonwealth, new functions might at some stage become exercisable by the Crown in that capacity. This recognition by India might be at least the foundation on which some new constitutional structure might, as time went on, be built.

(d) *The Attorney-General* said that, from the legal point of view, there was little content in the conception of the Crown as the symbol of the association of the Commonwealth peoples, once the element of common allegiance had been removed. If the constitutional basis of India's membership of the Commonwealth were challenged before the International Court, it was by no means certain that the position could be successfully upheld.

(e) A communiqué announcing the conclusions reached at the Meeting of Commonwealth Prime Ministers was to be released for publication in the Press on the morning of 28th April. There would be simultaneous publication in all Commonwealth capitals. This was not an occasion on which the announcement ought first to be made to Parliament. It seemed likely, however, that the Opposition would ask for an opportunity to debate the subject matter of the announcement; and the Lord President should be able to give some indication, in reply to the questions which were likely to arise on his Statement on Business on the following day, of the date on which a debate might be held.

The Cabinet:—

Approved the terms of the declaration, set out above, to be made by the United Kingdom Government jointly with other Commonwealth Governments regarding India's future relations with the Commonwealth.

404 CO 537/5202, no 26 17 Apr 1950

[Nationality of Indians in the colonies]: CO circular despatch on the citizenship clauses of the Indian constitution (1949). *Annex*

[The position set out in this despatch was as important for what it did not contain as for what it did. To the relief of the Colonial Office no substantial alterations were made in the position of Indian citizens overseas as a result of Indian independence. Previously, the great worry of the Colonial Office was that dual nationality might have been established; a circular despatch of 28 Nov 1947 had explained the difficulties and complications which would result from Indian subjects being able to appeal to Delhi. If Indians were given the option of British nationality a very large alien population might be created; in Mauritius with an Indian majority it was feared that this might have had serious consequences.]

I have the honour to transmit to you a copy of the India (Consequential Provision) Act, 1949, and a copy of the citizenship provisions of the new Indian Constitution, which came into operation on 26th January. The citizenship provisions of the Constitution do not constitute a complete citizenship law and it will be seen from Article 11 that further legislation by the Indian Parliament is contemplated.

2. Under its new constitution India was to become a Republic (and therefore ceased to be part of His Majesty's dominions) while remaining within the British Commonwealth. The India (Consequential Provision) Act, 1949, was passed to avoid any change in the legal position under United Kingdom law of India or of Indians, whether in regard to their rights, their liabilities, or their property until such time as it may have been decided, in the light of the then Constitution of India, and any additional relevant legislation which may be enacted there, that changes are necessary. India will, for example, still be counted a part of His Majesty's dominions

for the purpose of Acts of Parliament passed before 26th January, 1950, subject to any alteration which may be made by Order in Council under Section 1(3) of the Act. Citizens of India will be in the eyes of United Kingdom law British subjects, both as regards rights and duties. It follows that, for example, provisions in Constitutional instruments requiring voters or elected members of the Legislative Council to be British subjects, will not exclude Indian citizens from voting or from membership. It will however be convenient, and in accordance with the wishes of the Indian Government, that Indian citizens should not be referred to as British subjects, whether in future legislation or otherwise. The manner of effecting this in United Kingdom legislation is at present under consideration. It may be possible to make use of the alternative description "Commonwealth citizens" (see section 1 (2) of the British Nationality Act, 1948). The rules established by the Act extend to colonies, protectorates, and trust territories, but can be varied if necessary by the legislature, and they do not of course apply to legislation passed after India became a Republic on 26th January. When the Indian Parliament passes a citizenship law it may be necessary to introduce further legislation in this country in order to amend the British Nationality Act, 1948.

3. The important article of the citizenship provisions in the Indian constitution from the point of view of the Colonies is that numbered 8 which provides for the local registration of certain persons of Indian origin who thereupon are deemed to be citizens of India. Persons already citizens of the United Kingdom and Colonies who became Indian citizens under the new constitution will have dual citizenship. Those residing in a Colonial dependency will, owing to the operation of the master nationality rule, be unable to claim the intervention or protection of India.

4. The question whether Indian Government representatives in Colonial territories are entitled to canvass for the registration as Indian citizens or Indians domiciled in those territories is at present under active consideration by His Majesty's Government in the United Kingdom and the other Governments of the Commonwealth, and I hope it will soon be possible to inform you of the decisions which have been reached. In the meantime His Majesty's Government is in communication with the Government of India regarding the elucidation of certain nationality questions outstanding between the two Governments. These are largely, but not wholly, confined to the position of British subjects of European extraction living in India, but you will be kept informed of any developments which may affect Colonial territories.

Annex to 404: The Gazette of India Extraordinary, 26 November 1949: Part II: Citizenship

5. At the commencement of this Constitution, every person who has his domicile in the territory of India and—

(a) who was born in the territory of India; or
(b) either of whose parents was born in the territory of India; or
(c) who has been ordinarily resident in the territory of India for not less than five years immediately preceding such commencement,

shall be a citizen of India.

6. Notwithstanding anything in article 5, a person who has migrated to the territory of India from the territory now included in Pakistan shall be deemed to be a citizen of India at the commencement of the Constitution if—

(a) he or either of his parents or any of his grand-parents was born in India as defined in the Government of India Act, 1935 (as originally enacted); and

(b) (i) in the case where such person has so migrated before the nineteenth day of July, 1948, he has been ordinarily resident in the territory of India since the day of his migration, or

(ii) in the case where such person has so migrated on or after the nineteenth day of July, 1948, he has been registered as a citizen of India by an officer appointed in that behalf by the Government of the Dominion of India on an application made by him therefor to such officer before the commencement of this Constitution in the form and manner prescribed by that Government:

Provided that no person shall be so registered unless he has been resident in the territory of India for at least six months immediately preceding the date of his application.

7. Notwithstanding anything in articles 5 and 6, a person who has after the first day of March, 1947, migrated from the territory of India to the territory now included in Pakistan shall not be deemed to be a citizen of India:

Provided that nothing in this article shall apply to a person who, after having so migrated to the territory now included in Pakistan, has returned to the territory of India under a permit for resettlement or permanent return issued by or under the authority of any law and every such person shall for the purposes of clause (b) of article 6 be deemed to have migrated to the territory of India after the nineteenth day of July, 1948.

8. Notwithstanding anything in article 5, any person who or either of whose parents or any of whose grand-parents was born in India as defined in the Government of India Act, 1935 (as originally enacted), and who is ordinarily residing in any country outside India as so defined shall be deemed to be a citizen of India if he has been registered as a citizen of India by the diplomatic or consular representative of India in the country where he is for the time being residing on an application made by him therefor to such diplomatic or consular representative, whether before or after the commencement of this Constitution, in the form and manner prescribed by the Government of the Dominion of India or the Government of India.

9. No person shall be a citizen of India by virtue of article 5, or be deemed to be a citizen of India by virtue of article 6 or article 8, if he has voluntarily acquired the citizenship of any foreign State.

10. Every person who is or is deemed to be a citizen of India under any of the foregoing provisions of this Part shall, subject to the provisions of any law that may be made by Parliament, continue to be such citizen.

11. Nothing in the foregoing provisions of this Part shall derogate from the power of Parliament to make any provision with respect to the acquisition and termination of citizenship and all other matter[s] relating to citizenship.

405 CAB 134/55, CA 8(48)2 & 3 29 Oct 1948

'Constitutional reform in Gibraltar; constitutional development in smaller colonial territories': Cabinet Commonwealth Affairs Committee minutes

The Committee considered a memorandum by the Secretary of State for the Colonies (C.A. (48) 18) on the question of constitutional reform in Gibraltar.

The memorandum recalled that, when the detailed proposals set out in C.A. (48) 14 were considered by the Committee on 26th July, the general view of Ministers was that the area and population of Gibraltar were too small to justify the establishment of a Legislative Council in addition to the existing City Council; and the Secretary of State had been asked to consider whether it would not be possible to set up a single body with both legislative and municipal functions. The Minister of State for Colonial Affairs had since visited Gibraltar and had found that local opinion was unanimously opposed to any modification of the constitution or powers of the existing City Council. There was general agreement in Gibraltar that the powers and responsibilities of the central government and the municipality respectively were clearly defined and separated, and that there were no grounds for fearing that there would be political friction between the City Council and an elected legislature. The point had also been made that the municipality could be granted a degree of autonomy which, in a Fortress, could not be extended to the Legislative Council. If the two bodies were merged, it was hard to see how these two principles could be reconciled in practice. In the light of these findings, the Secretary of State sought approval for the proposals in C.A. (48) 14, subject to the modification that there should be a single electorate for the legislature and City Council. These proposals were fully supported by the Governor.

The Prime Minister said that he still felt very doubtful whether the establishment of two elected authorities in so small a community as Gibraltar could be justified. In his view, insufficient attention had been given in the past to the form of government that was most appropriate for the smaller colonial territories. United Kingdom models might not always be the most suitable, and it was not necessarily right to reproduce in these communities the full paraphernalia of representative bodies and administration appropriate to much larger territories. The present position in Gibraltar illustrated the tendency towards a needless multiplication of authorities and officials in small Colonies, which threw an excessive burden of overhead expenses on their limited resources. It was difficult to see why it should be necessary in Gibraltar for both the central government and the municipality to maintain health and public works departments, and there was no indication that any attempt had been made to co-ordinate the functions of these departments with the technical services maintained by the three Fighting Services. As far as he could judge, the cost of administration and the establishment of staff was out of all proportion to the area and population of the Colony.

Ministers were in general agreement with the criticisms made by the Prime Minister. In their view, the case for the creation of two representative bodies, each supported by a separate administrative machine, had not been adequately made out and they would have had no doubt, if it had been possible to consider the question without reference to the promise made in 1945, that the right course would be to make a further attempt to establish a single representative body with both legislative and municipal functions. But a formal promise of an elective legislature had been made and, though it had not been specifically stated that this body would be additional to and separate from the City Council, it was apparently clear that it had been generally assumed that this would be the case. It was also felt that it would be difficult to reconcile in one body the restrictions imposed on the powers of a legislature with the wide measures of autonomy appropriate to a municipality. In these circumstances, the people of Gibraltar would no doubt regard as a breach of faith any further attempt to press for the establishment of a single representative body. It was therefore agreed that there was no alternative to acceptance of the proposals put forward by the Secretary of State, but Ministers considered that a further investigation ought to be made into the allocation of responsibilities between the central government and the municipality with a view to eliminating any overlapping or duplication of functions and to securing maximum economy in the costs of administration. For this purpose, the services of someone with wide administrative experience should be secured.

In discussion, the following further points were made:—

(a) It was intended to extend the franchise to United Kingdom members of the Armed Forces who had resided for a reasonable period in the Colony.

(b) The question was raised whether it might not be advisable for the unofficial members of the Legislative Council to be elected by the City Council and *The Secretary of State for the Colonies* undertook to examine this suggestion.

The Committee:—

(1) Approved the proposals contained in C.A. (48) 18.

(2) Invited the Secretary of State for the Colonies to arrange for an investigation to be carried out into the allocation of responsibilities between the Central Government and the City Council in Gibraltar with a view to securing the maximum economy in the costs of administration and eliminating any duplication of functions between these authorities.

(3) Invited the Secretary of State for the Colonies to circulate a paper showing the number of officials and the costs of administration of the Central Government and the City Council respectively.

3. *Constitutional development in smaller colonial territories*

The Prime Minister said that the discussion of the question of constitutional reform in Gibraltar, as recorded in the preceding minute, had thrown into relief the need for an enquiry into the appropriate form which constitutional development should take in the small Colonial territories. The ultimate constitutional objective for these Colonies had not been defined; and it had been too readily assumed that the parliamentary and administrative system suitable to large countries should be reproduced in miniature in the smallest Colonies. In consequence, authorities and officials were needlessly multiplied and unnecessary costs incurred. Had not the time come for the whole problem to be authoritatively examined by a Royal Commission or an expert Committee?

In discussion, it was pointed out that the appointment of a Royal Commission might arouse hopes and expectations which could not be fulfilled. But there was general agreement on the need for further consideration of this question, and *The*

Secretary of State for the Colonies undertook to circulate a paper as a basis for the Committee's discussion.

The Committee:—

(1) Invited the Secretary of State for the Colonies to consider the proposal that a special enquiry should be undertaken into the question of constitutional development in the smaller Colonial territories.

(2) Agreed to resume their discussion in the light of the paper to be circulated by the Secretary of State for the Colonies in accordance with (1) above.

406 CAB 134/56, CA 1(49) 19 Jan 1949

'Constitutional development in smaller colonial territories': Cabinet Commonwealth Affairs Committee minutes[1]

The Committee considered a memorandum by the Secretary of State for the Colonies (C.A. (48)19)[2] on the question of constitutional development in the smaller Colonial territories.

The Secretary of State for the Colonies recalled that, at their meeting on 29th October, the suggestion had been made that a special enquiry ought to be undertaken into the question of the ultimate constitutional objectives and the probable trend of political development in the smaller Colonial territories. He thought that Colonial territories fell into three categories: (i) those which were potentially capable of achieving full independence; (ii) those which could combine with others to form units capable of full independence; and (iii) those which came within neither of these categories. Substantial constitutional progress had been made over the whole Colonial field during the past decade; and in C.A. (48) 19 he had given some information about the parallel progress made in developing closer union between groups of territories. But his paper was mainly concerned with the third category; and in their case he thought that it would be valuable to carry out an enquiry on the lines suggested at the previous meeting. He proposed that this should be undertaken by a small working party of experts; and in paragraph 8 of his paper he had suggested the general lines of their terms of reference. It was essential that the enquiry should be strictly confidential, since there was otherwise a risk that it might provoke widespread speculation and even political agitation in the Colonies.

The Prime Minister said that there had hitherto been no comprehensive study of the constitutional problems of the smaller Colonial territories; concessions were made *ad hoc* in the light of local developments without relation to an accepted body of principles. In consequence, no attempt had been made to define authoritatively the ultimate constitutional objective towards which these territories were moving and there was a serious risk that our policy might be found, perhaps too late, to be ill-advised and misguided. For instance, he thought that it was too readily assumed that the Westminster Parliament must be accepted as the appropriate objective at which Colonial peoples should aim; but experience showed that a constitutional system which had grown up slowly in response to the needs of the people of this country was by no means necessarily suited to the political genius of peoples in other

---

[1] Previous reference: see 405.

[2] See annex to 407.

countries and of other races. He had always thought, for instance, that it would have been wiser in India to have followed the model of the United States rather than the British constitution; serious dangers for democratic government were involved in the enormous concentration of power resulting from an excessive centralisation of authority in an area so large as India. It was important that this sort of mistake should not be repeated in the Colonies, and that the local peoples should not be encouraged to regard every constitutional change as a step towards the uniform goal of a constitution on the Westminster model. He attached great importance to the proper development of local government as the foundation for further constitutional growth, and he thought that this aspect of the question ought to be brought out more explicitly in the terms of reference proposed for the enquiry. Finally, he was doubtful whether a body constituted as proposed in paragraph 9 of C.A. (48) 19 could appropriately be expected to undertake so extensive an investigation, or whether it would have either the experience or the authority to deal adequately with the broad political and constitutional issues involved. Its membership ought not to be restricted to persons with only official experience; it was important that some at least of its members should bring wholly fresh and unprejudiced minds to their task.

There was general support for the proposal that a comprehensive enquiry should be carried out into the question of constitutional development in the smaller Colonial territories. Our Colonial policy should reflect the general trend in international affairs towards closer association and co-operation between individual Sovereign States; and we should not encourage the natural separation of small Colonial communities by an exclusive pre-occupation with the constitutional objective of self-government within the Commonwealth. Our aim should not be to create a large number of small political entities, technically independent but, in reality, isolated and feeble; but to develop new principles and methods of association and integration.

In discussion, the following further points were made:—

(a) While it might be hoped that the proposed enquiry might establish certain general principles for further constitutional development in the smaller Colonies, it was not desirable to aim at uniformity in the practical arrangements adopted to meet the needs of each individual Colony. *Ad hoc* solutions would have to be found for their special problems.

(b) The problem of inspiring the peoples of small and isolated communities with a general sense of partnership in the Commonwealth could not be solved by constitutional and administrative devices alone; it was equally important that they should feel that they were not debarred from sharing in the educational facilities and opportunities for employment available to fellow-citizens in other parts of the Commonwealth. The recent appointment of a West Indian to a Professorship at a United Kingdom University had, for instance, given great encouragement to the people of the West Indies.[3] These aspects of the problem could be better examined by an independent University enquiry than by an official Committee.

(c) Certain of the smaller Colonial territories were of special importance for defence purposes, and it was important that the enquiry should take defence factors fully into account.

---

[3] Prof W Arthur Lewis, Stanley Jevons professor of political economy, University of Manchester, 1948–1958.

(d) The people of Malta and Gibraltar were anxious for closer integration with the United Kingdom, and the enquiry should cover this point. The proposal that these territories should have the right to send a representative to the Westminster Parliament ought at least to be examined.

(e) It was already an accepted principle that constitutional machinery should be related to local conditions and circumstances, and no attempt was made to impose a uniform pattern on the Colonies. In the African Colonies, for instance, there was a very wide variety of constitutional forms.

Discussion turned next on the manner in which the enquiry should be carried out. There was general agreement that a larger and more authoritative body was required than that suggested in C.A. (48) 19. On points of detail, it was suggested that a Foreign Office representative should be associated with the enquiry; and that the membership of an enlarged Committee should include someone with a wide knowledge of the Commonwealth. On the question of procedure, Ministers thought that, as it would ultimately be necessary for the members of the proposed Committee to visit individual Colonies, it would not be possible to maintain secrecy regarding its existence indefinitely; on the other hand, the first need was to ascertain the facts and to consult persons with expert and first-hand knowledge of the Colonies, and visits to the Colonies by members of the Committee need not take place for some time.

The Committee:—

(1) Endorsed the proposal that an enquiry should be carried out into the question of constitutional development in the smaller Colonial territories.

(2) Invited the Secretary of State for the Colonies to submit detailed proposals to the Cabinet regarding the constitution and terms of reference of a Committee to undertake this investigation, and the procedure which they should follow.

(3) Took note that the Secretary of State for the Colonies would consult with the Prime Minister on the membership of the proposed Committee.

407 CAB 129/33/2, CP(49)62 10 Mar 1949

'Constitutional development in smaller colonial territories': Cabinet memorandum by Mr Creech Jones. *Annex* A: memorandum by Mr Creech Jones for Cabinet Commonwealth Affairs Committee (CA(48)19), 8 Dec 1948; *Annex* B: list of territories

1. The annexed paper C.A. (48) 19 (Annex A) was considered by the Commonwealth Affairs Committee on 19th January (C.A. (49) 1st Meeting).[1] The Committee endorsed the proposal that an enquiry should be carried out into the question of constitutional development in the smaller Colonial territories and invited me to submit detailed proposals to the Cabinet regarding the constitution and terms of reference of a Committee to undertake this investigation and the procedure which they should follow.

2. The Commonwealth Affairs Committee noted that the Colonial territories fall into three main classes:—

(i) Those which are potentially capable of achieving responsible Government;

[1] See 406.

(ii) Those which can combine to form units capable of responsible Government; and

(iii) Those which fall into neither of the above categories.

3. In regard to category (ii), considerable progress (of which examples are given in paragraph 5 of the annexed paper) has been made in associating British Colonial territories together in geographical regions. That process continues. But in a number of small territories internal constitutional developments have gone forward *ad hoc*. While these developments have engaged the constant attention of the Colonial Governments concerned and the Colonial Office, the ultimate structure and status of these territories has not been the subject of an enquiry, nor has there been any comprehensive study of the constitutional problems or of such questions as whether developments have been based on right principles, whether political and legal institutions are growing up on the lines most suitable to the needs of the individual peoples, and how far genuine local government is being made the foundation for further constitutional growth.

4. I recommend that the terms of reference of the new Committee should be as follows:—

(i) To enquire into the present constitutional position of the smaller Colonial territories* and the probable trend of their future political development, and in particular,

(a) to examine the suitability of various modes of constitutional structure and to consider whether it is desirable or practicable to define the ultimate constitutional objective in the case of particular territories or to lay down any general principles on which policy should be based;

(b) to examine the relationship of individual territories towards each other and towards the United Kingdom and to consider how far, by strengthening these relationships or by other means, it may be possible to mitigate the parochialism and other handicaps to which small and isolated communities may be subject and to give the Colonial peoples a genuine sense of partnership in the Commonwealth;

(c) to consider how far the present political, legal and administrative structures within the territories make for healthy political growth, and for efficiency and economy in administration, and in particular whether by adopting simpler forms of Government (such as following the pattern of municipal or local Government rather than the Parliamentary model), or by other means, unnecessary extravagance may be avoided, higher standards of efficiency attained, or fusion or combination made easier.

(ii) To make recommendations in the light of these enquiries.

5. The Committee should consist of an unofficial Chairman, three of four persons of experience in political and constitutional matters, the Legal Adviser to the Colonial Office and Commonwealth Relations Office, and a senior administrative officer of the Colonial Office.

6. For the reasons given in paragraph 10 of the annexure, the enquiry should, at any rate for the time being, be conducted in the strictest confidence. I suggest that the Committee should be left to determine its own procedure, bearing in mind that secrecy, at least in the early stages, is essential and is desirable throughout. Visits to

* Listed in Annex B to this memorandum.

individual Colonies at a later stage may well be found necessary, but this should be considered in the light of the initial progress made with the enquiry and the situation in the particular territories at the time.

Annex A to 407

1. At their 8th Meeting the Committee invited me to consider, and to circulate a paper dealing with, a proposal that an enquiry should be undertaken into the question of constitutional development in the smaller Colonial territories.

2. The latest general statement of our constitutional objectives is as follows:—

> "The central purpose of British Colonial Policy is simple. It is to guide the Colonial territories to responsible self-government within the Commonwealth in conditions that ensure to the people concerned both a fair standard of living and freedom from oppression from any quarter." (Cmd. 7433, paragraph 3).

3. This statement embodies by implication the obvious truth that full independence can be achieved only if a territory is economically viable and capable of defending its own interests. In fact, Colonial territories can be placed in three classes:—

(1) Those which are potentially capable of achieving full independence;
(2) Those which can combine with others to form units capable of full independence;
(3) Those which fall into neither of the above categories.

4. This paper is concerned chiefly with the third class. But I should point out that constitutional progress has been going on over the whole colonial field at an ever quickening pace during the last decade. These internal developments have gone forward *ad hoc*, and their pace had depended upon social and political conditions in the individual territories and not upon extraneous considerations such as are involved when the question of granting "Dominion status" arises. Changes in the political institutions of a territory have sometimes followed on the recommendations of Commissions, but, broadly, the individual position of each territory has been under the constant review of the Governor and the Colonial Office. Considerable thought has also been given to the grouping of territories, but the ultimate constitutional status of certain of the smaller territories has not been the subject of any enquiry.

5. My colleagues will know that some consideration was given to the grouping of territories by the Coalition Government, and much progress has been made since then. The form which grouping takes has varied according to the circumstances of each case. The principal developments are:—

(a) *West African Council* (includes Nigeria, Gold Coast, Sierra Leone and Gambia). No executive powers, but it secures co-ordination for certain common services and regional problems (e.g., research, transport, security, &c.).
(b) *East Africa Commission* (includes Uganda, Kenya, Tanganyika). Executive power in respect of transport, research, economic regional development, &c.
(c) *Central Africa Council* (includes Southern Rhodesia, Northern Rhodesia, Nyasaland). Advisory council of representatives of these three Governments.

Develops certain common services and co-ordinates policy, e.g. labour, communications.

(d) *West Indian Development and Welfare Organisation*, for advising and stimulating British West Indian Governments. *The Caribbean Commission*, representative of United States, France, Holland and United Kingdom also exists for advisory services and achieves a degree of co-operation in the Caribbean. A movement towards *federation* of the British West Indian territories is being pursued as a result of the Montego Bay Conference last year.

(e) *South-East Asia* (North Borneo, Sarawak, Brunei, Singapore and Malaya). A central government for the Malay States, &c., has been achieved. A Commissioner-General in South-East Asia has been appointed.

(f) *South Pacific Commission* (includes Fiji, Western Pacific High Commission Territories and Kingdom of Tonga). A consultative and advisory body, comprising representatives of the Netherlands, France, United Kingdom, United States, Australia and New Zealand, in matters affecting the economic and social development of the territories concerned and the welfare and advancement of their peoples.

6. Of the Colonial territories as at present organised, it is hardly likely that full self-government will be achieved under any foreseeable conditions (apart from association with other territories) by any except Nigeria, the Gold Coast, and the Federation of Malaya with Singapore. There are also territories where our aim is to promote closer union or federation in order that units capable of independence may be built up: (a) South-East Asia, (b) Caribbean Colonies, (c) East and Central Africa Territories.

7. I refer now to the smaller Colonies.

(i) *In Africa*

(a) Gambia. Is part of the West African Council and in several services is associated with Sierra Leone.

(b) Somaliland. Has affinities with both Kenya and Aden.

(c) High Commissioner's Territories in South Africa (dealt with by the Commonwealth Relations Office).

(ii) *In Mediterranean*

(a) Malta. Enjoys internal responsibility.

(b) Cyprus. Constitution in abeyance.

(c) Gibraltar. New Constitution recently considered.

(iii) *In Indian Ocean*

(a) Aden
(b) Mauritius
(c) Seychelles } In each case minor constitutional changes have been made in recent years.

(d) Maldive Islands. A Sultanate under British protection (now under the Commonwealth Relations Office).

(e) (The Sultanate of Muscat (Oman) and the Sheikdoms of Kuwait and Bahrein ought perhaps to be included in this list. These are independent States to which British protection is afforded through the Foreign Office.)

(iv) *Atlantic Ocean*

(a) Bermuda and Bahamas. They have ancient Constitutions conferring fairly complete local government and are not likely to seek an alteration of status.
(b) St. Helena (with Ascension and Tristan da Cunha).
(c) Falkland Islands (and Dependencies).

(v) *Pacific Ocean*

(a) Hong Kong.
(b) Fiji. It is doubtful if Fiji should be included in this list. Administration is assisted on education and medical side by proximity of New Zealand.
(c) Western Pacific High Commission Territories (Gilbert and Ellice Islands, Solomon Islands, New Hebrides, Tonga, &c.). (In the New Hebrides there is an Anglo-French Condominium).

8. I agree that some enquiry should be made into the present situation of these smaller territories and the probable trend of their political development. Such enquiry could advise whether it is practicable or desirable to define the ultimate objective in the case of particular territories or to lay down any general principle on which policy should be based, to examine any practical steps which might be suggested for promoting healthy political progress, for mitigating the parochialism and other evils to which small and isolated communities are subject, and for giving the peoples of these territories a genuine sense of partnership in the Commonwealth. It should also take account of experiments in the way of amalgamation which have been tried in the past (e.g., Gambia and Sierra Leone, Mauritius and Seychelles), and seek to discover whether the reasons for the abandonment of these experiments hold good in modern conditions. It should consider the present political, legal and administrative structures, and whether by fusion or combination unnecessary waste may be avoided and a higher standard of efficiency attained.

9. I suggest that the enquiry should be conducted by a small working party of experts. Three should suffice: a Chairman from outside, with a legal Adviser to the Colonial and Commonwealth Relations Offices and a senior administrative officer of the Colonial Office as members.

10. I regard it as essential that the enquiry should be conducted on a strictly confidential basis and that the fact that it is taking place should not be published even in official circles. Any hint which might reach the Colonies that such an enquiry was proceeding could only raise undesirable speculations and lead to political agitation.

APPENDIX

Territory	*Population*	*Area sq. miles*	*Status*
Aden	731,000 mainly Arabs	112,080	Colony and Protectorate
Bahamas	80,600 (62,300 Africans, (12,900 Europeans, (5,400 other races)	4,375	Colony

British Somaliland	700,000 Somalis	68,000	Protectorate
Brunei	48,000 mainly Malays and Dyaks	2,226	Protected State
Cyprus	449,500 mainly Europeans	3,584	Colony
Falkland Islands excluding Dependencies	2,200 mainly British and Scandinavian	4,618	Colony
Fiji	259,600 (120,400 Indians, 118,100 Fijians, 4,600 Europeans, 16,500 other races)	7,083	Colony
Gambia	249,300 mainly Africans	4,132	Colony and Protectorate
Gibraltar	21,200 mainly Europeans	1⅞	Colony
Hong Kong	1,800,000 mainly Chinese	391	Colony
Mauritius	430,000 (270,900 Indians, 148,300 of European, African or mixed descent, 10,800 Chinese)	720	Colony
North Borneo	330,000 mainly Borneans	29,417	Colony
St. Helena including Ascension Is.	4,700 mainly Europeans	80	Colony
Sarawak	500,000 mainly Malays and Dyaks	50,000	Colony
Seychelles	34,600 mainly Europeans, some Africans, Indians, Chinese	156	Colony
Western Pacific High Commission Islands—			
British Solomon Islands	95,000 mainly Melanesians	11,500	Protectorate
Gilbert and Ellice Islands	35,300 mainly Micronesians	333	Colony
New Hebrides	45,000 mainly Melanesians	5,700	Anglo-French Condominium
Pitcairn Island	200 of European descent	2	
Tonga	44,400 mainly Tongans	250	Protected State

Annex B: List of smaller colonial territories to be covered by the enquiry

Seychelles
Mauritius

Aden
British Somaliland
Zanzibar

Cyprus
Malta
Gibraltar

Gambia
St. Helena (including Ascension Island and Tristan da Cunha)

Falkland Islands

Bahamas
Bermudas

Hong Kong

Fiji
Western Pacific High Commission Islands (Gilbert and Ellice Islands, British Solomon Islands, New Hebrides, Pitcairn and Tonga)

408 CAB 128/15, CM 21(49)5 21 Mar 1949

'Constitutional development in smaller colonial territories': Cabinet conclusions

The Cabinet considered a memorandum by the Secretary of State for the Colonies (C.P. (49) 62)[1] on the question of constitutional development in the smaller Colonial territories.

The Secretary of State for the Colonies said that recent discussions by the Commonwealth Affairs Committee had drawn attention to the fact that there had hitherto been no comprehensive study of the constitutional problems of the smaller Colonies; in the past developments had taken place on *ad hoc* decisions without relation to an accepted body of principles or to an agreed policy regarding their ultimate structure and status. The Committee had reached the conclusion that a committee ought to be appointed to make an exhaustive study of the whole field and to submit recommendations on which future policy could be based. In C.P. (49) 62, he had made detailed recommendations regarding the composition and terms of reference of this committee. It was essential that the enquiry, at least in its first stages, should be conducted in the strictest confidence.

There was general support for the proposal that a comprehensive enquiry should be carried out into the constitutional problems of the smaller Colonies. In further discussion the following points were made:—

(a) Political unrest in the Colonies was often caused by economic and social discontents. If these could be dealt with first, there would be less immediate pressure for constitutional advance, and firmer foundations could be laid for liberal and efficient self-government. It was agreed that, while the scope of the committee's enquiry ought not to be unduly enlarged, the terms of reference suggested in C.P. (49) 62 should be amended to ensure that they gave adequate attention to the economic and social background of political and constitutional change in the Colonies. And, in this connection, it was suggested that at least one of the members of the committee ought to be selected with special reference to this aspect of the problem.

(b) Some Ministers expressed anxiety lest a committee constituted on the lines suggested in paragraph 5 of C.P. (49) 62 might be unduly academic in outlook, with the result that adequate weight might not be given to the defence and other factors unavoidably limiting the pace and scope of constitutional progress in some of the smaller Colonies. Might it not be preferable to appoint an interdepartmental committee of officials to undertake this enquiry under the general supervision of a special Ministerial Committee? Against this, it was pointed out that it was important that the committee would bring a fresh and constructive point of view to the problems covered by their enquiry; this could best be ensured by appointing both officials and non-officials to serve on the committee. It was intended that some at least of the unofficial members should have administrative qualifications, including experience of local government. There was no reason to suppose that a committee thus constituted would fail to make a practical approach to its task.

(c) The Foreign Office did not wish to be represented on the committee, but steps

---

[1] See 407.

should be taken to ensure that it was kept in touch with the progress of the enquiry.

(d) It was suggested that it might be useful if the committee acquainted itself with the administrative and constitutional machinery of the Channel Islands.

The Cabinet:—

(1) Subject to the point recorded in paragraph (a) above, approved the recommendations made in C.P. (49) 62 for the appointment of a committee to enquire into the constitutional problems of the smaller Colonies.

(2) Invited Ministers to communicate to the Secretary of State for the Colonies any suggestions they might wish to make regarding the composition of the proposed committee, and took note that the Secretary of State for the Colonies would consult with the Prime Minister regarding the membership finally proposed.

409 DEFE 4/26, JP(49)144 19 Nov 1949

'Constitutional developments in the smaller colonial territories—defence aspects': report to COS by JPS (annex), for reply to the committee of inquiry

It is important that full account of their likely role in the event of war should be taken in plans for constitutional development in the Colonies. We discuss below the part that the Colonies as a whole should play in Commonwealth strategy and then consider in turn the defence role of each of the following smaller Colonies.

- Malta
- Gibraltar
- Cyprus
- Gambia
- Sierra Leone
- Zanzibar
- Somaliland Protectorate
- Aden
- Mauritius
- Seychelles
- St. Helena with Ascension Island and Tristan da Cunha
- Falkland Islands
- Bahamas
- Bermudas
- Hong Kong
- Fiji
- Western Pacific High Commission Territories:
  - British Solomon Islands Protectorate
  - Gilbert and Ellice Island Colony
  - New Hebrides
  - Pitcairn Island
  - Tonga

General considerations

2. The pre-war conception of Imperial Defence as it affected the Colonies was founded upon command of the sea and of the air over the sea, the exercise of which required a chain of firmly-held bases, and implied the ability to move reserves at will, and to deny to potential enemies the opportunity for launching and sustaining oversea expeditions. Assuming that the only likely future war would be against the Soviet Union, this conception still applies. Only a few Colonies would, however, be

within range of any serious external attack. The main threat to most of the Colonies both in peace and in war will be one of internal security.

Whilst in general the future strategic role of the Colonies will remain unaltered the granting of independence to India and Pakistan has increased the importance of colonial manpower in war.

3. *Internal security*. It is a matter of principle that Colonial territories should be responsible for their own internal security. Serious disorders may, however, involve heavy demands on Imperial manpower and resources, and His Majesty's Government has, therefore, a continuing interest in measures designed to safeguard internal security in all Colonial territories.

This factor will remain constant irrespective of the stage of constitutional development reached: it would be inappropriate to attempt any categorisation of the degree of supervision over internal security matters which would be exercised by His Majesty's Government. The internal security factor has not, therefore, been taken into account [in] assessing the degree of authority which should be retained in the smaller Colonial territories.

4. *External defence*. Due to the comparative inferiority of the Soviet Union at sea only those colonies which can be reached by land or are within range of Soviet air bases will be subject to an appreciable scale of attack. The threat against such colonies will vary with their distance from the Soviet bases and their importance in the general scheme of Commonwealth defence.

5. It can be stated as a general principle that where a colony such as Gibraltar or Malta plays a vital part in Allied strategy it is essential that overriding powers in matters of defence are retained by the Crown. Where a colony is only of minor strategic importance the retention of some degree of authority will suffice, and in some cases even this reservation can be surrendered without prejudice to strategic plans of defence arrangements.

6. *Allied interests*. However, in the case of Colonial territories which may be of strategic importance to an Allied country, e.g. the Bahamas, due consideration should be given to this fact before any action is decided on to reduce the degree of authority held by His Majesty's Government.

Strategic importance of the smaller colonies

7. We set out below the strategic importance, as already assessed, of each of the Colonies listed above, and state the degree of authority in defence matters that should be retained by His Majesty's Government.

Malta

8. The importance of Malta is entirely strategic. Its role in war must be defined for two cases:—

(a) If Southern Italy and Sicily were accessible and friendly Malta would be:—

(i) A base for offensive air operations to gain and maintain air superiority in the central Mediterranean and to attack strategic objectives in enemy territory.

(ii) A base for maritime air forces.

(iii) An operational base for naval forces employed in controlling and using sea communications.

(iv) A trunk route staging post for aircraft in transit to and from the Middle and Far East.

(b) If Italy and Sicily were hostile, the role of Malta would then be:—

(i) To defend herself, bearing in mind that even should the enemy succeed in rendering the Island temporarily of little use to the Allies, it is important that its use should be denied to the enemy.

(ii) To provide advanced radar warning.

(iii) To provide refuelling and repair facilities for ships and aircraft in an emergency.

9. The military manpower requirements will include the following:—

(a) *Naval*

The Admiralty will not require a Maltese local naval force, but there will be a continued requirement for Maltese in the dockyards, and for service as cooks and stewards in ships of the Royal Navy, and also as seamen in tugs and other craft working from Malta.

(b) *Army*

Maltese troops:—

(i) To assist in meeting the Internal Security requirements.

(ii) To assist in manning the Anti-Aircraft and Coast Artillery defence of the Island.

(c) *Air*

R.A.F. (Malta). Maltese enlisted into this arm will have a general service liability in an emergency.

(d) Civilian labour for all military purposes.

10. *Authority to be retained*. In view of the great strategic value of Malta it will be essential for His Majesty's Government to retain overriding authority in defence matters.

Gibraltar

11. The importance of Gibraltar is entirely strategic and lies in its use as a naval and air base. It will be required as a base for the control of communications through the Straits, as well as in the Eastern Atlantic and Western Mediterranean. It will be needed as a staging post for aircraft in transit to the Middle East and beyond.

If the threat of a land attack on Gibraltar developed, its continued use as a base would be jeopardised and the requirements of the base would become secondary to the need to hold Gibraltar against such an attack.

12. The military manpower requirements will be for civilian labour for military purposes, particularly for the dockyard, and for locally raised troops to assist in providing the anti-aircraft and coast defence of the base.

13. *Authority to be retained*. In view of the great strategic value of Gibraltar it will be essential for His Majesty's Government to retain overriding authority in defence matters.

Cyprus

14. In war, the Island is strategically well placed to assist in the defence of our interest in the Middle East. It is the only British Colony in the Eastern Mediterranean and in the future, its importance may greatly increase, particularly as a forward air base, and/or a staging post; moreover, early warning Radar sets located in Cyprus

might provide a valuable extension of the Air Raid Warning system covering our bases in Egypt.

15. The military manpower requirements will include the following:—

(a) *Naval*

A minor naval organisation at Famagusta which will employ a small number of men recruited locally for harbour services, examination [sic] services, drivers, etc.

(b) *Army*

Cypriot troops:—

(i) To meet internal security requirements.

(ii) To provide Transport (both animal and motor) and Pioneer Units for use outside Cyprus.

(iii) To assist in manning the anti-aircraft and coast defences on the approved scale.

(c) *Air*

Cypriots will be required to replace Royal Air Force man-power in the Island to the maximum extent.

(d) Civilian labour for all military purposes.

16. *Authority to be retained*. The strategic importance of Cyprus necessitates the retention by His Majesty's Government, of a large degree of authority in defence matters.

Gambia

17. Bathurst is well situated to provide facilities for forces employed on the protection of our sea communications should a submarine threat develop in the Central or South Atlantic.

Gambia can also provide air bases for Maritime Air forces and for staging on the Trans-African route.

18. The military manpower requirements will include the following:—

(a) *Naval*

Small naval forces to undertake harbour defences, should Bathurst be used as a naval port.

(b) *Army*

West African troops:—

(i) To meet internal security requirements.

(ii) To provide the Army share of defences for Imperial naval and air bases.

(iii) To form part of a force for use outside West Africa.

(iv) To provide Pioneer and Labour units.

(c) *Air*

(i) Local personnel to assist in manning of airfields if required.

(ii) Local personnel to assist in the manning of anti-aircraft defences.

(d) Civilian labour for all military purposes.

19. *Authority to be retained*. Gambia has potential importance for the defence of sea communications. His Majesty's Government should therefore retain some degree of authority in defence matters.

Sierra Leone

20. Freetown is important as a base for the logistic support of escort forces employed on the protection of sea communications, and in certain circumstances might be required as a convoy assembly port.

Air bases may be required for Maritime Air forces and for staging on the Trans-African route.

21. The military manpower requirements will include the following:—

(a) *Naval*

Naval forces to undertake such duties as harbour defence, minesweeping and coastal patrols; these forces to be available for service outside the West African area, if necessary.

(b) *Army*

West African troops:—

(i) To meet internal security requirements.

(ii) To provide the Army share of defences for Imperial naval and air bases.

(iii) To form part of a force for use outside West Africa.

(iv) To provide Pioneer and Labour units.

(c) *Air*

(i) Local personnel to assist in manning of airfields if required.

(ii) Local personnel to assist in the manning of anti-aircraft defences.

22. *Authority to be retained*. The importance of Sierra Leone in the defence of sea communications necessitates the retention by His Majesty's Government of some degree of authority in defence matters.

Zanzibar

23. Zanzibar has no strategic importance.

24. *Authority to be retained*. It is unnecessary, for strategic reasons, for His Majesty's Government to retain any authority in defence matters.

Somaliland Protectorate

25. British Somaliland is well situated to provide air bases for the protection of the approaches to the Suez Canal.

26. Military manpower requirements will include the following:—

(a) *Army*

Local forces:—

(i) To meet Internal Security requirements.

(ii) For service elsewhere as required.

(b) Civilian labour for all military purposes.

27. *Authority to be retained*. Although British Somaliland is of minor strategic importance it would be advisable for His Majesty's Government to retain some degree of authority in defence matters.

Aden

28. The importance of Aden is entirely strategic. It will probably serve as a naval base, for the protection of sea communications, in advance of Kilindini and as an air

base for operations in the Red Sea, Persian Gulf and Indian Ocean. It will also serve as a staging post on the air routes across Africa to the Far East.

29. The military manpower requirements will include the following:—

(a) *Army*
A Labour Corps.
(b) *Air*
Certain local forces for:—
(i) Internal security duties in Aden Colony and Protectorate including Socotra.
(ii) Garrison duties at airfields.
(c) Civilian labour for all military purposes.

30. *Authority to be retained.* The importance of Aden in the defence of allied lines of communication necessitates the retention by His Majesty's Government of overriding authority in defence matters.

Mauritius

31. The strategic importance of Mauritius is that it is suitable as a fuelling base for the Royal Navy and could be used as an air staging post and an air base for maritime operations.

32. Military manpower requirements will include the following:—

(a) *Naval*
Local naval forces will be needed to undertake harbour defence and harbour services if Mauritius is used.
(b) *Army*
Local Forces:—
(i) To meet Internal Security requirements.
(ii) For service in Pioneer and ancillary units overseas.

33. *Authority to be retained.* It will be necessary for strategic reasons for His Majesty's Government to retain some degree of authority in defence matters.

Seychelles

34. The Seychelles are strategically well situated to provide a naval refuelling base and a Flying Boat Base for anti-submarine operations. In addition, they could be used as a staging post on an air route across Central Africa to the Far East via Diego Paicia [sic, ? Garcia].

35. The military manpower requirements will include a small Home Guard to assist in internal security duties and Pioneer Troops for service overseas.

36. *Authority to be retained.* It is unnecessary for strategic reasons for His Majesty's Government to retain any degree of authority in defence matters.

St. Helena with Ascension Island and Tristan da Cunha

37. The importance of St. Helena is small owing to the absence of a harbour. Ascension is important because of its Cable and Wireless Station and air base.

38. Military requirements for St. Helena and Ascension will include:—

(i) Provision of Police for internal security purposes.

(ii) Home Guards to man, in an emergency, any coast artillery installed to deal with isolated raiding parties.

39. *Authority to be retained.* It is not necessary for His Majesty's Government to retain any degree of authority in defence matters.

Falkland Islands

40. Port Stanley will continue to be of importance to the Royal Navy. As far as can be foreseen, the Falkland Islands and the Dependencies will be of no strategic value to either the Army or the R.A.F. Should the Panama Canal become blocked in a future war, shipping will have to be diverted round Cape Horn and the Falkland Islands will acquire a much greater strategic importance. It will be important to ensure that the enemy are denied the occupation, or occasional use, of the Falkland Islands and their Dependencies.

41. Military manpower requirements are that a Volunteer Force should be maintained for local protection against raiding parties; and Civilian forces will be required for internal security purposes.

42. *Authority to be retained.* Because of the importance of denying the Falkland Islands to the enemy it will be necessary for His Majesty's Government to retain some degree of authority in defence matters.

Bahamas

43. The Bahamas are important since they form part of an extended defence in the Atlantic for the Panama Canal Zone and for the United States itself. The air-fields in the Bahamas are of particular importance for use in connection with shipping protection and staging.

44. *Authority to be retained.* Because of its importance to the Allies it will be necessary for His Majesty's Government to retain some degree of authority in defence matters.

Bermuda

45. The naval base, dockyard and air facilities which Bermuda can provide are of importance.

46. Military manpower requirements will include the following:—

(a) *Naval*

Naval forces to undertake such duties as harbour defence, minesweeping and coastal patrols.

(b) *Army*

Local forces:—

(i) To meet internal security requirements.
(ii) To assist in providing the Army share of defences of the Naval Base.
(iii) To provide a proportion of any infantry units raised for service overseas.

(c) Civilian labour for all military purposes.

47. *Authority to be retained.* The facilities which Bermuda can provide, not only to the Commonwealth but also to the Allies, necessitate the retention by His Majesty's Government of a considerable degree of authority in defence matters.

Hong Kong

48. The retention of Hong Kong is strategically important in peace and it is vulnerable to external attack and internal subversion. It is an important base for the Fleet in carrying out its duties of protecting British interests in the China Seas. The holding of Hong Kong against Chinese Communists is essential to our plans for halting the spread of Communism.

49. The military manpower requirements will include the following:—

(a) *Naval*

A Local Naval Volunteer Force to undertake such duties as harbour defence, minesweeping and coastal patrols; these forces to be available for service outside the Hong Kong area if necessary.

(b) *Army*

Local forces:—

(i) To assist, as their primary duty, in ensuring the internal security of the Colony at all times.

(ii) To be prepared to fight together with the Garrison and under the same command in the immediate local defence of the Colony. These forces to be available, if necessary, for service outside Hong Kong.

(c) *Air*

(i) A fighter control unit equipped and trained as a fighter control and reporting centre.

(ii) An Auxiliary Fighter Squadron.

(iii) R.A.F. (Hong Kong)

(d) Civilian labour for all military purposes.

50. *Authority to be retained*. Because of the strategic importance of Hong Kong as a British outpost in the Far East it is essential that His Majesty's Government retain overriding authority on defence matters.

Fiji

51. Fiji is considered by New Zealand to be a key-point in the outer defences of that Dominion. It is an important centre for both sea and air communications and for cable and wireless. It has natural facilities for the operation of air and naval forces.

52. The military manpower requirements will include the following:—

(a) *Naval*

Fiji R.N.V.R. to provide such duties as harbour defence minesweeping and coastal patrols.

(b) *Army*

Local forces:—

(i) To meet internal security requirements.

(ii) For Anti-Aircraft and Coast Artillery defences; airfields defences.

(iii) For Administration and Training units.

(c) Civilian labour for all military purposes.

53. *Authority to be retained*. The defence arrangements for Fiji are at present, with the approval of the Defence Committee, co-ordinated under the New Zealand Chiefs of Staff. It is necessary for Allied plans that this arrangement should continue;

a degree of authority for defence matters should therefore be retained by His Majesty's Government.

Western Pacific High Commission Territories (British Solomon Islands, Gilbert and Ellice Islands, New Hebrides, Pitcairn Island, Tonga.)

54. The Australians consider that the British Solomon Islands are important as forming part of the outer defences of Australia. The Gilbert and Ellice Islands would only be of strategic importance in a situation comparable to that of the last war. The only Imperial defence requirement is the possible use of air staging posts in these territories.

The New Hebrides, Pitcairn Island or Tonga have no strategic importance.

55. *Authority to be retained.* The High Commissioner is responsible for co-ordinating the defence of the Western Pacific High Commission Territories and it has been recommended that he should receive strategic guidance from the Australian Defence Committee together with the accredited representatives of the United Kingdom and New Zealand. It is necessary for allied plans that this arrangement should continue and some degree of authority in defence matters will have to be retained by His Majesty's Government.[1]

[1] This report was signed by: T M Brownrigg, W S Cole, and H I C Cozens.

410 CO 967/146, no 1 Mar 1951

'Interim recommendations to the S of S for the Colonies by the Committee of Inquiry into Constitutional Development in the Smaller Colonial Territories' (chairman: Sir J F Rees)[1]

1. As our proposals gradually take shape, it has been borne in upon us with increasing force that the principles which underlie them would, to a very considerable degree, be dependent for their successful application upon a reorganisation of the central administration in London. The recommendations which we shall make are based on the conception of a new constitutional status to be recognised as something between a dependency and a fully self-governing territory under the title of 'Island or City States' and to which the smaller territories can aspire. But the proposals contain implications which must affect the whole of the Colonial Empire (and not only the smaller territories which have been referred to us) and consequently the position of the United Kingdom in relation to all territories. While we are not yet able to present our Report, or to complete our proposals, it has seemed to us that recent developments in the Gold Coast, and the statements in South Africa which these developments have engendered, raise broad questions concerned with membership of the Commonwealth and the relation of the members with the United

[1] Members of Committee: Sir J F Rees, principal, University College, Cardiff; Sir J Maude, deputy chairman of the Local Government Boundary Commission; Prof V T Harlow, Beit professor of the history of the British Commonwealth and fellow of Balliol College, Oxford, since 1948; Miss Margery Perham; Mr T Reid, Labour MP for Swindon and formerly of the Ceylon Civil Service; and Col A D Dodds-Parker, Conservative MP for Banbury and formerly of the Sudan Political Service. There were two representatives of the CO: Sir C Jeffries and Sir K Roberts-Wray, legal adviser to the CO and to the CRO.

Kingdom and with each other which we have found impossible to ignore in the course of our own deliberations and which are likely to demand early consideration by His Majesty's Government. Indeed, we understand that this is already being given and we are, therefore, submitting our recommendations on this subject in advance of our main Report in the hope that the thought which the Committee has given to the matter may be of value.

2. Wholehearted acceptance of the status of an Island or City State which we envisage for the smaller territories will depend, not only on making provision for the natural desire of all communities, however small, to exercise a large measure of control in the management of their own domestic affairs, but also on the extent to which the United Kingdom Government promotes a sense of privilege and pride in holding that status within the Commonwealth. In addition, we believe that the promotion of this sense of 'belonging' on the part of small communities cannot properly be achieved without adopting the central instrument of administration to meet a rapidly changing situation. We are aware that in approaching this question we may be going beyond our terms of reference; but, in fact, we cannot adequately fulfil the task referred to us with regard to the smaller Colonial territories without considering the wider implications of what we propose.

3. It is impossible to lay reforming hands upon twenty-one out of some forty territories without affecting the system as a whole. Moreover, the needs of Island and City States will be closely related to those of larger territories which are approaching complete internal self-government and may sooner or later achieve independent membership of the Commonwealth either as individual units or in a federation. Some of these, as, for example, Nigeria or the Gold Coast, may attain that status while they are still in need of aid and expert advice in their social and economic concerns. Yet under the existing system the achievement of independence would presumably imply the transference of their relations with the United Kingdom from the Colonial Office to purely diplomatic contacts through the Commonwealth Relations Office. There might, accordingly, be a sudden cessation of the many services which they may still require, since it would be difficult, after their change of status, to continue to use the accumulated knowledge of the Colonial Office and Colonial Service in their interests.

4. The severance of the connection between territories and, it may be, groups of territories and the Colonial Office would inevitably give rise to other problems. Recognition of independent membership of the Commonwealth becomes a matter of pride and emulation to the aspiring Colony but it also attaches the stigma of inferiority to those territories which have not secured that status. If the larger and more advanced territories were handed over, one by one, the remaining territories would become increasingly discontented, for they would be left to bear in a most marked and public way a status of permanent subjection under the Colonial Office.

5. The effect of this piecemeal promotion of territories from one department to another would be especially unfortunate in Africa. There is no need to marshal here the many reasons why the African continent is likely to be of such great political, economic and strategic importance during the next ten or twenty years. In every branch of government there will be a growing need for co-ordination of policy under British leadership in the African colonies with further development within the present regional organisations and between the regions. The African conference of members of Legislative Councils held in London in 1948 has already pointed the way

towards greater political contact between African leaders. The extension of communications, of higher education and many other influences will foster these inter-colonial relationships. It is quite clear that these colonies will not graduate into independent status simultaneously—it should be noted that three territories and one island dependency figure in the list of minor units presented to our Committee for consideration—and their division both in status and in departmental affiliation would gravely handicap the British Government in the evolution of a common African policy and in promoting self-government and co-operation.

6. Furthermore, the effect of the process of transfer in the conditions which have been described above, upon the Colonial Office itself, should not be overlooked. Its officials would labour under growing disabilities in striving to maintain the great tradition of the Department, as they witnessed their sphere of work being terminated section by section, their own numbers reduced and redistributed, and their remaining functions progressively condemned both by those remaining in their charge and by the world in general.

7. For the sake of clarity and brevity we have indicated in a diagram the kind of metropolitan reorganisation which we have in mind. We have suggested that (on the analogy of the Ministry of Defence) there should be a Minister for Commonwealth Affairs, who would be a member of the Cabinet, and under whose comprehensive supervision there would be three Departments—a Commonwealth Relations Office, a Commonwealth Services Office and a Commonwealth Territories Office, each under a responsible Minister.

8. These suggestions are based upon the following principles:—

(a) That the Commonwealth Relations Office should function as at present and the existing machinery for consultation and co-operation as between the United Kingdom Government and the Governments of the other autonomous Commonwealth Countries overseas should not be disturbed.

(b) That such Colonial territories or groups of territories as may in the future attain independence should continue to have available to them (to be used entirely at their own discretion) the advisory, central and research services which were previously provided under the aegis of the Colonial Office, and that to avoid the danger of affronted prestige such services should be provided through a new procedure on a 'Commonwealth' basis.

(c) That States within the Commonwealth which have achieved internal self-government, but which are not in a position to assume the responsibilities of sovereign States, should not be left in an obviously separate and inferior category and should have some opportunity also of expressing their views on those matters of general Commonwealth concern which affect them.

9. The proposal that all Commonwealth affairs should be brought under the aegis of a co-ordinating Minister would have positive advantages additional to those of avoiding serious difficulties over the political evolution of the colonies, and over the functions of the Colonial Office. It would demonstrate that in the eyes of His Majesty's Government not only is the relationship of the Commonwealth countries of a special character, but that the Colonial territories are included in that special relationship. It would offer to the older Dominions the opportunity (to be taken up or not, as each might determine) of associating themselves more closely with the continuing task of the United Kingdom in developing the dependent territories. To

the Colonial peoples it should give a sense of added prestige by blunting the distinction between their relationship with the United Kingdom and that of the independent Members of the Commonwealth. The division of departmental functions below the co-ordinating Minister would be seen as a domestic arrangement for the efficient handling of business within the United Kingdom government organisation, and the idea of "promotion" from one Office to another would lose significance. The present international situation, and the dangers which are obliging the Commonwealth, as part of the western alliance, to consolidate its position, make it essential that all its economic and strategic resources should be utilized to the fullest extent. The new arrangement could help all the Dominions and territories within the Commonwealth to act more closely together, and this opportunity, instead of derogating from the sovereign status of the autonomous members of the Commonwealth, would enhance it. We feel bound to point out that, from the point of view of the Colonies, the public recognition of their partnership in the Commonwealth is of the highest importance if the goodwill and co-operation of their peoples are to be retained. We would hope that this consideration would make a powerful appeal to the independent Commonwealth countries, who are equally concerned with the United Kingdom that the Colonies should remain in willing and loyal association with the Commonwealth.

10. For similar reasons to that influencing the proposal for one co-ordinating Minister, we would urge that every consideration should be given to the possibility of housing the C.R.O. (Commonwealth Relations Office) and the C.T.O. (Commonwealth Territories Office) in the same building, even if the C.S.O. (Commonwealth Services Office) would be physically separated. We feel that much of the value of our proposal would be lost if this could not be achieved.

11. Apart from this question of Ministerial responsibility, which we recognise is outside our province but to which we have felt obliged to invite attention, our main proposal is the creation of a new *Commonwealth Services Office*. The function of this Office would be to organise and co-ordinate all advisory, research and central services, and to act as a central recruiting organisation and clearing house for technical and administrative staff which any Commonwealth country might wish to recruit from other parts of the Commonwealth. The new Office would take over and develop on a Commonwealth scale, the advisory, research and recruitment organisations now included in the Colonial Office and also the work relating to the Commonwealth Agricultural Bureaux and other general bodies. Its services and facilities would be available to all Commonwealth governments which wished to make use of them. The older members might not all need or wish to use them extensively, but Australia, New Zealand and South Africa at least might find such an Office of value in certain fields, and all members of the Commonwealth could contribute staff, technical assistance and perhaps even funds. To the extent that they were willing to co-operate in this regard, so much would the general sense of corporateness within the Commonwealth be enhanced. The main consideration, however, is that the existence of such an Office would enable the countries which have recently achieved independence, or may achieve full or virtual independence in the future, to make use of central services of which they are undoubtedly in need, but which for political reasons they would not wish to seek through the existing Colonial Office machinery. We think also that the prestige of dealing with a "Commonwealth" Office over a large range of subjects would give satisfaction to the territories which

must remain in some degree of political dependence.

12. As already stated, our proposals envisage no change in the present structure or functions of the *Commonwealth Relations Office*. Ideally, it might be desirable to transfer the management of the affairs of the South Africa High Commission Territories to the Colonial Office (or Commonwealth Territories Office), but we recognise the political obstacles to such a course and assume that it will be best to leave these territories under the Commonwealth Relations Office while giving them full access to the Commonwealth Services Office and following to the greatest possible extent the pattern of administration laid down for the Colonial territories of comparable status.

13. It might also be argued that a Commonwealth Relations Office should deal with intra-Commonwealth relations affecting the Colonial territories and with all general questions of external affairs and defence. But such matters cannot be considered apart from the other administrative questions to the territories, and the selection of the most suitable departmental arrangements for securing coordination is best left to the experienced judgment of the officers concerned.

14. In our scheme, the *Commonwealth Territories Office* would carry on the responsibilities of the present Colonial Office, except in so far as these would be taken over by the Commonwealth Services Office. We consider that some change of title (though there may be better alternatives to the title which we suggest) is needed to mark the fact that our proposals involve a genuinely new departure in relationships for the smaller territories and must *a fortiori* affect the larger territories outside our terms of reference. But a mere change of title will not be enough. The keynote of the new relationship which we envisage is that emphasis should be laid upon the dignity and status enjoyed by each territory in its own right (though subject to necessary reservations) rather than upon the dependence of the territory on the United Kingdom. The larger territories will enjoy the dignity and status of major States looking forward to eventual independence. The smaller territories will enjoy the dignity and status of Island or City States of the Commonwealth endowed with a maximum of internal self-government. Both kinds of States, while not exercising sovereignty in external affairs, must be given solid grounds for regarding themselves as active Commonwealth partners, and the machinery of administration must be adapted to this end.

15. We do not feel in a position to make detailed proposals as to the methods by which this new relationship might be given practical expression. We have, however, given some thought to the possibility of these states being given the right of representation in London. We do not feel that it is practicable or desirable to apply to them the High Commissioner system which is in force in respect of the independent Members of the Commonwealth. The modified form of that system which, we understand, obtains in respect of Southern Rhodesia, would hardly be applicable except in the case of the largest Colonies. We think, however, that there should be a wide field for the appointment by Colonial Governments of London representatives (who might be styled Agents-General or Commissioners). The work of these officers would include that of the present trade representatives but it might be extended also to cover quasi-consular (though not diplomatic) activities, such as looking after the interests and welfare of people from the territories concerned when in this country. The representatives would naturally have close relations with the political departments concerned with their territories.

16. Furthermore, we feel that it might become a normal rather than an exceptional procedure for representatives of a State government to be invited to London for *ad hoc* discussions with the Secretary of State and other United Kingdom Ministers on important matters of policy relating to the territory. Similarly, we think that when the Secretary of State has an exceptionally important communication to make to a State Government, he might from time to time send a senior representative to put the case with any necessary explanations and to hear any representations which the State Government might wish to make in reply.

17. In making these suggestions, we do not wish to derogate in any way from the position of the Governor. He would remain the normal channel for correspondence with the Secretary of State and he would be entitled to be present or to be represented at discussions of the kind which we envisage. But we feel that there are times when the Governor would welcome the opportunity of being relieved of the duty of being the only spokesman of the Secretary of State to the Colonial government and *vice versa*, and the sole intermediary between them. An impartial counsellor of both sides, he would be in a stronger and less invidious position, while the representatives of the people of the territory would derive experience of responsibility as well as satisfaction of *amour-propre* from dealing directly as principals with His Majesty's Government.

18. Other modifications of technique will no doubt suggest themselves as the new relationship becomes established. The essential point is that territories which are not fully independent should be endowed not only with sufficient control of their internal affairs but with sufficient marks of external status to make the condition one in which their people will have real grounds for satisfaction and will be content to remain for a long time to come—in some cases indefinitely. In our submission this vitally important end cannot be attained without some rearrangement of the metropolitan administrative system such as we have suggested in the preceding paragraphs. Since political changes in the Colonial territories are taking place with such rapidity, it is, in the view of the Committee, essential that the central organisation should be adjusted and made sufficiently flexible to meet the situation before such re-planning is overtaken by events. Such adjustments, if made as a concession to pressure and after the critical moment for a gesture has passed, would be deprived of their grace beforehand and would accordingly lose much of their effect.

411 DO 35/2218, no 7A 1 June 1951

[Commonwealth implications of constitutional development of the colonies]: CRO note of discussion at an interdepartmental meeting with the CO. *Minute* by Mr Gordon Walker

[Following Griffiths's question in February 1951—had the Colonial Office considered the constitutional problem of a mid-way stage between colony and independent member of the Commonwealth? (see part 1 of this volume, 55)—a small Working Party was set up of CO and CRO officials under Sir C Jeffries and Sir C Syers. They concluded that a 'two-tier Commonwealth membership' was possible; they saw the object as in effect to try to preserve the 'inner ring' of old members, 'at any rate for as long as possible—by giving the "intermediate" an advanced status which would satisfy them and might prevent them from asking to join the inner ring' (CO 967/148, no 2, report, 29 Mar 1951).

Interdepartmental discussion took place at the meeting recorded in this document, but it was 'very inconclusive' (minute by Syers, 2 June 1951).]

During recent months two parallel examinations have been conducted by—

(1) the Committee established by the Colonial Secretary to examine the problem of the smaller Colonial territories, and
(2) the Working Party established by the Secretary of State and the Colonial Secretary to report on the broader question of the constitutional development of the Colonies and its implications from the point of view of the Members of the Commonwealth.

The Committee on Smaller Territories have produced an Interim Report on organisation problems at the Whitehall end; the Working Party its Report on constitutional development. The full Report of the Committee on Smaller Territories has not yet been produced and may not be available for some months.[1]

Before the Colonial Secretary left for his trip to Africa, the Secretary of State and he had a brief discussion of the position and agreed that, since the question of admission or non-admission to Membership of the Commonwealth of even the most forward Colonial territory (i.e. the Gold Coast) cannot be expected to become a live one in the immediate future, they should await the Committee's full Report before deciding what views on all these problems they should submit to their colleagues.

More recently, Sir Thomas Lloyd and Sir Charles Jeffries of the Colonial Office asked to meet Sir Percivale Liesching and Sir Cecil Syers for a purely exploratory talk at the Departmental level. Our meeting took place on the afternoon of Monday, the 28th of May, in the Commonwealth Relations Office. We had a long and full talk without of course attempting to reach any conclusions.

The following is a summary of some of the main points which came up:—

(1) *Smaller territories*. The Colonial Office Committee have been concerned to work out some special status for those smaller territories which, for one reason or another, cannot expect to come to full independent sovereign status either alone or in federation with others. There are a number of such territories, e.g. Gibraltar, Malta, Cyprus, the Seychelles, the Falkland Islands, Mauritius, and *possibly* Bermuda, the Bahamas, Zanzibar, the Gambia, the Borneo territories.

The Committee are working on the idea that such territories might be conceded full internal self-government and given such collective title as "City and Island States" to mark the status and satisfy local opinion. These States would continue in relations with the Colonial Office and would, of course, come under the United Kingdom for international and defence purposes. But in local affairs they would eventually reach full self-government.

The Committee think it important that, if the United Kingdom Government accept the policy they recommend, there should be full publicity of the new conception. This for very obvious reasons. But they recognise that this must raise problems in relation to the larger Colonial territories whose eyes are set perhaps on a larger goal and might expect a simultaneous public declaration about their precise future. For the purposes of this memorandum these territories may be described as the "intermediate territories".

[1] For interim report, see 410; the final report was presented in Aug 1951.

(2) *Intermediate territories*. These may be broken down into—

(i) Central Africa, if federation comes into force;
(ii) some federation of East Africa;
(iii) a federation of the West Indies, less probably Bermuda and the Bahamas;
(iv) the Gold Coast;
(v) Nigeria;
(iv) Malaya, less probably the Borneo territories.

In relation to these territories the governing doctrine is that the United Kingdom Government's aim is to lead them to responsible self-government within the Commonwealth. What does this mean? As the Working Party pointed out, it is within the competence of the United Kingdom Government to deal with its Colonies as it pleases and therefore to confer self-government on them; but admission to the inner Councils of the Commonwealth (i.e. the Prime Ministers' Meeting) has hitherto been, and must presumably remain, a matter for agreement between all the existing Members. There is thus the dilemma to which the Working Party have called attention. While it may be presumed that the day will come when these territories will have reached full nationhood (as Ceylon did three years ago) and may expect not only sovereign independence but all that sovereign independence has hitherto meant in relation to the Members of the Commonwealth, it is certain that one Member (South Africa) will refuse to sit round a Conference table with them and it is possible that other Members may withdraw rather than see the Conference table enlarged. Although it does not follow that a country which withdrew from the Prime Ministers' Meeting would weaken her links bilaterally with this country and with some or all of the other Members of the Commonwealth, the ultimate effect would be the destruction of the Prime Ministers' Meeting, which is—as it were—the outward embodiment of what is at present meant by "Membership of the Commonwealth". Moreover, it is not impossible that South Africa would withdraw from the Commonwealth on such an issue. Could we with equanimity face this as a price of bringing the Gold Coast to the Conference table?

(3) To meet this difficulty the Working Party suggested a special status for the intermediate territories rather like that enjoyed to-day by Southern Rhodesia. The Working Party hoped that some of these territories might be prepared to accept this status indefinitely and that even those who were not prepared to go so far as that would accept it for a time: if so the root problem would at least be postponed and might, with the passage of time, prove easier of ultimate solution.

At our meeting doubt was expressed whether this would be so, since experience shows that aggrandizement of status generally leads to further demands and that what was prepared as an advanced position for retention for some time has soon been over-run by progressive nationalism (e.g. the Soulbury Constitution in Ceylon). Would such territories as the Gold Coast in fact be satisfied by a half-way house? Might not Ministers who had pledged themselves to the whole road either have to lead their people to the end or give way to others who would? Moreover there is (as indeed the Working Party recognised) an anomaly in that Southern Rhodesia has already been admitted to the inner Councils on several occasions; true there were special reasons for this but they would not appeal to nationalists in e.g. the Gold Coast.

En passant there was a brief discussion at this point about the effect of the adoption (if they were adopted) of the Central African Closer Association proposals. Southern Rhodesia would presumably expect that the special position enjoyed by Sir Godfrey Huggins would continue. Would this mean that the Prime Minister of Southern Rhodesia would expect to be invited to Prime Ministers' Meetings? Or the Prime Minister of the Federation? Obviously, difficult questions arise here.

(4) We then discussed the question of solving the dilemma by some special arrangements for associating intermediate territories in the Councils of London. We rejected as impracticable the idea of some selective representation at the Prime Ministers' Meetings: this would require the full agreement of all other Members, which would not be obtainable. We wondered whether it would be possible to hold the position—

(a) by crystallising the present arrangements in the form of a Prime Ministers' Conference with a special Central Secretariat, and
(b) by arranging for special Conferences with those intermediate territories which came to full self-government.

The Colonial Office representatives pointed out that, apart from the obvious difficulties, there are special difficulties here under (b) by virtue of the fact that there is really very little in common between e.g. East Africa and West Africa; when the Colonial Office held an African Conference they in fact had to break into separate huddles. If this happened the system could hardly be defended as a satisfactory substitute, in the eyes of ardent nationalists, for attendance at the Prime Ministers' Meeting.

(As regards the smaller territories no question would arise of even selective representation at the Prime Ministers' Meeting. The Colonial Office Committee had rejected the idea of a Standing Conference in London for these territories and would probably recommend some intermittent form of consultation in London, possibly by way of an occasional Smaller Territories Conference).

Beyond examining all the difficulties of this side of the question we found ourselves unable to reach any conclusions.

(5) We also considered what in fact "responsible self-government within the Commonwealth" in relation to the intermediate territories would mean. Since it would imply abolition of all reserved powers, it would mean from the United Kingdom point of view complete absence of control—balanced no doubt by absence of obligations. In the international and defence spheres the United Kingdom might have rights to consultation etc.; but in the last analysis there was nothing (short of force—which was unthinkable) to prevent such territories from gaining full control of their destinies if they had the finance and manpower necessary (and in the case of e.g. the Gold Coast or Nigeria the day might well come when they had). We could not therefore argue that they could be excluded from Prime Ministers' Meetings on the grounds e.g. that they were unable to look after their own defence or that they were incapable of running their own international affairs with those countries with which they were especially concerned by the appointment of their own diplomatic staffs.

(6) We then discussed the organisational questions dealt with in the Smaller Territories Committee's Interim Report. The suggestion here was that there should be a special Minister for Commonwealth Relations to whom, on the analogy of the Minister of Defence, there would be subordinated a Secretary of State for Commonwealth Affairs, a Secretary of State for Colonial Affairs and a Minister for Common-

wealth Services. We thought it unlikely that this proposal would be acceptable, both on political and on manpower grounds. It was surely inconceivable that the Secretary of State for Commonwealth Affairs should not be a member of the Cabinet; the other Members of the Commonwealth would undoubtedly expect no less, and would hardly be satisfied by the explanation that in the Cabinet relations with them were in the hands of the co-ordinating Minister (the Minister for Commonwealth Relations). It was difficult too to envisage a situation in which the Secretary of State for Colonial Affairs was not in the Cabinet. Yet there could not presumably be three Ministers in the Cabinet (cf. the Defence analogy). The proposal also looked to two new Departments, two new Permanent Secretaries, and subordinate staff. Was it likely that this could—or should—be provided at a time like the present?

Nor, if our analysis of the aspirations of the intermediate territories was right, would the proposals meet one of the objectives of the Smaller Territories Committee—that of keeping the intermediate territories under the same umbrella (i.e. the Colonial Affairs Department) as the smaller territories. The intermediate territories would presumably expect to come eventually under the Commonwealth Affairs Department.

We thought, however, that there was much to be said for the idea of setting up some form of Commonwealth Services organisation, to which not only Colonies but independent sovereign Members of the Commonwealth could look for advice, guidance and expert help. Though the independent Members might not all avail themselves of this help and those who did might be slow to seek it, we thought it likely that some would come to avail themselves of it. Thus, it could form a focus in London for the activities under the Colombo Plan. It could also assume special responsibility towards such institutions as the Commonwealth Agricultural Bureaux.

We discussed the possibility of the organisation being not a Government Office under a separate Minister but rather a functional corporation under a Director-General who would be responsible to a Minister, possibly in the same way as is the Head of the C.O.I. This idea has obvious attractions and is clearly worth considering. The suggestion was made that the organisation might be given some such title as "Crown Services Office" (cf. the Crown Agents) to mark its Commonwealth-wide character.

Minute to 411

I think this has taken things about as far as they can go at the moment. It is abominably difficult—but some prospects open. I am inclined to the idea in the last 2 paragraphs. I also think it might be possible to treat the Island and City States as (at least in many ways) part of the Metropolitan area. We still need to solve the problem of some sort of Ministerial link with the Middle Group.

I am sure we must cling to the Prime Ministers' Conference as a touchstone.

P.C.G.W.
18.6.51

412 CAB 128/5, CM 45(46)8 13 May 1946

'South-West Africa': Cabinet conclusions on South Africa's proposed incorporation in the Union

The Secretary of State for Dominion Affairs said that he had discussed with Field-Marshal Smuts and his advisers the South African proposal to seek the incorporation of South-West Africa in the Union. Field-Marshal Smuts would be glad to have an assurance that in putting his proposal to the United Nations he would have the support of the United Kingdom and of some at least of the Dominions.

The Secretary of State recalled that after the last war the Governments of the United Kingdom, Australia and New Zealand had favoured the incorporation of this territory in the Union, but it had been placed under mandate because President Wilson had been opposed in principle to the annexation of ex-enemy territory. The mandate provided, however, that it should be administered as an integral part of the Union. The native administration in territory had not been subject to the criticism directed against the native policy within the Union itself. A large part of the territory was reserved for the natives, and councils of chiefs had been established which were working satisfactorily. The Union Government had recently sought to obtain the views of the natives on the proposal to incorporate the territory in the Union. The Herero tribe opposed it, but most of the rest of the natives appeared to favour it. Of the European population, two-thirds were citizens of the Union.

There had been opposition to the proposal from the neighbouring Protectorate of Bechuanaland; and Tshekedi, Paramount Chief [sic] of the Bamangwato tribe, was intending to come to this country to make representations against it, chiefly on the ground that it would set a precedent for the subsequent incorporation in the Union of Bechuanaland and the other South African High Commission Territories.

The Secretary of State said that, despite this opposition, it seemed to him that the balance of the arguments was in favour of incorporation. There was the further consideration that our support of Field-Marshal Smuts in this matter would strengthen his hand against the secessionists in South Africa, whose activities were causing him considerable difficulty. The Secretary of State therefore recommended that Field-Marshal Smuts should be told that the United Kingdom Government would support his application to the United Nations and would also be glad to arrange for him to discuss his proposal at a meeting of Dominion Prime Ministers.

The Secretary of State for the Colonies, while he admitted the force of the arguments adduced by the Secretary of State for Dominion Affairs, thought that there were also strong reasons why the United Kingdom Government should not commit themselves to support this proposal. There was much concern not only in Bechuanaland and the other High Commission Territories but throughout Africa, against the native policy of the Union Government, and there was likely to be strong opposition to any measure which would give the Union a greater control over the welfare of Africans. Nor would this opposition be confined to Africa. There was considerable feeling on the subject in this country, in some of the Dominions and elsewhere. South Africa would have to obtain a two-thirds majority in the United Nations Assembly and might not succeed in obtaining it. India might well object to the proposal, on account of her troubles with South Africa. There were also indications that the Soviet Government would oppose it.

The Secretary of State therefore recommended that the United Kingdom Government should not commit themselves to support the proposal, at least until United Kingdom Ministers had discussed the matter further with Field-Marshal Smuts and possibly also with the other Dominion Ministers now in London.

The Minister of State[1] said that the South African Government had had difficulties with the Hereros in the early days of their administration of the territory. The action they had then taken had occasioned much adverse comment, and when it became known that the Hereros were opposing the policy now proposed, this would no doubt influence public opinion against it. The Foreign Secretary thought that the case against the proposal was very strong, and it was his view that the United Kingdom Government should not commit themselves at this stage to support it.

In discussion it was recalled that when the matter had last been before the Cabinet[2] it had been considered that it would be reasonable to support the incorporation of South-West Africa in the Union if the consent of the native as well as the European inhabitants had been sought and obtained by methods agreeable to the United Nations. The view of the Cabinet was that this decision should be maintained. If Field-Marshal Smuts wished to ascertain the views of the United Kingdom Government before the matter was discussed at a meeting of Dominion Prime Ministers, he could be told that this was the line which this Government would take at such a meeting.

The Cabinet:—

Invited the Secretary of State for Dominion Affairs to inform Field-Marshal Smuts that the United Kingdom Government would support the incorporation of South-West Africa in the Union if the consent of the native as well as the European inhabitants had been sought and obtained by methods agreeable to the United Nations.

---

[1] Mr P J Noel-Baker.

[2] CAB 128/5, CM 37(46)3, 24 Apr 1946.

413 CAB 128/6, CM 85(46)5 10 Oct 1946

'South-West Africa': Cabinet conclusions: UK attitude at UN on proposed incorporation[1]

The Cabinet considered a memorandum by the Secretary of State for Dominion Affairs (C.P. (46) 371) regarding the attitude to be taken by the United Kingdom Government to the proposal which was to be made by the South African Government at the forthcoming Session of the General Assembly of the United Nations that South-West Africa should be incorporated in the Union.

The Secretary of State for Dominion Affairs said that the matter was one of great importance, in view of the political situation in the Union. After two previous discussions the Cabinet had decided that they would support the South African proposal if the consent of the inhabitants had been sought and obtained "by methods agreeable to the United Nations." Field-Marshal Smuts had been informed accordingly. The South African Government had consulted the natives by methods which were

---

[1] Previous reference: see 412.

set out in Annex I to C.P. (46) 371, and a substantial majority had declared themselves in favour of incorporation in the Union. He was himself satisfied that the methods of consultation adopted had been as fair as was practicable; and Lord Hailey, who was now in South Africa, had confirmed this view.

The South African Government had given notice of their intention to raise this question at the forthcoming Session of the Assembly; but the United States Government had suggested to them that it should be postponed for a year and that meanwhile a United Nations Commission of Enquiry should visit the country and make recommendations to the Assembly. This suggestion would not be acceptable to Field-Marshal Smuts, who would feel obliged by considerations of domestic politics in the Union to keep the subject on this year's Agenda.

The attitude of the United Kingdom Government must be reconsidered in the light of these developments. The Secretary of State believed that a most unfavourable impression would be created in South Africa if we showed any signs of sympathy with the United States proposal. He therefore suggested that a public statement should at once be made, in reply to a Question which was to be asked in the House of Commons on the 14th October, to the effect that we supported the South African case and were satisfied with the steps taken to ascertain the wishes of the inhabitants.

In discussion serious doubts were expressed about the expediency of committing ourselves at this stage to support of the application of the South African Government. It was unfortunate that the consultation of the inhabitants had been carried out under the sole responsibility of the mandatory Government without any independent observers. We might ourselves be satisfied that the consultation had been carried out impartially; but, if we argued that this form of consultation was sufficient, we might establish an embarrassing precedent. We might debar ourselves from proposing an independent enquiry, or the presence of independent observers, on future occasions when the United Nations wished to be satisfied about the views of a population under the control of a foreign country. It was not enough that such a consultation of the inhabitants should have been fair in fact; it must also be possible to prove to the world in general that it had been fair.

The Secretary of State for the Colonies said that at the first session of the General Assembly the United Kingdom Government had given a firm lead towards the maintenance of the trusteeship principle which had been the inspiration of the mandate system. Any apparent change of attitude on our part would create an unfortunate impression in the Assembly and might increase the difficulties of negotiating trusteeship agreements in respect of our own mandated territories. It would also have repercussions in those territories in Africa, particularly Tanganyika, where the terms of our draft trusteeship agreement had not been readily accepted by the European population. If the Cabinet felt that it was necessary to support the South African application, the Colonial Secretary hoped that it might at least be possible to secure from the South African Government a declaration that in the administration of South-West Africa the principles of the mandate system would continue to be fully observed.

After further discussion, the Cabinet decided that if they were pressed for an immediate indication of their views, use should be made of the following formula: "His Majesty's Government, for its part, expresses its confidence that the South African Government has sought to ascertain as accurately as possible the wishes of the inhabitants; but it will, of course, be for the United Nations to decide whether the action taken for this purpose by the South African Government is satisfactory to them." They understood, however, that Field-Marshal Smuts would be arriving in this country during the following week. This being so, the wisest course would be to explore the position further with him in the first instance. The Cabinet were most anxious to avoid action which might cause him embarrassment in South Africa, and the problem was to secure this without causing themselves embarrassment in other directions. To gain time for discussion with Field-Marshal Smuts, arrangements could no doubt be made to postpone the Question down for answer in the House of Commons on the 14th October.

The Cabinet:—

(1) Took note that the Prime Minister and the Secretary of State for Dominion Affairs would arrange to discuss this matter with Field-Marshal Smuts as soon as he arrived in this country.
(2) Asked the Secretary of State for Dominion Affairs to endeavour to arrange for the Parliamentary Question for the 14th October to be withdrawn from the Order Paper.

414 CAB 128/6, CM 88(46) 18 Oct 1946

'South-West Africa': Cabinet conclusions on UK attitude to proposed incorporation[1]

At their meeting on 10th October the Cabinet had deferred, pending discussions with Field-Marshal Smuts, a final decision on their attitude towards the proposal of the South African Government that South-West Africa should be incorporated in the Union. They had, however, considered that, if they were pressed for an immediate indication of their views, use might be made of the following formula: "His Majesty's Government, for its part, expresses its confidence that the South African Government has sought to ascertain as accurately as possible the wishes of the inhabitants; but it will, of course, be for the United Nations to decide whether the action taken for this purpose by the South African Government is satisfactory to them."

The Cabinet were now informed that the Prime Minister and the Secretary of State for Dominion Affairs had had an opportunity of discussing this matter with Field-Marshal Smuts. He had urged very strongly that, in the discussions at the forthcoming meeting of the General Assembly of the United Nations, the United Kingdom Government should support the incorporation of South-West Africa in the Union; and he had taken particular exception to the second part of the formula reproduced above. Apart from the fact that it indicated indecision, it would be inappropriate to suggest that the United Nations might prescribe other methods of ascertaining the view of the inhabitants. For the United Nations had not inherited all the powers of the League of Nations in respect of mandated territories; and the approach which the South African Government were making to the General Assembly was not an application for permission to incorporate South-West Africa in the Union, but merely a notification of the wishes of the inhabitants. Field-Marshal Smuts had made it clear that, whatever was said in the General Assembly, the Union

---

[1] Previous reference: see 413.

Government intended, in pursuance of their powers as mandatory, to proceed with their plan of incorporating this territory in the Union.

In discussion the view was expressed that, even though the United Nations had no legal right to prescribe procedure for ascertaining the views of the inhabitants in this case, the United Kingdom Government should on general grounds support the principle that transfers of sovereignty should not take place unless the wishes of the inhabitants had been ascertained by methods prescribed or approved by international agreement. It was also suggested that it was unfortunate that the Union Government should insist on proceeding with this proposal at the present time, before the Trusteeship Council had been established and laid down rules of procedure which would afford some guidance to Governments in such matters. The notification which the Union Government proposed to make at the General Assembly was likely to provoke debate in which the policy of that Government would be criticised, and other Governments of the British Commonwealth would be placed in an embarrassing position.

Despite these considerations, however, it was the general view of the Cabinet that it would be inexpedient for the United Kingdom Government to refrain from supporting the Union Government in this matter if the action which they proposed to take were contested in the General Assembly. As the matter was to come up in the form of a notification of the steps taken by the Union Government to ascertain the wishes of the inhabitants, there was no occasion for the United Kingdom Government to indicate in advance that they would support the South African case. The United Kingdom Government were, however, satisfied that the steps taken by the Union Government to ascertain the wishes of the inhabitants were as complete and satisfactory as was practicable; and their representatives could properly support the Union Government in resisting any suggestion which might be made in the Assembly for supplementary enquiries for this purpose.

The Cabinet were informed that the Union Government would be willing to make a declaration, in the course of the proceedings at the Assembly, that in the administration of South-West Africa the principles of the mandate system would continue to be fully observed.

In the light of the discussion recorded above, the Cabinet proceeded to consider the draft reply contained in Annex IV to C.P. (46) 371 to a Parliamentary Question by Lieut.-Colonel D.R. Rees-Williams, M.P., about the steps taken to ascertain the wishes of the inhabitants of the territory. It was agreed that, subject to the omission of the statement that the United Kingdom Government "supported the South African case," a statement in the terms of the draft answer annexed to C.P. (46) 371 should be made in the House of Commons before the meeting of the General Assembly.

The Cabinet:—

(1) Agreed that, if the proposal of the South African Government to incorporate South-West Africa in the Union were contested in the General Assembly of the United Nations, the United Kingdom Government should express their confidence in the measures taken by the Union Government to ascertain the wishes of the inhabitants, should oppose suggestions for any independent enquiry on this point, and should support the South African case for the incorporation of this territory in the Union;

(2) Agreed that, while there was no occasion to announce in advance this intention to support the South African case, the Parliamentary Question about the

consultation of the inhabitants of the territory should be answered in the terms of the draft annexed to C.P. (46) 371, subject to the substitution of the following, in place of the final sentence of that draft: "I take this opportunity to say that His Majesty's Government in the United Kingdom is satisfied as to the steps taken by South African Government to ascertain the wishes of the inhabitants."

415 AB 16/393, no 2B 7 July 1947

[Atomic energy]: possible construction of nuclear plant near the Victoria Falls: letter from Mr Creech Jones to Mr Alexander (Defence)

[At a staff conference, 11 June 1947, Bevin suggested that the possibilities of constructing large-scale atomic energy plants near the Victoria Falls should be investigated, and the PM agreed that Alexander should inquire into this. The advantages would be the strategic dispersal of industrial effort in the Commonwealth, the local availability of large supplies of Zambesi water for cooling purposes, and a secure location unreachable by enemy air attack, within convenient reach of the uranium deposits in the Belgian Congo. Prof J Cockcroft (director of the Atomic Energy Research Establishment) believed that the South Africans would wish to use some of their own newly-discovered uranium sources for the domestic production of industrial power from atomic energy, and that the UK might co-operate with them in building an experimental pile of the Harwell type. With Alexander's approval, Prof H Tizard (chairman, Advisory Council on Scientific Policy, and Defence Research Policy Committee) proposed to write to Dr B E J Schonland (president of the South African Council for Scientific and Industrial Research), if the scheme seemed a good one, asking him to come and discuss the possibility of South Africa's agreeing to take the initiative in sponsoring such a project in Rhodesia, providing a large part of the money. Alexander thought Lord Addison should be informed, and he in turn reported his anxieties to Creech Jones. In reply, Alexander agreed that 'we must be most careful not to put a foot wrong in a delicate matter of this kind', but the political issues would not arise until the technical feasibilities had been agreed (AB 16/393, no 2A, 9 July 1947). In the event the scheme collapsed on account of fear of annoying the Americans and a strong technical argument against the dispersal and duplication of the UK atomic programme, especially when it was realised that building a Rhodesian plant would be expensive and difficult because of the lack of local expertise in construction, supervision and inspection, which could only be met by export of scarce UK resources (ibid, no 6).]

My dear Bert

Addison has sent me copies of his correspondence with you about the possibility of constructing atomic energy plants in the neighbourhood of the Victoria Falls.

I thought that I had better write to you at once to say that I share the doubts which Addison has expressed in his letter of the 4th July about the desirability of approaching the South African authorities in the way you suggest. I do not, of course, want to pre-judge any discussion which we may have on the subject, but, on the facts given in your letter of the 3rd July, I feel bound to say at once that I think that there would be serious political difficulties in allowing the South African Government to sponsor a project in Rhodesia. If such a project were to go forward my personal feeling is that it would be much better for it to be undertaken by the United Kingdom Government, with such co-operation as the two Rhodesian Governments could provide. I do not suggest, of course, that the South Africans should be excluded; but I think that we should have to be very careful before suggesting that they should play the leading part in this project. Anything which gave them a major say in a territory forming part of the Colonial Empire would, I think, be politically dangerous and I imagine that the same objections would apply to

Southern Rhodesia. In any case, we ought certainly to consult the two Rhodesian Governments before approaching them. And apart from anything else, the Central African Council (which represents the two Rhodesias and Nyasaland) has under examination extensive schemes for the production of hydro-electric power in the Zambesi valley before the Victoria Falls. The bearing of an atomic energy project close to the Victoria Falls on this would have to be considered.

I notice that Addison says that he has no objection to private consultations with Brigadier Schonland, but I wonder whether it would not be advisable to have a meeting of those concerned with representatives of the Commonwealth Relations and Colonial Offices even before any such consultations take place, so that we may all know exactly where we are.

I am sending a copy of this letter to Addison.

Yours sincerely,
(Sgd) A Creech Jones

416 DO 35/3518, no 108 12 Jan 1948
'Gold loan from South Africa': CRO note

The idea of a loan from South Africa (though not necessarily in gold) was first put informally to the South Africans in July, 1947, when Mr. Strauss, the Minister of Agriculture, and Mr. Waterson, the Minister of Mines and Economic Development, with senior officials, were in London discussing steps that might have to be taken to reduce the outflow of capital from this country to the Union and to reduce our purchases of South African products. It was put to them that a credit would enable the U.K. to continue to participate in the economic development of South Africa and in particular in that of the gold mining industry, and to maintain her purchases of the major Union exports to this country. Later, when the dollar crisis came to its height, this suggestion was reinforced by a personal message from the Prime Minister to Field-Marshal Smuts emphasising on the broadest grounds of policy the importance to this country, and indeed to all Western Europe, of our receiving early and substantial help in the form of a gold loan which would assist in relieving the heavy strain on the U.K. and exert a steadying influence elsewhere. Field-Marshal Smuts at once expressed his willingness to help and after some negotiations and discussion an agreement providing for a loan of £80 million was signed on 9th October.

It appeared that there was not complete unanimity within the Union Cabinet over this proposal. Field-Marshal Smuts was in favour of a loan of £100 million (which was the figure suggested in Mr. Attlee's message to him), but the Union financial authorities maintained that the sum was more than the Union could afford and they suggested a very much lower total. It also appears that in some Union Government quarters there was considerable fear that the Nationalist opposition would violently oppose the loan, and that such an attack would seriously jeopardise the prospects of the Government at the general election which is due to take place in the latter half of 1948. In recent years the Union Government have as a matter of policy refused to hold large sums in sterling on the grounds that if they did so they would be criticised for committing their country to a currency the future of which was uncertain; there were some fears that a gold loan would lay them open to similar attacks.

In the event the total was fixed at £80 million and the U.K. gave assurances in the Agreement concerning the payment of interest, the continued participation of U.K. capital in the development of the Union and the continued purchase of certain South African exports, which (and especially the last) should go far to mollify opposition. Indeed we understand that a large section of Nationalist opinion is already reconciled to the Agreement. There has, however, been considerable criticism, both from the Nationalists and from supporters of the Government, that the Agreement did not safeguard exports of footwear from the Union to the U.K., and we may expect this ticklish question to cause the Government some trouble in Parliament.

In short:—

(a) a general election this year hangs over the heads of the Government and there is no certainty that they will win it;

(b) anything which commits South Africa to the support of sterling is politically dangerous;

(c) it is clearly important that nothing should be done on the U.K. side which would embarrass Field-Marshal Smuts' government in handling this matter in the Union Parliament.

The loan is subject to ratification by the Union Parliament and we understand that Field-Marshal Smuts intends to introduce the necessary legislation early in the new session; this starts on about 15th January.

417 CO 537/3608 16 July–28 Oct 1948

[Proposals for closer association in Central Africa]: minutes by A B Cohen, Sir T Lloyd and Mr Creech Jones

Sir T. Lloyd

I hope that you will be prepared to write to Sir E. Machtig as in the attached draft and to take part in the meeting with him some time next week.

There has been what I believe will prove to be a very important development in political alignments in Central Africa. The United Central Africa Association has become active in Southern Rhodesia under the leadership of Captain Harris, formerly Minister of Agriculture in the Southern Rhodesia Government, a post which he abandoned some time ago on the ground of ill-health. He is a close friend of Sir G. Huggins and indeed the latter held down his portfolio of agriculture as well as his own for a very considerable time in order to keep Captain Harris in the Cabinet while he was away.

This association has, sensibly enough, seen that there is no chance of amalgamation of the two Rhodesias and Nyasaland being agreed to by H.M. Government in the near future, even if it was agreed to by everybody else concerned. They are therefore now putting forward federation as a political aim, thus seeking to find a way round the strong differences in native policy between the territories. They have been up to Northern Rhodesia and talked to the elected members and Mr. Welensky[1] has now come round to the objective of federation. We do not yet know what Sir G. [sic]

[1] Roy Welensky, member of Executive Council, Northern Rhodesia, since 1940.

Gore-Browne's[2] views are. He is always opposed to amalgamation and if he changed his view on this would lose whatever shreds of confidence the Africans whom he represents may still have in him. He is probably for this reason not coming out too strongly in favour of federation since a large section of African opinion in Northern Rhodesia does not distinguish between it and amalgamation but I suspect we shall find when he gets here that he too favours federation as an aim.

I have asked Sir G. Rennie[3] for his views on this subject but these have not yet been received. I will however send on before the meeting with Sir E. Machtig a statement of our views. We are having a domestic discussion on Saturday morning to formulate these.

As far as I am concerned personally, I have myself for some time taken the view that federation of the three territories should be the ultimate aim of policy—I have expressed that view in various minutes which I have written. I have felt, however, that federation could not come until the Africans in Northern Rhodesia and Nyasaland had developed politically and were able both to take an intelligent decision on the question and to play an effective part in the federal arrangements. I am now, I must confess, beginning to wonder a little whether we are really right not to attempt to step forward towards federation (perhaps on the lines of the East Africa High Commission) in the fairly near future. The closer linking of a self-governing territory with two Protectorates would present very considerable administrative difficulties, but I do not believe that these would be insuperable.

There is clearly no possibility of getting a definite policy worked out before the discussions with the Northern Rhodesia delegation. All that Mr. Welensky wants to do is to put his personal views before the Secretary of State and the Secretary of State need, I think, only listen to them. But I do think it is rather important that we should clear our minds and discuss the matter with the C.R.O. before the delegation arrives and it is for that reason that we have raised the question. After the letter has gone off, if you approve, the papers should be recirculated urgently to Mr. Lambert[4] for further consideration of the important letter at No. 52.

A.B.C.
16.7.48

We are having a meeting at 10.30 tomorrow morning about the Northern Rhodesia delegation and at 12 with Mr. Gordon Walker and Sir E. Machtig about federation in Central Africa. I was not able to get hold of Mr. Clark[5] until this afternoon but Mr. Lambert and I have now had a general talk with him. Meanwhile Sir G. Rennie's letter of the 17th July has arrived and, as you will see, he is against any immediate move by H.M.G.

I think nevertheless that we shall have to consider our future policy pretty seriously. For the purposes of the Northern Rhodesia delegation we can, I think, advise the Secretary of State to do little more than listen to what Mr. Welensky has to say. I should prefer to explain to you orally tomorrow morning Mr. Clark's point of view. It is that federation is desirable as a fairly early objective, provided that the

[2] Sir Stewart Gore-Browne, member of Legislative Council, Northern Rhodesia, since 1935.
[3] Gov of Northern Rhodesia; formerly chief secretary of Kenya. [4] C E Lambert, CO assistant secretary.
[5] W A W Clark, chief secretary to Central African Council, 1945–1948; see also note on p 292.

Southern Rhodesia Government can get sufficient popular support for it in Southern Rhodesia and provided that it can be put across with Nyasaland and the Africans in Northern Rhodesia. What should be aimed at is a scheme generally similar to the East African inter-territorial scheme but perhaps extending to education as well as the other various subjects. Mr. Clark also is in favour of a Governor General for Central Africa (I cannot say that I share his view in this). I have discussed with Mr. Clark the real crux of the matter, namely how to get over the difficulty of retaining H.M.G.'s ultimate responsibility to Parliament in matters covered by any federal scheme in respect of Northern Rhodesia and Nyasaland while not infringing Southern Rhodesia's position as a self-governing colony. I have expressed the view to Mr. Clark that unless some means of safeguarding this ultimate responsibility could be found we should not succeed in putting over any scheme either in Parliament here or to the Africans of the two northern territories. Mr. Clark has not been able to produce any solution to this problem. His own view is, I think, that the retention of reserve powers in the ordinary sense is not necessary. It was no doubt this crux which led the Royal Commission of 1938–39[6] to the conclusion that federation was not a practical solution (see page 213 of their Report). I do not myself believe that the problem is insoluble but it will need a great deal of thought.

Perhaps I can develop this further orally when we meet.

A.B.C.
21.7.48

The Secretary of State in his note attached opposite has asked for advice as to the line to be taken in discussion with Sir G. Huggins on the question of closer co-ordination in Central Africa. To provide the necessary information Mr. Lambert has prepared the attached factual note, with three appendices, which I think gives the full background, and with which I am in entire agreement.

After Mr. Lambert's note was written Mr. Welensky telephoned to Mr. Lambert to say that he had had a talk with Sir G. Huggins, and Mr. Lambert and I have since had a talk with him. Sir G. Huggins has told Mr. Welensky that he now favours federation rather than amalgamation and that he wishes to discuss the matter with Mr. Creech Jones in Mr. Welensky's company. He has asked Mr. Welensky to approach the Colonial Office in order to arrange such a meeting. Mr. Lambert has at my suggestion asked the Private Office to proceed accordingly, subject to the Secretary of State's agreement, and to consult the C.R.O. as to a suitable time. We have also suggested that Mr. Gordon Walker, who, as you will remember, presided over our meeting with the C.R.O. last summer on this subject, might be invited to attend the meeting. In any case the C.R.O. would no doubt wish to be represented.

As regards the line to be taken with Sir G. Huggins, my views and those of Mr. Lambert are as follows. We think that in the interests of the development of Northern Rhodesia and Nyasaland, of defence, and of commonwealth relations some fairly early move towards the closer co-ordination of the Central African Territories is desirable. The last point seems to us particularly important in view of the somewhat uncertain attitude of the present Government of the Union and of the need to strengthen Southern Rhodesia's hand in dealing with the Union. Quite apart from

---

[6] *Report of the Rhodesia-Nyasaland Royal Commission* (chairman, Lord Bledisloe, formerly gov-gen of New Zealand), Cmd 5949, 1939.

that, Sir G. Huggins, who certainly uses his influence in favour of liberal policy towards Africans, has now been returned by the Southern Rhodesian electorate with a large majority and is therefore in a very strong position locally. His last Government fell over an issue connected with the Central African Council; in fact he went to the country on the principle that a Government which makes agreements with its neighbours must stick to them. The size of his majority is, I understand, mainly due to the solidarity of the ex-service mens' votes behind him. In other words he is largely supported by the new post-war immigrants who are inclined to take an unconventional and considerably more progressive line towards Africans than seasoned residents. These people are liable to become more Rhodesian as they live longer in Africa and it is in our interests to do everything we can to encourage them in a more liberal direction. Mr. Clark, after studying Central African relations during his time in Salisbury, has always emphasised that by wise influence through the medium of the Central African Council we can do much to encourage Southern Rhodesians to move gradually towards our conception of native policy. We believe that by strengthening the Central African co-ordinating machinery we could exercise a more powerful influence. For all these reasons we think that the policy of H.M.G. in the U.K. should be towards some form of closer co-ordinating machinery in Central Africa, provided that certain conditions can be fulfilled.

The conditions which must be fulfilled are those mentioned in the discussions with the Northern Rhodesia delegation last July, namely:—

(1) African opinion in Northern Rhodesia and Nyasaland must be prepared to accept whatever machinery it is proposed to set up and there must be provision for African participation in any central assembly. Mr. Welensky's view is that it should not be too difficult to persuade Southern Rhodesians to accept African participation. But it may well be difficult to persuade African opinion to accept closer co-ordination. That will be a matter in the first instance for local diplomacy.

(2) Some acceptable solution must be found to the problem of linking together a self-governing colony with two non-self-governing protectorates. This difficulty is brought out clearly at the end of Mr. Lambert's note. Either Southern Rhodesia must be prepared to accept some redefinition of her self-governing status in respect of the joint services—it is most unlikely that she would be willing to do this—or H.M.G. in the U.K. and the U.K. Parliament would have to accept the abrogation of the Secretary of State for the Colonies' reserve powers in respect of these joint services.[7]

There are two other points which would have to be covered:—

(3) Since Nyasaland would have to come into the federation in order to justify its setting up, Nyasaland opinion would have to be fully consulted and persuaded to accept this step. Mr. Welensky believes from conversations with the European unofficial representatives from Nyasaland who are in London that there should be no difficulty about them at any rate.

(4) The position of Barotseland would have to be secured. The Barotse were inclined to ask earlier in the year that they should become a protectorate like the High Commission Territories.[8] If any constitutional change affecting the status of Barotseland and its relations with H.M.G. were contemplated, the Barotse Council

---

[7] Sir T Lloyd wrote in the margin here against the second alternative: 'We can assume that [this] is the only practicable course; and Parliament's consent to this abrogation of responsibility is therefore essential to the plan'.

[8] See part 3 of this volume, 202 & 203.

would have to be consulted. It is doubtful whether a scheme of co-ordination within the limits which would be possible would in fact affect the status of Barotseland, but the point should not be lost sight of.

We think that the form of any machinery for closer co-ordination should be similar to that of the East African inter-territorial scheme, with a Central Executive and Central Assembly, but with the Territories retaining their identity and their own constitutions and with the Legislative Councils exercising control over the actions of the Central Executive and Assembly through the power of the purse. Mr. Welensky, while he felt that this might well be the right step to take, was rather doubtful whether Sir G. Huggins and Southern Rhodesian opinion would accept it as sufficient. Mr. Lambert and I feel that we should make it quite clear that this is the furthest that H.M.G. could contemplate going.

As regards the action to be taken to consider this matter further, we recommend that the suggestion should be made to Sir G. Huggins that some form of local representative committee under the aegis of the Central African Council should be set up to examine the whole problem, the difficulties involved, and possible methods of overcoming them. We are not in favour of a Royal Commission set up by H.M.G. in the U.K. and I know that Mr. Welensky will take the same view.

We do not feel that such a committee could be set up until Ministers here had considered the broad issues involved by federation. In other words it would not be sufficient merely to say to Sir G. Huggins and Mr. Welensky that they should examine the problem locally and submit their recommendations to H.M.G. It would, we feel, be necessary for H.M.G. to go as far as to say that they felt that there were strong arguments in favour of federation, provided that certain difficulties could be overcome, and then to ask that local representatives should consider these difficulties. If this course were adopted, it would follow that, assuming that reasonably satisfactory solutions were found by the local committee, it would not be easy for H.M.G. to refuse to proceed further.

The important point seems to us to be to make it quite clear to Sir G. Huggins and Mr. Welensky what we believe the difficulties to be and then to place squarely on them the task of finding solutions for these difficulties. The main difficulty is the probable opposition of African opinion, at any rate until the limitations on any central machinery had been explained. The important point is that the various European representatives in Central Africa should be made to realise that before any scheme for closer co-ordination can be entertained by H.M.G. it will be necessary for them to convince African opinion in Northern Rhodesia and Nyasaland that there is nothing to fear from the establishment of such central machinery.[9]

There is finally the question of bringing the two Governors into consultation. I think that we should certainly inform them by telegram of what is going on, but I suggest that the discussion with Sir G. Huggins and Mr. Welensky should be on a purely informal basis and that, if the Secretary of State agrees with the line which we have suggested, he should merely say to Sir G. Huggins and Mr. Welensky that this is the way in which his mind is working and that it will be necessary for him to consult not only with his colleagues but also with the two Governors. Following on the conversation a further communication should be sent to the Governors and that might perhaps be followed by a discussion with the Central African Council.

---

[9] Sir T Lloyd wrote in the margin against this paragraph: 'I agree'.

The Secretary of State may wish to discuss this matter with Sir T. Lloyd, Mr. Lambert and myself before talking to Sir. G. Huggins.

A.B.C.
12.10.48

I agree with the general lines of Mr Cohen's minute.

2. The more we can present this next move, if made, as 'closer association' and the less as 'federation' the better will be the chances of persuading African opinion to accept it. It is not 'federation' in the strict sense of the word.

3. Any local C'ttee set up to study the problems involved shd., of course, include African representatives from N. R. and Nyasaland. If Sir G. Huggins jibs at that the inquiry is not worth starting.

4. It might be well to consult with C.R.O., at the Ministerial level, before the proposed talks with Sir G. Huggins & Mr Welensky. . . .

T.I.K.L.
13.10.48

The British Govt. cannot at this point initiate discussions regarding the future of the Rhodesias & I have not discussed the matter with Sir Geoffrey [sic] Huggins. It is premature for me to initiate any discussions with the Commonwealth Relations Office as S. of State, although I have told Mr. Noel-Baker that the matter may come up & in that case he & I would confer. But as yet we, i.e. the C.O. should *not* prepare for the consideration of the C.R.O. any draft. I do not think it proper that I should bring Mr. Welensky, Sir G. Huggins & myself & Mr. Noel-Baker together to discuss the problem. The desire for such a meeting should come from Sir Geoffrey [sic]. There remains the difficulty that Mr. Welensky is pressing for some discussions. I will see him and explain the position. The political stuff is dynamite & must be handled with great care. We must go slow with such discussions.

A.C.J.
21.10.48

I saw Mr. Welensky & told him:

(a) H.M.G. could not initiate discussions;

(b) Neither C.O. nor myself could bring Huggins & Welensky & myself together for a discussion;

(c) Obviously the matter was one which (if he felt strongly about it) he should take up in the way he thought best;

(d) Huggins had seen me & we had talked about many things & had had chances of talking about this but Huggins had made no mention of it;

(e) H.M.G. had not considered Federation or any other course, & therefore I could not express their view & speak officially about the question;

(f) We were watching changes in Africa & the world, but were still conscious of the grave apprehensions of Africans about S. Rhodesia policy & alive to our own special regard for African interests. No scheme that failed completely to satisfy African interests or win African approval had slightest chance of success.

(g) I mentioned that U.K. was also interested in High Com. territories in S. Africa.

Mr. Welensky went off to keep appointment with Sir A. Vincent & with Sir G.

Huggins.[10] Huggins subsequently made a press statement about Federation. Welensky recognised the necessity, he said, of carrying Africans along any line of closer association proposed. He added that if S. Rhodesia was not interested then there was still E. Africa with which some arrangement might be worked out.

It was a friendly conversation.

A.C.J.
28.10.48

---

[10] Sir Alfred Vincent was a member of the East Africa Central Legislative Council.

418 CO 537/3608, no 45 8 Oct 1948

'Central African federation': minute by Mr Creech Jones to A B Cohen

The Central African Council has met regularly and secured a measure of genuine co-operation between Nyasaland and Northern and Southern Rhodesia. It has achieved results in the fields of research, labour, migration, roads and communications. Action depends on the willingness of the Governments to implement decisions.

The basic objections to Amalgamation set out by the Bledisloe Royal Commission remain. There continue in the two British Protectorates the strongest feelings among the Africans against amalgamation of the territories. The pronouncements of S. Rhodesia native policy are out of line with those of N. Rhodesia and Nyasaland.

Since the war however certain changes have occurred in the situation which suggest some revaluation of the existing arrangements. Our strategic needs in Africa, the importance of more thorough going development, the desirability of certain common services and regional approach suggest the need of a closer association of the three territories. I would add that a more intimate connection with the S.A. High Commission Territories ought also to be achieved.

The existing Council has no real executive power and the discharge of its recommendations depends on the resources available to the territories and the willingness of the respective governments to implement. Some loose form of federation might be within the realm of possibility which preserved native policy to the individual territories, fully recognised African interests in Central government and did no prejudice to the rights of the African populations in law and discrimination.

An effort was made to reach such a solution in East Africa and the experiment has aroused no opposition. There are considerable difficulties about the Central Africa idea because (a) the deep African dislike to native policy in S. Rhodesia and South Africa, (b) the desire of S. Rhodesia for dominion status and white domination and segregation (c) the trust and native protective obligations entered into by H.M.G. under treaty.

What then might be done?

419 DEFE 4/19, COS 3(49)10 — 8 Jan 1949

'Meeting with the UK high commissioner in South Africa': COS Committee minutes of discussion with Sir E Baring about effects on military planning of the change of government in South Africa

Sir John Edelsten[1] welcomed Sir Evelyn Baring and said that the Committee would be very glad of his views on the implications of the recent change of government in South Africa, particularly as regards Defence Matters and consultation on Commonwealth military planning.

Sir Evelyn Baring said that the present Government of the Union kept their own counsel, and to that extent they were incalculable. Compared with the previous Government they had certain drawbacks from the British point of view. Many of them had spent their lives in anti-British agitation, and during the last war the Nationalist Party had based its policy on the example of the neutrality of Eire. Also, whereas in dealing with the former Government all that had been necessary was to obtain the agreement of the Prime Minister, either directly or through his Service Advisers, the Nationalists were apt to take decisions without professional advice and it was no longer possible to hope to obtain the agreement of the Government by first approaching the Services Heads or any one Minister. The views of no one member of the Government could be accepted in advance as an indication of the policy which it was likely to adopt.

On the other hand, from the Defence point of view, the Nationalist Party had certain points in its favour. They were very anti-Communist. They had a strong regional consciousness, and maintained that the Union should be the leading country in the defence of Africa, or at any rate Southern Africa. In this respect, although in a future war they would probably side with the United Kingdom, they had made it clear that their first consideration was the local security of the Union; there was nothing they feared more than internal trouble in the Union itself and they would, therefore, not be likely to commit themselves in advance to sending forces to, say, the Middle East. A further point in their favour was that in spite of the difficult attitude they had adopted they might possibly prove to be more active in military planning than their predecessors.

Regarding the procedure for consultation on Commonwealth military planning, Sir Evelyn Baring recalled that the Union Government had not yet signified their approval of the conclusions of the recent conference of Commonwealth Prime Ministers. This approval would be necessary before any approach could be made for planning discussions to take place with the South African Service authorities and he suggested that, to this end, he might prepare the way by broaching the subject in personal conversation with members of the Government. He would put the view that the Middle East was really the first line of defence of the Union.

In the event of the Union agreeing to the talks being held they should take place, initially at least, in Pretoria at a time when Ministers would be available there. During the first half of the year the South African Parliament would be sitting in Cape Town, so he suggested that any talks should not take place until the session ended and Ministers returned to Pretoria. He agreed with the suggestion that it

---

[1] Vice-chief of the naval staff, in the chair.

might be possible to have a preliminary discussion in South Africa, on a broad regional basis, including the Middle East, the latter problem to be considered in detail at a subsequent conference in North Africa. The most that it could be hoped to obtain from the South Africans as a result of such talks would be an agreement to put certain facilities of the Union, including productive capacity and military installations, at the disposal of the United Kingdom and an agreement in principle to the sending of forces to the Middle East, without any commitment as to the actual numbers which could be sent. Even so, such an undertaking and agreement would be difficult to obtain.

In discussion it was pointed out that any plan arrived at after discussion with the South African Services would be tentative and would in no way commit the South African Government. This point could be made clear to the South African Government when permission to hold the talks was being sought. But any plan, however tentative, would result in a considerable saving of time in the event of a decision taken on the outbreak of war to send forces.

In discussion it was agreed that the Planning Team should if possible visit Pretoria in the second half of the current year after conclusion of discussions in Australia and New Zealand.

The Committee:—

Thanked Sir Evelyn Baring for giving them the benefit of his views.

420 FO 800/445, ff 29–30 20 Apr 1949
[Meeting with Dr Malan]: minute by Mr Attlee to Mr Bevin

1. When I saw Dr. Malan[1] this morning he said that he would be glad if he could have an opportunity, while he is in London, for an exchange of views with United Kingdom Ministers on some general questions of major policy affecting Africa as a whole. The three particular points which he mentioned were:—

(a) *Political*. He said that the Union Government were keenly interested in developments likely to arise from the Atlantic Pact, for many of the countries associated with the Pact had colonial possessions in Africa which, directly or indirectly, would become involved if any of those countries were at war. Apart therefore from any obligations arising from her position as a member of the Commonwealth, South Africa had this other interest in the possible implications of the Pact.

(b) *Native policy*. The Union Government were gravely concerned at the long-term consequences of Indian immigration into Africa. They were convinced that the unrestricted admission of Indians would hamper the natural evolution of the African native. The problems to which this would give rise were likely to become even more acute in Kenya than in South Africa. It would be helpful if a consistent policy could be applied in this matter throughout the whole of East Africa. But in any event they would welcome discussion with United Kingdom Ministers on what they regard as a problem common to themselves and us.

(c) *Militarisation*. Dr. Malan did not indicate precisely what he had in mind under

[1] D F Malan, Prime Minister of South Africa, 1948–1954, leader of the National Party.

this head; but he spoke generally of a need to consider whether the various parts of Africa were in future to be "militarised", as European countries had been.

2. I am sending copies of this minute to the Secretary of State for Commonwealth Relations and Secretary of State for the Colonies.

My own time is likely to be fully occupied during the next week with the main business of the Commonwealth meeting. I should be grateful therefore if, in the first instance at any rate, you could find an opportunity of seeing Dr. Malan (with the other Ministers to whom I have sent copies of this minute), and have a general talk with him on these subjects.

421 CAB 134/1, A(49)2 5 July 1949

'Co-operation with the Union of South Africa': CO memorandum for the Cabinet Africa Committee

In talks with United Kingdom Ministers during his visit to London in April Dr. Malan showed his anxiety for closer co-operation with this country and the other European powers concerned with Africa in defence, immigration, transport, economic development and 'native policy' (the vague phrase commonly current in the Union). Similar suggestions have been put forward by Mr. te Water the South African Ambassador at large, in discussions both with the East and Central African Governors and with Ministers in this country. Mr. te Water is particularly anxious to arrange a high level conference on natural resources and the preservation of the fertility of the soil.

2. The present Union Government has shown itself deeply interested, perhaps even more so than General Smuts' Government, in furthering a policy of co-operation with the other African powers. This is no doubt due to their fear of isolation from world opinion as a result of South Africa's difficulties with United Nations Organization and the almost universal unpopularity in other countries of the policy of apartheid. Internally South Africa has to face for the next few years the danger of political unrest among the Indian, coloured and native populations who are denied political rights and industrial unrest in the mining industry on which her whole economy is based. Externally she fears renewed pressure from the Government of India in connection with the Indian population of Natal and continued pressure in the United Nations on all or any of the questions over which South African policy is not accepted by world opinion. Moreover South Africa, like other parts of Africa, has to contend with Communist efforts to disrupt the existing order. In the face of these dangers it seems that public opinion in the Union increasingly realises that the future of South Africa is linked up with the future of Africa as a whole. Mr. te Water has recently said that isolationism is dead in the Union except among a small body of uncovertibles.

3. It appears desirable to consider in some detail what the attitude of His Majesty's Government in the United Kingdom should be to these recent South African suggestions for closer co-operation, not only on technical but also on political questions. The following factors have to be taken into account:—

(a) In the interests of Commonwealth relations it is desirable that we should co-operate as closely as possible with the Union on all matters of common interest to the African territories.

(b) Co-operation with the Union in defence matters is accepted policy. The more highly developed resources of the Union, particularly in the industrial sphere, and her large European population make it inevitable that South Africa shall play a leading part in African defence.

(c) In transport, research, campaigns against disease and the locust and economic development generally South Africa can play a leading part, again through her more highly developed economy.

(d) South African policy towards African development is fundamentally different to ours. South Africa aims at maintaining a stratified society in order to safeguard the economic and political domination of the European and, above all, the Dutch community. Our policy aims at the political, economic and social development of the tropical African territories to fit them for self-government.

(e) In West Africa we are seeking to build up politically and economically stable communities capable, at any rate in the case of Nigeria and the Gold Coast, of becoming states with internal self-government which will themselves choose to remain within the Commonwealth. When this policy was described to Mr. te Water in a recent conversation he said that it was fully consistent with the policy of apartheid, which recognised the necessity for developing African institutions in purely African areas. In fact our West African policy is radically different from the policy of the Union. Public opinion in West Africa is bitterly hostile to the Union, more so since the present Union Government came into power, and any suggestion that the Union should have a say in any question of policy affecting the West African territories would be entirely unacceptable to them.

(f) In East and Central Africa our policy aims at building up political experience among the African inhabitants, through local government and participation in central government, to the stage at which they can play an equal part with the immigrant communities in administration, politics and the economic and social life of the territories. At present, speaking generally, Africans in these territories cannot compete with Europeans and Indians in government, politics or business and the European leaders have so far accepted the general policy of African advancement. When, however, Africans reach the stage of competing with Europeans and Indians on equal terms, a delicate situation will have to be faced, since the immigrant communities will at that stage have to accept full partnership with Africans. South Africa has close links with the East and Central African territories and, particularly in Kenya and Northern Rhodesia, there is a danger that she might use her influence to oppose African advancement and might even seek to detach European opinion in East Africa and Central Africa from the loyalty to the United Kingdom. Such a move on the part of South Africa will meet with strong opposition on the part of larger sections of the local European Communities, but might none the less be embarrassing.

4. There are thus two opposing sets of factors to be taken into consideration. On the one hand we wish to remain on terms of close friendship with South Africa and we need South African help both in the defence of tropical Africa and in solving the technical problems of African development. On the other hand our political approach to African problems is fundamentally different. The South African attitude is intensely disliked by public opinion in West Africa. Any policy of close co-operation with South Africa in dealing with purely West African problems would be unaccept-

able to the West African territories. In East and Central Africa there is a danger that South African influence might be used against the policy of His Majesty's Government in the United Kingdom for the advancement of the African inhabitants.

5. This paper does not attempt to discuss policy in the sphere of defence and security; it is concerned primarily with the technical and political spheres.

6. In all technical matters it is suggested that we must continue to co-operate to the closest possible extent with South Africa. The Union already plays a leading part on the Southern African Air Transport Council. The South African Government was represented at the recent preparatory conference at Lisbon on rail, road and water transport. The main conference will take place next year in the Union and the preparatory secretariat will be organised by the Union Government. A full dress conference on African research problems will be held in the Union in October. South Africa has taken her full part in the international conferences on tsetse, locusts, rinderpest and soil erosion. She is now accepted by the French and Belgians as a full partner in the programme of conferences on technical co-operation in Africa and it is intended to invite her to be represented at the conference which it is hoped to hold during September in London to discuss the machinery for maintaining and promoting this technical co-operation. South African leaders cannot therefore argue that South Africa is left out of plans for technical co-operation in Africa and it is suggested that we should lose no opportunity of impressing this on them. We ought also to lose no opportunity of furthering co-operation on all technical subjects of common interest, since there is obviously a great deal to be gained by doing so.

7. There can clearly be no objection in principle to Mr. te Water's suggestion (see paragraph 1) for a high level conference on soil erosion; but it is suggested that this conference should be fitted into the general programme of technical conferences in Africa. The present programme covers the period up to the end of 1950 and it would be desirable if possible to avoid having any new conference arranged for a date before 1951. So many conferences are now taking place on African problems that there is a serious danger that, unless some limit is imposed to these gatherings, key officers working in the field will be unable to make effective progress with their real jobs. A conference on soil erosion at which the South Africans were represented was held in the Belgian Congo last year and there is to be a conference on rural economy in Nigeria this November at which they will also be represented.

8. In the sphere of political co-operation we are severely limited by the fundamental differences between South African policy and our own. To mention the three matters in which the South African Government is particularly interested, we can follow the same principle as the South Africans in connection with immigration, the principle of controlling immigration from outside in the interests of the existing inhabitants of the Territories concerned; but our policy in this respect must be entirely non-discriminatory; the South Africans may not be able to accept this. In connection with African forces we cannot accept South African ideas, which are entirely opposed to the arming of Africans. Both on defence, internal security and political grounds we are bound to maintain African fighting forces. In 'native policy' generally we are aiming at entirely different objectives, they at the maintenance of white domination, we at full African advancement. So long as South African policy remains as it now is there is nothing to be gained by the formal discussion of these fundamental differences. Indeed, if it were known publicly that we were discussing these matters with the South Africans, the most violent suspicions against our good

faith would be aroused throughout West Africa and among thinking Africans in the East African and Central African territories. Mr. te Water has stated in his most recent conversations in London that he fully recognises the uselessness of any general conference on these subjects.

9. While any attempt to reach agreement with the South Africans on these major political issues would be futile, and indeed harmful, it is suggested that there is much to be gained from the exchange of information with South African Ministers and officials, and indeed with all interested students of the problem in South Africa, on administrative and political problems. From our point of view it is important that South Africans should both know what we are doing in our African territories and understand, even if they do not agree with the reasons for our policy. We ought therefore to consider how best we can promote this exchange of information and ideas. The following methods are suggested:—

(a) The United Kingdom High Commissioner in South Africa should be provided with much more background material on our problems and policy in East, Central and West Africa, so as to enable him and his staff to discuss these matters more fully with South African Ministers and officials.

(b) Visits to the Union by suitable people from this country and from the African Colonial territories, whether official or unofficial, should be encouraged for the purpose of discussions with people in South Africa concerned with similar problems. Such discussions should preferably be private and informal.

(c) Suitable South Africans should be encouraged to visit African Colonial territories both in East and Central Africa and in West Africa to see what we are doing and to gain an understanding of our policy. In connection with this suggestion it should be noted that when the Nigerian Government were informed of Mr. te Water's proposed visit to Lagos, which was subsequently cancelled entirely on his own motion, they reacted strongly and said that such a visit would be very embarrassing and might do considerable political harm, since it would arouse suspicion of our motives and might lead to awkward incidents through leading Africans refusing to meet him. On the other hand, if South Africa is to realise that the fact of African political advancement in West Africa must be accepted, there is much to be gained from such visits by leading South Africans and it is felt that we must attempt to convince the West African Governments that on balance it is desirable that such visits should take place.

(d) South African officials from the Union Native Affairs Department engaged in field work should be encouraged to attend conferences in this country, such as the African Summer Conferences in Cambridge. So far the only South African who has attended is the official of the Native Affairs Department who represents South Africa at international conferences in Europe and the United States.

(e) Close contact should be maintained for the purpose of exchanging information and documents between the African Studies Branch of the Colonial Office and the appropriate government organisation in the Union. Mr. te Water said during his recent visit that he intended to recommend to his Government that an African Affairs Department should be set up.

(f) Closer informal contact should be maintained between the Colonial Office and the political officers at South Africa House. If these officers visited the Colonial Office regularly much current information could be given to them in the same way as information is given to the member of the United States Embassy in London who is concerned with Colonial affairs.

10. If a policy can be worked out on the basis of the above recommendations it is suggested they should form the subject of a despatch to the Governors of British Colonial territories in Africa. It may be, however, that, before this despatch is sent, the recommendations in this memorandum, subject to any views of the African Committee, should be communicated to Sir Evelyn Baring so as to obtain his comments.

422 CAB 129/36/1, CP(49)155 19 July 1949

'Bechuanaland Protectorate: succession to the chieftainship of the Bamangwato tribe': Cabinet memorandum by Mr Noel-Baker (CRO) on Seretse Khama

[On 30 Sept 1948 at a registry office in Kensington, Seretse Khama, heir to the chieftaincy of the Bamangwato in the Bechuanaland Protectorate, married Ruth Williams, a London secretary, and did so against all advice. Reversing its initially unfavourable reactions, the Bamangwato *kgotla* (assembly) decided in June 1949 that it would still accept Seretse as chief. As a result, Seretse's uncle Tshekedi immediately announced his intention of resigning as regent. Representations were then received from the Union government asking the British government not to confirm Seretse's formal designation as chief. Sir E Baring wrote to Sir P Liesching (CRO), 11 July 1949, taking an apocalyptic view. Prompt recognition of Seretse might provoke a disastrous and dangerous head-on collision with the Union 'at the worst possible time and for the worst possible reason': 'this incident on the edge of the Kalahari might lead to the complete secession of South Africa from the Commonwealth' (DO 35/4114, no 34). This undoubtedly set the alarm-bells ringing in the CRO: Gordon Walker (parliamentary under-secretary for Commonwealth relations) was quick to see that 'this is an extremely grave matter and can involve us in historic calamities if we are not careful' (minute, 15 July 1949). The high commissioner recommended holding a judicial inquiry, in order to buy time, and Creech Jones supported this: 'immediate refusal to recognise Seretse would be likely to have serious repercussions, and, from the Colonial Office point of view, is the worst possible course' (CO 537/4714, minute by Cohen, 20 July 1949). Noel-Baker's memorandum as printed here largely reiterated Baring's arguments, but expressed them even more forcibly. On 21 July 1949 the Cabinet agreed to hold an inquiry into Seretse's suitability for the chieftainship, which would 'allow time for reflection by all concerned'. It was agreed vigorously to rebut any suggestion that their attitude was determined in any way by racial arguments 'about mixed marriages as such'; their concern was for the stability and well-being of the Bamangwato people, and recognition of a chief with a white wife 'might have consequences gravely prejudicial to good government. . .'. (CAB 129/16, CM 47(49)8.]

A difficult problem, to which some prominence has been given in the Press recently, has arisen from the marriage to an English girl of Seretse Khama, the Chief Designate of the Bamangwato Tribe in the Bechuanaland Protectorate. This is the largest and most important tribe in the Protectorate. Owing to Seretse having been a minor when his father died, his uncle Tshekedi has been for a considerable time the Acting Chief of the Tribe and has achieved the position of being one of the most prominent Africans in South Africa. Under the local native custom the Chieftainship is hereditary, descending from the father to the eldest son, but the local Native Administration Proclamation provides that, upon the occurrence of a vacancy in the Chieftainship, the tribe must designate the former Chief's successor according to native customs and cause the name to be submitted to the Resident Commissioner, with a view to seeking the High Commissioner's recognition and the Secretary of State's confirmation of such designation.

2. Seretse, who is now a man of 27, has had an unusually prolonged education, which was arranged for him by Tshekedi at the cost of tribal funds. He was sent two years ago to England, where he spent a year at Balliol College, Oxford, and afterwards became a law student at London University. When in London he met an English girl—Ruth Williams—at some social function for Colonial students, and they were married last year, in spite of vigorous warnings given to both parties by interested friends that such a marriage would be resented by the Bamangwato tribe. Ruth Williams is, apparently, a fairly well educated girl, interested in Church matters, and there is nothing against her character personally.

3. Shortly after the marriage, Seretse proceeded by air to South Africa to discuss his position with the tribe. A series of meetings took place and the local Resident Commissioner reported that, although there was no opposition to Seretse's claim to be chief, there was almost solid disapproval of the marriage among the Bamangwato. This disapproval was based upon the following grounds:—

(a) General racial bias.

(b) Seretse's neglect to conform to the formalities required in an African marriage.

(c) Aversion to a possible half-caste heir.

The result was that Seretse returned to England to complete his law studies and the position remained unresolved.

4. Last month Seretse went out again by air to the Bechuanaland Protectorate and further meetings were held. Tshekedi and his chief followers reiterated their strong objection to the marriage which Seretse had made. At the final meeting, however, Seretse made an emotional appeal, which resulted in a very large majority of those present acclaiming him as the hereditary heir to the Chieftainship. The High Commissioner states that it would appear that constitutional questions regarding the marriage were rather submerged in the process and that the implications of the marriage were not defined. Tshekedi subsequently made a formal statement to the effect that tradition was being so severely flouted, and native law and custom so abused, that he proposed, having wound up his administration, to leave the Bamangwato Reserve, and he declared that he would never concur in acceptance of a white woman as the Chief's first or principal wife.

5. In the ordinary course, the signification of approval by the majority of the tribe would be regarded as an adequate ground for proceeding to recognise Seretse. It appears, however, that the recent meetings were not very fully representative of the tribe as a whole, since those present included more than half the men of the tribal capital, but only about one-fiftieth of those in the country districts. There had also evidently been a good deal of propaganda by certain members of the tribe who nurse various personal grievances against Tshekedi. Nevertheless, it is surprising that there should have been such a sudden reversal of the opinion expressed by the great majority of the tribe last year. The High Commissioner states that the local administrative aspects are such that he feels great hesitation about the immediate recognition of Seretse. In his opinion, the doubts cast upon the representative character of the assembly, the indefinite nature of the decisions taken at it, the

obscurities relating to the status and position of Seretse's wife and any children of the marriage, and the dangers of a split in the tribe and of a breakdown of native administration, are sufficient reasons for holding some further enquiry, which would allow time for a considered verdict.

6. There are, moreover, other wider considerations involved. The suggestion that we should recognise a chief who is married to a white woman has caused intense feeling among Europeans, both in the Union of South Africa and in Southern Rhodesia. Representations have been made to me by the High Commissioner for the Union in London, on behalf of his Government, to the effect that the repercussions in the Union of a white woman becoming the Chieftainess in an African tribe will be extremely grave. Similar views have also been expressed to our High Commissioner, Sir Evelyn Baring, by the Prime Minister of Southern Rhodesia. Sir Evelyn Baring reports that information which he has received, from such a reliable authority as the Secretary of the Department of External Affairs, has convinced him that this matter is the gravest which has faced us since he first went to South Africa. It is suggested that the more extreme Nationalists will argue that the recognition of Seretse would demonstrate the folly of allowing the existence side by side in Southern Africa of two systems of native administration diametrically opposed to one another. They would say that South Africans should not and cannot remain associated with a country which recognises officially an African Chief married to a white woman, and they would make Seretse's recognition the occasion of an appeal to the country for the establishment of a Republic, and not only of a Republic, but of a Republic outside the Commonwealth. Sir Evelyn Baring states that the South African Prime Minister is desperately worried and feels that he could not successfully oppose an extremist offensive on these lines. It must be remembered in this connection that the Union Government have a particularly close interest in the Bechuanaland Protectorate, since this is one of the territories which, in view of the provisions in the South Africa Act of 1909, they look upon as due to be transferred to the Union. The question of such transfer has been frequently raised by the Union Government and, quite apart, therefore, from the graver possibilities indicated above, the demand for the transfer of the High Commission Territories might clearly become more insistent if we disregarded the Union Government's views in a matter of this kind in relation to one of these territories. The fact that Dr. Malan is feeling extreme anxiety, rather than jubilation, at the present development, is evidence that the threat to the Commonwealth relationship must be taken seriously. Indeed, we cannot exlude the possibility of an armed incursion into the Bechuanaland Protectorate from the Union if Seretse were to be recognised forthwith, while feeling on the subject is inflamed.

7. In all these circumstances it seems clearly important that a decision in favour of Seretse's recognition, if it is ever to be taken, should not be rushed, and that there should be due time for reflection and enquiry. In the Bechuanaland Protectorate Native Administration Proclamation there is a provision to the effect that, if any doubt arises whether a person designated as chief is worthy or capable of exercising that office justly, or for any other sufficient reasons is a fit and proper person to discharge the functions of chief, the High Commissioner may direct that a judicial enquiry should be held to enquire into the matter and to report thereon to the High Commissioner, who shall then decide the matter. The High Commissioner accordingly proposes that use should be made of this provision and that an enquiry should be held, presided over by the Judge of the High Courts of the High Commission

Territories, to investigate Seretse's suitability for the Chieftainship and the true views of the tribe. During the interval the present Regency would continue. It is proposed that the Judge should be assisted by two other officers, one of whom might be the Government Secretary of the Bechuanaland Protectorate and the other possibly a retired administrative officer from one of the other two High Commission Territories.

8. There appear to be two possible courses of action. We could declare now that we could not recognise Seretse in view of his disregard of the native custom in the matter of his marriage. The Local Administration, indeed, feel that if we are ever to take this line, it would be better to do so now. Sir Evelyn Baring has, however, explained that he has assumed that the United Kingdom Government would not be prepared to declare forthwith that Seretse cannot be recognised as Chief simply on the ground that an African married to a European woman cannot successfully perform the functions of a Chief. The other course of a judicial enquiry, which Sir Evelyn Baring has advocated as an alternative to immediate refusal to recognise Seretse, would at least demonstrate, both in the Union of South Africa and in Southern Rhodesia, that the Protectorate authorities and the United Kingdom Government were mindful of the gravity of the issues involved. It cannot, of course, be assumed that the enquiry would result in a report unfavourable to the recognition of Seretse. But the eventual decision would still remain with the High Commissioner and a careful enquiry into all the issues should have resulted in the presentation of a report which would set out fully the pros and cons, and would provide clearer material for a decision than exists at present.

9. I am still in communication with the High Commissioner on various aspects of the matter, and I will shortly be able to present a further report to my colleagues. This preliminary paper has been prepared in advance of further advice from the High Commissioner, since it is important that a decision should be announced as soon as possible. Seretse's wife is likely to leave for South Africa within a short time, and if she joins him there before we have made any announcement, the position will have become much more difficult, since the press would sensationally represent this as the arrival of a white "Chieftainess". It would be very difficult to overtake the implications of this, and any subsequent announcement would look like a harassed rear-guard action. The High Commissioner is anxious therefore to be authorised to make an announcement by 23rd July, when he is visiting Mafeking, and will be able to see both Seretse and Tshekedi, and so could first inform them personally.

10. In the light of the above, and of the further report which I hope to make, a decision has to be taken between (i) declaring now that Seretse is not recognised, and (ii) announcing the appointment of a judicial enquiry.

423 PREM 8/1361 19 July 1949

'Simonstown': CRO brief on possible transfer of the naval base

It has been suggested that, in the context of the present defence discussions with the South African Minister of Defence, there might be advantage in offering to surrender Simonstown Naval Base to the Union Government provided

(a) there is a satisfactory financial settlement;

(b) the South African Government agree to make available to the United Kingdom repair facilities at Simonstown during peace-time and joint user of the base during war-time.

2. There could be compelling reasons for a gesture of this kind, such as:—

(1) A desire on the political level to do something which would impress the present South African Government and bring us into closer relationship with them. This can only be judged by Ministers but it is at least relevant to observe that, in dealings with Commonwealth and other countries, the history of such unilateral gestures of goodwill is not unchequered with disappointment (cf. the surrender to Eire just before the last war of the Irish Ports).

(2) An insistent demand by the South African Government for the revision of the Simonstown Agreement. Although, however, we know that the supporters of the present Government have no liking of the Simonstown position (regarding our rights there as an invasion of the sovereign rights of South Africa and as something which might involve South Africa against her will in war), there has been no approach—so far as the Commonwealth Relations Office are aware—for the revision of the Agreement.

(3) A decision by the United Kingdom Government either that Simonstown was unnecessary for our over-all strategic plan or that financial stringency precluded its maintenance. This is not a matter on which the C.R.O. can express an opinion. If this should be the case, then obviously the question would need examination and it might well be that the prudent course would be to offer the South African Government Simonstown and acquire some credit with them by so doing. But we should be justified in suppressing our reasons and getting the best possible deal in return for a concession which would undoubtedly appeal to the people of South Africa.

3. If none of these reasons operates then the proposal falls to be examined on its own merits alone. On this the following observations may be made:—

(i) Even Field-Marshal Smuts at the height of the war with Germany had his difficulties in retaining the Simonstown position. There were those, even among his followers, who were unhappy at the retention by the United Kingdom of an enclave in South Africa. The Nationalists of course regularly inveighed against it. It was for this reason among others that Field-Marshal Smuts in 1942 refused to allow the United Kingdom to acquire any land whatever in South Africa for defence buildings and, while undertaking to provide any land that was needed, made it a condition that such defence establishments must be wound up as soon as possible after the end of the war. But Simonstown was invaluable to us as our only effective base in the South Atlantic and our strategic needs were undoubtedly eased by the existence of the Simonstown Agreement.

(ii) An Agreement is an agreement and the South Africans are very jealous of their scrupulous observance of their agreements. In a future war, if the Simonstown Agreement should not have been challenged before, the existence of the Agreement would be of value. It might not be sufficient to secure our retention of the base—and, in face of a hostile Government we presumably could not maintain our position à outrance—but we should at least be in a strong position if we could invoke a Governmental agreement.

(iii) The present South African Government may be expected to honour any obligations undertaken by them. But it is significant that our High Commissioner has warned us that, forthcoming though they at present are on these defence questions, they may yet be unwilling to undertake any *public* commitments in the event of war with Russia. If therefore we surrender Simonstown, it does not follow that we shall necessarily get a favourable agreement in which they would undertake a public commitment to make it available to us in the event of war. Though we have been given to understand that in the event of war with Russia South Africa would not be neutral, the South African Government cannot be expected to commit themselves in a formal public document to a sufficiently precise promise to secure Simonstown for us at need.

(iv) We cannot be certain that the present team of Ministers will necessarily be in the saddle if and when (unhappily) war should break out. There are sufficient indications of stresses and strains in the South African Cabinet to suggest that the present compromise Government, with a moderate Prime Minister and a further moderating influence in the Finance Minister (neither of them young men), might be swept away by a Government of more extreme Nationalists, whose attitude to the United Kingdom would be less forthcoming. It is true that these men hate and are frightened of Russia as much as anybody in South Africa but at the same time they are by nature isolationists. It is not inconceivable that such a Government would remain neutral, thinking it prudent to leave the Western powers and Russia to fight it out and hoping (as they did in 1940) that, even if the powers of darkness prevailed, they would leave the happy land of South Africa alone. This may seem an exaggeration but at least it is fair to observe that from 1939 to 1945 one of those countries in Europe which most detested the Germans—and had cause to—was not prepared to join the common struggle (what is now the Irish Republic). In such a position it is inconceivable that we should be able to retain the use of Simonstown but at least we should be in a stronger moral position if we could invoke the Simonstown Agreement.

(v) Simonstown is an expensive proposition and it seems highly unlikely, particularly in her present financial position, that South Africa would be able or willing to take it on. Yet, by making the suggestion, we should have put them in a very strong position to secure a revision of the Agreement or possibly its cancellation. Simonstown might then fall into disuse.

(vi) There is a political argument which should be borne in mind. At this early stage of the Nationalist Government is it wise to make to it spontaneous concessions which we did not make to the man (Field-Marshal Smuts) who stood by us, at the risk of his political existence, in two world wars? It has been the feeling in the Commonwealth Relations Office that this is one argument in connection with the vexed question of the cession of Basutoland, the Bechuanaland Protectorate and Swaziland. Should we be wise, at a time when our friends in South Africa are in the doldrums, to blow this favouring puff on the sails of those who, whatever their merits, are less close to us? To secure the abrogation of the Simonstown Agreement would, of course, be a first class political triumph for them.

4. In short, it is submitted that, unless an approach from the South African Government forces us to discuss this matter, it would be preferable to retain the

substance and not risk it for a shadow. In any event, if it be decided to proceed with the suggestion, it would be right first to consult the United Kingdom High Commissioner who alone can advise on the basis of a really up to date appreciation of the position in South Africa.

424 CAB 128/17, CM 3(50)1 31 Jan 1950

'Bechuanaland Protectorate: chieftainship of the Bamangwato': Cabinet conclusions on Seretse Khama

[The judicial inquiry into Seretse's suitability for the chieftainship was held in Serowe in November 1949 under Sir W Harragin, chief justice of the High Commission Territories. The Harragin Report was not unfavourable to Seretse, but because of his 'unfortunate marriage' it found that he was 'not fit in present circumstances' to be installed as chief (DO 35/4123, 1 Dec 1949). Creech Jones believed the report came to the right conclusion—withhold recognition from Seretse for a period of years—by use of the wrong arguments (CO 537/5927). The danger of course was that non-recognition might seem to be dictated by South Africa. As Attlee put it after a careful reading of the report: 'The document is most disturbing. In effect we are invited to go contrary to the desires of the great majority of the Bamangwato tribe, solely because of the attitude of the governments of the Union of South Africa and Southern Rhodesia. It is as if we had been obliged to agree to Edward VIII's abdication so as not to annoy the Irish Free State and the United States of America' (PREM 8/1308, minute, 22 Jan 1950). It was indeed true that the main ground for deciding against Seretse's recognition was the need to avoid continuing friction with the Union, but this was for a very good reason—the danger that if opinion in South Africa became 'united and inflamed' on this issue, Dr Malan might demand transfer of the High Commission Territories or put economic pressure on them (CAB 129/38, CP(50)13, memo by Noel-Baker, 26 Jan 1950).]

The Cabinet considered a memorandum by the Secretary of State for Commonwealth Relations (C.P. (50) 13) on the succession to the Chieftainship of the Bamangwato Tribe.

The Secretary of State for Commonwealth Relations recalled that the Cabinet had agreed on 21st July that a Judicial Enquiry should he held under the provisions of the Bechuanaland Native Administration Proclamation into the suitability of Seretse Khama for the Chieftainship of the Bamangwato Tribe. The Judicial Enquiry had now completed their work and a copy of their report was annexed to C.P.(50)13. Their main findings were that the tribal meeting (Kgotla) at which Seretse had been designated as Chief had been properly convened and assembled, and that its proceedings had been conducted in accordance with native custom; but that, having regard to the interests and well-being of the Tride, Seretse was not a fit and proper person to discharge the functions of Chief. The reasons given for this second finding were that, as the headquarters of the administration was at Mafeking and Seretse was a probibited immigrant in the Union of South Africa, he would be unable efficiently to carry out his duties as Chief; that the friendship of the Union and of Southern Rhodesia was essential to the well-being of the Tribe and to the Bechuanaland Protectorate generally; and that recognition of Seretse would disrupt the Tribe. The Secretary of State said that, while he accepted the conclusion that Seretse was not a fit and proper person to discharge the functions of Chief, he did not consider that the reasons given by the members of the Enquiry in support of this conclusion could be endorsed by His Majesty's Government. In his view there were three main reasons for refusing to recognise Seretse as Chief. First, those closely acquainted with the

Bamangwato Tribe were agreed that the Enquiry had under-estimated the risk that his recognition would result in the disruption of the Tribe. At their previous discussions, Ministers had expressed the view "that the principal objective of policy must be to safeguard the future well-being of the Bamangwato themselves" and he was in no doubt that a decision to recognise Seretse would be incompatible with this objective. Indeed, various passages in the report showed that, in supporting Seretse, the members of the Tribe had been actuated by fear of Tshekedi, and the decision of the tribal meeting should not therefore be regarded as an endorsement of Seretse's claims. Secondly, Seretse had shown an irresponsibility, both in his marriage and in other matters, which made it doubtful whether he could safely be entrusted with the duties and responsibilities of Chieftain. Thirdly, liberal European opinion generally was convinced that Seretse ought not to be recognised as Chieftain, and this view was shared by a strong body of native opinion in Africa. He thought that these considerations would in themselves justify a decision not to recognise Seretse; but it would not be realistic wholly to ignore the effect which recognition might have on South African opinion and on future relations with the Union Government. From the point of view of African interests, the paramount need was to safeguard the position of the South African High Commission Territories. For the first time, there was a strong body of opinion within the Union itself which considered that the Union's claim to these Territories ought not to be actively pressed at the present time. Recognition of Seretse would weaken this opposition and strengthen the position of those who favoured the transfer of these Territories to the Union. In these circumstances he recommended that Seretse should not be recognised as Chief, and that the Government's decision should be announced in a White Paper on the lines of the draft annexed to C.P. (50) 13. In the first instance, however, he suggested that Seretse and his wife should be invited to come to England, so that a further attempt might be made to persuade him to relinquish voluntarily his claim to the Chieftainship. Finally, he recommended that the administration of the Bechuanaland Reserve should for the present be conducted directly by the Bechuanaland Protectorate Administration, and that the system of native government in the Reserve should, by gradual stages, be made more representative.

The Secretary of State for the Colonies said that he was in general agreement with the recommendations made in C.P. (50) 13. The decisive consideration was that the recognition of Seretse would undoubtedly endanger the stability and well-being of the Bamangwato Tribe. Although opinion in Africa was divided on this issue, it was clear that a substantial body of opinion was opposed to the recognition of Seretse. He also endorsed the proposals for reforming the system of native government in the Bamangwato Reserve; and he thought that every effort should be made to transfer the headquarters of the administration from Mafeking to some place inside the Protectorate.

In discussion there was general agreement that the handling of this problem had been seriously complicated by the terms of the report of the Judicial Enquiry. It was impossible for the Government to endorse the reasons on which the second conclusion of the Enquiry was based; and, if it became necessary to publish the report, the Government would have no alternative but to make this clear. There were other passages in the report which were likely to give rise to damaging controversy in this country or in Africa. On the other hand, there could be no doubt that Seretse's marriage had introduced into the affairs of the Bamangwato Tribe a persisting element of controversy and unsettlement, which would be further aggravated if he should have children. Indeed, the United Kingdom High Commissioner and his advisers considered that insufficient weight was given in the report of the Judicial Enquiry to the stimulus which recognition of Seretse would give to the disruptive tendencies already inherent in the Tribe. In these circumstances Seretse's continuance as Chieftain would involve great risks for the Tribe. It seemed likely that Seretse himself was not unaware of these considerations and that he might therefore be responsive to suggestion that, by relinquishing voluntarily his claims to the Chieftainship, he would serve best both his own interests and those of the Tribe. The general view of Ministers was therefore that, as a first step, Seretse and his wife should be invited to come to London for discussions with the Secretary of State. In these talks an offer of an allowance and other appropriate forms of help should be made to Seretse on condition that he should not return to the Bechuanaland Protectorate. Ministers hoped that it might then be possible to avoid publication of the report of the Judicial Enquiry.

Ministers considered that it was unnecessary to decide at the present stage what action should be taken if it should prove impossible to persuade Seretse to relinquish the Chieftainship.

The Cabinet:—

(1) Invited the Secretary of State for Commonwealth Relations to invite Seretse Khama and his wife to visit London with a view to persuading him to relinquish voluntarily the Chieftainship of the Bamangwato Tribe.

(2) Agreed that their consideration of the recommendations made in C.P. (50) 13 should be resumed in the light of the results of the talks held in accordance with Conclusion (1) above.

(3) Instructed the Secretary to recall all copies of C.P. (50) 13 from circulation.

425 DO 35/3588, no 36 [15 Mar 1950]

'Relations of the two Rhodesias and Nyasaland': memorandum by A B Cohen

[Before completing this paper, Cohen discussed it on 15 March with J P Gibson (assistant secretary, CRO) and G H Baxter (assistant under-secretary of state, CRO). Griffiths agreed generally with the suggested line of action, subject to Gordon Walker's views (minutes, 16 March 1950).]

1. The arguments in favour of some form of closer constitutional association between the two Rhodesias and Nyasaland are:—

(1) From the broad Commonwealth point of view the creation of a solid British bloc of territories in Central Africa would make it easier to resist economic and political pressure from the Union of South Africa and to prevent the undue spreading of South African ideas northwards. At the same time the existence of a strong unit in Central Africa would probably tend to ease relations with the Union in the future.

(2) From the strategic, economic and communications points of view there would be great practical advantages in establishing a stronger inter-territorial organisation in Central Africa. The planning of these matters on a regional basis represents

accepted policy and our current troubles over transport in Central Africa are an illustration of the difficulty of using the transport facilities to the best advantage while more than one Government is responsible. U.K. Ministers have on a number of occasions, including the recent talks with Mr. Beadle[1], recognised the practical advantages of some form of closer association in Central Africa.

2. The arguments against closer association are:—

(1) There are certain major differences between Southern Rhodesian and U.K. policy towards Africans. The Southern Rhodesian Government have no definite plans for the participation of Africans in the central political life of the Colony. There is an industrial colour bar against Africans in Southern Rhodesia in certain areas and in respect of certain trades. With regard to the second point it must be admitted that on the Rhodesia Railways and the Copperbelt in Northern Rhodesia there is effectively at present an industrial colour bar. This has always existed on the railways, which are managed from Southern Rhodesia, and was forced on the managements of the copper mines by the white trade union during the war at a time when production of copper could not be endangered. The colour bar is not recognised by the Government in Northern Rhodesia. The Government has encouraged the formation of African trade unions and will continue in its efforts to find some means of bringing the colour bar in Northern Rhodesia to an end in spite of the formidable difficulties. In spite of the major differences in Southern Rhodesian policy towards Africans referred to above, Southern Rhodesia's efforts for African advancement, particularly in agricultural matters, have been excellent, as has been recognised by many outside observers.

(2) Africans in Northern Rhodesia and Nyasaland are almost unanimously opposed to amalgamation or even federation with Southern Rhodesia. It would certainly be necessary to consult with African opinion through the African Representative Councils in the two Territories and the Provincial Councils before any final decision could be taken by His Majesty's Government to agree to any form of closer association with Southern Rhodesia. His Majesty's Government is, of course, under no obligation necessarily to accept African views and, if a scheme could be devised which His Majesty's Government regarded as fair, it would be reasonable for this scheme actually to be recommended to Africans. But it would be most difficult to proceed with any scheme in the face of strong African opposition. It must be noted in this connection that any scheme which subordinated Northern Rhodesia and Nyasaland to Southern Rhodesia would be objected to not only by Africans in the two northern Territories, but also by Europeans. This is a point which is often ignored by Southern Rhodesian proponents of closer union.

(3) Any scheme which failed to safeguard African interests in Northern Rhodesia and Nyasaland or which subordinated these two Territories to Southern Rhodesia in a unitary self-governing state would be strongly objected to by opinion in this country and would be similarly criticised internationally.

3. The most recent positive step in the direction of closer association between the Central African Territories was taken in 1944, when it was decided to set up the present Central African Council to promote the closest possible co-operation between the three Territories in matters of common interest. This Council has achieved a considerable amount and it is generally agreed that its Secretariat has

[1] T H W Beadle, minister of justice and internal affairs, Southern Rhodesia.

been most useful to the three Territories. But Southern Rhodesia Ministers have criticised the Council itself on the two contradictory grounds that it is purely consultative and that it infringes on the prerogatives of the Southern Rhodesia Parliament. The main reason why the Council has been less successful recently than in its earlier years has been the unwillingness of Southern Rhodesia Ministers to work its machinery properly and to recognise that for the purpose of wider co-operation in Central Africa Southern Rhodesia must be prepared to accept some derogation from its full right of independent action, just as the European countries do for example in O.E.E.C. and members of the United Nations do in that body and the specialised agencies. Underlying the attitude of Southern Rhodesia Ministers is the thought that so long as an inter-territorial body such as the Central African Council exists His Majesty's Government in the U.K. may use its existence as an argument against some form of closer association.

4. In the talks last November with Mr. Beadle, Mr. Noel-Baker and Mr. Creech Jones asked that the Southern Rhodesia Government should provide His Majesty's Government with their views on three points:—

(1) the limitations which they see in the existing machinery of the Central African Council;
(2) their views on some form of political association short of amalgamation;
(3) their views on the establishment of an effective body to deal with economic co-operation should closer political association not prove possible.

Mr. Beadle suggested that after these views had been sent to His Majesty's Government a conference should be called by His Majesty's Government to discuss the problem with representatives of the three Territories (including unofficial representatives from Northern Rhodesia and Nyasaland). This suggestion was favourably received, but U.K. Ministers said that they would first wish to obtain the information from Southern Rhodesia.

5. At the end of January it was agreed at the Central African Council that an inter-territorial organisation was necessary, but the Southern Rhodesia Ministers gave notice that they would not be prepared to continue membership of the Central African Council as at present constituted after a period of twelve months had elapsed. A committee of the Council was set up to examine the existing machinery and alternatives to it and to make recommendations to the three Governments. This committee has already met and presented its report to the three Governments. The report has not yet been received in London, but it will presumably provide the information about the Central African Council for which His Majesty's Government has asked (see paragraph 4 (1) above).

6. As regards the answers to questions (2) and (3) in paragraph 4 above, Sir Godfrey Huggins has stated that answers will be prepared after consultation with the elected members of the Northern Rhodesia Legislative Council. It is thought possible that a proposal will be put forward for the amalgamation or federation of Southern Rhodesia and the whole of Northern Rhodesia except Barotseland (the native state in the north-west part of Rhodesia which is in special treaty relations with His Majesty's Government). Nyasaland would also under this proposal be left out. The proposal is, of course, quite unacceptable. A close integration of the major part of Northern Rhodesia, including the Copperbelt, with Southern Rhodesia would be opposed by Africans generally in Northern Rhodesia just as much as the amalgamation or

federation of the whole Territory. Barotseland would be deprived of the necessary financial support. If this proposal is put forward by Sir Godfrey Huggins in London, it will, it is suggested, be necessary to make it clear that it would not be acceptable to His Majesty's Government.

7. It is suggested that in the solution of this problem the following three principles should be accepted:—

(1) On practical grounds much would be gained by some form of closer association between the three Central African Territories.

(2) Any scheme must be such as would safeguard the interests of the African people of Northern Rhodesia and Nyasaland and not in any way prejudice their advancement. Equally a scheme must be such as His Majesty's Government could wholeheartedly recommend to the Africans for acceptance.

(3) We should avoid giving the impression to Southern Rhodesia Ministers that there is no chance of His Majesty's Government agreeing to any form of closer association. Otherwise there is a danger of encouraging the tendency towards isolation which has shown itself in the recent unwillingness of Southern Rhodesia Ministers to work the Central African Council and in some of the statements made by Sir Godfrey Huggins in his speech at Gatooma last December. (No doubt Sir Godfrey Huggins was talking for political effect rather than on conviction; he has always been a good Central African). There is also the danger that a negative attitude on the part of His Majesty's Government might eventually lead Southern Rhodesia in the direction of a closer association with the Union of South Africa.

8. With these principles in mind it is suggested that the line to be taken by Ministers in the forthcoming discussions with Sir Godfrey Huggins might be as follows:—

(1) Ministers should, it is suggested, adhere to the line taken by Mr. Noel-Baker and Mr. Creech Jones in the talks with Mr. Beadle, namely that the next step is for Southern Rhodesia to provide His Majesty's Government in the U.K. with their views as to the existing limitations of the Central African Council and as to possible forms of closer political or economic association. It is important that Sir Godfrey Huggins should not succeed in avoiding the necessity of submitting these views.

(2) Ministers might frankly recognise the practical advantages of some form of closer association.

(3) They might say to Sir Godfrey Huggins that, in order to have any chance of acceptance, a scheme of closer association between the three Territories would require to satisfy Parliament in the United Kingdom that African interests in the two northern Territories would be safeguarded and to satisfy the Africans themselves. In the view of H.M.G. in the U.K. it is very unlikely that any scheme would satisfy either Parliament or Africans if it sought to fuse the two northern Territories into Southern Rhodesia or completely to subordinate their Governments and Legislatures, over the whole or the greater part of the field of administration, to some federal authority. It might be suggested, therefore, that further examination of the problem should address itself to studying a scheme under which inter-territorially executive machinery would be established for the existing inter-territorial services and others which have been under consideration but have been rejected by Southern Rhodesia (this would cover railways, air communications, currency, meteorology, research and perhaps certain other matters of common interest). Appropriate machinery for legislation on these subjects or at any rate for close consultation with the

Legislatures of the three Territories could also be considered. Under such a scheme the Central inter-territorial executive and legislative or consultative machinery would derive its authority and finance from the three Central African Governments and legislatures and would not be a federal authority super-imposed on them. If a scheme on these lines could be devised, it might perhaps be possible for Parliament in the U.K. to be persuaded to agree to some arrangement regarding their responsibility towards the inter-territorial services which would not infringe against Southern Rhodesia's self-governing status.

(4) Ministers might suggest to Sir Godfrey Huggins that after the information referred to in paragraph 4 (1) above had been supplied to His Majesty's Government in the U.K., a conference of officials of the U.K. Government and the three Central African Governments might be held in London for the purpose of narrowing the issues for further discussion by the Governments and preparing an analysis of the problem and recommendations for a solution.

(5) If this conference were fruitful it should be followed by another conference, also in London, at which U.K. Ministers would be prepared to discuss the whole problem with Southern Rhodesia Ministers and representatives of the Governments and Legislatures of Northern Rhodesia and Nyasaland. The conference of officials should be regarded as purely preparatory to this conference, but the final decision by the Governments whether to hold the main conference should await the outcome of the preparatory conference and there should be no publicity of the intention to hold the main conference until this decision had been taken.

9. The following points may be made on the above suggestions:—

(1) For the last eighteen months His Majesty's Government in the U.K. have deliberately refrained from taking the initiative in this matter and have left it to those in Central Africa who are in favour of closer association of the Territories to put forward their proposals for consideration. The results have so far been negative. The Victoria Falls Conference produced a scheme which, besides being half-baked, would clearly have been unacceptable not only to His Majesty's Government in the U.K., but also to the European as well as the African inhabitants of Northern Rhodesia and Nyasaland. A scheme for amalgamating or federating Northern Rhodesia and Southern Rhodesia, less Barotseland, if it is put forward, would be equally unacceptable to His Majesty's Government and at any rate to African opinion in Northern Rhodesia. The Southern Rhodesia Government and Mr. Welensky in Northern Rhodesia have had great difficulty in agreeing on terms of reference for further study of the problem locally. Mr. Beadle admitted this in the talks last November and his purpose in discussing the matter with U.K. Ministers was to find out how far His Majesty's Government would be prepared to go. Similarly Mr. Welensky introduced a motion in the Northern Rhodesia Legislature asking His Majesty's Government to take the initiative in the matter. The Chief Secretary of the Central African Council [Sir Arthur Benson] has also urged that His Majesty's Government should take the initiative.

It is suggested that there are good grounds for His Majesty's Government taking the initiative at this stage, but this must be done in such a way as to safeguard African interests and to avoid alarming African opinion. Hitherto the U.K. Government and the Southern Rhodesia Government have been working separately on this problem and the solutions coming from Southern Rhodesia have so far been quite unacceptable to H.M. Government in the U.K. What seems to be required now is to bring the parties together, but at the same time to make it clear what H.M. Government in the U.K. regards as the limits to any scheme of closer association at the present time. The suggestions in paragraph 8 (4) and (5) for a preparatory and a main conference in London are designed to bring the parties concerned in this problem together in devising a solution to it. The suggestion in paragraph 8 (3) that H.M. Government should indicate broadly the lines on which they think that further studies should proceed is designed to safeguard African interests and if possible to set the limits within which an attempt to devise a solution should be made.

(2) The proposal in paragraph 8 (3) that any form of closer association should be limited to the subjects which are already dealt with inter-territorially, with certain others which have already been considered for inter-territorial action, is based on suggestions made by Sir Gilbert Rennie, the Governor of Northern Rhodesia, who believes that it might be possible to arrive at some solution in this way.

(3) If the main conference proposed in paragraph 8 (5) takes place, it will be necessary for African representatives to be included in the Northern Rhodesia and Nyasaland delegations. It may be desirable to make this point clear to Sir Godfrey Huggins, if the suggestion for a conference is put forward.

426 DO 35/4018, no 79 [Apr 1950]

[High Commission Territories]: draft letter prepared by CRO in case the Union government asked for the transfer of their administration

In your letter of the Your Excellency communicated to me the representations of your Government on the question of the transfer to the Union of the Government of the High Commission Territories. These representations have been given the very full and careful consideration which they deserve, and I am now in a position to furnish you for communication to the Union Government with the views of the United Kingdom Government upon them.

2. The position of the High Commission Territories today has its roots in nearly a century of South African history. The historical factors are well known to your Government and I need not recapitulate them further than recalling that the issue now before our two Governments derives from the responsibilities which were assumed by the United Kingdom Government in response to appeals for protection received from the native populations. These appeals arose in the context of the relations of Europeans with the indigenous (native) peoples and it is in the light of relations between the two races in South Africa that the United Kingdom Government must seek an honourable performance of the responsibilities which have remained with them for so many years.

3. The United Kingdom Government, who are conversant with the racial problems arising in the many dependent territories of their own in the African continent, appreciate that South Africa, with its permanently resident yet greatly outnumbered white population, is in a unique position and, therefore, faces greater difficulties than any other country in Africa. The unusual, indeed the unique, pattern of life in the Union and the complicated nature of the problems facing any South African Government are *too*[1] often overlooked by those who are not familiar with the

[1] Italicised words were amendments or additions suggested by Sir E Baring.

situation at first hand. The United Kingdom Government fully recognise the nature and extent of the heavy burden of responsibility laid upon the Union Government and upon the people of South Africa. They realise that South Africans of European stock are determined to maintain their present standard of living and way of life *whilst fulfilling their duties as trustees for the welfare of all inhabitants of their country irrespective of race. The United Kingdom Government are also well aware that any increase in the wealth and well being of the whole community in South Africa will benefit not only all sections of the Union's own population but also the peoples of other parts of Africa*. They are, therefore, under no misapprehension of the special nature of the difficulties which face any South African Government in the formulation of policy, and they *like the Union Government confidently believe that these difficulties are of a temporary nature*.

4. At the same time as the United Kingdom Government appreciate the difficulties of the Union Government they hope that Union Ministers also will appreciate their difficulties. In weighing the representations of the Union Government the United Kingdom Government are bound to give heed to *non-European* opinion not only in the High Commission Territories but elsewhere in the Continent of Africa. The United Kingdom controls many African territories inhabited by various *indigenous* peoples at many different stages of development. It is the experience of the United Kingdom Government that *these peoples* in any one part of the Continent attach great importance to promises—or indeed to anything which may be interpreted as a promise—made to *other peoples of their race* elsewhere. Pledges, which were subsequently renewed on several occasions, were given in Parliament in 1909 in regard to the future of the High Commission Territories when the South Africa Bill was under consideration and thus became, together with the Act, part of a single political transaction regulating the procedure and the conditions in accordance with which the transfer of the Territories to the Union might be carried out. *Non-European* opinion will undoubtedly expect from us scrupulous observance of the letter and the spirit of the pledges.

5. It is against the general background described in the foregoing paragraphs that the United Kingdom Government view the specific problem of the future of the High Commission Territories. They will understand the disappointment *among South Africans that these Territories are still outside the Union*. For their part, they remain committed to the position of their predecessors in 1909 whose intention was that the way should be open for the transfer of the Territories. *There has been no retreat from or alteration of either that position or the position adopted by the United Kingdom Government in 1935. The spirit which animated the United Kingdom Government in 1935 is that of their successors today*. Transfer would in their view take place—and perhaps I might say here that the use of the word "may" at the beginning of S[ection] 151 of the South Africa Act has no greater or less significance than its use in the similar provision in S. 150 relating to Southern Rhodesia—subject to certain conditions and to the observance of the pledges that the population of the Territories and Parliament in London should be fully consulted before transfer takes place. Their attitude is in accordance with that set forth in the Aide Mémoire handed to General Hertzog on the 15th May, 1935. They feel confident that the Union Government would not dissent from the statement made by General Hertzog in the Union Parliament on the 25th March 1925 that the incorporation of any territory in the Union depends on whether the inhabitants are prepared to come in. If the Union

Government should wish the views of the inhabitants of the Territories on the question of transfer formally to be ascertained the United Kingdom Government will be prepared to make the necessary arrangements, which may take some time to complete, for that purpose.

6. *United Kingdom Ministers are bound to take into account the wishes and feelings of the inhabitants of the three Territories. Most of the Bantu in the High Commission Territories are in touch with relations or fellow tribesmen who are permanently resident in the Union, and, if males, they have usually themselves worked for one or for several periods in the factories, farms or mines of South Africa. They consider, whether rightly or wrongly, that they are well informed of the conditions of life of their fellow Bantu who are permanently resident in the Union. They are unlikely to alter their views regarding the constitutional position of the three Territories on account of anything said to them by European officials. No attempt has been made or will be made by Government servants in the High Commission Territories to discourage any movement of opinion in those Territories towards transfer to the Union; but it is unlikely that, even if they should wish to do so, Europeans would be able to influence such a movement either one way or the other*. Meanwhile the United Kingdom Government feel bound to point out that, while they have instituted no enquiries on the subject, the expressions of opinion which have been reported to them indicate no greater readiness than hitherto on the part of the Bantu population to assent to, or willingly acquiesce in, the transference of the administration of the Territories to the Union Government. In the circumstances it would seem to them a matter for the earnest consideration of the Union Government whether formal consultation of the inhabitants at this stage would in fact best serve the ends which the Union Government have in view.

7. In these circumstances of great difficulty for both Governments the United Kingdom Government will willingly explore any method of increasing points of contact between the administrations of the Union and the three Territories and of improving collaboration. They understand that the Union Government will shortly devote special attention and effort to the development and improvement of native areas in the Union. They feel that any information which might be given to them on this subject would be of great use. Should this suggestion appeal to the Union Government they would be glad to organise exchanges of visits between the administrative and technical officers and between prominent Bantu in the Union native areas and the High Commission Territories. A special purpose might be the explanation to Bantu inhabitants of the High Commission Territories of development work in Union native areas, since inevitably their views will be influenced by what they see themselves in the Union and by what they hear from their fellow Bantu in the Union.

8. In the field of administration the United Kingdom Government assure the Union Government that every possible effort will be made to improve administrative co-operation and to ease any of the administrative difficulties mentioned in your letter or any other difficulty which may arise in the future. They will sympathetically consider any proposals made to them, either by the Union Government or by their own officers, for the joint planning of schemes affecting those problems which are common to both the High Commission Territories and the Union; the possible uses of the waters of the Orange River basin mentioned by the Union Government is a case in point. If in furtherance of these ends the Union Government should wish to

institute discussions with United Kingdom representatives the United Kingdom Government will be glad to comply.

9. The Union Government have made reference to particular aspects of the administration and of the economic life of the Territories which are of special interest to the Union. The United Kingdom Government welcome the opportunity thus afforded to explain to the Union Government how these matters stand, and to put on record the relevant features of their policy in the future conduct of the affairs of the High Commission Territories. This has been done in the memorandum annexed herewith.[2] The United Kingdom Government would invite the particular attention of the Union Government to the expression of their readiness to collaborate in all matters of defence, to the record of achievement in the control of animal diseases and to the statement of what has been accomplished or is planned for the future in fighting the ravages of soil erosion in Basutoland.

10. In furnishing the enclosed memorandum the United Kingdom Government are anxious to demonstrate the attention which is given in the administration of the High Commission Territories to matters that are of concern both to the Territories and to the Union, and to emphasise the desire of the United Kingdom Government to collaborate actively with the Union Government in the promotion of their common interests. For indisputable reasons of geography and economics the future of the Territories is closely linked with that of the Union and until the difficulties which at present stand in the way of political association can be overcome the United Kingdom Government hope and believe that by joint discussion of common problems and by administrative co-operation the mutual interests of the Territories and the Union will be effectively safeguarded and advanced. *They are at any time prepared to join in discussions*.

[2] Not attached.

427 CAB 128/17, CM 28(50)3 — 4 May 1950

'South-West Africa': Cabinet conclusions on proceedings before the International Court of Justice[1]

[This major Cabinet discussion, with its finely balanced arguments, was important not least for the rejection of the inter-departmental advice tendered. The memorandum referred to, CP(50)88, had been many months in the drafting (CAB 129/39). Most of the work on this 'exceedingly difficult' issue was done by Sir E Beckett (the FO legal adviser), W G Wilson and A N Galsworthy of the CO, and the paper also took account of suggestions from N Pritchard of the CRO; it was also vetted by Cohen, Lloyd, Martin and Sir K O Roberts-Wray (legal adviser to the CO and CRO); and finally it was discussed with Sir Hartley Shawcross (the attorney-general) and Dugdale (minister of state, CO) as ministers. It was then signed by Griffiths, Gordon Walker and Younger, minister of state at the FO (FO 371/88565 and 88566). The Cabinet, however, feared that participation in the International Court proceedings, for whatever reason, and even to the limited extent of holding a 'watching brief', would, however wrongly, be misinterpreted as support for South Africa, and therefore a majority of ministers opposed it on political grounds. This was a position which Dugdale had all along argued for strongly: 'We are already in enough difficulty with the Seretse case without putting our head into a noose' by being represented at the International Court (CO 537/5708, minutes 10 and 15 Mar 1950). In

[1] Previous reference: see 414.

the event, the Court gave an advisory opinion which endorsed the view (which South Africa herself opposed) that the Union government could not divest itself of its obligations under the Mandate to render information while claiming the Mandate to administer still held good. The Court declared that the Mandate *did* still exist, with its attendant privileges and obligations. The Court did not say the Union was legally obliged to place South-West Africa under United Nations Trust; South-West Africa was therefore *not* declared to be a Non-Self-Governing Territory under Chapter XI of the UN Charter and Article 73—and to this extent British officials had much reason to be satisfied with the outcome (CO 537/5708). The next step was to advise the PM to urge Dr Malan to accept the Court's advisory opinion and co-operate with the UN by resuming the submission of reports. Attlee's letter to Malan is at 429, annex. No reply was received.]

The Cabinet considered a memorandum by the Secretary of State for the Colonies, the Secretary of State for Commonwealth Relations and the Minister of State (C.P. (50) 88) on the forthcoming proceedings before the International Court of Justice on certain legal aspects of the question whether South-West Africa should be placed under trusteeship.

The Secretary of State for the Colonies said that these proceedings were due to commence on 16th May, and the Registrar of the Court had asked to be notified by 6th May whether the United Kingdom Government intended to participate in them. The arguments for and against participation were nicely balanced. The Court would be asked to pronounce upon the international status of South-West Africa and the international obligations of the Union Government towards it. If it were to decide that South-West Africa had the status of a "non-self-governing territory," it was most important, from the point of view of our general interests as a Colonial Power, that we should have an opportunity of putting before the Court our views regarding the obligations of Colonial Powers under Article 73 of the United Nations Charter. In particular, it would be greatly to our advantage that the Court should endorse our view that Colonial Powers were not obliged by that Article to transmit to the United Nations information on political and constitutional developments in dependent territories. The Court would also be called upon to determine the second question whether the Union Government were competent to modify the international status of South-West Africa. If it should decide that this power did not rest solely with the Union Government, it would be of great importance to us that this opinion should related [sic] to the status of the territory as a former mandated territory; for it would be highly inconvenient to the United Kingdom Government if the Court should give an opinion implying that the International status of a non-self-governing territory could not be modified by the metropolitan country without the concurrence of the United Nations Assembly. If the Court were likely to make pronouncements on either of these questions which would embarrass us in our future dealings with the United Nations in respect of our own dependent territories, it was desirable that our views should be placed before the Court. On the other hand, there was undoubtedly a risk that any intervention on our part would be construed as support for the policy of the South African Government in respect of South-West Africa, or even for the native policy of the present Government of the Union.

The Secretary of State said that, on balance, he was inclined to the view that the United Kingdom Government should be prepared to intervene in the proceedings in order to safeguard their own interests. He therefore recommended that the Government should be represented in the proceedings, but that their representative should ask leave to reserve his right to speak later in the proceedings if any general points were raised which affected this country's interests. He also recommended that the Government should take an appropriate opportunity to make it clear that their appearance before the Court did not imply support for the native policy of the South African Government.

The Secretary of State for Commonwealth Relations said that the Union Government would take it amiss if, having supported the United Nations resolution referring these issues to the Court, we now failed to intervene in the proceedings before the Court. He agreed, however, that the question now before the Cabinet should be determined by reference solely to United Kingdom interests, and without regard to the feelings of the Union Government. On these grounds he supported the recommendations made by the Secretary of State for the Colonies. He had just received a summary of the submissions which the United States Government were proposing to put before the Court; and it was clear from these that the general issues mentioned in paragraph 3 of C.P. (50) 88 would in fact be raised in the arguments before the Court. This confirmed his view that the United Kingdom Government should be represented in the proceedings in order to protect their interests. He was, however, doubtful whether the Court would agree that our representative should hold a watching brief: he would be expected to express his views early in the proceedings.

The Minister of State said that the arguments were very evenly balanced, but he supported the proposals in C.P. (50)88 on the understanding that our representative would speak with great discretion and that we should do our best to make it clear that our appearance in the proceedings did not imply support of the policy of the Union Government.

In discussion there was general agreement that, if the United Kingdom Government were represented in these proceedings, it would be difficult for their representative to refrain from speaking until it appeared that the Court was likely to give an opinion adversely affecting the general interests of the United Kingdom as a Colonial Power. As representing one of the main Colonial Powers, he would be expected to assist the Court in general argument and would be pressed to speak at an early stage. Such intervention was bound to be represented, in political circles, as implying support of the South African case. Thus, we should certainly incur political odium by intervening in these proceedings. What hope was there that we should be able to persuade the Court to give a ruling favourable to our own interpretation of Article 73 of the United Nations Charter? The Court was most unlikely to be sympathetic towards the South African claim; and the particular issue of South-West Africa was, surely, a most unfavourable one on which to argue the general questions set out in paragraph 3 of C.P. (50) 88. By our intervention we should be inviting the Court to pronounce upon those general questions, in a context most unfavourable to our case. And, having entered an appearance and deployed our arguments, we should find it the more difficult to dissociate ourselves from an unfavourable decision. We were not ourselves directly concerned in the particular issue which had been referred to the Court, and were under no obligation to be represented in the proceedings. Would it not be better, therefore, to refrain from sending a representative, so that we might be the more free thereafter to argue that the Court's opinion was related to the special circumstances of this particular case, viz. a former mandated territory, and was not of general application to the relations between a metropolitan Power and its non-self-governing territories? We had already been forced to take the line that we could not accept, in relation to our dependent territories, the interpretation placed by the United Nations Assembly upon Article 73 of the Charter; and it would not be very much more difficult for us to take the line, if need be, that we were equally unable to accept, in relation to our dependent territories, the implications of an advisory opinion given by the International Court in respect of South-West Africa. There was undoubtedly a grave risk that the Court might give an opinion in terms which might be embarrassing to us in our future dealings with the United Nations in respect of our dependent territories; but it was the general view of the Cabinet that these embarrassments would probably be increased if the United Kingdom Government had been represented in the proceedings before the Court.

The Cabinet:—

Agreed that the United Kingdom Government should not be represented in the forthcoming proceedings before the International Court of Justice on certain legal aspects of the question whether South-West Africa should be placed under trusteeship.

428 CO 537/5710 18–25 Sept 1950

[South Africa]: preparation of draft Cabinet paper on relations with South Africa: CO minutes by W G Wilson, N B J Huijsman, W I J Wallace,[1] J M Martin, and Sir T Lloyd

Since the minutes above were written the draft Cabinet Paper on United Kingdom "relations with the Union of South Africa", prepared in the C.R.O. and referred to in paragraph 3 of my minute of 15/9 above, has been received and placed on top opposite. The paper was prepared on Mr. Gordon Walker's instructions: he also directed that it should be referred in draft to the Foreign Office and the Colonial Office. It will be seen that the last paragraph of the paper states that "the Colonial Secretary . . . (is) in general agreement with what is proposed". The paper is intended to provide members of the Cabinet with background information against which they can take decisions on the line to be followed by our delegation in New York when the questions of Indians in South Africa and South-West Africa are discussed at Lake Success.

2. The C.R.O. are thinking in terms of the paper being taken by the Cabinet on today week (i.e. the 25th September). The present draft has been approved at Departmental level in the C.R.O. and I have agreed that it should be held in this Office at Under-Secretary level until any amendments made by C.R.O. higher authority and Ministers can be incorporated in the draft, which can then be sent forward to higher authority in the Colonial Office as a final draft, including any amendments suggested in the Foreign Office and Colonial Office at Departmental

[1] Wallace was head of, and Huijsman a principal in, CO International Relations Dept 'B' which dealt with general international and Commonwealth relations, including political questions relating to the UN Economic and Social Council and its commissions and specialized agencies, colonial accession articles in international agreements and colonial representation in international organisations. Wilson was a principal in CO International Relations Dept 'A' (head, A N Galsworthy) which dealt with the UN on such matters as trusteeship and information from non-self-governing territories and international co-operation on colonial questions.

level and accepted by the C.R.O. The extent to which the C.R.O. is able to accept any amendment proposed by the Foreign Office or ourselves will, of course, determine the extent to which the Secretary of State and the Foreign Secretary can subscribe to the paper, and to the wording of the final paragraph.

3. Being a C.R.O. production, the draft paper is as lenient as possible on the Union. It lays great stress on the importance to the United Kingdom of good relations with the Union, but fails to bring out the fact that, unless we make it perfectly clear to the world at large that we hold no brief for Union policies, nor are we prepared to condone or overlook them for the sake of harmony with the Union, our position in the eyes of African and Indian opinion will be seriously weakened, and our credit in the United Nations on this matter will be completely destroyed. Unless we are prepared to make it clear beyond all doubt, for instance, that we cannot compromise in our opposition to the Union Government's policy towards Africans, our own "new policy" in the handling of colonial affairs in the United Nations will be completely ineffective.

4. In order to restore the balance in the draft paper suggested alternatives to paragraphs 5 and 9 of the paper have been inserted in the draft opposite. I.R.D.'B' may have comments on these and also on paragraph 7. It will be seen that the suggested amendments are closely linked to the proposals made in paragraph 6 of my minute of the 15th September for the handling of the South-West Africa issue at Lake Success. It will be seen also, from the record of Mr. Gordon Walker's conversation with Dr. Geyer[2] on the 13th September (at (136) opposite) that the C.R.O. are pressing Dr. Malan to make up his mind immediately as to whether or not he will accept the Court's opinion. Although this is a purely C.R.O. issue I should have thought that Dr. Malan is at present quite unable, because of his public utterances in South-West Africa, to agree publicly to a submission of reports. For this reason I feel that pressure on Dr. Malan to make up his mind now can only result in his taking a decision not to submit reports. I therefore suggest that if the tactics proposed in paragraph 6 of my minute of 15/9 and the amendments suggested to the draft Cabinet Paper above, are agreed in the Colonial Office, they should be sent in writing to the C.R.O. under the guise of a paper prepared for discussion at the forthcoming Inter-Departmental meeting.

W.G.W.
18.9.50

I agree with Mr Wilson that the UK should avoid being tarred with the apartheid brush and I also agree that some mention in the Cabinet paper of views such as are expressed in Mr Wilson's minute of the 18th of September (para 3) would be desirable. I think, however, that we should avoid over-emphasising these views.

For instance, I am not sure whether the vocal disapproval of S. African policies in the UN should be regarded as more important than obtaining the firm promise of a S. African contribution to the defence of the Middle East. The latter is after all, very nearly the biggest strategic interest of the UK. It would be folly to risk antagonising the S. African Govt on imperial defence for the sake of making doubly sure that HMG's policy is not confused with S. Africa's.

We should also bear in mind that the Nationalists are on present form unlikely to

[2] A L Geyer, high commissioner in London for South African government.

lose the next election. They may therefore be with us until 1958 or later, and outside condemnation of S. Africa's position is likely only to strengthen the present Government's hand. Being anti-British first and anti-Commonwealth second by origin, too public expression of our antipathy towards the Union Government's native policies would, in my opinion, only encourage the Nationalists to seek a break with the Commonwealth connection. The effect of that on the Commonwealth's (and more particularly the UK's) political and material influence would be considerable.

My own inclination is therefore to modify Mr Wilson's amendment to para 5 of (133), and to confine it to the substitution of the following sentences for the sentence "while we cannot . . . unnecessary polemics should be avoided" in the latter half of the paragraph under reference:—

> "In preserving good relations with the Union we should however bear in mind that any suspicion that the United Kingdom condones or takes a lenient view of the Union Government's native policies would be likely to embarrass us in our relations with India and Pakistan in particular; the United Nations, and the peoples of the Colonies. We cannot therefore in any way associate ourselves with S. Africa's native policies, and should explain our attitude to the South Africans as clearly and politely as possible, avoiding unnecessary polemics."

I have no comments on Mr Wilson's other amendments. . . .

N.B.J.H.
18.9.50

The treatment of Indians in South Africa

1. The C.O. has hitherto supported the U.K. line in the United Nations on this dispute between two members of the Commonwealth—viz., strict neutrality. In paragraph 7 of (138) the C.R.O. advocate a continuance of this policy—viz., avoid taking part in the debate and attempt to exercise a conciliatory influence from the background. It will be noted that Sir Zafrullah Kahn[3] has already indicated to Mr. Gordon Walker that Pakistan is not much interested in this matter (not indeed about South-West Africa either). As for India, we have hitherto managed to preserve neutrality on this matter without embittering our relations with her. I think we should continue to agree with the C.R.O. policy.

South-West Africa

(It appears that the agreement with Mr. Galsworthy referred to in my minute of 15/9 has not been carried out to the letter and that I.R.D.'B' has in fact been carrying on its files such things as Reports from the U.K. High Commissioner in South Africa. This does give us a responsibility to express a view here, for what it is worth; I am sorry for ducking under a misapprehension on 15/9.)

2. I agree that the U.K. ought to support the opinion of the International Court, ought not to support South Africa if they refuse to accept it, and ought to make clear to the world that that is our standpoint. Whether, however, we ought to go beyond this and join in actively in condemning South Africa is another matter. From the point of view of African opinion in our Colonies it may be that that would be the right policy. From the point of view of Commonwealth relations I must agree with the

[3] Foreign minister of Pakistan.

C.R.O. in thinking it would be the wrong one. It is just possible also that it might be the wrong one from the point of view of the Africans in the Union, to say nothing of the whites there. The U.K. is probably the only outside influence which can, however slightly, affect the attitude of the South African Government in this matter. But it is certain that we should lose what little influence we have if we joined the pack howling against them. This would merely drive them out of the Commonwealth into an outer darkness of their own and they would carry with them, not only the sympathy of their people of Dutch stock, but much of the sympathy of the 40% of their people which is of British stock.

3. With reference to Mr. Wilson's suggested amendment to paragraph 5 of (138), I doubt, *pace* African Division's views, whether the suspicion that we were prepared to condone South African apartheid policies for the sake of good relations with the Union would really inflame Indian opinion in our African colonies against us. And provided we left no doubt as to where we stood as to the Court's opinion, I very much doubt whether a failure to join in public condemnation of South Africa on this issue would seriously compromise our relations with India and Pakistan. (c.f. the matter of the treatment of Indians in South Africa referred to above). Viewing the problem, therefore, from the angle of Commonwealth relations rather than from that of the effect on African opinion in our Colonies, I find myself (naturally enough) nearer to the C.R.O. line than the I.R.D.'A's.

W.I.J.W.
19.9.50

The divergence of view between I.R.D.'A' and I.R.D.'B' expressed in the minutes of 18/9 and 19/9 within is apparent rather than real and is based on the assumption that I.R.D.'A' advocates "vocal disapproval of S.A. policies in the U.N." or active condemnation of these policies. This is not the case. We suggest only that:—

(a) in a Cabinet Paper designed to bring out the background to our relations with the Union, as much emphasis should be given to the disadvantages of close public alliance with the Union as to its advantages. For this reason the suggested new para. 5 to the draft Paper seeks to show that we should not be over-enthusiastic about clinging to the Union. It also, in my view necessarily, lays great stress on the effect in Africa of any appearance that the U.K. is co-operating with the Union to give the latter as easy a passage as possible on the S.W.A. issue. This view is put forward after discussion with Mr. Cohen and Mr. Gorsuch. I agree that we need not actively oppose the Union, in the U.N. or elsewhere, but we must at all costs attempt to avoid acting as the public advocate of a compromise solution on the S.W.A. issue.

(b) For this reason, if discussion of S.W.A. becomes heated in the U.N., we must side against the Union in our voting (see para. 6(c) of my minute of 15/9) and we must not allow ourselves to be manœuvred, either by the Union or the C.R.O., into the position of seeming to plead the Union's cause, as we would be obliged to do if the existing paragraphs 9(a) and (d) of the draft paper at (138) were to be adopted.

The amendments to paras. 9(a) and (d) are, of course, of more importance than that to para. 5, but I would nevertheless suggest that, if the paper is to present a balanced picture to the Cabinet, the rather more detailed summary in the proposed new paragraph 5 pinned inside the draft is preferable to the general expression of opinion suggested in Mr. Huijsman's minute of 18/9. The suggestion in the existing para. 5 that we should explain our attitude politely to the Union Government is, it seems to me, redundant at that stage, since it is made, more appropriately, in the conclusion to the Paper (para. 9(a)).

W.G.W.
19.9.50

At (147) is the draft of a Cabinet Paper, prepared in the C.R.O. and agreed at the Departmental level in the C.R.O., F.O. and C.O., which is intended to provide the Cabinet with the background to our relations with South Africa against which the decisions as to the U.K. line on the South-West Africa and Indians in South Africa questions in the United Nations can be taken. The Paper was, I understand, prepared as a result of an invitation by the Cabinet to Mr. Gordon Walker, who asked that it should be agreed with the Foreign and Colonial Secretaries. It is to be presented to the Cabinet on Thursday next (28th September) and must therefore be circulated tomorrow.

2. The original draft of this Paper (at (138)) was unacceptable to us since it did not emphasise the effect on African public opinion of any appearance that we were ready to overlook or condone South African policies, and it also suggested (in para 9) that we should be ready to act as mediators in any dispute between South Africa and other parties, and that we should seek a compromise between the U.N. and South Africa on the South-West Africa issue. Both suggestions might have obliged us to appear to defend the South African attitude over S.W.A. and would almost certainly have placed us, alone, between the Union on the one side and the vast majority of the U.N. on the other, incurring the enmity of both. After the discussions recorded in the minutes of 18/9 to 20/9 above, therefore, the letter at (135) put forward certain amendments for the consideration of the C.R.O. The purport of these amendments has now been incorporated in the underlined parts of paras. 3 and 9 of the agreed draft Paper at (137). In our request for the insertion of these amendments we had the full support of the Foreign Office officials.

3. As a result, the draft Paper now makes clear

(a) the effect on African public opinion of our siding too closely with the Union (para. 3);
(b) that we must stand by the opinion of the International Court on South-West Africa (para. 8);
(c) that we should press South Africa to comply with this opinion (para. 9(d));
(d) that we should make our attitude clear to South Africa (para. 9(a));
(e) that, while we should do all we can to reach a settlement on the South-West Africa question, we should not act alone in this, but should only move if we have the support of Canada, Australia, New Zealand and the United States. This should insure our activities against any suspicions of our motives on the part of the U.N. Assembly and African and Indian public opinion (paras. 9(a) and 9(d)).

4. I now submit the draft Paper for the consideration of the Secretary of State in order that he may decide whether he can associate himself generally with it in the terms of its paragraph 10. This invites him to express his "general agreement" with the Paper. It would be helpful if the Secretary of State's opinion could be recorded today since the Paper must be processed and circulated to the Cabinet tomorrow.

5. The Department's views on the tactics which might be adopted by the U.K. Delegation when the S.W.A. question is discussed in the U.N. are set out in paras. 2–5 of the letter at (144). These tactics conform with the proposals in the Cabinet Paper and have been well received by the F.O. and C.R.O.

W.G.W.
25.9.50

I think that the Secretary of State can be advised to express his general agreement with the draft paper as now amended. It is satisfactory as far as it goes; but it does not attempt to suggest details of policy and tactics at the United Nations (last sentence of paragraph 8) and I suggest that it is very desirable that, in the Cabinet discussion, the Secretary of State should say that he regards it as implicit in the paper that, X besides making clear to the South African Government that we must stand by the opinion of the International Court, we must also leave the Assembly in no doubt that that is our attitude.[4] Nothing less would be acceptable from the point of view of public opinion in the Colonies and in this country. (In (144) Mr. Wilson has made some suggestions about tactics to the C.R.O. which I understand the latter, at any rate at first sight, found attractive. The Secretary of State might care to read this before the Cabinet discussion.)

J.M.M.
25.9.50

S of S
I agree that (see para 10 of no 147) you could now properly agree with the dft of this paper. Also that the point as [sic] X shd if possible be made orally in Cabinet. The Cabinet is not likely to discuss tactics in any detail.

T.I.K.L.
25.9.50

The Secretary of State has spoken to me about this. Commonwealth Relations Office should be told that while he does not wish to dissent from the redraft of the Cabinet paper they should know that when this comes up in Cabinet he intends to express the view—and to stress it as a point to which he attaches great importance—that the representative of H.M.G. should make clear beyond all doubt in the United Nations Assembly, when this matter comes up there, that it is the strongly held view of H.M.G. that the Union Government ought to abide by the opinion of the International Court.[5]

The Secretary of State would like this view to be communicated to the Commonwealth Relations Office at once; they should be told by telephone and this should be confirmed by letter.

T.I.K.L.
25.9.50

---

[4] Sir T Lloyd marked this passage 'X' in the margin.

[5] The final version of the Cabinet paper follows at 429; the Cabinet discussion is at 431 below.

429 CAB 129/42, CP(50)214 25 Sept 1950

'Relations with the Union of South Africa': Cabinet memorandum by Mr Gordon Walker (CRO). *Annex*: telegram on South-West Africa from Mr Attlee to Dr Malan [nd]

[Following the rejection by the Cabinet of the advice on South-West Africa in CP(50)88 (see 427), a Cabinet paper was prepared in the CRO to clarify the more general issues of Anglo-South African relations. Again this was several months in preparation; it was drafted by G E Crombie, with a great deal of consultation (eg with R R Sedgwick, G H Baxter, C Syers and J S Garner), and it was 'much travelled' between departments too, so that in its final form responsibility for it was spread widely. It represented the conclusions of a considerable debate in Whitehall (for CO discussion see 428). In the process, the hostility of the CO to the CRO original drafting was much reduced. Griffiths for the CO and Younger for the FO signified their general agreement with it (DO 35/3839; FO 371/88566).]

The accession of power of the Nationalist [sic] Party in South Africa after the General Election in May 1948 has made the conduct of our relations with the Union a matter of some delicacy. As my colleagues will be aware, the Nationalist Party is Republican and its more extreme elements are anti-British. Although the Nationalists command only a minority of votes in the Union, weightage is given to the rural areas from which they draw their support, and with the nine votes of their allies, the Afrikaner Party, they have hitherto had a majority of seven votes in the House of Assembly over the combined forces of the Opposition. Their position has just been considerably strengthened by the elections in South-West Africa in which they have won all the six seats now allotted to that territory in the Union House of Assembly. Though they still do not possess an independent majority, there seems to be some doubt whether Mr. Havenga, the leader of the Afrikaner Party, who has hitherto been successful in preventing the Nationalists from carrying into effect their policy of reducing the political representation of the Cape coloured population and abolishing the three seats for representatives of the native populations of the Union, would now be able to rely on the solidarity of his own party should the Nationalists decide to go forward with these measures. By these means the Nationalist Party has consolidated, and hopes still further to consolidate, their hold on the country since the last general election in 1948 and there seems no likelihood that it will be overthrown in the near future. By contrast, the United Party, now that they have lost Field-Marshal Smuts as well as Mr. Hofmeyr,[1] may be unable for some time to produce a first-class leader or a sufficiently challenging policy to counter the Nationalist Party's appeal to the electorate.

2. The feature of the Nationalist Government's policy which has caused the greatest shock in their relations with the rest of the world is their programme of Apartheid—a stiffer form of the traditional South African policy of racial segregation. Their ultimate objective is the establishment in the Union of a Republican, white and predominantly Afrikaner, form of Government which would ensure the domination of the white race and postpone as long as possible, if not for ever, the rise to power of the native population. While the Republican aspect of their policy has recently been

---

[1] J H Hofmeyr, deputy prime minister, 1948, in the United Party government, died 3 Dec 1948; Smuts died 11 Sept 1950.

in abeyance, the Nationalists are pressing on with their racial programme. They have by legislation prohibited marriages between Europeans and non-Europeans, and have now passed the Group Areas Act, 1950, described by Dr. Malan as the "kernel of apartheid," which extends earlier legislation so as to provide for the segregation of different racial groups of the population into defined areas for both residential and commercial purposes. In all this they have gone much further than their predecessors, the previous United Party Government, but much of the strength of the Nationalists is derived from the general support for some form of racial segregation apparent among most sections of the white population, including those of British descent.

3. Public opinion outside the Union of South Africa is unmistakably hostile to the policies of the Nationalist Government, not least in the United Kingdom itself, where these feelings have recently been expressed in many quarters. Foreign criticism has been apparent in the United Nations and a similar hostility exists in the Colonies and in other Commonwealth countries, especially India. The attitude of India is of particular importance to us at this juncture since we wish to enlist her great influence in Asia to help in the solution of Far Eastern and other problems which are at present major issues in the United Nations. Any suspicion that the United Kingdom sympathised in any way with South Africa's native policies would so deeply disturb African and Indian public opinion in our African Colonies as to constitute a threat to their internal security.

Importance to the United Kingdom of good relations with South Africa

4. Though there is thus a great deal in the policy of the present South African Government with which we in the United Kingdom clearly cannot associate ourselves, it is important for the following reasons that the United Kingdom should continue to preserve good relations with South Africa:—

(i) From the general strategic and defence points of view South Africa's good will is of particular importance to us. If, as seems likely at present, the Mediterranean is closed to us in any future war, the naval base at Simonstown, where the South Africans have granted us special rights, will be of vital importance to the Royal Navy, and other South African ports will be indispensable to our shipping and as staging bases for our troops. Apart from this the Union can contribute considerable military forces and we hope shortly to obtain from them a firm commitment to send troops to the Middle East in the event of war. The contribution envisaged would consist of one Armoured Division together with aircraft and naval forces. There are believed to be important deposits of uranium in the Union and the Union Government have stated that they have recently developed processes for its extraction.

(ii) The Nationalists are staunchly anti-Communist and Dr. Malan himself has more than once publicly pledged South Africa's support in any war resulting from Russian aggression; he repeated this pledge at Durban on 19th September, when he is reported as having said that they "would ally themselves with the Commonwealth and other like-minded nations of the world in the event of a major war." The Union Government provided air crews to assist in the air lift to Berlin when it was blockaded by the U.S.S.R., and, despite the unpopularity of the United Nations in South Africa, they have now agreed to send a squadron of the South African Air Force to co-operate with the United Nations Forces in Korea.

(iii) South Africa is by far the largest gold producer in the world and it is of the utmost importance for the viability of the Sterling Area that the United Kingdom should be able to obtain a substantial part of her gold output. During friendly discussions with the South African Minister for Economic Affairs this summer an agreement was reached which guaranteed that the United Kingdom will obtain from the Union at least £50 million of gold per annum. South Africa is, moreover, an important market for United Kingdom exports, and several hundred millions of pounds of United Kingdom capital is invested there.

(iv) The High Commission Territories of Basutoland, the Bechuanaland Protectorate and Swaziland could at any time be economically strangled by the Union Government withholding essential facilities.

(v) Finally, we have obligations to South Africa as a fellow-member of the Commonwealth, and even if South Africa decided to become a Republic, we should hope that she would remain with the Commonwealth. Though we have many points of difference with South Africa we have also many in common and 40 per cent. of the white population is of British stock. The Commonwealth partnership rests on the principle of tolerance; any attempt to secure complete identity of view between all its members would break up the association overnight.

5. In spite of difficulties and differences our relations with the Nationalist Government have, in practice, been surprisingly good. Thus we held successful economic talks with them last summer and prospects for the present defence talks are promising. While we cannot in any way associate ourselves with South Africa's native policies, our attitude should be explained to the South Africans as clearly and politely as possible and unnecessary polemics should be avoided. It should, moreover, be remembered that, in general, Nationalist Party leaders are new to office, parochial in their outlook, and without much experience of the outside world. If our relations with them are carefully handled there is some reason to hope that they may gradually modify their extremer views in response to world opinion. This is more likely to happen if we for our part show in our dealings with them that we appreciate the problems confronting them and do not simply adopt an attitude of condemnation.

6. Against this background we now have to consider the United Kingdom's policy in dealing with the specific issues of the treatment of Indians in South Africa and the question of the Union Government's Mandate for South-West Africa, both of which are once again on the agenda of the forthcoming session of the United Nations General Assembly.

7. *The treatment of Indians in South Africa*. This is a problem of long standing, but the present quarrel between the Union Government on the one hand and the Governments of India and Pakistan on the other originated with the Asiatic Land Tenure and Indian Representation Act, 1946, which was passed by Field-Marshal Smuts's United Party Government. This Act restricted the ownership or occupation of residential property by persons of Asian descent in certain areas. The Nationalist Government have extended these restrictions and applied them to the occupation of property for trading purposes as well as for residence. Indians are also affected by the other recent Apartheid legislation mentioned in paragraph 2 providing for the segregation of racial groups and the prohibition of "mixed marriages." The Union Government claim that these are all matters of domestic jurisdiction with which the

United Nations and other Governments have no right to interfere. These "Indians" are of course South African citizens who would not be happy if they were "repatriated" to India. The United Kingdom Government obviously cannot support the Union Government's policy on the treatment of citizens of Indian origin. In the past, when the matter has been considered by the United Nations, we have maintained an attitude of strict neutrality and avoided being drawn into the merits of the dispute. It is recommended that, at this session of the Assembly, we should continue the same policy, avoid taking part in the debate and attempt to exercise a conciliatory influence from the background. We should abstain from voting on any Resolution against South Africa of a strongly condemnatory character. The question last came before the General Assembly in 1948 and there is no likelihood that further discussion at Lake Success will lead to any useful result. Even the Indians realise this. As regards Pakistan's attitude, Sir Zafrullah Khan told me the other day that his Government's general relations with South Africa were good and that, while the Pakistan Delegation would have to vote in favour of previous Resolutions, they would cause as little trouble as possible at the Assembly over this problem. He did not think there was any solution to the matter and the sooner it could be dropped the better. Pakistan's attitude over South-West Africa is similar.

8. *South-West Africa*. The recent Advisory Opinion of the International Court of Justice on this subject is briefly to the following effect:—

(i) South Africa is not obliged to submit a Trusteeship Agreement for South-West Africa.
(ii) The status of the territory remains the same as was laid down by the original League of Nations Mandate of 1920.
(iii) South Africa is under an obligation to transmit reports and petitions on South-West Africa to the United Nations, which the Court regards as having inherited the rights of the League of Nations in this respect.

The Foreign Office Legal Advisers endorse the legal correctness of (i) and (ii) but have expressed doubts concerning the soundness of (iii). It is recommended, however, that His Majesty's Government should support the Court's Opinion as a whole (without actually endorsing its legal correctness). The arguments for this are:—

(a) It is our policy to support the authority of the International Court and to accept its Advisory Opinions.
(b) Whatever the strictly legal position, there is a strong case on moral and political grounds for the continuance of the same sort of international supervision in respect of South-West Africa as existed under the League of Nations.
(c) Failure to support the Court's Opinion as a whole, including the part about the submission of reports and petitions to the United Nations, would encourage other parties to contest the section of the Opinion favourable to South Africa on the question of submitting a Trusteeship Agreement.

If, in the face of the Court's Opinion, the South Africans should persist in refusing to submit reports and petitions to the United Nations, it is likely that they will find themselves completely isolated at the Assembly and, for the reasons mentioned above, we ourselves in that event would be unable to give them any support. This is a position which we are most anxious if possible to avoid. On the recommendation of the Parliamentary Under-Secretary of State for Commonwealth Relations, therefore, and with the concurrence of the Foreign Secretary and the Secretary of State for the Colonies, the Prime Minister recently sent a message to Dr. Malan (copy annexed), the object of which was to attempt to persuade the Union Government to agree to act in accordance with the Court's Opinion as a whole, on the understanding that reports (and by implication also petitions) submitted to the United Nations would be deal[t] with by the latter under a procedure conforming as far as possible with the procedure of the former Mandates Commission. The adoption of such a procedure would in itself accord with the Court's Opinion, which states:—

> "The degree of supervision to be exercised by the General Assembly should not therefore exceed that which applied under the Mandates System, and should conform as far as possible with the procedure followed in this respect by the Council of the League of Nations. These observations are particularly applicable to annual reports and petitions."

At the same time Mr. Attlee's message will serve to warn Dr. Malan, as courteously as possible, that if he refuses to make any concession over submitting reports, &c., the United Kingdom Government will not be able to give South Africa any support at the General Assembly of the United Nations. Although the message made it clear (see paragraph 2 (c) and paragraph 5) that we considered that the Court's Opinion should be taken as a whole, partly for reasons of tactics, the question of petitions was not specifically mentioned, but when the point arises we propose, if necessary, to explain to the South Africans that under our proposals we should expect them to transmit petitions as well as reports to the United Nations. The Prime Minister has not yet had any reply from Dr. Malan. We know that it will be very difficult for him to accept our suggestions since he and his colleagues have already committed themselves publicly against sending reports to the United Nations. I have myself talked to Dr. Geyer, the High Commissioner for the Union of South Africa in London, and strongly pressed on him the importance of South Africa accepting the Court's Opinion and sending reports to the United Nations. Meanwhile, we cannot decide on the details of our policy and tactics at the United Nations at least until we have had Dr. Malan's reply. It may be that there will be several draft Resolutions on this subject before the General Assembly, in which case our line would be to back the least violent that supported the Court's Opinion. If some Members of the General Assembly should seek to enforce on the Union the sending of reports and petitions to the United Nations without giving her the benefit of the reservations quoted above regarding the procedure which should be followed and the degee of supervision to be exercised, the United Kingdom Delegation should do their utmost in that case to secure that the Assembly itself, as well as the Union, accepts the Court's Opinion as a whole.

9. *Conclusions*. In the light of the above considerations my conclusions in regard to our relations with the South African Government are:—

In general

(i) We clearly must not associate ourselves with South Africa's native policies and apartheid, which are repugnant to public opinion in this country, but we should state our own attitude as politely as possible and thus avoid antagonising South Africa. At the same time we should attempt, in concert with the older Commonwealth countries and the United States, to exercise a moderating influence on disagreements between South Africa and other parties, ensuring that we do not act alone as a mediator in these disputes.

(ii) We should do all we can to retain South Africa as a member of the Commonwealth—preferably as one owing direct allegiance to the Crown.

On the specific issues before the General Assembly

(iii) We should remain neutral and avoid being drawn into the merits of the dispute over the Indians in South Africa, and

(iv) We should continue to bring pressure to bear on the Union Government to act in accordance with the Advisory Opinion of the International Court of Justice on South-West Africa and, again in concert with the Commonwealth Governments and the United States, attempt to secure agreement if possible between the Union Government and the United Nations General Assembly.

10. The Secretary of State for the Colonies and the Minister of State have seen this memorandum and are in general agreement with what is proposed.

Annex to 429

United Kingdom Government have been considering recent Advisory Opinion of International Court of Justice on South-West Africa. Situation arising therefrom in forthcoming session of United Nations General Assembly is bound to be most difficult and delicate and I feel I should acquaint you with our present ideas.

2. Greatest difficulty is likely to be caused by opinion of Court that Union Government is under obligation to submit reports to United Nations. While Union Government objections to this course are understood, I feel I should warn you frankly that United Kingdom Government would see great difficulty in supporting the Union Government should latter feel themselves unable to take any action to conform with Court's Opinion. Reasons for our view are as follows:—

(a) We are on principle anxious to uphold authority of Court and have welcomed its increased use recently, e.g., in case of human rights in Hungary, Bulgaria and Roumania and on competence of General Assembly in admission of new members. Even though in present case we realise that some of Court's Opinions are open to question, we would generally be disinclined to do anything to call in question authority of Court. Further strong argument for upholding authority of Court in this case is desirability of inducing members of General Assembly to think along legal rather than political or emotional lines.

(b) Whatever the strictly legal position, we believe it would be wrong and contrary to principle of international Mandate to take unilateral action which would have effect of denying any international interest in South-West Africa.

(c) Opinion of Court should in our view best be taken as a whole. Satisfactory feature is majority opinion that Union Government are not obliged by United Nations Charter to negotiate Trusteeship Agreement for South-West Africa. We fear that failure on part of Union to accept Opinion as a whole would encourage Assembly to reopen this issue, on which Court pronounced only by narrow majority in favour of South Africa, and to persist as strongly as ever in demanding that South-West Africa should be placed under trusteeship.

(d) We believe that arrangements are possible whereby your Government could accept substance of Court's Opinion while at the same time avoiding more objectionable features of United Nations methods of dealing with earlier report submitted on South-West Africa. These arrangements are outlined below.

3. Page 138 of the Court's Opinion reads:—

"The degree of supervision to be exercised by the General Assembly should not therefore exceed that which applied under the Mandates System and should conform as far as possible to the procedure followed in this respect by the Council of the League of Nations."

Main points of difference between Permanent Mandates Commission and Trusteeship Council would seem to be as follows:—

(a) Commission normally worked in private though it had right to operate in public if it so desired.
(b) Members of Commission were not Government representatives (although the Commission throughout included a British subject) and could not be connected with national delegations.
(c) Comments of Mandatory Power might accompany Commission's report to the League Council.
(d) Commission sent no Visiting Missions to Mandated Territories.

4. We would earnestly suggest for consideration of your Government possibility of agreeing to some arrangement whereby *ad hoc* committee of independent experts might be set up to receive reports on South-West Africa operating as closely as possible on lines of the Permanent Mandates Commission. This Committee would doubtless report to Fourth Committee of Assembly, but latter should have no more rights in this case than Council of League and Union should not be called upon to report in any different manner from previous procedure under Mandates system. If it were felt, however, that it would be preferable not to increase number of U.N. bodies already existing, it would be worth considering whether reports might not be received by a sub-committee of one of existing U.N. bodies or by an existing U.N. body itself under strict proviso that procedure followed in any such body conformed as closely as possible to that of Permanent Mandates Commission.

5. Arrangements on these lines would in first place involve agreement by other parties to act in accordance with Advisory Opinion of Court as a whole and would therefore entail dropping of demand made at all previous sessions of General Assembly that South-West Africa should be placed under trusteeship. Agreement of Union to accept international supervision to extent provided for under League of Nations Mandate would be best answer to any allegations that international status of territory is being altered by Union legislation as has been alleged, for example, in case of South-West Africa Affairs (Amendment) Act, 1949. Moreover, arrangements on these lines in accordance with Court's Opinion would strengthen authority of Court and help to wean General Assembly away from purely political or emotional approach to this problem and induce them to deal with it in future on more sensible and dispassionate legal basis. I would emphasise that it would not be necessary to accept the validity of the Court's Opinion as correct or binding, but rather to consent to take action in conformity with it provided the General Assembly also agree. If this

arrangement can be established as we believe is possible without embarrassments that attended consideration of earlier report by Trusteeship Council, I am sure that necessary concession of agreeing to submit reports on this restricted basis would help greatly towards settlement of this difficult problem. If events proved that critics of Union were not prepared to accept Court's Opinion on question of negotiation of Trusteeship Agreement, then clearly South African position would be greatly strengthened.

6. I should let you know frankly that, if in face of Court's Opinion Union Government should still feel obliged to persist in attitude of complete refusal to submit reports, United Kingdom Government themselves, for reasons given in paragraph 2, would find it impossible to continue that measure of support which we have hitherto been able to give Union in this matter. In that event we are most gravely concerned lest Union may find itself in dangerously isolated position at United Nations, and I need hardly say how anxious we are to avoid this. I earnestly hope, therefore, that you will be able to give favourable consideration to our proposals coming as they do from a friendly Government which has always endeavoured in the past to give you such assistance as we could in this most difficult problem. If you feel able to accept proposals on these lines it goes without saying that the United Kingdom Government will do their best to persuade others to support them.

7. I realise that elections are now proceeding in South-West Africa and are likely to make it difficult for you to engage yourself publicly at this stage to agree to any arrangement for submission of reports. I hope nevertheless that it will meanwhile be possible to avoid any statements likely to increase difficulty later on of coming to an arrangement such as I have proposed. Naturally we for our part will avoid any public disclosure here at present stage that we have made any approach to you whatever on this subject and will treat as most strictly confidential any interim reply which you may feel able to send me in answer to this telegram.

430 PREM 8/1346 26 Sept 1950

[High Commission Territories]: minute no 56/50 by Mr Gordon Walker to Mr Attlee about administrative arrangements

I apologise for a long minute. I have summarised at the end the questions for decision.

2. As I have told you I am far from satisfied with our arrangements for administering the High Commission Territories. This is the only bit of direct administration that has to be done in the Commonwealth Relations Office. In the past the Territories caused very little trouble and we never had to face up to the extremely difficult problem of creating a machinery by which we could properly discharge our responsibilities. Since Malan came to power the problem of the Territories has become a critical and potentially explosive one.

3. The problem is two-fold: we have to find the right organisation both in London and on the spot. Inside the Commonwealth Relations Office we must find means by which we can keep the problem of the Territories under continuous and direct

attention and by which the Secretary of State can receive the advice necessary for the discharge of his administrative duties. After careful consideration I have decided against my original idea that we should bring Baring in to advise the Secretary of State. He is really too big for the job. It would be hard for any Secretary of State to reject his advice: it would also cause difficulties for the next High Commissioner. Moreover, Baring would in effect be an unattached Adviser who did not fit properly into the Office: and this I think is nearly always a mistake. What we want is a new post in the Office of Head of the Territories Department. It should be held by a man who functions as a normal Assistant Secretary. He should if possible have had direct experience of the Territories. I think the right man would be Clark who has been Chief Secretary[1] and responsible under Baring for the Territories and who has handled the Seretse affair particularly well. There would be a number of questions about secondment etc. to be settled about which I need not trouble you. I would like to speak to the Colonial Secretary about securing Clark's services.

4. A further necessary change at the London end concerns our Legal Advisers. I was appalled when I got back to find the sort of advice we had been given throughout the Seretse affair. It was casual to the point of irresponsibility. As you know the Government might have been put into serious difficulty if Seretse had persisted in his legal challenge to the validity of what we had done. The arrangement up to now has been that we call when needed on the services of the Legal Advisers to the Colonial Office. This arrangement I would like to bring to an end.

5. One difficulty is that we may not have enough work for a full-time Legal Adviser of our own. However, besides the sort of work that arose out of the Seretse case we do have a good deal of quasi legal work (e.g. in connection with the status and immunities of High Commissioners, Kashmir, the High Commission Territories, etc.) and we have plenty of constitutional, nationality, citizenship and similar questions, especially in relation to the new Members of the Commonwealth. On all that it would be a great help to have a Legal Adviser at hand to consult from day to day.

6. The best arrangement, I think, would be that Mr. Dale, the second Legal Adviser to the Colonial Office (and a good man) should sit in the Commonwealth Relations Office and that we should have first call on his time, the Colonial Office having second call. One improvement would result, namely that Mr. Dale could regularly read the telegrams and files that provide the necessary background, political as well as legal, for the opinions that he would be called on to give. No such arrangement is possible at the moment: nor is there any way in which we can be warned of unexpected legal difficulties that may arise.

7. I would of course bring any important legal point to the Law Officers: but we must have some machinery for dealing with lesser legal matters and for properly preparing submissions to the Law Officers. One of the defects in the Seretse case was that this was never adequately done.

8. What to do in South Africa and the Territories is a very difficult problem. One solution would be to create a new High Commissioner for the Territories separate from our High Commissioner in the Union. This would be administratively convenient, but would I am sure be a mistake. Our aim is not only to administer the Territories but to preserve them from incorporation in the Union. Half the job must

[1] Mr Attlee wrote 'I agree, CRA' in the margin here. W A W Clark was appointed in Dec 1950.

therefore be diplomatic. It would be fatal to separate off our administration of the Territories from our relations with the Union. The two things are part and parcel of one another.

9. If, however, we decide that we must have a single High Commissioner who is responsible both for the Territories and for our relations with the Union, we must face the consequence that there is no neat administrative solution of the problem of making our control from London effective. I am tempted to appoint a second Deputy High Commissioner who should have special responsibility for the Territories. He would work through the High Commissioner but would spend much of his time touring the Territories and he would not move down to Capetown with the High Commissioner and the Union Government. This arrangement might however make difficult the position of our Resident Commissioner in each of the three Territories. It might be regarded as a reduction of their status and responsibility and it would certainly bring another person into the official hierarchy and perhaps reduce the natives' respect for the Resident Commissioners. We have a real problem here and one that I would not like to make a final decision about until I have had a chance to see things on the spot for myself.

10. The matter is not urgent and I am not worried so long as Baring is there. He has special knowledge and, during the war, was able to spend a great deal of time in the Territories. Since the advent of Malan, our High Commissioner has had to devote nearly all his time to relations with the Union Government. Future High Commissioners, I fear, will not be able to acquire Baring's special acquaintance with the Territories and, for half the year will have to discharge their responsibilities from a great distance from them.

11. There is one other matter that has caused me concern and on which we should make a decision of principle. The simple fact is that these three Territories are not administratively viable. They do not yield enough money to finance their own proper administration. Were we concerned only with economic considerations we would certainly yield the Territories to South Africa. We hold them for political and not for economic reasons. But in that case we must accept the consequences of our political decision which is that we must, within reason, ourselves make good the expenditure needed for decent administration. Otherwise we will be committed to the impossible position of sticking to these Territories for political reasons and being unable to administer them properly. We would thus be cutting the ground from under our own feet.

12. I don't think any very considerable sums are involved. We do quite well out of the Colonial Development and Welfare Fund and out of the Colonial Development Corporation. The sort of problem I have been faced with is that we have no Court of Appeal for the Territories. This amounts to a denial of natural justice, especially in capital cases. In trying to find a solution I have constantly come up against financial difficulties and, indeed, on analogy from ordinary colonies, rightly so. Another example might arise out of the creation of a new Deputy High Commissioner. I have found that, for lack of money, the offices of Legal Adviser to the High Commissioner and of Judge in the Territories have both been held by one man. Similar problems may arise in the future.

13. What I would like is a decision in principle that we must contemplate expenditure on a scale which would not be justified if the conditions peculiar to the Territories did not exist. Each particular proposal would of course have to be judged

on its merits: but should not be decided by strict analogy with comparable Territories in the Colonial Empire. The principle should be that we must pay enough to administer the Territories properly. It could be clearly laid down that the Territories were exceptional and that they must never be used as a precedent for other territories.

14. If you agree with this last proposition the question will arise of how to make it effective. The creation of a Court of Appeal, for example, is urgent as death sentences may be passed in Ritual Murder cases [in Basutoland]. What I suggest is that I prepare a separate minute to you on this matter and secure the views on it of the Treasury and the Colonial Secretary. The question could then, as you decide, come up to you or to Ministers for decision.

15. *Conclusions*

(a) I would like your consent to approach the Colonial Secretary about the appointment of Mr. Clark (or some similar person) to a new post in the Commonwealth Relations Office of Head of the Territories Department.

(b) I would like to bring to an end the arrangement by which we use the Legal Advisers to the Colonial Office and instead to have a Legal Adviser who sits in the Commonwealth Relations Office and on whose time I would have first call and the Colonial Office second call. The man I have in mind is Mr. Dale, Second Legal Adviser to the Colonial Office.

(c) To leave the question of a new Deputy High Commissioner for the Territories or other similar arrangement until I can look at things on the spot.

(d) I should prepare a minute to you embodying the principle that we must pay for the proper administration of the Territories.[2]

[2] Mr Attlee wrote 'I agree' against each of the conclusions (a), (b) and (c), and against (d) 'Discuss this with Treasury before submitting minute, 26.9.50'.

431 CAB 128/18, CM 62(50)4 — 28 Sept 1950

'Relations with South Africa': Cabinet conclusions on general position and on issues at the UN [Extract]

The Cabinet considered a memorandum by the Secretary of State for Commonwealth Relations (C.P. (50) 214)[1] on the general state of relations between the United Kingdom Government and the Government of South Africa, and on the particular issues affecting South Africa which were likely to come forward for discussion at the United Nations.

The Secretary of State for Commonwealth Relations said that the task of preserving good relations with the Union Government was one of the most difficult of the problems now confronting him. The native policy of the South African Government was one which the United Kingdom Government could not approve, and one which caused them serious difficulties both with their political supporters in this country and with public opinion in Colonial territories. On the other hand, from the strategic point of view, South Africa's goodwill was of special importance to us;

[1] See 429.

and on defence questions we were making very satisfactory progress towards a better understanding with her. Our economic relations were also satisfactory. And South Africa's attitude towards her Commonwealth membership was less difficult than it had previously been. It was important that in all these matters we should retain South Africa's co-operation as a member of the Commonwealth; and it followed that, while we should avoid expressing sympathy with the native policy of the present Government, we should refrain from publicly condemning it.

The Secretary of State for the Colonies said that he was seriously disturbed by the effect which the domestic policy of the Union Government was creating in Colonial territories, and also by the indications of South African ambitions for control over other parts of Africa. There were, for example, signs that South Africa was encouraging the immigration of Afrikaaners into Northern Rhodesia. While therefore he appreciated the economic and strategic advantages of our present relations with South Africa, he feared that a time might come when we should be forced to weigh these against our Colonial interests in other parts of Africa. *The Minister of Health*[2] supported this view. He referred to the embarrassments which the domestic policy of the Union Government caused to United Kingdom Ministers, both in their relations with their supporters in this country and in their international relations in the United Nations; and he suggested that, if these continued, the United Kingdom might have to consider whether she lost more than she gained by her present association with the Union Government.

Other Ministers, on the other hand, stressed the strategic importance of securing South Africa's support in any struggle against communism, and the great value of the military support which she now seemed likely to promise in the Middle East. Good progress was being made in the current discussions with the South African Minister of Defence, who seemed more ready to enter into defence commitments than any of his predecessors had been. Emphasis was also laid on the importance of retaining South Africa within the Commonwealth.

The Cabinet:—

(1) Endorsed the general policy outlined in paragraphs 1–5 of C.P. (50) 214 on the relations between the United Kingdom Government and the Government of South Africa.

Treatment of Indians in South Africa

The Secretary of State for Commonwealth Relations recalled that, on previous occasions when the treatment of Indians in South Africa had been discussed in the United Nations, the United Kingdom Government had maintained an attitude of strict neutrality and had avoided being drawn into the merits of the dispute. He recommended that, if this question arose at the current meeting of the United Nations, the United Kingdom Government should follow the same course, avoiding participation in debate and attempting to exercise a conciliatory influence from the background. In particular, we should abstain from voting on any resolution which was strongly condemnatory of South Africa.

The Cabinet:—

(2) Approved the proposals in paragraph 7 of C.P. (50) 214 regarding the attitude

---

[2] Mr A Bevan.

to be adopted by the United Kingdom Government towards any discussion of the treatment of Indians in South Africa at the meeting of the United Nations.

South-West Africa

The Secretary of State for Commonwealth Relations said that the International Court had delivered their Advisory Opinion on South Africa's obligations to the United Nations in respect of South-West Africa. The Court had found (i) that South Africa was not obliged to submit a trusteeship agreement for South-West Africa; (ii) that the status of the territory remained the same as was laid down by the League of Nations Mandate; and (iii) that South Africa was under an obligation to transmit reports and petitions on South-West Africa to the United Nations. The Prime Minister, in a telegram reproduced in the Annex to C.P. (50) 214, had urged the South African Government to accept to Court's Opinion; and the Secretary of State recommended that, when this matter came before the United Nations, we should vote in favour of acceptance of this Opinion. Some Governments might seek to lay it down that the reports and petitions should be forwarded to the Trusteeship Council; but we should argue that the Court's findings should be accepted as a whole and without amendment. If, as was likely, various forms of resolution were proposed, we should support whichever of the resolutions advocating acceptance of the full report was the least objectionable to the South African Government.

The Cabinet:—

(3) Endorsed the proposals in paragraph 8 of C.P. (50) 214 regarding the line to be taken by the United Kingdom Government in the discussions on South-West Africa at the United Nations. . . .[3]

---

[3] Attendance of Rev M Scott at UN omitted.

432 CO 537/7100, no 2 24 Feb 1951

[Statement by Dr Malan criticising British policy for the Gold Coast and the Commonwealth (23 Feb)]: inward tel [unnumbered] to CRO from Sir P Liesching in Cape Town

[Gordon Walker was in Johannesburg when Dr Malan made this statement, and he could hardly avoid reference to it at a press conference held on 26 Feb. His defence was that there was nothing novel in the British policy of self-government, and new nations were going to arise whatever anybody did; the Commonwealth was 'the only good bridge in the world' between these new and the older nations—'the fact that there are Eastern nations within the Commonwealth provides a solid bridge between the nationalism of Asia and the nationalism of the West' (CO 537/7100, no 16).]

The following are main points of Press interview by Dr. Malan published in *Die Burger* to-day.

(a) Nkrumah Party in Gold Coast want the same sovereign independence and right of self determination as other members of Commonwealth possess and want to be admitted into that circle on an equal footing. British Government through Mr. Griffiths has in advance cordially agreed to that. Native peoples of Africa are in a state of ferment. What is happening in West Africa must therefore affect all other native territories and indirectly South Africa. If these other territories are now going to demand with the same success what negroes of British West Africa have obtained, it means nothing less than expulsion of white man from virtually everywhere between South Africa and Sahara. White man's leadership and work of civilising which has only just begun and which for generations will be indispensable will then be at an end. What this means for us in the South but even more for Europeans to North of us need not even be conjectured.

(b) Personally he has no doubt of failure of West African experiment. It is unrealistic and shows lack of knowledge of human nature and must result in tragedy. But rights once given have come to stay and a failure which cannot be made good is usually more dangerous than failure itself.

(c) South Africa is faced with accomplished fact and with general statement of policy regarding Commonwealth's future if it still has one. Mr. Griffiths has welcomed new West African Negro State in advance as member of Commonwealth and went on to announce a policy of making British Colonies free independent members of Commonwealth one after the other presumably on equal footing in all respects with present members. At Durban Mr. Gordon Walker had also forecast entry into Commonwealth of British West Indies. According to Mr. Griffiths' statement we must expect that within measurable time succession of new Commonwealth members will be completed with addition of other territories such as Indian controlled East Africa, Uganda, Nyasaland etc. to speak only of Africa.

(d) Commonwealth is closed shop. Everyone free and everyone equal and consequently one would expect that everyone would have equal say in admission of new members because it may affect whole nature and character of the group. But acting off her own bat and without consultation with or [sic] the approval of other members, England a short while go added India, Pakistan and Ceylon to Commonwealth and she now proposes to continue process indefinitely. As Colonies territories are England's concern only but as possible members of Commonwealth there are others who have just as much interest in their position and who should have equal say as to their admission, this absurdity should be cleared away without delay.

(e) A change is taking place in nature and character of Commonwealth. Commonwealth can only exist as result of sense of solidarity between all its members, based on specific common interests and sufficient similarity of culture and political outlook. Link of common Kingship was not strong enough in case of Ireland, India and Burma and in any case is too remote and vague to exercise any real effective force in the long run. Insofar as it affects Commonwealth as a whole it has become a symbol separated from fulfilment of any constitutional function. When Commonwealth consisted of five members position was simple but question now arises what greater solidarity or common interests or uniformity exists for example between South Africa and India than exists between South Africa and the Netherlands, Belgium, France or Germany. Or for example between Australia and Negro State of West Africa than between Australia and United States.

(f) Newly announced policy of British Government signifies nothing less than undermining of foundations of Commonwealth and its gradual liquidation. Between United Nations which with its policy of interference makes it possible for one member of Commonwealth to interfere in domestic affairs of another via that Organisation and new British Commonwealth policy Commonwealth cannot last. We who value its survival may regret but blame is fortunately not ours. New situation promises no good for South Africa. But it may bring two European races closer together. In their consolidation on sound basis in genuine South African national unity lies in the end our common good.

433 CAB 129/45, CP(51)109 16 Apr 1951

'Visit by the Secretary of State for Commonwealth Relations to the Union of South Africa, Southern Rhodesia and the three High Commission Territories of Basutoland, the Bechuanaland Protectorate and Swaziland': Cabinet memorandum by Mr Gordon Walker

I am circulating this report for the information of my colleagues. I am afraid it is long, but I visited three different and difficult areas. I have sub-divided the reports as follows:—

(i) Southern Rhodesia (paragraphs 3 to 11).
(ii) High Commission Territories (paragraphs 12 to 21).
(iii) Union of South Africa (paragraphs 22 to 34).
(iv) Problems of Policy (paragraphs 35 to 55).

Some of my colleagues may prefer to read only the conclusions I have formed. These are in section (iv).

2. I spent six weeks in January and February this year travelling in the Union of South Africa and Southern Rhodesia as the guest of the two Governments and in the Bechuanaland Protectorate, Basutoland and Swaziland. In that time I travelled by air, road and rail some 17,000 miles.

(i) *Southern Rhodesia*

3. Southern Rhodesia is still in many ways like an enlarged County Council. Its white population is 129,000. The general level of Ministers and Civil Servants and business men is not high: but there are a few outstanding exceptions in all these classes. Trade Union and Labour leaders are not impressive. The Labour Party is small and split. The Trade Unions are extremely colour-conscious and enforce a rigid colour bar in the fields they control (particularly housing). They seek to exclude Africans from all skilled and semi-skilled building labour (and indeed from what we would here classify as unskilled labour) in the towns. Through training schools, African builders are becoming quite good though they cannot yet, in any numbers, work as well as the whites and they lack persistence. Nevertheless, I saw some excellent African-built houses, schools and hospitals. Their cost is about half as much as similar buildings put up by European labour. With the exception of the small Labour element the whole of Southern Rhodesia seems to be pro-Churchill and conservative in British politics, in which they are very interested. Even many of the Labour people think the British Labour Party has innocent and utopian ideas about race-relations. In their own internal affairs they are, however, quite radical and readily create State industries in fields such as iron and steel and railways in which they think we are stupid to have done so.

4. In general Southern Rhodesia is a happy and prosperous country. It has very considerable resources (doubtless much more than have yet been discovered). The population is pretty vigorous and virile. The country is suffering now from the effects

of unco-ordinated development and lack of foresight: for example, the railways were long neglected and are now inadequate to the economy; too many unimportant secondary industries were started; the immense coal resources at Wankie were slackly developed. All these things have been realised and are now being taken in hand. There is a tremendous housing shortage both for Europeans and Africans, aggravated by the colour bar in the building industry. Some ingenious experiments are being made with new building materials. As far as I could judge houses cost about twice what they would in England. On the average, general prices seemed about the same as in England.

5. One of Southern Rhodesia's main problems is white population. If they build this up fast it imposes a great strain on their resources: but if they do not, their potential resources cannot be developed. In recent years they have somewhat restricted immigration by insisting upon a high standard of quality and upon deposits by each immigrant. At the current rate South African immigrants outnumber British immigrants by 2 to 1. This is much discussed and argued about in Southern Rhodesia. It is hard to analyse the motives behind the immigration from the Union and there are no figures about its make-up. A fair proportion are *British* South Africans and not Afrikaners. Some of these and some of the Afrikaners, too, are leaving a country whose policy and Government they do not like. Not every Afrikaner by any means is a bad immigrant; indeed, the loyal Afrikaner who accepts King and Commonwealth is an admirable citizen. Most of these immigrants probably came in for simple economic reasons. Land is relatively cheap and tobacco is a quickly profitable crop; farmers and employers find it much cheaper to bring in a man from the Union than from the United Kingdom; also much easier to send him back if he is unsuitable. Many who come to work for others soon settle down on their own. There is, however, an element in this immigration (no one can say how large) that is political; various organisations in the Union deliberately foster immigration in order to bring Southern Rhodesia increasingly within South Africa's sphere of influence.

6. Sir Godfrey Huggins, the Prime Minister, spoke to me about this. He said that he had resolved to tackle the matter radically. He wanted to allow unrestricted immigration from Britain (with an assisted passage scheme) and to impose quotas on all other countries (in fact South Africa). He had not yet put this to his own party—but would soon do so. If he does bring this forward it will cause great controversy in Southern Rhodesia. I myself met many different views on this matter. It will certainly greatly annoy South Africa. Huggins had got the agreement of his Cabinet to his policy.

7. As far as I could in the time I went into the question of native policy in Southern Rhodesia. I saw Native Reserves and many schools, hospitals and housing schemes for Africans. I also discussed the question with all sorts of people. There is certainly a genuine distinction between the native policy of Southern Rhodesia and the Union. There is nothing in Southern Rhodesia to compare with the racial hatred and tension in places like Johannesburg in the Union. There have been some strikes by African workers but these have been purely economic and conducted in an orderly way. As in the Union, a good deal of money (almost all raised by taxes on the whites) is spent on African education, health and housing. All the officials I met concerned with these things impressed me. African food production in the Reserves and from farms and market gardens is relatively much higher than in the Union and makes an important contribution to the country's food supply.

Southern Rhodesia has largely been able to avoid the urban native problem that has arisen in towns like Johannesburg in the Union and steps are being taken to prevent it by building separate African townships that will have complete local self-government.

8. The Southern Rhodesian Government and its officials are well ahead of public opinion. Although one can meet people whose views are indistinguishable from the Nationalists in South Africa, they are not dominant. The general attitude, I think, is one of kindly superiority—the Africans must be helped but must keep in their places. There is a vague but widespread apprehension about the future when there will be increasingly large numbers of educated and trained Africans. At the moment, the vast majority of Africans are primitive and illiterate and ridden with superstition. Only a very small number is educated or politically conscious. Only some 30 per cent. attend even primary schools. About 4,000 were qualified for the electoral roll before the qualifications were recently raised. The Government, under Huggins, has steadily pressed for, and often secured, better treatment for the Africans than they would otherwise have got. For example, the Government is overcoming the resistance of towns (and Trade Unions) against African drivers and conductors for buses. The Government would like to break down or weaken the ban on African building workers. Against a good deal of criticism a maternity home for Africans was opened recently in Salisbury that is more modern and better than the home for Europeans and this at a time when the European maternity home is greatly overcrowded. Huggins is thinking of starting a University for Africans before one for Europeans. Of course, the social provision for Europeans is beyond comparison better than for Africans; I doubt if any Government has a better record in the provision of schools—including many State-financed boarding schools.

9. The most debatable question concerns the franchise. There is a common electoral roll open to all who meet certain qualifications. These qualifications have recently been raised, the property qualification from £150 to £500 and the annual income qualification from £100 to £240. There is also a simple English language test. This will undoubtedly postpone the day when Africans can play a significant part in elections and still further the day when any of them can hope to be elected to Parliament. On the other hand, only 800 out of the 4,000 already qualified ever actually put themselves on the roll. Moreover, the English language test will exclude a number of undesirable Afrikaners. The qualifications have been fairly administered and Europeans are excluded as well as Africans. Huggins had considerable difficulty in resisting pressure to exclude Africans altogether. He has preserved the essential principle of a single electorate and avoided the blind-alley of separate communal electorates. Constituencies, though immense in area, have very small electorates, and if Africans show a greater keenness to get on to the roll they should in less than a decade be able to play an important part in some constituencies. In about 25 years there should be African M.Ps.

10. The gravest Southern Rhodesian problem concerns the pull towards South Africa. This problem is as old as Southern Rhodesia itself: when in 1922 there was a plebiscite on whether Southern Rhodesia should join the Union or become an independent self-governing colony the voting was no more than 8 to 5 in favour of independence.

I discussed this question with a number of leading people and was surprised to find how considerable is still the readiness and desire to join the Union. Those who hold this view have many and mixed motives. Some want it for economic reasons; some to strengthen the pro-British element in South Africa; some out of genuine approval of the Union; some from dislike of what nearly everyone in Southern Rhodesia calls "Colonial Office policy." Perhaps as many as a third would vote for incorporation to-day. But the two-thirds on the other side would be very determined and adamant. The general sentiment in Southern Rhodesia is very powerfully in favour of the British connexion. There is no immediate danger of any change of loyalty. Present policies in the Union have weakened what feeling there is in favour of incorporation.

11. Sir Godfrey Huggins is outstandingly the ablest man in Southern Rhodesia and it is hard to see who can take over when he goes. The second man in the Cabinet is Davenport, Minister of Mines, Transport and Education, who is solid and reasonable, but lacking in personality. Whitehead, the Minister of Finance, is the cleverest member of the Government, but he is deaf and half-blind and an aloof man, not at all popular. Nor is his political judgment sound. The best man after Huggins is, I think, Greenfield, the Minister of Internal Affairs and Justice. He is new in the Government and will need some years to develop. (Incidentally he told me that he had always been in favour of the incorporation of Southern Rhodesia in the Union and had only changed when Malan had come into power.)

(ii) *High Commission Territories*

12. I was greatly impressed by what I saw of developments in our three High Commission Territories: the Bechuanaland protectorate, Basutoland and Swaziland. The High Commissioner, Sir Evelyn Baring, has in his seven years of office done a magnificent job. In the past these Territories were sadly neglected on the ground that it was not worth spending money on Territories that would one day go to the Union. From all accounts relations between the Africans, the Europeans and the Administration were all bad. To-day they are all pretty good. The loyalty of the Africans is very high. They are overwhelming against incorporation and cling to their allegiance to The King, as they pointed out in every single public speech they made to me. The only exceptions are a very few Africans in posts in which they would be paid at a higher salary in the Union. Salaries are commonly higher in the Union, but this consideration influences only a handful of people. I think the great majority of the Europeans are also against transfer.

13. The change in the temper of these Territories is partly due to the direct interest taken in them by the High Commissioner, who has frequently visited them, understands their problems, and personally knows many Africans and Europeans. It is essential that future High Commissioners should take the same interest. It is also desirable that the Secretary of State should sometimes visit the Territories. The population is inclined to feel isolated and ignored, and much appreciates any concern shown by His Majesty's Government. A firm attitude on transfer to the Union has also raised the morale of the Territories.

14. Another main cause of the general good feeling lies in the recent plans for economic development. About £1 million is being spent on each of the three Territories out of the Colonial Development and Welfare Fund. This is being spent in the main on raising the basic wealth of the Territories—(e.g. on water supplies and anti-soil-erosion work). At the same time the Colonial Development Corporation has undertaken some very important projects. In Swaziland there is a big afforestation scheme that should yield considerable dividends in 12 to 15 years. Previous

experience in afforestation makes this project a very safe investment. The Corporation is also developing a big irrigated farming project pioneered by private enterprise in the north of Swaziland. In Bechuanaland there are two schemes—one for mixed farming and cattle-raising in the North; one for an abbatoir in the South. The abbatoir seems very sound economically, as it will enable stock to be killed at its prime and sent to market in South Africa where it can fetch good prices; there should be a sufficient through-put of cattle to sustain it comfortably. The other scheme in the North seems sound, but I am looking into it again in order to be as sure as one can. By these means the Government revenue in each Territory should steadily increase and permit schools, hospitals, &c., not only to be started but to be adequately sustained.

15. The High Commissioner's aim, with which I wholly agree, is to find in each Territory some new major economic resource and develop it so that each Territory may become largely self-sustaining and much less dependent upon sending workers to the South African gold mines. In Bechuanaland (ranching) and Swaziland (timber) this policy is being carried out. But in Basutoland there is no corresponding potential resource. The only hope here is to dam the source of the Orange river, build subsidiary hydro-electric dams and sell water and power to the Union. This would be a costly undertaking, and it might arouse political difficulties as it concerns the headwater of one of the main South African rivers. It would enable the Orange river to be made silt-free and would remove one of the Union's best arguments for the incorporation of Basutoland. (This project—which has been carefully explored and checked—is still confidential, the Union Government is aware of the investigation, but the timing and handling of any official approach to them will be a delicate question.)

16. The major immediate problem in Basutoland and Swaziland is soil-erosion. Excellent work is being done by our officials. But only if this work is stuck to and pushed ahead, with adequate funds, can soil-erosion be conquered. If it is not, the two Territories will be economically ruined. Successful anti-erosion work depends upon the goodwill of the Chiefs and headmen: the whole work can go to pieces unless a large number of minor infringements of the law are promptly punished (e.g., breaking down a contour furrow or ploughing in a grass-strip). Only the Native Courts can look after this. Their powers are being steadily increased, and African co-operation in this work is steadily improving. The most difficult task still lies ahead, which is to persuade the people to de-stock. Everywhere there is serious over-grazing which kills out the grass by preventing re-seeding. It is hard to persuade these Africans, who regard cattle as wealth, that their wealth will increase by reducing their stock. It is like persuading our people of the benefit to themselves of a wage and dividend freeze.

17. The immediate problem in Bechuanaland (besides de-stocking) is the provision of water both by surface dams and bore-holes. The head of cattle that can be carried is a direct function of the water available. Moreover, the railway that runs through this Territory and provides most of its revenue must have increased water-supplies if it is to carry increased traffic. Unless this is done there is danger of an alternative line being built outside the Territory. For political reasons South Africa is pressing such a project. This would pretty well ruin Bechuanaland. Improving water-supplies is an expensive undertaking in itself and there seems to be no certain way of ensuring that every bore-hole will in fact tap water.

Ultimately Bechuanaland may become extremely prosperous cattle-country. Apart from the Colonial Development Corporation project, large parts of the Kalahari desert have underground water; but to develop this desert, roads and railways would have to be built.

There seems to be no prospect of any of this Bechuanaland meat coming to Britain. The demand for meat in Africa is rapidly mounting. Indeed, a meat shortage (and general food shortage) is one of Africa's most pressing problems.

18. I do not deal in this section of my report with the problem of how we can keep the Territories out of the Union (that problem can only be properly considered in relation to the Union). But, if we are to keep these Territories, we must be prepared to put money into them. One of South Africa's best arguments for incorporation has been their general backwardness. The three Territories are shop-windows in the midst of the Union and we must keep them economically strong and progressive. We cannot hope to spend as much on them as South Africa spends on her corresponding Native Reserves—nor is this necessary in order to hold their loyalty. Their African inhabitants feel themselves to be free men, and they rate this above mere material prosperity. Nevertheless, we must develop the Territories if we are to hold them. They must get at least their fair share of whatever money we are putting into our Colonies. The decision to hold the Territories is a political decision which cannot possibly pay us economically. We must therefore be ready to face the economic consequence of our political decision.

19. I gave special attention in the Bechuanaland Protectorate to the Bamangwato tribe (from which Seretse and Tshekedi came). I attended a Kgotla that was said to be the biggest to assemble for the conduct of business. A Kgotla is theoretically the assembly of the whole tribe: every male inhabitant is entitled to attend. In fact, some 10,000 attended, most of them coming in lorries from outlying districts. All this occurred during the ploughing season—which is the one time when the men (as distinct from the women) work and when they all want to be in the fields.

The Kgotla was a friendly one and I was greeted in an enthusiastic way on my arrival and before it could be known what I was to say. Before I spoke there was one main speech and nine subsidiary speeches—all on the same theme—and all in a broiling sun. They wanted Seretse back: above all they wanted Tshekedi and all his followers excluded for ever from the Territory. There was, of course, some organisation and rehearsal behind all this—but it is quite impossible to stage a Kgotla of 10,000. Moreover, each of the nine subsidiary speakers came from one of the "allied" or "subject" peoples who are ruled over by the Bamangwato and whom Tshekedi had claimed were on his side.

I had already discussed the whole situation with the first-rate officials who are now in charge. They had produced overwhelming evidence of Tshekedi's extreme unpopularity. This seems to rest partly on the feeling that he is seeking to usurp the Chieftainship to which he is not lineally entitled; but mainly on sheer fear. He is an extremely able, ruthless and unforgiving man, and everyone is frightened that if he comes back into the Reserve in any capacity he will get back to power and revenge himself on all who have either supported Seretse or failed to support Tshekedi.

I am quite convinced that the tribe cannot settle down nor can the newly instituted system of councils be got to work until the Bamangwato are convinced that Tshekedi will not be allowed to return to the Tribal Reserve. Once this is made clear the tribe will settle down and will begin to make up its mind about Seretse. (It was significant that the desire to exclude Tshekedi was even more strongly expressed than the desire to have Seretse back, and that not a single mention was made at any time of Ruth.)

In these circumstances I made a speech to the Kgotla saying that His Majesty's Government adhered to the White Paper policy (under which both Seretse and Tshekedi are excluded); that we would reconsider the matter in about five years; that this did not necessarily mean that Seretse would then return; and that neither Tshekedi nor anyone else would ever be imposed as Chief against the will of the people.

I saw Tshekedi later, but he produced so many documents and talked at such length that I agreed to continue the talks in London. I intend to tell him that the White Paper policy must be enforced and that he must not enter the Reserve save for the most exceptional reasons. I will make this decision public so that it shall be known to the Bamangwato. I hope Tshekedi, who is extremely able, will accept some useful job in connexion with the economic development of the Territory.

This whole affair is tricky. I am hopeful that the Bamangwato will settle down and develop a more democratic council system. I have received reports (including letters from leading tribesmen to people in this country) that the Bamangwato are prepared to accept the decisions I announced to them and to get on with the job of getting the Native Administration going again. They received my speech at the Kgotla well. All signs of non-co-operation have disappeared.

20. I met a good many of the Chiefs in all three High Commission Territories. I have no doubt that the institution of Chieftainship in these Territories is essential. It is very strongly established, and only through it can the administration (e.g., in anti-erosion work) be carried out. There are stirrings against the old order due to the emergence of a small minority of able and well-educated Africans, who are usually more capable than the Chiefs. The widened experience of the thousands of Pioneers who served overseas in the war has also led to a desire for greater participation by the people in their own administration. We must therefore prevail upon the Chiefs to work with elected councils and to decentralise their authority to local councils. I stressed this in all my speeches in the Territories and in my private talks with leading Chiefs. These developments are already in hand. They will need delicate and skilful handling.

The ablest man among the Chiefs is Sobhuza, Paramount Chief of the Swazi. He is well educated and speaks excellent English. His general policy is to be very progressive in the establishment of schools, &c., and in pressing on anti-erosion work; and at the same time to preserve and share in all the old tribal customs and traditions. When I first met him in his own tribe he was naked to the waist and decked in gorgeous feathers, beads and a skin-kilt. Later [that] afternoon he turned up at the Resident Commissioner's garden party and was the best-dressed man there in a beautifully cut suit. He has ten wives.[1] I had a long talk with him and found that he was very satisfied with the way things are going. He is strongly against Seretse's marriage, and thinks that he should be compelled to choose between Ruth and the Chieftainship. If he wants to stick to Ruth, he should abdicate. Sobhuza plans to have a meeting of all the leading Chiefs of the three Territories (including the leading men of the Bamangwato) to discuss the whole matter.

---

[1] Later increased to 117 (editor's note). Sobhuza II ruled from 1921 to 1982.

The Paramount Chief of the Basuto is a lady called 'M'antsebo Seeiso. She is famous for her smart Western hats (no-one knows how she keeps them on her short, frizzy hair) and highly coloured shoes. She is, unfortunately, not a very strong ruler, and like too many Chiefs is rather too fond of gin. She was almost certainly involved in a number of medicine murders, though the proof was never complete. She became very scared when two other Chiefs were hanged for such murders and she is now co-operating in stamping them out.

Unfortunately Bechuanaland has no Paramount Chief, but consists of a number of separate and equal tribes. On the whole, the level of the Chiefs is not very high. Tshekedi was the outstanding one when he was Regent of the Bamangwato.

21. I was impressed by the calibre of our senior officials in the Territories, though I think it will be necessary for the junior officials to acquire more experience of administration in other of our African territories.

As His Majesty's Government, through the Secretary of State, is directly responsible for the administration of these three Territories, I gave particular attention to the question whether the machinery for discharging this responsibility can be improved. I found little that need be done. But I think the three Territories need to be treated rather more as a single entity than has been the case in the past. I am making detailed arrangements to secure this. I am also considering the enhancement of the status of the Chief Secretary by making him a Deputy High Commissioner. He could then, on the one hand better co-ordinate policy in the three Territories, and on the other hand better serve as a channel between them and the Secretary of State. The Deputy High Commissioner would, of course, be under the High Commissioner—but he would have greater authority over the Resident Commissioners in each of the Territories.

I intend also to send out to the Territories for short terms officials in my Office who deal with the Territories and bring back for short terms to London some of the officials in the field. I discussed all these matters with the High Commissioner who is in agreement with me about them.

(iii) *The Union of South Africa*

22. South African politics are extremely sharp and bitter. The Nationalist [sic] Party (Malan's) has many of the characteristics of a devoted movement of liberation. It uses Afrikaans as a political weapon; it puts its own people in every possible office; and it believes unshakably in its cause. The leaders have long been in the wilderness and live and dream politics: their wives are as much in the movement as they are.

To some extent the Nationalists are still fighting the Boer War—or rather they have just won it. (When they say "the war" they mean the Boer War.) They regard as their enemy not so much the United Kingdom as the British in South Africa and they are taking a long-delayed revenge for what they regard as oppression.

A main motive behind the Nationalist faith is that the Afrikaner has no other home but Africa. He resents the way in which the British can look to Britain and often send their children to be educated here. The Afrikaner glories in South Africa and is filled with a desperate determination to keep it as his home and to be master in his own house.

23. I was extremely disappointed in the British in South Africa. They undoubtedly regarded the Boer War as their victory over the Afrikaners. For a generation they have been (and still are) very arrogant and despise the Afrikaners. They refuse to

learn or use Afrikaans. They have kept all jobs in the great industries they control for British people. They have excluded Afrikaners from their clubs. Worst of all, they have completely failed to go into national public life. Recently an attempt was made to find a British candidate for Smuts's seat—a safe seat. But not one could be found. The British in South Africa deserve the "persecution" that is now being visited upon them by the Nationalists.

Incidentally, the worst race relations of all are in cities dominated by the British—Johannesburg and Durban. On the other hand, the best relations I saw were in another British town—Port Elizabeth, the only town without Pass Laws for the Africans. The early English settlers are much better than the British who came in to open up the gold mines of the Transvaal and the sugar estates of Natal.

The British still have a very considerable influence. They command great wealth and they are very efficient indeed in business. The English Press is much larger and more influential than the Afrikaans Press. Nevertheless, the Afrikaners are steadily advancing and colouring the whole nation. They are dominant in the countryside and are gradually entering all the towns, which used to be British preserves.

24. The best people in South Africa seemed to me to be the Afrikaners in the United Party (Smuts's party). They are well-educated, self-confident and have in many respects sensible policies. They are loyal to the British connexion and know much more about the world than the Nationalists. There are a great many Afrikaners who oppose the Nationalists—even in its strongholds. This infuriates the Nationalists, who regard them as traitors.

25. The Nationalists have two main objectives which tend to be contradictory: this makes their policy unstable and difficult to predict. In a nutshell, the two objectives may be said to be to pursue simultaneously an anti-Black and an anti-British policy. (The anti-British policy always being more against the local British than against the United Kingdom—though the two become confused, as the local British want to preserve the realities and the symbols of the British connexion.) So long as the Nationalists concentrate on an anti-Black policy they get a good deal of British support in elections. And this they need to keep them in power. But if they push their anti-British policy too far they will lose their British support. It is not always realised how far the Nationalists get British votes and the United Party gets Afrikaner votes. If the Nationalists stressed too strongly their Republicanism or any policy that involved a breach with the United Kingdom, practically the whole British population would vote against them.

Moreover, the present Government in South Africa is very conscious of its isolation in the world and of the value of the friendship and support of Britain, which tends to carry Commonwealth support with it. They are also highly conscious of the Russian Communist danger. They tend, therefore, to cling to their good relations with Britain and to flinch from actions that would involve an open breach. In defence, for instance, they are more forthcoming than Smuts ever dared be in peace-time.

In consequence, the Nationalists tend to limit their anti-British actions to the domestic field and to keep their anti-Black policies more pronounced than their anti-British policies. Typical of this is the appalling Voortrekker Monument outside Pretoria. This is designed as a national shrine—and though it is very ugly and rather hysterical—it has some of the characteristics of such a shrine. It is, however, completely Afrikaner. You would not know from seeing it that there were any British in South Africa. It emphasises the struggle between Afrikaner and Bantu and outside this "national shrine" is a notice that non-Europeans are admitted only on Tuesdays.

The Nationalists are steadily putting their own supporters into places of authority and into the Police and Army. Their strict application of the rule of bi-lingualism is in effect excluding the British. They are very effectively rigging the electorate in their favour. This underlies their present bill to exclude the Cape Coloured from the electoral roll—they all voted for the United Party. It also explains the large representation given to South-West Africa.

On the whole the Nationalists are far better and keener politicians than the United Party and much more ruthless. The United Party is fairly confident of winning the next election, but in my view they are wrong—unless the Nationalists do something that involves a breach with Britain.

26. It must always be remembered, however, that the Nationalists are highly emotional and absolutely convinced of their rightness. They are apt at any time to do something stupid and completely against their own real interests. It would be easy to provoke them into actions that they might later regret but would, nevertheless, do with intransigent obstinacy. They are in some respects comparable to the Irish Nationalists: they have a logic of their own that is grounded on emotions and hatreds that it is practically impossible for us to understand.

27. Personalities are very important in South African politics.

Amongst the Nationalists, Malan is (comparatively) a moderate. He is 76 and is an old Reformed Dutch preacher and has all the longings and hatreds of an extreme Predikant. He is, however, a very shrewd old boy and has some grasp of political realities. He is inclined to satisfy the more extreme Nationalists by gestures—often foolish ones. The things he does actually carry through are measures against Africans and Indians and measures that give him electoral advantage. He has some qualities. He has been ready to spend most of his political life in the wilderness for his convictions: he is very religious: he keeps his word. He has a very high regard for Mr. Attlee and wants to have close relations with Britain. He is very conscious of the danger of world communism.

Malan does not seem to have a very good hold over his Cabinet and tends to be pushed along by the extremists. This has become more marked since the Nationalist victory in the South-West Africa elections which gave them a majority that makes them independent of the support of Havenga and his followers (the Afrikaner Party). Havenga is another "moderate" and Malan relies much on him. He has been longer Finance Minister than any other in the Commonwealth and is extremely orthodox. He is also extremely ambitious. He has always said that he would not agree to the disfranchisement of the Cape Coloured: but directly he lost his grip on the balance of power (through the South-West Africa elections) he changed his tune. One motive was his desire to be Prime Minister after Malan: another was probably to maintain the "moderate" control of the Cabinet. If Malan dies I think Havenga will be the next Prime Minister. He would be a useful "moderate" cover for the extremists: and these are not yet ready to engage in the fight amongst themselves for leadership that must soon come. The leaders of the extremists in the Cabinet are Dönges[2] and Strydom[3]

[2] Dr T E Dönges, minister of the interior, 1948–1958; finance minister, 1958–1967; and state president elect at the time of his death early in 1968.

[3] J S Strydom (Strijdom), minister of lands and irrigation, 1948–1954, prime minister, 1954–1958.

(pronounced Stray-dom). They are both outstandingly able and it is generally assumed that one or other will be Prime Minister. A great many people on the United Party side hope that Dönges will win: he is regarded as less extreme and more realistic. It is also thought that his attendance at the last Prime Ministers' Meeting in London may have widened his horizons (as it undoubtedly did). In my view he would make the worse Prime Minister of the two. He is much cleverer than Strydom and more supple and adroit. He can put on a reasonable face. But he is extremely bitter and would always be working, by however indirect means, to make South Africa completely Afrikaner.

Strydom is much more direct and fundamentally honest. He, too, is extreme and might well do a number of foolish things, especially at first. But I think he would learn in the same way that Malan has, and one would know where one was with him. It is most important that he should be prevailed upon to visit England. I worked on him (and on his wife) and I think they will in due course respond to an invitation.

Though I think Strydom would be the better of the two from our point of view—the prospect of either is very disquieting.

If Dönges and Strydom deadlock for leadership or shrink from splitting the party, it is possible that Sauer[4] may get the Prime Ministership. He is the most human of the Nationalists and a man of considerable ability. But it is hard to say what sort of a leader he would make. He would probably be relatively "moderate" and aware of South Africa's position in the world.

I was much impressed by Strauss,[5] the new leader of the United Party. He has long been overshadowed by Smuts and is much under-rated. He does not try to imitate Smuts, but he is developing his own character, which is confident, calm and farsighted. He will never be a great orator or world-figure—but he is rapidly becoming a leader with in some ways greater moral courage and directness than Smuts. He stands head and shoulders above the rest of his party, which is most undistinguished.

There are a few good Civil Servants who are likely to play an important rôle. Outstanding amongst these is Forsyth, the Secretary for External Affairs. He is the child of British and Afrikaner parents and is a solid man, very friendly to us.

28. The South African policy towards African Natives is fundamentally different from Southern Rhodesia's. It is based on the theory of permanent exclusion of Africans from any share in government or political rights. In theory Apartheid involves the material and social development of the Africans—and to some extent this is carried out in practice. For instance, African school teachers, nurses, &c., receive considerably higher wages than in our High Commission Territories and (so I was told) in the Colonies. Very considerable sums (almost wholly raised by taxes upon the Whites) are spent on the material welfare of Africans. Very large areas are set aside as Native Reserves. In these, extremely costly anti-erosion work is carried out—hundreds of miles of wire-fencing at £100 a mile.

The officials of the Native Affairs Department are mostly keen and devoted workers, who clearly do not like the policies of the present Government. They treat the Africans as permanent children—but they put great energy into their welfare and development. Most of the Africans in the Reserves are still very primitive with very

---

[4] P O Sauer, minister of transport, 1948–1953; minister of lands, forestry and public works, 1954–1964.

[5] J G N Strauss, leader, 1950–1956.

low standards of cultivation. Faction fights of great fierceness are fairly frequent and sometimes result in a good many deaths.

Treatment of the Africans by these officials in the Native Reserves is wholly different from the treatment in the towns like Johannesburg, which I have already mentioned.

29. It was hard to form an opinion about the attitude of Africans in the Reserves. I saw some who were extremely primitive and seemingly happy and unconcerned. I saw others who were being trained in agriculture and domestic science—and those seemed at least eager to raise the standards of their own people. I was introduced to one Chief in the Transkei—Chief Poto, who is regarded as rather a show-piece and who co-operates very well in anti-erosion work and runs his court competently. His proudest possession was a picture of The King and Queen. I got him to myself for a moment and asked him his attitude to the High Commission Territories. He said that Africans in South Africa regarded the inhabitants of the Territories as having superior rights and we must on no account let them be incorporated until conditions were as good in the Union.

I also asked Chief Poto about Seretse. He said we had taken the only possible course.

30. I spoke with African political leaders in Johannesburg and Indian leaders in Durban. The Union authorities knew that I was having these talks but the talks themselves were private and confidential and the confidence has been strictly kept. Both sets of leaders impressed me by their moderation and responsibility. With all they have had to put up with one might expect them to be extreme and bitter men. They are firmly anti-Communist and believe in constitutional methods. Although denied all political rights, they do indeed possess some means of expressing their views—mainly through their press, which is free. The very wealthy Indian leaders in Durban and Natal get much that they want by bribing Councillors and officials.

The African leaders talked to me mainly about the High Commission Territories. Their information about economic and social progress in the Territories was out of date and they were inclined to assume that it was our intention to yield them up. I did my best to reassure them.

The Indian leaders were mainly concerned about the Group Areas Act (which enables the Government to set up by law segregated racial areas). They were convinced that this Act is primarily aimed at the economic destruction of the Indian community in order to force them to repatriate themselves to India. They all said that they would, under no circumstances, go to India, where economic conditions were far worse than in the Union. They emphasised that they were South Africans. If there were no social segregation in *economic* affairs they would themselves be quite prepared to arrange voluntarily that all Indians should reside in special areas.

Both the African and Indian leaders wanted His Majesty's Government to intervene in one way or another on their behalf, and I had to explain the limitations imposed by the conventions of Commonwealth relations. I have since had appreciative letters from both sets of leaders.

31. Owing to the ever more acute labour shortage in all Southern Africa it is quite possible that the material standards and education of Africans in the Union will be improved. Only by improving the output of Africans can the labour shortage be solved. This will, of course, make it increasingly difficult for the Whites to hold the Africans down. I saw, however, no signs of violent opposition. I doubt whether the

Africans are, or for long will be, capable of any sort of organised underground movement. If there is violence it is more likely to take the form of a sudden spontaneous blood-letting by the Africans of the Reserves and the slums.

32. I spent some time looking at a Compound on a Rand gold mine, as considerable numbers of Africans from Bechuanaland and Basutoland work there. The compounds are extremely efficiently run, with excellent food supplies and kitchens, water-borne sewage, baths and provision for recreation. Every African recruit is X-rayed, and if any of them lose 5lb. of weight in a month he is at once medically examined. The hospitals provided are very good. If gold is to be produced at all, and if this is to be done by workers who are separated from their women, it is hard to think of a better way than these compounds—to which many of the workers return many times during their lives. As far as we are concerned it would not be in our interests were married quarters substituted for compounds as this would depopulate the High Commission Territories. We have an arrangement by which the interests of High Commission workers in the mines are looked after by our own agents; a proportion of the wages earned is paid to the worker *after* his return to the Territory. This has largely done away with the drift of our workers from the mines into the great cities; it also brings considerable sums into the Territories and ensures that the wives have a chance of getting their fair share.

So long as we need to supply this labour, the present system works well. Our policy should be to help it work, and steadily to reduce our need for this labour-outlet by developing the economic resources of the Territories.

33. Our High Commission Territories (and for that matter Southern Rhodesia too) are largely dependent on the Union for the secondary and higher education of Africans. The ban recently imposed by the Union on all non-Union Africans entering their schools and Universities threatened us with very grave difficulties. The ban has been suspended for three years and may not be reimposed. We must, however, prepare alternative forms of education, though this will cost money. I discussed with Sir Godfrey Huggins an idea he put forward for an African University to be established in Francistown (in Bechuanaland) to be jointly financed by the two Rhodesias and the three Territories. The High Commissioner is now sympathetically considering this idea amongst several others.

34. I visited our naval base at Simonstown. In view of what Erasmus, the Minister of Defence, said whilst he was in London and of a factual memorandum he gave me whilst I was in the Union it was rather surprising that he never raised the question of the transfer of this base to the Union, though I had several talks with him on defence matters. The base is very well run: it is the only corner of the Union where the colour [bar] is wholly absent and skilled workers of all colours work happily side by side.

Although we will have one day to face the question of the transfer of this base and may have to make some concessions to South African sovereignty, I think this day is a good way off. The Union is quite incapable of running a great base like this (its Navy is a sub-department of its Army). I think we may hope to play this problem very long.

(iv) *Problems of policy*

35. Our relations with the Union of South Africa raise appallingly difficult problems, for which there can be no simple solutions.

36. It seems to me that one of our prime aims must be to *contain* South Africa. By this I do not mean that we should pursue a hostile policy towards the Union:

indeed, as I argue later, I think we must be friendly. By containment I mean that we must prevent the spread of its influence and territorial sovereignty northwards. This will not be at all easy to achieve as South Africa is infinitely the most powerful political unit on the whole African continent. Its economic, and therefore its potential military, strength is rapidly increasing. There are, moreover, in Central and East Africa settled white populations that the Union may hope to bring under its political leadership and protection. It would be illusory to count on internal racial tensions frustrating South Africa's plans of expansion. These internal tensions may indeed one day become insurmountable, but we cannot simply sit back and reckon on this happening in time to prevent South African expansion.

37. We can only succeed in containing South Africa and playing the very strong cards that we have in our hand if we seriously set this objective of containment as a genuine aim of our policy. This would mean that we do not regard as our sole objective the emancipation and political advancement of the African in all our African colonies. That must of course remain a major objective, but we must not subordinate all else to it.

If we wish to contain South Africa we must succeed in keeping the white communities in Southern Rhodesia, Northern Rhodesia and even Kenya independent of, and distinct from, the Union. This should not be too difficult to do as they are all very British and very loyal. They like neither Afrikaners nor Republicans. But here too we must have a positive policy. We cannot count on this loyalty alone and for ever. If we do not shape our policies aright there is a very real danger indeed that, to avoid domination by Africans, these white communities will in the end throw in their lot with the Union.

38. We must in our long-term African policies reckon this as a grave danger to be set alongside the danger of some African (and Indian) discontent. Should we, [un]intentionally or by default, throw British communities in East and Central Africa into the arms of the Union our whole work in Africa would be undone. The policies that we detest in the Union would be established far to the North and in the heart of this part of our Colonial Empire. Millions of Africans would be subjected to oppression. Terrible wars might even be fought between a white-ruled Eastern Africa and a black-ruled Western Africa.

39. It would be a fatal mistake to count on our power to prevent these things happening if in fact our policies tend to bring them about. In the last resort we do not control these British communities by power. As they grow richer and more numerous they will become potential American colonies—very loyal, but very determined to have their own way. If we are in due course faced by defiance of our will in the Rhodesias or Kenya there will in effect be nothing that we can do about it. Certainly our power on the spot would be inferior to South Africa's.

40. Fortunately these dangers are not imminent. But they will come upon us if we allow the impression to arise that we are committed to a policy of subordinating Whites to Africans. Rather than face that the Whites will in the end revolt. I am not at the moment concerned about the morality of their possible actions but about their possibility. It would be small comfort to us to have been right, if the consequence were the effective end of our position in Africa and the effective frustration of all our well-intentioned policies. Certainly tens of millions of Africans for whom we are responsible would be calamitously worse off.

41. The test-case will be Southern Rhodesia. This country already has practical

independence. The day is not far off when it could defy us with impunity if we sought to interfere improperly, as its white inhabitants would think in its internal affairs. We certainly could do nothing to prevent Southern Rhodesia's accession to the Union were they to decide on such a course. As it seems to me the whole fate of our policy in Southern Africa turns on whether Southern Rhodesia is drawn Northwards or Southwards. It is not big enough to remain for ever a separate unit without access to the sea. At the moment its loyalties are with Britain—but if we do not succeed in attaching Southern Rhodesia to the North, it will inevitably turn ultimately to the Union. As I say above (paragraph 10) there is even now a force in Southern Rhodesia in favour of incorporation with South Africa, that it would be folly to ignore. We must, therefore, it seems to me, adopt a deliberate policy of attracting Southern Rhodesia to the North. If we do not, we will fail to contain South Africa and in the end all our good work and all our influence will be ruined.

42. I would therefore propose that it should become one of our cardinal policies to keep Southern Rhodesia out of the Union. This is a key-stone of the policy of containing South Africa. This should be a policy of *equal* weight and importance in our eyes with the political advancement of the Africans in our Central and East African colonies. It should not be a secondary or subordinate policy, but an equal one.

43. This would involve a shift in the emphasis of our policy and it would not be popular or easy. It is very easy for Africans and many in Britain, and especially many in the Labour Party, to say that there is no difference between Southern Rhodesia and South Africa in respect of Native policy. Anyone who stands up for a policy of binding Southern Rhodesia closer to our colonies in the North will have to face a pretty vocal chorus of abuse, both from Africans and from sections of British opinion. It is, of course, true that Southern Rhodesian Native policy is different from ours: but it does not follow from that that it is identical with the Union's. It is, in fact, different (see paragraphs 7, 8, 9 and 28 above). It is about as good a Native policy as one can expect at this stage from any considerable settled White population. If we insist on treating it as being identical with South African Native policy we shall in the end succeed in making it so. By driving Southern Rhodesia into the Union we would allow a fatal shift of the balance of power and immensely increase the attractive power of the Union's policy for White communities in neighbouring colonies. By listening to the protests of Africans and others against any truck with Southern Rhodesia we would in the end betray our trust to the Africans by being unable effectively to protect them against South African Native policy. It would not be against South African expansionism as such that we would have to contend but against the will of our own white communities.

44. We will soon be faced by a practical problem that will raise this very issue in an acute form—namely, the question of some form of closer association between Southern Rhodesia, Northern Rhodesia and Nyasaland. I do not here wish to argue the merits of this question; the recommendations of the recent officials' conference will have to come before Ministers. But one issue that will have to be decided may well be whether Southern Rhodesia is to go Northwards or Southwards. Closer union may now encounter some opposition: but if we fail to face it, the result may be that Southern Rhodesia finally loses hope in any possibility of closer association with her Northern neighbours. Moreover, were we at some later time to attempt again to achieve some sort of a Central African Union, we would certainly find African opinion

even more strongly against it.

45. Apart from positively drawing Southern Rhodesia northwards it should be our policy to widen in every possible way the gulf between Southern Rhodesia and South Africa. South Africa's economic and other influences upon Southern Rhodesia are bound to remain strong and Southern Rhodesia must live in peaceful and neighbourly relations with the Union: nevertheless, there are natural differences between them.

46. One of these concerns South African migration to Southern Rhodesia (paragraph 5 above). Here we should give Southern Rhodesia all possible support in her desire to restrict migration from the Union and to encourage it from Britain.

47. Another example is to be found in railway development, which is a highly political problem. Further railway lines and links are certain to be developed in Southern Africa and are badly needed. Where they are built will largely determine the balances of political influence. There is at this very moment a dispute between Southern Rhodesia and South Africa about a projected new railway link. South Africa wants to see built the link that would be most economical: but this route would put Southern Rhodesia at the mercy of South Africa and powerfully advance South African influence over Southern Rhodesia. (Incidentally, it would also largely ruin the Bechuanaland Protectorate—see above, paragraph 17). This is a case where we should, as we are doing, use our influence against the economically desirable and obvious solution.

48. We should also do what we can to help direct capital into Southern Rhodesia. Very considerable sums of private British capital are going into the development of the Union—particularly into gold mines and secondary industries. This is, of course, important: but, other things being equal, it would pay us to see a proper proportion of our capital going to Southern Rhodesia. It is not in our long-term interest to see South Africa's economic development altogether outstripping Southern Rhodesia's.

49. Into this general framework of policy must fit our intentions about the High Commission Territories. These cannot be indefinitely held unless there is behind them a solid block of British territory that is distinct from and independent of the Union. The three Territories can be indefinitely held as outposts or bastions of such a block. Their fate will be sealed if South Africa's influence and area spreads further North. As outposts or breakwaters the Territories, indeed, can play a coherent part in our policy. Otherwise we can at best hope for a hand-to-mouth policy of holding them as long as we can against great odds.

50. I have returned very much more confident of indefinitely holding the Territories, on condition that our whole Southern and Central African policy is far-sighted, and on condition that we do not make any foolish mistakes. South Africa is very conscious of its need for British friendship and there are in South Africa powerful forces that positively desire to retain the British connexion (see above, paragraphs 23 to 25). This means that we should be able to keep South African internal opinion divided on the issue of the incorporation of the Territories. Every White South African, of course, wants to see the incorporation of the Territories, and will always declare himself to be in principle in favour of incorporation. But a very large section of the population does not want to break with Britain on the issue and will always find that the moment is not opportune for pressing the demand. I was surprised to find how strong was the reaction in the British Press in the Union against Malan's Cape Town speech about incorporation. I was surprised, too, to find

how fairly the whole Press (including the Afrikaans papers) reported my version of the meaning of the relevant Acts. There is a pretty widespread realisation that it would be unwise to take over wholly hostile populations. Strauss, the leader of the United Party, said privately that he did not see how the Territories could ever be taken over by South Africa. The populations of the Territories were to a man against it, and even if the United Party got back to power and improved the lot of the African in the Union, the fear would be present that the Nationalists would once again get back to power.

51. I think we can therefore fairly confidently adopt a policy of indefinitely holding the Territories. *But only if South African opinion continues to be divided.* If anything happened that both united and inflamed South African opinion on this issue, we would be helpless. The influences that we can exercise over the Union because of her need for us and because of her material and political interests, would become quite feeble. In certain moods South Africa will do things that are pig-headedly doctrinaire and against all her best interests. (See above paragraph 26). If the Union put the incorporation of the Territories above every other interest, we could not resist her economic and even perhaps military power. The Territories are not large enough even to be administered as wholly distinct units. The railways that run through them belong to the Union: the currency is South African: the customs are joint. The frontiers are unguarded and such things as control of cattle disease and anti-erosion work must be done in co-ordination. Nearly all the consumer goods needed by the Territories must come through the Union: all the Territories' exports must go out into or through the Union.

52. If we are to hold the Territories, we must, therefore, as an integral part of this policy, take public opinion in the Union into account and so direct our actions as to play upon it. (This is, in my view, the decisive reason why the Territories should be administered by the C.R.O.)

53. This means that we cannot in what we do in the Territories ignore reactions upon South African public opinion. There are many things we can and should do that they do not like. For instance, they do not like the way we are putting development funds into the Territories. Nor will they like it when we set up an independent Post Office in Swaziland, as we intend to do. What we must refrain from doing are those acts that would unite and inflame Union public opinion. That is a luxury that we cannot afford if we seriously want to hold the Territories and use them as part of our policy of containing the Union.

54. Amongst acts that would unite and inflame Union opinion would have been the recognition of Seretse and Ruth. This view was confirmed by several leading Africans in the Union with whom I discussed the matter. After seeing things on the spot for myself, I am more convinced than ever that our decision about Seretse was right. Quite apart from internal Bamangwato considerations, a decision to recognise Seretse would have very gravely endangered our tenure of the Territories.

So probably would a decision to arm the Africans in the Territories. We can once again very usefully raise Pioneer Corps amongst them, but were we to arm Africans in the midst of the Union, we would run a very grave risk of losing the Territories.

55. While we firmly announce our intention to keep the Territories—by reiterating our established policy about consultation—and while we develop them economically and refrain only from extremely provocative actions—at the same time we should be ready to develop those relations with the Union that bind her to us and

make her unwilling to risk a break with us. These relations are also in our own direct interest. Chief amongst them come co-operation in defence and in economic matters. Also important is to give the Union what help and guidance we decently can at the United Nations. Those who argue that because we dislike the Union's Native policy we should ostracise her and have nothing to do with her completely fail to understand the realities of the situation. Such a policy would not only gravely harm us in the defence and economic field, it would also weaken our power to deter South Africa from foolhardy acts from fear of breaking with us. It would immediately and directly reduce our chances of holding the Territories, which form a vital part in any policy of containing and confining the Union's influence and territorial expansion in Southern Africa.

434 CO 537/7203, no 7 18 Apr 1951

'Note on Central African closer association proposals': memorandum by A B Cohen on the case for it and the safeguarding of African interests

[Cohen wrote this memorandum after two meetings with Griffiths and Cook on 16 and 17 March. It should be read in conjunction with 435, annex.]

In view of the doubts which have been expressed about the proposals of the recent Conference on Closer Association in Central Africa, I have thought that it might be helpful, in preparing for the further discussions which are to take place, to set out the main considerations affecting the problem as I see them. These fall into two groups:—

(1) Is there a sound case for some form of closer association between the territories?

(2) Are African interests in the northern territories suitably safeguarded in the proposals put forward?

I. *Case for closer association* (see paragraphs 25–33 of the main report).

The main arguments are as follows:—

(a) *Economic and communications*

There is no need to enlarge on this because the Secretary of State said at our meeting on April 17th that he agreed that the economic arguments for closer association were very strong. I take it that the same would apply to communications, in view of the close road, rail and air links between the territories.

(b) *Strategic and administrative*

Admittedly under their present constitutions the territories can be counted upon, as they are doing, to make their full contribution to defence. Nevertheless, given the economic and transport links, the general defence effort would be more effective under closer association, especially as Southern Rhodesia adopts our policy and not that of the Union with regard to African military forces. Equally I assume that the administrative arguments in paragraphs 29 and 30 of the report would be accepted.

(c) *Development*

Nyasaland and large parts of Northern Rhodesia are much less developed than

Southern Rhodesia. Paragraph 31 of the report argues that through the increased prosperity which closer economic integration would bring more revenue would be made available for the expansion of social and economic services, particularly for Africans. I think that this is undoubtedly true and I would draw attention to the important statement in paragraph 56 of the report that it should be one of the primary objectives of the Development Commission to secure that proper attention is given to the more backward areas. This would assist Northern Rhodesia and particularly Nyasaland.

(d) *Current inter-territorial difficulties*

The Central African Council, through having no executive powers and no machinery for enlisting the support of public opinion, has been ineffective in ironing out inter-territorial difficulties. Coal from Southern Rhodesia for the Copperbelt has been the salient example. It is not so much that the Southern Rhodesia Government has been selfish; but that their Ministers have only to answer to Southern Rhodesia public opinion through the Southern Rhodesia Parliament. If coal for the Copperbelt were dealt with inter-territorially and Central African Ministers had to answer to Central African opinion in a Central African Legislature, Northern Rhodesia (and incidentally the United Kingdom through its demand for copper) would be very much the gainer. This is merely an illustration of the general need for a Central African legislative body to deal with genuinely inter-territorial matters.

(e) *Political*

It is on the political aspects of the problem that the discussion at the meetings on the 16th and 17th April centred and it is with these aspects that the present note must mainly deal.

In the confidential minute submitted after the Conference great emphasis has been laid on the urgent necessity of countering South African and Afrikaner immigration into Central Africa (paragraphs 5–8). It is there argued that immigration could be controlled far more effectively by a federal Government than by the three territories acting separately. The main arguments in support of this view (which are given in paragraph 7 of the appendix to the confidential minute) are that a single quota system is easier to operate; that, since people move fairly frequently from territory to territory inside Central Africa, only a single Central African immigration system can exercise effective control; and, most important, that a Government exercising self-governing powers in internal affairs would be in a far stronger position to take the necessary measures against South African immigration than colonial territories subject to H.M.G. in the U.K., which must be cautious in its relations with the Union. This last argument is borne out by experience hitherto; Southern Rhodesia, as the appendix to the confidential minute shows, has been much more effective in controlling Afrikaner immigration than Northern Rhodesia.

It has been suggested that the three territories individually ought, if the will exists, to be able to control immigration as effectively as a single federal Government. Theoretically it may be true that the Northern Rhodesia Government, with the support of the Colonial Office and African representatives, could force through as strong an immigration control ordinance as it wished. Even if this is the case—which is by no means certain—I do not believe that the Northern Rhodesia Government would over a period have the necessary strength and authority to operate an immigration control system effectively and in fact to resist persistent attempts to immigrate from the south. It must be remembered first that the

Copperbelt necessarily relies on a large amount of white South African workers, who it has been found cannot in practice be replaced from the U.K. at the present time and could not under any policy be replaced by Africans, except over a considerable period; secondly that there is already a considerable South African population in Northern Rhodesia which would resist control measures; and thirdly that the rest of the European population of Northern Rhodesia, although it is very nervous about Afrikaner immigration, tends in a colonial community, where there is a premium on united action among the Europeans, to be unwilling to risk a serious split with the South African elements over an issue of this kind. The Northern Rhodesia members of the Conference were extremely doubtful whether under any system of immigration control the Northern Rhodesia Government would in fact be able over a period effectively to control Afrikaner immigration. I agree with this view and I feel sure that the Conference was right in reaching the conclusion that the only really effective method of control would be one exercised by a federal Central African Government. I think, therefore, that this is a very strong argument for the proposals.

But it is possible that the confidential minute did not lay enough emphasis on the other aspects of South African pressure. It is not simply a question of immigration by individuals. There is also pressure of ideas through the press and in other ways and, more important still, economic pressure which the Union is in a particularly strong position to exercise through its geographical situation and its much more advanced development. Above all there is the pressure of the stronger neighbour against the relatively weak. In any major clash of ideas South Africa through its geographical proximity has a very great advantage over the U.K.

All the members of the Conference, including the U.K. members, felt strongly that the major task in Central Africa at the present time is to make sure that Union influence can be resisted. None of us believed that this could be done effectively by three separate territories. At the moment Southern Rhodesia is certainly the most powerful counter in Central Africa to South African influence. Most of the European population is very strongly attached to the British connection—this applies to Sir G. Huggins and his party and to a growing more liberal element composed of younger people who have settled in Southern Rhodesia from the U.K. since the war. The presence of this newer element will ensure the continued development of more liberal ideas even after Sir G. Huggins retires, but only provided that H.M.G. is prepared to see a closer link developed with the northern territories. If H.M.G. is not prepared to agree to closer association on any terms, then the less liberal and more pro-Union elements in Southern Rhodesia are bound to grow in strength and resistance to Union pressure will be correspondingly weakened. Northern Rhodesia is not at present in a strong position to resist Union pressure. African opinion is immature and unorganised politically. A large section of the Europeans is South African. Nearly all politically-minded Europeans, whether South African or British, absorb most of their political energies in resistance to so-called Colonial Office rule rather than in resistance to Union pressure. In these circumstances the official Government, while it can exercise negative safeguards, is not in a position to take a strong and vigorous positive line against Union influence generally—a line which would in any case be most difficult for a Government directly dependent on H.M.G. in the U.K. to take in view of our own relations with the Union. The point must also be made that, given the geographical and other circumstances, it is not possible for the U.K. Government to enforce in Northern Rhodesia the ideal policy which it would like to see followed for African advancement. Progress has in fact been made over the last fifteen years but we and the Northern Rhodesia Government have had to act in co-operation and agreement with the European community. If on any issue there was a major clash with the European community, the U.K. Government would not be in a strong position in view of influences from the south, particularly from the Union.

If the proposals for closer association which have been made are turned down by H.M.G. in the U.K. the effect on Southern Rhodesia is bound to be very bad. Closer association in one form or another has been under discussion for more than fifteen years and U.K. Governments have recognised the need for closer association between the Central African territories to the extent of establishing a Central African Council, although this has in the event proved ineffective. The turning down of a scheme with provision for African representation and safeguards for African interests would be interpreted in Southern Rhodesia as closing the door to closer association for an indefinite period. It is, I believe, generally realised in Southern Rhodesia that they must either look north or south; they are too small to carry on alone. If they cannot look north, those who want to look south will inevitably gain influence and, although there will be solid resistance to them from those in Southern Rhodesia who abhor Malan and are devoted to the British connection, yet in that event we must, I think, look to a greatly increasing Union influence in Southern Rhodesia with the possibility of absorption sooner or later. If South African influence or even power extends from the Limpopo to the Zambesi, the task of preventing Northern Rhodesia from being absorbed would of course be immeasurably more difficult. It would not be a question of a High Commission territory like Bechuanaland, which is a native reserve from which Europeans can be virtually excluded. Northern Rhodesia has a considerable European population and depends on Europeans for its main industry. The economic and other links between the two Rhodesias are already so close that if Southern Rhodesia succumbed Northern Rhodesia would, I am sure, succumb sooner or later. In that event Nyasaland would, I believe, follow suit. All her links are with the south and, although theoretically she could link up with East Africa, the distance from Zomba to the nerve centres of East Africa is so great that I am extremely sceptical of such a development.

The above is a gloomy picture but not, I believe, taking the long view, an excessively gloomy one. Now, with the general dislike of Malan on the one hand and the urgent need to limit Afrikaner immigration into Central Africa on the other hand, is the psychological moment to take a really effective step to safeguard the future of Central Africa. At present the Africans cannot themselves provide an effective counter influence because, as I have said, they are immature and disorganised. In my view the only effective counter influence available is the strong attachment to the British connection of a large section of the Europeans in Central Africa. Given a willingness on the part of H.M.G. to agree to closer association and to entrust increased powers, although over a limited range of subjects, to a federal Central African Government and Legislature, I believe that we could certainly count on such a Government being firmly attached to the British connection and on its providing an effective counter to the influence of the Union.

But it is not only in connection with the Europeans that advantages would follow; there would also, I believe, be important advantages in the sphere of native policy in Southern Rhodesia. Whatever criticisms may be made against the recent electoral

Bill, there is no doubt (as is shown by the Comparative Survey of Native Policy) that native policy in Southern Rhodesia has become more liberal over the last ten years. This applies particularly to local government in all its forms and to education and agricultural measures. The practical achievements by Southern Rhodesia in this field have been recognised by a number of authoritative visitors. This is due to the fine work of the Native Affairs Department with the continuous support of the Prime Minister, and the new liberal element of U.K. settlers should ensure the continuance of this trend, provided always that the links with the north can be developed. Under a scheme of closer association I have no doubt at all that the trend would continue to be in the direction of closer approximation by Southern Rhodesia to the policies of the northern territories (one of the functions of the African Affairs Board would be to promote liaison between the three territories in any matters—not only federal matters—dealing with African affairs). I think it is fair to claim that it is one of the advantages of the proposals that, while closer association would have this effect, African political advancement and the development of local government and of the main social and economic services would remain in the hands of the territories. The effect of this arrangement would be that as Northern Rhodesia and Nyasaland Africans advanced further there would be strong pressure for Southern Rhodesia to follow suit. The influence of the north on Southern Rhodesia has been apparent below the surface ever since the war; now is our opportunity to strengthen that influence. If we miss this opportunity the effect is almost certain to be to reverse the present trend. I have talked of the advantages from the point of view of native policy in Southern Rhodesia, which is not a direct concern of the Colonial Office; but of course what is done in Southern Rhodesia must in the long run have a bearing on what happens in Northern Rhodesia. In other words, if Southern Rhodesia were to reverse the present trend and pursue an illiberal policy, it would be more difficult for us to develop liberal ideas in Northern Rhodesia. I believe it is fair to claim, therefore, that because of the necessity of countering Union influence African interests in the northern territories as well as in Southern Rhodesia would in the long term certainly benefit from closer association.

II. *The bearing of the proposals on African interests*

In the proposals we have aimed at three things in relation to Africans; first to keep services intimately affecting African life away from the federal authority; secondly to provide safeguards for African interests under the federal scheme at the present stage of African political development; and thirdly to provide for the representation of African interests in the Legislature immediately. I will deal with these points below.

(a) *Functions of the federal authority*

There is no need to go into this at length, because the Secretary of State said at the meeting on the 16th and 17th April that he regarded the division of functions between the federal and territorial authorities as a sound one. But it is worth pointing out that all the services most closely affecting Africans are kept to the territories (health, education, agriculture, etc., police, native administration and local government). The subjects to be dealt with by the federal authority fall into four categories; those already dealt with inter-territorially (census, railways, civil aviation, broadcasting, etc. and research); those which do not directly affect politics and can usefully from the practical point of view be dealt with inter-territorially (trunk roads, electricity, posts and telegraphs, surveys, major water development, national parks and inter-territorial trade); those which in any federal scheme must necessarily be federal (external affairs, defence, external trade and customs); and those for which there is a special reason for making them federal (immigration, as explained above, European education, which can far more conveniently be dealt with inter-territorially, and higher education). Higher education was included at our instance because it can only be provided inter-territorially and without an inter-territorial scheme we do not see how Northern Rhodesia and Nyasaland Africans can effectively get higher education. Moreover we believe that an inter-racial scheme for higher education in Central Africa would be a powerful liberalising influence. Most of the subjects to be dealt with federally are highly technical and would not be of the closest interest to Africans. We believe that the reservation of all the subjects which mainly interest Africans to the territorial Governments would be a powerful argument in favour of the scheme with African opinion in the north.

(b) *The African Affairs Board*

This was included in the proposals entirely at the U.K. instance. Apart from promoting co-operation between the territories in native policy generally and in keeping a watching brief for African interests over all the activities of the federal Government, the Board would have the function of considering all federal legislation, whether principal or subsidiary, before it was published. Any legislation which was considered by the Board to be detrimental to African interests would have to be reserved for H.M.G. in the U.K. before coming into force and it can be taken for granted that such legislation would not be accepted by the U.K. Government. The Board would in effect, therefore, have a power of veto and it is most important to note that this power goes very considerably further than the existing reservation in the Southern Rhodesia constitution, which only applies in the case of legislation actually discriminating against Africans. The recent Electoral Bill and the Industrial Conciliation Act do not discriminate in terms. The Africans Affairs Board would moreover become a powerful focus for liberal ideas in Central Africa. Another advantage of the arrangement would be that whenever it was suggested that any subject should be added to the federal list—which could only be done with U.K. agreement—this would involve bringing it within the purview of the African Affairs Board; thus a check on the desire of, say, Southern Rhodesia to add new subjects would be created.

The membership of the Board would also in our view be a very important gain. It is entirely novel for Southern Rhodesia to agree to an African member of such a body, but this Board would have an African from each territory. It would also have the Secretary for Native Affairs from each territory; they would in my view be even more effective than Africans in actually safeguarding African interests and many Africans would, I am sure, agree with this view. Of the ten members of the Board, three would be Africans, another three (the S.N.A.'s of Northern Rhodesia and Nyasaland and the Minister for African Affairs) would be appointed directly by or in agreement with H.M.G. in the U.K. Of the remaining four, two would be appointed directly by the northern Governors. We could, I am sure, safely rely on the Board to exercise the necessary safeguarding powers and it was the view of the two northern S.N.A.'s that African opinion would have confidence in the Board.

(c) *Minister for African Interests*

This was the proposal about which we had most difficulty in the Conference. The Southern Rhodesia representatives, while they themselves recognised the merit of the proposal, felt considerable doubt whether they could secure its acceptance and it was only after very great pressure by ourselves that they did in fact accept it. It is clear from the latest telegram from Southern Rhodesia that Sir G. Huggins expects difficulty in putting it across, but the telegram also gives the impression that he is prepared to try. The proposal involves importing what is, I believe, an entirely new kind of safeguard, namely the power of H.M.G. under certain circumstances to veto executive action by a Government as well as legislation. This greatly increases both the range and the force of H.M.G.'s reserve powers and still more important, perhaps, is having a Minister appointed by H.M.G. inside the Cabinet and able directly to influence his colleagues in favour of African interests.

Admittedly the arrangement is novel and admittedly the Minister's position would be difficult. But novelties are unavoidable in colonial constitution-making and the Minister's position would be no more difficult, for example, than that of the European Ministers in the Gold Coast Government. The Minister would be supported powerfully by the existence of the African Affairs Board, of which he would be chairman, and the fact that he would be a member of the Legislature and not be appointed from outside it would, I believe, strengthen his position. The importation into the federal Cabinet of a Minister specifically representing African interests seems to us to be a very important step forward in breaking down the purely European character of institutions in Southern Rhodesia.

A great deal would turn on the personality of the men appointed and in this respect we should be in a favourable position. The Minister would be drawn from the members representing African interests in the federal Legislature and would no doubt at first be a European, although it is an important point in the proposals that the appointment of an African is not in terms ruled out. The European members representing African interests are to be nominated by the three Governments. Since the appointment of the Minister would require the Secretary of State's approval, it is clear that the practice which would in fact be followed would be for the three territorial Governments to consult with H.M.G. in advance to make sure that at least one of the members nominated to the Legislature by them would be suitable to be appointed Minister.

(d) *The federal legislature*

It has been pointed out that the method of appointment proposed for representatives of African interests in Southern Rhodesia is to be different from that in Northern Rhodesia and Nyasaland. But it must be remembered that in Southern Rhodesia there is no African Representative Council at present, so that it is necessary to go to the bodies which do exist and it will be noted from Appendix VII (page 61) that some of these bodies include African members. The ultimate choice is to be made by the Governor, the same arrangement as in Nyasaland. Although it is not specifically stated that any of the three Southern Rhodesia members would be Africans this is not ruled out and the fact that the other territories are to have Africans would, I believe, sooner or later compel Southern Rhodesia to do the same.

The number of representatives of African interests, 9 out of a Legislature of 35, is also a point of importance. I suggest that this ought not to be compared with an ideal representation but with the existing situation in the territories. Northern Rhodesia has two Africans, two Europeans representing Africans and ten European elected members. As against this she would have two, one and eight in the federal Legislature. Nyasaland has two African and six non-African unofficials as against two

Africans, one European representing Africans and four Europeans in the federal Legislature. Southern Rhodesia, of course, has no representatives of African interests in her Legislature at present.

The inclusion of Africans in Central African Legislatures is an entirely new thing; it is less than three years since the first African took his seat in Northern Rhodesia and Africans were appointed in Nyasaland still more recently. The African representatives have not yet made their way and the subjects to be discussed by the federal Legislature are highly technical and not those of most interest to Africans. In the circumstances it would not have been possible to secure the agreement of any of the Central African delegations to a larger representation of Africans, nor, I believe, would it be easy to put across a larger representation with European public opinion in the territories at the present time. But we have made it clear at the end of the report that the constitution is not intended to be immutable (page 42). It is also stated on page 17 that political progress for Africans must be maintained and that Africans must be enabled to play a proper part according to their qualifications in the government and political institutions to be established. Still more important is the last sentence on page 23 of the report, which makes it clear that the Conference agree that Africans can eventually aspire to play a full part in the federal Government and Legislature. In other words the present African representation must be regarded as transitional; as African representation in the territorial Legislatures increases, so it must be increased in the federal Legislature.

I suggest that we have gained two very important points indeed in getting the Southern Rhodesia representatives to agree to the inclusion of Africans from the northern territories in the federal Legislature and to the representation of African interests from Southern Rhodesia. Neither of these points has been accepted in any past discussions on the subject—the Victoria Falls Conference talked of representatives of African interests in the Senate, which would not have been the body with main powers. Once the principle of African representation is accepted [,] that representation must in Central African conditions inevitably grow in time and I believe that it is of first-class importance that we have got the principle into our recommendations. If after the report has been ventilated publicly Africans ask for larger representation, that will be a matter for negotiation with Southern Rhodesia at the time; but I suggest that we should not be in a strong position to raise the point now.

(e) *Dominion status*

It has been suggested in discussion that the federal scheme would amount to something like granting dominion status. This, I submit, is not the case; indeed the adoption of the scheme would, I think, make it more difficult for Southern Rhodesia to get dominion status. It is true that a certain section of public opinion in Southern Rhodesia favours this and that a Select Committee of the Southern Rhodesia Parliament has put forward a scheme with this end in view. But Sir G. Huggins himself does not support the idea and is taking steps to have the Select Committee's report pigeon-holed. In any case dominion status could not be achieved by Southern Rhodesia without the agreement of the U.K. Government. Clearly with two more backward territories with relatively smaller European populations linked with Southern Rhodesia in a federation there would be a much stronger case for H.M.G. resisting any demand that there might be for dominion status. My own view is that it would be impossible for H.M.G. to agree to dominion status until the Africans were in a position to play a much fuller part in the political life of the country and European opinion accepted this and allowed them to do so. So far from bringing dominion status nearer I think that the present scheme would make it more remote.

(f) *Political development of the territories*

Under the proposals the Northern Rhodesia and Nyasaland Governments and Legislatures would retain their existing status and powers within the spheres assigned to them and their relationship to H.M.G. in the U.K. would be exactly as it is at present (paragraph 48 of the report). The political development of Africans in the territories would go forward as at present (paragraph 47). I believe that it would be an important advantage of the scheme that it would make it easier for H.M.G. in the U.K. to resist pressure from the Europeans in Northern Rhodesia for increased responsibility inside the territory. At present the Europeans claim that their political progress is frustrated by the fact that H.M.G. will not allow them to advance until the Africans can advance as well. Under existing arrangements it is not going to be easy to resist their pressure for the comparatively long period until Africans can play their full part. But under the closer association proposals Europeans would get their outlet through the federal Government and Legislature, which would be dealing with a range of subjects not of the most direct concern to Africans. The existence of such an outlet would, I believe, greatly strengthen our hand in insisting that in territorial matters in Northern Rhodesia (as in Nyasaland) the constitutional position should be held until Africans have progressed to the stage when they can play a much fuller part.

(g) *The Development Commission and Central African Loans Council*

Although these proposed institutions do not bear directly on the political aspect of the problem, I think it is just worth calling attention to the importance of the Development Commission and the Loans Council in promoting the economic and general progress of Central Africa. I believe that by the creation of these bodies as part of the federal scheme we should be giving a great impetus and encouragement to development throughout the area to the general benefit of its inhabitants, both European and African.

435 CAB 129/45, CP(51)122 3 May 1951

'Closer association in Central Africa': joint Cabinet memorandum by Mr Griffiths and Mr Gordon Walker. *Annex*: confidential minute by G H Baxter and A B Cohen to the secretaries of state, 31 Mar 1951, with appendix on immigration policy

We circulate herewith, for the consideration of our colleagues, the Report of the Conference of officials recently held in London to consider the question of the closer association of the Central African territories of Southern Rhodesia, Northern Rhodesia and Nyasaland (Annex II).[1] The substance of the Report is summarised in the following paragraphs. There is no question of committing ourselves at this stage to a final view on the proposals of the Conference and we do not ask our colleagues

---

[1] Annexes II and III not printed. The Conference, chaired by Baxter, opened on 5 Mar. The report was published as Cmd 8233.

now for a decision on the substance of the recommendations. But we do recommend, for the reasons given below, that His Majesty's Government

(1) should, if the other Governments concerned agree, publish the Report for general information; and
(2) should, without being committed to acceptance of the proposals in the Report, commend them in general terms for the careful consideration of all the peoples concerned as embodying a constructive approach.

We should, of course, propose to report further to the Cabinet when there has been time for public discussion of the proposals both here and in the Territories.

Review of recommendations of the recent conference

2. The question of the closer association of the three British territories in Central Africa has been under discussion for many years. It has recently become more urgent; and last year it was decided to hold a conference of senior officials of all the Governments concerned, to re-examine the problem and endeavour to formulate proposals that might be generally acceptable. This was announced in Parliament on 8th November.

3. The Conference took place during March. Its Report (Annex II), which is addressed to all four Governments, was unanimous on all points. The Conference also agreed on the terms of a Confidential Minute, to be addressed by each team of officials to its own Government, setting forth certain considerations not suitable for publication (Annex I).

4. The Report (paragraph 35) reaches the definite and unanimous conclusion that "closer association between the three territories ought to be brought about, and that the need for this is urgent." The reasons for this conclusion are set forth under the headings "Economic" (paragraphs 25–26), "Strategic" (paragraph 27), "Communications" (paragraph 28), "Administrative" (paragraphs 29–30), "Moral and Social" (paragraph 31), and "The urgency of the problem" (paragraph 32). In the Confidential Minute closer association is held to be the only effective means of countering the increasing pressure of the Union of South Africa on the Central African Territories.

5. While thus decisively recommending closer association, the Report adds: "But in any scheme of closer association certain conditions must be fulfilled. Account must be taken both of Southern Rhodesia's self-governing status and of the special responsibilities of His Majesty's Government in the United Kingdom towards Northern Rhodesia and Nyasaland. Political progress for Africans must be maintained and Africans must be enabled to play an appropriate part, according to their qualifications, in the Government and the political institutions to be established. At the same time, until their partnership with Europeans becomes fully effective, there must be adequate provision in the constitution for African welfare and advancement. Finally, the unit of government which is established for the Central African territories must be able to stand on its own feet economically; and it must be autonomous financially." The detailed recommendations in the Report are designed to satisfy these conditions.

6. The Report rejects amalgamation and recommends that association should be on a federal basis; in paragraphs 35–45 it gives reasons for this and for the belief that on such a basis adequate safeguards for the interests of Africans can be provided.

Subject to these safeguards, the federal Government would have full responsibility within the sphere allotted to it under a Ministerial system and with a federal Legislature. The federal subjects would include defence, external affairs, immigration (but *not* land settlement and alienation), economic development planning, customs, posts and telecommunications, railways, and civil aviation. The authority of the Centre, however, would be limited to the specified subjects declared to be "federal," and the whole sphere of government in all three territories would, apart from these specified subjects, remain with the Governments and Legislatures of the territories constituted as at present. The Territorial subjects would include all those matters that are most closely related to the life of the African inhabitants: for example, African education, health, agriculture, land and settlement questions, local government and native administration generally, police, mines and labour. In respect of all subjects not made federal the relationship of each territory to the United Kingdom Government would remain exactly as it is now and African political development would go forward as at present in the two territories. (The Conference assumed that the federal State would come, and Southern Rhodesia would remain, within the scope of the Commonwealth Relations Office, while Northern Rhodesia and Nyasaland would remain within that of the Colonial Office. There would be the closest consultation between the two Offices in all important questions affecting Central Africa.)

7. Thus in all matters most closely affecting Africans existing safeguards would remain unaltered and the control of the Colonial Office in respect of Northern Rhodesia and Nyasaland would continue as at present. But in federal matters (e.g., customs or railways) decisions would have to be taken affecting African interests. To meet this the proposals provide, in the federal field, for African representation in the Legislature; for an African Affairs Board including an African member from each Territory (with the duty of scrutinising all projected federal legislation which, if the Board considered it detrimental to African interests, could not be brought into force without the approval of the United Kingdom Government); and for a Minister for African Interests in the federal Cabinet (with power to defer executive action proposed by the federal Government, if he considered it detrimental to African interests, pending reference to the United Kingdom Government who could, if they thought it necessary, refuse agreement to such action). The Minister for African Interests would be appointed and dismissed not by the Prime Minister of the federal Government, but by the Governor-General acting in his discretion and then only with the approval of the Secretary of State; the Minister would thus be responsible through the Governor-General to the United Kingdom Government.

8. To secure co-ordinated planning over Central Africa as a whole, to minimise friction between the federal and territorial authorities, and to promote from the outset a habit of co-operation rather than rivalry, the proposals (paragraphs 53–56, 70, and 77) provide, in the spheres of economic and development policy and of finance, for the establishment of consultative machinery through joint federal-territorial bodies.

Our conclusions and recommendations

9. For the reasons given in paragraph 4 above and particularly because of the need to counter South African pressure, we are satisfied that closer association is urgently desirable in the interests of the Territories (including those of the African

inhabitants) and of the Commonwealth. The scheme put forward appears to us to be constructive and workable; whether it can be brought into force will depend on the reactions to it of European and African opinion in the Territories and to that we will revert below. We do not at present ask our colleagues for decisions on the specific recommendations; we will therefore confine our comments on these to certain points affecting the safeguards for African interests.

10. His Majesty's Government in the United Kingdom have special responsibilities towards the African inhabitants of Northern Rhodesia and Nyasaland, which they have an inescapable obligation to fulfil. The safeguards proposed in the Report are necessarily different, within the limited federal field only, from the existing methods of exercising our responsibilities in respect of the two northern Territories; but we see no reason why they should not be effective. And it is noteworthy that they would apply to the Africans in Southern Rhodesia, who would thus acquire, again in the federal field, safeguards which they have not now.

11. The linchpin of the proposed federal safeguards is the "Minister for African Interests." Though a member of the federal Cabinet, and appointed to it as a Member of the federal Parliament (from those nominated thereto to represent African interests), he would be outside the ordinary political field and would be appointed with the approval of, and be ultimately responsible to, the United Kingdom Government. The arrangement is certainly unusual, but we do think it would be workable and we regard it as an essential part of the scheme. It is only by being within the Cabinet that the guardian of African interests could be fully effective; and a Minister appointed—ostensibly to protect African interests—on ordinary party grounds would not necessarily be an adequate safeguard.

12. It should be recognised that if the Southern Rhodesian Government agree to the scheme recommended they for their part will be accepting, within the range of subjects proposed to be made federal, the reimposition (through the safeguards already referred to) of a measure of control from London which would amount to an appreciable curtailment of Southern Rhodesia's degree of independence. From their standpoint this would be a very severe concession which it would require a great effort to commend to their Legislature and contituents [sic]. His Majesty's Government in the United Kingdom would also be making an important concession, although only within the limited federal field, in respect of our responsibility for Northern Rhodesia and Nyasaland; but we should at the same time secure powerful safeguards within this field for African interests. We should also gain the acceptance by Southern Rhodesia of the representation of African interests in the federal Legislature—a most important and a new step for Southern Rhodesia. In the allocation of seats in the federal Legislature between the three territories, we understand that it only just proved possible—with no margin—to find a basis that the members of the Conference felt might be capable of acceptance by their respective Governments. Indeed, it seems evident that, as regards the main lines of the recommendations, there is very little scope for manœuvre, and that any attempt on our part to push the Southern Rhodesians still further would probably wreck any hope of securing a practical outcome.

13. Amalgamation being ruled out (paragraph 38 of the Report), the only form of closer association worth considering is federation; and it is therefore a choice between federation and doing nothing. If we do nothing, and so prevent the Southern Rhodesians from linking with their northern neighbours, they will

inevitably tend more and more to look southwards. The absorption of Southern Rhodesia into the Union would then probably be only a matter of time. If Southern Rhodesia were absorbed, Northern Rhodesia, through its geographical position and economic circumstances, would be exceptionally vulnerable to Union pressure and eventual absorption and it is most doubtful if Nyasaland, at present a backward territory, could in those circumstances stand out against encroachment by the Union.

14. That the danger is real and urgent can be seen by a perusal of paragraphs 5–8 of the Confidential Minute. Afrikaner infiltration into both Southern and Northern Rhodesia is proceeding apace—at present the flow of immigration from the Union is almost double of that from the United Kingdom. Not all the immigrants from the Union are Afrikaners, and not all the Afrikaners have strong political views; but those who do obviously form a base for the extension of Nationalist South African influence. There has always been an appreciable minority body of opinion in Southern Rhodesia which would not be averse from incorporation into the Union, and indeed we have just heard from Southern Rhodesia of a reported movement there for the formation (under local Afrikaner auspices) of a new political party with incorporation as its main plank. The rejection of closer association would enable this party to increase its influence.

15. Our task must in fact be to take every possible step to induce Southern Rhodesia to look northwards rather than southwards and to strengthen those in Southern Rhodesia who favour a more liberal policy towards Africans. Much progress has been made by Southern Rhodesia in recent years in services for the benefit of Africans and a more liberal attitude is developing, particularly among settlers from this country since the war; we must do everything we can to encourage this process. In the absence of an organised African public opinion in Central Africa, the most effective counter to Union influence is the attachment to the British connection of a large section of the Europeans in all three Territories. By forging a constitutional link between them and creating a strong Central African block we shall at once put Central Africa in a better position to resist Union pressure and strengthen the British connection.

16. Economically the Union overshadows Central Africa, and if the Central African territories were to encounter a serious slump in production or the export of their products the danger of the economic attraction to—and pressure from—the Union would be aggravated. A Central African block, forming a strong economic unit, would be in a better position to resist this pressure than three separate units.

17. It will be a difficult and delicate matter to enable these vital considerations to play a part in convincing Parliamentary and public opinion here of the need for positive action to keep Southern Rhodesia out of the Union. They cannot well be stated publicly by United Kingdom Ministers. We shall have, by one indirect means or another, to endeavour to bring them to the notice of influential quarters in the Press and of others, including certain members of the Parliamentary Labour Party, who will seek to lead public opinion. We must aim at persuading those who are concerned for the welfare of Africans that if we do nothing—with the consequence of driving Southern Rhodesia into the Union—we are likely to expose the welfare of the Africans to much greater dangers than any that may arise from the pursuit of closer association, specially if the latter includes the important safeguards embodied in the Conference's proposals.

18. The Governments concerned, including our own, have given assurances that before any decision is taken to bring about closer association adequate opportunity will be afforded for public discussion of any proposals that may be put forward. This can only be done on the basis of a set of concrete proposals. For this reason the Conference has framed its Report in a form suitable for publication. We recommend that, if (as expected) the other Governments agree, the Report should be published here for general information in the form of a White Paper early in June, shortly after the Secretary of State for the Colonies returns from East Africa. (Two separate documents that provide relevant background—a factual survey of the territories and a comparative survey of native policy—would be published at the same time.)

19. In addition to publishing the Report, we consider that His Majesty's Government should also (on the broad lines of the draft statement at Annex III) commend it in general terms for the careful consideration of all the peoples concerned as embodying a constructive approach. As no decisions would be taken until after public reactions have been obtained, this would in no wise conflict with our undertakings.

20. In the public discussion of the proposals in Central Africa the crucial factors are likely to be the attitude of Europeans in Southern Rhodesia and of Africans in Northern Rhodesia and Nyasaland; the latter is bound powerfully to affect the reaction in this country and in Parliament. Vocal African opinion in the northern Territories has expressed itself as opposed to closer association with Southern Rhodesia and the conference recognised (paragraph 20) that this is a serious obstacle to closer association. But the Conference took the view that in the last resort the African reaction in the northern Territories would depend on the nature of the scheme put forward. They thought it unlikely that Africans would withdraw their opposition to amalgamation, but they felt that, provided that some form of closer association could be designed containing adequate provision for African representation and adequate protection for African interests and provided that the services more intimately affecting the daily life of Africans were outside the scope of a federal Government, Africans might well come to realise the very substantial advantages of closer association from their point of view.

21. It is fairly certain that Africans do not at present realise that it is only by setting up a strong Central African block that Union influence, which they greatly fear, can be effectively countered. It is clearly most desirable that before His Majesty's Government in the United Kingdom have to make final decisions they should be fully aware of African opinion in the northern Territories; it is equally desirable that there should be opportunity for full discussion of the proposals between representatives of His Majesty's Government in the United Kingdom and Africans in the northern Territories and Europeans, as well, of course, as the three Central African Governments. The matter is of such importance to Central Africa and the Commonwealth as a whole that we think that, if this proves practicable, we should both proceed to Central Africa during the summer recess after there has been sufficient time for consideration of the proposals by the public for the purpose of such discussions. A Conference could then be held in which we should take part and which would settle the form of the proposals which the Governments would formally sponsor for the consideration of the Legislatures and the public in Central Africa and, of course, of Parliament here. The holding of such a Conference, whether here or in Central Africa, could of course only be decided upon with the agreement of the Governments

concerned, and subject to the approval of our colleagues we propose to seek this forthwith. In our view it is most important that the intention of holding such a Conference and if possible of a visit by ourselves should be referred to in the announcement accompanying the publication of the proposals; this would discourage public opinion in the Territories, whether European or African, from reaching premature conclusions, pending our visit, either for the acceptance or rejection of the proposals or particular features of them pending the opportunity of discussion with ourselves.

Annex to 435

On behalf of the United Kingdom members of the Conference we have the honour to submit, for the consideration of the United Kingdom Government, a Report embodying the views and the unanimous recommendations of the recent Conference on the problem of the closer association of Southern Rhodesia, Northern Rhodesia and Nyasaland.

Confidential considerations

2. The Report has been drawn up in terms suitable for publication if the four Governments concerned agree that it should be made public. It consequently does not fully report all the detailed deliberations of the Conference. In reaching their conclusions members were influenced by certain considerations which might well, if developed fully in a published document, be a cause of offence to the Government of the Union of South Africa. They also discussed freely and at length a variety of proposals for the future of Central Africa, but the full publication of their discussions might result in confusing public opinion instead of focussing it upon consideration of the solution they wish to recommend. The Conference felt, however, that these matters should be brought separately and confidentially to the notice of the four Governments and they are therefore set forth in the following paragraphs of this minute, which is in agreed terms and of which identical copies are being addressed to the other three Governments by their own officials. It was, of course, understood by the Conference that the submission of the agreed minute would not preclude members from giving such further explanations of the work of the Conference as they might wish to their respective Governments.

Scale of report

3. The Report has purposely been made as brief as possible. We are anxious that those who will have to form a judgment upon it should be induced to read not only the recommendations but the considerations leading up to them. In order therefore to maintain a continuous thread we have relegated to annexes much of what might more conventionally have been in the body of the Report. Two documents that might have been added as annexes, namely the Central African Council's most valuable comparative survey of native policy and a comprehensive factual summary prepared for us by some of our members, have been excluded. We assume that if the Report is published the factual summary will be published at the same time, and we think it essential that the Survey of Native Policy should also, with the agreement of the Governments concerned, be made public simultaneously. We recommend that both

documents should be published separately from the Report, partly because they would be out of scale if incorporated with it, and partly because we think that the Report volume should be small and therefore low-priced, so as to secure a wide circulation among the publics concerned.

Acceptance of closer association

4. The Conference had no hesitation in agreeing that in principle and for practical reasons the closer association of the three Central African territories was desirable and indeed urgently necessary. These three continguous territories, within the dominions or under the protection of His Majesty, have a wide range of common interests and common problems. In many respects their economic needs and products are complementary. Closer association would enable them to utilise more efficiently their capital resources in natural products, in man-power, in technical skill, and in finance, with benefit to all the inhabitants of all races.

The danger to Central Africa

5. The force of these considerations has been felt for many years, but Central Africa is now exposed to a special danger which, in the view of the Conference, makes it of compelling urgency that the three territories should combine in defence of their way of life. The danger lies in the extension of Union influence over the Rhodesias. The expansionist aims of certain Union politicians are well known. Allied with the alarming increase of Afrikaner immigration in recent years into Southern and Northern Rhodesia they are felt to constitute a serious and imminent threat to the independent existence of the two territories. The motives behind this movement northwards may not be wholly insidious; economic ambition and the love of adventure play a large part. The fact remains that the flow of migrants from the Union into the Rhodesias is now well in excess of that from the United Kingdom. The ties of blood, and the Nationalist loyalties of many of them, will make the migrants responsive to political intrigue and pressure from the Union. Many of them show little inclination to become assimilated to the British way of life and outlook that characterise the remainder of the European population. If early steps are not taken to slow down the movement the Afrikaner element (particularly in Northern Rhodesia with its smaller total European popultion) will before long undermine the British way of life in these territories, destroy the progress that has been made in both the Rhodesias in the economic, cultural and political advancement of the African, gravely prejudice race relations, and sooner or later lead to the absorption of the territories in the Union. In that event the future of Nyasaland would also be seriously jeopardised.

6. Linked with this danger of infiltration is another danger. The facts of geography and communications render the Rhodesias uncomfortably susceptible to economic pressure from the Union. Any onset of economic depression might at once make this pressure difficult for the individual territories to withstand; but the larger and stronger unit resulting from closer association would be in a better position to offer effective resistance.

7. The Conference was impressed with the gravity of the situation and felt it essential that there should be a strong British Central African Government, which would be better able to stand up to outside pressure than the territories individually, and which would remove the existing fears that internal pressure in any one of the

territories might enable the Union Government to extend its political influence over the area by a piecemeal technique. Acting in virtue of its own powers it could enforce a common immigration policy for all three territories and could control immigration without the embarrassment which the United Kingdom Government would experience in the field of Commonwealth relations. The Report makes clear that federal control of immigration policy would not include control over land settlement and alienation. The problem of Afrikaner immigration and the suggested means of dealing with it on a Central African basis are discussed at greater length in the Appendix to this Minute.

8. In the view of the Conference the increase of the danger of penetration from the Union if there is no closer association is imperfectly realised by Africans in Central Africa and by public opinion in the United Kingdom. If the threat to both African and British interests were clearly recognised opposition in those quarters to the closer association of the Central African territories would soon be transformed. The matter, moreover, is urgent. Delay at this juncture in establishing an effective scheme of closer association would probably be fatal to hopes of creating a British *bloc* in Central Africa, and the opportunity of commending such a scheme to Southern Rhodesian opinion should be taken now, under the leadership of Sir Godfrey Huggins.

Form of association

9. Convinced, therefore, for this and other reasons mentioned in the Report of the urgent need for some form of closer association, the Conference examined with great care several proposals in order to discover the scheme which would be most effective and command the greatest measure of agreement. The proposals considered were: the amalgamation of the three territories; amalgamation of part of Northern Rhodesia with Southern Rhodesia; a form of league; and a federal arrangement.

Amalgamation

10. The case for amalgamation as the most desirable and, apart from political considerations, the most practicable form of closer association, was stated with great force and clarity by the Southern Rhodesian members, who stressed the need for a bold and imaginative approach. It was, in their view, essential that a strong central government should be set up capable of inspiring the loyalty of the inhabitants of Central Africa and of defending the territories from the dangers that threatened them from within and without. Federal schemes were open to a variety of objections, e.g., complexity, cost in money and man-power, and relative weakness; amalgamation alone would ensure the full advantages of the closer association that was agreed to be necessary. The Southern Rhodesian members recognised the difficulties, notably opinion in the United Kingdom. The objections of Africans, they felt, could be faced and overcome; for example, examination showed that the native policies in all three territories were much closer than critics had supposed. In their suggestions they incorporated a number of features designed to operate as safeguards for African interests when His Majesty's Government divested itself of its responsibility.

Rejection of amalgamation

11. The Conference, appreciating the sincerity with which the case for amalgamation had been stated, examined it with great care and sympathy. Members were

impressed by the advantages claimed for amalgamation and by the endeavour made to meet its difficulties. On the other hand, it was equally strongly argued from the point of view of Northern Rhodesia and Nyasaland that, given the different stages of material and political development of the territories, amalgamation in existing circumstances would not be the right solution. In any case the Conference found itself forced to the conclusion that, despite the safeguards suggested, there was no hope that, even with the utmost exercise of explanation and persuasion, amalgamation would be accepted either by Africans in the Northern territories or by Parliament and public opinion in the United Kingdom. That being so, to propound a scheme which was certain to be rejected in so many quarters would set back indefinitely all hope of forging a constitutional link between the territories; progress could only be made possible by recommending the most practicable scheme that had a reasonable chance of winning general assent.

Amalgamation with the Copperbelt

12. A scheme had been put forward in certain quarters for amalgamating with Southern Rhodesia the Copperbelt and Line of Rail in Northern Rhodesia (the principal area of European settlement), leaving Barotseland and the remainder of Northern Rhodesia to be administered as native areas on the lines of the High Commission Territories. The scheme was considered by the Conference and rejected without dissent; apart from the financial difficulties which it would create for the non-amalgamated areas it was condemned as a scheme of vivisection, not of closer association; it was completely at variance with the policy of partnership between European and Arican; and it would be bitterly opposed by both Europeans and Africans in Northern Rhodesia.

League

13. Since amalgamation, despite its practical advantages, had to be excluded, the problem before the Conference was to decide what advance could be made towards an effective form of closer association without forfeiting the chance of acceptance by African and European opinion. One solution considered was the establishment of some form of league between the territories under which they would set up machinery for co-operation in matters of common interest without surrendering any part of their sovereignty or affecting the channels for the discharge of the responsibilities of His Majesty's Government in the United Kingdom towards the Africans. Under this scheme there would be an inter-territorial organisation which, without disturbing the existing channels of responsibility, would provide—on the basis of delegated powers—for the direction and administration of a specified list of common services by means of a legislature elected by the territorial Legislatures, a small executive consisting of members of the territorial Cabinets or Executive Councils, and a central secretariat and Departments. Assent to legislation would rest with the three Governors.

14. There was general agreement that this scheme would not prove satisfactory. There were grave doubts whether the cost of such a scheme would be justified by the results or whether indeed it would really work. Not the least difficulty would be the establishment of an effective ministerial framework. The central organisation would be weak and continually dependent on the goodwill of the individual territories. The Conference had to recognise that it would provide no effective link between the three

territories and would amount to little more than the shadow of a central Government that would fail to attract the respect and loyalty of the inhabitants of Central Africa. It might, indeed, prove a source of weakness rather than of strength. Southern Rhodesia would not be prepared to share its authority with such an organisation, and the Southern Rhodesian members saw no prospect of securing its acceptance by their Government and Legislature.

A federal scheme

15. The Conference then turned to consider whether a solution might not be found on a truly federal basis. The problem was fourfold:—

(i) could agreement be found for the inclusion of a sufficient range of subjects in the federal field to make it a reality;
(ii) could agreement be found for a form of federal Government possessing sufficient power and authority to further the development and enhance the prestige of the three territories;
(iii) could adequate provisions be devised to satisfy Parliament and public opinion in the United Kingdom that the discharge of His Majesty's Government's responsibilities towards the African population in the Northern territories would not be impaired;
(iv) could these provisions be such as to be acceptable to the people of Southern Rhodesia, who have been self-govering since 1923.

The Conference, while very conscious of the difficulties of the task, feels entitled to claim that these desiderata have been met by its recommendations.

The federal field

16. In devising the list of subjects which are recommended in its Report for inclusion in the federal field, the Conference was guided by the broad principle that matters which closely affected the everyday life of the African should as far as possible be left within the control of the territories. These subjects, such as local government, education, health, agriculture and allied subjects, would therefore remain the responsibility of the territorial Governments. Nevertheless, in addition to the minimum federal content of external affairs, defence and communications, a wide range of authority has been assigned to the federal Government, sufficient, in the view of the Conference, to make it an effective force for the protection and furtherance of common interests in Central Africa.

The safeguards

17. We believe, moreover, that in the possibly more difficult side of its task the Conference has succeeded in devising arrangements which will satisfy opinion in the United Kingdom that the interests of the African have been safeguarded and the discharge of His Majesty's Government's responsibilities assured. Certain features which have been included in the scheme for this purpose will also, we consider, make a positive contribution to the welfare of British Central Africa. That is, of course, notably the aim of the proposed Development Commission and the Loans Council, which it should be noted would be joint federal-territorial institutions. The African Affairs Board is to include three Africans in its membership as well as the three Secretaries for Native Affairs, and in addition to the safeguarding of African interests

its periodic meetings will provide a forum for the discussion of common problems, leading, we believe, to mutual understanding and a closer approximation of the native policy of all three territories with results which cannot fail to be of benefit to Africans.

The Minister for African Interests

18. In the scheme of safeguards we attach special importance to the position of the Minister for African Interests who would also be Chairman of the African Affairs Board. The definition of his status and functions was a signal example of the spirit which animated the Conference in seeking means whereby, without compromise of principle, the proposals might satisfy the apparently conflicting requirements imposed by the need for obtaining acceptance in different quarters. While the functions of the Board would provide a means of ensuring that legislation detrimental to African interests should not be enacted, the United Kingdom members felt that it was no less important to have a similar procedure with regard to the executive actions of the federal authority. This could only be attained by associating the Chairman in some way with the activities of the federal Cabinet. It seemed that the United Kingdom Government's responsibilities would best be satisfied if the Chairman were inside the Cabinet. He would thereby obtain a full knowledge and understanding of proposals discussed by the departmental Ministers and would be in a position to make his views known before decisions were reached. The Conference therefore decided to recommend that there should be a Minister for African Interests in the Cabinet. He would have no departments operating under him, and his independence would be secured by the provisions for his appointment and dismissal. He would admittedly occupy an anomalous position in a body which in other respects would conform to the usual type of Cabinet Government; but the Conference, after thorough discussion, agreed to accept the anomaly as justified and inevitable in the circumstances. In the recommendations which were eventually adopted everything possible was done to assimilate the Minister's position, consistently with his independence, to the normal requirements of parliamentary government by ensuring that he should be a member of the Legislature. It should be emphasised that as a member of the Cabinet it would be his duty, subject to his special responsibilities for African interests, to co-operate with, and assist his Cabinet colleagues in the conduct of the affairs of the federal Government. It is proposed that he should be drawn from the number of members appointed to the Legislature to represent African interests, i.e. from those who are nominated for the purpose. This arrangement would avoid the difficulty which would arise if an elected member, responsible to his constituents, were appointed to the post. In the form of closer association of the Central African territories which we have recommended we can think of no more effective device for the protection of African interests, and we are confident that the efficacy of our proposal will be generally recognised.

19. In conclusion we wish once again to record our sense of the urgent need for bringing the Central African territories by some effective constitutional link into closer association with one another. Our recommendations offer, we believe, a solid framework for the purpose, and we think that they will be found to be in the best interests of the peoples of British Central Africa. It is of great significance that they have been unanimously agreed to by responsible officials of the three territories who will have the duty of operating them if the new constitution is brought into being,

and some of whom will be called upon to explain and commend them to the African inhabitants. It is the earnest hope of all members of the Conference that as soon as may be after receipt of the Report all four Governments will be able to agree to the simultaneous publication of the Report for general information and to commend it for the favourable consideration of all the peoples concerned as a fair and workable scheme. We believe in particular that nothing is better calculated to secure favourable reception of the Report by Africans than to have this measure of support from His Majesty's Government and we trust that their support may readily be made known. His Majesty's Government in the United Kingdom, like the other Governments, are committed to consultation with the peoples concerned before arriving at final decisions, but this is no bar to their commending the Report for favourable consideration.

APPENDIX: IMMIGRATION POLICY

Present position

At the present time immigration into Southern Rhodesia, Northern Rhodesia and Nyasaland is subject to legislation and regulations which differ from territory to territory. In all three territories, however, though to a differing degree in each, the immigration legislation and regulations have proved inadequate to solve immigration problems which are common to the whole area. In particular, they are not effective in restricting the numbers of Afrikaners included in the immigrants from the Union of South Africa, which represents a grave political threat to the future of Central Africa.

2. The problem of Afrikaner immigration is at present much more serious for the two Rhodesias than for Nyasaland, and probably more serious for Northern than for Southern Rhodesia. In Southern Rhodesia, up to 1946, immigrants born in the Union of South Africa outnumbered those born in the British Isles. During the period 1946 to 1949 this trend was reversed and immigrants born in the British Isles were in the majority. But in 1950 the old position was restored and Union-born immigrants were once more in the majority. In Northern Rhodesia immigrants born in the Union of South Africa have always since the war exceeded those born in the British Isles and have also represented a higher proportion of the total immigrants than have those entering Southern Rhodesia. Detailed figures are as follows:—

	1938		1946		1947	
Born in	*Southern Rhodesia*	*Northern Rhodesia*	*Southern Rhodesia*	*Northern Rhodesia*	*Southern Rhodesia*	*Northern Rhodesia*
British Isles	1,237	660	3,582	974	6,320	1,446
South Africa	1,534	1,263	4,654	2,221	5,104	2,361

	1948		1949		1950 (Jan–Oct)	
Born in	*Southern Rhodesia*	*Northern Rhodesia*	*Southern Rhodesia*	*Northern Rhodesia*	*Southern Rhodesia*	*Northern Rhodesia*
British Isles	8,574	1,990	5,908	2,197	3,959	1,929
South Africa	4,410	2,392	5,173	3,146	7,041	3,360

No reliable emigration figures are available, but it is known that a considerable number of immigrants from the Union do return there after a short stay in the Rhodesias.

3. It is not easy to determine how many of the Union-born immigrants are Afrikaners and what proportion of these are Afrikaner nationalists. A fairly reliable

guide is provided by the figures for membership of the Dutch Reformed Church. In the 1946 census in Northern Rhodesia 18 per cent. of the entire European population were members of the Dutch Reformed Church. In Southern Rhodesia in 1946 the proportion was 14 per cent., but it is now believed to be about 16 per cent. In both territories there are now areas where Afrikaners are in the majority. There is, moreover, reason to believe that steps are being taken by Nationalist organisations in the Union to encourage the emigration to the Rhodesias of persons of Nationalist outlook, though there is no evidence to show that the Union Government are associated with these moves.

4. Under existing legislation in force in Northern Rhodesia the Government has little power to prevent anybody entering the territory unless he falls within the narrowly defined category of prohibited immigrant; and the powers available in Nyasaland are not much greater. In Southern Rhodesia the position is in several respects different. Not only can a potential immigrant be excluded on the grounds of his general undesirability, but all immigrants have to deposit or to have an employer's guarantee for £100, or have a private income of £500 a year; they must also satisfy certain health requirements. Furthermore there is a quota system for aliens.

Future proposals

5. The Southern Rhodesian Government are at present examining the subject of immigration with a view to a possible restriction of immigrants from the Union of South Africa and it is understood that they are inclined to favourr the extension of the quota system. They do not feel that they could apply it to the Union alone of Commonwealth countries and it would therefore have to extend to all immigrants from Commonwealth countries except the United Kingdom; the intention is that there should not be any quota limitation on immigration from the United Kingdom. If criticised by the Union the quota could be justified by the argument that the Union itself operates such a system and on the ground of the general desirability of creating stability among the European population within Southern and Central Africa.

6. The extension of a quota system of the kind now contemplated by the Southern Rhodesian Government to the other Central African territories appears to be the best way of dealing with this problem of Afrikaner immigration and also the most effective way of relating immigration to the absorptive capacity of the territories. There are two main reasons for this view. Other systems have been tried elsewhere and have not proved a success. Nyasaland, for example, has been working legislation on the East African model, under which a person can be refused entry not only if he is shown to fall within the strictly limited class of prohibited immigrants, but also if his entry can be shown to be prejudicial to the interests of the existing inhabitants of the territory. This is difficult to establish except in the case of individual immigrants or persons in particular professions and it could not be used effectively to keep out persons of any given race such as Afrikaners without attracting embarrassing attention. Similar legislation was introduced into the Northern Rhodesian Legislative Council over twelve months ago, but has never been passed owing to the opposition of some elected members. A second argument in favour of the quota system is that it enables a Government to operate an immigration policy to determine the composition of its population in the most positive manner which can be devised.

7. If a quota system is to be adopted for dealing with this matter in Central Africa, it will be much more effective if operated on a federal basis for the whole area than if each territorial Government has to operate it separately. First, a single quota structure is easier to operate than three separate systems. Secondly, it is useless for the Southern or Northern Rhodesian Government to limit Afrikaner immigration if the other Government is not taking the same action, since movement between the territories is not easy to control. Thirdly, since Union-born immigrants cannot be excluded altogether, the operation of a single Central African quota would make it easier to reduce the influx of Afrikaners into those parts of the territories where further settlement is not desired by counting against the full quota those Afrikaners at present essential to the economy of certain limited areas. For example, a certain number of Union-born immigrants are essential at present to the working of the Copperbelt; this necessary immigration counting against a limited quota should of itself do much to cut down the number of Union-born immigrants to be admitted to other parts of Central Africa. Fourthly, it would be easier politically for a Central African Federal Government to impose and operate a quota system than for Colonial Governments in respect of which His Majesty's Government in the United Kingdom still exercise full responsibility. Finally, Northern Rhodesia alone would have great difficulty in operating a quota system against Afrikaners in view of their increasing influence in that territory.

8. For these reasons it has been recommended in the Conference Report that immigration should be a federal responsibility. In making this recommendation public it would be important to emphasise, as the Report does, that immigration policy and regulation is quite distinct from land settlement policy, which under the recommendations in the Report would remain a territorial responsibility. The alienation of land would be controlled by the authority responsible for land settlement (i.e. the territorial Government) and not by the authority responsible for immigration.

436 CAB 128/19, CM 39(51)3 31 May 1951

'Central Africa: closer association of Southern Rhodesia, Northern Rhodesia and Nyasaland': Cabinet conclusions

The Cabinet resumed their consideration of the memorandum by the Secretary of State for the Colonies and the Secretary of State for Commonwealth Relations (C.P. (51) 122)[1] on the closer association of Southern Rhodesia, Northern Rhodesia and Nyasaland. They had also before them a further memorandum by the Secretary of State for Commonwealth Relations (C.P. (51) 144) regarding the desire of the Prime Minister of Southern Rhodesia that the United Kingdom Government should commend the proposals in the report of the conference of officials as a suitable basis for the closer association of these territories.

The Secretary of State for the Colonies said that there would be many economic and political advantages in the closer association of these territories. Immigration into the Rhodesias from South Africa was increasing, probably with unofficial encouragement from the Union Government, and some counter-action should be

[1] See 435.

taken to check this northward expansion of the Union. It was, however, essential that any form of closer association should provide adequate safeguards for the African population of Northern Rhodesia and Nyasaland. He believed that the proposals made in the report, if they were workable, would afford such safeguards. In the first place, African affairs would remain the responsibility of the individual Governments and so subject to his control. Secondly, the plan provided for a Minister for African Interests who, though a member of the Federal Cabinet, would be ultimately responsible to the United Kingdom Government. Thirdly, the plan provided for the creation of an African Affairs Board, with three Africans among its members. No plan on these lines could succeed unless the Africans could be convinced that it would offer them effective protection. The draft statement in Annex III of C.P. (51) 122, which was to be made when the report was published, while it made it clear that the United Kingdom Government were not committed to the plan, would commend it as a constructive approach to the problem which deserved careful consideration by all concerned. We should go no further than this until we could gauge the effect of the proposals on African public opinion.

The Secretary of State said that he favoured the proposal that he and the Secretary of State for Commonwealth Relations should visit the territories in the autumn and hold a conference there; but he was not sure that it would be possible to reach final conclusions at that conference, and he would prefer that in the final sentence of paragraph 4 of the draft statement the conference should be described as one at which the proposals would be further considered.

The Secretary of State for Commonwealth Relations endorsed the views expressed by the Secretary of State for the Colonies. There was a real danger that Southern Rhodesia might be absorbed by the Union of South Africa, especially if her economic position became difficult, and in his view closer association with the northern territories provided the only effective safeguard against this. The establishment of a Central African *bloc* opposed to the native policy and republicanism of the present South African Government would be of great value in encouraging the proper development of our African territories. There was great danger that public opinion in Southern Rhodesia might reject the proposals, which involved a diminution of her present autonomy, in favour of an attempt to attain full Dominion status; but he hoped that this danger could be averted if we were able to give to the present Prime Minister some measure of the support for which he had asked.

If it was agreed that the report should be published, and the statement made as proposed, every effort must be made to ensure that the proposals were not condemned without proper consideration, either here or in Central Africa; and he proposed, in consultation with the Secretary of State for the Colonies, to discuss them on publication with representatives of all political Parties and with the press.

The Minister of Defence said that the Chiefs of Staff considered that from the point of view of defence there would be advantage in promoting a closer association between these three territories.

In further discussion some Ministers expressed doubts lest the provisions for the proposed federal association might prove too complicated to work smoothly in practice. It was, however, the general view of the Cabinet that the plan was worthy of careful consideration and that a public statement should be made in the terms proposed, subject to the amendment suggested by the Secretary of State for the Colonies in the reference to the purpose of the proposed conference.

The Cabinet:—

(1) Approved the publication of the report annexed to C.P. (51) 122.
(2) Approved the terms of the draft statement annexed to C.P. (51) 122, subject to an amendment making it clear that the purpose of the conference mentioned in paragraph 4 would be to give further consideration to the proposals in the report.

437 CAB 131/10, DO 17(51)3 18 June 1951

'Defence policy in Africa': Cabinet Defence Committee minutes on co-operation with the Union government

The Minister of Defence said that before embarking upon a meeting of Commonwealth Defence Ministers he wished to bring a general point of policy before the Defence Committee. The Union of South Africa expressed itself as anxious to contribute forces to the defence of Africa, while at the same time the United Kingdom Government were building up local native forces in East and West Africa, and had recently agreed to send two battalions from East Africa to Malaya. There appeared to be a conflict of policy behind these practical moves. The South African Government had adopted a repressive native policy which found no favour in the United Kingdom, and they would no doubt look with suspicion upon the efforts of the United Kingdom Government to arm native forces in East and West African territories. Conversely, opinion in East and West Africa might find it difficult to approve the pressure which the United Kingdom Government was exerting upon the Government of South Africa to build up her forces, even though they were ostensibly for the defence of the Middle East. It might be supposed that this indicated that the United Kingdom Government had given tacit approval to South African native policy.

The Minister of Defence admitted that he had sometimes wondered whether, in their eagerness to build up forces, the South African Government were not keeping an eye upon internal security more than on the Middle East.

The Secretary of State for Commonwealth Relations said that on figures the South African contribution to the defence of the Middle East was an essential element which we could not forgo. He thought that the South African Government were now convinced that Africa must be defended in the Middle East and the fact that they were proposing to raise an armoured division was evidence of this. He agreed with the Minister of Defence that our attitude might be misunderstood in East and West Africa, though these territories were still immature and were not in a position themselves to make any contributions to the defence programme as a whole. He had always hoped that we might find it possible to raise much larger African forces to replace the Indian Army which had proved such an important element of defence, particularly at the outbreak of major wars. If that policy were ever adopted, it would no doubt be met with great resentment in the Union of South Africa. For the moment, he held the view that we should continue both with our pressure upon the South African Government to raise larger forces for the Middle East and with our present policy for Colonial forces in the East and West African territories.

The Secretary of State for War[1] said that he agreed that we must look upon the

---

[1] Mr John Strachey.

Union of South Africa as an ally and attempt to obtain the largest contribution we could towards the defence of the Middle East. At the same time, he did not think that we should go to the length of buying a South African contribution to Middle East defence at the expense of retarding our own policy in our East and West African territories.

The Prime Minister said that the point raised by the Minister of Defence was of great importance and should be discussed more fully at a meeting at which the Secretary of State for the Colonies was present. In the meantime, he agreed with the points made by the Secretary of State for Commonwealth Relations and the Secretary of State for War, and suggested that the Minister of Defence should keep this general line of policy in the back of his mind during the meeting of Commonwealth Defence Ministers.

The Committee:—

Invited the Minister of Defence to proceed as indicated by the Prime Minister.

438 PREM 8/1361, M 18/51 21 June 1951

'Simonstown': minute by Mr Gordon Walker to Mr Attlee on discussions about the future of the base

Mr. Erasmus, the South African Minister of Defence, is now in London for the Defence Ministers' Conference. He has told the Minister of Defence and myself that he wishes to discuss with us during his visit the question of the future of the Royal Naval base at Simonstown. At his urgent insistence officials on both sides had a meeting yesterday strictly on the basis that the question of policy was completely reserved for Ministers but that the United Kingdom were ready to provide facts and figures about the cost and effort involved in maintaining the base in terms of finance and trained personnel.

2. The Union Government presented us with an aide-mémoire last February proposing that they should take over the Simonstown base (Sir Percivale Liesching's minute to you serial No. PL/5/51 of the 7th February), and Mr. Erasmus spoke to me about the aide-mémoire in Cape Town on the 9th February as reported in the High Commissioner's telegram No. 64.

3. I am sure that we should not for the time being envisage handing over the management of the Simonstown base to the Union. We would suffer political damage both in the Union and elsewhere; our position in Egypt and Gibraltar would be weakened. We have two main desiderata:—

(a) we wish to be assured that we would always have full use of Simonstown in peace and in war;

(b) we must know that the base would be maintained in the fullest possible state of efficiency.

4. In his talk with me at Cape Town Mr. Erasmus several times emphasised that we would always have the full use of the base. But there is no direct commitment to this effect in the aide-mémoire and we should probably have great difficulty in securing a really satisfactory undertaking.

5. While it was apparent from the discussion yesterday that Union officials were pretty well aware of the facts, it is doubtful whether Union Minister[s] personally

have as yet any conception of what is involved in the way of finance, personnel and organisation in keeping such a base running at full efficiency. The South African Naval forces as at present organised would be hopelessly inadequate to carry out the task. This is clear from papers prepared by the Commander-in-Chief, South Atlantic on the present state of the South African Naval forces and the organisation at Simonstown.

6. We ought therefore to aim at avoiding, for as long as possible, any need for taking a decision in principle about the future of Simonstown and we should play our cards with that end in view. It is not yet certain how far the South Africans themselves really intend to press us on this, though Mr. Erasmus himself spoke very firmly and his Government must of course go through the motions in order that they may have an answer for their followers. It would therefore be a mistake for us to adopt a purely negative attitude; this might well only provoke pressure from the Union Government which otherwise we might avoid. From this point of view the most useful line to take with Mr. Erasmus is to see that he is informed of what is involved in the maintenance of a really efficient naval base; to emphasise to him that the training of officers capable of managing such a base and the proper organisation of the South African Naval forces must come first; and to offer South Africa help in providing training facilities.

7. I would propose therefore that the following points should be made to him:—

(a) we can understand that the Union Government might regard transfer of the control of Simonstown Dockyard as an objective in keeping with their natural aspirations;

(b) nevertheless, it is impossible to give any realistic consideration to the question of the future administration of the base without both Governments knowing precisely what would be involved, and we would be prepared to authorise the Commander-in-Chief, South Atlantic, to have talks with the appropriate South African authority so that he could supplement in full detail what has already been said to South African officials here about the organisational and administrative requirements of an efficient naval base and the cost of administering Simonstown efficiently. Such talks would be specifically without commitment on either side and would be designed merely to ensure that the Union Government fully appreciated the magnitude and the wide range of the responsibilities involved in running a complex technical organisation like a Dockyard plus such adjuncts as the W/T Stations, those in the Simonstown area having special problems and importance because they form part of our world-wide communications network. (The Commander-in-Chief, South Atlantic, would, of course, be instructed to proceed in very close touch with the United Kingdom High Commissioner; but we need not go into this domestic aspect with Mr. Erasmus);

(c) it should be pointed out to Mr. Erasmus that without anticipating the full explanation which the Commander-in-Chief, South Atlantic, would be able to provide, a very substantial effort in terms of finance, personnel and administration would be required on the part of the Union if they were to take over the base and that the training of South African personnel would in any case be a necessary prerequisite. This would take time both because of the nature of the training and because of the substantial numbers required. We should hardly expect the necessary evoluation [sic] of naval and civilian officers with the right experience

and knowledge to be possible unless the S.A. Naval Force were first to become autonomous;
(d) we should express our readiness to assist to the utmost of our ability in the training of South African personnel. (The South African Naval forces, unlike other Commonwealth Navies, are not in fact taking advantage of existing facilities for training in the Royal Navy);
(e) if the S. African authorities appeared to be rather shaken upon realising what would be involved for them in their suggestion, the Commander-in-Chief should be free, with due discretion, to hint that from a purely practical point of view the present arrangements may be more advantageous to them than the assumption of responsibility for the base. Something might be made of the point that the formal title to most of the land the Royal Navy occupy in that part of the Union is now vested in the Union Government.

8. I have been in consultation with the Minister of Defence and the First Lord of the Admiralty and they are in agreement with the above suggestions as to the line which we should take in our discussion with Mr. Erasmus. We shall have to see what sort of a case he has to make and how we can best deal with it. If he presses us hard we should of course refer to you again. I should be glad to know whether you approve.

9. There is one point which does not arise at this stage but which might cause great difficulty if the transfer of Simonstown were to become an issue. You ought therefore to be aware of it. At Simonstown we award Dockyard apprenticeships without restriction as to colour and some of our highly skilled craftsmen, as well as a proportion of the existing apprentices, are coloured. We have obvious moral obligations towards these men but we have some reason to fear that it would be contrary to Union Government policy to employ any but whites in a skilled labour force in their direct employment. If there were any sign that transfer of the control of the base was likely to be agreed, we should need to consider carefully whether to insist on safeguards for the coloured craftsmen and apprentices.[1]

[1] Mr Attlee minuted: 'I approve. C.R.A., 22.6.51'.

439 CAB 129/46, CP(51)173 — 22 June 1951

[Bechuanaland Protectorate]: 'Bamangwato affairs: Tshekedi Khama': Cabinet memorandum by Mr Gordon Walker

[On 6 Mar 1950 the Cabinet decided to exclude Seretse from the Bamangwato chieftainship for a period of not less than five years, and to control his uncle Tshekedi on a more or less equal footing, hoping that the situation in Bechuanaland would then settle down (CAB 128/17, CM 8(50)2). Unable to admit publicly the South African factor, which alone would make its policy intelligible, the British government met strong and continuing criticism of its decision. Tshekedi arrived in London in March 1951, and in the course of the next few months orchestrated his protest. A 'no confidence' motion against the government was scheduled for 26 June 1951. Gordon Walker's paper was discussed at the Cabinet on 25 June, Attlee expressing himself satisfied that Gordon Walker had shown them 'that a strong case could be made in support of the Government's policy in this matter'. If the government now reversed that integrated and defensible policy under pressure from the House of Commons, 'their authority would be gravely weakened both in this country and in Africa' (CAB 128/19, CM 46(51)4). The Labour government survived the censure motion in the Commons, but was defeated in a Lords debate. As a concession to backbench opinion, three independent observers were dispatched; they confirmed the government's view that Bamangwato majority feeling was strongly against Tshekedi (CAB 128/20, CM 60(51)8, 27 Sept 1951).]

The Conservatives and Liberals have tabled a Motion for Tuesday's debate in these terms:—

> "Banishment of Tshekedi Khama,—That this House deplores the decision to continue the banishment of Tshekedi Khama from the Bamangwato Territory without hearing or inquiring into the grounds for such banishment; and calls upon His Majesty's Government to rescind the order of banishment and allow him to dwell freely within the territory of his tribe."

2. We must face the possibility that the Government may be defeated if it resists this Motion. I would like to consult my colleagues on whether we should stand and fight or give way.

3. In my view the policy we have adopted over Tshekedi Khama is the right one. Quite apart from the advice of my officials on the spot, we have considerable evidence of the explicit view of the Tribe that if Tshekedi Khama were now allowed to go back unconditionally to the Bamangwato Reserve there would be considerable danger of disorder and almost certainly non-co-operation by the Tribe with the Administration. The Tribe has already shown itself to be adept in non-co-operation. When I offered Tshekedi Khama limited and conditional access to his cattle posts I went as far as I felt safe without provoking too much hostility from the Tribe.

4. I don't think we can find any compromise between standing firm and abandoning our whole policy of excluding both Tshekedi Khama and Seretse Khama. Even if we gave way to the extent of having an enquiry into our whole policy this would call into question the Government's policy and would make it look as if Tshekedi Khama was more powerful than the Government. The effect on the Tribe would be deplorable. In any case the Motion is for Tshekedi Khama's unconditional return and this is the issue we have to face. If Tshekedi Khama goes back it would be quite impossible to continue to exclude Seretse Khama. It would be most unjust to do so and we would be faced with very grave problems of maintaining order in the Tribe which wants Seretse Khama but does not want Tshedeki Khama. Pressures would develop in Seretse Khama's favour at least as strong as those at present in Tshekedi Khama's favour. The White Paper policy under which both are excluded rests on connected arguments and it cannot be partially or selectively applied. Therefore if Tshekedi Khama goes back, Seretse Khama goes back too.

5. I am not sure what will happen in the Tribe if both go back together: after a year's exile they may manage to get on together at least for a time. Much more serious would be the possible reactions in South Africa. It is, of course, impossible to be certain about hypothetical situations and the Union is at the moment in a very curious and unpredictable mood.

A year ago, when we made our decision about Seretse, I have little doubt that the reaction to the installation of Seretse Khama as Chief would have been to inflame and unite all white opinion in South Africa against us. No man can be installed as Chief of a Tribe without a positive act of confirmation on our part. This would have been regarded in the Union as giving the official seal and blessing of His Majesty's Government to the principle of mixed marriage, and this, as they would see it, in the midst of their national territory. We would have had to face an angry wave of emotion that would have been as strong amongst nearly all the British as amongst Afrikaners and would have united both political parties. (The late Field-Marshal Smuts was strongly against the recognition of Seretse.) Our relations would have been strained to breaking point and we would probably have had to face a demand for the transfer of the Territories that would have been very hard to withstand.

6. We must assume that if Seretse Khama now goes back to the Tribe it will wish to make him Chief. We could not, if we gave way on our main policy, withhold our assent and would thus (as South Africa sees it) put our seal of approval upon mixed marriage. This would still produce a very grave reaction upon opinion in the Union. But today the political parties are bitterly divided, as they were not a year ago, over the question of the entrenched clauses. The United Party is all out to attack Malan. It may be, therefore, that white opinion would not be inflamed and united as it would have been a year ago. But I think we must reckon upon a very fierce reaction from Malan's Government and although the Opposition might not now positively join with him, they would be extremely unlikely on this issue to oppose him.

7. Malan can do a number of very awkward things. In particular, he might (at the very moment of Commonwealth Defence talks) refuse to co-operate with us and more strongly press South Africa's claims for Simonstown. He might also make things very difficult for us in the three High Commission Territories. Each of these is a small territory that cannot stand on its own and is dependent on day-to-day co-operation with South Africa in such matters as customs revenue, railways, veterinary arrangements, the movement of trade, cattle and African labour. This is particularly true of Basutoland, which is wholly surrounded by South African territory. We might nonetheless be able to hold the Territories as the Union might flinch from an ultimate breach with us. But we might well find that we could no longer administer the Territories properly. Unless we were ready to put a very great deal of money into them to keep them going, they might fall into economic and social stagnation. Thereby South Africa's case for transfer would be greatly strengthened. Some Nationalists would probably also use the episode to assist their campaign for a republic and severance of their connection with the Commonwealth.

8. On the merits of the case I therefore think we should stand and fight in the House. I cannot calculate the chances of success. Our case has never been put whilst Tshekedi Khama has been most able and active in putting his. I think we have a very good case and answers to most of the points with which Tshekedi Khama has influenced opinion; indeed I think the case we can put is really more convincing and more easily arguable than a year ago over Seretse. I think the bulk of the Party would come with us if we are resolute but there would, I suppose, be an irreconcilable core that could not be moved by any arguments. On the other hand, it is possible that some Conservatives would abstain or stay away.

9. We must consider what we could do if we should stand and nonetheless be defeated. I suppose that we would then announce that we would accept the views of the House, reverse our whole policy and let both Seretse Khama and Tshekedi Khama go back. This would gravely weaken the Administration in all three Territories; imperil our relations with South Africa; and perhaps have serious effects upon Commonwealth relations. We would have to do our best to cope with these consequences.

10. The alternative is to give way and announce a reversal of our policy either

before the debate or during its course. This would have the unhappy results set out in paragraph 9, but in addition it would be a heavy blow to our prestige, heavier perhaps than being defeated in the House. We would also have endangered the chance of winning through and adhering to our policy. All this must, however, be weighed against the consequence of a possible defeat in the House.

11. My colleagues may prefer to await the outcome of the Party Meeting that will consider this matter on the morning of the debate. But if we are to do this, we must, I suggest, show great firmness between now and then and at the Party Meeting.

440 DO 35/4133, nos 302 & 312 22 & 23 June 1951

[Seretse Khama]: inward telegrams nos 257 and 265 from High Commissioner's Office (Cape Town) to CRO on likely South African reaction to allowing Seretse's return to Bechuanaland

No 257

I have had a word with High Commissioner by telephone and with his consent have discussed position with Strauss who confirms accuracy of following assessment of likely Union reaction in circumstances you forecast.

2. Anti-British feelings would be more and not less repeat more and not less inflamed and political reactions fiercer than they would have been in 1949. To this following recent developments contribute:

(1) Events in Gold Coast and Dr. Malan's interview on subject.
(2) Dr. Malan's attack on British Press.
(3) His recent open advocacy of Republicanism.
(4) His statement that he is prepared to make future of High Commission Territories an election issue.

3. Fundamentally white South Africans are at one on colour question. Return of Seretse with Ruth would be hot "news" and English language press, however reluctantly, would be forced to feature it in some way as would Afrikaans press with resultant high feelings among all sections of white population.

4. United Party differs from Nationalists on question of future of Territories only on one point that Strauss has no wish to be provocative. He would be able to do no more than counsel moderation among his friends. He could not openly oppose any action taken by Nationalists in consequence of Seretse's recognition. To do so would drive at least some loyal South Africans over to Nationalists and give them that measure of local British support without which they cannot hope to achieve a republic.

5. Having confirmed all this Strauss added that in certain circumstances, i.e. (1) if South Africa were criticised in approaching United Nations Organisation debate (2) if Supreme Court declares separate Representation of Voters Act *ultra vires* and (3) Seretse is recognised Malan might even go to country on basis of "no outside interference in Southern Africa". He added that "issue before British Government is in short whether it is more important that Khamas should return or that South Africa should remain with the Commonwealth".

6. It has occurred to me too that though Malan has been very correct over

possible Central African Federation he may wish to seize an opportunity to force issue of Territories before a potentially powerful state with claims on one of them comes into existence on his borders.

7. It is impossible with any real hope of accuracy to forecast whether Nationalists will take measures to embarrass actual Administration of Territories. That they could do so is certain but Territories possess at least two weapons, labour and meat supplies, which though their use would make things even more difficult in Territories would be very disturbing to Union and likely to make Malan lose votes if he provoked their use. The one, labour, would seriously affect industry and the other, meat, would make even more difficult a matter which is already the object of political criticism. Moreover Malan only this week dissociated himself from the threats of economic sanctions used by Hertzog. I would expect that very helpful co-operation which we have recently received from Union Government Departments would be withheld but at a guess repeat at a guess I would expect Malan to hold major measures in reserve for use to force hand of His Majesty's Government after he had received mandate from country on issue of Territories.

8. I have repeated your telegram to High Commissioner and it may reach him this evening but meanwhile you may be assured that foregoing substantially represents his views. Rumbold[1] is already en route to Pretoria and I cannot consult him.

9. You are aware that Forsyth Secretary for External Affairs is in London and perhaps you would be prepared that someone should sound him on your behalf. Strauss thinks it would be safe to do so.

10. I will reply about possible situation in reserve when I have been able to consult [Resident Commissioner] Beetham.

No 265

Message from High Commissioner makes following points additional to those in my telegram No. 257.

2. Reasons why reactions today would be worse than in 1949:

(1) whereas in 1949 Dr. Malan was anxious to preserve the position of the Union within the Commonwealth, today he is threatening to leave. (This explains his strong reaction to Gold Coast events.)

(2) Afrikaans press is suspicious of reasons behind Rhodesian plan and talks of "encirclement".

(3) Nationalist legislation now provides for maximum racial separation, e.g. Immorality Act and Group Areas Act. It follows that recognition of Seretse while married to Ruth would run even more obviously counter to their racial policy now than in 1949.

(4) Since South-West Africa elections Nationalist Party is stronger. Within it the extremists are also stronger. Party is therefore less anxious to avoid clash with us.

(5) Possibility of exploiting Seretse's recognition for purposes of Party politics is greater now than in 1949 for reasons given in paragraph 4 of my telegram No. 257. Dr. Malan recently said (in speech in which he raised question of transfer of Territories) that before a Republic could be achieved it would be necessary to attract a number of English speaking South Africans to the cause.

---

[1] H A F Rumbold, formerly India Office; deputy UK high commissioner in South Africa, 1949–1953.

3. Deterrents to clash with United Kingdom are now less strong for following reasons:

(1) With deterioration in world situation feeling of South Africa's importance to Western defence is keener and Union Government now knows more of defence matters than in 1949.

(2) Economic position is stronger than in 1949 immediately following devaluation. Since then Union has borrowed outside London.

(3) Increasing dislike of United Nations Organisation.

(4) High Commissioner says these views were shared by General Smuts. *Ends*.

441 DO 35/3140, no 55 25 July 1951

'South Africa: review of affairs, 1944–1951': CRO confidential print: memorandum by Sir E Baring to Mr Gordon Walker (30 June)

On my approaching departure from South Africa, I have the honour to submit the following comments on developments here during my period as High Commissioner:—

Internal affairs

2. The South Africa of 1951 is very different from the country I saw on arrival seven years ago. There is a difference both in the relationship between the two sections of South Africans of European origin, and in that between the whites and the non-Europeans. In the past, the attitude of the two sections of the European population to one another and also to the British connection has fixed the line of cleavage in politics. This is still broadly true. But in the future, it may well be that South African voters will divide on their attitude to Africans and to the two other non-European communities, the Indians who are mainly in Natal and the coloured people who are mainly in the Western (Cape) Province.

3. Since the Nationalists came to power in May 1948, a great and, to many, a surprising change has occurred. To understand its nature some mention of South African history is essential. Even since the days of the Great Trek there have been two attitudes of mind among white South Africans. The one has been that of those who hope in good times to dominate the other section of the European population, and in bad times to live in isolation. The other attitude is that of South Africans of both sections who have striven patiently for co-operation.

4. On the British side the first school of thought was in the early 19th century that of Lord Charles Somerset and the Cape Governors who would have nothing of either the Dutch language or the way of life of the *burgers*. In more recent times it was represented by Lord Milner's determination, at least in the later part of his term of office, to extirpate "Krugerism," to bring British settlers on to the land of the Transvaal, and British teachers into its schools. On the Afrikaner side, there has been the belief in the "Volk" as a separate and all-powerful entity, in the Afrikaans language as the symbol of identity preserved, and in the soil of South Africa as the inspiration of its only true sons, the members of the "Boer Nation." These ideas have led, in times of comparative political weakness, to a desire for isolation and a vague nostalgic longing for the perpetuation of the conditions of the old pastoral Republics. In times of comparative political strength there has developed from them a resolve to

attempt to absorb all other white elements in South Africa, so that the loss of identity may be as complete as was that of the Huguenots in the 17th Century Cape and the Scottish settlers of the early 19th Century in the Orange Free State. If absorption is not complete, then, according to this school of thought, the white South African, with divided loyalty, must be kept as firmly from all political power as were the Uitlanders of Kruger's time.

5. But, both among English and Afrikaans-speaking people, there has been another point of view. It has attracted the best minds and the most balanced personalities in the country. This school has numbered among its adherents those who saw clearly that in the new world no land can prosper unless there grows in it a new patriotism for the new country appealing to all its inhabitants regardless of origin. It has also made an appeal to others through the hope that political settlement would improve trade and, more recently, through the belief that only by such a settlement can white supremacy be saved.

6. The ideas of this school of thought appeared in mid-Victorian times when Sir George Grey, in the Cape Colony and, later, Lord Carnarvon in London, worked with the aim of establishing a Confederation of the two British Colonies and the two Republics. Later, they grew in importance when Rhodes adopted them, and when, in the days before the Jameson Raid, he made a greater appeal to Afrikaners than has any other man of British origin.

7. But it was in 1910 that they came right to the forefront of South African life, and, with perhaps one break, animated those in power for nearly 40 years. The spirit of 1910 was one of co-operation and optimism. It was felt that a return had been made to the period before the Boer War and the Raid, to the days when Rhodes and Jan Hofmeyr, then leaders [sic] of the Afrikaner Bond in the Cape Colony, together saw the same vision of a united South Africa. The Afrikaners of 1910 seemed to be borne forward on a wave of gratitude for self-Government. All South Africa apparently felt a surge of hope for the new nation just born. The old assertions of domination from the United Kingdom were abandoned, and the unextinguished flame of Republican sentiment was not mentioned. Everyone felt that a new South African patriotism had been born; and that pride in their newly united land would lead white South Africans towards an increasingly just and liberal treatment of non-Europeans.

8. In the event there has been much disappointment and more disillusion. Only two years after the National Convention General Hertzog formed the Nationalist Party. From 1924 to 1933, in alliance with the Labour Party, he was in power. But after 1933, when he joined General Smuts in the Fusion Government, it seemed that the effects of his break with General Botha in 1912 would be wiped out and that there would be co-operation between Britain [sic] and Boer more complete than anything known since that year. Yet, during all this period, quietly, insidiously, almost out of sight of the world, purely sectional ideas of the type believed in 1910 to be dead, had gradually grown in strength. They had slowly but surely drawn very many Afrikaners away from acceptance of the ideas of 1910 and back to the attitude of the unyielding Republican zealots of Kruger's day, an old attitude but one touched by the infection then spreading abroad from Germany and Italy.

9. This movement has waxed strong on the exploitation of two fears; and in the minds of its followers the two merge into one. The first is the fear that the Boer nation may lose its identity. This has grown in intensity with increasing indus-

trialisation and the constant flow of people to the towns, with the rise in the number of immigrants from Europe, and with the increase in the number of points of contact with the outside world caused by the development of modern inventions and the improvement of communications. The Nationalist creed is well suited to men and women living in isolated pastoral communities. To-day it must be preached to many sons and daughters of General Hertzog's original followers, living in factory towns, in mixed communities in touch with the outside world. The Nationalist desire to develop secondary industries, build a balanced economy to replace one based on farming and mining only, and finally to attain self-sufficiency, is not entirely attuned to the other Nationalist desire jealously to maintain "true" Afrikaners as a people apart.

10. The second fear is that of a threat to white supremacy. This has become sharper in the years since 1945. White South Africans have watched inside their own country the growth in the number of Africans living with their families in towns and working in the new factories; and, outside South Africa, they have observed with concern the surge of Asiatic Nationalism and, with a mixture of rage and terror, recent developments in West Africa.

11. The progress made recently by the movement based on these two fears has been remarkable. At the end of the war there was a brief moment of hope faintly recalling 1910. It seemed then that a Nationalist Party, imbued with the bitter hatreds of a backveld people, would never gain power. It was assumed that the cause of South African unity had increased in strength as a result of the war. More than half the South Africans who fought in the Western Desert and in Italy were Afrikaans-speaking and it seemed that experiences shared during the war would help the progress of a true and broadly based South African patriotism. Secondly, there was no doubt that, as long as General Smuts' Party remained in power, war-time co-operation between the Union Government and that of the United Kingdom had strengthened the Commonwealth link. In 1945 General Smuts frequently told individual Southern Rhodesians that a new approach by the Union to their country was now justified since Republicanism was manifestly dead. Thirdly, and of great importance, was the attitude among soldiers and airmen to the non-Europeans of South Africa. Africans and coloured men served in North Africa and Italy. White South Africans, as they discussed their country with soldiers of other lands, felt the need to reform the less admirable side of South Africa, and to improve the conditions of life of non-Europeans. Hence the demand made by serving soldiers and airmen that money subscribed by them should be used to establish a National Health Fund for use exclusively on native health.

12. In the early days of peace, it seemed, not only that the two sections of Europeans were drawing closer together, but that a tide of liberalism was flowing. In 1910, problems affecting natives had been somewhat neglected. General Smuts, when in opposition, once said to Lord Athlone: "I never turn my attention to native affairs unless I have to." In 1945 all this was changed. A strong feeling among those young South Africans, who were growing up in the towns, that greater justice should be done to the non-Europeans, claimed the attention of the Government and in 1948 General Smuts accepted the recommendations of the Fagan Commission. It was an important move. Mr. Fagan was an excellent chairman. The weakness of South African Liberals is a tendency to make proposals very far in advance of public opinion for fear of accusations of being illiberal. Mr. Fagan, who had held office as Minister

for Native Affairs, had no such fear and he avoided proposals which were politically impossible of acceptance. But the implementation of his proposals implied the clear acceptance of his premise that industrial development in South Africa must lead to the growth of an African population of both men and women permanently resident in the towns. From this it followed, according to the report, that by measures taken to improve housing, transport to work, and social security, by the relaxation (though not the abolition) of the vexatious Pass Laws, and finally by the grant of a degree of municipal self-Government in African townships, life must be made tolerable for the urban African.

13. But the hopes of 1945, renewed in 1948, were vain. The tide of patriotism and of liberal feeling left many islands uncovered. The whole of rural South Africa outside perhaps Natal and the Eastern (Cape) Province was untouched. So were the Nationalist Universities in Stellenbosch, Pretoria, Bloemfontein and Potchefstroom, the Dutch Reformed Church and the Afrikaans medium schools staffed by teachers imbued with Nationalist ideas. The movement, started by General Hertzog, had not only quietly gained in strength: it had also changed its nature. Its objective was now domination and absorption. The proof of this lies in the inability of the Nationalists to win over any appreciable number of English-speaking people. Afrikaners may well join the United Party since, even if the balance may be at times too tilted towards things English, it is a Party of co-operation. Very few English-speaking people can join the Nationalists, for they are a Party of domination.

14. The Nationalists of 1951 believe, without thought but with intense feeling, that only by the dominance of the nationally-minded section over all other people in South Africa can the survival both of the Boer Nation and of white supremacy be assured. The Afrikaner people, they feel, are too few in numbers to preserve their identity unless they are the dominant group. English-speaking South Africans they regard as allied to a people who give self-Government to Africans and whose missionaries have attacked Afrikaners ever since the first years of the 19th Century. They also feel that when their opponents are in power the vested interests of the gold mines count for too much. The only alternative is then a monopoly of political power in the hands of those who are nationally-minded.

15. The new Nationalist State implies a check on immigration and therefore perhaps the weakening in the long run of white supremacy. It implies also a migrant African labour force and, therefore, a check to the expansion of secondary industries and to progress on the road to self-sufficiency. Few Nationalists are seriously worried by these apparent inconsistencies. They are vote-catching politicians above all else, their eyes turned inwards to the politics of their own country, as inept in external relations as they are skilled in the management of South African elections. Moreover, there is another explanation of their neglect of these aspects of their policy. Young Nationalists do not learn to think. They strive to be loyal to the family, the State and the Church. They trust and obey their leaders, and they distrust anybody who exercises his or her critical faculties. Young men and women of this type are coming in increasing numbers from the Nationalist Schools and Universities and the comparison with pre-war Germany and Italy or, indeed, with Russia, is obvious.

16. In brief, General Smuts is dead and the ideas of 1910 are in eclipse. The country's rulers think with the blood and emotion prevails over reason. It is easy to criticise the Nationalists, but their strength should not be under-rated. A formidable force has gained control of the country and the South African Sinbad will find the

unseating of his old Man of the Sea very difficult. The modern Nationalist has virtues. He believes in God, in the strength of family ties and he strives to stay close to the soil. If he rejects liberal thought, he also turns away from an entirely material outlook and from the more tawdry side of the American way of life. He is no believer in small families and consequently the percentage of Afrikaans-speaking children in school considerably exceeds that of Afrikaners in the population as a whole. He feels that he is a crusader and that he is winning. But to South Africa's misfortune he is crusading for a false god, for an all-powerful State controlled for ever by a comparatively small number of men and women and decked out with the attractive trimmings of a simple Republican people whose emblem was the ox-wagon. The growth in the southern tip of the African Continent of this strange force gives rise to many questions. It is often asked whether it is entrenched for ever, whether it will alter its nature, whether it will spread north and what will the United Kingdom's relations be with a South Africa controlled by men of the Nationalist type?

17. The strength of the Nationalist hold on power may be best explained by using a South African slang expression, to "white ant," i.e., to undermine someone. By exploiting the apathy of English-speaking voters, the complacency of the men who surrounded General Smuts, and the aloofness in his later years of their great opponent, they gradually gained adherents. The small secret and well-organised Broederbond followed with great success its policy in infiltration, until the Nationalist doctrine was heard from every pulpit and expounded in the classroom of every Afrikaans medium school. In politics, the weightage given to country seats was of great advantage to the Nationalists. In 1948, at a time when developments outside their country had alarmed white South Africans, when they were smarting under criticism at the United Nations, and when they were exercised inside their own borders by the growth in the number of urban Africans, the Nationalists emphasised White Supremacy rather than Republicanism. The cry "Vote White" was most effective and the consequent wave of emotion carried them to power; continuation of the two fears which they so well exploited and of material prosperity in a period of rising prices has maintained them in office.

18. By the grant of heavy weightage to South-West Africa and by the removal of Coloured voters from the common roll in the Cape Province, the Nationalists hope to strengthen their position. They hold a number of urban seats. The United Party may win back some but not all of these. Such gains are unlikely, by themselves, to counter-balance the effects of South-West Africa, of the Franchise Bill, and of various minor acts of gerrymandering. The key to the next General Election lies, therefore, in the rural seats, particularly in the Eastern Transvaal, traditionally the stronghold of Botha and of Smuts, yet completely lost to the Nationalists in the 1948 landslide. But farmers are prosperous and to my mind the outlook for the United Party is poor unless some change occurs before the date of the next Election.

19. On the other hand, the finances and the organisation of the Opposition have been improved. Many Nationalist majorities are very small. The core of the United Party supporters still exists in many rural constituencies and only a small part of the floating vote in the countryside—mainly Afrikaans-speaking—need be turned in order to enable the United Party to regain power.

20. Much has been said of various developments which might loosen the grip of the Nationalists. Their position might be damaged by a depression and a fall in farm prices; but rearmament seems to imply the continuance of high prices for South

African farmers and especially sheep farmers. The Nationalists have long memories, and are determined to avoid the type of split which, in the past, has so often damaged them. Mr. Havenga, after obtaining some benefits for the Coloured People, appears to have surrendered completely. He is but a shadow of General Hertzog, a follower rather than a leader, and the United Party must stand on its own feet and not look to him to save it. The third possibility of relief derives from the nature of the Nationalists themselves.

21. This requires some explanation. The root and branch school led by the blunt, austere and uncompromising Strydom has gained strength inside the Party, especially since the South-West African Elections. Even the apathetic English-speaking business man is beginning to understand something of the Nationalists aims. If these are fulfilled the non-European will be deprived of all political rights; the maximum of separation of races in every walk of life will be enforced by draconian legislation. Residence of African women in the towns will be discouraged by tightening up the administration of the Pass Laws, by a possibly deliberate slowness in providing houses for urban Africans and by the cancellation of unemployment insurance benefits for the greater part of them. The English-speaking South African will be treated better. He will be allowed to lead a happy life and to become rich, provided he steers clear of politics. But public life in Parliament and in Government service will gradually become the preserve of the ruling section who, inside their own ring fence, will no doubt preserve the greatest equality of opportunity.

22. If, on the other hand, the English-speaking South African is willing to accept *in toto* the Nationalist creed, to forget all his links with Britain, his loyalty to the Crown and all other things British, and to become, in fact, an Afrikaner of British origin, he will be readily accepted. He must, in fact, be absorbed as were the early English-speaking settlers in the Free State, and not try to live in a community of his own, as did the Uitlanders who came to the Transvaal after the discovery of gold.

23. Once the English-speaking South African has grasped the nature of the fate in store for him, he may come to understand also the only method of avoiding it. The Nationalists are the heirs of Krugerism who have caught some of the infection of Nazi Germany. Their appeal is strong. In South African history the only other appeal which has successfully opposed it is that of a patriotism for South Africa as a whole. If Afrikaans-speaking members of the United Party are questioned on the reason for their adherence to the Party, the answer will often be, that in the days before 1910 they or their fathers were fired with this enthusiasm. It is often said that in Asia the emotion of national patriotism is the only effective counter to the emotional appeal of Communism. In South Africa the emotional appeal of true patriotism is probably the only answer to that of sectional interests. The call to wider patriotism and to the defence of individual liberty can alone provide enthusiasm sufficient to roll back the Nationalist flood. Unfortunately the United Party is, at the moment, an organisation which can reason with people but cannot inspire them. The most vital task of the future for all true patriots in South Africa will be to remedy this weakness.

24. Fortunately there is some hope. Their nature is such that, though the Nationalists profess to be constitutionalists, yet they may eventually go so far that they will arouse against them a really strong feeling among their disunited and inert opponents. It is arguable that this has happened already. Many, who could by no stretch of the imagination be classed as liberals, deplore the breach of faith which is

the new Franchise Act. They realise, dimly but rightly, that if a Government with a small Parliamentary majority and a minority of the votes cast, can use a legal quibble to go against what nearly every child has been taught is the Constitution of the country to the detriment of the Coloured People, then there is no reason why that same Government should not at some future date go against it again to the deriment [sic] of those white South Africans who are not "nationally-minded."

25. Expression has been found for these fears aroused by the Nationalists in the surprising, sensational and spectacular protest in Cape Town and other centres against the Coloured Franchise Bill made by the War Veterans Action Committee. This movement has grown suddenly and without organisation by political leaders. Its leaders have been the first opponents of Nationalism who have raised enthusiasm and drawn large crowds. It may come to nothing. But when seen in its historical setting, it may also become a development of great importance. The explanation of this view is that apparently there are at least signs that possibly an enduring enthusiasm has been roused to match that so often exploited by the Nationalists. This enthusiasm and the ideas behind it may seem new to the younger men among the Veterans and may appear to them to be something born during the war years. In point of fact they represent a return to the broadly based South African patriotism with an appeal to all, inherited from Grey, from Rhodes and from the members of the National Convention in 1910. It is for this reason that the new organisation may at last provide a rallying cry for the opponents of the fierce but sectional enthusiasm of the Nationalists.

26. From all this the conclusion on the internal position is that for the first time since 1910 South Africa has stepped back in time. It is now dominated by an oligarchy. Its rulers are strongly entrenched. They control the thoughts and ideas of many young Afrikaners. They evoke strong feelings and are served with devotion by many. The Ministers of to-day are at the head, less of a political party prepared for alternating victory and defeat at the polls, than of a movement probably determined to retain power permanently. Their overthrow will be a very difficult though not impossible task. For their opponents the hopeful signs are few, and what there are, are of recent date and uncertain importance.

External reactions

27. From this darkening of the South African scene flow several results for Great Britain. First, the strong tie of sentiment binding many South Africans to the United Kingdom may well be broken. A Republic may be declared. Following its establishment, interest in and love for all things British, may, with the active encouragement of the Union Government, suffer gradually a process of decay. As the tie of sentiment weakens, our political relations will inevitably suffer.

28. Secondly, South African Nationalism may be for export in the African Continent. The ideas of the Nationalists are those of a Frontier and the "Trek Boer" still exists and still feels an urge to move North. It is a feeling inherited from his ancestors of the 17th Century who moved inland away from the Netherlands East India Co. and its trading monopoly, and from his other ancestors of the 19th Century who crossed the desert to the new Canaan of the two Republics away from the British, away from close Government and away from the liberation of slaves.

29. It is undeniable that, if Nationalist ideas spread over the Limpopo, the hopes of the peaceful development of partnership between Europeans and Africans in some

northern Territories may well dwindle. Much was amiss with the treatment given to Africans by the predecessors of the present Government; and it is often said that for Africans there is nothing to choose between the two political parties. This is a misleading statement. It is no doubt true that both political parties are determined to maintain white supremacy and to prevent the development of a mixed race. All the same it is possible to refuse to share political rights equally and yet in other ways to treat Africans not unfairly. Under the United Party the climate was one of change and the leaders of the country were, like those of Southern Rhodesia, open to persuasion on matters affecting non-Europeans. Expenditure on native education was increasing. Attempts were being made, not only to improve agriculture in the rural reserves, but also to provide better houses for Africans in urban areas, and the United Party Government had it in mind to grant a form of local self-Government for Africans in the towns, and to expand that already existing in the native reserves. The country was on the move and in the right direction. Nearly all the Nationalists on the other hand fear and hate Africans. As a result they cannot refrain from threats and insults. What they say has often a worse effect on the African than what they do. They not only refuse to share power but also in all the activities of government they treat Africans harshly.

30. They have closed minds. The theory of "apartheid" dominates Nationalist thinking and, what is more important, Nationalist feeling on race problems. Yet, considered as a programme of action, it is useless and little more than a pipe dream. The theorists imagine that, with some exceptions, all African women might live in an African state carved out of modern South Africa. Some African men would work on the farms and in the factories of that state, many others would come as migrant labourers into the white state. This is impracticable. The new land Africans might obtain is insufficient, and the suitable sites for factories totally inadequate. The Government are already running away from the implementation of the theory. In point of fact, whatever the wishful thinking of the Government may be, an increasingly large number of Africans will live with their families in towns and, possibly following the increase in the number of family quarters provided in the new Free State area, on mines. The existence of the theory of maximum separation merely serves to check the improvement in the living conditions of these people. Thus, under the heel of the Nationalist Government, progress for Africans stagnates. No new contracts are placed for African housing, the enforcement of the Pass Laws becomes more strict, important social security benefits are withdrawn and there is every prospect that educational facilities may be curtailed. Nationalists would bring these ideas north with them and, if they attained political power north of the Limpopo, would probably attempt to copy the actions in the Union of Dr. Malan's Government.

31. The third result is less depressing. It is that a Government has come to power which, on certain subjects such as resistance to Soviet Russia, can enlist the support of more South Africans than General Smuts ever could either in resistance to Germany or in measures of international co-operation. There need be little fear, provided they are properly handled, that the Nationalists will refuse to co-operate with the United Kingdom and with other countries on defence, on security and on transport matters. At one time it was felt that, by organising African Conferences, first on non-contentious matters and then gradually on those with a more and more delicate political flavour, South Africa all the time taking the lead, they might come

to exercise an undue influence beyond the Union's borders. The lesson of the South African Transport Conference of 1950 is that the suspicion of the motives and aims of the present Union Government felt in other Territories, for example, the Portuguese Colonies, is so great that this fear is groundless.

32. To despise or to ignore the strong and expanding force of South African nationalism in 1951 would be as unwise as it was to decry in March 1933 the power of Hitler to do harm. The strength and threat of Nationalism derive partly from the nature of the leaders themselves and partly from that of the country they rule. Of the men I have written sufficient. The country, like Egypt, is and perhaps always will be a key point in the world. Since it has been proved that warships cannot operate within range of shore-based aircraft and that consequently the Mediterranean will be denied to our ships once an enemy holds its northern shores, South Africa has resumed the degree of importance in war attached to it before the construction of the Suez Canal. Should war come, it will be needed as a transit base, as an arsenal for the countries surrounding the Indian Ocean and as a contributor of land and air forces to the vitally important fighting in the Eastern Mediterranean area during the first critical days. South African uranium, manganese, chrome and coal will be very badly needed. South Africa is the only African country fairly far advanced on the road to industrialisation. Its steel production is rising. It can now manufacture trucks and will soon make locomotives. It is the one African country which could in war time provide a large body of trained European technicians. Finally, Britain is in dire need of its gold; and owing to the new discoveries in the Orange Free State the life of the gold mining industry has been greatly increased.

33. South Africa will provide vital war-time needs. With very cheap and plentiful coal and consequently cheap electricity, with large iron ore and limestone deposits and with some of the steel alloys, it has the basis for heavy industry. Shortage of water and shortage of skilled men are at present the two bars to progress. It will prosper in times either of war or of rearmament. With high prices for wool, export coal and other minerals the country is adding to its financial and economic strength, in spite of the uncertain future of South African farming under the threat of erosion.

34. A result of growing economic strength is that South Africa will continue to act as a magnet drawing African labour from the north. White South Africans will continue to invest in the north. The growth of schools and universities in South Africa will enable increasing numbers of students to come to the Union from northern territories. The expansion of South Africa will increase the volume of trade with northern territories; and it is already surprising to note how large a part of the traffic north on the Rhodesian Railways line through the Bechuanaland Protectorate is of Union origin. In short, Nationalist fanatics control a strong and important country. However unpalatable may be the political and social theories of the present rulers of South Africa, it will be useless to attempt to draw a complete cordon sanitaire round South Africa and to cut ourselves and our African dependencies off from the Union entirely.

The future

35. But if it is idle to hope that South Africa may be ignored, it is essential to take measures to meet the new position. These, as I see it, may be divided into three parts. There are those to counteract the impact of the new Nationalism on territories north of the Limpopo, there are those to preserve, as long as their inhabitants wish it, our

outposts in the three High Commission Territories, and finally there are those to regularise as well as we can our relations with the Union itself.

36. Looked at from this point of view, the proposals for a Federation of the two Rhodesias and Nyasaland are very much a step in the right direction. But it would be necessary to follow the promulgation of the new constitution with positive measures to control the flow of Afrikaner immigrants and the activities of Afrikaners already residing in the Rhodesias. The great instrument of the Nationalist movement is the Broederbond and the great talent of the Broederbond is the planning of infiltration. At no one moment could its activities in the teaching profession and the police in the Union be proved, yet finally both have been completely captured. It would therefore be a mistake to await proof of the entry into the Rhodesias of large numbers of Nationalist supporters before taking action to control immigration. Inside the Rhodesias the key move will, in Nationalist eyes, be the establishment of Afrikaans medium schools. If this is resisted and if watch is kept against schools in predominantly Afrikaner areas being staffed entirely by Nationalist supporters, then it should be possible to check the activities of the Broederbond inside the two Rhodesias.

37. On the High Commission Territories perhaps one remark will suffice. If Britain wills the end of maintaining the Basuto, the Bechuana and the Swazi under her control as long as they themselves wish for this, then she must also will the means. This implies two decisions. The first is to develop the resources of the Territories and, once this has strengthened their financial position, to improve the social services in them. Basutoland has so few natural resources that it is now the weak spot. But at last there is a hope—and it is an only hope—from the storage of the waters of the Orange River, for use partly for irrigation in the Union and partly for the generation of electricity to be sold at a profit. The second decision is to maintain reasonably friendly relations with the Union. If South Africans become united and inflamed on the issue of transfer, our position in Swaziland and the Bechuanaland Protectorate would become very difficult indeed. In Basutoland not only would it be necessary to abandon the Orange River scheme, since it requires the close co-operation of South Africa, but the day-to-day administration of the country and, in a dry year, the feeding of its people would become impossible. Experience shows, I think, that the United Kingdom can continue to govern the High Commission Territories and can develop their resources, but only on condition that the limitations placed on us by their geographical position are realised and that nice judgment is exercised in distinguishing those acts, which are so violently provocative to all but a very small minority of South Africans, that they will remove the deterrents to a clash with the United Kingdom, from those other acts which are merely irritating to some South Africans.

38. As for South Africa itself, there is our attitude to the present Government and there is our attitude to our friends, both English and Afrikaans-speaking. With the Government we should seek to co-operate as often as possible. We can join with them in the defence of the West, in security measures against Communist agents, and in international co-operation in the development of the Continent—an easy task if scientific research is in question and a very difficult one if railway matters are under discussion. Finally we can develop our economic connections, remembering that the South Africans need British capital goods and prefer London to all other markets for the satisfaction of their very great need of capital and that the farmers who sell us

fruit and wines are mostly Nationalists and are politically important in the country. In general, the Nationalists would be happy if they could convert the country into a Republic, dominated by the "nationally-minded," yet maintaining very friendly relations with the United Kingdom in economic and defence matters. But at intervals some act of ours, such as the recent constitutional reforms in the Gold Coast, revives old grudges and causes a surge of emotional anti-British feeling followed by a series of ill-tempered outbursts. Our best policy is to ignore these and to await the moment when a reasonable consideration of the interests of South Africa displaces the emotions of hatred and fear as the guiding force of South African policy. Timing is therefore the essence of the successful conduct of affairs with the Nationalists. Patience is the quality most needed, not only in those who work with Africans but also in those who deal with Nationalist Afrikaners, most of whose ancestors have lived for many generations among Africans on the African Continent.

39. Finally, Great Britain should not despair of her friends in South Africa. In politics they have for long been complacent and supine. They have allowed the reins of power to slip through their fingers. But they still outnumber the Nationalists. There are signs that they might at last be stirred to activity if the right stimulus could be given. The facts of economics and the problems of race are both in favour of the broadly based patriotism of which they should be the champions. The immediate political future is gloomy, but the prospect as a whole is not hopeless. Our aim should be to avoid making more difficult than it is already the task of the opponents of the Nationalists. We should be very careful of sweeping condemnation of white South Africans as a whole or of Afrikaners as a people. The first assists the Nationalists in their efforts to win English-speaking voters or at least to induce them to abstain. The second alienates the friendly Afrikaners who support the United Party; and the important floating vote is rural and Afrikaans-speaking.

40. I am sending copies of this Despatch to the United Kingdom High Commissioners at Ottawa, Canberra, Wellington, Delhi, Karachi, Colombo and Salisbury, to the United Kingdom Ambassador at Dublin, the Chairman of the East African Commission, the Secretary of the West African Council and the Governors of Northern Rhodesia and Nyasaland.

442 PREM 8/1361, DO(51)96 28 July 1951

'Simonstown naval base—proposed transfer of control to the Union government': joint memorandum for Cabinet Defence Committee by Mr Shinwell,[1] Mr Gordon Walker and Lord Pakenham.[2] *Annex*: draft statement

Mr. Erasmus, the South African Minister of Defence, made certain proposals to us during his visit to this country last month in regard to the Royal Naval base at Simonstown.[3] Before setting out his proposals and our recommendations we give below a historical introduction indicating what is the nature of our present tenure and the long term security it provides for our strategic requirements and what our requirements are.

---

[1] Secretary of state for defence.

[2] First lord of the admiralty since 24 May 1951.

[3] See 438.

Historical introduction

2. In 1921 the United Kingdom Government agreed to hand over to the Union Government responsibility for the land defences of the Cape Peninsula including Simonstown, and to complete the transfer to the Union Government of "war department" properties in South Africa. This agreement was reached following discussions and correspondence in London between the Secretary of State for the Colonies (Mr. Churchill) and the Prime Minister of South Africa (General Smuts). In making these arrangements the United Kingdom Government formally requested (in a despatch signed by Mr. Churchill) and received from the Union Government, an assurance that the Union Government would keep the Naval station in such a state of defence that it would at all times be able to discharge its functions as a naval link in the sea communications of the British Empire, and that the Union Government would for this purpose consult with the Admiralty and conform to their requirements.

3. As regards lands and property it was agreed that the freehold of all lands hitherto occupied by the United Kingdom services should be transferred to the Union Government with the reservation that the Admiralty would be secured in the right of perpetual user for naval purposes of such lands and buildings as they required. The arrangement as to the Admiralty tenure of such lands was subsequently set out in a formal agreement between the Admiralty and the Union Minister of Defence dated the 23rd June, 1930 which specified in detail the lands reserved to the Admiralty. This agreement contained a provision that the reservation in favour of the Admiralty could be cancelled at any time upon a notification from the Admiralty that such lands or any portion thereof were no longer required either by the Admiralty or by the Imperial Government for defence purposes.

4. In looking at the security which we have inherited from this Agreement, we must bear in mind that such an agreement is no longer in line with normal Commonwealth development under which Canada and Australia, for instance, have long since taken over complete control of former Royal Navy bases in their countries. If the Union Government chose to challenge in the international forum our continued occupation of their territory they could make things very difficult for us; in face of such a challenge we could probably not for long stand on the letter of a legal document.

Background to discussions with Mr. Erasmus

5. In September, 1950, Mr. Erasmus, the Defence Minister in the South African Government, raised with the Secretary of State for Commonwealth Relations the future of the base at Simonstown. Mr. Erasmus was informed that the United Kingdom Government would be prepared to have discussions on the subject if the Union Government wished to raise it, but that the Union Government should first let us have detailed proposals in writing.

6. The Union Government's proposals were received in February. After summarising the history of the South African Naval Forces and the provisions of the Simonstown Lands Agreement of 1930, the memorandum proposed, as a basis for negotiations, that the naval control of the Simonstown Base should be assumed by the Union Government; that South Africa should maintain the Dockyard and its repair facilities in proper condition and that, where necessary, officers and technicians should be seconded to help South Africa carry out this undertaking until their

own personnel had gained the necessary experience. The only reference to the future use of Simonstown by the Royal Navy was contained in a passage to the effect that the facilities at Simonstown would have to be retained "in order that repairs can be effected to our (South African) ships and that facilities of a fully equipped Naval Dockyard are available to our allies in the event of war."

Admiralty views

7. The view of the Admiralty, in the light of the views of Commander-in-Chief, South Atlantic, briefly stated, is that, while there is no over-riding operational reason why we must retain control of the base in peace, it is most important that its war potential should not be allowed to deteriorate and that it should be freely available to the Royal Navy and its allies in peace and war. The South Africans would not, however, be capable of running the Dockyard efficiently entirely with Union personnel for a long time to come. Moreover, the present South African naval Command structure and general state of efficiency of the Union Naval Forces must be much improved if South Africa is to be capable, unaided, of assuming full responsibility for her own naval defence in war and of operating the base.

United Kingdom requirements

8. The four main requirements on the United Kingdom side may be summarised as follows:—

(a) we must be assured that the Royal Navy will have unrestricted use of the base in peace and war;

(b) we must know that the base would be maintained at its present level of efficiency and that to this end there would be skilled staff at the base backed by a properly run Naval service;

(c) we should need to secure special safeguards for the interests of the coloured craftsmen and apprentices at Simonstown before there could be any question of transferring them to Union control;

(d) politically, if there were to be a progressive assumption of control of the Simonstown base by the South African Naval Force, it would need to be a gradual process in keeping with the growth of South Africa's own forces and responsibilities and not a sudden or dramatic act of transfer.

Discussion with Mr. Erasmus

9. During his recent visit, Mr. Erasmus pressed for an early decision. According to his explanation the Union Government would wish to take over all the naval Establishments in the Cape Area i.e. the W/T Stations and Store Depots, as well as the Dockyard proper. He made it clear that the Union Government were aware of the financial and administrative commitments which would be involved and would be willing to assume them. We accordingly explained frankly to him the four main prior requirements on the United Kingdom side. Mr. Erasmus proved very receptive. We understood him to say that we could count on such facilities as we might require in peace and in war. He emphasised that South Africa wished to maintain the base at full efficiency and for this purpose would need to take over or borrow the appropriate personnel. He accepted our suggestions that the S.A.N.F. needed strengthening at the top and he did not appear to rule out the idea, which was mentioned to him, of

the appointment of a Flag Officer, Royal Navy, as Head of the South African Naval Forces. He said that safeguards for the rights of the coloured employees would be acceptable. He recognised the need for avoiding any dramatic announcement and he accepted a draft statement (see paragraph 15 below and Annex I) which would be satisfactory from this point of view.

Considerations involved

10. Mr. Erasmus' assurances, if confirmed by his Government would indicate a striking advance on the part of the Union. An assurance of the use of Simonstown by the Royal Navy in peace and war would be of great importance to our defence relations with South Africa beyond the narrow issue of Simonstown itself. We should have made a major step forward if a Nationalist Government in South Africa, which has hitherto dangerously weakened its armed forces by a narrowly Afrikaner policy, were to follow the example of all other Commonwealth Governments in accepting the guidance of a Flag Officer from the Royal Navy at the formative stage in the growth of their Navy.

11. We must recognise, however, that there may be political difficulties and dangers in this country. South Africa does not stand high in public esteem. The existing arrangement stems from an agreement between Mr. Churchill himself and the late Field-Marshal Smuts. Our unhappy experience over the Irish Ports may be quoted in this context. We pointed out these considerations frankly to Mr. Erasmus and warned him of the damage to his own objectives if the matter were to become the subject of acute political controversy here in the same way as the question of the appointment of an American Admiral to the Atlantic Command. We explained, and Mr. Erasmus accepted, that for these reasons any changes at Simonstown must be very gradual and unspectacular. But the fact remains that, if we start such a process, we are admitting to the Union Government that we do contemplate handing the base over to them at some future but unspecified date.

12. We may expect the Union Government to press us hard. They have a case which, in the international forum, we should find some difficulty in countering. They will reaffirm that they would be ready to take over all the technical and other experts and accept the full cost involved. They will recall that other Commonwealth Navies (the Canadian and Australian) developed and took over responsibility for naval bases in their own countries, and that the British Army, which also had been stationed in South Africa, had handed over completely to the South African Army in the period 1914 to 1921. We could probably not for long stand on the letter of a legal document.

13. A firm guarantee that the Royal Navy must have full use of the base *in peace and in war* is fundamental for us. We made this very clear to Mr. Erasmus. It is disturbing that, in a letter to the Minister of Defence written after his return to South Africa, he speaks of facilities "in peace and in war against Communism". We should not accept any ambiguity about this and we should reject any suggestion for amending the words used in discussions with us. In any case a phrase linking the guarantee to a war against Communism would provide obvious opportunities for Cominform counter propaganda.

Action proposed

14. In all the circumstances it seemed to us at the end of our discussion with him

to be right to take Mr. Erasmus at his word and to follow up our talks with him in an endeavour to reach agreement between the two Governments on a basis which would fully meet our requirements as set out in paragraph 8 above.

15. We accordingly agreed with Mr. Erasmus that we would recommend to the Cabinet, and that he would recommend to his Government, action as follows:—

(i) When the general approval of both Governments had been given talks would be started between experts in South Africa, with the object of examining in detail the various technical, administrative and financial problems which would be involved in the progressive assumption by the Union Authorities of effective control over the Simonstown base.

(ii) As soon as these talks had produced inter-Governmental agreement on two main points, a joint statement would be issued in the terms of the draft at Annex I. These two points are:—

(a) mutually satisfactory arrangements for the Higher administrative direction of South Africa's naval forces;

(b) arrangements to safeguard the legitimate expectations of the existing European and non-European staff and apprentices at Simonstown;

(iii) After the issue of the agreed statement, the talks would continue on the remaining issues involved. Among these would be such matters as arrangements for the loan of Royal Naval officers and United Kingdom civilian personnel; arrangements for the training of South African personnel; the future of the Commander-in-Chief, South Atlantic and his squadron; the implications of transferring control over the W/T stations; the properties to be included in transfer under the application of the 1930 Agreement, and the terms upon which these properties and others would be transferred. In effect, the object of the second stage of the talks would be to produce proposals, to be considered by both Governments, for at least the first steps in the progressive assumption of control by the Union.

16. Two points arise on the above "programme":—

(a) There may be a danger of leakage at stage (i) and we should agree with the Union Government on the line to be taken should a leakage occur.

(b) We need firm and definite undertakings of a specific kind on the two matters under (ii). Neither will be easy for the Union Government; and we must expect negotiations on them to take time.

17. At the close of the discussions, Mr. Erasmus in fact asked for some early indication of the time factors envisaged on the United Kingdom side. The most we should say would be to point out that, in practice, timing must depend on the outcome of the contemplated talks between experts, but that we for our part would certainly do our best to expedite the carrying-through of these talks. Mr. Erasmus also threw out the suggestion that, so urgent was the need of the South African Navy for some facilities at Simonstown, if it was to develop as planned, an arrangement for joint use might be adopted as an immediate interim measure. This also will have to be examined from the practical stand-point.

Recommendation

18. We recommend that:—

(a) the question of the assurance regarding use "in peace and in war" should be taken up with Mr. Erasmus in reply to his letter (para. 13);
(b) if, but only if, a satisfactory reply is received from him, he should be informed that the Cabinet have approved the agreement provisionally reached with him and set out in para. 15.

Annex to 442

The United Kingdom and Union Governments have discussed the latter's plans for the expansion of the South African Naval Force and their desire progressively to assume control of the base at Simonstown at present under the control of the Royal Navy. The United Kingdom Government made it clear that they welcome the Union Government's policy of expanding South Africa's own forces and working towards the assumption of wider naval responsibilities in accordance with the normal pattern of development in Commonwealth countries. The progressive assumption of control of the Simonstown base by the S.A.N.F. and related problems of organisation require full and expert examination, and for this purpose arrangements have been made for talks to take place in the Union.

The Union Government have assured the United Kingdom Government that, if South Africa assumed responsibility for the base at Simonstown, such facilities there as the United Kingdom may require in peace and in war would be made available.

443 CAB 131/10, DO 22(51)1 10 Sept 1951

'Simonstown naval base—transfer of control to Union government': Cabinet Defence Committee minutes

The Minister of Defence said that his memorandum (D.O. (51) 100) traced the course of negotiations with Mr. Erasmus, the Minister of Defence in the Union of South Africa, about the transfer of the control of the Naval Base at Simonstown to the Union Government. Mr. Erasmus had now offered a form of words—given in the Annex to the memorandum—which appeared to him unsatisfactory. While it was no doubt probable that at some future date it would be necessary for control of this Base to be transferred to the Union Government, it would only be done in return for an unambiguous guarantee that the United Kingdom and her Allies should have the use of the Base in war, whether or not the Union of South Africa were neutral. It was politically and practically impossible to accept anything else. His own personal view was that any weakening on this point would create political difficulties for us both in South Africa and in the United Kingdom.

The following points were made in discussion:—

(a) From the naval point of view it was important that the Base at Simonstown should be available to us and should be effective. The use of Durban, which possessed the largest dry dock in the area, and of Capetown were equally desirable. Our object should therefore be to ensure that the Union of South Africa did not remain neutral in a war in which the United Kingdom was involved, since the neutrality of South

Africa would affect the provision of facilities, not only in Simonstown, but in Capetown and Durban also.

(b) If possible, the assurance should make it clear that facilities at Simonstown would be granted to the United Kingdom and her Allies in any war. The Allies of the United Kingdom would, of course, be understood to include the other members of the British Commonwealth. If it was difficult for the Union of South Africa to agree to the grant of facilities to Allies, then we must still insist that they should be made available to the United Kingdom and to the other members of the British Commonwealth in war.

(c) Although Mr. Erasmus had appeared to be optimistic about being able to give the guarantee required when the negotiations were first opened, his position had subsequently hardened and there seemed little prospect of obtaining what we wanted from the present South African Government.

The Prime Minister said that the sense of the Committee was that we should insist upon the firm guarantee. He thought, however, that no reply should be made to Mr. Erasmus at the present time and that we should delay dealing with this problem as long as possible. On the other hand, it was important not to alienate the sympathy of the Union Government over the matter of the defence of the Middle East. There would be advantage in the United Kingdom High Commissioner in South Africa discovering privately what the attitude of the Opposition party in South Africa was likely to be towards this question.

The Committee:—

(1) Agreed that no reply should be made to the letter from Mr. Erasmus (Annex to D.O. (51) 100) for the time being.

(2) Invited the Secretary of State for Commonwealth Relations to ask the United Kingdom High Commissioner in South Africa to make the approach referred to by the Prime Minister above.

(3) Agreed to reconsider the question when the High Commissioner's views had been obtained.

444 CAB 129/47, CP(51)265 12 Oct 1951

'Closer association in Central Africa': joint Cabinet memorandum by Mr Griffiths and Mr Gordon Walker on the Victoria Falls Conference, Sept 1951

[This memorandum appropriately enough rounds off this collection. It was the last CO/CRO memo issued by Attlee's government before the election of 25 October. The last Labour Cabinet meeting was on 27 Sept 1951, so this paper was not discussed by ministers. It was called for by Attlee to leave behind 'for the record'. The two secretaries of state were prepared to commend the federal scheme as it had emerged from the Victoria Falls Conference in September as in the best interests of all the inhabitants; but there was a very important proviso against any attempt to force the proposals through in the face of the existing strong African opposition.]

We circulate herewith for the information of our colleagues the final communiqué issued on 21 September by the Conference on the Closer Association of the Central African Territories which we attended at the Victoria Falls with representatives of the three territories. No immediate decisions are required on the conclusions of this conference; but early decisions will be needed after the General Election and we wish to place our views on record. Our main recommendations are that—

(1) as soon as possible after the General Election His Majesty's Government should publicly endorse the conclusions of the Victoria Falls Conference, including the proposal to resume the conference in London about the middle of 1952;
(2) at the same time His Majesty's Government should state publicly that it would favour in principle a scheme of federation between the three territories on the general lines recommended by the London Conference of officials, and considers that such a scheme is in the best interests of the Africans as well as of the other inhabitants of the territories; that it recognises that African opinion in the two northern territories has declared itself as opposed to those proposals; but that, in the light of the assurances agreed upon at the Victoria Falls Conference and of the economic and other advantages of closer association, it trusts that Africans will be prepared to give further and favourable consideration to the proposals; His Majesty's Government should also endorse the statement in paragraph 11 (i) of the Victoria Falls Conference communiqué that any consideration now or in the future of amalgamation of the three territories is excluded unless the majority of the inhabitants of all three territories desire it, and should make it clear that a similar principle would apply equally to amalgamation of two of the territories or any part thereof;
(3) we should regard the federation of the three Central African territories as an essential measure for preventing non-British influences from the Union of South Africa from encroaching on and eventually engulfing British Central Africa. In our public statement we should endorse the agreed declarations of the Victoria Falls Conference that the British connection and British traditions and principles in the Central African territories should be so strengthened as to ensure that they continue to prevail.

Background of our visit to Central Africa

2. In our memorandum of 3rd May[1] we submitted to our colleagues the report of the London Conference of officials, which recommended that closer association between the three territories ought to be brought about urgently and that this should be done not by amalgamation of the territories but on a federal basis. On 31st May[2] our colleagues approved our proposals that the report should be published and that His Majesty's Government, without being committed to acceptance of the proposals, should commend them in general terms for the careful consideration of all the peoples concerned as embodying a constructive approach. The report was duly published and a statement to this effect made on 13th June when our intention to visit the Central African territories during the summer recess was also announced. Since then public discussion of the proposals has been proceeding in the three territories.

Our visit to Central Africa

3. We duly visited Central Africa during August and September. The Secretary of

[1] See 435.

[2] See 436.

State for the Colonies left London on 24th August and spent eight days in Nyasaland and twelve days in Northern Rhodesia before proceeding to the Victoria Falls. In Nyasaland he held discussions with the Acting Governor and his Executive Council; with members of the Legislative Council, European, African and Indian; with representative European bodies, both commercial and agricultural; with certain missionaries; with representatives of the Indian and Coloured communities; with the three African Provincial Councils and the African Protectorate Council, which are the recognised bodies for the expression of African opinion; and with the Nyasaland African Congress, which corresponds to a political party. In Northern Rhodesia the Secretary of State for the Colonies held discussions with the Governor and his Executive Council; with the members of the Legislative Council, European and African; with representative European bodies, commercial, agricultural, municipal and trade union; with representatives of the Indian and Coloured communities; with the Barotse National Council, the African Provincial Councils in the five other provinces or representative members of them, and the African Representative Council; with the Northern Rhodesia African Congress (a body similar to the Nyasaland Congress); and with representatives of African urban councils, welfare societies and trade unions. The Secretary of State attended over eighty meetings during his tour and thus obtained a complete picture of public opinion on the proposals in Northern Rhodesia and Nyasaland.

4. The opinions which were expressed to him may be summarised as follows:—

(a) *European, Indian and Coloured opinion*

European opinion in Northern Rhodesia and Nyasaland is generally favourable to the proposals, subject to some minor reservations on points of detail. Europeans recognise the economic advantages of federation and the need to create a strong British *bloc* to resist pressure from the Union of South Africa and they believe that the proposals would safeguard their own future. The European leaders in Nyasaland, in view of African opposition to the proposals, expressed the hope that if the proposals were put into effect this might be done in such a way as to carry African opinion with them, indeed they would regard a measure of African support for the proposals as a necessary basis for their own agreement that the proposals should be carried into effect.

Indian and Coloured opinion is at present generally suspending judgment on the proposals. Indian and Coloured people recognise the economic advantages of the proposals but, before they make up their minds finally, wish to see how any detailed scheme would affect their own interests and future in Central Africa.

(b) *African opinion*

African opinion in Northern Rhodesia and Nyasaland, as expressed to the Secretary of State for the Colonies during his visit, was almost unanimously opposed to the proposals. This opposition has been organised by the two African Congresses, bodies which are mainly although not entirely composed of the comparatively small educated elements in the two territories. In Northern Rhodesia the Congress has been influenced and assisted by a local European resident known to be a Communist. In Nyasaland in particular the campaign has been much influenced and indeed largely directed from outside by Dr. Hastings Banda, a Nyasaland doctor in London,[3] who is rigidly opposed to federation and issued a pamphlet

[3] Subsequently life president of Malawi.

against it directed not against the report of the London Conference of officials but against the earlier proposals for federation produced in 1949 by the unofficial conference at the Victoria Falls; this pamphlet, although published after the London Conference, was written before it. The administrative staff in Northern Rhodesia and Nyasaland, although they have very fully explained the proposals to the African population over a period of weeks, have been bound, because His Majesty's Government is not yet committed to them, to refrain from any attempts at persuasion. This position has been scrupulously observed, with the result that the two Congresses have had the field open to them for three months. Although the organised campaign by the Congresses has powerfully influenced the course of events, it would be a grave mistake to regard the opposition as representing nothing more than the views of the educated minority. The chiefs and other Africans who have considered the matter also expressed themselves as opposed to the federal scheme, partly as a result of the organised campaign against it and of their dislike of change, but largely also because of their fear of Southern Rhodesia and in Northern Rhodesia of domination by the local Europeans. It must be admitted that at the time of our visit African opposition to the scheme was both general and deeply felt. This opposition ignores the advantages of federation, both economic and political, and, as some of the more intelligent Africans admitted, is based not on the proposals in the officials' report itself, but on their fear of what might follow if federation came into being. Africans are afraid that in that event their land would be taken away, that their political advancement would be endangered, that the Protectorate status of Northern Rhodesia and Nyasaland would be abolished and that federation would before long be changed into amalgamation; many of them also confuse the two terms since the same word covers both in a number of native languages. These fears are not justified by the terms of the officials' report, which contains full safeguards for African interests, specifically reserves land and political advancement, and indeed all other services closely affecting the lives of Africans, to the Northern Rhodesia and Nyasaland (and not the federal) Governments under the general supervision of His Majesty's Government as at present, and clearly lays down that the Protectorate status of the two northern territories would be preserved under the scheme; while no change in the federal scheme could be made except by His Majesty's Government with the consent of Parliament. Reassurances to this effect were given by the Secretary of State to the Protectorate Council in Nyasaland in a formal statement which was repeated at other meetings. But by the time of the visit African opinion had hardened and the African representatives at the Victoria Falls Conference were given a definite mandate to oppose federation. Indeed, it was only with great difficulty that the Africans in Nyasaland were persuaded to be represented at the Victoria Falls at all. In Northern Rhodesia there was a favourable development just before the conference; as a result of the patient arguments of Mr. John Moffatt, unofficial representative of African interests on the Executive and Legislative Councils, the African leaders authorised their representatives to inform the conference that, while the Northern Rhodesia Africans opposed federation, they would be willing to consider the question of federation again on the basis of the officials' report after the policy of partnership between Europeans and Africans in Northern Rhodesia itself had been defined and, as so defined, put into progressive operation. This very important statement means that Africans in Northern

Rhodesia are likely to be willing to consider the federation proposals more favourably if as a result of discussions to be held between their representatives and Europeans during the next few months they are satisfied that their own political future in Northern Rhodesia is secured. In Nyasaland also there are now signs of a more favourable development of opinion which is referred to in paragraph 14 below.

5. The Secretary of State for Commonwealth Relations arrived in Salisbury on 10th September. During the next few days he had talks with the Cabinet, with Opposition Leaders, and with a number of representative people. The Southern Rhodesia Government had arranged for him to have meetings at Salisbury and at Bulawayo with representative Africans, urban and rural. Some of the Africans were in favour of federation, but the preponderant opinion was against it for a variety of reasons, of which some were mutually inconsistent. The Southern Rhodesia Government appeared to be prepared to come out in favour of federation, though there were certain specific points (see paragraph 16 below) on which they expressed themselves as dissatisfied. European opinion generally seemed to be in favour of closer association, with a tendency in some cases to prefer the complete amalgamation of the Territories rather than federation. As the result of the discussions with the Commonwealth Secretary, it was hoped that the Southern Rhodesian representatives at the Conference would observe care in putting forward their suggestions for varying the London proposals and would do their best to avoid a breakdown of the Conference.

The Victoria Falls Conference

6. It was made clear in the statement to Parliament on 13th June that the Victoria Falls Conference was not expected to reach decisions binding on Governments, but was regarded as a further stage in our consultation with local opinion. As a result of the differing views expressed to us in the three territories, it became evident before the Conference that we could not hope to reach agreed conclusions on the substance of the officials' report. We therefore decided to aim at preventing a breakdown of the consideration of the proposals and at securing that there should be an adjourned conference next year in London where Africans had made it plain that they would always be glad to attend discussions. We also decided to aim at securing general agreement as to the economic advantages of closer association between the three territories and at persuading the Southern Rhodesia delegation to join with us in assurances which would make it easier to carry the discussions further with Africans after the conference. All these objectives were achieved.

7. The conference was not easy to handle. The Southern Rhodesia delegation consisted not only of Sir Godfrey Huggins and three of his Ministers, but also of the leaders of the Opposition parties; they were therefore a somewhat rigid body. They were anxious to secure some tangible results at the conference which they could present to their public opinion, hesitant as much of it is, about the advantages of federation. They were irritated that African opposition to the principle of federation, based on grounds which they did not regard as reasonable, prevented the discussion at the conference of the specific recommendations in the officials' report. It was only with some difficulty and with the support of the Governors of Northern Rhodesia and Nyasaland, of Mr. Welensky and Mr. Moffatt, that we were able to keep the conference

on an even keel and to bring it safely into port with satisfactory conclusions. The communiqué which was eventually agreed to was based on our own draft with minor amendments by the Central African delegations.

8. The main points in the communiqué are:—

(a) There was unanimous agreement that the conference should be adjourned until next year when it would meet in London; it was also agreed that in the interval there should be discussions within each territory and exchanges of views between the four Governments.

(b) Certain assurances to African opinion were unanimously accepted and it was agreed that, if any form of closer association is eventually decided upon, all these should be enshrined as an integral part of the constitution. The most important of these assurances is that the Protectorate status of Northern Rhodesia and Nyasaland should be preserved under any federal scheme and that any consideration now or in the future of amalgamation of the three territories is excluded unless a majority of the inhabitants of all three territories desired it. This represents a very substantial concession by Sir Godfrey Huggins and his colleagues and means that federation cannot lead on to amalgamation unless a majority of the Africans accept amalgamation at some stage in the future. An absolutely watertight answer to what is undoubtedly the main objection of the Africans to the scheme is thus provided. An assurance was also agreed to that the political advancement of the peoples of Northern Rhodesia and Nyasaland must remain the responsibility of the Northern Rhodesia and Nyasaland Governments (subject to the ultimate authority of His Majesty's Government) and not of any federal authority; this provides the answer to the African fear of interference by a federal authority in their own internal political advancement. Finally it was agreed that land and land settlement questions in Northern Rhodesia and Nyasaland should remain the responsibility of the Northern Rhodesia and Nyasaland Governments and not of any federal authority.

(c) There was unanimous agreement that the policy of economic and political partnership between Europeans and Africans was the only policy under which federation could be brought about; on the need for countering the dangers which would flow from any weakening of the British connection in the three territories; and on the advantages of closer association for the common handling of problems transcending territorial problems such as communications, research, defence, higher education and the planning of economic development.

(d) We joined with the conference in declaring ourselves favourable to the principle of federation; the African representatives naturally abstained from this declaration. The conference as a whole recognised that African apprehensions are one of the main obstacles to the general acceptance of federation. The Northern Rhodesia Africans, in accordance with the decision referred to in paragraph 4 above, recorded their agreement to consider the question of federation again on the basis of the report of the London Conference after the policy of partnership in Northern Rhodesia had been defined and, as so defined, put into progressive operation.

9. The concrete conclusions of the conference were themselves of considerable importance and will in our view materially contribute to the solution of the problem. The conference had an equally important intangible value as the first occasion on

which Europeans of all three Central African territories have sat down with African representatives to discuss the relations between the three territories. The African members of the conference, particularly those from Nyasaland, were generally recognised to have made an important contribution to it. All the Africans expressed their deep gratitude for the arrangements made for them at the conference and the Nyasaland Africans, who had with so much difficulty been persuaded to come, volunteered at the end to other members of their delegations that it had been well worth while. The African representatives were certainly impressed by the attention paid to their views and they cannot have failed to be impressed also by the extent to which the African attitude to the scheme dominated the discussions and the differing views expressed on this subject by the various European representatives. It is significant that Sir Godfrey Huggins had already informed us before the conference, and repeated at it, that if Africans from the two northern territories were to sit on a federal Legislature Africans from Southern Rhodesia would have to sit there also. We can regard the conference as an important precedent for the inter-racial discussion of major problems in Central Africa.

Our conclusions and recommendations

10. So far His Majesty's Government has not declared its attitude towards the proposals in the officials' report, but if the discussion in Central Africa of those proposals is to go forward it will be necessary for an early statement of the views of His Majesty's Government to be made. We believe, for reasons given in the following paragraphs, that this statement should be favourable to federation.

11. From the economic point of view we believe that there is an unanswerable case for federation. The economies of the Central African territories are linked by a common port at Beira for all three of them, a common railway system for the two Rhodesias, the dependence on coal from Southern Rhodesia of the copper mining industry which is the life-blood of Northern Rhodesia, the prosperity which copper mining in Northern Rhodesia brings to a number of industries in Southern Rhodesia, the dependence of the two Rhodesias on manpower from Nyasaland, the many commercial connections between the three territories and, last but not least, the Zambesi and Shire River basin with its great potentialities for the development of hydro-electric power and irrigation facilities if handled on a Central African basis. The population of the three territories will double itself within twenty-five years so that a vast effort in economic development will be needed if food supplies are to be adequate and living standards are to be progressively improved. For this purpose economic planning on a Central African basis is needed so that the resources of the whole region may best be devoted to economic advancement. There must be effective machinery for settling priorities in transport, supplies of coal, &c., between the competing claims of the three territories. Industrial development must proceed on a Central African basis if adequate markets are to be available as a basis for new industries and the more backward areas are to secure the advantages of this form of development. The present units of government are too small to sustain the vast expenditure needed for hydro-electric development and large-scale water control schemes and difficulties are already appearing between the two Rhodesias in connection with the plans for the harnessing of the Zambesi and its tributaries. With its enormous potentialities the Zambesi should be the centre of economic activity rather than a frontier. It may be argued that theoretically all these matters could be

handled by co-operation between the three existing Governments. Experience over the past few years has shown that this not so and the only effective method of handling them is by a single federal authority answerable to a single Central African Legislature. There can be no doubt, moreover, that in external economic relations Central Africa operating as a single economic unit would be more effective than the three territories operating separately, while from the long-term point of view a Central African federal state with a more broadly based economy would be in a stronger position to face a world recession than the three territories individually.

12. Important as the economic arguments in favour of federation are, we are convinced on the basis of our recent experience in Central Africa that the political arguments are still stronger. We referred in our memorandum of 3rd May to the urgent need to counter South African pressure on Central Africa. Immigration from the Union into the two Rhodesias is almost double that from the United Kingdom. Not all of this is Afrikaner immigration, but we have definite evidence that Afrikaner immigration is being officially inspired, while, as a sign of the political interest being taken by the Nationalist Party in Central Africa, a census of all South Africans in the Rhodesias and their political sympathies is now being conducted through the Dutch Reformed Church. In Southern Rhodesia a new party has just been formed under the title of the Democratic Party; it is directed by a Mr. Cloete, who receives his salary from South Africa and described himself to *The Times* correspondent as an Afrikaner extremist. In Northern Rhodesia the position is still more serious in view of the comparative smallness of the European community and the dependence of the mining industry on white South African labour and owing to the difficulty of getting suitable people from this country. It is thought probable that at the next General Election in 1953 the Afrikaners will obtain five of the ten European seats on the Northern Rhodesian Legislative Council if the present electoral arrangements remain unchanged. There is a general fear among Europeans of British stock that the Afrikaners will gradually prevail, but the British element among the unofficial European community has so far shown little willingness to take active steps against this menace. The leading Southern Rhodesian Ministers are gravely apprehensive that the Afrikaners will succeed in dominating Northern Rhodesia and will then turn back on them. In Nyasaland there are so far few Afrikaners and the danger is less immediate; but if the two Rhodesias were absorbed or dominated by the Union Nyasaland could hardly stand out against such encroachment.

13. Southern Rhodesia has tightened up its immigration control law and made two years' residence and Southern Rhodesia citizenship a necessary qualification for the vote. The Northern Rhodesia Government is hoping to introduce similar legislation before the end of this year and the Colonial Secretary took the opportunity of emphasising the urgency of this to the Governor and leading unofficials. But the geographical and economic circumstances of the two Rhodesias make it impossible to keep out Afrikaners entirely and in any case immigration control and tighter conditions for the franchise, important though they are, are not sufficient by themselves to resist encroachment by the Union. We are faced in Central Africa with pressure by a country far stronger economically and industrially than any of the Central African territories, led by a militant Nationalist party with expansionist aims, anxious to strengthen its influence in the north. This pressure can be countered only by an equally firm policy of resistance to it both in the political and economic spheres—a policy which must have the support both of the European

and African populations of the Central African territories, and which in our view has little chance of succeeding unless we can establish a British *bloc* of territories in Central Africa knit together by constitutional ties. To secure our objective we must establish conditions in Central Africa under which the British element in the European population will remain not only substantially greater in numbers than the Afrikaners but able and willing to assert their loyalty to the British connection, and at the same time conditions in which the relations between Europeans and Africans will be progressively improved and the share of the Africans in the political and economic life of the territories will be progressively increased under the policy of partnership. In our view the proposals for federation are well designed to achieve these conditions. Political development for Africans in the two northern territories is secured under the scheme to their territorial Governments and His Majesty's Government. The Victoria Falls Conference has accepted the principle of partnership as an essential condition for federation; the federal legislature would contain African representatives from all three territories; and the federal constitution would have full safeguards for African interests. The prevention of excessive Afrikaner immigration could be far more effectively secured on a Central African basis than by the three territories acting separately. The creation of a Central African federal state would greatly strengthen the confidence in themselves of the British elements in all three territories and their willingness to resist Afrikaner encroachment and by increasing the political and economic strength of Central Africa as a whole and reducing friction between its component parts would provide a much firmer foundation on which that resistance could be based. On the other hand, if owing to African opposition federation had to be abandoned, relations between Europeans and Africans in the two Rhodesias would be seriously damaged and particularly in Northern Rhodesia a political vacuum would be created which would open the way for Afrikaner infiltration on a still more powerful scale. Signs are not lacking that the South African Government, although openly its attitude is correct, is anxiously hoping that the federation proposal will come to nothing.

14. We cannot too strongly emphasise the danger to British and African interests at present assailing the Central African territories. In our view we cannot continue to adopt a negative attitude towards this danger. It is incumbent on us to take positive steps to resist it. The establishment of a federal state in Central Africa is by far the most effective step that could be taken and this, combined with the economic advantages, convinces us that positive support for federation should be given by His Majesty's Government. The Afrikaner pressure, moreover, makes early action urgent; but we should be strongly opposed to any attempt to force the federation proposals through in the face of the present solid African opposition. Fortunately the Victoria Falls Conference conclusions, with the adjournment of the conference until the middle of next year, give time for further discussions with Africans in Northern Rhodesia and Nyasaland. The African leaders in Northern Rhodesia have already indicated that they will be prepared to consider the proposals again provided that their own political future inside Northern Rhodesia is secured and discussions to this end between Europeans and Africans are shortly to begin. The African members of the Nyasaland delegation at the Conference revised their views materially after hearing the discussions although their mandate prevented them from saying so publicly and since the Conference, they have already succeeded in persuading one of the three Provincial Councils in Nyasaland to give further consideration to the

scheme. The Governor of Nyasaland considers that, provided that His Majesty's Government will publicly state its general support of the federal scheme there is a distinct chance, given a period of from six to nine months, of persuading Africans to take a less negative line. Both he and the Governor of Northern Rhodesia[4] are convinced that if further progress is to [be] made a favourable statement by His Majesty's Government is an essential prerequisite to it. If therefore our opinion of the advantages of federation is accepted it is clearly important that an early opportunity of announcing this should be taken by His Majesty's Government.

15. We accordingly recommend that, at as early a date as possible after the General Election, the following action should be taken:—

(1) His Majesty's Government should publicly endorse the conclusions of the Victoria Falls Conference, including the proposal to hold a further representative conference in London about the middle of next year.

(2) His Majesty's Government should at the same time state publicly that it would favour in principle a scheme of federation between the three territories on the general lines recommended by the London Conference of officials and considers that such a scheme would be in the best interests of the Africans as well as of the other inhabitants of the territories; that it recognises that African opinion in the two northern territories has declared itself as opposed to those proposals; but that, in the light of the assurances agreed upon at the Victoria Falls Conference and of the economic and other advantages of closer association, it trusts that Africans will be prepared to give further and favourable consideration to the proposals. His Majesty's Government should also endorse the statement in paragraph 11 (i) of the Victoria Falls Conference communiqué that any consideration now or in the future of amalgamation of the three territories is excluded unless the majority of the inhabitants of all three territories desire it, and should make it clear that a similar principle would apply equally to amalgamation of two of the territories or any part thereof.

(3) The Governors of Northern Rhodesia and Nyasaland should be authorised to arrange further discussions on the proposals with Africans in the two territories on the basis,of His Majesty's Government's statement that they favour the scheme in principle and in the light of the assurances agreed to at the Victoria Falls Conference.

(4) The discussions envisaged in paragraph 5 of the final communiqué of the Victoria Falls Conference between His Majesty's Government and the three Central African Governments, or between the three Central African Governments themselves, should be undertaken in due course with the object of elucidating points of detail in the officials' report in preparation for the London Conference.

(5) We should regard the federation of the three Central African territories as an essential measure for preventing non-British influences from the Union of South Africa from encroaching on and eventually engulfing British Central Africa. In the public statement referred to above we should endorse the agreed statement of the Victoria Falls Conference that the British connection and British traditions and principles in the Central African territories should be so strengthened as to ensure that they continue to prevail.

[4] Sir Geoffrey Colby, gov of Nyasaland, 1948–1956; Sir Gilbert Rennie, gov of N Rhodesia, 1948–1954.

16. No detailed examination of the proposals in the officials' report is needed at this stage, but there are certain important points on which we wish to record our views. The final communiqué of the Victoria Falls Conference records that there are certain proposals in the officials' report relating to the federal Legislature with which the Southern Rhodesian Government do not agree; these are known to concern the number of nominated members proposed for the Legislature, the African Affairs Board and the Minister for African Interests. Our views on these points are as follows:—

(a) The Southern Rhodesia difficulties about the nominated members in the Legislature can to some extent at any rate be met. The officials' report (paragraph 90 and Annex VII) proposes that the federal Legislature should consist of seventeen members from Southern Rhodesia, eleven from Northern Rhodesia and seven from Nyasaland, three of whom from each territory would represent African interests. Of the twenty-six general members the fourteen from Southern Rhodesia and the eight from Northern Rhodesia would be elected, while the four from Nyasaland would be nominated by the Governor from a panel selected by the Convention of Associations (the body officially representing Europeans in the territory). The Southern Rhodesia Government take the view that on the basis of twenty-two elected members it would be difficult to operate a party system effectively. In our view we can meet them over this by arranging for the four Nyasaland representatives to be elected, either directly or indirectly. Of the African representatives those who are actually Africans could also be elected indirectly, leaving only three European representatives of African interests to be nominated.

(b) It is possible that Southern Rhodesia will suggest a bicameral legislature with a Senate consisting partly of members representing African interests as a substitute for the African Affairs Board proposed by the officials. Our view (which was made clear to the Southern Rhodesian Cabinet by the Commonwealth Secretary) is that any such suggestion should be opposed, first because a second chamber would make the constitution cumbersome, and secondly because we do not believe that a second chamber, however composed, could be as effective as a safeguard for African interests as the African Affairs Board proposed in the report. Powers of delaying legislation would not be sufficient, while it would be hard to secure a second chamber with an absolute veto.

(c) The Southern Rhodesia Government is likely to suggest that the Minister for African Interests should be appointed in the ordinary way on the recommendation of the Prime Minister rather than by the Governor-General subject to the approval of His Majesty's Government. We think that such a proposal should be rejected, since a Minister responsible to the Prime Minister rather than to the Governor-General and His Majesty's Government could not effectively exercise the safeguarding powers proposed for the Minister for African Interests in the report, which are the lynch-pin of the proposed federal safeguards. Such a change would moreover be strongly objected to by African opinion and would make it more difficult to convince Africans in the northern territories that the scheme does not prejudice their interests. The Commonwealth Secretary sought to persuade the Southern Rhodesian Government that, with good will on both sides, the appointment of the Minister of [sic] African Interests need cause no constitutional difficulties. They could be assured that His Majesty's Government would for its part work the system reasonably.

17. It will also be open to His Majesty's Government at the conference in London next year, and indeed to the African representatives at that conference, to put forward any amendment of detail to the proposals which may appear necessary from the African point of view since, owing to African opposition to the principle of federation, there was no opportunity at the Victoria Falls Conference of obtaining the views of Africans on the details of the scheme. The way for this is kept open by the statement in paragraph 14 of the Victoria Falls Conference communiqué.

Biographical Notes: parts I–IV

Addison, 1st Viscount of Stallingborough cr 1945 (Christopher Addison) 1869–1951
MP (Lib) 1910–1922, (Lab) 1929–1931 and 1934–1935; S of S for dominion affairs, 1945–1947 (for Commonwealth relations, 1947); lord privy seal, 1947–1951; lord president of Council, 1951

Alexander, 1st Viscount of Hillsborough cr 1950 (Albert Victor Alexander) 1885–1965
MP (Co-op) 1922–1931 and 1935–1950; first lord of Admiralty, 1940–1945, 1945–1946; member of Cabinet mission to India, 1946; minister of defence, 1946–1950

Arden-Clarke, Charles Noble, 1898–1962
Kt 1946; CAS from 1920; administrative officer, Northern Nigeria, 1920–1933; acting principal assistant secretary, Nigerian secretariat, 1934–1936; assistant resident commissioner and government secretary, Bechuanaland Protectorate, 1936, and resident commissioner, 1937–1942; resident commissioner, Basutoland, 1942–1946; gov and C-in-C, Sarawak, 1946–1949, Gold Coast, 1949–1957; first gov-gen and C-in-C, Ghana, Mar–July 1957; member of Monckton Commission on Central Africa, 1960

Attlee, Clement Richard (1st Earl cr 1955) 1883–1967
MP (Lab) from 1922; member of Indian Statutory Commission, 1927; leader of Labour Party in House of Commons from 1935; S of S for dominion affairs, 1942–1943; lord president of the Council, 1943–1945; deputy prime minister, 1942–1945; prime minister 1945–1951 (+ minister of defence to 1946); leader of the Opposition, 1951–1955

Baring, Evelyn (1st Baron Howick of Glendale cr 1960) 1903–1973
KCMG 1942; ICS 1926–1934; gov of Southern Rhodesia, 1942–1944; UK high commissioner in Union of South Africa and high commissioner for Basutoland, Bechuanaland Protectorate and Swaziland, 1944–1951; gov and C-in-C, Kenya, also chairman of East Africa High Commission, 1952–1959

Baxter, George Herbert, 1894–1962
India Office from 1920; assistant under-secretary of state for India, 1943–1947 and for Commonwealth relations, 1947–1955; chairman, Conference on closer association in Central Africa, Mar 1951; visited Central Africa for Victoria Falls Conference, Sept 1951

Bennett, John Sloman, 1914–1990
Royal Liberty School, Romford and Magdalene, Cambridge; CO from 1936; seconded to office of minister of state in Middle East, 1941–1945; CO assistant secretary from 1946 (International Relations Dept, 1946–1947, Mediterranean Dept, 1947–1952); seconded to Imperial Defence College, 1953; returned to CO in 1954 and continued in service with Commonwealth Office, subsequently FCO, after merger with CO in 1966, where he remained in charge of Gibraltar and South Atlantic Dept until 1971

Bevin, Ernest, 1881–1951
General secretary, Transport and General Workers Union, 1921–1940; member, General Council of TUC, 1925–1940; MP (Labour) 1940–1951; minister of labour and national service, 1940–1945; S of S for foreign affairs, 1945–1951; lord privy seal, Mar–Apr 1951

Bourdillon, Henry Townsend, b 1913
Son of Bernard Bourdillon (gov of Nigeria, 1935–1942); Rugby and Corpus Christi, Oxford; CO from 1937; seconded to FO (1942), Cabinet Office (1943) and Ministry

of Production (1944); CO assistant secretary from 1947; assistant under-secretary of state, 1954–1959; deputy UK commissioner for Singapore, 1959–1961

Brook, Sir Norman Craven (1st Baron Normanbrook cr 1963) 1902–1967
KCB 1946; Home Office 1925–1940; personal assistant to lord president of the Council, 1940–1942; deputy secretary (civil) to War Cabinet, 1942; permanent secretary, Ministry of Reconstruction, 1943–1945; additional secretary to the Cabinet, 1945–1946; secretary to the Cabinet, 1947–1962; joint secretary of the Treasury and head of the Home Civil Service, 1956–1962

Caine, Sydney, 1902–1991
KCMG 1947; Harrow County School and London School of Economics; CO from 1926 (from Inland Revenue); secretary, West Indies Sugar Commission, 1929; financial secretary, Hong Kong, 1937; CO assistant secretary from 1940; member, Anglo-American Caribbean Commission, 1942; financial adviser to S of S for colonies, 1942; CO assistant under-secretary of state from 1944; joint deputy under-secretary of state, 1947–1948; 3rd secretary, Treasury, 1948

Cartland, George Barrington, b 1912
Kt 1963; Manchester Central High School, Manchester University and Hertford, Oxford; Colonial Service, Gold Coast, from 1935; district commissioner 1943; seconded to CO 1944–1949 as head of African Studies Branch; editor, *Journal of African Administration*, 1945–1949; secretary, London African Conference, 1948; served in Uganda, 1949–1962 (chief secretary, 1960; deputy gov, 1961)

Clauson, Gerard Leslie Makins, 1891–1974
KCMG 1945; Eton and Corpus Christi, Oxford; oriental scholar; CO from 1919 (from Inland Revenue and army); assistant secretary, 1934; assistant under-secretary of state, 1940–1951; chairman, International Wheat Conference, 1947, and International Rubber Conference, 1951; retired, 1951; chairman, Pirelli Ltd, 1960–1969

Cohen, Andrew Benjamin, 1909–1968
KCMG 1952; Malvern and Trinity, Cambridge; CO from 1933 (from Inland Revenue); served in Malta, 1940–1943; CO assistant secretary (East and Central African Dept) from 1943; assistant under-secretary of state (Africa Dept), 1947–1951; Gov of Uganda, 1952–1957; permanent UK representative, UN Trusteeship Council, 1957–1961

Creech Jones, Arthur, 1891–1964
MP (Lab) 1935–1950; executive member, Fabian Society; member, CO Education Advisory Committee, 1936–1945; chairman, Fabian Colonial Bureau and Labour Party Imperial Advisory Committee; vice-chairman, Higher Education Commission to West Africa, 1943–1944; parliamentary under-secretary of state for colonies, 1945–1946; S of S for colonies, 1946–1950

Cripps, (Richard) Stafford, 1889–1952
Kt 1930; MP (Lab) 1931–1950; lord privy seal and leader of House of Commons, 1942; minister of aircraft production, 1942–1945; president of Board of Trade, 1945–1947; minister for economic affairs, 1947; chancellor of Exchequer, 1947–1950

Dawe, Arthur James, 1891–1950
KCMG 1942; Berkhampsted and Brasenose, Oxford; CO from 1918; secretary, Malta Royal Commission (1931) and mission to Malta, 1933–1934; assistant secretary, 1936; assistant under-secretary of state, 1938; deputy under-secretary of state, 1945–1947

Fisher, Mary Letitia Somerville, b 1913
Daughter of H A L Fisher; Oxford High School and Somerville, Oxford; BBC, 1941–1945; CO principal, 1945–1956; married J S Bennett (qv) 1955; principal of St Hilda's College, Oxford, 1965–1980

Franks, Oliver Shewell (Baron of Headington, life peer, cr 1962) b 1905
KCB 1946; academic career to 1939 when temporary civil servant, Ministry of Supply; permanent secretary, Ministry of Supply, 1945–1946; provost, Queen's College, Oxford, 1946–1948; British ambassador at Washington, 1948–1952; chairman,

Lloyds Bank Ltd, 1954–1962; provost of Worcester College, Oxford, 1962–1976; served on various government committees including chairmanship of Falkland Islands Review, 1982–1983

Galsworthy, Arthur Norman, 1916–1986
Emanuel School and Corpus Christi, Cambridge; CO from 1938; assistant secretary from 1947; assistant under-secretary of state, 1956–1965; deputy under-secretary of state, 1965

Gater, George Henry, 1886–1963
Kt 1936; Winchester and New College, Oxford; local government from 1912; CO permanent under-secretary of state, 1939–1947 (seconded to Ministry of Home Security and Ministry of Supply, 1940–1942)

Gordon Walker, Patrick Chrestien (Baron, life peer, c 1974) 1907–1980
MP (Lab) from 1945; parliamentary under-secretary of state for Commonwealth relations, 1947–1950; S of S for Commonwealth relations, 1950–1951

Gorell Barnes, William Lethbridge, 1909–1987
KCMG 1961; Marlborough and Pembroke, Cambridge; served in HM Diplomatic Service (1932–1939) and offices of War Cabinet (1939–1945); assistant secretary, Treasury, 1945–1946; personal assistant to prime minister, 1946–1948; seconded to CO as assistant under-secretary of state, 1948–1959; joint deputy under-secretary of state, 1959–1963

Grantham, Alexander William George Herder, 1899–1978
KCMG 1945; called to the Bar, 1934; chief secretary, Nigeria, 1941–1944; gov of Fiji and high commissioner for Western Pacific, 1945–1947; gov of Hong Kong, 1947–1957

Griffiths, James, 1890–1975
MP (Lab) from 1936; minister of national insurance, 1945–1950; S of S for colonies, 1950–1951

Hall, 1st Viscount cr 1946 (George Henry Hall) 1881–1965
MP (Lab) from 1922; parliamentary under-secretary of state for colonies, 1940–1942; financial secretary to Admiralty, 1942–1943; parliamentary under-secretary of state for foreign affairs, 1943–1945; S of S for colonies, 1945–1946; first lord of Admiralty, 1946–1951

Jeffries, Charles Joseph, 1896–1972
KCMG 1943; Malvern and Magdalen, Oxford; CO from 1917; assistant under-secretary of state from 1939; joint deputy under-secretary of state, 1947–1956

Jones, Arthur Creech, *see* **Creech Jones, Arthur**

Liesching, Percival, 1895–1973
KCMG 1944; Bedford and Brasenose, Oxford; CO from 1920; transferred to DO 1925; seconded to Board of Trade (1942) and Ministry of Food (1946); CRO permanent under-secretary of state, 1949–1955; UK high commissioner in Union of South Africa and high commissioner for Basutoland, Bechuanaland Protectorate and Swaziland, 1955–1958

Listowel, 5th Earl of (William Francis Hare) b 1906
Parliamentary under-secretary of state for India and Burma, 1944–1945; postmaster-general, 1945–1947; S of S for India (Apr–Aug 1947) and for Burma (Apr 1947–Jan 1948); minister of state for colonial affairs, 1948–1950

Lloyd, Thomas Ingram Kynaston, 1896–1968
KCMG 1947; Rossall, Gonville and Caius, Cambridge; CO from 1921 (from Ministry of Health); secretary, Palestine Commission, 1929–1930; secretary, West Indies Royal Commission, 1938–1939; CO assistant secretary from 1939; assistant under-secretary of state from 1943; permanent under-secretary of state, 1947–1956

MacDonald, Malcolm John, 1901–1981
Son of J Ramsay MacDonald; MP (Lab) 1929–1931, (Nat Lab) 1931–1935, (Nat Govt) 1936–1945; parliamentary under-secretary of state for dominion affairs, 1931–1935; S of S for dominion affairs, 1935–1938 and 1938–1939; S of S for colonies, 1935 and 1938–1940; minister of health, 1940–1941; UK high commission-

er in Canada, 1941–1946; gov-gen, British territories in South-East Asia, 1946–1948; commissioner-general in South-East Asia, 1948–1955; subsequently gov/gov-gen/UK high commissioner, Kenya, 1963–1965

McNeil, Hector, 1907–1955
MP (Lab) Burgh of Greenock from 1941; parliamentary under-secretary of state, FO, 1945–1946; minister of state, FO, 1946–1950; S of S Scotland, 1950–1951; vice-president, UN Assembly, 1947; leader of delegation to Economic Commission for Europe, 1948

Macpherson, John Stuart, 1898–1971
KCMG 1945; Malayan civil service, 1921–1937; seconded to CO, 1933–1935; served in Nigeria, 1937–1939; chief secretary, Palestine, 1939–1943; member, Anglo-American Caribbean Commission, 1943–1945; comptroller for development and welfare in West Indies and British co-chairman, Caribbean Commission, 1945–1948; gov of Nigeria, 1948–1954; gov-gen, Federation of Nigeria, 1954–1955; permanent under-secretary of state, 1956–1959

Makins, Roger Mellor (1st Baron Sherfield cr 1964), b 1904
KCMG 1949; FO from 1928; assistant under-secretary of state, 1947; deputy under-secretary of state, 1948–1952

Marquand, Hilary Adair, 1901–1972
Prof of industrial relations, Cardiff University College, 1930–1945; MP (Lab) East Cardiff, 1945–1950, Middlesbrough East, 1950–1961; secretary for overseas trade, 1945–1947; paymaster-general, 1947–1948; minister of pensions, 1948–1951; minister of health, Jan–Oct 1951

Martin, John Miller, 1904–1991
KCMG 1952; Edinburgh Academy and Corpus Christi, Oxford; DO from 1927; seconded to Malayan civil service, 1931–1934; secretary, Palestine Royal Commission, 1936–1937; private secretary to prime minister, 1940–1945 (principal private secretary, 1941–1945); CO assistant under-secretary of state, 1945–1956; deputy under-secretary of state, 1956–1965; UK high commissioner, Malta, 1965–1967

Mitchell, Philip Euen, 1890–1964
KCMG 1937; served in Nyasaland, 1912–1919 and Tanganyika, 1919–1935 (chief secretary, 1934–1935); gov of Uganda, 1935–1940; deputy chairman, Conference of East African Governors, 1940; political adviser (on conquered Italian territories in Africa) to Field-Marshal Wavell, 1941; British plenipotentiary in Ethiopia and chief political officer to GOC-in-C, East Africa, 1942; gov of Fiji and high commissioner for Western Pacific, 1942–1944; gov of Kenya, 1944–1952

Morrison, Herbert Stanley (Baron Morrison of Lambeth, life peer, cr 1959) 1888–1965
MP (Lab) from 1923; home secretary and minister of home security, 1940–1945; deputy prime minister, lord president of the Council and leader of House of Commons, 1945–1951; S of S for foreign affairs, Mar–Oct 1951

Noel-Baker, Philip James (Baron, life peer cr 1977) 1889–1982
MP (Lab) 1929–1931 and from 1936; minister of state, FO, 1945–1946; S of S for air, 1946–1947; S of S for Commonwealth relations, 1947–1950; minister of fuel and power, 1950–1951; Nobel Peace Prize, 1959

Ogmore, 1st Baron cr 1950 (David Rees Rees-Williams) 1903–1976
MP (Lab) 1945–1950; chairman, Burma Frontier Areas Committee of Inquiry, 1947; parliamentary under-secretary of state, CO, 1947–1950; parliamentary under-secretary of state, CRO, 1950–1951; minister of civil aviation, June–Oct 1951

Poynton, (Arthur) Hilton, b 1905
KCMG 1949; Marlborough and Brasenose, Oxford; CO from 1929; seconded as private secretary to minister of supply and minister of production, 1941–1943; CO assistant secretary, 1943–1946; assistant under-secretary of state, 1946–1948; joint deputy under-secretary of state, 1948–1959; permanent under-secretary of state, 1959–1966

Rees-Williams, D R: *see* Ogmore, 1st Baron

Robinson, Kenneth Ernest, b 1914
Monoux School Walthamstow and Hert-

ford, Oxford; CO 1936–1948; assistant secretary, 1946–1948 (West African Dept, 1946–1947, Economic Intelligence and Planning Dept, 1947–1948); reader in Commonwealth government, Oxford, 1948–1957; professor of Commonwealth affairs, University of London, 1957–1965; vice-chancellor, University of Hong Kong, 1965–1972

Sargent, Orme [Garton], 1884–1962
KCMG 1937; FO from 1906; permanent under-secretary of state, 1946–1949

Strachey, (Evelyn) John (St Loe), 1901–1963
MP (Lab) 1929–1931 and from 1945; parliamentary under-secretary of state for air, 1945–1946; minister of food, 1946–1950; S of S for war, 1950–1951

Strang, William (1st Baron of Stonesfield cr 1954) 1893–1978
KCMG 1943; HM Diplomatic Service from 1919; transferred to FO as assistant under-secretary of state, 1939–1943; permanent under-secretary of state, 1949–1953

Thomas, Ivor Bulmer, b 1905 (Ivor Bulmer-Thomas, 1952)
MP (Lab) 1942–1948, (Con) 1949–1950; parliamentary under-secretary of state for colonies, 1946–1947; first UK member, UN Trusteeship Council, 1947; acting deputy editor *Daily Telegraph*, 1953–1956

Williams, John Basil, (1906–1953)
Marlborough, McGill University, and Trinity, Cambridge; CO from 1930; assistant secretary from 1943; assistant under-secretary of state, 1949–1953

Wright, Andrew Barkworth, 1895–1971
KCMG 1948; Civil administration, Cyprus, from 1922 (colonial secretary, 1937); colonial secretary, Trinidad, 1943–1946; gov and C-in-C, the Gambia, 1946–1949; gov and C-in-C, Cyprus, 1949–1954

Bibliography 1: Public Record Office sources searched

Unless otherwise indicated, runs of files listed below cover approximately the period of the Labour government from 1945 to 1951, but the organisation of the archives does not permit references to be made exactly congruent with changes of government. Nor can it be assumed that all files in the runs are actually available.

1. *Cabinet*

(i) *Cabinet committees*

Ad hoc Committees: Gen and Misc series: CAB 130/20, 31, & 45
Defence Committee: CAB 131/1–11
General series from 1945:
Africa Committee: CAB 134/1–5 (1949 only)
Colonial Affairs Committee: CAB 134/52 (1945–1947)
Colonial Development Committee: CAB 134/64–67 (from 1948)
Commonwealth Affairs Committee: CAB 134/54–56 (1947–1950)
Commonwealth Relations Committee: CAB 134/117–119 (1947–1949)
Economic Policy Committee: CAB 134/215–230 (from 1947)
Malaya Committee: CAB 134/497 (1950–1951)
Overseas Reconstruction Committee: CAB 134/594–601 (to 1950)

(ii) *Cabinet Office*

Cabinet conclusions (minutes) from 1945: CAB 128/1–20
Cabinet memoranda from 1945: CAB 129/1–47
Cabinet Office registered files:
[Committees & conferences]: CAB 21/1848, 1976–1978, 1982–1984, 2879, 2888, 2915–2916
Prime minister's minutes: CAB 21/2277–2281B

(iii) *Other papers*

Lord president of the Council's secretariat: CAB 124/122–124, 1007–1020, 1078–1099
Private collections: ministers & officials: CAB 127/91, 94 & 344
Various ministers' files: CAB 118/29 (colonial affairs: constitutions of various colonies, 1945–1947) [Lord Privy Seal's Office]

2. *Chiefs of Staff Committee*

(i) *COS records, 1945–1946*
Memoranda: CAB 80/97–101

(ii) *COS records, 1947–1951*
Minutes of meetings: DEFE 4/1–48
Memoranda: DEFE 5/1–34
Joint Planning Staff reports: DEFE 6/1–18
Papers: registered files, general series: DEFE 7/413–423, 934–936
Secretariat's registered files: DEFE 11/1–51

3. *Colonial Office*

(i) *CO original correspondence, 1945–1951: geographical classes*
Aden: CO 725/86–106
Africa: CO 847/24–55
Africa, East: CO 822/113–158
Africa, West: CO 554/134–171
Barbados: CO 28/331–343
Bermuda: CO 37/295–301 (to 1949)
Ceylon: CO 54/986–1003 (to 1947)
Cyprus: CO 67/319–373
Eastern: CO 825/44–90
Falkland Islands: CO 78/217–265
Fiji: CO 83/239–253
Gambia: CO 87/256–269
Gibraltar: CO 91/519–545
Gold Coast: CO 96/777–830
Honduras, British: CO 123/385–409
Hong Kong: CO 129/591–629
Jamaica: CO 137/857–906
Kenya: CO 533/534–569
Nigeria: CO 583/264–317
Nyasaland: CO 525/193–221
Rhodesia, Northern: CO 795/126–170
Sarawak: CO 938/1–12 (from 1946)
Seychelles: CO 530/654–782
Sierra Leone: CO 267/685–702
Tanganyika: CO 691/186–217
Trinidad: CO 295/628–656
Uganda: CO 536/211–225
West Indies: CO 318/456–515
Zanzibar: CO 618/80–88

(ii) *CO original correspondence, etc, 1945–1951: subject classes*
Appointments: CO 877/23–34

Circular despatches: CO 854/132–153, 183–191
Colonies, general: CO 323/1869–1924 (1944–1946)
Colonies general supplementary ['secret']: CO 537/1209–7862
Confidential print, Africa: CO 879/150–155
Confidential print, Miscellaneous: CO 885/113–118
Defence: CO 968/169–201
Economic: CO 852/534–1364
Establishment: CO 866/41–62 (from 1947)
International relations: CO 936/1–67 (from 1944)
Private Office papers: CO 967/25–52, 58–67, 84, 143–151
Public relations and information: CO 875/20–75
Research: CO 927/1–198
Social service: CO 859/83–246
Welfare and students: CO 876/94–276

4. *Dominions Office and Commonwealth Relations Office*

Original correspondence: DO 35/1172–1190, 1383–1386, 2126–4231
Private Office papers: DO 121/15–157

5. *Ministry of Food*

[For East African groundnuts scheme and Overseas Food Corporation]
Supply dept: dairy produce & fats group: MAF 85/588–589 (1946–1949)
Supply dept: supply secretariat (overseas production): MAF 83/1746–2010 (1946–1951)

6. *Foreign Office*

(i) *FO original correspondence, political*

Africa, general: FO 371/45905–45909, 53223–53231, 62936–62938, 69150–69153, 73740–73774, 80124–80134, 90059–90072
Commonwealth liaison: (from 1947): FO 371/65574–65597, 70172–70204E, 76345–76375, 84801–84833, 91148–91173
Dominions intelligence, and general political: FO 371/50363–50377, 50912, 54701–54730 (1945–1946)
Planning: FO 371/124941, 124968 (1950–1951)
Southern, Greece [for Cyprus]: FO 371/48451, 58760–58761, 67081–67084, 72294–72297, 78420–78427, 87715–87724, 95132–95134
United Nations: FO 371/88560–88570 [South-West Africa, 1950]
Western, general: FO 371/60001, 67718, 73036–73043 [European colonial territories, 1946–1948]

(ii) *FO private collections: ministers and officials*

Ernest Bevin papers, 1945–1951: FO 800/434–522

7. *Prime Minister's Office*

Correspondence and papers, 1945–1951: PREM 8/1–1577

8. *Ministry of Supply*

Atomic energy division: AB 16/261, 379–383, 393–394, 514, 978, 1514, 2001 [South Africa]

9. *Treasury*

Agriculture & food division: T 223/17, 84–86 [groundnuts, 1946–1950]
Chancellor of Exchequer's Office: misc papers: T 172/2037
European Economic Co-operation Committee: T 232/4–265
General economic planning section: T 229/119–331, 711–712 [colonial development]
Imperial & foreign division: T 220/26–223, 357–359, 366
Overseas finance division: T 236/497–3303
Supply [sections on 'Countries' and on 'Materials (food)']: T 161/1249, 1371, 1402 (1946–1947)

Bibliography 2: Unpublished private papers, published documents and secondary sources

1. *Unpublished collections of private papers*
   A V Alexander papers (Churchill Archive Centre, Cambridge)
   Attlee papers (Churchill Archive Centre)
   Dalton papers (British Library of Political and Economic Science, LSE)
   Gordon Walker papers (Churchill Archive Centre)
   Morrison papers (Public Record Office, FO 800)
   Noel-Baker papers (Churchill Archive Centre)

2. *Published selections of documents*
   R Bullen & M E Pelly, eds, *Documents on British policy overseas,* series I vols I & III (London, 1984, 1986); series II vol I (London, 1986)
   N Mansergh *et al,* eds, *Constitutional relations between Britain and India: the transfer of power, 1942–7* vols VI–XII (London, 1976–1983)
   N Mansergh, ed, *Documents and speeches on British Commonwealth affairs, 1931–1952* vol II (Oxford, 1953)
   A N Porter & A J Stockwell, eds, *British imperial policy and decolonization*, vol I *1938–51* (London, 1987)
   H Tinker, ed, *Constitutional relations between Britain and Burma: the struggle for independence, 1944–1948* 2 vols (London, 1983 & 1984)

3. *Select list of published books*

Only books which draw substantially on archival materials are listed here.

A Bullock, *Life and times of Ernest Bevin* vol III *Foreign secretary, 1945–1951* (London, 1983)

A Cairncross, *The years of recovery: British economic policy, 1945–1951* (London, 1985)

J Darwin, *Britain and decolonisation: the retreat from empire in the post-war world* (London, 1985)

R Edmonds, *Setting the mould: the United States and Britain, 1945–1950* (Oxford, 1986)

M Gowing, *Independence and deterrence: Britain and atomic energy, 1945–1952* vol I *Policy making* (London, 1974)

Lord Hailey, *An African survey, revised 1956: a study of problems arising in Africa south of the Sahara* (Oxford, 1957)

J D Hargreaves, *The end of colonial rule in West Africa* (London 1979)

J M Lee, *Colonial development and good government: a study of the ideas expressed by the British official classes in planning decolonisation, 1939–1964* (Oxford, 1967)

W R Louis, *The British empire in the Middle East, 1945–1951: Arab nationalism, the United States and post-war imperialism* (Oxford, 1984)

R J Moore, *Escape from empire: the Attlee government and the Indian problem* (Oxford, 1983)

R J Moore, *Making the new Commonwealth* (Oxford, 1987)

D J Morgan, *The official history of colonial development* vol II *Developing British colonial resources, 1945–1951* (London, 1980)

R D Pearce, *The turning-point in Africa: British colonial policy, 1938–1948* (London, 1982)

R H W Reece, *The name of Brooke: the end of white rajah rule in Sarawak* (Kuala Lumpur, 1982)

A J Stockwell, *British policy and Malay politics during the Malayan Union experiment, 1942–1948* (Kuala Lumpur, 1979)

D W Throup, *Economic and social origins of Mau Mau, 1945–1973* (London, 1987)

H Tinker, *Separate and unequal: India and the Indians in the British Commonwealth, 1920–1950* (London, 1976)

M Wight, *British colonial constitutions, 1947* (Oxford, 1952)

J W Young, *Britain, France and the unity of Europe, 1945–1951* (Leicester, 1984)

4. *Select list of published articles*

M Cowen, 'Early years of the Colonial Development Corporation: British state enterprise during late colonialism' *African Affairs* vol 83 (1984) pp 63–75

D R Devereux, 'Britain, the Commonwealth and defence of the Middle East, 1948–1956' *Journal of Contemporary History* vol 24 (1989) pp 327–34

D K Fieldhouse, 'The Labour governments and the Empire-Commonwealth, 1945–1951' in R Ovendale, ed, *The foreign policy of the British Labour governments, 1945–1951* (Leicester, 1984) pp 83–118

J E Flint, 'Scandal at the Bristol Hotel: some thoughts on racial discrimination in Britain and West Africa and its relationship to the planning of decolonisation, 1939–47' *Journal of Imperial and Commonwealth History* vol XII (1983) pp 74–93

P S Gupta, 'Imperialism and the Labour government of 1945–1951' in J Winter, ed, *The working class in modern British history: essays in honour of Henry Pelling* (Cambridge, 1983) pp 99–123

A E Hinds, 'Sterling and imperial policy, 1945–1951' *Journal of Imperial and Commonwealth History* vol XV (1987) pp 148–169

R Hyam, 'Africa and the Labour government, 1945–1951' *Journal of Imperial and Commonwealth History* vol XVI (1988) pp 148–172, repr in A Porter & R Holland, eds, *Theory and practice in the history of European expansion overseas: essays in honour of Ronald Robinson* (London, 1988)

R Hyam, 'The geopolitical origins of the Central African Federation: Britain, Rhodesia and South Africa, 1948–1953' *Historical Journal* vol XXX (1987) pp 145–172

R Hyam, 'The political consequences of Seretse Khama: Britain, the Bangwato and South Africa, 1948–1952' *Historical Journal* vol XXIX (1986) pp 921–947

J Kent, 'Bevin's imperialism and the idea of Euro-Africa' in M Dockrill & J W Young, eds, *British foreign policy, 1945–1956* (London, 1989) ch 3

J Kent, 'Anglo-French colonial co-operation, 1939–1949' *Journal of Imperial and Commonwealth History* vol XVII (1988) pp 55–82

H Laracy, 'Marching Rule and the missions' *Journal of Pacific History* vol VI (1971) pp 96–114

E Lerman, 'British diplomacy and the crisis of power in Egypt: the antecedents of the British offer to evacuate, 7 May 1946' in K M Wilson, ed, *Imperialism and nationalism in the Middle East: the Anglo–Egyptian experience, 1882–1982* (London, 1983) pp 96–122

W R Louis, 'British imperialism and the end of the Palestine Mandate' in W R Louis & R W Stookey, eds, *The end of the Palestine Mandate* (Austin, Texas, 1986) pp 1–21

W R Louis, 'Libyan independence, 1951: the creation of a client state' in P Gifford & W R Louis, eds, *Decolonisation and African independence: the transfer of power, 1960–1980* (Yale, 1988) pp 159–184

C C S Newton, 'Sterling crisis of 1947 and the British response to the Marshall Plan' *Economic History Review* vol 37 (1984) pp 391–413

R Ovendale, 'Palestine policy of the British Labour government: I, 1945–1946' *International Affairs* 55 (1979) pp 409–431; 'II, 1947' *ibid* 56 (1980) pp 73–93

R Ovendale, 'The South African policy of the British Labour government, 1947–1951' *International Affairs* vol 59 (1983) pp 41–58

R D Pearce, 'Governors, nationalists and constitutions in Nigeria, 1939–1951' *Journal of Imperial and Commonwealth History* vol IX (1981) pp 289–307

R Rathbone, 'The government of the Gold Coast after the Second World War' *African Affairs* vol 67 (1968) pp 209–218

R E Robinson, 'Andrew Cohen and the transfer of power in tropical Africa, 1941–1951' in W H Morris-Jones & G Fischer, eds, *Decolonisation and after: the British and French experience* (London, 1980) pp 50–72

A I Singh, 'Keeping India in the Commonwealth: British political and military aims, 1947–1949' *Journal of Imperial and Commonwealth History* vol XX (1985) pp 469–481

R Smith & J Zametica, 'The cold warrior: Clement Attlee reconsidered, 1945–1947' *International Affairs* vol 61 (1985) pp 237–252

A J Stockwell, 'British imperial policy and decolonization in Malaya, 1942–1952' *Journal of Imperial and Commonwealth History* vol XIII (1984) pp 68–87

H Tinker, 'Burma's struggle for independence: the transfer of power thesis re-examined' *Modern Asian Studies* vol XX (1986) pp 461–481

J Tomlinson, 'The Attlee government and the balance of payments, 1945–1951' *Twentieth-Century British History* vol II (1991) pp 47–66

Index of Main Subjects and Persons

This is not a comprehensive index, but a simplified and straightforward index to document numbers, together with page references to the Introduction in part 1, the latter being given at the beginning of the entry in lower-case roman numerals. It is designed to be used in conjunction with the summary lists and chapter headings of the preliminary pages to each volume-part. It provides a quick finding-aid to the main references to the principal subjects (countries and broad themes) and the leading British policy-advisers and decision-makers. As far as persons are concerned, only in the case of key figures (Attlee, Bevin, Cohen, Creech Jones) are the entries subdivided by subject; a preceding asterisk indicates inclusion in the Biographical Notes at the end of part 4. Where necessary (eg, in particularly long documents), and if possible, paragraph numbers are given inside round brackets. The following abbreviations are used:

A – appendix or annex
N – editor's link-note (before main text of document)
n – footnote.

Documents are divided between the volume-parts as follows:

nos 1–73 part 1
nos 74–194 part 2
nos 195–343 part 3
nos 344–444 part 4.